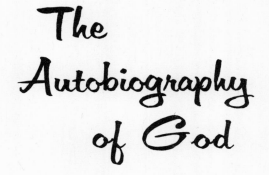

The
Autobiography
of God

C. G. Kindred

THE AUTOBIOGRAPHY OF GOD

By

C. G. KINDRED

Publishers

MISSION SERVICES ASSOCIATION PRESS

Joliet, Illinois

PHOTOLITHOPRINTED BY CUSHING - MALLOY, INC.
ANN ARBOR, MICHIGAN, UNITED STATES OF AMERICA
1959

The contents of this book are the result of Bible study and preaching by C. G. Kindred over a period of more than a half-century. The outlines of Bible study, the charts and bibliography quoted in footnotes and appendixes grew through the years and were recorded in carefully prepared notes and articles. For twenty-five years Nancy Berg served as Mr. Kindred's secretary, and her careful preservation of these notes, has made them available for this book.

Robert Lillie was closely associated with Mr. Kindred as a personal friend for twenty-three years, and for many of these years he heard Mr. Kindred teach a weekly Bible Study Class for ministers. Mr. Lillie worked closely with Mr. Kindred for one year before his passing on to be with the Lord, and in this year, Mr. Kindred developed the complete outline for this "Autobiography of God."

Following Mr. Kindred's passing, Miss Nancy Berg and Mr. Robert Lillie were asked by his daughter and son to complete this work begun so many years ago. After two years of daily labor on these notes and outlines, this work and dream of Mr. Kindred's life is now made available to students of God's Word everywhere.

With the exception of only a few necessary connecting sentences, the entire wording and exact language of this work is Mr. Kindred's.

FOREWORD

Jeremiah Black, the great jurist, said of Alexander Campbell:

> "The clinching fact was always in its proper place, and the fine poetic illustration was ever at hand to shed its light over the theme."

This same word might be fitly spoken of C. G. Kindred and his ministry with the Church of Christ, Englewood, Chicago. Brother Kindred wrote for SPEECH rather than for LITERATURE. To be best appreciated, it should be *heard* rather than *read*. But once one enters in to the realm of the Word Pictures which he paints, the beauty of the sentences and ideas become both visible and audible.

Robert M. Lillie, *Compiler*

BOOK INDEX

PHOTOS and ILLUSTRATIONS

Drawings by ARTHUR BUSSIAN, Tinley Park, Illinois

BIBLE VERSIONS USED

SCRIPTURES herein quoted or referred to, will follow one of three different headings:

1. References without any letter markings are quoted from the King James or Authorized Version.
2. Quoted Scripture verses followed by the letters A.S.V. are from the American Standard Version published by Thomas Nelson & Sons, New York, for which permission to quote has been granted.
3. Those references followed by the letter N. are quoted from the Newberry Bible (*The Englishman's Bible* by Thomas Newberry, printed in England by Oxford University Press, and published in New York by George H. Doran Company).

The Newberry Edition was found most suitable for its marginal and text markings; its indication of the verb forms and tenses, and particularly the Aorist Tense. These are more accurate translations of the original Greek text and therefore the Newberry Edition has been preferred in this book, though the verb *forms* have not always been quoted.

What enhances this use of the Newberry Edition? A number of the folks in the Englewood Christian Church used the Newberry Bible; and one of our members related the following:

"One Sunday morning the Englewood minister was reading direct from his Greek New Testament. I followed with the Newberry Bible and was really surprised at how precise were the verb markings of the Newberry Bible; the omissions, inclusions and the exact marginal-preference translations of this edition were in accord with the Greek text from which he was reading. I think this makes for easier and clearer picture reading, both as to Scripture time (verb form), and as to the intended Scripture definiteness."

The *Newberry Bible* INTRODUCTION (p. iii) has this to say:

"This Edition (Newberry) of the Bible is intended for the use of all who read the English language; and is founded on the text of the Authorized English Version.

"The plenary inspiration of the Original Scriptures is taken for granted; and it is believed that the minute attention to every 'jot and tittle' which this work enables the ordinary reader to bestow, if availed of, will lead to full conviction on the subject.

"In the Hebrew and Greek Scriptures there are precisions, perfections and beauties which cannot be reproduced in any translation.

"The design of the present work is to indicate many of these, by means of marginal readings, and by signs which are both simple and complete.

xiii

"In connexion with the DIVINE TITLES, there are treasures of precious truth which cannot be discovered in ordinary versions. One object of this Edition of the Bible is to present to the eye of the reader the Titles as they really exist in the Inspired Originals.

"The varied words used in Scripture for "MAN," no less than six of which are employed in the Old Testament, have also peculiar significance, and often throw light on passages.

"By means of MARGINAL EMENDATIONS an effort is made to show important distinctions between other words of frequent occurence, such as *Assembly, Congregation, Tent, Taberncale*, and renderings are thus made more correct and uniform.

"At the end of the Old and New Testaments a LIST OF THE SIGNS employed is given on a fly-leaf for easy reference.

"The value of many of these signs will without effort be at once appreciated, and the force of the verb-signs will soon be apprehended.

"Without interfering with the revered and loved text of the Authorized Version, much information which cannot be particularized will also be found."

This version of the Bible would be of special help and value to the interested Bible students.

THE AUTHOR

CHARLES GRANVILLE KINDRED was born in Naples, Scott County, Illinois, August 27, 1866.

When quite young, he moved with his parents to Mosier, Calhoun County, and when he was fourteen, they moved to Pittsfield, Illinois.

While still a student at Eureka College, Eureka, Illinois, Mr. Kindred preached for the Sciota Christian Church, and then accepted a pastorate at Vermont, Illinois. Still remaining in Illinois, he went from Vermont to Lewistown, and from there to the Englewood Church of Christ, Chicago, which was then located at 6417 Dickey Street (Eggleston Avenue).

With his family he came to Chicago in 1899, beginning his ministry with this Church on November 5, 1899. In 1904 the Englewood congregation moved to Stewart Avenue at 66th Place.

Under Mr. Kindred's leadership the Englewood Church grew spiritually, numerically and influentially. Not one loyal Christian Church building was erected in the Chicago territory but what the Englewood Church had a part in it; her missionary zeal reached into all parts of the world.

Mr. Kindred and the congregation celebrated his Fortieth Milestone together. With unbounded love for each other and an unquenchable faith in the Head of the Church, even the Lord Christ Jesus, they faced yet another decade together.

Not wishing to celebrate his Fiftieth Anniversary with the Englewood Church for fear the occasion might honor him rather than the Lord Jesus Christ whose bond-servant he sought to be, Mr. Kindred retired on April 18, 1948, after a consecutive ministry of forty-nine and one-half years with this Church.

Official retirement—June 30, 1948
Home-going—December 12, 1954, 7044 S. Perry Ave., Chicago.
Interment—Burbridge Cemetery, Pittsfield, Illinois

(Compiled from *Fortieth Anniversary Calendar Program,* November 5, 1939)

From a painting
by

Sudduth Goff. 1936.
portrait artist.

THE AUTOBIOGRAPHY OF GOD

THE BIBLE is not a system of facts or congeries of doctrines but it is the Biography of The Great Lover besieging our intelligence that He might capture our hearts, and make all things new—just as a lover ever does. So facts and ordinances are dissolved into a Temple for God.

GOD IS LOVE (I John 4:8) and this is His love story (John 3:16) and therefore it is His Autobiography. It is His Story, the field notes of a Father to His children from the campaign.

The Bible, to be understood, must be taken up as any biography. It is the *norm* of all biographies; It is the *incentive* of all that follows; It is the *teacher copy*. This *Auto*biography can be profitably studied; but to be fully understood, its Seven Divisions or Portions must be related to the purpose of the whole. Therefore I think that THE AUTOBIOGRAPHY OF GOD is about as good a name as I can think of for the Bible's related story.

I have no other ambition in my ministry than to create a love for His Holy Book. For these two reasons, popularity, preferment and audiences have been put aside; and upon this choice I face the "soon putting off" of II Peter 1:14, in a peace so satisfying that I know the choice is of Him (Galatians 2:20).

C.G. Kindred.

AN EULOGY ON THE SCRIPTURES

"For Thou hast magnified Thy Word above all Thy Name."

Psalm 138:2

AN EULOGY ON THE SCRIPTURES

THE BIBLE, The Mount of Transfiguration in literature, is plenary inspired in all Its parts; Its appeal is universal. Moreover, it is the God-breathed Word of the Living God, Maker of the heavens and the earth, Who sitteth in the midst of the Seraphim upon the Sapphire Throne dwelling in Light unapproachable (I Timothy 6:16).

This Book, the Bible, is not a scholarly volume; it is the Father's child-story for His children, written not in the classic school room speech but with words which the Holy Spirit chose out of the *common* speech; words worn smooth, like David's pebbles, in the every day use of daily events. These Bible *words* are the pigeon holes of heavenly events, and it is not until we all "become as little children" and cease striving for the high and mighty, the deep and profound, that He can reveal Himself to us. We must "be still" if we would know Him; we must "let go and let God."

This Book is lord of all libraries of the world and it is a *critic* "of the thoughts and intents of the heart" (Hebrews 4:12). Of what other text book could such language be used? Note that the *Written* Word *is* a Sword (Ephesians 6:17), and that the *Living* Word (Christ) *has* a sword (Revelation 19:15). The Bible is not just literature, but it is *THE* literature of *A* people. There is no worthy subject but what something evolves from within this spiritual world's library; and the Word of God is not bound but everywhere *It* takes precedence, and kings and leaders are haled before it.

This Book is an inspired revelation and its subject matter is of superhuman origin. With it as the model and the culture of the ages in contrast, there is not a rival or even the suggestion of one.

The Bible is *holiest* among the *mighty*, and *mightiest* among the *holy*. It is the Holy Spirit-produced Book (I Corinthians 2:13). So, He was compelled to compel His prophets to write beyond their understanding (I Peter 1:11).

In an article written by Dr. A. T. Pierson,[1] he says concerning the distinctive character of the Bible:

(Re: Psalm 19—Isaiah 55:8—9)

"For My thoughts are not your thoughts,
Neither are your ways My ways, saith the Lord,
For as the heavens are higher than the earth,
So are My ways higher than your ways,
And My thoughts than your thoughts."

"We must be ready to meet at every point in Bible study, the evidences

---

[1] *The Sunday School Times,* (Philadelphia, Pa.) Vol. 94, No. 33, August 16, 1933

that we are communing with an Infinite Being, and, as Coleridge discriminatingly said, 'we consent to apprehend much that we cannot comprehend . . .'. We shall find evidence that He has His own *lexicon*, using language in a unique sense and defining His own terms; that He has His own *arithmetic* and *mathematics* not limited to man's addition and multiplication tables; His own *calendar*, reckoning time in His own fashion, and dividing all duration into ages and dispensations, to suit His eternal plan; that He has His own *grammar*, using all the nice distinctions of conjugation and declension, voice and mood, tense and person, gender and number, with discrimination and design. In a word everything about God and His methods, shows that He lives on a different plane from man and cannot be either restricted to man's notions or judged by man's standards."

Dr. Pierson points out that there are:

"Three *standards* of *measurement* . . . as indexes of His divine power:
1. The wonders connected with the exodus from Egypt referred to hundreds of times (Micah 7:15)
2. The miracle promised in the regathering of the scattered tribes of Israel, a second time out of all lands (Jeremiah 16:14—15)
3. The supreme marvel of the raising of Christ from the dead and exalting Him to His own right hand (Ephesians 1:19—23; Philippians 2:9—11)."

Dr. Pierson concludes with:

"It is because The Word of God belongs to a super-human level that man's investigation of it never reaches its limit of new discovery. Every new study of it brings new unveiling. How thankful we should be that we live in a land where everyone may have his own copy of the Bible, and that there are in it always new, golden nuggets of truth to be discovered! And we have this promise of the Lord Jesus:

'Howbeit when He, the Spirit of Truth is come,
He will guide you into all truth . . .'."

The Bible is ONE Book, *The Autobiography of God*, the Almighty Creator of heaven and earth and "all that in them is"; the God of every and all "The Impossibles." It is the source Book of the knowledge of Him, and "the fear of Him is the beginning of wisdom." It is His Story of the universe, its creation, elements and the purpose for which it came into being. It is the record of the tragedy of defection for in it are recorded those who sin as having "missed the mark" (Romans 3:23). The defection begins with Satan and all mankind follows in his steps. It is the divine anabasis of heaven's redemptive invasion of sin-saturated earth, an invasion which was not a single battle but a campaign. It contains the Father's field letters from the campaign back to His children, believers in every age, that they reading, may understand, take hold of, and participate in His purpose. The issue appears doubtful oftentimes, but like it was said, "England loses every battle but the last," so Gog and Magog records the ultimate triumph of God. The whole Bible is a "Book of beginnings" from the Spirit brooding over chaos until that glorious victory foretold by Daniel (Daniel 9:24) and realized in Revelation 21 and 22.

The Bible was "sent from the heart of God" to a lost, cultured world, to Hebrew and to Greek. It contains the purpose (Gr. *Prothesis*) of God, "An Highway of Holiness" that reaches from every man's door up to God, though the unclean shall not pass over it. His Scriptures are each to its appointed place, broken up into sections best fitted to His purpose for which they were inspired to reveal unto us "upon whom the end of the ages is come."

The Bible is a Purpose-FULL Book. Its longevity and up-to-dateness should cause us to study expectantly. The purpose of the Bible is to persuade men of the futility of sin and the long suffering patience of the redeeming love (John 3:16) of our God and Father Who is striving to draw up into understanding fellowship with Himself, like as the sun draws water to the attraction of clouds (Romans 10:21, *Sept.* Isaiah 65:2). The reader of the Old Testament has missed "The Way" if he has failed to grasp that struggle to implant holiness into the mind and practice of the Hebrew race, while the New Testament (Ephesians 2:21—22) envisions "a new man" with the "stature of the fulness of Christ" whose citizenship is in heaven (cf. John 3:13).

The Bible is supreme in literature as Jesus is in the world of men. This Book contains the alphabet of all writings, the standards for all histories, all biographies, the bars and notes of all music, all emotions; it comprehends every science, philosophy and knowledge, beyond which there is none, for the human mind has never attained further. It is the self revelation of God, His Story. Searchers, whose delight is in the Scriptures, shall not walk in darkness but shall have the light of His life—a life that groweth brighter and brighter even unto the perfect Light.

H. G. Wells wrote *An Outline of History*; a book which is colossal, ambitious, inaccurate and out of date. But the Bible tells the Story of Redemption and is self-validating. Travelers, historians, and archaeologists use the Bible as a guide book, a source book and a survey. In this Book:

 a) The Builders of Governments and Constitutions find
   principles of the same
 b) The Astronomer finds the secret of the stars

c) The Geologist finds creation's story

d) The Surgeon finds circulation of the blood

e) The Archaeologist finds the frozen history of dead races

f) The Theologian finds the Presence of the Living God

g) And to crown all of these

    Isaiah 60:5 reveals the treasury of The Millennium:

> "Then thou shalt see, and be lightened together,
> And thine heart shall fear, and be enlarged;
> Because abundance of the sea shall be turned unto thee,
> And wealth of the nations shall come unto thee."

If the Bible be taken as an auto map for travel, geography and survey; or if used for digging or calculating, you will never be confounded.

God is a God of approved precision, order and meticulous accuracy. He moves resistlessly according to schedule. To avoid confusion, we must steer straight for with God there is "no variableness, neither shadow of turning." The Bible is uniquely THE Book of *The*'s, the definite article. It stands apart in autocratic humility as the service station devoted solely to broadcasting the Mind, the Will, and the Love of "The Father of (ALL) Lights" (James 1:17). Its "In a beginning," so far back of man or angels, compelled the indefinite, but after man arrived with his imparted, initiative faculties, its utterance "goes up into the mountains" and asserts *"The* Way, *The* Truth, *The* Light," and "speaks as one having authority." It is the voice from another world, "from above, not from beneath." It calls from *Ultima Thule*, unto an apocalyptic destiny to those "having ears to hear."

The Bible is the "world text," and is accurate in contemporary events, reliable in the records of the past, remarkable in depicting the unfolding of history, and is emotion-arousing in the expectance of things to come. The only explanation meeting the solution to many baffling incidents in the Bible, arises from its matter of fact utterances; that which to us is phenomenal, to Divinity is ordinary. The statements of the Bible are most plausible, rational and satisfactory; they have stood the test of time; they have survived all attacks; and the Bible speaks with sureness and assuredness upon the signs and events of these present times. It comprehends every science, philosophy and knowledge beyond which there is none. Critics like skin specialists, have so often been found in error; they deal with surface things; but the Scriptures, like unto Christ survived to rule! The vital, organic intent is not even deflected. "The firm foundation of God standeth sure" (II Timothy 2:14—21).

My conviction concerning this Book can be found in Hebrews 4:12,

II Timothy 3:15–17, Isaiah 55:10–11 and Matthew 24:35. Therefore, my concern is to preach the Word (II Timothy 4:1–5), and I believe that the preacher's sole task is:

a) To FIX unforgettably THIS WORD in the minds of his flock
b) To URGE persistently the claims of THIS BOOK
c) To WORSHIP, LOVE, and ADORE THE LORD of this Book

> "Preach the word;
> Be instant in season, out of season;
> Correct, rebuke, exhort
>   with all longsuffering and doctrine."
>
> II Timothy 4:2 N.

Would you know all mysteries and all knowledge? Then search the Scriptures, — for

> "Blessed is the man that walketh not in the counsel of the ungodly,
>   Nor standeth in the way of sinners,
>   Nor sitteth in the seat of the scornful.
>   But his delight is in the law of the Lord;
>   And in His law doth he meditate day and night."
>
> Psalm 1:1–2

Thus the Scriptures declare the blessing of God on that one who will dwell in this literary Garden of Eden where grow all manner of fruit good for food.

C. G. Kindred

PREFACE

𝕿 ODAY, there is a hunger-bitten spirit in men longing to be fed. "The common people" still "like sheep without a shepherd" would read the Bible, were it divided into digestible units. The Bible, Majestic River of Life, like the Mississippi, splits into ignominous shallows when it reaches the lowlands of man's daily life. It is God's Book of instruction for the children of men seeking the way of life eternal. It is plain, simple, direct, bringing the wisdom from above down to the every-day life of man.

"Many have taken in hand" and have made valuable contributions to the "Rightly Dividing" and profitable understanding of the Holy Scriptures —yet there remains much to be possessed. The findings within this book make no claim to finality or any attempt at a new channel of interpretation. But we are persuaded after re-study and critical and reverent approaches to each section of the conclusions, that herein will be found suggestions that will appeal to and aid in edifying the ordinary reader of God's Word of revelation. Should the book help toward the understanding of God's Purpose (Gr. *Prothesis*), as it has unto our group, then the effort at preparing this manuscript, a tedious and reluctant task, will have been a blessed compensation.

The findings arrived at in this book were of slow growth. They were begun more than sixty years ago in a mind then recently escaped from infidelity, which was baffled by any definite method or instruction as to a right understanding of The Way of Life. Later searchings left much to be desired, and this too, concerning the most important question of life. A ministry of well over a half century has been motivated by the attempt to meet this need toward the understanding of the Scriptures and is not extemporaneous but comes out of years of searching.

For a long time it was a lonely path. As the need grew more insistent, the Good Father Who always hears, answered the prayer for those of like minds. First a devout and cultured business man came alongside with valued findings. Later a college room-mate was led into a nearby pastorate, and for twenty-seven years nothing was permitted to interfere with our Wednesday morning "Searching The Scriptures." This became known, and one by one of like need came also, until there was a goodly group of seekers. These too, enriched by our studies, "many of whom are with me until this day," ascribe God's blessing upon the lengthening of their pastorates through this Berean fellowship.

For more than fifteen years, a devoted group of "honorable women not a few"—the Englewood Bible Study Class (some of whom "are fallen asleep)—in the Englewood congregation which has made much of Bible teaching and prayermeeting attendance, adjusted their program to become laborers together in the Lord. The atmosphere has been inductive to and productive of growth of Christian character; and surely must have had its benign influence upon "opening the Scriptures" so that we "would be without excuse." Each session of the class began in and with prayer, and closed in the same manner. We pleaded for frustration, should we have ventured beyond His leading. As it happened, we were being led in the only way that carried the solution to a "rightly divided" Bible. Our annual return to the book of Revelation had so familiarized us with its text (the Authorized, the many versions, and the Greek), that its allusions and its cross-references had produced a fairly good understanding of texts and teachings of the "other Scriptures."

One eventful class hour devoted to the Lord's speech in Matthew 24 and Luke 21, especially to His statement of the "abomination that maketh desolate, spoken of through (Gr. *dia*) Daniel, the prophet," expanded our horizon and brought nearer our appreciation of the unity of God's purpose, that it included the whole of the Scriptures. Without this door opening, there could have been no advance. The overlooking of the unity of these two books, *Daniel* and *Revelation*, because of the critical fires upon the book of Daniel, occasioned much of the difficulty experienced by not a few devout and gifted students of the Word. Had our *findings* been through ability, these lines would not have appeared. But what is to be set forth in this book came more from accidentals than planned investigation. For instance, the second "abomination" committed by Medo-Persia, which is not to be found in the text, rose up out of an evening's idling through *Josephus.* [1] The Lord's reference to "the blood of righteous Abel" (Matthew 23:35) and to the two prophecies given to Daniel concerning "The Times of The Gentiles," and, "Seventy Weeks are determined upon thy people," required *the whole surface of the Bible for a stage to work out so vast a drama.* From here we began to "lift up our eyes and beheld the fields white unto harvest." Our group is committed to "the soon-coming of our Lord," and this conviction is the urgency driving the pen never before used in attracting attention.

Within this book are produced charts and diagrams foot-noted with their portion of the Scriptures. Should any be led to studiously follow through, we are sure it will be well worth the hours set apart to its understanding.

There is no claim to scholarship, just belief in His promise: "Call unto Me and I will answer thee" (Jeremiah 33:3); based upon "the common people heard Him gladly"; and confirmed in I Corinthians 1:18 to 3:9; "not that we are sufficient of ourselves" (II Corinthians 3:5). Microscopically, there is opportunity for criticism, but few people carry microscopes, while

---

[1] Josephus, *Antiquities of the Jews,* Bk. XI, chap. VII, p.342

most have a hunger to walk in the ways of the Lord. And to such, these suggestions are offered to increase the group of "like precious faith."

Had our studies led to a questioning of II Timothy 3:16—17, there they would have ended. Two tests were rigidly applied to every text considered.

1. II Timothy 2:15,
   "Rightly dividing or steering a straight course."
   We asked:
   "Does it conform to 'a straight course' through the Scriptures?"
2. Matthew 5:48 "Be ye therefore perfect, even as your Father which is in heaven is perfect."
   Again:
   "Does it agree with our Lord's statement: 'Your Father which is in heaven is perfect'?
   Is God's perfection revealed in this text?"

"On these two hang all" satisfying study of the Scriptures and worship of God as a Person.

Let no one expect comfort in his doubtings in this volume. Not one jot or tittle of a shadow is allowed upon the text, nor is there any departure from the received text of the Authorized Version. We accept the Canon of Scriptures as placed under the illumination of the Holy Spirit. Our findings are insertions before suggested divisions. We would urge whoever takes up this volume, to give thought and prayer to the judgment rendered. It was not conceived in an attempt to produce a book, but it came forth out of the confusion from jangling voices of His divided people. May it carry conviction only as far as His blessing accompanies.

The urgency of II Timothy 2:15, particularly to those of Psalm One who appreciated and "gladly received" the instruction herein offered, has been wrought in over fifty years of study, meditation, and in fellowship and conference with like-minded believers, many of whom were members of the Christian Church congregation of Englewood, Chicago, Illinois.

I have also been strengthened, helped and enriched by a few Berean-minded ministers of the Chicago-Calumet District Evangelistic Association whose understanding, sympathy and approval, have made possible the issuance of this work.

Unto you now, this labor of love is laid reverently before our Father's Throne, as the tribute of love at the feet of His sacrificing Saviour in thankful recognition of His sustaining grace and enduement of the Holy Spirit. With expectant hearts let us approach this—the Thesaurus of another world.

> The arresting beauty of its language;
>> The altogether loveliness;
>>> The sweet reasonableness;
>>>> The haunting appeal to our better dreams;
>>>>> The mystic sense that one is not alone;
>
>>>>> — these all are sensed as one reads through even the first books.

> May the One Whose Word has been "searched,"
>> And without Whose approval it ought not be launched,
>> Place upon it His accolade.

C. G. Kindred

June 15, 1949

INTRODUCTION

to

THE AUTOBIOGRAPHY OF GOD

THE BIBLE to be understood, must be considered as ONE BOOK with ONE AUTHOR, and for ONE PURPOSE, set forth intelligently between Alpha and Omega (Revelation 1:8, 22:13). Arising out of a perfect beginning, it challenges and eventually defeats "principalities and powers in the heavenlies" (Ephesians 3:5, 6, 9, 10 and 17—21).

THE ONE AUTHOR

This Book will not yield its secret or mystery, as no real writing will, until a study is made of its Author, especially if that Author provides a Key under His own dictation (Revelation 1:1). The Bible is the norm of all *writing*, the pattern of all *books* or *autobiographies*, and the standard or teacher copy from which all *histories* are made. It is not a jumbled assembly of separated writings, addressed to different peoples and brought together by a fortuitous concourse of unplanned circumstances. Instead, the Bible is the product of sixteen centuries of writers, and rises into eternal relationships, welded into its present form "by a force not ourselves." It was produced by one Mind—even God's—and so is His Autobiography. When considered in this way, it will become both readable and appreciated as its Author unfolds His purpose. Thought put upon any portion soon discerns a current setting toward the definite goal objectives, and encompasses the WHOLE purpose and the WHOLE revelation of God.

THE ONE PURPOSE

This earth is the product of a designed plan of the Master Mind's purpose whose object is for it to be peopled by like-minded folks as Himself (Genesis 1:26). His purpose and plan of redemption (Romans 8:28) are directed toward the world that "lieth in wickedness" (I John 5:19; Galatians 1:3—4), and that purpose "without shadow cast by turning," is moving sublimely on toward a definite objective. God enters our world—and exits—without change or pause (James 1:17); He is on schedule, and obstacles are evanescent. God's *prothesis* or purpose, is to call men to repent toward Him (Revelation 3:18—22; Acts 20:21), and thereby repentance becomes the open door through which man must pass to participate in God's purpose. Within this purpose of God, there will arise heights and depths of continual challenge (Isaiah 55:8—9). We are challenged day by day with the majesty and power of God revealed through His Word; and we grow in understanding, so our knowledge of God advances and unfolds.

The Bible is the recounting of the earth's fall and reclamation; the joining together once more of the Alpha and Omega of Deity; "The beginning and the ending" of salvation (salvaging) of Jesus, Savior; "that God may be all in all." Amen and Amen.

THE ONE BOOK

The ghastly bone-marrow cancer of Satan's separation of the New from the Old Testament has been his masterpiece. Such division creates malignant bars that are impassable until taken away. The present method of division separates *Malachi* from *Matthew* which ought not to be since both are of the "Old Testament." The Spirit's method is to separate and to "render to each their due portion." The Jew, the Gentile and the Christian will each find provision made for him here (I Corinthians 10:32). The ONENESS of the Book is continually evident to those who follow the purpose of God from Alpha to Omega. Paul instructed Timothy to "rightly divide," or steer a straight course "through the Word of Truth," (II Timothy 2:15); not that the Bible might be divided into sections but rather that the purpose of God in the ONE BOOK might be discerned in every dispensation. To rightly divide these writings, is to open the mystery of eternity and to use aright the keys of the Kingdom of Heaven. This present work is what is hoped to be a pioneering toward rightly understanding the Omniscient God's effort to lay hold upon our attention; that, like as Moses, we may turn aside long enough to be led of the Holy Spirit.

CONCLUSION

May I state again that the Bible to be understood, must be considered as ONE BOOK, with ONE AUTHOR, and having ONE PURPOSE.

With our minds set on these three, may we expectantly approach the pages of this Book. It is essential to keep in mind the Master's prayer: "I thank Thee, O Father, Lord of heaven and earth, because Thou hast hid these things from the wise and prudent, and hast revealed them unto babes," (Matthew 11:25);—"But God hath chosen the foolish things of the world to confound the wise; and God hath chosen the weak things of the world to confound the things which are mighty," (I Corinthians 1:26 —31). Believing that God means and says what this book is setting forth in the chart[1] and its accompanying statements, it has become an analysis easy of apprehension, and satisfying to a group of seeking students who spent years together in a weekly attempt to "know the mind of Christ." Over these divisions we have copied the testimony of Paul, one of the Lord's own saints: *"Proved!"* It is for such that this chart and its analysis were prepared, for from such most of my knowledge of the Scriptures was derived. When I "joined the church," I was given a Bible and advised to read it. In later preparation for the ministry, it was my desire to make

---

[1] See Chart: *The Seven Sections of the Word of God*, p. 140

Bible reading understandably attractive to others of like confusion which I had experienced in the beginning. This is but suggestively introductory to those who have encountered like confusion!

> May the One Whom we love and seek to serve,
> In Whose Book I found the Way of Life;
> Bless or blot out the results of a life-ministry.

For those with seeing eyes and burning hearts, the Lord leads the way, opening up our understanding that we might understand the Scriptures,[1] (Luke 24:32, 46, and Matthew 24).

C. G. Kindred (Compiled Notes of 1947–1952)

---

[1] To receive the full value and understanding of the contents of this book, it is necessary to "run the references" and refer to the APPENDIXES when indicated. Though much inspiration may be received by rapid reading, the fuller understanding and appreciation comes only in tarrying with the Scripture references which accompany the statements on the many subjects included.

6

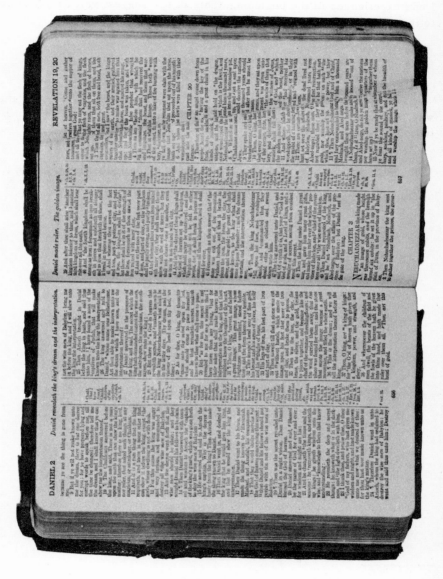

Brother Kindred emphasized that the Bible should be read as ONE Book. His study Bible shown above is pictured opened at DANIEL and folding to REVELATION, symbolizing that it is an *unbroken* story of God's Love and Redemption.

RIGHTLY DIVIDING

from

ALPHA to OMEGA

"Be diligent to present thyself approved unto God,
A workman that needeth not to be ashamed,
Rightly dividing the word of truth"
(steering a straight course through).

II Timothy 2:15 N.*

"And knowest his will, and approvest the things
that are excellent . . ." (Dost distinguish
the things that differ).

Romans 2:18 A.S.V.*

*see page *xiii*

7

TABLE of CONTENTS

RIGHTLY DIVIDING from ALPHA to OMEGA

INTRODUCTION

MY last work is upon RIGHTLY DIVIDING the Scriptures in which I think I have made clear how to shake off the confusion that now exists in the minds of people when they take up the Word of God and the Testimonies of Jesus Christ. As a young man, I fully accepted this "Way of Life" but nevertheless it lacked emotional power because of the confusion occasioned by the failure of the *method* of instruction. With this emotional appeal lacking, a definite obedience was frustrated and therefore failed in the divine assurance that accompanied the gospel plan of salvation.

After much "searching of the Scriptures" and research into commentaries and giving thoughtful attention to lectures, not neglecting current discussions, the notes accompanying these charts will resolve most of the problems within. The approach must be through faith in a Creator of love, wisdom, and power with a benevolent purpose as a Father. Every problem is tested in this alembic: "If any of you lack wisdom, let him ask of God, that giveth to all liberally, and upbraideth not; and it shall be given him" (James 1:5).

I. THE SURVEYED LINES of the PURPOSE of GOD

Our business is to pick up the surveyed lines of the purpose of God. To set this forth, and to "rightly divide" or to "steer a straight course through the Word of God"—this chart has been devised. Though exceedingly simple, it requires a desire "to know the mind of Christ" and a willingness to put forth effort; to concentrate upon it until you have mastered. To bring channelled, fixed opinions is to pre-judge and thus render futile your time and the chart's findings. This is not seeking an advantage; it is only fair that your formed opinions be kept in abeyance until you have completed your study of this chart. Then let them face each other complete rather than putting your whole against its dismembered statements.

This Seven-Fold Chart of the Ages, (viz. *The Seven Sections of the Word of God*[1]), was not planned but arose out of the experience of a group of quite ordinary believers who had spent years in the effort to know the mind of Christ, and who have arrived in complete unity at these findings. Gradually, the unfolding of His purposed plan became discernible ("first the blade, then the ear, then the full corn in the ear"); and along with this came the growing apprehension of the lowliness of the Scriptures ("a lamp unto our feet"); together with the awe-fullness of "Thou hast magnified Thy Word *above* all Thy Name" of Psalms 138:2. The depths

---

[1] See Chart: *The Seven Sections of the Word of God*, p. 140

and heights of The Word of God became more clear though we had read, "He hath given Him a Name which is above every name," and, "there is none other Name given among men whereby we must be saved." Even Saul of Tarsus was not privileged to claim exemption from the written requirement (Romans 10:6–8; Acts 26:22; 28:23). Here is no attempt to make light of learning, only to call attention to its futility in the affairs of the soul life. These "findings" of devout scholarship have brought forth vast stores of information to the enrichment of "seekers after God." But the value of their researches is to be summed up in the conclusions that have arrived at the simplicities of the Word. The archaeological excavations at Jericho[1] in 1930–1936 have shown that houses were built on the walls of Jericho, thus giving archaeological light on, and confirmation of, the Biblical indication that Rahab's house was on the wall. Many other such confirmations could be cited. The one attempting to know the mind of Christ must make Mary's choice (Luke 10:42) for only to such can the purpose of God be discernible in every age. The dispensational emphases are often helpful, but His "purpose" is essential to those who would "ask for the old paths"—the Highway of Holiness—the "untrackable" section of the universe of God's sin-free domain: "the Kingdom of God."

His purpose is much more clearly seen when each portion of the Bible is separated off into its significant purpose; each portion introduces the people addressed; every section has truths for all, the main thought is a doctrine (a teaching) for THE people of THAT dispensation. It is here that failure to "render to each their portion in due season" has raised the conviction that is vexing the perplexed minds of those who are searching for the Truth. Two common misapplications will serve to illustrate:

1. The blessings of the prophets taken over from Israel and then applied to the Church
2. By not giving attention to the *last* sentence of Micah 6:8 N.:

"He hath showed thee, O man, what is good;
And what doth the Lord require of thee, but to do justly,
And to love mercy, and to walk humbly with thy God,"—

And this actually calls men of each dispensation to an obedience of *the doctrine of their dispensation.*

The three sons of Noah have run true to the prophecies that went before. Through *Shem* came the nation of Israel, God's chosen people. The *Hamites*, Canaanites, et al, had a high degree of *inventiveness* that groveled in fetishness; the *Japheth*ites sought intellectual satisfaction,

---

[1] George A. Barton, *Archaeology and The Bible* (Philadelphia: *American Sunday-School Union*), pp. 135–136; and works of John Garstang.

"the work of men's hands," in their approach to God. There is an evolutionary philosophy expressed in *architecture* today, (but "God dwelleth not in temples made with hands," Acts 17:24), and this same evolutionary philosophy is influencing *organizations* as we see it expressed in the Latin, Romanist and State Churchex, and most recently, in the Federation Movements for pressure power. These three theories are fast approaching a new Babel of confusion. Only a return to God's way which is written plainly in His Word has hope as seen in Isaiah chapter 55, particularly verse 11.

II. DIVIDING THE GREAT LINES OF GOD'S INTENTION

When one arrives at unconditional promises made to Abraham, it becomes necessary to use reverent care in searching out and so dividing the great lines of God's intention. Dispensations direct the attention to the rapprochement of human and divine. Our plan seeks to point out the emphasis of each group in the process. This, like tithing, requires a completed revelation from which to start, (the tithe must be taken from the whole). The method which the Spirit appears to have adopted in Paul's urging upon Timothy in his last letter (II Timothy 2:15), yields more satisfactory solution than any tried. "The common people heard Him gladly" (Mark 12:37*b*), and Jesus said, "The word which ye hear is not Mine, but the Father's which sent Me" (John 14:24*b*). If the Word of Truth be rightly divided, then His Word will still be received gladly. The Bible is plain, simple, direct, bringing the wisdom from above down into the every day life of men. For what saith the Scriptures, "The spoken word is nigh thee . . ."—not in the heavens, but nigh thee (Deuteronomy 30:14; Romans 10:8), and when the great Teacher walked with men, He demonstrated its simplicity, "The common people heard Him gladly," while the learned in "the wisdom of this world could not take hold" upon: "how knoweth this man letters *never* having learned" (John 7:15).

> "Study to show thyself (N. 'be diligent to present thyself') approved unto God, a workman that needeth not to be ashamed rightly dividing the Word of Truth."
> II Timothy 2:15

The phrase "rightly dividing" is the Greek word *orthotomounta* which comes from the words *ortho-o*, set straight, and *temno*, to cut, hew, wound, maim, use the knife, to cut up, slaughter, sacrifice. *Temno* is also translated, "to cut lengthwise, plow, make a road, or as for ships, *cutting through* the waves." *Orthotomeo* is the classical Greek, "to cut into a straight line." From these usages, we may see the reason or possibility of translating this phrase "steering a straight course through," or, "rightly separating the Word of Truth."

There is a need for a rightly divided Word. As the Lord commanded those who stood by when Lazarus was raised, "Loose him and let him go," so He would have His Body, the Church, rightly divide His Word to Jew, Gentile and Christian, thus letting each portion go to its place. To rightly divide is to unravel or separate, to dis-entangle or interpret. The rightly separating of the Word of Truth as a good steward (Luke 12:42–43; I Corinthians 4:2) calls for prayerful spiritual discernment in the one who takes up the two-edged Sword for the purpose of rendering to each his portion. The Lord's admonition through Paul (Hebrews 4:12), "For the Word of God is quick and powerful (N. living and effectual), and sharper than any two-edged sword, piercing even to the dividing asunder both of soul and spirit, and of the joints and marrow, and is a discerner of the thoughts and intents of the hearts," cautions us as to the delicacy with which we are to handle this two-edged Sword.

The Church, the body of Christ, stands as a priest at the altar rightly dividing the Holy Story, rendering most solemnly in Almighty God's own Words, to each their portion in due season, for there is a curse appended to those who dare change. As the priest at the altar dissects a lamb for the sacrifice, cutting the sacrificial victim, leaving all parts and organs in-tact; so the Church, His Body, (Colossians 1:18, 24; II Corinthians 5:18) is to take up the Sword of the Spirit which is the Word of God, and rightly divide to Jew, Gentile and the Church, their portion of God's revelation, leaving each vital division of truth for its own function. Such rightly dividing can be intelligently done only by starting at the beginning. From here the Scriptures "go to their own place" carrying their own convictions with them. When the Spirit has "made the pile complete," then speculations and hypotheses give way before the exquisite simplicity and majestic grandeur which make for the abiding supremacy of the old Authorized Version. Whether we use the figure of *rightly dividing as a priest at the altar, or of steering a straight course,* we find that neither figure does violence to the text but rather adds vividness to the events and incidents therein. It neither twists nor distorts, adds to nor takes from the Bible.

"Rightly dividing" is the separation of the spiritual from the natural, the "discerning of spirits" and the conditions are unvarying: "if any man will come after Me, let him deny himself, take up his cross and follow Me"; then the glorious recompense, "and where I am, there shall also my servant be." To do this understandingly, one must begin at the beginning, else why the admonition "steering a straight course through?" This suggests a steersman holding his ship in mid-channel with an awareness, quick eye and firm hand. Likewise must there be also the completed ending, else where is the goal toward which you steer? The Spirit's admonitions pre-suppose the end (Gr. *telos*) objective which invites and also requires re-study. We are prepared to expect Genesis 1:1, "In a beginning—God!"

And who, familiar with the Bible but eagerly would do as John urged his disciples in John 1:29—37? That paragraph is enough to commit us to His leading in spite of any or all allurements which might arise between Alpha and Omega. "I'll follow Him through earth and sky."

Searching the Scriptures is as the man described by the Lord in John 10:9, one who was to go in and out and find pasture. So we might say that the good steward in rightly dividing or separating to each his portion, goes in and out and finds pasture for all. The church is the body of Christ and He has gone away; He has left us to do this task. To Paul He said, "Go into Damascus and it shall be told thee what thou must do." He could not tell him from heaven because He was already beyond a personal dispensing of the gospel, but the church could do so and this is our business.

Therefore, believing the Scriptures to be a dependable record of the events reported, and that the instructions therein are for our admonition (I Corinthians 10:11—12), we take the text, II Timothy 2:15, as urged upon the church, and give attention to the preparation required in "rightly dividing." First, there must be a *finished* work to view, for it is not possible to *rightly* divide until the *completed* whole has been viewed. Ponder therefore Revelation 1:1—3 and 5:1 wherein the Bible was given complete to the Lord to give to John to pass out to His servants as the revelation of God's purpose.

There must be at least a four-fold rightly dividing of the great lines of God's intention. These will be evident to the thoughtful, observant reader as he advances in this study (Romans 2:18 A.S.V.; Philippians 1:10 A.S.V. margin).

Though the *books* and *events* (dispensations) of the Bible are interrelated, yet when we rightly divide, we avoid a confusion of the two:

a) RIGHTLY DIVIDING *the Books* of the Bible

(1) The UNSEALED Division:
   Genesis through *The Song of Solomon*

(2) The SEALED Division:
   Isaiah through *Revelation*

b) RIGHTLY DIVIDING *the Events* of the Scriptures

(1) The Seven-fold Chart, showing
   "The Seven Sections of the Word of God"

c) RIGHTLY DIVIDING *the Record* of the Scriptures

(1) HIS Story   (History)
(2) MY Story   (Mystery)
(3) SATAN'S Story   (The Destroyer)

d) RIGHTLY DIVIDING *to Peoples* (I Corinthians 10:32)

    (1) To the Jew   (Israel)
    (2) To the Gentile (Nations)
    (3) To the Church (The Body of Christ)

To rightly divide can be the only basis for unity; and the reason for "the falling short" of our Plea to attain unto such unity has been our own failure to produce spiritual lives and spiritual writers. My own ministry has been a long search for this "Rightly Dividing" and for the consequent fruit-producing and peace-imparting life that "Our Plea" should bring forth.

With the glorious outcome of God's plan for His saints before us— how can hearts remain unmoved by the passionate plea of the church which is His body, carrying on His vicarious ministry (Colossians 1:24)?

> *O Church!*
> Incarnate this latest text of our sainted leader!
> II Timothy 2:15.
> Take up your cross;
> Return to the beginning —
> The only place from which to understand
> "Steering a straight course through the Word"
> Dividing aright;
> "As good stewards of the Grace of God."

THE UNSEALED)

    and   )   DIVISIONS of the SCRIPTURES

THE SEALED   )

RIGHTLY DIVIDING

THE BOOKS OF THE SCRIPTURES

The UNSEALED Books are GENESIS to THE SONG OF SOLOMON. These books are universal in scope and are easily understood by all.

I. THE BOOKS OF LAW

Genesis
Exodus
Leviticus
Numbers
Deuteronomy

II. THE BOOKS OF HISTORY

Joshua
Judges
Ruth
I and II Samuel
I and II Kings
I and II Chronicles
Ezra
Nehemiah
Esther

III. THE BOOKS OF POETRY

Psalms
Proverbs
Ecclesiastes
The Song of Solomon

ELOHIM is the significant name used for GOD in the UN-Sealed Division.

The SEALED or CLOSE-SEALED Books are ISAIAH to REVELATION. These books are the revelation to spiritually-minded people.

I. THE SIXTEEN RAPTURED VISIONERS— ISAIAH to MALACHI

1. *The Universal Gospel*
Isaiah
Jeremiah (and Lamentations)
Ezekiel
Daniel

2. *"To The Jew First"*
Hosea
Joel
Amos
Obadiah

3. *"Also to The Greek"*
Jonah
Micah
Nahum
Habakkuk

4. *"The Desire of All Nations"*
Zephaniah
Haggai
Zechariah
Malachi

II. THE GOSPELS

Matthew
Mark
Luke
John

III. THE GOSPEL OF THE HOLY SPIRIT

The ACTS of The Apostles

IV. PAUL'S CHURCH EPISTLES

1. *The Salvation Group*
Romans
I and II Corinthians
Galatians

2. *The Sanctification Group*
Ephesians
Philippians
Colossians

3. *The Glorification Group*
I and II Thessalonians

V. PAUL'S PASTORAL EPISTLES

I and II Timothy
Titus
Philemon

VI. THE GOSPEL TO THE REMNANT ACCORDING TO THE ELECTION OF GRACE

Hebrews
James
I and II Peter
I, II, III John
Jude

VII. THE OBSERVATORY FOR THE WORD OF GOD

The Book of Revelation

EMMANUEL (God with us) is the significant name used for the SEALED Division.

INTRODUCTION to (UNSEALED
(and DIVISIONS
(SEALED

OR

RIGHTLY DIVIDING the BOOKS of the SCRIPTURES

MY OWN GROUPING or dividing of the Scriptures to which I have come from many hours of my own study through long years, has brought me to this satisfying conclusion: that there are in the Bible UNSEALED books and SEALED books. Brevity has been studied so that the suggested divisions might bear the testimony unbiased by opinions. Thus the books of the Bible divide into TWO groups:

1. The UNSEALED books:
    GENESIS to THE SONG OF SOLOMON

    These books are universal in scope and are easily understood by all. ELOHIM is the significant name used for God in the UN-Sealed Division of the Bible books.

2. The SEALED or CLOSE-SEALED books:
    ISAIAH to REVELATION

    These books are the revelation to spiritually-minded people. EMMANUEL (God with us) is the significant name used for the Sealed Division of the Bible books.

While these two divisions are generally accurate, yet within the UN-sealed division, there are prophetical utterances that are as "Sealed" as those in the division from *Isaiah* to *Revelation*. But the *major emphasis* of the Unsealed division is upon the revelation of God's power, upon the historical facts and the movement of peoples which are easily discernible. It is also true that the "Sealed" division contains historical statements which are easily read and understood, but the *major emphasis* here is upon sealed prophecies which are difficult to comprehend.

These prophecies became "opened or Unsealed" when in Luke 24:27 and verses 44—45, Jesus began at *Moses* (in the Unsealed division) and in all the *prophets* (the Sealed division) and expounded unto them in ALL Scriptures, the things concerning Himself. He opened the apostles' understanding to *every* prophetic utterance in the Old Testament which concerned Him, but out of necessity, the larger number of these interpretations would come from the *Sealed* division, that of *Isaiah* to *Malachi*.

(left) The open Scroll of the Torah, showing the division of the writing into columns; (above) a miniature Torah owned by the Jewish Theological Seminary

The "Open" or "Unsealed" Book

(right) The encased scroll of the Torah showing how it was preserved and carried.

The "Closed" or "Sealed" Book

DIVISION ONE: ((UNSEALED DIVISION
((GENESIS to THE SONG OF SOLOMON

"And I saw on the right hand of Him that sat on the throne
a roll of a book written within and on the backside, having
been sealed with seven seals."

Revelation 5:1N.*

*see page xiii

TABLE of CONTENTS

THE UNSEALED DIVISION of the SCRIPTURES

Page

ENESIS to THE SONG OF SOLOMON is the Division "written on the backside" for all men to read and understand. It is a history of human experience and especially that of the Hebrew. *Genesis* is the historic baseline[1] visited frequently by visitants from above, enough to attract and seize the attention of disturbed minds upon a future life:

- *a*) Enoch is translated
- *b*) Methuselah is named:
     "When he dies, it (the flood) shall come"
- *c*) The Ark survives to the Tower of Babel
     and the dispersion of nations
- *d*) Abraham rises to prophetic vision
- *e*) And Joseph's hope is fulfilled as Moses takes the bones
     of this great patriarch up from Egypt (Exodus 13:19).

The Hebrews with psalms on their lips emerged as a nation from Egypt which was a land of death and embalmers (Hosea 11:1; Matthew 2:15). Job, the Gentile, heard the distant music of this nation raised from the grave of Egypt and uttered his conviction: "I know that my Redeemer liveth" (Job 19:25). From this prepared people Isaiah rose to apocalyptic utterance. Scattered through time and distances, they came to such a spiritual compactness, that the canon of their Scriptures became "fixed" as of today and only a guiding Mind explains it. The final adjustment of the canon was under Divine control as each book "went to its own place." Within this Book there lies open to "those having eyes to see" the revelation from God. Here the Father gives to His children His Story. John 3:16 is assuredly the text which is most applicable to the Unsealed Division of the Book:

> "For God so loved *the world*, that He gave His only begotten
> Son that every one that believeth in Him should not perish,
> but have everlasting life."

Genesis to *The Song of Solomon* is for everybody. All can study it and come to an apprehension of God as they take hold of things mentioned therein. *Job* and *Psalms* while written *by* and *for* the Jew are yet for all mankind. To those accepting the call of Abraham and his posterity, to *every* seeker after God in *every* age—the history of Israel, the philosophy of *Job*, the adoration of the *Psalms*, and the wisdom of the *Proverbs* would be the thesaurus of divine wisdom. Herein is found every resource for the intellectual development and the approach to the spiritual development of the whole human race.

To anyone having eyes to see, the opening of the Bible contains the most awesome and majestic of all events; yet these events are so simply

[1] See *Seven-Fold Chart of the Ages*, Sections ONE, TWO, THREE and FOUR, p. 140.

worded (Genesis 1:1) as to leave us unaware of the power which is adequate to produce them. The same is true of so much of God's mystery in creation and revelation. God's power is the open secret for all men to see (Proverbs 25:1–4; Romans 1:19–20).

In I John 5:19 we read, "*the whole world* lieth in the wicked one." This is *the world* of John 3:16 and it is not "sealed." That "God so loved the world" is clearly evident in the revelation which has been profitable to all men of every age and nation through the writings which God gave in these books. Redemption is written in love. The orderly process of God's purpose is seen through the Bible. It begins with God's glory, then Satan's fall, earth's sin, and finally, restoration's prothesis as given in Genesis 3:15. Information, consolation and comfort as well as inspiration, have all been received by those who have read these pages.

To bring man to God, we must begin at the beginning of the Scriptures; and as man advances in his study through the whole Book, he finds:

> God in *Genesis*
> God in *Exodus*
> God in *Deuteronomy*
> God in *Job*
> God in *Psalms*
> God in *The Song of Solomon*
> And God throughout all of The Scriptures.

I. THE BOOKS OF LAW – "Beginning at Moses"

> Genesis
> Exodus
> Leviticus
> Numbers
> Deuteronomy

A. GENESIS is the beginning of things; this is the mental process by which God, the loving Father, invites the participation of every soul of like desire in every generation and dispensation to see His purpose. This is the book which begins with the words:

"In beginning God created the heavens and the earth."

And this same book comes to a close with the words: "a coffin in Egypt." This coffin in Egypt is a symbol of the death which was produced by the sin beginning in Genesis 3.

B. EXODUS is the going out; – "A nation emerges out of Egypt." Israel was begotten in Ur, born in Egypt, and disciplined in Babylon. God is taking the people of Israel out of Egypt; but this book also enables all people to know God.

C. LEVITICUS contains a clear statement on the feasts of the Lord
(Leviticus)[1]

D. NUMBERS records the numbering of the people of Israel.

E. DEUTERONOMY is the repeating of the Law. To whom did they
repeat it? It would be to some of the folk that had inherited the *power*
given in *Genesis*, to whom it was *demonstrated* in *Exodus*, and then *developed* in these other books, *Leviticus* and *Numbers*. And now in *Deuteronomy* He says, "Go over that again." In Deuteronomy 32:8 N., we find
the direct connection with the book of Genesis:

> "When the most High divided to. the nations their inheritance,
> When He separated the sons of Adam,
> He set the bounds of the peoples
> According to the number of the sons of Israel."

The man who begins to believe in God and begins to see the place
of the Jew in relation to God, will recognize that here in the world, the
Jew is important in the eyes of God. That is why the gospel today was
commanded "to the Jew first." These books will show to the whole world
the Jew's place before God, that he is in the *blackboard* on which God
is writing His revelation.

II. THE HISTORICAL BOOKS:

Joshua
Judges
Ruth
I and II Samuel
I and II Kings
I and II Chronicles
Ezra
Nehemiah
Esther

Here are recorded God's dealings with the people that He is using
in His blackboard demonstration. These books might be compared to the
"Acts of the Apostles" of the New Testament.

III. THE POETICAL BOOKS:

The Pastoral Shepherding of the Old Testament
Job

---

[1] See Section FIVE, MY Story, VI. *Things . . . Established,* E. 1.*b*) p.441; and E. 2.
The Lord's Table Established in The Upper Room, p. 446

>   Psalms
>   Proverbs
>   Ecclesiastes
>   The Song of Solomon

These books are adaptable to the enlightened of the Jewish race, the chosen people, but are also universally adapted to all mankind and the problems they face.

A. JOB was God's attempt to prove the futility of rebellion and we led to consider Satan as the Old Testament parallel to the brother of the prodigal son (Luke 15:25—32). The book of Job is before its time in the personalities and languages of God, of Job, and of Job's friends; but as an appeal to one of another realm, they attract to the least cynicism.

B. PSALMS is intended for the comfort of folk through all ages who will trust God and come to Him. I am acquainted with a man who found his way to peace out of that portion of the Bible, and to comfort and to the answer to his problems by reading the Psalms. The Nineteenth Psalm is the universal apostrophe. Moses first wrote our convictions in his prayer of Psalm 90:1:

>   "Thou hast been our dwelling place in all generations."
>   God!   God!!   God!!!

This augments the truth that this division of the Bible is for all the peoples. Back of *Psalms* is *Job* who has all of the marvelous things that the scientific mind is interested in.

C. PROVERBS is on the other side of *Psalms*, for these things which it contains are practical.

D. ECCLESIASTES might be well summed up in chapters 1:1—3 and 12:13—14 N.:

>   "The words of the Preacher, the son of David, king in
>   Jerusalem. 'Vanity of vanities,' saith the Preacher,
>   'Vanity of vanities; *all is vanity*. What profit hath a man
>   of all his labour which he taketh under the sun'?"
>   . . . . .
>   "Let us hear the conclusion of the whole matter:
>   Fear God, and keep His commandments;
>   For this is the whole duty of man.
>   For God shall bring every work into judgment.
>   With every hidden thing whether it be good,
>   Or whether it be evil."

E. THE SONG OF SOLOMON shows that love goes in to a bad situation. The love-God and Israel are allegorically set forth in this book, and though Israel was unfaithful and is therefore separated from Him now, yet she is to be restored as a nation and as the Bride of Christ at His second coming to earth (Song of Solomon 2:8—17). For the present Israel has been "broken off" and is in rejection. Blindness in part has happened to Israel during the times of the Gentiles, and Israel has suffered persecution and wounding from the Gentiles, but when they call for the Lord (Matthew 23:39), He will come to them, and she will be restored (Song of Solomon 5:6—8).

SUMMARY

As we complete the reading of this open, unsealed division of the Word of God, we realize that we have been "thinking God's thoughts over after Him"; and having come to the knowledge of God, we are ready to advance further into the Sealed Division of this Book. We join our voices to the voice of the Psalmist:

"Lord, Thou hast been our dwelling place in all generations.
Before the mountains were brought forth,
Or ever Thou hadst formed the earth and the world,
Even from everlasting to everlasting Thou art God."

Psalm 90:1—2

Eternity, Eternity, Thou boundless, boundless
    Tideless sea of Mystery — The Mystery,
I will hew me great windows into Heaven
Hew with intensity, the windows of immensity!
"Behold, I will build me a nest on the greatness of God."

DIVISION TWO: ((SEALED DIVISION

(ISAIAH to REVELATION

"But thou, O Daniel, shut up the words, and seal the book,
even to the time of the end: many shall run to and fro, and
knowledge shall be increased."

"And I heard, but I understood not: then said I, 'O my Lord, what
shall be the end of these things?' And he said, 'Go thy way,
Daniel: for the words are closed up and sealed till the time of
the end'."

". . . And none of the lawless shall understand;
but the wise (instructed) shall understand."

Daniel 12:4, 8, 9, 10b, N.*

See page *xiii*

27

28

TABLE of CONTENTS

THE SEALED DIVISION of The Scriptures

Note: The above subdivisions of this SEALED DIVISION have their own
Tables of Contents on pages 31, 85 and 94.

INTRODUCTION to SEALED (or CLOSE-SEALED) BOOKS ((ISAIAH
                                                 (to
                                              (REVELATION

                      (Revelation 5:1—10
Texts: (Revelation 6:1
                      (Daniel 12:4

"And I saw on the right hand of him that sat on the throne a book written within and on the back, close sealed with seven seals. And I saw a strong angel proclaiming with a great voice, Who is worthy to open the book, and to loose the seals thereof? And no one in heaven, or on the earth, or under the earth, was able to open the book, or to look thereon. And I wept much, because no one was found worthy to open the book, or to look thereon: and one of the elders saith unto me, Weep not; behold, the Lion that is of the tribe of Judah, the Root of David, hath overcome to open the book and the seven seals thereof . . . . And I saw when the Lamb opened one of the seven seals, and I heard one of the four living creatures saying as with a voice of thunder, Come (and see)."

                                    Revelation 5:1—5; 6:1 A.S.V.

WE COME NOW to the Sealed Portion of "God's Autobiography," the Bible, which only the Strong Son of God is able to open, and "to loose the seven seals thereof." The blood of the Son of the woman (Genesis 3:20) contained enough dynamite—enough to blast the Gates of Death—and after His resurrection, the Lord opened and interpreted the Scriptures to His disciples (Luke 24:27, 44—45). The prophetic words which began in *Isaiah* and went through the sixteen volumes of the Old Testament Scriptures, are the work of Jesus Christ as Prophet. These were veiled before He opened the Scriptures to His apostles (Luke 24:44). The eunuch said to Philip, "How can I (understand) except some man guide me." These Scriptures or words of prophecy are now opened to us through the writings of the inspired apostles in the New Testament, (". . . holy men of God spake . . ."). The testimony of the prophets is found in Joel 2:1—11, 28—32, vs. 3, "The scorched earth"; John 5:39; Jeremiah 25:31. The prophets in the Old Testament are the best authenticated of all ancient or modern literature. They are more so than the New Testament for critics are blind to its authority. There are two witnesses: The Lord's approval and appeal; and the accuracy.

Through the books of the Sealed Portion of the Scriptures, our Lord fulfills three distinct offices: that of prophet, priest and king. His prophetic work takes place from the beginning of *Isaiah* and goes through the sixteen volumes of the books of prophecies concluded with *Malachi*. His earthly ministry begins with the Gospel when "The Word became flesh" and this introduces His work as priest. As priest, He offered His own body upon the altar on the cross for the atonement of the sins of the world, and He continues His work of priestly ministry through His Body, the Church, today. His priestly office will continue until the church is caught up to be with Him and the body of Christ is made complete. He shall come as king of kings and Lord of Lords and His feet shall stand upon the Mount of Olives and His Kingdom shall reach around the world. His kingly office shall last one thousand years and then having put down all enemies, the last of which is death, He shall turn over all things to the Father that God may be all in all.

This Sealed Portion of the Book begins with ISAIAH and continues through the book of REVELATION. Here are found the prophecies which are hidden from the world, but which are revealed unto spiritual people (I Corinthians 2:1—16). The wisdom of the world cannot by its wisdom, find the meaning which God has here revealed. The revelation is available to those who search the Scriptures and "compare spiritual things with spiritual." Now begins that portion of the Divinely Inspired and prophetic Scripture which grows brighter and brighter unto the perfect day of Consummation; for the Highway of Holiness (Isaiah 35:8) transverses the entire revelation of God from Alpha to Omega.

When in the wisdom of God, He brought the message of the stars, (the Zodiac) into the speech of man,[1] He called out men[2] whom He breathed upon and burdened with His Love, which had provided for the freighted task of the world's redemption. These were holy men, Spirit-moved, who "spake as the Spirit gave them utterance": prophets, revealers of God, faith-producers who gave light along the Way to Him (John 1:45; 1:11—22). *Sixteen* of these God-called-out men—*Isaiah* to *Malachi*—carried out and laid upon the speech of man, the message "of whom the prophets did write": "The Only Begotten Son,"—The Savior of the believing world.

God spoke through Amos saying (3:7—8):

> "Surely, *Adonahy* (Sovereign Lord Jehovah), will do nothing, But He revealeth His secret counsel unto His servants the prophets. The lion hath roared, who will not fear? Adonahy Jehovah hath spoken, who can but prophesy?"

The Bible emerges from the vast unknown antiquity with momentum and direction which is unrivaled. This is as we would expect. Because It arises from outside our experience, It is open to challenge; and It does not evade but rather invites our challenge. The chronology of the written Word is exhausted in the local needs, yet it yields in importance to the canonical. The same divine readjustments are seen in the New Testament for God's Word is both local in time and is also universal or timeless; and thus the prophets are prepared to utter the note of eventual victory.

---

[1] See Appendix "E" *Zodiac*, p. 609 ff.

[2] See Section FOUR, *Abraham to Christ's Spiritual Body*, MY Story, II. The Growing Cloud of Testimony Bearers, p. 232.

TABLE of CONTENTS

SEALED DIVISION—SIXTEEN PROPHETS

I. ISAIAH to MALACHI

Introduction to SIXTEEN PROPHETS; THE RAPTURED VISIONERS

"Knowing this first, that no prophecy of Scripture is its own
solution. For prophecy was *not at any time by will of man:*
but holy men of God spake borne along by Holy Spirit."

I Peter 1:20—21N.

𝕿 HE GROUPING of the prophets is of very great significance to
anyone who would know God's purpose for "men spake as they were
moved (borne along) by the Holy Spirit." God had something to say and
the canon was compiled under His supervision. A survey of the writing
prophets will prove profitable to those interested (I Corinthians 10:11—12;
12:4—7). These world-compelling, raptured visioners are cleansed and
sent forth. Isaiah chapter 6; Jeremiah 1:9; Ezekiel 3:12—15. The whole
story of redemption is panoramated by this world-illumining galaxy of
Isaiah, Jeremiah and Ezekiel. It now remains to be worked out historically;
so Daniel is given the base line upon which it is worked out to palin-
genesis by nations, kings, peoples and the Sanhedrin who are wholly unaware of what is occurring (Psalm 76:10). In *Daniel* is set forth in plain
historical events "in the midst," the consummation "to those having eyes
to see" through in *Daniel* and *Revelation.*

The Postscript to prophecy is the subscription voucher and is the
Lord's very own endorsement as found in Matthew 24:1—31; John 5:39;
and Luke 24:27N.:

"And beginning from Moses and from all the prophets,
He expounded unto them in all the Scriptures the things
concerning Himself."

As He interprets to His disciples "in ALL the Scriptures" He links Himself with Daniel and Jonah, the two prophets most severely critized who
are "the despised and the rejected men" (Isaiah 53:3).

The Bible is the world text and is accurate in contemporary events,
reliable in records of the past and is remarkable in depicting unfolding
history, and is emotion-arousing in "things to come." Consider its accepted accuracy of the creation process: its order, *gens* and adaptability.
We see the prophetic etchings of "THE Coming One." He is "A Man of
sorrows acquainted with grief"—yet they say, "Behold, your King!" These
are not twisted or contorted texts, but are limned outlines of "One not
seen" save by the Artist before the easel; yet He is exact when He steps
forth; "in the Old Testament, the New is concealed, and in the New, the
Old is revealed." We see "Mystery," the Holy Spirit, salvaged Israel, the
saved church, redeemed nations, and restored heaven, for "Behold! I make
ALL things new." The above is the Purpose, Pledge and Promise of our

God! And in this Book, God puts Himself on record and invites a check-up. As an expert marksman, He calls His shots.

These SIXTEEN PROPHETS are a double octet and correspond to the doubling method in Bible utterances as a reading of the *Psalms* or *Proverbs* will illustrate. The harmony of these books is elevating and the study of each part (each group of FOUR), will simplify and enable our understanding. The two end groups: the first and the fourth groups are concerned with the world and its Savior; while the two center groups, the second and third, address themselves "to the Jew first and also to the Greek." These books are em-bosomed in God and their division is indicated at the very beginning of prophecy. All prophecy of the Scriptures is based upon the two themes: first, "Seventy weeks are determined upon Thy people"; and second, "The times of the Gentiles." These two phrases mark the divisions,[1] and as always, these carry the theme or purpose, while the ends or fulfillments elaborate and round out the harmony.

God's plan of the ages is monotheistic, spiritual and universal, in the midst of Polytheism, sensual and tribal communities. The Scriptures are a power in themselves made for cleanness. Heathen, even the pagan practices are a copying of the divine with human concessions added, but they are not the originals and do not antedate the Bible events.

The sixteen prophetic *books* from *Isaiah* to *Malachi* fall into four unique sections of individual and peculiar, prophetic testimony:

1. The first group of prophets is ISAIAH to DANIEL, containing the Universal Gospel. The Majestic Isaiah, Jeremiah and Ezekiel with Daniel, are the "Way-Builder," "An Highway of Holiness." Its message is universal and it is the Proto-Evangel. It proclaims a world-saving Savior in language which the Holy Spirit teaches, written by Spirit-guided men, raised up and called of God.

2. The second group, HOSEA to OBDAIAH, is "to the Jew first"; "the Chosen People"; the John 3:16 group. Here, first adapted to the apprehension of a people, indulging in the looseness of sin, we see their God's abhorrence of their practices, yet He is bound to them with a "love that wilt not let go." Hosea, as we shall see, is called to share His sorrow.

3. The third group, JONAH to Habakkuk, is to the Gentiles, or "also to the Greek." This is "The Twilight of the Gods" Group. Alexander The Great scattered the Greek language all over the world and even today it survives as both language and philosophy. But failure of the nations is again revealed, for they are A-Theos, with gods many but a people without vision.

---

[1] See Section FOUR, *Abraham to Christ's Spiritual Body*, MY Story, Daniel, Prophet and Statesman, p. 240

4. The fourth group is ZEPHANIAH to MALACHI containing "The Desire of all nations." Here we have the "Behold! He cometh" group. Here both Jew and Gentile in words in the minor key utter their cry of defeat (I John 5:19; Romans 3:23; Haggai 2:7).

A. INTRODUCTION TO GROUP ONE:

THE WORD FLESH; THE UNIVERSAL GOSPEL

This group[1] contains the books of ISAIAH, JEREMIAH, EZEKIEL, and DANIEL; and it is the Universal Gospel, the open vision of the prophets for a world of sin; love seeking the lost (Isaiah 53) through sacrifice; it is love's greatest and most prevailing power for "WHOSOEVER." The main message of the first three books of each group of four prophets, is the spiritual message dealing either with Israel or with the other nations; but always the fourth book in each group deals with the prophecies concerning the affairs of men on earth which can be verified with historical reference. The other events are spiritual things, some of which have come to pass and some of which are yet in the future but they are in the spiritual realm rather than in the political and historical realm. Within this group:

ISAIAH presents the *Pre-Eminent Son*; "the Word made flesh"; whose "name shall be called Wonderful, Counsellor, Mighty God, The Everlasting Father, The Prince of Peace."

JEREMIAH presents the *Pre-Eminent Sinner*, Israel. He presents also the indefeasible promise of God to Israel (Luke 9:62, God cannot deflect upon *His* promise).

EZEKIEL presents the *Pre-Eminent Salvation* and he depicts the Universal Temple.

DANIEL, the fourth of the group, presents the *Pre-Eminent History* of the Course of Empires.

We must test "Rightly Dividing" by the prophets. ISAIAH, JEREMIAH, and DANIEL were chosen to be the prophetic messengers of the Major (John 3:16), the Universal Gospel which was to span the ages from Genesis 3:15 to Revelation 11:17, and these are the only prophets who do. *Isaiah* to *Daniel* are concerned with the Four Empires and the Seventy Weeks. These are separate and apart, and are unique in matter and time. *Isaiah* begins with Israel but looks out and up to the nations with whom the Lord will deal; so Isaiah writes of the Universal Gospel which is not opened or released until Christ, the Key, comes in His earthly ministry and opens

---

[1] See Section FOUR, *Abraham to Christ's Spiritual Body*, MY Story, II. The Growing Cloud of Testimony-Bearers, "The Era of Prophecy is opening . . . ." p. 232, paragraph 5.

the Scriptures (Luke 24:44—49). The Universal Gospel would include both the *Sufferings* of Christ and the *Glory* that should follow, and would not be completed until Israel is restored and the Seventy Weeks of Daniel have been accomplished. The Universal Gospel is for all the peoples of every age.

1. THE PROPHECY OF ISAIAH

"Hear, O heavens, and give ear O earth:
For Jehovah hath spoken, ..."

"In the year that king Uzziah died I saw also the Lord sitting upon a throne, high and lifted up, and His train filled the temple. Above it stood the seraphim . . . And one cried unto another, and said, 'Holy, holy, holy, is Jehovah of hosts: the whole earth is full of His glory'."

Isaiah 1:1a; 6:1—3 N.

As a pilgrim's first sight of the City of Jerusalem from the Mount of Olives, or as Balboa's first sight of the out-stretched Pacific,—so was this revelation an *Ultima Thule* to Isaiah. His ecstacy and emotion raised speech into apocalyptic utterance. He had experienced Uzziah's death and had seen "the Lord high and lifted up"; he had been touched with a divine fire and received God's pledge to set His Hand a second time to recover the remnant of His people (Isaiah 11:11; 12:6). Under this afflatus he sweeps the horizon of rivals and assesses Babylon, Damascus, Arabia and Tyre, as he picks up and analyzes, despises and casts out; like as, "small dust of the balance" is all summed up in Magog. In chapter 53 is the apocalyptic vision when "the desert shall blossom as a rose" and "sorrow and sighing shall flee away." In Job 38, God reared a pulpit for the Sermon on the Mount and Isaiah ascended.

Isaiah was a court favorite; a patron of culture, a formal religionist, one familiar with ambassadors and so spake of countries and their weaknesses. The conditions existing are found in Isaiah 1:3—4; 5:23; Hosea 4:6; Isaiah 1:5b; and II Chronicles 26:16.

There are TWO Isaiahs as there were TWO Pauls;—and as also there are TWO of EVERY born-again person (Galatians 2:20). When Christ lives in me, then I change eyes with God and I love as God loves.

Isaiah contains all of the elements of the Gospel; he is the gospel writer of the Old Testament; he wrote, "for unto us a child is born, unto us a son is given: . . ." (Isaiah 9:6—7). The four gospels are the record of Jesus' ministry to the lost sheep of the house of Israel (Matthew 10:6; 15:24), but there are still many things within them that are adaptable to us for our profit. We must be careful to note that the plan of salvation is not introduced in the gospels until *after* Jesus' death, burial and resurrection. We will profit from the Gospels if we are careful to rightly divide. This is also true of *Isaiah*: in this book (52:7–10), the Lord leads the way to "understanding the Scriptures" (Luke 24:45; Matthew 24); and Isaiah writes to a world sunk in sin to the depths of murdering the sinless Son of God; but he closes his prophecy in apocalyptic glory: that of, "so will I comfort you" (Isaiah 66). There is no wonder that critics have sawn him asunder for his recording is that of both the *sufferings* and the *glory* that should follow."

In the Isaiah Dead Sea Scroll there is no break between the 39th and the 40th chapters and there are no markings to indicate that it is not the writing of one man. Note in Isaiah 42:9:

> "Behold the *former* things are come to pass, and *new things* do I declare: before they spring forth I tell you of them."

And the Scofield Reference Bible marginal note (p. 750) says:

> "'Former' that is, Isaiah's prediction of Sennacherib's invasion and its results, Isaiah 10 and 37. See also Isaiah 41:21–23; 43:8–12; 44:7; 48:3, 5, 16. This appeal of the prophet to the fulfillment of his former predictions strongly confirms the unity of the book."

Isaiah is the rising Sun over Balaam's "Star" (Numbers 24:17) and the prophecy of Balaam reads thus:

> "I shall see him, but not now: I shall behold him, but not nigh: there shall come a Star out of Jacob, and a Sceptre shall rise out of Israel, and shall smite the corners of Moab, and destroy all the children of Sheth."

As also John saw before the event happened (Revelation 1:1–2 N.):

> "The Revelation of Jesus Christ, which God gave unto Him, to show unto His bond servants things which must shortly come to pass; and He sent and made it known
>
> by signs through His angel unto His bond servant John: Who bare record of the word of God, and of the testimony of Jesus Christ, and of all things that he *saw*."

2. THE PROPHECY OF JEREMIAH

> "Is it nothing to you, all ye that pass by? Behold (look attentively), and see if there be any sorrow like unto my sorrow, which is done unto me. Wherewith Jehovah hath afflicted me in the day of His fierce anger."

Jeremiah, the weeping prophet of Israel (Lamentations 1:12), has watered the centuries with his tears as he sorrows for back-slidden Israel (Jeremiah 5:14). He epitomizes Israel's history (Jeremiah 31:31) but also includes some things that concern the nations. His was a patriotic sorrow caused by the failure and defection of the favored nation. His story is reduced to the chosen people who were in unbelief, and it is a message concerned with their sin and redemption.

The book of LAMENTATIONS is included with Jeremiah's prophecy for he wrote both books.

Jeremiah "plods" their way even down into Egypt. The Light, as it falls upon sinful Israel, sees Jeremiah sharing with his people Israel, in their degradation.

3. THE PROPHECY OF EZEKIEL

"Then He said unto me, 'Son of man, these bones they are the whole house of Israel: . . . .'."
"And I will set My glory among the nations, and all the nations shall see My judgment that I have executed, and My hand that I have laid upon them."
"When I have brought them again from the peoples, and gathered them out of their enemies' hands, and am sanctified in them in the sight of many nations:"

Ezekiel 37:11*a*; 39:21, 27N.

Ezekiel is the prophet of the Restoration; he gives the apocalyptic glory of the end of sin; the departing glory of the nation and its final return as the majestic city-temple-nation. This is the Sun drawing up into the temple; and the glory upon the new nation.

Ezekiel walked on wheels to great prophetic power, even to the glorious consummation of chapters 40 through 48. He calls Jerusalem the *navel* of the earth (Ezekiel 5:5); and it is here that the final events center concerning Magog and the Apocalyptic Temple.

Ezekiel's vision of the Valley of Dry Bones (chapter 37) looks to the time when the nation of Israel shall rise again. His graphic description of the Universal Gospel in the Regeneration, matches that of Revelation 21 when God says, "I will make all things new." Ezekiel portrays the Restoration of Israel and their eventual redemption. He shows the depths of degradation, but also depicts earth's restored people and the eventual triumph of love. His story is coming back to awe humanity and runs up to the great temple and the winding up of all things there. The Universal Gospel of this section (*Isaiah* to *Daniel*) includes the city which Abraham saw in his vision in the dawn of the Scriptures and which is referred to again in Hebrews 11 and is finally brought to fulfillment in Revelation chapters 21 and 22.

4. THE PROPHECY OF DANIEL

"And behold, a hand touched me, which set me upon my knees, and upon the palms of my hands. And he said unto me, 'O Daniel, a man greatly beloved, (delighted in), understand

the words that I speak unto thee, and stand upright: for unto
thee am I now sent'."

                                                    Daniel 10:10—11N.

INTRODUCTION

The book of Daniel is as the Acts of the Apostles of the major prophets, for here God is at work. This book contains the Way of Holiness,
the Purpose of God, and the Revelation Terminii of God: The Seventy
Weeks,[1] and The Times of the Gentiles.

The book of Daniel is the pre-written history or historic chart containing the course and end of religion for Israel with their eventual restoration (The Seventy Weeks' prophecy); and the course and end of the
political rule of Gentiles (The Metal-Image Prophecy of the Four Empires).
So *Daniel* is a demonstration as a cemetery in which we see the tombstone
epitaphs of nations showing the Bible futility of all times, races and continents.

Daniel is the road-builder bringing prophecies to earth, and showing
history to be *His Story*. The Old Testament books contain the readjustment
of long accepted assignments. *Daniel* is among the major prophets and
deals with empires and revelation, which carry rational explanations of
events of time and the rise and fall of empires. Thus *Daniel* participates
in and carries to a satisfactory conclusion in time, the everlasting, un-
defectable purposes as set forth in the major Word of God brought nearer
our comprehension in the minor prophets, and to a full explanation of expression, in the Gospels when "The Word became flesh and dwelt among
us." In the four Gospels is set forth Israel's setting aside (Matthew 23:39)
for a season, for a period of Universal Grace when His Body, the church,
is set forth having hitherto been hid in God (Romans 11:33—36).

a) THE AUTHENTICITY OF THE BOOK OF DANIEL

Jesus recognized that the book of Daniel is authentic and Holy Spirit
inspired, by His reference to *Daniel* in Matthew 24:15N.:

> "When ye therefore shall see the abomination of desolation,
> spoken of *through* Daniel the prophet, stand in the holy place,
> (whoso readeth, let him understand:)"—(understand: observe,
> or mark attentively).

Note His careful use of the words when He says, "The abomination of
desolation spoken of *through* (Gr. *dia* not *by* or *in*) Daniel THE prophet."
Daniel was the means through whom God spoke to His people Israel. There
can be no mistake as to Jesus' recognition of the inspiration of the book
of Daniel.

---

[1] In Daniel's prophecy, one day is counted as a year; therefore the Seventy Weeks
would represent 490 years.

The ferocity of the attacks upon the book of Daniel reveals the Satanic animus to discredit the Spirit and to dethrone God (Isaiah 14:12—14). The attacks are marked by continuous ignominious defeat which proves the divinity of the book's authorship, and seals believers while it condemns enemies.

There are three undesigned witnesses to the authenticity of this book:

(1) The composition of the book:

There are *two* languages, *Aramic* and *Hebrew*
(Daniel 2:4 to 7:28, and 8:1—12:13).

There are four empires which are seen as metals and beasts. There are two divisions: one is *political*, and the other is *ecclesiastical*. There is ascendance of the ecclesiastical until intolerant brutality destroys it (Revelation 17, beast and the woman).

(2) The book is *Dispensational* and not *Chronological*, and this is a characteristic Bible custom seen in *Isaiah, Matthew, Romans* and other books.

(3) The events of the book are undesigned, yet the design is perfect. It is utterly impossible of forgery to create situations in Asia, Greece or Rome, that when fitted together, will make sense. The author would need to build cities and call out and develop situations that would be preposterous.

We are therefore entering *Daniel* assured of its veracity and accuracy as to the time, place and persons, and so of course, we are assured of its prophetic utterances. Daniel's historical reality is "founded upon the Rock'" (Luke 6:48) that this admitted corallary is inspiration from an Omniscient Mind. Therefore its statements are authoritative amid a flux of our time; here is refuge, "as the shadow of a great Rock in a weary land" (Isaiah 32:2*b*). The book of Daniel is of the Jewish kingdom. It is not Christian but is Messianic (note: "*Thy* people": chaps. 7:13—14, 18 and 27; chap. 9, Daniel's prayer; and 10:14 through 12:1).

Daniel's historical prophecies are being fulfilled to the letter. The Syrian Neoplatonic philosopher Porphyry[1] claims *Daniel* is *post facto*

1

Porphyry was a Greek scholar and Neoplatonist born at Tyre in Syria 223 A.D., died 304 A.D.; he was a violent opponent of Christianity and a defender of Paganism (*Encyclopedia Britannica*, Vol. 18, Ed. 1944, p. 243). "A distinctive character of his treatise against the Christians seems to have been its occupation with questions of historical criticism. Very little of it has been preserved even in fragmentary form, the set replies of apologists, as well as the treatise itself, being lost; but the view he took about the Book of Daniel is on record. According to Jerome, he maintained that it was written in the time of Antiochus Epiphanes; so that the historical events supposed to have been predicted were really events (concluded on page 40).

writing because it is so accurate. The *Matthew* context shows that not even the destruction of Jerusalem in the year 70 A.D. met the description of "The Abomination of Desolation spoken of *through* the prophet Daniel." This prophecy of Daniel has its first *application* to Antiochus Epiphanes; its *fulfillment* is still future. Antiochus Epiphanes is set forth in Daniel chapter 8:9—14 and this prophecy is admittedly authentic since the prophecy is dated 555 B.C. In 250 B.C. the Septuagint was translated and the book of Daniel was and still is *in* the critic's copy, yet the critics did not recognize that this Greek translation of *Daniel* completely destroys their charge that *Daniel* was written *after* the events recorded. The fulfillment of this prophecy occurred about 75 years after the Septuagint was translated between 175 and 170 B.C.

In His earthly ministry Christ emerges from the authentic facts of the Old Testament prophecies such as Daniel 9:25—even as the church today emerges from the historic facts and events of the New Testament, from birth at Pentecost to rapture.

(TWO STRONG MEN

b) DANIEL and NEBUCHADNEZZAR—THE (TWO DREAMERS

(TWO WRITERS

> For East is East, as West is West, and never the twain shall meet;
> Till Earth and Sky stand presently at God's Great Judgment Seat;
> But there is neither East nor West, Border, nor Breed, nor Birth,
> When *Two strong Men* stand face to face though they came from the
> ends of the earth. [1]

These two dreamers (see Daniel chaps. 2, 4, 7) received from heaven the pattern of the four empires as also David received the temple pattern (I Chronicles 28:12, 19). From Alpha to Omega "The Highway of Holiness" runs through this Bible up to God. Consider how great were these two men, Nebuchadnezzar and Daniel. Hammurabi, Croesus, Alexander, the Caesars and the story of Thermopylae, help to make up our history;— Xenophon's "Anabasis," Gibbon's "The Decline and Fall of the Roman Empire," Stobart's "The Glory That Was Greece," and his "The Grandeur That Was Rome,"—all record their deeds. Emerging above these peaks of history, are these two "Dreamers" who rise to God.

Though sophisticates ignore, the wise patronize, and theologians explain away, yet the Bible outsells this year as usual, and prophecy is in

(Conclusion of footnote 1 from preceding page):

that had taken place before the time of the writer. This, Jerome says, proves the strength of the case in favour of its genuinely prophetic character; for if events subsequent to the time of Daniel had not been very clearly prefigured, Porphyry would not have found it necessary to argue against the ascription to him of the authorship" (Thomas Whittaker, *The Neo-Platonists*, Cambridge, Macmillan, 1928, 2nd ed. pp. 107—108).

[1] Rudyard Kipling, *The Ballad of East and West*, (Doubleday and Company, Inc.)

first place. Worlds are regimented in ether (Job 26:7); schools of fish swim about in the sea; solar systems cluster in the Universe; thus this Book, the Bible, also is distinct, apart, and separate, even though it is all of One Divine Plan. In *Romans* we learn of sinners and salvation; and in *Ephesians,* of the church His body; in *Revelation* of the new heavens and the new earth. Here are galaxies or dispensations of redemption. In this Bible my very being is revealed (Psalm 139:14—16).

Daniel and Nebuchadnezzar are the *Microcosm,* the smaller revelation of the whole purpose of God and His one divine plan, which is the *Macrocosm.* They are the *visible* which live within and by the *invisible* (Acts 17:27—28). To Daniel and Nebuchadnezzar were given as the *microcosm,* the revelation of the seventy weeks for Israel and the four empires of the nations. This little book of Daniel, the *microcosm,* sets forth events whose fulfillment covers centuries and continents, and their fulfillment is the *macrocosm.* The Seventy Weeks' prophecy for Israel and the course and end of the Four Empires are both a part of the one divine plan.

(1) *Daniel, The God-Occupied Man*

The Lord's endorsement and approval of Moses, Daniel and Jonah is recorded in the Gospels. These and other prophets were inarticulate humanity who broke into emotion-satisfying expression for God, and life takes on meaning as we read them. God's men were men of stature who could be seated at the council table, yet their humbleness permitted their walking with the common man. Daniel had been made ruler of the vast province of Babylon, so we must consider his national prominence (Ezekiel 28:1—3). Daniel's book of prophecy is of the first magnitude even as Washington's farewell address. God always has His man.

Daniel set his heart to seek after God, and all heaven got into motion (Daniel 9:20—23). When any blood-earnest soul storms the flesh, then the heavens bow down:

> "And it shall come to pass, that before they call,
> I will answer;
> And while they are yet speaking, I will hear."
>
> Isaiah 65:24

Daniel's example should call us to worship and prayer; he is the beginning place, and his book is the prophetic base line. Earth and heaven are the negative and the positive: "The eyes of the Lord run to and fro through the whole earth" (Zechariah 4:10), and wherever a need attains unto persistent prayer, He sees and brings together questioner and answerer.

(2) *Nebuchadnezzar, The God-Troubled Dreamer*

The book of Daniel is the answer to the first Gentile king seeking

God's help in a worthy cause, to establish government; but Nebuchadnezzar sets himself against the "certain and sure" of God, and God "keeping
watch above His own," compels his confession of defeat (Jeremiah 29:22).
Let us read earnestly this fourth chapter of Daniel for this is the personal
confession of Nebuchadnezzar's conversion. This chapter is written *after*
he had experienced his conversion; it is dictated by this Gentile king and
comes out of the Syriac or Aramaic portion of the Hebrew literature. Hear
him tell from "Peace" (4:1) through his degradation (vs. 31), to his "excellent greatness" of verse 36. For a decade he was at war with Tyre; then
Tyre and Egypt and Jerusalem had all been given into his hand; and then
comes this troubling dream (Daniel 4:5).

After victory, we must often beware of pride (I Corinthians 10:9–12).
The Master warned, "What I say unto you (through Nebuchadnezzar's example), I say unto ALL: WATCH!" Before this time, Nebuchadnezzar had
met God's manifestations:

> (*a*) Daniel had revealed and interpreted for King Nebuchadnezzar
> the forgotten dream of the four Kingdoms' image: "Then
> King Nebuchadnezzar fell upon his face, and worshipped
> Daniel, and commanded that they should offer an oblation
> and sweet odours unto him" (Daniel 2:46).
>
> (*b*) The three children of Israel (Shadrach, Meshach and Abed-
> Nego) were delivered by God from the fiery furnace:
>> "And the princes, governors, and captains, and the king's
>> counsellors, being gathered together, saw these men, upon
>> whose bodies the fire had no power, nor was a hair of their
>> head singed, neither were their coats changed, nor the
>> smell of fire had passed on them" (Daniel 3:27).

In these Nebuchadnezzar had witnessed God's protection and approval
of faithful men which protection had been withheld from *un*faithful prophets
like Ahab and Zedekiah:

> "Thus saith Jehovah of hosts, the God of Israel, concerning Ahab
> the son of Koliah, and concerning Zedekiah the son of Masselah,
> which prophesy a lie unto you in My name; Behold, I will deliver
> them into the hand of Nebuchadrezzar king of Babylon; and he
> shall slay them before your eyes; And of them shall be taken up
> a curse by all the captivity of Judah which are in Babylon, saying
> Jehovah make thee like Zedekiah and like Ahab, whom the king
> of Babylon roasted in the fire"; (Jeremiah 29:21–22 N.).

But these manifestations to Nebuchadnezzar by God had been forgotten,
and now he is given a dream concerning the tree that reached to the (dual)
heavens (Daniel 4:4–18). Again the interpretation of the dream is given by
Daniel in verses 19 through 27. Twelve months (vs. 29) after the dream had
been given, nothing had happened, and "all things continued as they were"

(II Peter 3:19; 2:1—7). *Then* came the boasting: "Is not *this* great Babylon which *I* have built for the royal dwelling place by the might of *my* power and for the honour of *my* majesty?" (4:30 A.S.V.). This boasting sets self against God's "certain and sure" (2:45) prophecies for God puts Himself on the spot! *Then,* "While the words were still in the king's mouth. . ." (4:31 R.S.V.), the sentence fell: "the kingdom is departed from thee." The band of iron and brass which was placed around the tree stump (4:23) symbolizes the fear of Greece (brass) and Rome (iron) which kept the adversaries or enemies of Babylon (4:19) in check during the seven years of Nebuchadnezzar's insanity as he received God's protection. Any invasion of Babylon by the adversaries would have made them open to attack by Greece or Rome.

Then, "at the end of the days, I Nebuchadnezzar, lifted up mine eyes unto heaven, and mine understanding returned unto me, and I blessed the Most High . . . ." Nebuchadnezzar had seen the ages of the Four Empires but he had not understood, for they are spiritually discerned ages (Hebrews 11:3) which were unveiled through Daniel, God's prophet. We today must be careful to distinguish the "ages" that differ (Philippians 1:10). Note the time of the beginning of Nebuchadnezzar's spiritual victory (cp. vs. 34 with vs. 36): "at the same time my reason returned unto me." And now hear the great king's benediction to his chapter:

> "Now I Nebuchadnezzar praise and extol and honour the King of heaven, all whose works are truth, and His ways judgment: and those that walk in pride He is able to abase."

c) DANIEL, THE BASELINE OF HISTORY—THE FOUR EMPIRES[1]

The fourth and last book in each group of the prophets contains the *historic baseline.* Daniel, the Visioner, fits this portion for he deals with the development, or the rise and fall of nations down through history. It is the way that humanity has gone through from the beginning of their creation to the end of time. The rise of history is in the four great empires of which some is *apart* from God and some is *with* God; for the most part, it is a godless situation, but ends in the ultimate victory for God.

Daniel records the long road, the *baseline of empires,* the attempt of man to do the thing that only God can do; and thus there are four great nations which began with Babylon (Nineveh) and continued with Medo-Persia, Greece, and then Rome. All of these empires are under Satanic domination (Matthew 4:8—9; Luke 4:5—6). The historic baseline is the development of these world-ruling nations. Man's vital interest in these nations is indicated by his study of them to which the writing of histories attest. Nations go up and come down but always there is a continuing. Daniel is great because he gives the history of world-ruling nations from

---

[1] See Section FOUR, *Ibid.,* HIS Story, IV. The Four Empires, p. 210.

the very beginning to the end of all time, and through him we have expanded our horizon as the baseline across the centuries is foretold. Daniel deals with the way in which nations have organized themselves, and the way in which they undertook to do things and failed. It is *His Story* showing the marvel of God's redemptive power, for "who can bring a clean thing out of an unclean" (Job 14:4). We see forces at work through the Seventy Weeks, the Four Empires, and God's peculiar people, Israel.

d) DANIEL, THE BASELINE OF PROPHECY—
THE SEVENTY WEEKS

The transition from the *historical* to the *prophetical* baseline is so accurate that critics insist that it was written AFTER the events recorded,[1] not considering that it was contained in the Septuagint which was translated in the third century B.C., while Antiochus Epiphanes is dated 175—170 B.C. In the *Chaldaic* or Syriac language, chapter 2:4 to 7:28 (see Jeremiah 10:11), is recorded the *political course* of the world. In the *Hebrew* language in chapters 8 through 12 is the unfolding of *the plan of the ages, God's purpose.*

Daniel is the Alpha and the Omega, the foundation upon which rests all interpretation (Daniel 2:31—35; Acts 4:10—12). All of the prophets must be summoned up before Daniel. If they are passed here, they will be unchallenged anywhere; in like manner, all of the books of the New Testament must pass through the Gospels (John 14:6; Mark 4:13).

As the little lake at the foot of the Jungfrau of the Swiss Alps mirrors all—just so the book of Daniel nestles in the midst of the history of the nations and is the pre-history of God. Isaiah and the other prophets are clearly seen within the chapters of Daniel. Through this book the veil is taken away and we turn to God's message given through him (II Corinthians rinthians 3:14—16). This little volume of Daniel contains the whole and all other prophecy but elaborates. This is the structure, the rest merely enhances it to our good. The characters depicted and the presence of heaven's great, (Gabriel and Michael; 4:23; 8:26; 10:6, 13), show God's estimate of the events of *Daniel.* Dare we ignore? (Acts 10:15; Ezekiel 1:18). How can we be insensitive to these things? This is none other but the Book of God! Here men who are God-occupied are speaking! What set or series of books so vividly fixed so much of history as the Bible, and yet the Bible was not written as history (John 5:39).

(1) *Daniel's Seventy Weeks' Prophecy*

"Seventy weeks are decreed upon Thy people
and upon Thy holy city"

Daniel 9:24 A.S.V.

---

[1] *Ibid,* Prophyry, footnote 1, p. 32

Great events from God are before us; let us face them! They are embedded in the text of this book and Daniel records them as a printing press upon a roll of paper. Are men so indifferent to life and its future? Would a Creator of what we know is here, be unconcerned about their investment? Surely, He has a plan to "gather up the fragments in order that nothing be lost." We find here a people defiled by sin and a city polluted by idols (II Chronicles 28:19—25), and no other people had such depths and heights of experience.

Daniel, so greatly burdened for Israel, goes up to Jeremiah and upon reading the prophecy, is wrought up by his words (cp. Jeremiah 25:12—14 with 29:10—13), for this seventy years of captivity which he prophesies, is near an end and no one is concerned. Hear his words:

> "O Lord, hear; O Lord, forgive;
> O Lord, hearken and do; defer not, for Thine own sake,
> O my God:
>   for Thy city and Thy people are called by Thy name."
>
> Daniel 9:19

As Daniel prays, let us wait expectantly for this man who moves heaven:

> "And whiles I was speaking, and praying, and confessing my sin and the sin of my people Israel, and presenting my supplication before the Lord my God for the holy mountain of my God; Yea, while I was speaking in prayer, even the man Gabriel, whom I had seen in the vision at the beginning, being caused to fly swiftly, touched me about the time of the evening oblation. And he informed me, and talked with me, and said, 'O Daniel, I am now come forth to give thee skill and understanding. *At the beginning of thy supplications* the word came forth, and I am come to show thee; for thou art greatly beloved (desired): therefore understand the matter, and consider the vision."
>
> Daniel 9:20—23 N.

"SEVENTY WEEKS are . . .

Decreed":
  Literally this means:
  (1) To bring to a full stop, even as God stopped and rested in Genesis 2:1—3 (cp. Hebrews 4:4)
  (2) The purpose for which the seventy weeks are "decreed" is to introduce "A new heavens and a new earth wherein dwelleth righteousness" (II Peter 3:13). This is the full end, The Consummation, which is the acme of perfection at the end of the seventieth week.

Somewhere in the seventy weeks occur the six items of Daniel 9:24; they did not occur in the sixty-nine weeks that are past (Hebrews 2:8) and therefore they must all be related to the last week, the seventieth, and to it alone. The first two groups of weeks (the seven and the sixty-two weeks), run up to the Triumphal Entry, A.D. 30. In Daniel 9:26 we read:

> "After three score and two weeks shall Messiah be cut off,
> but not for Himself: and the people of the Prince that shall
> come shall destroy the city and the sanctuary";

Thus the king is crucified and the capital is destroyed *after* the sixty-ninth week.

The seventieth week must include all of these following six events:

"To finish (to complete or shut up, Revelation 20:10, 14) *THE Transgression."*

The following Scriptures suggest to us that *"the* transgression" is idolatry in its many different forms. The effect of it on Israel and the grief caused by it to God's prophets are in evidence throughout the Scriptures. See Daniel 8:12—14; Ezra 10:6; II Chronicles 28:22—25; Psalm 19:12—14; Isaiah 53:5. The burning of candles before saints today is no less a part of the great transgression of idolatry than these. Therefore the seventieth week cannot come to pass until all idolatry has been put away. The great cleansing of Israel in the seventieth week will include these things (Ezekiel 39:9).

"And to make an end (to seal up) *of sins."*

Though there is sin *after* the Kingdom Age (Revelation 20:7—9), there will be no more sin *after this seventieth week.*

"And to make reconciliation for iniquity."

This is to cover up, to atone. It occurs in the Kingdom Age (Hebrews 10:16) and God says, "their sins and iniquities I will remember no more forever" (Hebrews 10:17).

"And to bring in everlasting righteousness"

This is characterized completely in the Holy City (Revelation 21:1; Hebrews 11:10).

"And to seal up the vision and the prophecy" (Prophet)
(I Corinthians 13:8, 12).

"And to anoint the Most Holy" (the Holy of Holies).

This is the temple which Ezekiel saw in the twenty-fifth year of the captivity (Ezekiel chapters 40 through 46), and which will be built during the Kingdom Age (one thousand years) and anointed at its completion during the Seventieth Week.

The prophecy then recapitulates and to each is assigned a portion.

"Know therefore and discern that from the going forth of the commandment to restore and to build Jerusalem UNTO THE ANOINTED ONE, THE PRINCE shall be *seven weeks*. It shall be built again with street and moat even in troublous times."

All prophecy is of *sure events* (Genesis 3:15; Isaiah 53; Micah 5:2; Psalm 2:8); but the book of Daniel when it is fitted together, gives the *exact* timing. The three sections of these seventy weeks are: seven weeks; and three score and two weeks and one week; and are so plain that one can fit any prophecy into its proper place and it will be as accurate as a surveyor's chart. Many events fit the words of the seventy weeks' prophecy and their magnitude is global. Note carefully:

(a) In seven weeks, forty-nine years, the city is built or restored (see Ezra and Nehemiah)

(b) The sixty-two weeks (434 years) go to the Triumphal Entry of Jesus:
    i. The children and others said, "Hosannah"; and Jesus said, "Except ye become as little children"
    ii. The nation had been challenged to "Behold your God!" (Isaiah 35:4), but instead they said, "We will not have this man to reign over us" (Luke 19:14)
    iii. Note His words: "Ye shall not see Me henceforth till ye shall say, 'Blessed is He that cometh in the name of the Lord'." This has not yet been said by Israel. When He came at the Triumphal Entry, He rode upon the colt of an ass. When He comes again to Israel, He shall be upon a cloud.

"And after three score and two weeks"
(Up to the seventieth week we move with assurance for the landmarks are all fulfilled prophecy)

(a) "Shall Messiah, the anointed One, be cut off and shall have nothing" (A.D. 30); the Cross of Christ stands

(b) "And the people of the Prince that shall come, shall destroy the *city* and the *sanctuary*" (A.D. 70). That this has been done, makes these two facts indisputable. "And the end thereof shall be with a flood and even unto the end shall be war; desolations are determined" (9:26 A.S.V.). In Matthew 24:6 Jesus said, "And ye (Palestine) shall hear of wars and rumors of wars, See that ye be not troubled for all these things must come to pass, but the END is NOT YET." What more vivid description could be given of that land up to and including today?

(c) Daniel 9:27 N.: "He shall make a firm covenant with many for one week and in the midst of the week, He shall cause sacrifice and oblation to cease. And upon the wing of abominations shall come one that maketh desolate, and even unto the full end, and that determined, shall wrath be poured upon the desolator." God's avenging wrath is poured upon the desolator during this "Covenant week" of seven years.[1]

It is important to note that all of Daniel 9:24 happens in the last week. The seventieth week is the acme of the perfect (I Corinthians 13:10). It is the *Ultima Thule* of all revelation and of all prophecies and of all of God's love (Matthew 24:15–21; Daniel 9:24; II Thessalonians 2:5–8). As the Kleig lights are turned upon the Wrigley Building in Chicago, so the expectations of all the prophets are focussed toward this seventieth week; and the attitude of reverent modesty is the open sesame to "Mystery," especially to those who accept it as God's divine revelation. No Pilates may enter (John 18:38). One thing we know: that there are TWO parentheses within this prophecy, the Church Age and the Kingdom of Christ.[2] The use of parentheses in Scripture is not uncommon:

(a) The law of Moses was added (Galatians 3:19), and then taken away (Colossians 2:14)

(b) *Isaiah 61:1–3:*

There is a parenthesis between the "Year of Jehovah's favor," and the "Day of Vengeance of our God." Jesus noted this parenthesis when He read from Isaiah 61 in Luke 4:18–19; He omitted the latter half of verse 2

(c) *Joel 2:28–32a:*

This deals with Pentecost in part, but also includes events which are to be fulfilled beyond the parenthesis of the church, and these shall come to pass in verse 42*b*

(d) *Acts 2:34–35* and *2:19–21*

(e) *Acts 15:16–18*

The long and pregnant parenthesis between the sixty-ninth and the seventieth week (Matthew 24:15–31; Revelation 20:1–10, especially vss. 7–8), is broken by the events of Matthew 24. This set me to thinking while meditating upon the Old Testament prophets and I was compelled to raise

---

[1] See Section SIX, *The Kingdom Age,* II. The Tribulation, p. 551.

[2] There is no *word* in this prophecy *to* or *of* the Church, for the Church is not in the Old Testament or Covenant. The Church Age is from A.D. 30 to the Rapture and the Kingdom Age is from the Lord's Second Coming to earth following the rapture, and lasts one thousand years. Then follows the Seventieth Week. The Church and Kingdom Ages are both parentheses between the sixty-nine weeks and the Seventieth Week.

my sites for the Seventieth Week from Armageddon to Magog. My study
lifted the Seventieth Week *beyond Armageddon*, for Armageddon is not
mentioned by name in Old Testament prophecy. There is no place for it
in the sixty-nine weeks nor in the seventieth week, but there is a place
for it in Matthew 24:15—31, especially verse 21. For Israel was distinctly
told that they would not see Him again until they would say, "Blessed
is He that cometh in the Name of the Lord" (Matthew 23:39); and this will
be brought to pass by the "Great Tribulation," "and after that" comes the
thousand years, with the rod-of-iron-reign by Christ. There will be no
"everlasting righteousness" until the end of the thousand years when
Satan is cast into the Lake of Fire. Then can begin the Seventieth Week
and "Everlasting Righteousness." In Malachi 3:1*b* we read:

> "And the Lord, whom ye seek, shall suddenly come to His temple,
> Even the messenger of the covenant, whom ye delight in;
> Behold, He shall come, saith the Lord of Hosts."

Here reference is to the Parousia, the second coming to earth, and
does not refer to the Seventieth Week. This requires verification which
easily and convincingly is at hand once the difficulty is confronted and
interest is aroused. Who could be indifferent before God's attempt at His
most important revelation?

"To the Law and to the Testimony. If they speak not according to
this word, *surely* there is no morning for them" (see Isaiah 8:20; 21:11).
And surely none are so indifferent as not to hear in the presence of such
a world condition and such a mental confusion. Especially also, in the
presence of the Bible's accuracy and Its winnowed morality which has
outridden all storms both mental and sensual, and has never needed to
apologize nor recede; nor has It ever been successfully contradicted, but
silently, even as Christ before Pilate, and as majestic before all other
books, this Book still asserts "Heaven and earth shall pass away but
My words shall in no wise pass away" (Matthew 24:35 N.). The earthly
Messiah faded from earth's view at the ascension; libraries crumble and
fade away into dust (Ecclesiastes 12:12), but HIS WORD never.

> "The grass withereth, the flower fadeth:
> But the word of our God shall stand for ever."
>
> Isaiah 40:8

Even as "The Mystery" (the "Joint Body" in the New Testament) is
NOT revealed in the Old Testament—so the Seventieth Week is nowhere
revealed more so than here in Daniel 9, for it is not even spoken of elsewhere in the Old or New Testaments. Although other prophets (Isaiah,
Jeremiah, Ezekiel and others) refer to incidents occurring within the Seventieth Week, yet there is but one clear sign given and that is through Daniel.
Even as to Paul alone was given the understanding of the events occurring

at the rapture of the Church, just so here in Daniel 9:24, to Daniel is given the details of the Seventieth Week. These details mark the Seventieth Week as Post-Millennium, and it is:

"That far off divine event to which all creation moves."

The careful reading of *Ezekiel*, chapters 36 through 39; of *Zechariah*, chapters 9:12 through 14:21; of *Matthew* 24:15 through verse 31; and of *Revelation* 20:6—9, will take us through the Millennium and the judgment on Gog and Magog at the end of the thousand years. These above passages have been chosen from many to show how long it is from the rejection of the Messiah (A.D. 30) to Armageddon, (the beginning of the Kingdom Age), and then from Armageddon to Magog (one thousand years); *after which* follows the Seventieth Week.

(2) *The Church's Telescopic View of Israel's Seventy Weeks*

"Seventy weeks are determined upon Thy people and upon Thy holy city"

Though the *fulfillment* of this is limited to the *Jews* and *Jerusalem*, yet this is for *our admonition* upon whom the ends of the Ages are come (I Corinthians 10:11). Christians in Jerusalem escaped the destruction in A.D. 70 because they knew how to discern the signs of the times. When John states in Revelation 6:1, "I saw," he is saying that it is the church that sees (Revelation 21:2). As a traveler notes signs on a journey, warning him to "Watch," so the church has a preview of *end time events* which were denied even to Daniel (Daniel 12:9—10), and we are urged to "Watch," for the sealed book of prophecy has been opened by the Son of God (Revelation 5:5). Let us *also* emphasize that the church is shown signs for which they are to watch as the Day of the Lord approaches, and then we are also given a revelation of the events *during* the Day of the Lord (one thousand years) that lead up to the Seventieth Week. As we see these signs of the approaching "Day" coming to pass before our eyes, then we note the progress toward that event for which all of the ages have been waiting.

The events of the Sixty-Nine Weeks (of years) include:

    (a) "*Restore* and *build* Jerusalem" (Daniel 9:25)
    (b) "Until Messiah, The Prince" (Daniel 9:25)
    (c) "AFTER (Daniel 9:26) Sixty-nine weeks":
       i) Messiah shall be cut off
      ii) The city and sanctuary shall be destroyed;
          These were destroyed by Titus A.D. 70; and
          there has been no temple since A.D. 70.
      iii) He (the prince) shall confirm a covenant for
          one week (Daniel 9:27)
          During this " Covenant Week," these occur:

(aa) "In the midst of the week" (three and
one-half years)

(bb) "He (the desolator-Anti-Christ) shall cause
My sacrifice and oblation to cease"

(cc) "He (Christ) shall make desolate" (Daniel 9:27*b*)

(dd) "Even until the Consummation . . .
upon the desolator."

Leading up to Armageddon there will be:

(a) A Mandatory covenant

(b) A Psuedo peace (Daniel 11:27)

(c) Desecration of the new temple in Jerusalem

(d) Israel resists the desecration of the temple
which brings on the war resulting in Armageddon
(Matthew 24:21)

(e) The Messiah comes and sets up His Kingdom
(Revelation 19:11; Daniel 7:13—14)

  i) The destruction of world empires is at Armageddon.
The Stone smites the image of the Four Empires in
the feet, destroying it; and grows into a Mountain
(Kingdom) which fills the whole world (Daniel 2:34, 44—45)

  ii) " And I saw another angel fly in mid-heaven having the everlasting Gospel to preach unto them that dwell on the earth
and to every nation and kindred and tongue and people"
(Revelation 14:6). Here we find God's over-all mercy as a
judgment on the nations is announced (Revelation 14:7),
and as Israel is brought back again to the Holy land

  iii) The one thousand years' reign of Christ extends from
Armageddon to Magog which is followed by the Seventieth Week

   (aa) At the beginning of the thousand years, Satan is bound
and cast into the bottomless pit (Revelation 20:1—3)

   (bb) The Kingdom of Christ increases (Daniel 2:35)

   (cc) The temple revealed through Ezekiel is begun and the Lord
dwells within it in Jerusalem and reigns on His throne
(Ezekiel 43)

   (dd) Israel evangelizes (there are some who will need to be
evangelized; Revelation 14:7; Zechariah 8:20—23)
Then after the thousand years are ended, Satan is loosed
for a season and Magog, a world rebellion, begins with the
mightiest army ever mobilized, *but they never fight a battle!*
The victory of the Lord over this army is seen in Revelation
20:9 and Zechariah 14:12 (cp. Isaiah 37:36)

   (ff) Ezekiel 39:9 occurs AFTER Magog and lasts "One week"

or seven years. During this time, Israel is cleansing the land, and the Messiah is cleansing the people. These seven years (The Seventieth Week) are being used to bring to conclusion the Seventy Weeks' prophecy which was "decreed" upon Daniel's people.

The Seventieth Week *could not occur anywhere else,* and *nowhere* in the Scriptures or in the plan of the ages are the six events of Daniel 9:24 possible *until* we reach this point of the Lord's victory over Magog at the end of the thousand years.

(3) Distinguishing The Things That Differ (Philippians 1:10)
    The Seventieth Week:

(a) Applies to Israel, for it is "upon *Thy people*" and therefore it it cannot apply to the church age.

(b) Does not occur during the thousand years Kingdom reign of Christ

 i) During the Kingdom, the Lord reigns with an iron sceptre, but the Kingdom Age ends in a great *rebellion* (Magog); while the seventieth week ends in *perfection* (Day of God—Omega)

 ii) The Stone of Daniel 2:35:
 "became a great mountain and filled the whole earth." This occurs *during* the thousand years reign. Though Christ Himself is perfect, yet not till His Kingdom is world-wide can He bring in Everlasting Righteousness, bringing forth fruit after its kind; and perfection is not indicated in the Scriptures until the end of the thousand years; this will introduce the Seventieth Week

(c) Is a Mystery even as the Church, for it is beyond the experience of even good men

(d) "Decreed" in Daniel 9:24 is in contrast to the Covenant Week in that the latter comes at a time of war and overspreading abominations, while the Seventieth Week brings in Everlasting Righteousness.
    The Covenant Week is *"confirmed"* whereas The Seventieth Week is *"determined"* or *"decreed."*

CONCLUSION: The End (*Telos*) of the Seventy Weeks' Vision

Daniel's Seventieth Week is the first ecstatic and rapturous view of Palin-Genesis when the cleansed heaven and earth and the New Jerusalem are opened for occupancy. This is the archipelago of Palin-Genesis into "The Age (of all) the Ages." The time is immediately following the Judgment of fire upon Gog and Magog (Revelation 20:9). This is the week, the Seventieth, of Ezekiel 29:9 and Daniel 9:24. Then follows the Consummation, Omega, when God again enters into His rest (Genesis 2:2).

Still is the admonition to the Church: "WATCH"

B. INTRODUCTION to SECOND GROUP—HOSEA through OBADIAH

The second division of books include HOSEA, JOEL, AMOS and OBADIAH. This group is "to the Jew first" for "the chosen people' are a peculiar people when in relation to Jehovah's purpose (Exodus 9:16; Isaiah 43: Ephesians 3:8—12; II Thessalonians 1:7—12), and herein is the winning back of the lost radiance of God's presence with His people (Ezekiel 1:27—28; 8:3—4; 8:12; 9:3—4, 18—19*a*; 11:23; 43:1—5; Psalm 67:1—2).

These books take up the Jew in his adulterous separation from God, his Father, but also show God's indefectible love and this second group becomes the "John 3:16—God is love."

The departure of "The Glory of God" from Israel is earth's greatest tragedy—a blind Samson pulling down the foundations of society. The most brilliantly gifted race of all time is busy at debasing schools, pleasures, and holy days. The nation is like a Rembrandt in a junk shop. Israel is as an adulterous cast-off wife. The departure was in FACT:

a) The crucifixion and the veil rent (Matthew 27:35, 51)

b) Acts 28:23—29; 26th vs.: ". . . 'Go unto this people and say, Hearing ye shall hear, and shall in no wise understand; And seeing ye shall see, and in no wise perceive'"

c) The destruction of Jerusalem, A.D. 70, which lasts until their return when they shall say, ". . . blessed is He that cometh in the name of the Lord' (Matthew 23:39).

1. THE PROPHECY OF HOSEA

"For the children of Israel shall abide many days without a king (Hosea 10:3; John 19:15), and without a prince, and without a sacrifice, and without an image, and without an ephod, and without teraphim: *Afterward* shall the children of Israel return, and seek the Lord their God, and David their king; and shall fear the Lord and his goodness in the latter days."

Hosea 3:4—5 (cp. Matthew 23:39)

Hosea is as Lot in Sodom and Jesus in Nazareth. Hosea is the heavy hearted replica (model) of God, proof of the indefectible love of God. When the Church loves as Hosea, God will be compelled to work. Hosea's book reveals a will which is reflected in his great heart, his set face and his endurance. To such God entrusts His burdens.

This is the story of the prophet who was told by God to become the lover and husband of an adulterous woman; and Hosea was taken up into heart-breaking fellowship with God so that God could deliver His Own message to the prophet, even as our Savior did in Luke 22:44, when He became sin for us. Thus Hosea becomes a type of national Israel.

His prophecy pictures Israel as the adulterous wife whom a great prevailing love would not let go. The redemptive power of God's love was set out in the prophet's domestic life. We see in this book the Jew in sin (3:1 and 1:10) and the end of all unredeemed sinners (Revelation 20:15). Hosea joined with God in suffering as must all fellow-workers with God. Like unto Jeremiah, Hosea has "sorrow like unto my sorrow." He is called to share God's sorrow and only such a love-experience can understand.

Through Hosea, God says:

"I will go and return to My place,
Till they acknowledge their offences and seek My face
In their affliction, they will earnestly seek Me."

Hosea 5:15

2. THE PROPHECY OF JOEL (Jehovah is God)

"Blow ye the trumpet in Zion,
And sound an alarm in My holy mountain:
Let all the inhabitants of the land tremble:
For the day of Jehovah cometh, for it is nigh at hand;"

Joel 2:2N.

Joel is the rhythmic beauty poet of the out-of-doors; he is the oldest of the prophets; his book contains 73 verses, 27 of which are recorded by eight of the other prophets. Joel's voice rises above the local horizon to Pentecost and Revelation. It is "the Day of Jehovah" (1:15; 2:11; 3:14), and the setting is THE plague of locusts, a calamity of vast proportions, ranking with World War II, where civilization was destroyed, none were spared, and houses were despoiled. He calls upon the aged men to search the past for comparison; then he urges the children to tell their children; and then to pass it on.

This is the beginning of the prophetic:

"And ye shall know that I am in the midst of Israel,
And that I am the Lord your God, and none else;
And My people shall never be ashamed."

Joel 2:27

This is beyond the horizon, "And it shall come to pass AFTERWARD" (2:28). There is a gap from Pentecost to the Last Days as here shown in the history of Israel to the coming of Christ. On Pentecost, their sons and daughters prophesy. Pentecost was to Israel *only*, and the Acts of the Apostles were to Israel *first* (Acts 2:16). Note again in *Acts*: "Ye men of Judea" (2:14); "ye men of Israel (2:22); and then "let ALL the house of Israel"(2:36). There were no others and they were undone at the Crucifixion; they were *A-Theos* and now Acts 2:40 warns: "Save yourselves from this untoward generation." At the Crucifixion the Jews' clock stopped and time ceased as one who is sleeping, notes not the passage of time . . . till they return to the land.

And now the close of the gap "in the last days," old men shall dream dreams, young men see visions. The picture is from dreams of the past to visions of the future (Ezra 8:12; Haggai 2:1–9, and including Luke 1:17), "blood, fire, pillars of smoke." Even then, "Whosoever shall call upon the Name of the Lord shall be saved."

> "Proclaim ye this among the Gentiles;
> Prepare war, make up the mighty men,
> Let all the men of war draw near;
> Let them come up;
> Beat your ploughshares into swords,
> And your pruninghooks into spears;
> Let the weak say, I am strong."

Joel's revelation is of the last days of this present age, the times of the Gentiles, and it includes the battle of Armageddon, the restoration of the nation of Israel, and the establishing of the Kingdom. Joel, one of the first of the prophets who wrote, sees beyond the earlier events of the Kingdom to the Consummation of all things.

In *Joel* note the frequent phrase, "In the last days" and this takes in the purifying fire of "that great and notable day of the Lord." Through the understanding of these things, there is lifting vision and so we have patience.

The prophecy closes with, "I will sit in judgment" (cp. Matthew 25:31) upon "multitudes, multitudes in the valley of decision" (Joel 3:14). These are those who have maltreated Israel; and, as Israel, "They shall look upon Him whom they pierced." Then is fulfilled Amos 9:11–15 when "the plowman shall overtake the reaper."

E. THE PROPHECY OF AMOS

> "Then answered Amos, and said to Amaziah,
> 'I was no prophet, neither was I a prophet's son;
> but I was a herdman, and a gatherer of sycomore fruit;
> And Jehovah took me as I followed the flock, and Jehovah
> said unto me, 'Go, prophesy unto My people Israel'.
> Now therefore hear thou the word of Jehovah:"
>
> Amos 7:14–16*a*

Amos is the Gospel of the regathering.

After warning Israel in chapter 6:2, "Woe to them that are at ease in Zion, . . .," he prophesies in 7:17*b*: ". . . and Israel shall surely go into captivity forth of his land." But his finale "regathering" is in chapter 9:9*ff* as he closes:

> "For lo, I will command, and I will sift the house of Israel
> among *all* nations, like as corn is sifted in a sieve, yet shall

not the least grain fall upon the earth." (And compare Revelation 20:15; Isaiah 27:12; Deuteronomy 28:64; Ezekiel 37:11;
12:15).

"All the sinners of my people shall die by the sword, which
say, The evil shall not overtake nor prevent us. In that day
will I raise up the *tabernacle of David* that is fallen, and
close up the breaches thereof; and I will raise up his ruins,
and I will build it as in the days of old: That they may possess the remnant of Edom, and of all the heathen which are
called by my name, saith the Lord that doeth this. Behold,
the days come, saith the Lord, that the plowman shall overtake the reaper, and the treader of grapes him that soweth
seed; and the mountains shall drop sweet wine, and all the
hills shall melt. And I will bring again the captivity of my
people of Israel, and they shall build the waste cities, and
inhabit them; and they shall plant vineyards, and drink the
wine thereof; they shall also make gardens, and eat the fruit
of them. And *I will plant them upon their land, and they shall
no more be pulled up out of their land* which I have given them,
saith the Lord thy God."

4. THE PROPHECY OF OBADIAH

"The pride of thine heart hath deceived thee, thou that dwellest
in the clefts of the rock, whose habitation is high; that saith
in his heart, Who shall bring *me* down to the ground? Though
thou exalt thyself as the eagle, and though thou set thy nest
among the stars, thence will *I* bring thee down, saith the Lord."

Obadiah 1:3—4

Obadiah has words of warning for Edom for sin against Jacob. Here
again is the historic base line, "so perish all enemies" under God's vengeance. Esau has been reaping during the times of the Gentiles while
Jerusalem is trodden under foot of the Gentiles till her enemies are destroyed.

The enemies of Jacob are warned concerning "the day of the Lord,"
and that "though thou set thy nest among the stars, thence will I bring
thee down." Herein must have been the boast of the city of "Petra" and
to this ruined city uncovered by the archaeologists might well be applied
the lines: "Lo, all our pomp of yesterday
                 Is one with Nineveh and Tyre!"

The book closes with the final victory of the Lord,

"And the kingdom shall be the Lord's."

C. INTRODUCTION TO THE THIRD GROUP: JONAH to HABAKKUK

The third group of prophets is JONAH, MICAH, NAHUM, and HA-
BAKKUK, and these are "to the Greek also" and deal with lapsed but

prosperous Gentiles. The Isaiah group contained the universal gospel and the next group beginning with *Hosea* is "to the Jew first"; and now this group beginning with *Jonah* is "also to the Greek," and announces the doom of idolators, "The Twilight of the Gods."

The Greek language shares with the Hebrew the immortal glory of introducing "The Mind of God to the heart of man." To Nineveh the proto-type of rebels, the God, whose nature is love (I John 4:16), insists upon sending even a reluctant and sulking prophet with His amnesty (Acts 11:18) and, as seems His custom, God's amnesty is presented through four pro-phets, Jonah, Micah, Nahum and also Habakkuk. This last of the four is the historical base line of this group.

Athens was the greatest intellectual center in its time and in the age of these prophets its Greek influence had reached out even to these nations and Nineveh where Jonah was sent.

1. THE PROPHECY OF JONAH
"Yet forty days and Nineveh shall be overthrown."

Jonah 3:4*b*

"The people that walked in darkness have seen a great light: they that dwell in the land of the shadow of death, upon them hath the light shined."

Isaiah 9:2 (cp. Matthew 4:13—15)

The third group begins with Jonah a prophet from the Jewish nation who knew God and who was sent to Gentiles, for both Jew and Gentile have fallen short of the glory of God (Romans 3:23). Both the Jew and Gentile world of Jonah's time had gone into idolatry and it was evident everywhere, but within the hearts of the men of the nations, there was still this hope, "the desire of all nations shall come."

Jonah is the only Bible writer who continuously put himself in a bad light. The Master's use of him with His own resurrection makes the intui-tive unbelief of the book understandable, for His resurrection is now also explained away. Jonah's historicity can be maintained.

Tobit of the Apocryphal book (Tobit 14:4) made a dying request of his son: "Go into Media my son, for I surely believe those things which *Jonas the prophet* spoke of Nineveh, that it shall be overthrown . . . ." His re-quest was obeyed and Tobit lived to see Nineveh destroyed (14:15).

Jonah, the prophet of the Lord, prophesied in the days of Uzziah, king over Judah, and Jeroboam II, king over Israel; and his relationship to these two kings might well be compared to Christ Himself before Pilate and Herod. Both Jonah and Christ ministered to Israel in peace times and lived in very similar settings. First consider the historical setting for Jonah: the date was about 800 B.C.; Uzziah, king of Judah, was the Teddy Roosevelt of that day; and Jeroboam II, king of Israel, was as the

Kaiser Wilhelm of his day; this is the most martially glorious period of Israel's history. These double *suns* (Uzziah and Jereboam II) swung around the prophets of God and are recorded among the *kings* but are not in the book of Chronicles which are the *priestly* writings. This in itself is most significant.

Next let us consider the man himself. At the heart of any great event is God's man. Isaiah was converted at the death of Uzziah, but it was Jonah who helped to make Uzziah. In the 53rd chapter of Isaiah is predicted the suffering of Christ, and the book of Jonah foreshadows the Lord's resurrection. These are both of one piece and they are fragments of the eternal. As Elijah swayed Ahab, Jonah swayed Jeroboam. John the Baptist, like these, preached to Herod. The trumpets of the Lord stabbed the supine tranquility of kings and nations! Here in *Jonah* is no single-barreled, one-cartridge derringer, but a "Big Bertha." This is not a Billy Sunday breaking chairs; but it is a Martin Luther moulding a nation. Jonah wrought enlargement in his King; and repentance in Nineveh and its king without a press agent! He was no peeved shrimp such as Balaam, else God would not have tolerated him, but he was an heroic patriot ready to die for his nation. Syria had been beaten to the earth by Assyria; both were exhausted by the effort and were as game cocks, dying and bled white. Jonah saw the opportunity and urged Jeroboam to the enlargement of their sea coast facilities, and soon commerce and industries developed, flooding gold into the nation, but only into the pockets of the few to the prophet's own chagrin. Then comes the shock out of the blue, and God said to Jonah:

> "Arise, go to Nineveh, that great city, and
> cry against it;
> for their wickedness is come up before me."

Jonah 1:2

The unexpected surely happened to Jonah. He is sent to Nineveh, the capital of the enemy against whom he had urged, and now he is to evangelize them! *They* were ready, but the prophet was not; yet isn't that the way? Here a worldly repentance was produced in Nineveh by an unrepentant preacher (1:14 cp. Romans 10:12). The Gentiles were reprieved at Nineveh and the just were reconciled to Habakkuk (1:5; 2:4) and Zechariah (2:11). Jonah was the rebellious prophet who resented the ravages of his own nation. Yet Jonah became the greatest evangelist of all time. He converted sailors and a city. The sailors at first were skeptics (1:10) but they were noble (1:13); and also they were reverent (1:14); and in 1:16 we find that they were converted. Nineveh became a whole city in sackcloth. God knows when to commission His men, and so Matthew 28:19 comes "in the fulness of time." Gospelizers know what Jonah knew:

". . . for I knew that THOU art a gracious God, and merciful,
slow to anger, and of great kindness, and repentest Thee of
the evil."

Jonah 4:2b

They knew the God back of the order to "go, teach, baptize, . . ." for He
is "The Lord working with them" (Mark 16:20), and God wanted Nineveh
evangelized. I wonder if we have not been stubborn in our time? The repentance of Nineveh reveals the value of positive preaching in Jonah's
day and in the whole world in this age.

We read, "he (Jonah) rose to . . . flee." Here is a real tragedy for he
is fleeing "from the presence of the Lord." Some say that he was afraid
of the city, or that he disliked the Gentiles. These motives are not sufficient! Here is a renunciation exceeded only by One other, even Jesus
"bearing His Cross, He went forth" in renunciation for US. Cain (Genesis
4:16) and Satan (Job 1:12) both "went out from the presence of the Lord"
but for *themselves*; Jonah and Paul (Romans 9:3) were willing to go out
"from the presence of the Lord" for *others* ("their kinsmen according to the
flesh"); with eyes open they too chose, even as Adam chose Eve. Jonah
knew that Nineveh would repent and that God would pardon (4:2) as did
also David (Psalm 86:5), and Hosea (11:8—9), and Joel (2:13) and Micah
(7:18); but if Jonah failed God, he knew that he might frustrate the plans
of God, even though it meant infinite personal loss to himself. Maybe there
would be infinite national gain for Israel. Nevertheless he tried to frustrate
God at a terrible cost to Himself. He was ASLEEP for SORROW like the
sleeping disciples of Luke 22:45. Jonah took a ship and God hurled a wind
upon it, and then was Psalm 139:5 proven:

> "Thou hast beset me behind and before,
> And laid Thine hand upon me."

God's presence was sensed by the sailors, the nation, and the Ninevites. Here is a man upon whom rests down the Spirit of God; for though
he is wrong, he is Godlike in it for he has no selfish ends. Now we understand his lack of pity for the city of Nineveh. Nineveh's salvation would be
Israel's loss, and, "having loved *His own*, He loved them to the end." What
matters if they are not worthy; Love is measured by the Lover, and not by
the object of it. Has any people ever been so loved (or so hated as Israel)?

Jonah was a "foreign missionary" in thought and desire, passion and
prejudice. The repentance of the city meant death to his people and so,
hardened under this burden, he went through the city but would not retrace
his steps even to be nearer his own. Their sack cloth was an abomination
to him and brought no pride even of his successful preaching. His anger
is of one who feels that God has failed His own.

There were two men in the Scriptures who said, "I knew Thee"; one,
the unprofitable servant of Matthew 25:24, said, "Lord, I knew thee, that

thou art a hard man reaping where thou hast not sown and gathering where
thou hast not strawed." And the second is Jonah who said, "THOU art
gracious . . ." (Jonah 4:2). The first man was given a responsibility but
he kept his talent and disobeyed his lord. The second, though reluctant,
still obeyed for he knew what the result would be because of the character
and gracious mercy of God. This is the crux of the whole account of Jonah
and when once it is apprehended, it takes Jonah away from the sneer and
joke, and puts him among those "of whom the world is not worthy." We
would as soon joke of the Cross of Christ, for Jonah is the Lord's fellow-
yokeman whom the Master deliberately chose (Matthew 12:38—41). Jonah
and Jude are as the cherubim over the Mercy Seat of His blood where atonement is made for sin. The blind world is now vomiting Jews again on the
Homeland.

The city of Nineveh to which Jonah preached had not as yet adopted
the Greek tongue but with the conquests of Alexander, these same peoples
adopted the Greek language and culture and it was to these that the messages of these prophets were delivered.

The prophecy of Jonah closes with these words of God:

> "And should not I spare Nineveh, that great city, wherein
> are more than sixscore thousand persons (babies) that can-
> not discern between their right hand and their left hand; and
> also much cattle?"

> *"Oh, love that wilt not let me go."*

2. THE PROPHECY OF MICAH

> "But in the last days it shall come to pass, that the mountain
> of the house of Jehovah shall be established in the top of
> the mountains, And it shall be exalted above the hills; And
> peoples shall flow unto it."

Micah 4:1 N.

Micah like Amos in Group Two and Zechariah in Group Four, continues
the Gospel of the regathering and reveals the eventual glory which is to be
Israel's. In Micah 1:12 we read, "But evil came down from the Lord unto
the *gate* of Jerusalem" (and no further) (cp. vs. 9 also). This evil came
through Lachish whom Micah describes by saying, "she is the beginning
of sin to the daughter of Zion and the transgressions of Israel were found
in thee" (Micah 1:13, cp. II Kings chaps. 18 and 19; Isaiah 37:14—37).
Lachish gave hospitality to Sennacherib and his army. The army was destroyed at the gate of Jerusalem but Sennacherib returned to his capital
in Nineveh where he died at the hand of his sons.

Micah's prophecy for Israel was also directed to the well-to-do social
leaders who were heedless, selfish and covetous. Micah exhorts them and
says in 2:10: "Arise ye, and depart: for this is not your rest: because it is

polluted, it shall destroy you, even with a sore destruction.*" But though they were warned to arise and depart, yet he gives to them the promise of verse 12, "I will surely assemble, O Jacob, all of thee; I will surely gather the remnant of Israel; . . . ."

Two things are prophesied:

1. Zion shall become a plowed field (3:12)—
   and it remains so even today
2. Armageddon, the gathering of the nations
   to destroy Israel (4:11).

The result of Armageddon is in chapter 4:3:

"And he shall judge among many people, and rebuke strong nations afar off; and they shall beat their swords into plowshares, and their spears into pruninghooks; nation shall not lift up a sword against nation, neither shall they learn war any more.*"

How is this to be done? —Micah 5:2:

"But thou, Bethlehem Ephratah, though thou be little among the thousands of Judah, yet out of thee shall He come forth unto Me that is to be ruler in Israel; whose goings forth have been from of old, from everlasting."

The ruler in Israel (Jesus) will bring to pass judgment for this is the post-Armageddon text, the John 3:16 for Israel.

In Micah 7:16—20 he describes the nations coming before the Lord as:

"They shall lick the dust like a serpent, they shall move out of their holes like worms of the earth: they shall be afraid of the Lord our God, and shall fear because of Thee."

Rightly dividing of the Scriptures will prevent us from misusing them. There are those who have quoted Micah 6:8 to excuse their lack of faithfulness at the Lord's Table or in other relationships to the Church. We must always note the purpose and the age in which each Scripture is given. Another illustration might be used in Micah 4:3 compared with Joel 3:10. Some would use wrath or fear to produce repentance but II Corinthians 7:10 tells us, ". . . for Godly sorrow worketh repentance to salvation not to be repented of.*"

3. THE PROPHECY OF NAHUM

"The Lord is good, a strong hold in the day of trouble; and he knoweth them that trust in him, but with an ever-running flood he will make an *utter end* of the place thereof, and darkness shall pursue his enemies.'

Nahum 1:7—8

Now we go back to Nineveh with Nahum. A hundred years before, through the preaching of Jonah, the city and king had turned to God (Jonah 3:3—10), but now it had apostasized and was "drunk with the sight of power."

The moral description of Nineveh can be found in Romans 1:21—23:

> "Because that, when they knew God, they glorified him not as God, neither were thankful; but became vain in their imaginations, and their foolish heart was darkened. Professing themselves to be wise, they became fools. And changed the glory of the uncorruptible God into an image made like to corruptible man, and to birds, and fourfooted beasts, and to creeping things."

The bull god was the chief deity of Nineveh. It had the face of a man and the wings of a bird and fits the description by Paul as "an image made like to corruptible man, and to birds, and fourfooted beasts and creeping things."

Nahum's prophecy which came about one hundred years before Nineveh was destroyed, is a warning of judgment rather than a call to the city to repent (cp. vss. 1:8—9; I Samuel 26:8). The complete destruction of Nineveh and its power, is attested to by history and archaeology. Two hundred years after the destruction of Nineveh, Xenophon passed by and thought the mounds of Nineveh were the ruins of some Parthian city. In 331 B.C. Alexander the Great fought the battle of Arbela near the site of Nineveh, and he did not know there had ever been a city there. It has never been rebuilt and the judgment of God still stands which was pronounced by Nahum seven hundred years before Christ,—"He will make an utter end" (Nahum 1:8—9). "Ichabod" might well be written over this city which Nimrod builded from whom the glory has departed even as it shall also be written of the nations in the judgment at the beginning of the Kingdom Age (Revelation 19:11—16).

Again the lines of Kipling's *Recessional* re-echo:

> Lo, all our pomp of yesterday
> Is one with Nineveh and Tyre!
> Judge of the Nations, spare us yet,
> Lest *we* forget — lest *we* forget!

4. THE PROPHECY OF HABAKKUK

> "For the earth shall be filled with the knowledge of the glory of the Lord, as the waters cover the sea."
>
> Habakkuk 2:14

We come to another fourth in the group of prophets and so to another base line. Habakkuk is praying through the chapel along the way and his prophecy includes the course and end of the nations and the problem he faces as he speaks for God is seen in chapters 1:1—4; 2:1—3; and 3:1—2 (cp. Romans 3:23; I John 5:19; Psalm 14:3). The question arises: "Is God just? What shall we choose to do?" And the prophet answers for himself in chapter 2:1:

> "I will stand upon my watch, and set me upon the tower,
> and will watch ("look out" N.) to see what He will say
> unto me, and what I shall answer when I am reproved."

He waits expectantly for the Lord's answer and it comes. He was as confused as Jonah. But the perplexed prophet prayed through as he sought the solution by prayer.

Like tall pine trees upon a mountain side which the poet has called *The Harps of God*, making music as the winds surge through them; so the Harps of God, the prophets, were moved to music by the storms of baffling calamaties.

Isaiah wrote, "In the year that King Uzziah died . . . ." This was at the time that Josiah was passing and Jehoiakim was coming upon the scene. The music of his prophecy partially arises out of the problems he faced in his day.

And now we come to Habakkuk, this sensitive lad of clinging embrace, a poet whom discord hurt as a lash on quivering flesh. Sin broke his heart and tore him from the embrace of God for a bit. Then separating himself, he resolves, "I will set me upon my watchtower, (my look-out) which became his Holy of Holies; and as Jehovah speaks, he is "in the secret of His Presence." See his sensitiveness and his painfulness as he writes, "The burden I did SEE" (1:1). Here is another Jonah or a Jeremiah in tears! The heathen-brutishness was triumphant in those days (1:2—4) with "Right forever on the scaffold, Wrong forever on the throne." And Habakkuk is concerned that God does not seem to hear. But God tells him that the Chaldeans shall be cut off through their atheistic pride (vs. 5 ff.). Habakkuk cannot see how, so he resolves to pray, and God speaks to him further and gives him the vision of the first chapter. How prayer clarifies! How much would be corrected if *we* prayed! Consider this young, poetic, diffident prophet at prayer (James 3:5). Like mothers of great men who though themselves un-noted, were yet much in prayer; so this boy-prophet "climbing altar stairs up to God" will bring back a message whose trumpet-tones will call Luther from Rome's "Via Scala"[1] to Habakkuk's "hidden way." Luther also ascended a watch tower, and this German monk made Rome tremble and put to work faith in God. Habakkuk said, "I will set me upon my watch tower" ("fortress" A.S.V.), and Luther moved by Habakkuk's

---

[1] *Via Scala* refers to the *Scala Sancta* (*The Holy Stairs* of 28 white marble steps) to the church of Saint Salvatore, Rome, near Lateran. According to tradition, the staircase leading once to the praetorium of Pilate at Jerusalem, hence sanctified by our Lord during His Passion. Historians relate that the Holy Stairs were brought from Jerusalem to Rome about 326 by St. Helena, mother of Constantine the Great. (*The Catholic Encyclopedia*, Vol. 13, p. 505).

vision wrote, "A Mighty Fortress is our God." In a lesser way, but to us equally vital, may the grasping of this text come to us today, "The just shall live by faith."

His prophecy closes with:

> "The Lord God is my strength, and he will make my feet like
> hinds' feet, and he will make me to walk upon mine high
> places. To the chief singer on my stringed instruments."

D. INTRODUCTION TO THE FOURTH GROUP OF PROPHETS: ZEPHANIAH to MALACHI

The fourth and final group of the Minor Prophets contain the books of ZEPHANIAH, HAGGAI, ZECHARIAH and MALACHI; and this last book of the four is concerned with great expectations of the TWO Comings of Jesus. Both Jew and Gentile in minor-key words utter their cry of defeat (Romans 3:24; Haggai 2:7; I John 5:10). Those were dark days and sad times but their messages set to music in the minor key, are "the songs of Zion":

> "By the rivers of Babylon, there we sat down,
> Yea, we wept, when we remembered Zion.
> We hanged our harps upon willows in the midst thereof.
> For there they that carried us away captive required
>   of us the words of a song;
> And they that wasted us required of us mirth,
> Saying, 'Sing us of the songs of Zion.'
> How shall we sing the Lord's song on a stranger's ground?
> If I forget thee, O Jerusalem, let my right hand forget
>   her cunning.
> If I do not remember thee, let my tongue cleave to the roof
>   of my mouth;
> If I prefer not Jerusalem above my chief joy."

Psalm 137:1—6 N.

These four books contain the prophecies of Him Who is to come, "The desire of all nations" (Haggai 2:7), and they include the "latter glory" of Jehovah's universal reign and the *two comings* of Jesus to the defeated. This is the voice of the "feelers after God" (Acts 13:47), the common voice of Jews and Greeks. This section is the literary forerunner of the Gospels as was John the Baptist of Jesus. The seed of the great hope planted at the beginning of prophecy (Isaiah 9:6) fructifying through *Hosea* to *Obadiah* ("to the Jew first"), and from *Jonah* to *Habakkuk* ("also to the Greek"), is united in the world's desire; all men are in expectancy. Heaven has loosed "His star in the East." The "family" genealogical tree of Israel is like Aaron's rod that burst into bloom; angels and temple devotees break forth into "Unto us a Child is born"—"And thou shalt call His

Name Jesus, for it is He that shall save His people from their sin." Men compare themselves with the God who is their Creator, and they recognize their own sinfulness and realize that their hope of salvation is in Him only.

Under each of these groups of four, the fourth book of the group becomes the historic base line and ties in directly with the events of history occurring at the time of the prophecies of each book. We will note that this is true of *Malachi* just as it has been of the fourth book in the three previous groups. Thus by ignoring the *chronology* of this fourth group, and the rather giving attention to its *purpose*, it becomes intensely significant and credible. As the New Testament Epistles have been grouped according to their purpose rather than their chronological order, so also the prophets. There are two events to come:

> Out of the shadows of night
> The world rolls into light;
> It is daybreak everywhere. [1]

To study this fourth group and its main outline, is to be prepared for current events and also to avoid the catastrophic debacle!

1. THE PROPHECY OF ZEPHANIAH

> "For then will I turn to the peoples a pure language (lip)
> That they may all call upon the name of the Lord,
> To serve Him with one consent.
> The remnant of Israel shall not do iniquity, nor speak lies;
> Neither shall a deceitful tongue be found in their mouth:
> For they shall feed and lie down,
> And none shall make them afraid.
> Sing, O daughter of Zion;
> Shout, O Israel;
> Be glad and rejoice with all the heart,
> O daughter of Jerusalem."
>
> Zephaniah 3:9, 13—14 N.

Zephaniah might well be called "the voice of the day of the Lord" (1:14) for herein is described something of the wrath and darkness of this time of judgment when the Lord says, "I will *utterly consume* all things" (1:3). The immediate reason for His pronouncement of judgment is found in 1:4—6. The Jewish nation had intermingled with those worshippers of Baal; and the "black-robed" priests of Baal, the Chemarims, were fraternizing with the priests of God. Some were worshipping the hosts of heaven and others were swearing by Malcham, the Ammonite idol Molech (Luke 16:13). There were those who had come to the conclusion that the Lord was an indifferent conscience-less God of "do-nothing-ism" (1:12). These who were settled on their lees find themselves under God's judgment even

---

[1]
Henry Wadsworth Longfellow, *From The Bells of San Blas*, 11th stanza

as those today of whom Paul writes in II Timothy 3.[1] This should serve as a warning to princes and kings' children and all such clothed in some "strange" apparel. We must arouse back to the Bible, prayer, and to God. We must arouse back to the Bible, prayer, and to God. Though the nations are to be judged and the ungodly "utterly consumed," yet Israel is to be remembered (2:3; 3:8—20).

The significant position of the Lord "with His people" despite their degrading moral state in the nation, is set forth for the future restoration in Zephaniah 3:2—4:

a) The *people* "obeyed not the voice . . .; received not correction; trusted not in the Lord; drew not near to her God."

b) Her *Princes* within her were as roaring lions; corruption of government and religion were rampant

c) Her *Judges* were evening wolves "deferring till tomorrow" to gnaw the bones after consuming the flesh, so complete was their corruption

d) Her *Prophets* were "light and treacherous persons," deceitful, prophets prophesying peace "when there is no peace."

e) Her *Priests* had polluted the sanctuary, they had done violence to the law, and were teachers of falsehoods corrupting the law.

Yet in contrast, the very next verse 5 says, "for God, the *just* Lord is in the midst thereof"; and this verse refutes every iniquitous work of the foregoing; for God was "in their midst"; He will not do iniquity; His judgment was righteous; He was dependable and impartial; He faileth not (cf. 3:11—17).

And the result for those that mourn (Matthew 5:4) concludes the book of Zephaniah:

". . . And I will get them praise and fame in every land where they have been put to shame.   At that time will I bring you again, even in the time that I gather you: for I will make you a name and a praise among all people of the earth, when I turn back your captivity before your eyes, saith the Lord."

Zephaniah 3:19b—20

2. THE PROPHECY OF HAGGAI

"For thus saith Jehovah of hosts; Yet once, it is a little while, And I will shake the heavens, and the earth, and the sea, and the dry land;

---

[1] King Josiah destroyed idolatry outwardly but the people clave to it inwardly (Thynne, *Student's Commentary*).

> And I will shake all nations, and *the desire of all nations*
>   shall come:
> And I will fill this house with glory, saith Jehovah of hosts.
> The silver is Mine, and the gold is Mine,
>   saith Jehovah of hosts.
> The latter glory of this house shall be greater than of the former,
>   saith Jehovah of hosts:
> And this *place* will I give peace,
>   saith Jehovah of hosts."
>
> Haggai 2:6—9N.

Haggai begins with the rebuke of the nation of Israel as the prophet lashes out at the luxury of their ceiled houses while the temple "lies waste" (Haggai 1:4—9). Their excuse was that it was not the time that the Lord's house should be built. Haggai presents a parable to the priests of Israel concerning the matter of being clean or unclean and he uses this parable (2:11—14 *ff*) to teach the nation of Israel that a neglected house of worship is a contagious defilement. Awakened to their duty before God, they lay its foundation. As the old men saw the structure grow, they wept (Ezra 3:12) for they remembered the glory of the former house, Solomon's temple, but Haggai points them to the future at the time when the "desire of all nations shall come" and shall bring to the nations their desired things (2:6—9).

This latter house must refer to the temple which Ezekiel reveals to be erected during the Kingdom Age when Israel has been regathered to the land (Ezekiel chaps. 42 through 45). It does not refer to the temple of Zerubbabel nor that of Herod.

The Lord who came as perfect man on earth and is today perfect God in heaven, says through the prophet:

> "I will shake the heavens and the earth;
> And I will overthrow the throne of kingdoms,
> And I will destroy the strength of the kingdoms of the heathen;
> And I will overthrow the chariots, and those that ride in them;
> And the horses and their riders shall come down, everyone by
>   the sword of his brother.
> In that day, saith the Lord of hosts, will I take thee,
>   O Zerubbabel, my servant, the son of Shealtiel,
>   saith the Lord, and will make thee as a signet:
> For I have chosen thee, saith the Lord of hosts."
>
> Haggai 2:21*b*, 22—23

Again and again God promises the overthrow of Gentile kingdoms and the restoration of His people Israel.

In Hebrews 22:26—27, a further application of the prophecy of Haggai 2:6—7*a* will take place at the end of the Kingdom Age when the things that can be shaken are removed (the heavens and the earth that are now), and they shall be replaced with the new heaven and the new earth wherein dwelleth righteousness which are those things which come by "shaking." That there is to be no temple in the new heaven or new earth or the new city of Jerusalem is indicated in Revelation 21:22. The double application of this prophecy must be noted and rightly divided or there is confusion in arranging the eschatology.

3. THE PROPHECY OF ZECHARIAH

"In *that day* shall Jehovah defend the inhabitants of Jerusalem;
  And he that is feeble among them *that day* shall be as David;
  And the house of David shall be as God,
As the angel of Jehovah before them.
And it shall come to pass in *that day*,
That I will seek to destroy all the nations that come
    against Jerusalem,
The Spirit of grace and of supplications:
And they shall look attentively upon Me whom they have pierced,
And they shall mourn for Him, as one mourneth for his only son,
And shall be in bitterness for Him, as one that is in bitterness
    for his firstborn."

Zechariah 12:8—10 N.

, Zechariah's prophecy is Messianic, mystical and eschatological. As we study the book, the figures used (chap. 1:11—21) may be hard to lay hold of and I urge you to grasp the facts set forth and overlook for the present the figures.

The angel that communed with Zechariah said unto him: "Cry thou saying, thus saith the Lord of hosts, 'I am jealous for Jerusalem and Zion with a great jealousy, and I am very sore displeased with the nations that are at ease'" (Zechariah 1:14—15a). These nations are unconcerned over the suffering of the Lord's people (Lamentations 1:12). The prophet points to the latter rain of spiritual blessings that shall fall upon Israel and in the 9*th* and 10*th* verses, he shows the dispersion of the nation and its restoration to the land. The nation is sown in dispersion but the blessing of the latter rain makes possible the reaping of harvest, the regathering, and the restoration. The result of this regathering is further seen in 8:20— 23 when "the inhabitants of many cities shall say, ... let us go speedily to pray before the Lord ...."

"Thus saith Jehovah of hosts;
  In those days it shall come to pass that ten men
  shall take hold of all languages of the nations,
  even shall take hold of the skirt of him that is
  a Jew, saying, 'we will go with you; for we have
  heard that God is with you'."

Such will be the evangelization of the nations by the Jews in the Kingdom Age. [1]

When we come to chapter 12:3, we find the prophecy of Armageddon when the people of the earth are gathered against Jerusalem. A world league has not yet become possible but it can become so. Assurance is given to Israel of the Lord's protection and care in 12:8—10.

The great concluding 14*th* chapter of this book begins "Behold the day cometh" and as we envision the events of this chapter, we see the return in glory of the Lord when (vs. 4) "his feet shall stand in that day upon the Mount of Olives" and the experiences of that day of His coming are described together with the physical effects. And the 9*th* verse brings us to the result of His coming: "The Lord shall be king over all the earth: in that day there shall be one Lord, and his name one."

Verses 16—21 conclude the chapter and the great prophetic book showing the worship of the nations before the Lord in the Kingdom Age and the absence of the Canaanite. It forever damns all other *A-theos* which includes Cain, the angels of Jude 6, Nimrod and Nineveh:

> "And in that day there shall be no more
> the Canaanite in the house of the Lord of hosts."

4. THE PROPHECY OF MALACHI

> "Then they that feared Jehovah spake often one to another:
> And Jehovah hearkened, and heard it,
> And a book of remembrance was written before Him
> For them that feared Jehovah,
> And that thought upon His name.
> And they shall be Mine, saith Jehovah of hosts,
> In that day when I make up My jewels (peculiar treasure);
> And I will spare them, as a man spareth his own son that
> serveth him."
>
> Malachi 3:16—17 N.

The prophetic base line of the fourth prophet in each of the four groups of sixteen prophetic books continues in *Malachi*. God's judgment on the nations and His eventual victory over them is clearly set forth in this book of Malachi (1:4—5, 11).

After dealing with the sins of Israel and their careless attitude toward God, the prophecy begins with the burden of the word of the Lord TO ISRAEL by Malachi, and after assuring Israel of the Lord's judgment on Edom, he cries out, "Oh priests that despise My name, . . . ye offer polluted bread upon Mine altar . . . ye say the Table of the Lord is contemptible" (1:6—7), and he further rebukes them by saying, "I have no

---

[1] See Section SIX, *The Kingdom Age*, III. The Day of The Lord, E. The Reign of Righteousness and Peace, 5. The Nations come up to Jerusalem to seek favor . . . p. 567.

pleasure in you" (1:10). Their insincerity is now rebuked with, "Ye have wearied the Lord with your words . . . when ye say everyone that doeth evil, is good in the sight of the Lord and He delighteth in them, where is the God of judgment" (2:17). And finally in the third chapter he rebukes them for "robbing God of tithes and offerings" which have been withheld (3:7—10).

This is the book of the *two comings* and the two messengers: The first is to be announced by John the Baptist, who came in the spirit and power of Elijah, God's prophet in the day of the Lord's first coming to the nation of Israel.

The second coming to the earth is to be announced by Elijah "before the coming of the great and dreadful (notable) Day of the Lord" (Malachi 4:5).

At His first coming, Christ came to Israel, not to the Gentiles, but at His second coming in the day of the Lord, we find the course and end of His Story brought into completion as He answers the "call" of Israel and as He calls the nations before Him for judgment of blessing. These two comings are those spoken of by Peter (I Peter 1:11), "the *sufferings* and the *glory* that should follow." The first coming immediately follows in the Gospels and *Mark* (1:2) fulfills Malachi 3:1; but the second coming (Malachi 4), remains to be fulfilled beyond this age of grace—the Church Age. Thus it is a continued story of the "One Book."

Again there is a four hundred year interval[1] when the silence of God sets in, awaiting the coming of THE PROPHET when "The Word became flesh and dwelt among us" (John 1:14), and *The Key* to the Scriptures opened to men the understanding of these prophets (John 5:39; Luke 24: 44—45).

JESUS CHRIST, THE Prophet, THE Priest, THE King, fits each promise, prophecy and description of the Old Testament, and as each is opened, we are enabled to see God (John 14:9).

---

[1] See Section FOUR, *Abraham to Christ's Spiritual Body*, MY Story, II. The Growing Cloud of Testimony Bearers; list of the prophets, pp. 233—235.

TABLE of CONTENTS

THE SEALED DIVISION of The Scriptures (Continued)

"Jesus in the Workshop"—Cameron
(In the Shadow of the Cross)

For a half century, this picture hung in Bro. Kindred's study.

II. THE GOSPELS: MATTHEW, MARK, LUKE, and JOHN

GOD'S GREATEST of PARABLES; A MIGHTY PARALLEL

A S WE enter the SEALED Division of the NEW TESTAMENT, may I share with you an experience that I have entitled:

GOD'S GREATEST OF PARABLES—A MIGHTY PARALLEL

I stood within the Canadian Rockies before a tiny stream issuing from the snow-capped, heaven-touching peaks above me. Across this rivulet was a title: "The Great Divide," and I was informed that a drop of water divided here, would find its way to two oceans, the Pacific and the Atlantic. The fragment going west, by easy descent would go into a slumberland of paradise as intriguing as that which caused Lot to "pitch his tent toward Sodom." The other segment of the drop would be beaten, tossed and hammered by falls and rapids, always "encompassed about" by the ever-present rock obstruction, and brought to a condensation of the mightiest rapids on the Eastern Seaboard; thence going on into the seeming stagnancy of the whirl-pool. From there on through lake-calm and island-beauty, it goes until swallowed up into the great Atlantic.

It came to me then though more forcefully now, as I have been looking upon the relief map of the Bible, that here is a parable of the Divine Inspiration even as Psalm Nineteen. Both of these parallels are embedded in the two lands of Promise: America, and, the eventual great David's Empire. The Canadian Rockies whose snow-crowned heights appear to meet and mingle with the low-bending heavens—these answer to the prophets of God in the Old Testament who send down their spiritual waters from the heights of Inspiration; these descend into the Four Great Lakes, just as "The Word became flesh" in the Four Gospels—the many condensed into the Four, becoming incandescent in "The Light of the World." From within and around the shores thereof, is summed up the resources of "The Everlasting Hills." These four again narrowed into the book of Acts and Pentecost, and are parallel to the Niagara River, the Falls, and the Whirl-pool. The resistless, dynamic Gospel, resistless advance to conquest, is worthy to be put alongside Niagara's display.

Over the Niagara hangs a rainbow written in the rising spray; and here the Church is being caught up into "the heavenlies" of Paul's epistles. After that, the glorious Hope for Israel in all of the prophets comes into its own, as is unfolded in the book of Hebrews and through the book of Revelation. The Lake of Ontario answers to "The King and Kingdom unto Israel"; the thousand islands in their ravishing beauty, could present no better picture than of the Lord's Millennial Reign, "When He shall reign from sea to sea"—"Nations shall learn war no more"—and each shall "sit under his own vine and fig tree" with none "to molest or make afraid."

So that it might be crystal clear to us, let us consider this outline:

1. Abraham is given the promises
2. The Prophets (the Mountains of God) stored these up in their heavenly heights
3. The Lord came in the Four Gospels (Lakes Superior, Michigan, Huron and Erie), condensing the prophets into His incarnation (Luke 24:25—44) which became "The Light of the World."
4. Pentecost and the Acts of the Apostles together correspond to the Niagara River
5. The spread of the Gospel by the Church is seen in the Niagara Falls and the Rapids
6. The Jews in rejection are pictured in the Whirlpool below the Falls and the Rapids of Niagara
7. At a long but glorious last, we see Israel restored (Romans 9 through 11) pictured so beautifully in Lake Ontario which flows peacefully toward the eventual end of the fulfillment to Abraham
8. And as the St. Lawrence River gemmed by its thousand islands, goes steadily on to the great Atlantic, we see "The New Heavens and the New Earth."

As the Lord found parallels and parables in earth of the things of heaven, may it not be, that He has fashioned this parable in the heart of America—this political "Land of Promise" patterned after that first spoken to "Abraham and thy seed forever" (Psalm 19)? I love to think of it as so—

> "Before the mountains were brought forth, or ever Thou
> hadst formed the earth and the (habitable) world, even
> from everlasting to everlasting, Thou art God."—

that even "before the mountains were brought forth," so it was in God's great heart, to put this most glorious of parables at the very heart of this America, written in such large characters, that even the half-blinded might see. And this treasure we have in full splendor of His resurrection!

"Blessed be the Name of the Lord forever and forever." Amen!

INTRODUCTION TO THE GOSPELS:
THE SIXTEEN PROPHETS PROJECTED UPON THE FOUR GOSPELS

The four prophet groups of *Isaiah* through *Malachi* "became flesh and dwelt among us" in the four Gospels (Matthew 1:1, 18—25; 27:37). The meeting of God and Abram at Mamre (Genesis 13:14—18) is the place where heaven implanted Hope in the heart of humanity (Hebrews 11:8—27) and nourished it with visioners and prophets whose utterances, incarnated in Christ, have become "the desire of all nations." He alone is their adequate, fitting climax "of whom Moses and the prophets did write." Of Him, God the Father could say, "This is My Son"; and Pilate said, "Behold! the Man."

The Hebrew Scriptures are the source and the resource of the four Gospels (Isaiah 55:1—3a; Amos 8:11—13), and they stand in solitary splendor as God's Tabernacle, visible to ALL the world, (Psalm 121:1—2). But the resources of the eternal flow out from their inner Holy of Holies. They are God's borderland and the warehouse of His mercies. The currents have never been in reverse (Isaiah 40:12—17). Cosmologies, jurisprudence, letters and religions are grouped impotently at the base of them (Matthew 17:14—21). Archaeologists have spaded all over Bible lands. And "Earth-Scraper" (in contrast to "sky-scraper") cities are uncovered layer upon layer. Dead language and lost Arts are being resurrected; and the Sphinx is again seen above the sands, but still there towers *"ho Biblos"*—The Bible—for no lowliest part is buried, obscure nor obscured:

"Holy Bible, Book divine,
Precious treasure, thou art mine;"

The Bible is the inspiration of all aspirings, the dynamic of all reforms, and the regenerating influence of the born again. For four centuries that Book, compact of prophecy stood apart in unscalable, awesome grandeur; while

"Humanity with all its fears,
With all the hopes of future years, ..."

hung breathless upon Its promises. Athens was attempting to scale the heights of knowledge when she fell; and Hammurabi with his "code," and the priests of Egypt with their "Book of the Dead," had long before tried and failed. The impediments of ambitious attempts to destroy the Book, lie about It—yea, even *lean* against Its side! Its truthfulness, accuracy and inspiration have all been questioned. Christians, once timid, trembled at each new expedition, but those fears are gone forever for the Old Book still stands though time-tested, fire-tried, and critic-attacked.

Joined to the prophets of the Hebrew Scriptures is a companion volume with a Cross within its heart which arises like "a root out of dry ground." Isaiah 53 is incarnated, "saying none other things than Moses and the Prophets" (Luke 24:27). These two (the Old and New Testaments) immediately were bound together and the affinity was never questioned. Bethlehem began the ascent to Golgotha. We discover that the first, the Old Testament is unfinished, when the Holy Spirit starts once more to write the sequel; and only He could do so. We lacked a revelation, the happy ending required of a book, and so the four Gospels are the revelation of the Old Testament as if the message of the prophets were projected upon a steropticon curtain. Prophecy is incarnated:

"The Desire of All Nations" is come; "Behold, the Lamb of God"; and, "Behold! The Man." And the tradition-barred gate of prophecy is opened: "To him the porter openeth."

The flood tide of John 5:39 is filled full in MATTHEW. MARK, the lad, wonder-eyed, looks upon this One "of whom Moses and the prophets did write," and he records the immediacy ("straightway") and wonder of His mighty acts. His is the child's story of God's Immanuel. LUKE, matured, professionally trained, and with scholarly accuracy, lays down in words the Highway of Holiness over which this glorious, suffering (Isaiah 53), "Son of God" (Luke 4) goes forth to all the world, bearing His Cross, the propitiatory for the sins of the whole world. Then follows JOHN, catching up into transfiguring glory in his gospel, this Jesus of the "Synoptics" into "The Christ of God." His is the glory light, the Shekinah cloud of God's Presence, abiding upon His Incarnated-One until withdrawn for "The Mine Hour" of the Cross, returning to receive Him up at the ascension from Olivet (Acts 1).

Thus, prophecy yields to Personality (John 1:14), and Haggai 2:7 yields to Matthew 2:2; 3:17 and John 19:5.

THE FOUR GOSPELS
ARE NEITHER REDUNDANT NOR TAUTOLOGICAL

As was noted in the prophets (Amos 3:7–8), chronology is exhausted in the local needs but yields in importance to the canonical needs; just so, the same divine re-adjustments are seen in the New Testament. God's Word is local in time, and universal or timeless. God is a God of precision, order and accuracy. His Scriptures are for His Purpose, with each going to its appointed place as Abraham and Judas. So, the Scriptures were written to *reveal* and were not a jumble of books thrown together. A rightly dividing throughout the Scriptures between that which is natural and that which is spiritual, makes possible our understanding of God's purpose.

The four Gospels focus upon the incarnation. They are NOT synoptic but rather were written for a purpose which explains why for the same event different terms were used, as in the use of "The Kingdom of Heaven" and "The Kingdom of God." It is said, "Shakespeare never repeats"—but never does anything else repeat!—see the plots and situations of his plays. Likewise, read carefully the record in the four Gospels, of the ministry of our Lord. Many events which did not occur at the same time have been forced by commentators into a federation even as churches today have been federated through man-made plans.

The four prophet groups are incarnate in these four gospels and therein is revealed the righteousness of God, "who for our sakes became poor that we through Him might become rich." There are two ways of emphasis:

a) Collectively, the writers of the four Gospels "all speak the same things"

b) Individually, they may say as John, "I was in Spirit on (Gr. *en*) the Lord's Day." When one is separated unto the work whereunto the Holy Spirit calls him (Acts 13:2), he follows the leading of the Holy Spirit.

In the affirmative statements of the four Gospels concerning Christ's Deity and Purpose, there is agreement. But in the assertive record of His words which He speaks and the work which He did, there is pioneering and therefore difference. This pioneering is of importance to the author's purpose as he writes under the Holy Spirit's leading. Thus at both places there is special stress.

Why are there four Gospels? Because the Holy Spirit required it. The "Synoptists," (Matthew, Mark, Luke—those who see together), and John may speak of the same event but they are under different terms, and there is a reason to be found in the purpose of each. Each book and grouping is of divine origin, significance and importance. Nothing must be over-looked or put aside; for there is no tautology or redundance in this God-breathed volume (John 5:39; 20:30—31; 6:63*b*). The thought and language of the Bible are as their Lord, a servant, despised and rejected (Matthew 10:25; Philippians 2:7), but never forget, that to both the Word and the Lord, there is a restoration. The Lord's glory was seen of John (17:5; Revelation 1:17); and the Word of God, like the two prophets of Revelation 11:12 who were raised up, shall be raised from ridicule and fulfilled as He has promised in Matthew 24:35. "It is enough that the disciple be as his teacher and the servant be as his Lord." The Bible also is stripped till "there is no beauty or comeliness that we should desire Him." All is severely vital, never ornamental. The four Gospels are four revelations each sufficient "unto the work whereunto called"; their diversity adds greater emphasis to their unity. The "Synoptists" SEE; John SOARS. The "Synoptists" are as the apocalypse of the Old Testament. As a painting has depth, coloring and pose, *plus* lighting, so *John* is the light which follows upon the three-fold painting of *Matthew, Mark* and *Luke*; or the three Gospels are as the tabernacle and *John* is as the Shekinah.

In John 12:15 we read, "Behold, thy king cometh." He presents double credentials: *The Throne*, David's Son; and, *The Land*, Abraham's heir. To prove His claim to these two, He has legal, factual and literary credentials:

1. The genealogy drives through the most jealously guarded of Israel's documents. There is no chance for fraud:
    a) Joseph and Mary enroll at Bethlehem
    b) Jesus, eight days old, is presented at the temple and enrolled upon the family tree

2. The facts: ". . . this was not done in a corner."
    a) Jesus' teachings
    b) His miracles
    c) A Life—perfect and sinless. He stood the scrutiny then, and the test now!

3. The literature: *Matthew*, the book nearest to the Old Testament,
    is full of Hebraisms and Jewish customs while *John*, the far-
    thest away of the Gospels from the Old Testament, is given
    over to parenthetic explanations. Matthew makes more quo-
    tations from the Old Testament than the other three combined.
    He translates from the Hebrew originals and they quote from
    The Septuagint. *Matthew* is more related to the Old than to the
    New Testament.

    Matthew presents the facts of inherence while *Luke* presents
    the facts of the Inherent, the documented act of One who met
    the inner needs of the world. *Mark* presents the wonder-worker.
    He gives questions through facts but not the answer. And *John*
    reveals the Shekinah glory (the seamless robe) of the "logos."
    Matthew tells of the coming of the Messiah proved by fulfilled
    prophecies (Matthew 1:1); *Mark* shows the coming of the Gospel
    (Mark 1:1 and 16:16); *Luke* demonstrates the coming of Faith
    (Luke 1:1—4; Acts 1:1—5): "that thou mightest know the cer-
    tainty." And *John* reveals the coming of the Word, and shows
    His nature, His work, and its effect (John 1:1—14).

The most effective method for understanding the Gospels is to determine the purpose of each; and then to study the one nearest *your* need.
Do not use a so-called Harmony! The "Synoptists" are observing the same
events though reporting to different people, and though for the same ends:
to convince, to convict, and to SAVE. The wisdom of the Holy Spirit is
nowhere else so discernible as here. *Matthew* is written to the Semitic
mind; *Mark* to the Latin mind; and *Luke* to the Greek mind; each "sticks
to his text"; and we find the origin of:

1. A Race—Abraham and David
2. Law and Order—Malachi 4:4
3. Man

A few hours of comparing will enrich you in Philippians 1:10; the failure
to distinguish is the occasion of the mental fog that has wrought confusion
and wreckage. Once started aright, there is pleasure and profit and it will
create a thirst which is quenched only by the "Living (Word) Waters" of
Psalm 42:1 and John 4:14.

If you are studying the *Messiah*, read *Matthew*; if studying the *Savior*,
read *Mark*; if you would study *Christ*, then read *Luke*; and if studying *The
Christ of God*, read *John*. Use as helps all of these books, but "each in
its own order." These "Synoptics" give the human side of Emmanuel,
"the *Candle* of the Lord," (Proverbs 20:17), while *John* is the *flame* (Spirit)
that rests down upon these (Ecclesiastes 4:12; John 1:4—5).

To the Jew   —MATTHEW writes presenting Jesus as the
                                                          Messiah
To the sinner   —MARK records Jesus as the Savior
To the world citizen   —LUKE introduces Jesus as the Christ
To an immortal (Christian)—JOHN reveals Jesus as God

Note in Matthew 1, Jesus is *descending* out of heaven into the earth. His Name is to be *Jesus* and He is to be the *Savior*; these things are recorded in *Matthew* and *Mark*. Then note in John 20:17, He becomes the One who is *ascending*, and this is revealed in *Luke* and in *John*, "The Christ of God.

MATTHEW   was a banker, an accurate keeper of records
                       (the genealogy)
MARK   was a servant, (an attendant, Acts 13:5)
LUKE   was a surgeon, and writer of Christ as
                       being of one structure and nature
JOHN   was the visioner (John 1:18; 13:23)

Our salvation is all compact of these elements which flow bank full into the *Acts* of Salvation.

A. THE GOSPEL OF MATTHEW

> ". . . 'Where is He that is born King of the Jews? for
> we have seen His star in the east, and are come to
> worship Him . . .'."
>
> Matthew 2:2

MATTHEW, the Messiah Gospel, is the genealogy and records His Name and mission (1:21). This Gospel is among the challengers where indisputable facts are resisted (as in Acts 4:16). Through this book a king moves; the Lion of Judah (Matthew 4:17——16:.1). It began with "the kingdoms of the Earth and their glory," and ends with "All authority——Go!" Though there is the absence of the trappings of royalty (I Corinthians 1:26), yet there is no mistaking Him. I have never been so impressed by His being "every inch a King" as when I read His trial before the Sanhedrin.

Matthew writes of "The Kingdom of Heaven" where Abraham and David have earthly hopes which are yet to be realized by Daniel's Seventieth Week.[1] This is the reason why *Harmonies* do not harmonize; cp. the Sermon on the Mount (Matthew chaps. 5—7) with the Sermon on the Plain (Luke 6:12—49).

After His rejection the Gospels are fused together. Here His Deity shines through as He gives the Great Commission of "ALL the NATIONS," *sic* "Teaching THEM to *observe* all things whatsoever I have commanded

---

[1] See SEALED DIVISION, I. A. 4. *d*), (1) Daniel's Seventy Weeks' Prophecy, p. 44.

you." This is the order of our *mission* and Luke gives us our *commission*. Confusion comes from not *observing*, and from trying to synopticize where the record is *not synopticized*.

Jesus as presented in *Matthew* is too big to be only "The King of the Jews." Though some day He shall reign over them, yet His reign will be extended over all the nations during the Kingdom Age. Matthew's Commission (Matthew 28:18—20) is our "burden" to take care of them (the Jews) who are "scattered among the nations." Thus the discipling of the nations will produce a benevolent spirit toward Israel while they are scattered, and nationally they shall be saved, preserved, until the Lord's return. Our efforts must also be to win them to Christ *now*. The "sheep" of Matthew 25:31 will be God's test of our efforts of evangelism today.

B. THE GOSPEL OF MARK

> ". . . They that are whole have no need of a physician, but they that are sick: I came not to call righteous ones, but sinners to repentance."
>
> Mark 2:17*b*N.

MARK presents Him as Savior to the sinner. He includes "THE WHOLE CREATION" in the Gospel of our Salvation (Mark 16:15—16 A.S.V.). Should you will to read *Mark*, you will often find *yourself*; for this is a human document though divinely occupied. Mark is the pragmatist so things must be gotten done.

The young man Mark is likely the son of Peter (I Peter 5:13). Mark's Gospel is as impetuous as Peter and the two were always together. Mark had access to the acts and events near Jesus at Capernaum and Jerusalem. The real battleground of the ministry of Jesus was *not* in His miracles or His teachings, but rather it was in the power to forgive sin; and this was first demonstrated in Mark's own home, Peter's house, where the paralytic was healed (Mark 2:1—7—12). *Mark* is the first to mention this. To forgive sin He demonstrated His authority over nature, even the nature of man. Now the real battle, "the last for which the first was planned," is here conjoined into one mighty stream. The Gospels flow together and the Cross sweetens the stream (Exodus 15:25). The Gospel is en-dynamited in *Mark*, companioned by *Matthew* and *Luke*, one on the right hand and the other on the left. *Luke* (24:44) stresses the pre-salvation basis and the endue-ment of the Gospelers; while *Matthew* (28:19) stresses the Post-Salvation teaching which is a plea to us for the Jew (Romans chaps. 9—11); but *Mark* (16:15—16) is upon the individual, "every creature" (Romans 8:19).

Mark's Gospel is the shortest for it has no preface or postscript. It is the most dynamic and we find the word *straightway* used 19 times; the word *immediately* which is the same Greek word, used 15 times; and the same Greek word translated by such words as *forthwith, anon, as soon as,* used seven times, making a total of 41 times in the short book of Mark. There is no waste of words or any preliminaries. Salvation and a Savior are presented and there is no time for dressing up, for men are lost. A *life-saver needs no introduction.* The genealogies on each side are given in *Matthew* and *Luke,* but *Mark* is concerned that a generation is dying and he avoids genealogies (I Timothy 1:4; Titus 3:9). His description of the five thousand is vivid where he said they looked like a garden (Mark 6:40, Gr. *prasia*). He was a city lad and had seen the formal gardens of the city.

Luke consults Mark (Luke 1:1, 2, 4); Paul finds Mark "profitable" (II Timothy 4:12) for Mark was the metropolitan, having lived in Jerusalem, Babylon, Ephesus and Rome, while Capernaum, his home, was itself upon a world highway.

C. THE GOSPEL OF LUKE

> "And He said unto them, 'But whom say *ye* that I am?'
> And Peter answering said, 'The Christ of God'."
>
> Luke 9:20 N.

LUKE presents the ascending Lord, the Christ of God, and gives the early events surrounding His birth, youth and baptism. This Gospel comes *after* "to those that received Him."

Luke is the only Gentile writer of the Bible and he writes in the books of Luke and Acts to Theophilus, the only Gentile thus singled out. These books are a series of "human interest stories" "from faith unto faith," or "from friend unto friend." None others can tell it, for we must love before we can impart (cf. 1:3–4). Luke only (24:49) uses the term *endued,* i.e. emotioned. It is the Gospel for man, all of man: the adolescent, the adult, and the re-teller (Acts).

Luke was of Antioch of Syria; he is called the beloved physician (Colossians 4:14; II Timothy 4:12).

> *Renan* said that the book of Luke is "the most beautiful Gospel that was ever written"
>
> *Dr. Philip Holmes* said that the exquisite delicacy and the virtuous elevation could proceed only through a cultured mind and a clean heart"
>
> *Sir William Ramsay* called Luke "the greatest of all historians, not excepting Thucydides"
>
> *Dr. A. T. Robertson* said of Luke, "but if we had only Luke's Gospel, we should have an adequate portrait of the Lord Jesus Christ"
>
> *Dr. William MacClure* of Drumtochty said that next to ministry

is medicine; that the doctor is the beloved one to whom all
is told; that when the doctor comes into the home where there
is sickness, his presence changes the very atmosphere.
The doctor opens and closes our eyes. He counsels in health
and fights off the death which we have encouraged. Who better
than a doctor would be so disciplined to harmoniously cooper-
ate with the Holy Spirit to produce such exquisite delicacy,
in narratives of the Nativity? His Gospel groups events as
orchestrated parts, "to make one music as before, but vaster.'

Luke, like a troubadour who collects folk songs and folk lore and dis-
seminates these to his listeners, might well be called the Shakespeare
of the Gospelers to the Church. He is a poet of facts which are touched
into beauty. His accuracy is meticulous:

a) His information comes from those who have been eye-witnesses
(Luke 1:2). Luke uses the Greek word *autoptai* for eye-wit-
ness; and he is the physician probing for facts in an autopsy.
Each case in his writings has been *post-factum-ed.*

b) Luke used events, dates, names of places, cities, coins and
official titles in the books of Luke and Acts and *never* is there
an inaccuracy. This a fabricator would not have dared to do.

Luke was not conscious that he was under control of the Spirit but he put
his best into it. So every Christian is under the Holy Spirit as far as he
yields.

Antioch was named after Antiochus Epiphanes who produced the a-
bomination referred to in *Daniel.* The city was a place where the disciples
were first called *Christians* and it was also the mission center of the early
Church. Luke joined Paul for the second time in Acts 16:10 (note "we"
and "us"), and for the third time in Acts 20:5—6 (note "us" and "we").
He spent the two years in Palestine during Paul's imprisonment (see Acts
21:18 "us" and 27:1 "we"). How was this time spent? Luke 1:1—4 gives
the answer: "consulting with eye-witnesses and ministers of the word."
The Bible is as any other book, so it is documented with time, nations,
and cities (Luke 1:5; 2:1—2); but as *no* other book, it is inter-woven with
many nations. God has exhausted proof in producing the Bible. The Bible
was so produced that it could be said, "This was not done in a corner"
but it was done in Egypt, Babylon and Rome and when these were in their
glory. No other book has been so produced. It is ONE Book written in
two languages, and upon *three* continents during *Four* Empires.

D. THE GOSPEL OF JOHN

"In a beginning was the Word, (Gr. *logos*)
and the Word (*logos*) was with God,
and the Word (*logos*) was God."

John 1:1

John's is the Glory Gospel as the Shekinah over the Tabernacle of the Ten Words (LAW).

"The Word became flesh and tabernacled among us
and we beheld His glory,
The glory as of the only Begotten of the Father."

This is spoken of Him only, and is used by John only (7:15; 12:12; 13:6; Revelation 19:11–16; 21:3); "this is the Son of Man who is in heaven." The "tabernacled Logos" is the glory over *Matthew, Mark* and *Luke*. When they meet, it is not by appointment but at transcendant, heaven-touching events and the three are taken up (as Matthew 17:1–2). St. Augustine said that in the Gospels there are "varieties not contrarities."

In the events of the Cross, Jesus moves as the Master: GOD. Never was He more so: "I lay down My life and I take it up again"; He takes control: "I thirst" — "it is finished"; — "He gave up His Spirit." And He compels service and readjustments. The Greek word, "*Ho logos*," is from the root word "*leg-o*," that is, to lay, pick out, gather together." And here it is used of the thoughts in mind, materials and expression. Here it is used of picking out of God's mind, as a book reviewer before a Literary Society (14:24), and adjusting men and materials into divine purpose (John 20:23). "As many as received Him, to them gave He authority to become children of God" (John 1:12). "If any willeth he shall KNOW" (I Peter 5:6–11). When one yields to the form or pattern with honest intent, he is "changed."

John's *Gospel*[1] is "much more" profound than his *Revelation*. Stalker in his *Life of St. Paul* said, "His thoughts to this day remain the property of only the finest minds." John's Gospel is the worshipper's manual where prayer as incense rises. And yet seekers and Greek students begin with *John*! The limpid heights are deceiving even as mountain atmosphere or siderial suns. The sounds and sights of the earth are about the events

---

[1] From Robertson's *Word Pictures*: "The test of time has given the palm to the fourth Gospel over all the books of the world. If Luke's Gospel is the most beautiful, John's Gospel is supreme in its height and depth and reach of thought. The picture of Christ here given is the one that has captured the mind and heart of mankind . . . . This is the Holy of Holies of the New Testament. Here we find the Heart of Christ, especially in chaps. 14 to 17. The language of the fourth Gospel has the clarity of a spring, but we are not able to sound the bottom of the depths. Lucidity and profundity challenge and charm us as we linger over it."

of the other Gospels, but in *John*, Life, Light and Love lie mirrored in its fathomless heights. Nicodemus fits into this silent majesty. Personalities rise into unsuspected dignity: John the Baptist; the woman of Samaria; the man born blind.

CONCLUSION

Having thus completed our survey of the four Gospels, we have seen that the relation of the three Gospels to *John* is like that of the sixteen Prophets to all four Gospels. All through the first three Gospels, the writers SEE through the incarnation and the ministry, (though also looking beyond as did the prophets—as though each were writing in his particular dispensation, yet seeing through unto the *Telos* (end). Yet John sees beyond these three writers; he SOARS. Such comparison can be seen throughout the whole Bible:

SEES	SOARS
The sixteen Prophets looked forward to His first coming	— And in the Gospels, the Incarnation is fulfilled
Matthew, Mark and *Luke* see Him as Jesus, Savior and Christ	— And *John* sees Him as God
These three are as painting with depth, color and pose	— And *John* adds the lighting
These three are as the Tabernacle	— And *John* is as the Shekinah
These three are as the Candle	— And *John* is as the Flame.

We now move into the *Acts* of the Apostles, and a like parallel exists between the book of Acts and Paul's Epistles. Through the framework and examples of *Acts*, we are made to SEE, but "in the heavenlies" of Paul's Epistles, we find that we SOAR.

Later, in the study of the "especially Jewish" Epistles which will be of unusual significance after the rapture of the Church, and after the "blindness in part" has been removed from Israel,—then the Jewish nation again SEES, and the Gospel at that time becomes *Hebrews* through *Jude*.

And the book of Revelation, like John's Gospel and Paul's Epistles, SOARS in its description of the ages which end in an incomparable and inescapable judgment, out of which comes the Restoration of all things when God is again over all (I Corinthians 15:28).

TABLE of CONTENTS

THE SEALED DIVISION of The Scriptures (Continued)

III. THE BOOK OF ACTS

> "And when the day of Pentecost was fully come, they were all with one accord in one place."

> "And they were all filled with Holy Spirit, and began to speak with other tongues, according as the Spirit gave them to utter" (in short weighty sentences, or apothegms).
>
> Acts 2:1, 4 N.

The Book of Acts is the most completely GOD-occupied, GOD-controlled, and GOD-directed of the Bible books and peoples:

> ". . . Lo, I am with you all the days, unto the completion of the age."
>
> Matthew 28:20*b* N.

> "And they went forth, and preached everywhere, the Lord working with them, and confirming the word with signs following."
>
> Mark 16:20, cf. Luke 21:15—17

ACTS is the Gospel of the Holy Spirit in which Stephen is the forerunner of Paul. *Acts* is "THE WAY," the "Isthmus of Panama" between the Gospels and the Epistles, and this "Way" stretched from the Incarnated Jesus ("I am the Vine . . .") to the In-churched Christ, for this "Way" was rooted in the Cross and Pentecost, and fruited in jail!

A. ACTS VINDICATES GOD

This is the book of the ever-present, unquenchable, incandescence of God's glory. And no wonder: for it is preceded by sixteen prophets and four Gospels; and the "I AM" is accompanying this book and it is Holy Spirit indwelt. Nowhere else in all of God's world is there the like. It is the "Lying-In" hospital of the new creation. The Holy Spirit grooved the Church to be as definite and as accurate as the siderial bodies (Psalm 19). Therefore, let US be very definite:

1. At Sinai, Israel was set apart from the nations
2. In like manner even more so, at Pentecost is the Church set apart
3. Matthew 23:39 ended Christ's personal offer of the Kingdom to Israel
4. The two appeals: "The restoration of all things" (Acts 3:17—21), and "this salvation" (Acts 28:28) were individual; they are not national; and they are positively NOT the Kingdom.

Added to the above facts, ALL of the prophets surface in the Acts.

To the two disciples of Emmaus and to the eleven in the Upper Room, Jesus opened the prophetic Scriptures (Luke 24:27, 44); but these were not to be preached until the disciples had been endued with power from on high which came in Acts 2:4. The book of Acts alone explains the relationship: of the Old to the New Testament; of the Gospels to the Epistles; and of Philippians 2:11 to Ephesians 3:10; and thus *Acts* vindicates God! The sermons preached in the book of Acts to those who had the prophetic Scriptures, point out how Christ fulfilled those things which testified of Him in the prophets.

The book of Acts is a book of illustrations from Africa (the eunuch), Asia (Saul), and Europe (Cornelius) along the Highway of Holiness (Isaiah 35:8) showing God's Omniscience and compassion unto the highest degree. God uses all within His power to make it plain. A studied approach to this book will enhance its value. So much of unwise discussion from both sides has obscured its beauty. You open the Bible to study the Scriptures upon some one of these dispensations that you might be able to rightly divide, and you find that each book has its own purpose. The Prophets produce faith; the Gospels produce expectancy; the *Acts* produce love of Him; and the Epistles produce our Salvation and Hope. How can these be transposed without resulting confusion since the Holy Spirit "set them in order" (John 14:12; 16:12—13):

1. Consider what is *poured into* the *Acts*:
    a) The "Mystery process"; the "hid treasure" in the field of the Old Testament
    b) The rejected Lord; "the stone which the builders rejected . . ."
    c) That which was washed down of the wealth of God's love (Luke 24:27)

2. And consider what *arose out* of the book of Acts:
    a) The great chapters of Romans 8, 13; I Corinthians 13 and 15; II Corinthians 3 through 5; I Thessalonians 4:13 and II Thessalonians 2
    b) The great characters emerging from this book, and their impress upon conduct, art and life ("He that saveth his life shall lose it")
    c) The Joint Body, Jew and Gentile believers (Ephesians 3:6)

He who meditates upon this book will appreciate fully that "there is a power not ourselves which makes for righteousness" (Arnold).

And finally, the book of Acts is the Divine Demonstration of the Holy Spirit's work of salvation (Acts 6:2—8; 8:4—24; Romans 10:14). Today men are citing text books and re-writing them to become up-to-date; also, men are writing creatively. In contrast to these books, here is the church's book of Acts: "the same yesterday, today and forever" translated into every known tongue and NOT revised. The underlying text "abides" unaltered. The revisers of text books work on prior translations as revisers of revisions! This is not Bibliolatry for we are not stressing the book, but the Holy Spirit, the Author. It is not the Acts of Conversions, but it is the Acts of Persons. The Bible is a transcript of LIFE (John 6:63; 8:28). Its accuracy is Its only value and that is guaranteed by Its Author. This is the book of demonstrations that the Gospel applied to individuals, to nascent congregations, to diverse solidarities, and to amalgamations (Acts 2:28), is to "every creature," to "All nations," "That they may all be one." That same power is operating today and where it is applied, it produces like results.

B. ACTS and RIGHTLY DIVIDING

The Acts of the Apostles is the book of the Restoration of the Image of God (John 16:7—15; 14:12; Acts 1:1—5; and 2:4). It is the Assembly Room (Plant) where the parts (Dispensations) are assembled into the plan of salvation. It is "that FORM of Doctrine," the baptistry ("the bath of regeneration"); it is the Holy Spirit's Workshop where He is working this Transformation (Acts 4:13). Peter and Paul are as Bezaleel and Aholiab (Exodus 31:1—11), for we find that Peter is working upon the visible structure while Paul is working upon the spiritual body; and *Acts* becomes the transition experience where we pass from death into life. Such a transition period was witnessed in Acts 2:1—47 as we note the speech, the result, and the effect.

Acts is the story of another great transition—that of the transfer of leadership from Jewish to Gentile (Acts 3:17—24; 14:44—47; 15:13—18; 22:17—22; and 28:23—29). These are well-known facts:

1. That the Lord we worship spent His whole earth-
    life as a Jew and in a mission to them
2. That He was rejected by them and crucified
3. That the Jew still awaits His Messiah while the
    Christian now enjoys Him as Savior and Lord
4. That the Jewish Christians of the First Century
    were gradually estranged from the Gentile
    Christians (Galatians 2:11—14).

The book of Acts is the record of this; and it was also foreshadowed by the Lord (Matthew 14 and John 12) in His own break with the rulers. Now the emphasis changes from the Tables of the Law to the Table of Love;

and it becomes the fading-out of the Kingdom (John 3:30) and the shining-forth of the Church (Matthew 16:18). In the *Acts* He is still rejected. As the rulers rejected Jesus, so the people rejected the Gospel (Acts 3:17—23). The Divide is in Acts 11:19. Prior to this time, Peter had received the spotlight, but from this point on, Paul comes to the fore, and he meets two currents: the reluctant Jewish Christians, and the vindictive Jews. To one "having eyes to see," this book of Acts is the spiritual battle-ground of Esdraelon. It is not between the apostles but between the people. The Twelve were restricting their preaching to Israel, but Paul was forced from Israel unto the Gentiles. Thus, Peter decreased as Paul increased, but in II Peter 3 we are shown that they are at one following the change in leadership. Paul's stature was thrust upon him! (Acts 22:17—21; I Corinthians 9:16); there was no jealousy in Peter.

The transition in the church from Jewish to Gentile is clearly stated by the Holy Spirit (vs. 28) through James before the whole church (Acts 15:13—21). This working agreement (vss. 23—29) between the Twelve and Paul was published (Acts 15:30; 16:4—5) and it was observed by both parties. Barnabas went back at the cleavage. From here on, the battle was with the rulers and it was political and they pursued Him even unto death. Jesus as the Messiah was rejected and so he was banished from the land for it is Israel's land in perpetuity, indefectible and unconditioned. But the offer was not finally withdrawn until Acts 28:28 though it was threatened at 13:46 at Antioch of Pisidia. This closing curse is hurled from heaven at Israel's three tragic apostasies:

1. From God (Isaiah 6:9—10)
2. From Christ (Matthew 13:14)
3. From the Holy Spirit (Acts 28:25).

The Gospel began to be proclaimed "to the Jew first," and for at least eight years it was preached to none others (Acts 10). That priority remains their's until this day, and until His coming again. The Holy Spirit devoted unto them the book of Hebrews as their portion of the New Testament to be used for conversion to Christ now, but also with a future use after the rapture of the Church. The church age opens, and there is no place for it on earth, so it is "in the heavenlies" and is "called out." This prepares us to understand the literature of the New Testament. To the Church-Gentile is given *Romans*, and to the Church-Jewish is given *Hebrews*. Both are portals into glorious vistas, and these divide aright Paul's letters which arise from "dead in sin" to "seated in the Heavenlies."

Luke's Gospel witnessed to facts in the ministry and suffering of Jesus (Luke 1:1—4), while *Acts* is concerned with those things which occurred "after He had suffered" (Acts 1:1—5). The Gospel of Luke was a record of "the things that Jesus *began* both to do and to teach"; and the "do" in the book of *Acts* is the assembling, while the "teach" is the group of Epistles which are edifying (I Timothy 3:14—16; II Timothy 2:14—15; 3:16—17). These *Acts* call us to action, and "now why tarriest thou! Arise and be baptized and wash away thy sins." Don't copy Naaman's reluctance to obey the prophet's command, but the rather "go bathe" in the Acts of the Apostles.

C. GOD'S TWO WITNESSES: ISRAEL and THE CHURCH

The Acts of the Apostles is the Church set apart unto the work of salvation. It is a blackboard demonstration (13:38—41; 17:16—34), where those being saved are added. The *board* is not the answer but it carries the answer. The demonstration is stated and solved in chapter 2 and is the basic copy. There is no other place to which we can go (4:12). *Acts* is the common denominator, the "sheet" of chapter 10:10—15, and tells us that there is no distinction between Jew and Gentile. It is the story of "to the Jew first and also to the Gentile," up to the falling back upon traditions and Mosaism (2:39; 3:20—21; 28:25—28). God's Two Witnesses are Israel and the Church, both of whom are dispersed through both disobedience and obedience, and these two witnesses are as undebatable as the sun. Restoration and Rapture are their goals. *Acts* is the Red Sea of the Church where Israel was left "forsaken until" the Grace Age is finished. Nothing of Egypt passed through. Even so, nothing of the Kingdom enters the Church. When across the Red Sea, Israel sang of victory; in like manner, the Apostle Paul's triumph epistles are given, but these are embedded within Romans 9 through 11.

D. A MEDITATION UPON THE BOOK OF ACTS

ACTS begins the Church Age of Grace (cp. Revelation 2:3, seven churches) and it contains the church that arose out of Mystery, Theophanies, and the Incarnation. And herein is the Gospel which produces the Body. My effort is to fix attention upon the vital change. This is a new age for peoples, institutions and ordinances, and of necessity it must have a new terminology. The *doctrines* of Acts will produce the *Church* of Acts. Creeds are departures from these which are common to all believers. The simplicity of *Acts* is deceptive for it seems so obvious even as is mountain air or crystal water. God studied to make it so (Habakkuk 2:2) as did also the Lord in His parables (Matthew 13:12—13). Here—apart, unique and alone—is "The Mystery." We must be explicit in language for there is no "Kingdom" here. In *Acts* man is entering into God! (Galatians 3:27; II Corinthians 5:17). He becomes *in Christ* (cf. *Ephesians*). This book must be brief, simple, documented, reasonable and explicit; and above all, it must produce results, i.e., it must make good, for the Lord said, "If any is willing to do His will, he shall know concerning the doctrine, whether it be of God, or I speak from Myself" (John 7:17).

ACTS is the book of "The Way"; the "going down from Jerusalem" to Rome. *Along the way* are Antioch, Ephesus and Athens, and *upon the way* are pray-ers, the crippled beggar, Stephen, the Samaritan half-breeds, the eunuch, Saul, Cornelius—all of whom make up a common brotherhood from Jerusalem to Antioch. Take careful note that, "this was not done in a corner," but amidst the most cultured and religious of the earth in Jerusalem, Athens and Rome.

Our Plea, the Restoration of the Church of the New Testament, is as the re-opening of a long lost gold mine. It is not our task to convince denominations of sin, but to convince ourselves *by* Scripture searching (Jeremiah 6:16) until observers shall say:

> "But we desire to hear from thee what (things) thou thinkest; for indeed as concerning this sect, we know that everywhere it is spoken against."

Acts 28:22 N.

E. ACTS: GOD'S LABORATORY OF SALVATION

ACTS is the laboratory of salvation. In *The New Epoch* George S. Morison says, "the highest tool is an engine which manufactures power." A new Age of Power was introduced when Edison came to the door of the laboratory and said, "I have found and tested it and it works"; and then he revealed the formula, so that men were no longer dependent upon water-falls, but that this power was available in every place. So the apostles' formula of chapter 2 is tested out in *Acts*, Salvation's laboratory. It is no longer *of* the Jews nor *for* them *exclusively*, but is available anywhere (1:8). Now that it lies directly across our way, it is the "must" of God's Ages' long purpose. *The Acts* opens up a new and living way of "The Whosoever" Salvation (Isaiah 35:1—10; Acts 4:1—20; Hebrews 10:19—20); the Cross challenges each; the test is put to all. The value that a man places upon the book of Acts, containing God's formula of salvation, is his estimate upon his own soul. So let us explore its margin and meditate upon the before and after,—for *Acts* blocks the way; there is no detour through the book of Acts, nor any place to stop to turn back. We are buried and raised with Him and as at the Transfiguration, we hear, "This is My Beloved Son . . . hear ye Him."

The *Acts* are the record of God on the *offensive* as He goes out to seek and to save the lost. Here is His vindication before principalities (Ephesians 3). Up until now God has been on the *defensive*, pleading: "All the day long have I stretched out My hands unto an unbelieving and gain-saying people" (Romans 10:21). But now to the Church, the word is "GO!" This is an *offensive*. "It is finished"—God's part—and here the Lord "turns again Home." He turns from "if any man willeth . . ." to the now, "take up his cross and follow Me" (cp. Acts 4:12).

The down-plunge of Acts 2 and its transformations were miracle events and are of "the assured results." These phenomena of Pentecost are not of our experience, though they are not alien to it. We come in upon another level where the incidents are familiar and the items are invariable.

The Church was thrust out into the world as an eagle stirs its next to make her fledglings fly; or as a student who enters upon his commence-ment. Amid ethnic antagonisms, social inequalities, and Babel polyglotism the Church is compelled to edify itself with conquered enemies, those who are born-again!

CONCLUSION

F. ACTS and CHRISTIAN DOCTRINE

The contents of *Acts* are the acts of the Father (Romans 1:4), and The Son (John 16:13—14), and the Holy Spirit (Acts 1:8; 2:4) through the obedient acts of the apostles. It is the book of Spirit-controlled orators, and of heaven-revealed salvation, together with divine imperatives where men "spake as the Spirit gave" that which *I* also have received. It is THE book of THE way. It is the Inter-Spirit Bridge like the International Bridge of Niagara. It is THE Milky Way, THE solo aria, THE radio producer, THE incandescent filament that brings in to man's comprehension the total elements of the whole Bible, divinely stated, didactically imparted, and realistically re-enacted. The Simple can understand; the Wise can impart; and the Caviller is without excuse. The book of Acts is the child's illustrated primer, the adult's divine demonstration of the new birth, and the sinner's worked-out plan of salvation through grace.

Acts is "the only way"; it is the book without a parallel or codicil. As all voices were silenced on the Mount of Transfiguration when God, the Father said, "Hear Ye Him," so at Pentecost, "they all spake as the Spirit gave them utterance"; but when Peter stood up, others ceased when he said, "This is THAT" and the "keys"-man under the Holy Spirit's control set forth the Savior and the Salvation.

As all other mouths were closed, and all other authorities silenced at the Transfiguration, so Pentecost is the second Transfiguration with like divine inhibitions. Souls, each of whom are above the whole world in value (Matthew 16:26), cost too much in planning and patience from Eden to Pentecost, and in the pain and passion of the Cross, to allow room for even a shadow upon the path of a Christ-pleasing Christian's faith, baptism and Memorial Table. So each of these (faith, baptism, and communion table) are doctrinally stated, humanly illustrated, and historically verified.

At the close of *Acts* there rises the finished product: Antioch. The elements are so mixed in that congregation that the Holy Spirit can say, "this is the Church." The Church in Bible study is seen in Acts 11:26:

> *a*) In Name, it is "Christian"
> *b*) In Missions, are recorded Paul's travels, letters
>   and the "My Gospel"

A return to these "living oracles" is "The Way" of "The Restoration."

THE SEALED DIVISION of The Scriptures (Continued)

IV. PAUL'S CHURCH EPISTLES: ROMANS through THESSALONIANS

ROMANS   EPHESIANS
I–II CORINTHIANS   PHILIPPIANS
GALATIANS   COLOSSIANS

THESSALONIANS

"But I certify you, brethren, that the gospel which was preached by me is not according to man. For I neither received it of man, neither was I taught it, but through revelation of Jesus Christ."

"But when it pleased God, who separated me from my mother's womb, and called me through His grace, To reveal His Son in me, that I might preach Him among the nations; . . . . ."

Galatians 1:11–12, 16–16*a* N.

My time has been much spent upon Paul. His divisions have suggested and made profitable my study and illuminated other Scriptures. These outline divisions are suggested that they might stir you up to rightly dividing. From Paul's epistles I have preached expository sermons in the attempt to direct those who are interested as to where to look and what to look for. This type of preaching is not the assumption of wisdom or sanctity, but rather is the report of a worth-while finding. To accomplish the purpose for which expository sermons are intended, exacts study from the listeners.

In his epistles, in language of rare beauty and exquisite accuracy, Paul sets forth this "inheritance" from God (Ephesians 1:11) as being the Temple, the Church, the Body, and in terms and figures too subtle for theologians and too advanced for scientists.

A. PAUL, THE VISION-DOMINATED SLAVE OF CHRIST

Paul's call (Acts 26:15–19; Romans 1:1; Ephesians 1:1) and his place (I Corinthians 15:10) are of extra-ordinary nature and circumstance, and accompany his preparation (Galatians 1:15). His call and his literature impressed the ablest minds. His conversion and the Lord's resurrection stand alone. God's work required a super-man, a God-occupied and God-dominated personality. He was a free-born man, a scholar of rarest attainment (Acts 22:3), one with transcendant emotions, with a love-servitude that is the rarest freedom. The Lord laid hold upon Paul whose own personality was so dominant that he is credited with Paul-inizing the church. Look upon Elohim's work up to Acts 11:26; can you imagine *that* God being over-shadowed or colored by one or all men? God's stature in the eyes of men increases with His Universe (Isaiah 40:12–17). The real explanation of Paul's place in the church is seen only in God's purposed Plan of The Ages at whose consummation "The Age of The Ages" will be the new heaven and the new earth wherein are Nations, Israel and "The Heaven-lies," and where God shall be all and in all (I Corinthians 15:28). To achieve such an Age and to form such institutions are worthy of such a Savior and must require a Paul. Dr. Moffatt says, "We miss the cascade because the whole stream is moving forward with resistless force under a surface of apparent calm." Mighty souls are under emotion, and when God called Paul, the babe leaped as John the Baptist, and heaven had a holiday like unto the church's Christmas, for the Lord's chiefest of architects "was come" (I Corinthians 3:10).

> There are hermit souls that live withdrawn
> In the place of their self-content,
> There are souls like stars, that dwell apart,
> In a fellowless firmament;
> There are pioneer souls that blaze their paths
> Where highways never ran— . . . . [1]

Nebuchadnezzar "fixed" the norm for governments; yet Daniel dominated him and "fixed" a great hope of a Deliverer. Even so in the days of the Roman Empire, Paul stood before Caesar. This great apostle "caught a-way" (II Corinthians 12:1—4), was shown the Body, the Church, being raised (Gr. *egeirantos*), and as he comes back from Paradise, he states "to die is gain" (for me), but to remain is far better for you (Philippians 1:22—24).

Paul is the vision-dominated slave of Christ whose conversion, in-spiration, and epistles are all unique and apart from others (Acts 9:1—19a; 22:12—15; 26:12—19; 22:17b—18; I Corinthians 9:1; 15:3; and Galatians 1:1). Paul was the emotional one of the apostles. You could gather all of the love of John and all of the tears of Jeremiah and put them up before the passion of Paul and they would be lost sight of in the greatness of this man's love and emotion. A study of Paul removes him from the other a-postles for his speech and his letters have unique revelation elements. Only Paul visioned the church as a third body (separate from Jew or Gen-tile; Galatians 3:28), which is visible only to re-born ones. Other of the apostles preached the gospel and those who received it were added to the group of believers; but "to the Jew first" became a sect ("Way") within Israel, and this misconception occasioned Galatians 1:6—9. Peter and the others saw the Christ risen while Paul alone saw the Body of Christ, the church, rising (Gr. *egeirantos*, Galatians 1:1) from amongst the dead (in sin) ones. He saw this continuum miracle of God's ever-present and ever-operating resurrection power. Here is explanation which is luminous and satisfying of why God kept Jesus and Paul apart in the flesh so that there would be no slightest taint of Messiah-ism which might veil Paul's eyes

---

[1]
    Sam Walter Foss (1858—1911), *The Book of American Poetry*, Selected by Edwin Markham, (N.Y., William H. Wise & Co., Inc.) 1934, p. 301.

(II Corinthians 3:18). The proof of this is in I Corinthians 15:8; and in Paul's question on the road to Damascus when he asks "who art thou Lord?" Inasmuch as he was "separated" from his mother's womb, Paul is "A Chosen Vessel" and his epistles contain "The Mystery." He was born out of due time but into the apostolic family. It is profitable to examine his call and the contents of his epistles. Concerning his call, he says, "they of repute added nothing to me" (Galatians 2:6); and also, "I was not a whit behind the very chiefest apostles" (II Corinthians 11:5). Paul's every contact with the Lord was immediate through miraculous, heavenly initiative. No other was ever so, nor ever received that same attention. He is like the United States of America flag which never touches the ground. Every new advance in Paul's ministry was prefaced by a vision or appearance of the Lord.

a) Stephen, (Acts 6:55—56)
b) Damascus, (Acts 9:12; 22:14; 9:16; 26:16)
c) Arabia, " conferred not with flesh and blood" (Galatians 1:17)
d) Jerusalem in the Temple, "I fell into a trance" (Acts 22:17)
e) Antioch, "Holy Spirit said" and "Sent" (Acts 13:2 and 4)
f) In Asia, "forbidden of Holy Spirit" (Acts 16:6)
g) At Troas, the vision of "a certain man" (Acts 16:9)
h) In Corinth, "In a vision . . . much people" (Acts 18:9—10)

When he finally went up to Jerusalem by revelation (Galatians 2:2) he preached on the way up (Acts 15:3; Galatians 2:6, 9).

Paul was a man of very great prayer. No other of all the Bible so prayed, Daniel excepted. But Paul saw, he visioned and he revealed the flood gates of heaven in knowledge and love of Him, until like Enoch, he rises in Philippians 1:23 N.:

> "For I am in a strait betwixt two, having a desire
> to depart, and to be with Christ; which is very
> far better;"

This was spoken by no other apostle. John was ordered up (Revelation 4:1), but Paul was *"caught up"* (II Corinthians 12:2). John was ordered up for the purpose of revealing, but Paul was caught up beyond speech and this was just for love's rare rapture, as though God had impulsively drawn him away from some lonely experience. Moses was taken up into the Mount and given the Law. The Savior at His Transfiguration talked about His decease; and Paul was given *Romans* through *Thessalonians* (II Timothy 1:13). After being shown the pattern, Moses was ready to die for his people (Exodus 32:32); the Savior did die; and Paul was willing to die (Romans 9:1; 10:1); no others in the Scriptures were like unto these save Jonah.

B.   PAUL, THE HYPERBOLIST, SHIFTING INTO HIGHER TERMS

"How that he was *caught up* into Paradise, and heard
unspeakable words, which it is not lawful for a man
to utter."

II Corinthians 12:4

The Living Words of the Living Scriptures are as a portfolio of pen
sketches or pictures (I Corinthians 2:1—14; Proverbs 25:11; Ecclesiastes
12:11; John 6:63). Words are the mosiacs and the pigments of artists, and
the nails of builders. With words Ezekiel drew the Temple and Shakespeare
limned the theatre.

To get your intelligence directed to and interested in the higher terms
of Paul, is my prayer. Jesus said, "My Church" and likewise He spoke of
"The Way"—"The Mystery"—"The Body." Paul used all of these terms;
he joined those in "The Way"; he was caught up (II Corinthians 12:4) into
"The Mystery" and he visioned "The new man."

1. "The Way" (Acts 9:2) has land marks easy to follow and easy
   to demonstrate (Acts 2:37). Men received definite instructions
   and easily practiced ordinances, imparting a quick sense of
   refuge as it did when the eunuch "went on his way rejoicing."
2. On the other hand, "The Mystery" (Romans 16:25) is an ocean
   navigable only to those tying to the stars and to those who
   participate in an "heavenly calling" (Philippians 3:14). The
   wind and the mildest tide may deflect these.
3. The term "The Body" describes the close, intimate relationship
   of "the new man" with Christ the Head of the Body (Colossians
   1:18—24).

These higher terms are a piling up of compounds. Even as when we
approach mountains we note that boulders become more rugged and massive.
Super-thought and speech are inviting the searcher into "the heavenlies"
of spiritual wealth. Scholars speak of Paul's *words.* Dante in his *Divine
Comedy* describing Paradise wrote:

> The glory of Him who moveth everything
> Doth penetrate the universe, and shine
> In one part more and in another less.
> Within that heaven which most his light receives
> Was I, and things beheld which to repeat
> Nor knows, nor can, who from above descends;
> Because in drawing near to its desire
> Our intellect ingulphs itself so far,
> That after it the memory cannot go.
> Truly whatever of the holy realm

> I had the power to treasure in my mind
> Shall now become the subject of my song. [1]

So Paul as he was "caught up" into the true Paradise, returns from "the heavenlies" and like Dante could say, "truly whatever of the holy realm I had the power to treasure in my mind shall now become the subject of my song," and through him God makes known the hidden mystery, the Church.

Paul, the hyperbolist, ascends to prayer (Ephesians 1:15—23; 1:19), and *Ephesians* contacts a world beyond. Note the use of the Greek *huperballo* in II Corinthians 3:10; 9:14; Ephesians 1:19; 2:7 and 3:19. The Church is God's "hyperbole,"—beyond, apart, above, separate in every way from "every several building" and "principalities and powers" and residence (Ephesians 2:22), for the Church is like the Governor's residence in a State Capital. We have noted that Paul writes of the "exceeding greatness of His power to us-ward who believe." Here is a massing of elements, powers, and persons that exhausts language and compels Paul to the use of a hyperbole which is a poetic figure: "for we are God's poem" (Ephesians 2:10*a*). Concerning Paul's use of this word, Vincent says:

> ". . . Compounds are characteristic of Paul's intensity
> of style, and mark the struggle of language with the
> immensity of the divine mysteries."

This hyperbole, "exceeding," is not an exaggeration but it is *aorist*. [2] It is beyond our horizon. Imagine yourself on an island whose beach is pebbled with pearls! No matter what you take, you will leave fabulous wealth. You say, "Go back and get it!" That is what I am trying to do in *Ephesians*. We go from the known "Christ and Him crucified" to the un-realized, "head over all things." What we have received is but "earnest" money, the good-faith or down payment pledge.

> ROMANS   is the Cross propitiatory
> GALATIANS is the battle before the Cross
> EPHESIANS is beyond the Cross

And these three books reveal Paul in his greatness as:

> *a*) The scholar, secluded with his parchments
> *b*) The polemic, the contender for "the faith"
> *c*) The mystic, "the prisoner of the Lord,"

No other New Testament writer except Paul elaborates a system of doctrine. In the Old Testament Moses did this, and, like Paul, was divinely

---

[1] *The Divine Comedy of Dante Alighieri,* translated by Henry Wadsworth Longfellow, (N. Y., Houghton, Mifflin and Company), *Paradiso,* Canto I, p. 493

[2] See Appendix A. *Aorist Tense,* pp. 590—592

admonished (Exodus 25:40; II Timothy 1:13). Of them all:

 a) Paul alone ascended into *unscalable* heights (II Corinthians 12:2)
 b) Paul alone traveled an *untrackable* way (Ephesians 3:8)
 c) Paul alone heard *unspeakable* words (II Corinthians 12:4)
 d) And Paul alone was stabbed with *unescapable* weakness
    (II Corinthians 12:7).

There was "purpose" in all of this and that purpose was "to reveal His Son in me." As the deltas of great rivers divide into mouths, but always one is open and deep; so the twelve apostles and Paul are like that. The twelve slowed down for they were shallowed by the Lord's human side, and they had been His familiars. Paul on the other hand, had not been one of these for he had met Him on foreign soil on the road to Damascus.

C. FROM THE PRIMITIVE CHURCH
TO THE RESTORATION MOVEMENT

The primitive church aflame with zeal and "saying none other things" (Acts 26:22), in fifty years had laid the "Way" (Acts 19:9) from Antioch to Rome. Paul wrote in II Timothy 1:15, ". . . all they which are in Asia be turned away from me; . . ."; and again in 4:16, ". . . but all forsook me . . ."; and Paul's name still is not honored in Rome today. It was with difficulty that I obtained a picture of Paul there; but it would have been easy had I been looking for one of Peter. The absence of Paul's teaching produced the Dark Ages. Darkness is the absence of light; "Thy Word is a lamp . . ." and to remove this Word, is to stumble. ". . . If therefore the light that is in thee be darkness, how great is that darkness!" (Matthew 6:23). After the Scriptures were taken away, teaching became obscured and interpreters explained them *away*. They explained away first the Thessalonian truth of the *Hope*; second, the Ephesian truth of the *Mystery*; and third, the Roman truth of *faith-salvation*. Darkness settled down upon the Church and it was lost during these Dark Ages.

We must take up the "My Gospel," "The Mystery," epistles of Paul. This is that body of teaching to which the Lord referred in John 16:7—15; 14:12—17; and to which Satan has blinded the Church quite too long (II Corinthians 4:4).

If this salvation is not here in Paul's epistles, then there is nowhere else even a suggestion of it and His promise has never been fulfilled. Just as Israel never fully occupied the Promised Land (Genesis 13:14—17; 15:*18*) though it was opened and surrendered at their entrance (Joshua 9); so the Pentecost Gospel began in "great power," and in a half century had reached unto Rome where the church lost its passion and settled back into institutionalism. So also our "Plea" stopped at the borderland before truce flags of sectarianism and forfeited our cultural leadership as the Jews did their religious supremacy. We have preached the Gospel plan of Salvation with unrivaled clarity and power; we have made creeds impossible and this has required logic and enthusiastic dogmatism and we have furnished these of a high order. Our very success has blinded us. We were so much beyond sectarianism that we did not sense our own falling short which is just being revealed in these acid times. More than *logic* and *dogmatism* are essential if we are to have "fellowship with Him."

The going apart "with Him" with transforming intent, the deliberate going into His Presence not to *beg* but to be *made over*, must become the in-betweens of the activities and arguments of primary obedience; "forgetting those things which are behind" and "leaving the doctrine of the first principles of Christ, let us press on unto perfection." This is not found in the *ordinances* in *Romans* but "in Him" in *Ephesians*. We are children of eternity, and our "meat" is to do His will, and our conversation is prayer. We must search out all defiling leaven; we must know all sin and we must reject, judge and cast out every (even pet) weaknesses. "Much," "great," "continuous" prevailing prayer must share time and strength with our preaching. Preaching is reaching out to *men* with a "once for all" delivered Gospel while prayer is reaching to *God* with an upward sky-striving groaning of the Spirit. These are parts of *one* whole and it is not possible to separate them. We are called to "teaching them to observe all things," but we must pay the price. Denominations have reversed the order and are teaching *us* as we use their Bible helps, quarterlies, essays and books. These things ought not and must not be, else our Candle of Testimony will be removed, and the creed-less principles of our Plea will be forfeited. The devisive bickerings among us announce our lost condition because we have stopped short and would not go on to perfection.

This church age must be grasped ere we can understand Paul, and ere we can explain the ordinances of death and new life. His great chapters are Romans 12, I Corinthians 13, Ephesians 4, and I Thessalonians 4. Think of Paul's blood ancestry, his religion, mentality, and how he moved the great: Felix trembled, Festus cried out, and Agrippa said, "Almost." His emotional perorations convince and move until this day. Here is no ordinary soul-weakling, but instead a giant forging the logical thunderbolts, or a Vesuvius throwing its lava stream up and out, shaking both the Roman Empire and Judaism. Watch him, as facts conquered his mind and the consequences leered upon him. The determining factor had not yet entered, but at Damascus, his imagination grappled; he became vision-mastered and the events of his life reveal it.

Paul was a *see-er* for he saw the Church rise in Christ's stead. He is "the chosen vessel" and we would expect that one so chosen would be given a high station, but instead the Lord tells him "how great things he must suffer." Paul carried Christ to man. He was the ambassador of God to the human intellect. It takes an adequate mind with which to rear an invisible temple and Paul was fully able to describe the "breadth, length, depth, height" of the Church (Ephesians 3:18). A book built an empire in Napoleon's brain (Caesar's *Commentaries*) but the necessary statesmanship was not seen by Napoleon for he was blinded to it. Paul looked upon Stephen and then upon Stephen's Lord, and he rears the Church after the Divine pattern.

The Scriptures as any text book must be properly approached and explained if there is to be an intelligent response and spiritual growth. I have long felt our confusion. With the greatest Plea, we have failed to evangelize cities, or to unite His dis-severed Body. Such colossal failure drove me to study. The Scriptures are a text book and our failure to e-vangelize and unite, is seeking an explanation and an efficiency to vindicate the claim of Hebrews 4:12 and the assertion of Isaiah 55:11. And I believe I have found the lost way, and the reverse order of teachings emphasized, confirms my conviction. As we have said, church history shows that the first doctrine surrendered was the RAPTURE, followed by the surrender of the ONE BODY, and then of SALVATION by FAITH. The movement in the New Testament leads to the same conclusion:

a) The closing of the Gospel of John prepares for ACTS
  b) The closing of *Acts* prepares for ROMANS
a) The Gospels present CHRIST
  b) The *Acts* present the HOLY SPIRIT
    c) And *Romans* through *Thessalonians* present the CHURCH

From the close of *Romans* through *Thessalonians*, there is left no trail, as though *tracks* give way to *wings* of rapture. Here is progress:

a) ROMANS closes on "The Mystery" (16:25)
b) EPHESIANS opens on "The Mystery" (1:9)
c) PHILIPPIANS is "forgetting the things . . . behind" (3:13)
d) COLOSSIANS calls us to the fact that "if we have been risen with Him," then "*seek* those things which are above where Christ is" (3:1)
e) THESSALONIANS points to the Rapture (4:13—18)

I have long felt that the "Restoration" was unfinished. To follow the fathers and to go on is to honor their efforts. The present trouble among us has been caused by the incompleteness of our Plea. My faith in God's Grace, Christ's Deity, and the Word's Inspiration, make bold in the face of any save "Thus saith the Lord."

Our fathers stopped short of a *full* study of the Scriptures. They said "we have reached the place of *Ne plus ultra.*" The plan of salvation and the pattern for the church was clear to them, but *we* must "steer a straight course," and we must launch out and "Sail on!"—into all of the Christ, who is above all other anointed ones; and into all of THE Book which all other truth; for all other is searched out (Proverbs 25:2), but this salvation to the dead ones, must be brought to them.

D. FROM THE GOSPELS TO *ACTS,* TO THE EPISTLES

Across these New Testament pages as across a continent, through the Gospels from the Manger to the Cross, through *Acts* from the Cross to *Ephesians* and through the Epistles to II Peter 3, "moves the Church of God"—foundationed in faith, washed in blood, and seated "in the heavenlies." To those who in the love of the Bible hold communion with its divisible dispensations, the Bible speaks.

The Shekinah glory upon Paul's epistles is discernible to the Spiritually-minded. But recently to me appears a God-ordered, Spirit-controlled, wonder-provoking advance marked in Paul's three and one-half journeys. These fit in to the pattern of the Great Commission and are developments of the elements therein. Take the *Acts* and go over these journeys of Paul and note where the *emphasis* falls:

In Journey *One*, it is upon FAITH

In Journey *Two*, the emphasis is upon BAPTISM

In Journey *Three*, it is upon the LORD'S SUPPER

And in the *Half Journey*, to Rome as a prisoner, the emphasis is upon "THE HEAVENLIES" which as a Jacob's ladder, is set up in prison out of which come his prison epistles, and especially the book of Ephesians.

Peter and Paul were both given the Gospel message and the same terms of salvation for all, and both preached the same message. Peter was shown that the Gentiles were to be received into the Church; but he did not grasp the fact that the Church is a distinct Body which is not related to the Jew, Judaism, the Law, or the Jewish community. Paul, in his epistles clearly draws the line between those who would continue under the law while claiming to follow Christ and those who are free from the bondage of the law and who are in heavenly places in Christ Jesus. The differences are not in the revelation made to these two apostles, but rather in their *willingness* to receive and to preach that which they were given. God's man follows God's plan.

Paul's "My Gospel" church letters are most fascinating and wonderful in their analysis and revelation of the Bible. And why should not this be so to us Gentiles to whom Paul was an apostle? To appreciate and understand them, to be able to teach others, is that whereunto we are called. The impersonal-essay quality of *Romans* and *Ephesians* sets them apart as fundamental, as initial documents. *Romans* is a workshop for the evangelistic; the church at work in the harvest field there. *Ephesians* is a prayer room for transformation (Luke 9:29). The church is at home—at ease—"in Him." Here it is possible to "take time to be holy, speak oft with thy Lord." *Romans* is Christ's public ministry while *Ephesians* is like the times of His retirement—apart to pray. *Romans* is the place where Christ (the Gospels) is in practical operation, as He wrought wonders upon matter here which was "greater" because it was upon dead souls (John 14:12). *Ephesians* is the church in *Acts* banishing the fear of those "who through fear of death were all their lifetime subject to bondage" (Hebrews 2:15). Here *Ephesians* is like that place where Jesus said to His disciples, "I have yet many things to say unto you but ye cannot bear them *now*" (John 16:12). He is speaking to us "in the heavenlies" for this is the battle-field of those who are Spirit-driven, Spirit-forbidden, and Spirit-guided before they fully understood. The Scriptures were written for "our learning" and require no extraordinary ability to understand; but even the Authors of the Transition Epistles could not grasp (I Peter 1:10). Bullinger and others missed this understanding. In the *Acts*, men "spake as the Spirit gave them utterance." Paul said, "I have lived in all good conscience" and here in *Acts* there were Jews who had a "zeal but not according to knowledge." Peter of Pentecost who was *right* as he preached the first Gospel sermon, was *wrong* at Antioch later. It took his second epistle to show that he had not seen clearly the first gospel sermon and the terms of salvation. In the book of Acts the campaign is Spirit-directed and we find "being filled with the Spirit" to be an occasional experience for Peter. Then the driving, visible power of the campaign retires to within the Church, His Body, to prepare it for the future demonstration of Ephesians 3:8—11. At the close of *Ephesians*, Paul speaks of "peace" and at once the marvelous "filling" of *Acts* gives way to "abiding." As the Gospels' Transfiguration closes the miraculous, and *John* chapters 12 through 17, "straightway" opens, so *Acts* is "The Way"—as the Spirit leads the Church from the Gospels to the Epistles. Men are Spirit-controlled through the *Acts* because they are moving out from one method into another. What an anabasis! They are moving from the Gospels to *Romans*.

The *local* occasion for these letters soon passed though as a shower they brought local relief. Then began their *real purpose*. They are as a system of graded steps from *Atheos* and worse, up to I Corinthians 2:9—10. These letters are prepared as were the materials for the Temple of Solomon:

"And the house, when it was in building, was built of stone made perfect before it was brought thither; so that there was neither hammer nor axe nor any tool of iron heard in the house, while it was in building."

E. RIGHTLY DIVIDING PAUL'S CHURCH EPISTLES

". . . Rightly dividing (steering a straight course through) the Word of truth."

II Timothy 2:15

INTRODUCTION

This is a severely and frugally planned Universe and Bible (Psalm 8:1–5; 19:1; John 5:39). The more accurately any of God's elements are searched out, the more we become aware that while there is always plenty, there is never a wasteful surplus. God's economy is a vast one wherein there is never lacking an abundance. There is a fear-allaying, satisfying supply for every need to all those who walk in "The Way" of trust. The occasion for this statement is that attention is being addressed to Paul's revelation which calls for "location" in the book of the Church. And this requires "Rightly Dividing" which is only acquired through "searching the Scriptures." Those who will to do this will "not walk in darkness" but will be able to "save themselves and those who hear them." How many are blind who just read with no aim or understanding!

Israel's Red Sea experience fits this text marching straight between crystal walls which the unbelieving Egyptians assaying to do, did drown. This steering a straight course is also like the experience of seamen venturing between the two dangers of Scylla and Charybdis. This "Rightly Dividing" is the "Of Mine" of John 16:14. It is not the dividing of the Old from the New Testament nor the dividing of dispensational ages, though these too are most profitable, but the Church is "added" as was the Law, and though invisible, yet it is spiritually discerned by those who rightly divide. The church epistles were revealed to Paul and these open out at the end of *Acts* where "The Way" yields to "The Mystery" even as the Pillars of Hercules front the Atlantic. Here the breath of the Spirit is filling the soul of Paul. This one was called and Spirit-qualified as a specialist in church literature. There is no explanation of Paul on other grounds. Scholarship recognizes the Spirit's use of John which shows "God is able," but the mind of Paul is the refined instrument for this subtle "Mystery."

The Scriptures are not the temple but are the revelation light therein. "Thy Word is a lamp unto my feet and a light unto my path" (Psalm 119: 105). Their symbol is the candle stick (lamp stand) and this was the only source of light in the Holy Place of the Tabernacle and today that Holy Place is the Church. Of itself this alone would emphasize unto those who are thoughtful of life and its concerns. An outline survey of the Bible is essential for no other text or book is ever intelligently considered aside from its relation to the whole volume. Microscopic parts must "go to their own place" in the whole and fit. This rule would save from blunders. This is my profound conviction as my knowledge of the Word enlarges, and this is why there is so much of expository preaching upon Paul's group which is peculiarly ours.

> "In every great mechanism, whatever the number or complexity of its parts, there must be unity of design. Every part bears a given relation to every other part, and the perception of that relation is necessary to a proper understanding of the whole.[1]

See the beauty and symmetry of the Bible groupings which are so familiar to all: Law, Prophets, Psalms, Gospel, History, Doctrine, Hope. These are suggestive of yet further sub-divisions, each revealing a like beauty and symmetry even as students also will discover in nature; and accepting the leading of the Holy Spirit, we are quickly amid wonders (I Corinthians 15:46). The Lord takes Paul apart (Romans 15:23; I Corinthians 3:10) and sends him to release "My Gospel." His ministry up until now was the Cross, the Propitiatory, from I Corinthians 2:2 "the sea of the dead," to Romans 8:39, the Communion Table. It is the Gospel of Salvation, i.e. the Great Commission, till the Church was called to its *Prothesis* (purpose) that is, "seated in the heavenlies." Having advanced from the first (*Romans*) to the sixth (*Colossians*), we are eager for the seventh (*Thessalonians*) and this growth is like Shakespeare's *Seven Ages of Man,*[2] or like the progress of man depicted in Lorado Taft's *Fountain of Time* (Chicago). The *outward*, the physical, goes through the stages of senility, but the *spiritual* does not (II Corinthians 4:16). Within this house of God we "come unto" a living fountain of *seven* springs whose waters, bursting from the Throne, carry life to all who will come and partake:

> ROMANS will bring forth baptism and salvation
> EPHESIANS brings forth holiness and sanctification
> THESSALONIANS brings forth hope and glorification.

An audience seated in a room is first given an explanation and then

---

[1] Charles Hodge, D.D., *Systematic Theology,* (*Church Polity,* Selected, Arranged by the William Durant), (New York, Scribner's Sons).

[2] Shakespeare, *"As You Like It,"* Act II, Sc. 7, line 143 ("All the world's a stage . . .") "His acts being seven ages. At first the infant, . . . whining school-boy, . . . lover, . . . soldier . . . justice . . . lean and slipper'd pantaloon, . . . last of all, is second childishness and mere oblivion."

the call is for "lights out" and the revelation starts, so here in the church epistles, the lecture opens and "The Mystery" begins:

a) In *Romans*, he is feeding them with "milk," preaching Jesus Christ
   (1) In *Ephesians*, he gives them "strong meat," the revelation of the mystery
b) In *Romans*, wonder of wonders, the dead are raised to life
   (1) In *Ephesians,* mystery of mysteries, saved sinners are seated in the abode of God! This (God) receiveth sinners! and eateth with them!

From here on Paul proceeds alone on the way that leads straight on to the inheritance of Ephesians 1:11. Paul descended from that experience of II Corinthians 12:1—4, veiled in mystery as was Moses.

Every dispensation comes to fruitage and from the fruit of each comes a succeeding dispensation as in any other seed-propagated species. The first advance is dividing and grouping. Next we will consider the group teaching, but first we must see the cleavage and affinities within these seven church letters, and we must divide aright if we are to get light. The first step is to isolate and study to discover the reason for such cleavage. I am not seeking to do away with any of the Bible. All Scripture "is profitable" (II Timothy 3:16—17), but it is necessary to adjust them to us that there may be light. Even the Ten Commandments were placed on *two* tables of stone, for they contained *two* sets of relationships. Why should we not expect like departments in church teaching?

In the building of a home, plans are first made and usually there is one thing uppermost that we wish to see within the home. It may be enough closets or a den or something else. Whatever it is, we call in an architect, for the rest of the house must be in proportion and harmonious and inter-related. So is there in these seven epistles just such proportion and a harmony. At the start they seem to be a jumble for *Thessalonians, Corinthians, Galatians* and *Romans* are widely scattered and not related, just as all building materials are widely scattered. Try to think of the chaos of Genesis 1:2 which was over the world and for the same reason. Paul was not conscious that a church library was being written and that divisions were being placed within it (I Peter 1:11); but here they are and they are each as orderly as heavenly systems. Paul grew with these revelations, but these are the Spirit's letters, for God, all-wise, foresaw the need and ordered out salvaging agencies even before the wreck. The problems which the church was to face were prepared of God in Paul's letters even before the need occurred. A train dispatcher knows that two trains going toward each other on the same track will be wrecked and therefore orders doctors and nurses to the scene before the wreck happens. So God ordered Paul before he was shown Galatians 2:15; and He ordered "My Gospel" (the Mystery) as the instrument of power with which to raise the dead. Paul's "My Gospel" became the vision beckoning past all pain. As Abraham sought "the City" and the Lord "for the joy set before Him" endured the Cross, so Paul said:

> ". . . . forgetting indeed those things which are behind,
> and reaching forth unto those things which are before,
> I press toward the mark for the prize of the up-calling of
> God in Christ Jesus."
>
> Philippians 3:14N.

This Gospel was common to all but particularly to Paul. If the Bible be "rightly divided," it will be "rightly" understood and will become popular. The secret of "Our Plea" was that every man carried his Bible and was able to give a reason (I Peter 3:15). My hope is to see Bible School boys carrying their Bibles along the street to church, for these will be the armed legions of the Church (Revelation 19:15).

1. Seeing the SYSTEMS in Paul's Epistles

The "Synoptics" plus *John* are the Lamp of the Lord; then fire falls at Pentecost and the Church moves down through to Romans 1:17 where the Pentecost "Lamp" sheds its light upon all. From Pentecost the Church traveled along "The Way" until it opened into the central suns of ROMANS and EPHESIANS and THESSALONIANS, and the Planets of CORINTHIANS with GALATIANS and PHILIPPIANS with COLOSSIANS. There are two easily discernible currents: Positive and Negative, and as a cracked mirror so the Negative reflects the Positive:

a) The Positive (the suns):
   ROMANS, EPHESIANS, THESSALONIANS
b) The Negative (the planets):
   CORINTHIANS and GALATIANS,
   PHILIPPIANS and COLOSSIANS
c) THESSALONIANS stands apart, without planet, for its
   central theme is the Rapture, and it is still future.

Then there is a further "dividing" of the Positive group: here, there is an "ascent," and an unveiling of "things of MINE." These are easily discerned by those seeking:

> ROMANS is concerned with SALVATION
> EPHESIANS, with SANCTIFICATION
> THESSALONIANS, with GLORIFICATION

Wouldn't you expect system and progress here? And that it would be hid

to the indifferent? All other truth of God is so kept from defiled or indifferent minds (Matthew 11:25; Isaiah 6:9—10; Ephesians 3:9).

ROMANS and its satellites, CORINTHIANS and GALATIANS, are the
SALVATION Group; and these are exactly in their right order. The first,
Corinthians, is the correction of the *Practice* of Salvation. At Corinth,
men were going wrong in heart as Eve in Genesis 3:6, and as the Ephesian
Church of Revelation 2:4. The second, *Galatians*, is the correction of the
Doctrine of Salvation. Here man's head is following his heart; he is in-
venting a theory to fit the practice. The brain, no matter what its quality,
is ever the apologist of the heart. This Romans group quotes the Old Testament the most of any of Paul's writings, for "Salvation is of the Jews"
through the Christ of John 5:39. There is no "Mystery" at the first, for it
is hidden till Romans 8:26.

EPHESIANS and its satellites, PHILIPPIANS and COLOSSIANS, are
the SANCTIFICATION Group. These three are in a rarer spiritual en-
compassment, but the movement is of like direction and import. The
secondary letters of this group deal with the vagaries which are inherent
within the indifferent discipleship: the half-hearted, the half-interested,
and the half-informed.

THESSALONIANS is the GLORIFICATION Epistle. This book is the
exception, and is without satellite, for those who attain unto glorification
are at the journey's end.

This grouping of books is not peculiar to Paul's letters but is found
in the Pentateuch, as well as the Gospels, and seems to be the orderly
process of God's mind which is revealed in nature, in a thought, or in King
Solomon's Temple (I Kings 6:7). Can you imagine such results doubted
or disputed? Why then should the arrangement of these letters be doubted?

No other wrote to THE Church. The readjustment of Paul's letters
admits him into the society of the prophets (I Peter 1:10—12; II Peter 3:
15—16). The perfection of their order leaves no place (Galatians 1:8—9)
for "any other Gospel." The rightly dividing of these is the necessary
preparation for the spiritual understanding of any unit of the group. In
Romans, Ephesians and *Thessalonians* is set forth the Gospel of Faith,
Love and Hope, the immortal trinity of the human emotions. Here is a complete homogenous body of salvation doctrine, the open "Mystery" that the
"Man of God may be thoroughly furnished (lacking in nothing) unto EVERY
good work." To understand these there must be much study in *Romans*,
much prayer in *Ephesians*, and much meditation upon *Thessalonians* (I Corinthians 2:14).

These church letters of Paul's set forth simply:

                            Man — lost
                            Christ's Gospel
                            Man — saved

All are within God's ages-long purpose (Ephesians 1:5; Philippians 2:13; II Thessalonians 1:11) and they are motivated through Grace and adjusted to the eventually perfect (Hebrews 2:10; 12:2). "Why should it be thought a thing incredible with you that God . . ." should personally be in control of His Literature, His Church and His Universe?

In *Romans* the church is like an organization, a machine, an instrument, a vehicle to evangelize, and as such it must ever be. But in *Ephesians*, the church is an *organism*, a body, and it is vital (2:21). Organization is as essential for the Roman *job* as Organism is essential for the Ephesian *living*. In the Roman group, men could say, "I am of Peter, of Paul or of Apollos," and there was sectarian separation; but in the Ephesian group which is an indivisible group, a people are as distinct as the Gulf Stream and as ameliorating. The Body in the Roman group (I Corinthians 12) is composed of parts which are prideful and conscious of rivalry. That divisive rivalry is the bane of missionary and evangelistic work today. While in *Ephesians* (chap. 4), the parts of the Body lose their (own) lives in the over-life functioning as ONE Body:

> "From whom all the body fitly joined together and compacted through that which every joint supplieth, according to the effectual working in the measure of each one, maketh increase of the body unto the edifying of itself in love."
>
>   Ephesians 4:16 N.

> "But strong food belongeth to them that are of full age, even those who by reason of use have their senses exercised to discern both good and evil."
>
>   Hebrews 5:14 N.

This "building up of itself in love" is as a bearing working in oil. The ideas, language and operation are different for here is the language and atmosphere of two planes of life.

Chart out the result as the revelation of the Mind of God upon man's supreme quest for Salvation, Sanctity and *Telos* (The Consummation), in an intellectually satisfying, a heart-peace imparting, and a worth-while outcome, that will encompass and "supply your every need," even as the land of Eden did Adam's.

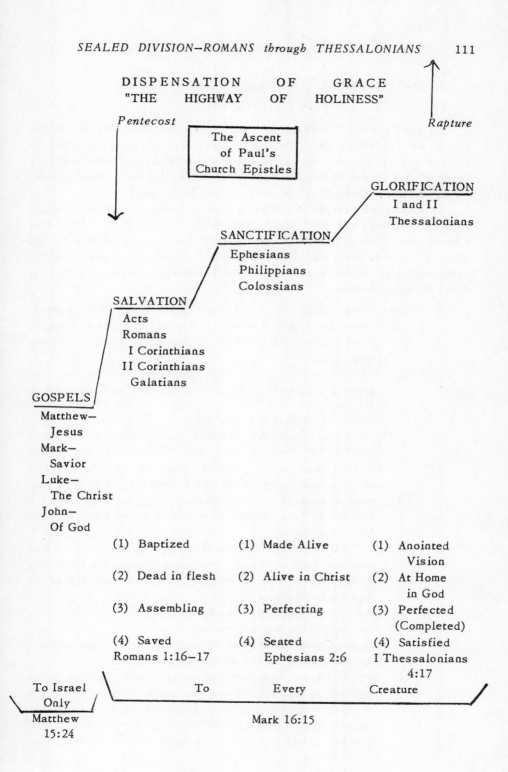

DISPENSATION   OF   GRACE
"THE   HIGHWAY   OF   HOLINESS"

Pentecost   *Rapture*

The Ascent
of Paul's
Church Epistles

GLORIFICATION
I and II
Thessalonians

SANCTIFICATION
Ephesians
Philippians
Colossians

SALVATION
Acts
Romans
I Corinthians
II Corinthians
Galatians

GOSPELS
Matthew—
Jesus
Mark—
Savior
Luke—
The Christ
John—
Of God

(1) Baptized	(1) Made Alive	(1) Anointed Vision
(2) Dead in flesh	(2) Alive in Christ	(2) At Home in God
(3) Assembling	(3) Perfecting	(3) Perfected (Completed)
(4) Saved	(4) Seated	(4) Satisfied
Romans 1:16—17	Ephesians 2:6	I Thessalonians 4:17

To Israel
Only   To   Every   Creature
Matthew   Mark 16:15
15:24

2. The DOCTRINAL Ascendancy of Paul's Epistles

INTRODUCTION

To rightly divide is the first move toward the understanding of the Bible. We can divide and subdivide within a dispensation but when we confuse and mix the two, we are hopelessly confused. The order of Paul's seven church letters is never changed though they are not chronologically arranged. Here is enough to "Selah" (stop and think upon).

That there are degrees in Christian growth, steps in spiritual development, both Christ and Paul teach (Mark 4:28; Romans 2:27). The Great Commission, "Going, PREACH the Gospel" is dynamite (Romans 1:16) which is used to raise the dead (as drowned bodies in a lake). It is "to every creature," the lost, the dead in sins and worse (Romans 2:32), for these are only creatures.

a) This Great *Commission* contains steps, levels and degrees, and these agree with *Romans, Ephesians* and *Thessalonians*:

(1) As the fruit of the GOSPEL is planted, it produces *Roman* truth

(2) ROMANS' truth is laid upon the Great Commission. The articles of Mark 16:16 are illustrated and enforced in *Romans*:

   (a) *Faith* in Romans 1:17 and 5:1

   (b) *Baptism*, "Buried," "Planted and Raised" in chapter 6

(3) EPHESIANS' Truth is laid upon Romans 8:31 when faith (raised) appropriates, trusts (and not before), and sits down in the presence of "mine enemies." The "teaching them to observe . . ." (Matthew 28:19), not only to do but to intently look, results in the "full grown man" with the fulness of Christ.

(4) THESSALONIANS' Truth is laid upon Ephesians 4:16. The complete body of Christ when it has finished its earth stay is raptured to where there is "telos," and the Age of the Ages meet (Matthew 28:20).

b) The *foundation* Scriptures of the New Testament are:

(1) The GOSPELS, *Matthew* through *John.*

   In these are briefed the element of God, Christ's Deity, and the purpose of His coming into the world

(2) The ACTS, the demonstration period where doctrine is developed, tested and worked out during which *Romans* and the other practical Scriptures are produced. Here those like unto the prodigal son "come to themselves, arise and go." *Romans* is on the way back home as the prodigal son.

(3) EPHESIANS is the place of peace. Here the prodigal is back home: robed, ringed and seated "in Him" at peace. He is as a group of refugees who, when taken aboard a United States ship and placed back of its guns, sail amid dangers "in the heavenlies."

(4) THESSALONIANS is the sight of land for refugees, and home for the prodigal. As Abraham looked for "the City," so we look for "the Hope."

Jesus said, "He (the Holy Spirit) shall receive of Mine" and "He will guide you into all truth" (John 16:14, 13). At Nazareth, Jesus read from Isaiah 61:1—2*a*:

"The Spirit of the Lord is upon me,
Because he anointed me *to preach the Gospel* to the poor;
He hath sent me *to proclaim release to the captives,*
And *recovering of sight* to the blind,
To set at liberty them that are bruised,
To proclaim the acceptable year of the Lord."

Luke 4:18—19*a* A. S. V.

This event furnishes a parallel to illustrate the rightly dividing of Paul's epistles:

Romans   —"to preach the Gospel"
Ephesians   —"to proclaim release to the captives"
Thessalonians—"the recovering of sight."

And then the general statement covering the above three follows: "to set at liberty the bruised, to proclaim the acceptable year of our Lord." This would enable man to see what Abraham saw—"the City" which would have been the common vision had there been no sin.

c) Paul's epistles guide us into all:
           truth about Salvation in *Romans*
           sanctification in *Ephesians*
           glorification in *Thessalonians:*

(1) In the ROMANS group is Justification and Salvation.
    The *conduct* of the CORINTHIANS, and the *doctrine* of the GALATIANS denied these above teachings of Justication and Salvation

(2) In the EPHESIANS group is the headship of Christ and the Unity of the One Body.
    Here the *conduct* of PHILIPPIANS, and the *doctrine* of COLOSSIANS denied both of these facts.

(1) ROMANS faces the *world*, and is evangelistic, "making disciples" of its great doctrines which are for man coming into Christ.

(2) EPHESIANS faces *God* and here is the position of personal, spiritual development into Christ as men are "being transformed." All of its great statements have to do with Ephesians 4:1—16, "growing up into Him."

The unchanged order and doctrinal ascendancy of the books of Romans and Ephesians, are the most obvious out-croppings of wealth within these seven church letters. ROMANS must be the first. It opens with man dead in sins, and it hits his pride (evolution). There is no least bit of life in the men of the world and the Gospel faces the world on that proposition. To yield here is to fill the church with still-born factionists: "Ye must be born again." The lapse is always first MORAL, then DOCTRINAL, and men seek out a religion to comfortably fit their lapse.

    d) The Romans (Salvation) Group
    (1) ROMANS

The book of Romans deals with things which are much talked about but are little studied. Here is study, culture, and PEACE. These doctrines of *Romans* have been so distorted that they are distasteful to many; and *Corinthians* deals with sins, delinquencies and failures which are common today. Like broken mirrors which distortingly reflect the "heavenlies" here the truth of God is mixed with the practices of men. It is as though our church building, a thing of beauty at dedication, were visited years later and found to be cracked, soiled, defaced, and still recognizable, but marred and neglected. It is in these lower, more human documents that the soul's hunger for escape is enkindled. They are like a Jacob's ladder where commerce with heaven (going up and down) is maintained (I Corinthians 15).

Romans is "The Way" into (Gr. *eis*) the heavenlies where the redeemed (Saved), seated "In Him," are delivered unto God's workshop where we "let go and let God" (Ephesians 2:10) "for we are His workmanship"(poem).

    (2) I and II CORINTHIANS

The Romans' group doctrine is in regard to Salvation, and both books of the *Corinthians* are the practical lapse from *Romans'* dogma (Jeremiah 31:27—34; Acts 5:19—20).

We are entering a book dealing with "men of like passions" and problems as ourselves (I Corinthians 1:1—9). Let us enter under the conviction that God is under the same compulsion that drove the Lord and then Hebrews 13:8 is still true. *Corinthians* is a planet of *Romans* that deals with human limitations (John 8:23). The approach is not down a shining phalanx of angels, but up out of the hot abyss of man's weakness. These statements transcend human wisdom and have met the educated of each age and race and still are the most read, discussed and obeyed. We are going to school to Deity and we would do well to heed.

Note especially that in *Romans*, Paul calls himself a bond-servant, a called apostle. In *Corinthians* he uses only the term "called apostle." In *Romans* he speaks of salvation which was of God alone and the apostle was but a servant, a steward; but in *Corinthians* there is bickering and division and he needs authority to rebuke. While considering these, note that in *Romans* and *Ephesians* alone, where he is receiving revelation, there is no mention of sharing with others even as Moses was taken up into the Mount alone. In *Corinthians* and *Galatians* he emphatically asserts, "I received from the Lord." In these latter epistles he was dealing with "sources," while in *Philippians* and *Colossians* he is striving for "the things which were *before*" and *above*—the ultimates and the aspirations. As I studied these books, I was baffled at first. *Romans* was analyzable but *Corinthians* was not. Then came the solution, the one is positive, the other remedial. In *Romans*, the Spirit leads and is therefore logical and consistent; while in *Corinthians* man leads and is capricious, illogical "driven by wind and tossed"; or is as a mother chasing a child who is dodging and turning. Corrective teaching must follow the meander line of the wrong doer; a criminal never keeps to the highway but twists and turns and dodges. *Corinthians* requires "staggering," zig-zagging, as one who is intoxicated and defies both forecasting and logic. Dummelow said concerning *Corinthians*:

> The doctrines of Christianity are not set forth here in a formal way, but are brought forward incidentally, as they bear on life and practice . . . . It is mainly the dark side of the church life which is disclosed in this epistle . . . .

From this position let the Christian test his own soul. Do you function? If not, descend into *Corinthians* and find the image of your sin and the remedy.

Mountains, physical and spiritual, are God's pulpits, and Paul's letters are especially so. They are from the mouth "of the great high God." *Romans* and *Corinthians* are very different; one is *positive* and the other is *punitive*:

(a) In *Romans*, doctrine is revealed by the Holy Spirit when "men spake as they were moved." So it is logical. cumulative and climactic. The steps are from death through to new life, and the ordinances go to Romans 8:39 (The Communion Table). It is easy to follow because the Spirit has something to say and says it.

(b) While in *Corinthians*, the message is punitive, remedial; man in sin leads as an erring child. The steps are neither charted

nor analyzable, and the pathway, is that of ingenious twist-
ings.

(3) GALATIANS

The book of Galatians continues the doctrinal lapse from *Romans'*
teaching (Acts 14:8—20). In the first group, *Romans* presents the doctrine
of Salvation while *Corinthians* is the *correction* of the practice or *living*
of Salvation. *Galatians* follows and it is the doctrinal correction answering the attempt to discredit the Gospel and demonstrates that the mind is
ever an apologist for the conduct.

Creeds are made to fit desires, but the Bible is ever rebuking sins.
Galatians is the doctrinal denial. The character of the people addressed
fits the subject matter discussed. Paul's letters and people fit from *Romans* to *Thessalonians*, but no more so than *Galatians* for we could not
change the titles. If the teachings of *Galatians* are studied, they contain
the correctives for today. Herein Luther on his knees started the Reformation. *Galatians* is the restored inner temple of *Romans* where Abraham
and Paul replaced the cherubim of the Tabernacle which looked down at
the Mercy Seat. They are at the propitiatory where is the enthroned and
exalted and glorified Lord and Christ. Paul the contender appears to guard
"The Way" of the Cross. He bows in worship, then faces *Galatians* with
unscabbarded sword, as Genesis 3:24 or Moses in Exodus 32:15—20. He
comes brusquely as a warrior and we can understand his abruptness as
when a doctor would come to a hospital and find departure from his pre-
scribed treatment, for the Galatian Christians were inserting Mosaism
between the disciple and his Lord.

God's saved (salvaged) man is the sample of the Salvation Group
(Galatians 5:1——6:10). At the close of the Gospels we hear "Behold!
The Man." But here in the close of *Galatians*, we behold the new man
"in Christ Jesus." As at a beginning, the apparently *one* element is soon
revealed as *many*. So at the close of this book, "the elements are so mixed
in the purpose" of the author as to stand forth a vindicating unity of His
purpose (Ephesians 3:10—11).

This Romans—Salvation Group opens "the Gospel of God," the "Power
of God," and ere the problem is stated (Romans 1:18), a remedy before has
shown the problem not to be over-discouraged. Now closing on a victory
note with Paul and his man, as Peter and John with the healed man (Acts
4:14), this problem material and man is found nowhere else in the Scriptures. The next group of Paul's is even of a different structure and content.
Now it only remains to gather these separate elements into a combination
and to see the transformation where duties are becoming privileges.

From *Galatians* let us take our leave of Paul as he enters into E-
phesians' Glory. Play the flood-lights upon him and we see the colossal

storm-beaten, battle-scarred immortal whose light we shall never again see. There is a sense of holy ground and divine presence as the lights go down to rise upon the fairer shores and the heights of *Ephesians'* Glory (Matthew 25:21). I know that he lived on; that he wrote, that he missionized and established churches after this, but the writings were grouped to show *action (Romans)* closed; and that *being (Ephesians)*—trust and quietness—followed; and that *hope* beckoned.

> "Home is the sailor, home from the sea,
> And the hunter home from the hills."

e) The Ephesian (Sanctification) Group
  (1) EPHESIANS

> "The Ephesian Epistle presents the clearest philosophy of Christian unity in the New Testament, excepting the treatment Jesus accorded the subject at the Last Supper. 'Emerging from the Galatian letter,' said Harnack, 'we leave the tumult of the battlefield. In *Ephesians* it is as though a door of heaven were opened and we breathe the air of meditation'."

> Walter M. Haushalter

We are now to look upon the "little flock" within the green pastures for *Ephesians* is the Twenty-Third Psalm of the New Testament. Compare the two most beautiful spots in the Testaments (Psalm 23 and *Ephesians*), and see how alike they are. These *Ephesians* "green pastures," high and lifted up, are a place of surpassing loveliness, inviting to refreshment and restoration.

Ephesians is the greatest of all writings. It is the only section which carries punctuation and analysis by prayer. At the Transfiguration of Jesus, we read, "And as He prayed . . . spake of His exodus . . ." (Luke 9:29, 31). After this came Gethsemane. In *Ephesians* there are two prayers:

(1) The first prayer is for the spirit of revelation (1:15—23); vss. 16—17 N.:

> "Wherefore I . . . cease not to give thanks for you, making mention of you in my prayers; That the God of our Lord Jesus Christ, the Father of glory, may give unto you the Spirit of wisdom and revelation in the full knowledge of Him;"

(2) The second prayer is that they might apprehend the dimensions of the Church (4:14—19); vs. 3:18 N.: "May be fully able to comprehend with all saints what is the breadth, and length, and depth, and height;"

And the doxology is 3:20—21 N.:

> "Now unto Him that is able to do exceeding abundantly above all that we ask or think, according to the power

that worketh in us, Unto Him be glory in the church in Christ Jesus unto all the generations of the age of the ages."

Both the Lord and Paul went alone (John 16:32 and II Timothy 4:16). They are one in agony and prayer and loneliness. Their only escape into peace was upward in the heavenlies. The prayer travail of Moses brought forth the Tabernacle; that of Jesus in Gethsemane, the Cross; and Paul through the prayers of *Ephesians* brings forth the Church.

The Mystery initiates the Head and the Body (Matthew 24:36; 28:18; John 13:7; Matthew 13:11; Ephesians 3:9). We thus are fellow work-men of God in the restoring of the redeemed, fallen section of the Universe (I Corinthians 3:9; Ephesians 4:1—16; Romans 8:22). The Church is the vindication of God (Ephesians 3:8—11; Colossians 1:17—18; Hebrews 1:2—3). This "Ephesian"cy group is the elect group, having "The Mind of Christ" to whom by revelations are made known the "unspeakable" glory of God's *"Telos"* PURPOSE as seen in *Ephesians*, chapters 1—3.

Ephesians contains:
  (i) The overshadowings of the *"egeirantos"* (rising)
  (ii) The ones who were "in Christ"
  (iii) The dimensions of the Church

These are as the clustered colors which the sun drapes across the horizon as he moves into another world.

Ephesians sets forth "The Mystery of His Will" (1:9). Here is a full-statured man above false doctrine in the heavenlies not disturbed by every wind of doctrine.

(2) PHILIPPIANS

The book of Philippians is the *practical* denial of the doctrine of Sanctification, and this is seen in the personal rivalry of its members and the disputing as to which is the greatest (1:10, 23—24; chap. 2:1—4; 4:2—3). In *Philippians* 1:10 reference is made to the more subtle factions and their rivalries.

(3) COLOSSIANS

The book of Colossians is the doctrinal denial of Sanctification,— seeing rivals of Christ in "gods" and "mysteries" (1:13—17; 2:8). They were surrendering the Hope; in fact they were accepting false philosophy.

f) THESSALONIANS (Glorification)[1]

We have labored through the Romans and Ephesians Groups and are

---

[1] See Section FIVE, MY Story, THE CHURCH, VI. *"Things . . . Established"* I. The Rapture, pp. 515—516

now come to the apocalyptic hope of *Thessalonians*. To go forward, we must first go backward as sky-scrapers must "dig deep" to solid rock (Luke 6:48). For the Thessalonians hope is rooted in apocalyptic literature and "in the fulness of the times" at a set time, the good Father God, seems to lay it upon burdened hearts to search out.

Thessalonians is a bridge; it is hope's observatory. Here the apocalyptic heights of *Daniel* and *John* and the Scripture foundation of *II Peter* and *Jude* become "the far off interest of tears." With such a faith and hope, our watchword should be "Watch ye, stand fast in the faith, quit you like men, be strong" (I Corinthians 16:13).

SUMMARY

Paul's epistles might well be set forth as a house with several doors:
ROMANS dealing with Salvation, is a *closed* door. Sin has been shut out and the saved are shut in and the Cross stands between. EPHESIANS presents Sanctification and it is *within* doors "in Him" set apart. This is the "now" of Jude 25, the Holy Spirit's hour. THESSALONIANS which is concerned with Glorification, is the *open* door (Revelation 3:7—8; 4:1). It opens upon eternity into immensity. It is the outlook upon "things to come."

We see the steps in the soul's ascension. Men are raised from the dead into "the heavenlies" awaiting the rapture. Paul is as an "angel in the sun" (Revelation 19:17) as the New Testament opens revealing things "hid in God." There are no quotations from "the other Scriptures" in either *Ephesians* or *Thessalonians*. In "this beginning" of inspired New Testament writings (*Thessalonians*), Paul began and manifested forth the glory of the Church. According to Moffatt, Paul was the first Christian that the Thessalonians had ever seen, and he was the only interpreter of church truth ever ordained. Because of this, every word and phrase will repay microscopic analysis. Revelation 22:18—20 surely applies here. With a sense of solemn eagerness let us push forth to its "waters of life' in full confidence "that He which hath begun a good work in you, will perform it until the day of Jesus Christ" (Philippians 1:6). Here we will find words, some with new meaning, some of new birth that are as wonderful and as evidencing as the Spirit's work within human lives.

"The first shall be last" and "hope," *Thessalonians*, was written first. Now the last is first:

The ROMANS group shows the *Son's* FAITH (Galatians 2:20)

The EPHESIANS group shows the *Father's* LOVE (Ephesians 1: 4—5) — we are edified in LOVE

THESSALONIANS shows the *Spirit's* work (II Thessalonians 2:7) — we are sustained by HOPE

FAITH produces Salvation, a *Roman* result based upon Romans 1:16
LOVE brings Sanctification (John 17:19); and this is an *Ephesian* result,
motivated solely by John 3:16
HOPE (of glory) is a *Thessalonian* promise.

The order in I Corinthians 13:13 of Faith, Hope, and then Love, is
because the need there was of *Love* (I Corinthians 3:3; 2:2). Now the need
is the HOPE of His Coming.

> Our FAITH is in the *Lord*
> Our LOVE is in *Jesus*
> Our HOPE is in *Christ*
>
> (I Corinthians 15:19).

3. Paul's Twenty-Third Psalm

The *Ephesians* (Group) is Paul's Twenty-Third Psalm (The Lord's
Fold), and the two most beautiful spots in the New Testament are Psalms
Twenty-Three and the Ephesians Group. See how alike they are:

Psalm 23:1   "I shall not want"
    "My God shall supply your EVERY need"   Philippians 4:19
Psalm 23:2a "He shall make me to lie down"
    "Made to sit in the heavenlies"   Ephesians 2:6
Psalm 23:2b   "He leadeth me"
    "We should walk" (in good works)   Ephesians 2:10
Psalm 23:3a   "He restoreth my soul"
    "Not having spot or wrinkle"   Ephesians 5:27
Psalm 23:3b   "He leadeth me . . . for His name's sake"
    "To the end that we should be to the praise
    of His glory"   Ephesians 1:12
Psalm 23:4   "Yea though I walk . . . I will fear no evil"
    "Put on the WHOLE armor . . . and STAND"   Ephesians 6:1
Psalm 23:5   "Thou settest a table before me"
    "Purpose" (Presence bread)   Ephesians 1:11
Psalm 23:6a   "Goodness and mercy shall follow me"
    "Grace and Peace"   Ephesians 1:2 and 6:24
Psalm 23:6b "Dwell in the house of the Lord"
    "Builded together for an habitation"   Ephesians 2:22
Psalm 23:6c   "FOREVER"
    "Unto THE Age of (All) Ages"   Ephesians 3:20—21

V. PAUL'S PASTORAL EPISTLES: TIMOTHY through PHILEMON

I and II TIMOTHY

TITUS

PHILEMON

The Holy Spirit's warning and exhortation to the Church and particularly to its bond-servant ministry, is the text of II Timothy 2:15 N.:

> "Be diligent to present thyself approved unto God,
> a workman that needeth not to be ashamed, rightly
> dividing the word of truth."

In these four pastoral epistles, Paul gives guidance and teaching for oversight and correction within the churches. To Timothy he exhorted II Timothy 2:1—2 N.:

> "Thou therefore, my child, be strong in the grace that is
> in Christ Jesus. And the things that thou hast heard from
> me among many witnesses, the same commit thou to faith-
> ful men, who shall be competent to teach others also."

Such exhortation continues in *Titus* concerning the setting of the churches in order and in *Philemon* concerning the relationship of Christian brethren whether slave or master.

> "Wherefore, having much boldness in Christ to enjoin
> thee that which is convenient, for love's sake I rather
> beseech, being such an one as Paul the aged, and
> now prisoner of Jesus Christ."
>
> Philemon 8—9 N.

These four epistles conclude this portion of the New Testament which deals exclusively with the Church as the "Mystery" which must be rightly divided from all other teaching. And as Paul here is able to complete his writing, the Holy Spirit leads him yet further into one more book which is to his brethren according to the flesh, the Hebrews' book.

VI. THE EPISTLES of HEBREWS through JUDE

HEBREWS   I, II, III JOHN
                JAMES
                I and II PETER   JUDE

> "God, having of old time spoken unto the fathers
> in the prophets by divers portions and in divers
> manners, hath at the end of these days spoken
> unto us in a Son, ..."

> Hebrews 1:1—2a A.S.V.

A. THE AUTHORSHIP and PURPOSE of HEBREWS

In the New Testament there are two great un-named ones: the writer of *Hebrews* and the Holy Spirit, and both are un-named because of a great love. To Israel the book of Hebrews is written out of a great love, as great as that of Moses and Jonah. Think of the love involved in Romans 9:1—3 which is like John 3:16 itself. Only *one* could write this book and he could not do so until after "The Mystery" letters to the Church had been re-vealed,—and that one is Paul.

In *Hebrews* is condensed for the Hebrew people that which is:

> ". . . Profitable for doctrine, for reproof, for cor-
> rection in righteousness that the (Hebrew) man
> of God may be perfect (complete), thoroughly
> furnished unto all good works."

> II Timothy 3:16—17

This book was written by Paul[1] who was following his own admonition to Timothy:

> ". . . In meekness instructing those that oppose
> themselves, if God peradventure will give them
> repentence to the acknowledging of the truth. . ."

> II Timothy 2:23—26

Paul had Luke, Titus and Timothy as his helpers. Why then would he need Mark (II Timothy 4:11)? He did not need him until *Hebrews* was to be written.[1] Timothy was exhorted "to divide," but until the group of books particularly for Israel in the New Testament was completed, there was nothing to divide! Paul is urging Timothy to hurry to Rome with his manuscripts and parchments and to bring Mark with him also. His life is being cut short and he has only a little time. The beautiful love-God, as He always does, has told him: "Now you have been praying for your people and you have been begging Me to let you go to them, and I have told you

---

[1] See Sec. FIVE, *Church*, MY Story, III. Growth . . . B. 1. *c*. Paul . . . Jewish brethren, p. 355.

that they won't hear you (Acts 22:21). Now then, you can write to them the book of Hebrews and they will go over all those livid things that are in the Old Testament but it will have a new meaning; it will be a new version and there will be a new significance."

It is to this group of Hebrew folk that Paul is writing through his book to Mark who now has become profitable unto him, and the old apostle will pour the wonders of his educational advantages through the language and style of Mark. Today when you are reading commentaries about the book of Hebrews, one will say Apollos wrote it and others will say some-one else. Why is this? Because the Holy Spirit intended that its *writer* should be hidden from the Jews until Paul had told them the story.

As *Genesis* and *Acts* are complimentary—*Genesis* reveals the first creation, and *Acts* the second or the new creation,—so the church epistles of Paul and *Hebrews* compliment one another. In Paul's church epistles we find life rising up from among the dead ones; and *Hebrews* is "to the Jew first," the chosen people, and it calls them to repentance before God who is the only Omnipotent, Omniscient, and Omni-*agape*nt One. All life is small that is "without God" (Ephesians 2:11). Only *The Autobiography of God,* the Bible, meets the need as our text.

In Acts 26:16—23 Paul is commissioned by the Lord to open the eyes of both Israel and the Gentiles and "to turn them from darkness to light and from the power of Satan unto God." And it is *the book of Romans* which opens the eyes of the *Gentiles* (Romans 1:20), and it is *the book of Hebrews* which opens the eyes of *Israel* (Hebrews 1:1—2; Romans 3:1—2). And then with open eyes they both advance into all the truth of the Word of God.

B. THE GRACE-ELECTED REMNANT FROM ISRAEL

In Romans 11:1*ff* we see that Paul includes himself among those from the nation of Israel who become "a remnant according to the election of Grace," obtaining salvation through the Gospel. Israel as a nation had not obtained "salvation" *nationally* although this was their "hope"; but the election, those out of Israel who heard the Gospel and believed it, like those of Pentecost and Paul, obtained "grace salvation" and the rest of the nation of Israel were blinded (hardened; II Corinthians 3:13—16). Nevertheless when they shall turn to the Lord, their blindness shall be taken away.

It was to this group who obtained the election of grace and were under persecution that the books of Hebrews through Jude were written during the first century. To such a group down through the church age, these books make their appeal in each generation; but after the Church is taken away at the rapture, *Hebrews* through *Jude* will be of special interest and value to the *nation* of Israel whose blindness (hardness) shall be healed and whose eyes shall be opened by the events surrounding the rapture. In that day they shall see and understand the things to which Israel has been blinded since the first century and before.

The Church's Scriptures for this Age of Grace are from *Acts to Philemon*, though we are not derrogating for "every Scripture . . . is profitable . . ." (II Timothy 3:16); but rather we are "rightly dividing" the Word of God. Confusion comes through neglect of these Scriptures. To Israel was given the Old Testament, but to the Remnant, following the rapture, their Scriptures for their Age are from *Hebrews* through *Jude*; and here again, we are not derrogating or debarring from "every Scripture . . . is profitable . . . ."

The Church, the Body of Christ, is preaching the Gospel to both Jew and Gentile today. In preaching repentance toward God to the Gentiles, the Church should use especially Paul's church epistles; but in preaching this same repentance to the people of the nation of Israel, they would use particularly *Hebrews* through *Jude*. This is "becoming all things to all men, that I might by all means save some" (I Corinthians 9:19—22). Thus we see that in these epistles as in the prophets, there is a local, immediate application, and then a future use as well.

C. THE BOOK OF HEBREWS and RIGHTLY DIVIDING

> "For the word of God is living, and powerful, and sharper than any two-edged sword, and piercing even to the dividing asunder both of soul and spirit, and of joints and marrow, and is a discerner of the thoughts and intents of the heart. Neither is there any creature that is not manifest in His sight: but all things are naked and opened (laid bare) unto the eyes of Him with whom we have to do."
>
> Hebrews 4:12—13

Three times in Paul's epistles, the apostle challenges us to distinguish the things that differ and to rightly divide, or steer a straight course:[1]

Romans 2:18 N.: ". . . and triest the things that differ"
Philippians 1:10 A.S.V.: ". . . distinguish the things that differ"
II Timothy 2:15: ". . . rightly dividing the word of truth."

These three calls to rightly dividing are all within the *church epistles* which indicate that their placing or location in this group of letters shows its special importance over and above all other portions of the Scriptures. It is also significant to note that the first of these three admonishings

---

[1] See *Rightly Dividing,* pp. 9—11.

appears near the beginning of the church epistles (Romans 2:18); and the second is near the center of all the seven church letters (Philippians 1:10); and the third is near the close of Paul's epistles (II Timothy 2:14).

Paul's epistles present "The Mystery," how Jew and Gentile become a Joint Body in Christ (Ephesians 2 and 3). This "Mystery," the Joint Body, does not appear in prophecy. The prophets' writings include the facts of the Gospel, i.e. death, burial, resurrection and the Holy Spirit; and these fulfillments are clearly set forth in the book of Acts. *Hebrews* takes up the proof of the fulfilling of the Old Testament prophecies concerning Christ and the Gospel and those from Israel who believe this, become the "Election of Grace" and are added to the Joint Body which is spoken of in *Ephesians*. First in importance is that these Israelites believe the *facts* of the Gospel which are prophesied by the Old Testament prophets, and then are they readied for "Mystery" truth. After the rapture when the Church and the Holy Spirit have been taken away, there is no longer a Joint Body to which Israel might be added. Then the books of Hebrews through Jude will convince those of that generation of Israel who remain, that the prophecies concerning Christ's *sufferings* were fulfilled in the first century, and those prophecies concerning His *glory* are about to be fulfilled at His second coming to earth.

Many brethren today have used the Jewish epistles of the New Testament for church teaching, even as they have used the Jewish promises of the Old Testament prophets for the Church today. Thus the Church, about to complete her stay on earth, has robbed Israel of her rights by taking *Hebrews* out of its proper place, as has also been done to those promises of the Old Testament. These Jewish epistles contain the gospel of Christ but they are written for the understanding of those who have the background of the Old Testament teachings. Paul's preaching in the book of Acts shows him entering into a synagogue and turning to the Old Testament Scriptures, "opening and alleging" through them, that Jesus is the Christ, the Messiah; but in going to the Gentiles, as at Athens, no reference is made to the Old Testament, but rather he preaches to them directly concerning the Man whom God ordained and raised from among the dead ones (Acts 17:31). A close, thoughtful reading of *Hebrews* giving attention to the illustrations and references, will put the book in its rightful place (II Timothy 2:15) in relation to Israel who in turn will be brought to their Savior-Messiah-King (I John 3:1–5; Hebrews 8:4 and 1:2).

The book of Hebrews is rooted in the Law and the Law-giver (Deuteronomy 18:18–20; Hebrews 1:1–2; 2:1–4; 3:1–8; Isaiah 11:11). In like manner of "remembrance" the eleventh chapter of *Hebrews* is the Westminster Abbey of God's taking care of His people. These are not Christians but are some of the Old Testament saints; and this calling to remembrance in the hall of memory of these "by faith" saints, has the idea of a suspension in music which acts as a pause before a climax; or like unto a "Selah"; "stop and consider this." These saints of Hebrews 11 looked away for the Leader or Captain of those who "seek," and endure "as seeing"—those who "look for a new heaven and earth wherein dwelleth righteousness." This transfigured group is about Him even as were the twelve disciples during His ministry, and with this group:

> He roams the fields of the Universe and turns the hearts,
> hopes and aspirations of those "willing-hearted" out toward
> the Infinite; He is the Minister of that great people Israel
> He is the Holy-izer of that land Palestine
> He is the satisfying Revelator of Life
> He is the Flower of creation
> He is the Glory of man
> He is the Son of the Living God.

The mental, moral and heroic stature of these saints of Hebrews 11, is too secure to doubt their sanity or judgment; and the consequences are too tangible to be explained away. These are separated from the world by their "other worldliness"; they confessed that they were strangers and pilgrims for they sought a City and they endured as seeing Him.

The Bible, as seen through this book of Hebrews, is the Jews' from first to last:

Hebrews 1:1   "God . . . spake . . . unto the fathers by the prophets"
      5:5—14   "First principles, the oracles of God" (vs. 12), cp.
                  Isaiah 28:9—11
      11:2, 39 "The Elders . . . obtained a good report through faith";
      12:1   "We (Christians) are compassed about with so great a
                  a cloud of witnesses" (Old Testament saints of Hebrews 11).

After His resurrection Jesus taught His disciples:

> "'Was it not needful for Christ to have suffered these things,
> and to enter into His glory?' And beginning from Moses and
> from all the prophets, He expounded unto them in all the
> Scriptures the things concerning Himself."

Luke 24:26—27 N.

What a sermon it must have been! Its outline is the same as that of *Hebrews* which begins with a reference as to how God spake unto the fathers by the prophets and "hath in these last days" spoken "in Son." All illustrations and types in *Hebrews* are Jewish: e.g. the high priest, blood of sprinkling, and the examples of faith of Old Testament saints in chapter eleven.

D. ISRAEL'S NEW TESTAMENT: HEBREWS through JUDE

After the mystery heights of the church letters, there is no contribution for *Hebrews* through *Jude* to make concerning "The Mystery." These books will be the means of opening the eyes and the understanding of the nation of Israel to the prophets and to their fulfillment in Christ (Luke 24:27, 44). *Hebrews* through *Jude* are epistles "of the last days" written within the shadow of 70 A.D., and the fall of Jerusalem, and reach in their fulfillment to the age of the ages. These books contain short, sharp, staccato trumpet blasts for their messages were urgent when written and in their future use after the rapture, the time will also be short, not more than seven years.

> The message of HEBREWS was there from the beginning until Israel put it aside
>
> The book of JAMES pleads for the Gospel of Grace, but they went went back to Moses
>
> The books of PETER held before them their second chance, and Peter tells them that Paul's writing of *Hebrews* is to them
>
> The book of JUDE warns and pleads.

The New Testament books for Israel *begin at Pentecost* and do not let go of His people until the *Seventieth week of Daniel.*

HEBREWS is *doctrinal*, the book of typology

JAMES is *hortatory*, the pleading, urging, persuading and warning book. As Ezekiel, James remains with his people from their lapsing into "works."

> This book is a kind of postscript to *Hebrews* and is the book of the Law of the New Testament. The Law restrictions, ending in the dispersion, and eventuating in Romanism's pagan practices, is to be finally joined by the protestant "falling away" (Revelation 13).

In the Hebrews' epistle the text, the typology, the personalities, the incidents, and the references are all Jewish. *Hebrews* is the beginning of the New Testament to Abraham's seed. This section of *Hebrews* to *Jude* is devoted to the fulfillment of the promises made to Israel. The whole Bible was produced through the Jews and was written principally for them. The Church is not a subject of prophecy nor is it clearly understood in the New Testament apart from Paul's writings.

A slow careful reading, weighing the words used in *James* through *Jude*, will suggest the items of the Sermon on the Mount, thus bridging past the church epistles and taking up the "promise unto the fathers." To the Jew first was given opportunity to become a "Star" descendant of Abraham's[1] to receive the promise given to Abraham's seed. Now the gospel of the grace of God would have brought in the Kingdom (Acts 3:18–26). Individually some received it, but nationally they refused it and so compelled God to turn unto the Gentiles until after the rapture of the Church (John 17:23) when "the fulness of the times of the Gentiles shall be come in," and Israel shall cry out for their Messiah (Matthew 23:39).

In I Peter 1:13 we find the up-pushing into spiritual results. The elements of this life are being woven into the Personality of that Life, even as stone and tree are woven into a temple:

> "That the trial of your faith, being much more precious than of gold that perisheth, though it be tried through fire, might be found unto praise and honour and glory in the revelation of Jesus Christ."
>
> I Peter 1:7 N.

The prophets searched diligently, i.e. they were girded but it was beyond them; now gospel preachers have "announced" the fulfillment of those things which the prophets searched out diligently. It is an open secret needing only "girding" up of the loins of the mind through rightly dividing the Word of truth (I Peter 1:13).

As we move along in Israel's New Testament books, we come to the epistles of John, the aged apostle. He with his brother James had been called the "sons of thunder" who wanted to call down fire from heaven in the Samaritans. But now we start in to read and we see that John begins to define love and to prepare our minds to understand that "God is love"; and in the next chapter (I John 5), in contrast we read that "the whole world lieth (is lying down prostrate) in the evil one."

It was not stated in the Old Testament that God is love. It did not appear that He was a God of love. Men were afraid of Him. They were trying to propitiate God in the prophets: "The burden of the Word of the Lord came to me." The prophets hurled anathemas upon the enemies of God and they were not rubbing salve on those that were trying to walk before God. The *Psalms* gave indication of this love but there was no explanation of it such as we find in I John 4:8.

But John 3:16 states "God so loved" and this describes the manner and action of His love. In I John 4:19, we read, "We love Him because He first loved us." Literally it is we *love* because "He first loved us." My attention was called to that when I was a student in Eureka College: Concerning it, Henry Drummond wrote: "We love because He first loved." And love (Gr. *agape*) did not come in to our apprehension until after He loved. God is love; He so loved us that we learned to love folks. The great commission was "going into all the world, preach the Gospel,"—love people.

---

[1] See Section FOUR, My Story, I, Prophets, E. *The Indefectible Promises to Abraham*, p. 226

We are getting the understanding of the tremendous significance of what love is.

No thoughtful and reverent mind can read the books of Jude, II Timothy or II Peter by the light of today's events and remain unmoved to the significant co-incidences. These are "Minor" epistles and they are short, clear, vivid and "these three agree in one." The "Minor Prophets" are the same; they are named such because they are shorter books; that name Minor, a device of Satan, has caused their neglect. These books II Timothy, I and II Peter and Jude are trumpet-calls "to those having ears to hear." Jude who denied His Deity, Peter who denied at the Cross, and Paul who denied His Lordship,—all having been redeemed and forgiven,—unitedly sound the alarm as Habakkuk on his tower (2:2), "that he may run that reads."

Jude grew up in the home in Nazareth with Jesus and knew His hardships. He begins "a servant of Jesus" and "brother of James." Jude is like Paul who said he was not worthy to be called an apostle (I Corinthians 15:9). Jude and his brothers were under the same roof with Jesus and were unbelievers. If ever salvation by character is found wanting, it is here. The Lord's family was the most exposed to Him personally, and yet were the least effected. Of Jude it is written, "for even His brethren did not believe on Him" (John 7:35; Mark 6:3).

Both Paul and Jude exalted faith and they both were "second chance" men as also were Peter and Mark. When Jude began to plan and collect material on the human home life of Jesus, the nearly thirty years in Nazareth, the text shows a re-coiling:

> "Beloved, when I gave all diligence to write unto you
> of the common salvation, it was needful for me (con-
> straint was upon me) to write unto you . . . ."

> Jude 3*a*

—for this material could be seized upon and used by the "Jesus way" philosophers. A pulpit centered "curriculum" would have been helped by the inciting of the curiosity seekers who would be more interested in His earthly life rather than His Deity. The Holy Spirit knew it must be stopped.

E. THE POST RAPTURE USE of *HEBREWS* through *JUDE*

As *Romans, Ephesians* and *Thessalonians* prepare the Church as the *Body* of Christ, so after the rapture, *Hebrews* through *Jude* will prepare the living generation of the nation of Israel at that time, as the *Bride* of Christ. Would the Lord overlook blinded Israel when He has been so careful to prepare the Church to expect His coming again? To what and to whom is He coming *to earth* again? He is to take His Body away at the rapture and He will then come back with His Body[1] to receive His Bride. The Gentiles are now saved by grace even as are Israelites and both become one Joint Body, the Church (Ephesians 3:6). Both Jew and Gentile are now saved by grace, but Israel as a nation will be saved by restoration at the time indicated in Acts 3:21.

The rapture of the Church is the answer to the Lord's prayer for the world will come to "know" (John 17:23) and Israel will be brought to realization and "provoked" by a great victory of a Son of Israel. Where then can they turn for guidance? The Old Testament prophets are fulfilled in Christ. The New Testament literature is fulfilled in the Church's rapture. There remains only *Hebrews* through *Jude*. Consider the evidence arising out of a rightly dividing of the Scriptures:

The book of Hebrews is Israel's New Testament written for their instruction upon whom the end of the ages is to come. This book does not contain certain terms that are found in Paul's church epistles:

  a) The terms "mystery," "the body" are not mentioned in *Hebrews*, nor are the terms "Jews and Gentiles," nor "one new man"

  b) The three great characters of the book of Hebrews are Abraham, Melchizedek and Christ, and each is in a different role.

The present day *organized* church is "Jewish" in its dependence upon "works," and these "organized religionists" will be left at the rapture. As the Gentiles are to be present in future blessings of the Old Testament, so *now* the Christ is to be for Israel also (Romans 3:28—30). These following parallels may be seen:

  a) In the first century the Jews rejected the Messiah and as a nation they were set aside

  b) The apostate church rejects the Head and they are spewed out (Revelation 3:16).

God emerges in *Hebrews* to bring in everlasting righteousness, and the Consummation of His purpose to carry out to Israel His unconditional promises to Abraham which are carried on through woman (Genesis 3:15; Revelation 12:1—6).

The Roman trail ends with *Thessalonians* and the tracks cease, for His Body, the one making the tracks, has taken unto itself wings. Both ends of the trail are equally marked:

  a) From *Thessalonians* to *Hebrews* are as from the *Acts* to *Romans*

  b) Though the language, officers and appeals are different, yet the theme of *Hebrews* joins on to *Acts*

  c) *Hebrews* is an explanatory parenthesis which also helps toward

---

[1] See Section FIVE, MY Story, VI. "Things . . . Established," I. *The Rapture*, 502

supplying the Scriptures in the regeneration

d) As *Acts* is "laid upon" the gospels, so *Hebrews* is "laid upon" *Romans*.

Hebrews will be the "Roman letter" for Israel for that age following the rapture of the Church. Did not God catch up His Son at the ascension following His resurrection and forty days of appearances? Why then should it be thought a thing more incredible that God should rapture His Church which is His Son's Body? And why should we doubt that a body of growing truth would be compiled for this Church which would include the Gospel, the Body, and the Out-Resurrection (Rapture)? Again, why could God not have prepared prophetic truth in one age to be unveiled in the succeeding age? It was so done in Daniel 9:2 and John 16:25—30. *Hebrews*, written through Paul to convert his "brethren according to the flesh" of the first century, will be unveiled in further meaning and use after the rapture. There must be unused and mystery portions written to us which will become plain to them then; just as Christ emerged to us from the Old Testament prophecies of His sufferings and glory, so, in that day *Hebrews* truth will come forth clearly. If it is not clear today, it is because we lack time to sit quietly and "wait upon the Lord."

> "Jesus Christ the same yesterday, and
> to-day, and for ever" (the ages).
>
> Hebrews 13:8N.

F. THE NEW COVENANTS: CHRISTIAN AND JEWISH

The contrast between Christian Jew and the national Jew is also seen in their obtaining of New Covenants. The key to understanding the "New Covenants" is found in the institution of the Communion Table. In Matthew 26:28—29, Mark 14:25 and Luke 22:18, the reference is to the New Covenant which shall be established by the Lord in the Kingdom of Christ between the Lord and the nation of Israel. This is the same covenant referred to in Hebrews 8:7—13. In Luke 22:20 and I Corinthians 11:25, the New Covenant which is made with the Church is set forth in the Table of Remembrance, and salvation to the Christian comes in this New Covenant through the blood of Christ which was shed upon the Cross.

There has been confusion concerning the use of the term "New Covenant" which is used in the New Testament with reference to the Lord's dealing with both the Church and Israel. The following alignment shows the contrasts and similarities between the Two Covenants:

The New Covenants:

I Corinthians 11:25 and Luke 22:19—20	Hebrews 8:7—13
1. To the Church (The Body of Christ) Includes both Jew and Gentile who become One Joint Body	1. To Israel (The Nation)
2. Effective beginning at Pentecost, A.D. 30	2. Will become effective after the rapture of the Church, and when Israel calls for the Lord (Romans 11:26—27)
3. Sins are forgiven by the obedience of faith (Acts 2:38)	3. Sins will be forgiven by the Word of the Lord—as were the sins of the paralytic (Mark 2:5—11)
4. This covenant is eternal.	4. This covenant is for the Kingdom Age of one thousand years.

SUMMARY

God's ages-long concern for His people Israel and His mercy upon them is demonstrated more in the church age than in any other. To Abraham He had given unconditional promises which He is to carry out toward Abraham's seed, and to the nation of Israel is yet to be given the fulfillment of these promises, some of them during the Kingdom Age, some during the Seventieth Week and the rest upon the new earth. But to the people of Israel, who have been set aside as a nation during this church age of Grace, He is offering salvation through the gospel, and is giving to them the same opportunities and blessings that He is extending to the Gentiles, that they *both* might become a Joint Body, the Church of Jesus Christ (Ephesians 2:14—18). These from the nation of Israel who receive the gospel today and become a part of the Joint Body, participate in *heavenly* blessings which Paul describes as being "unutterable" (II Corinthians 12:4; Ephesians 1:3) and which are far greater and more precious than the *earthly* blessings promised to the nation of Israel. Israel will become *subjects* of the King for this thousand year reign, but the Church, His Body, are to be *fellow-heirs* and *sons*, and these reign with Christ. The advantage of these Jews who receive the gospel today in contrast to the rest of the nation of Israel who reject it, is described by Paul in Romans 11:7N.:

> "What then? Israel hath not obtained that which he seeketh
> for; but the election hath obtained it, and the rest were
> hardened . . . unto this day."

We have now arrived at the closing book of the SEALED DIVISION of the Word of God. This is by no means an analysis of the whole book but rather an attempt to understand and recognize the place which this remarkable book has in relation to all the rest of the Word of God:

VII. REVELATION, THE OBSERVATORY FOR THE WORD OF GOD

The book of Revelation is uniquely set apart in the statement as being "The Revelation of Jesus Christ which God gave to Him." No one of all the other books makes such a claim. Its position at the close of the canon; its assertion "God gave"; its unique contents; its accuracy in agreement with the facts of history, together with its striking forecast of days and events—all of these lift its utterances above comparison and set it apart for serious consideration. With such reverence we approach this most solemnly introduced book of the Holy Scriptures, expecting to receive the key to the Scriptures through the "Word of God and the testimony of Jesus Christ," (Revelation 1:2) and to share the blessings of all those who "read and hear" (1:3). This book is the glorious *climax* of *God's Autobiography*. His age-long vindication came *before* and can be seen *from* Genesis 1:1 to the palin-genesis (Revelation 21 and 22), (cf. Ephesians 3:1, 10, 21). Looking to this long awaited "end" (Gr. *telos*) for His first and only time, the good Father, having finished the work He set Himself to do, takes time to dictate the only book to which He affixes His Name: "The Revelation (unveiling) of Jesus Christ" and through Him to His bond-servant John (John 21:23) to give to His bond servants who have been prepared through faith and love and hope, to receive.

John wrote "And many other signs truly did Jesus in the presence of His disciples which are NOT written in this Book" (John 20:30). Now I would like to say that "many other things did Jesus" that ARE written in this inspired Word. Exceedingly and unbelievingly strange is the neglect visited upon this one New Testament book in the most wonderful Book ever written, especially as it asserts that its Author is God Himself, Who sets forth His design for the book (Revelation 1:1—4). The book of Daniel in the Old Testament suffers a like neglect and criticism for like service in our world-Empires. [1] To one familiar with the volume, He presents a most rational and satisfying "finis" in its two endings: chapters 2 through 11 is the historical; and chapters 12 through 22, is the consummation or the unveiling of all between the Alpha and the Omega, the summing up of the Bible as His *Autobiography*.

---

[1] See Division TWO, THE SEALED DIVISION, I. Isaiah to Malachi, A. Group One, 4. The Prophecy of Daniel, p. 37

There can be no just estimate of the Scriptures until they are completed. First, the place of beginning is of importance, as is any attempt toward understanding. The seeker after God, the man who is not a Christian, begins at *Genesis*; but the saved man who has learned of God and has found Christ and is ready to rightly divide to others this Word of God,— his starting point is not in *Genesis* but is in the book of Revelation. Allow your antipathy time to cool off! Nineveh, a city of atheism, was a rival of Babylon. Babylon is where Jews and Gentiles came to grips that developed each. Here the prophet voice of Daniel mapped out the ages-long struggle: "The Times of the Gentiles," and, "Seventy Weeks are determined upon thy people." All history and all prophecy, the whole of the Scriptures have to cope with the struggle of these stage-occupying antagonists. Further illustrations which indicate the importance of starting with the book of Revelation will follow.

Unless we enter the Bible through this book of Revelation, there is no clarity. No matter how much you can explain, and how beautifully you can make the interpretations, or give an exegesis of the books of the Bible, it is not possible to enter into the vision of the whole Bible except through the book of Revelation. "The last shall be first" (*Revelation*), that the perfect will of God may be light upon your pathway. The command is to "rightly divide" but this lacks cogency short of the whole; thus *Revelation* is THE MUST. Its first sentence 1:1–3 is of like authority as Genesis 1:1–3 and is vastly more important, for without this book there is no dividing the Word aright. He who would master the Scriptures must enter upon his quest through this God-given revelation else he will lack the guidance promised. That God is able to make Himself understood, is demonstrated in this His only book in which He names Himself as the Author.

The book of Revelation is THE Observatory to which one must mount up in order to be in position to rightly divide the Word of Truth.

God has defined Himself: "I am The Alpha and The Omega" (Revelation 1:8, 22:13). This is accompanied by His reason for writing (1:1), to be validated by signs and those signs being limited to three: chapters 12:1 and 3, and 15:1, (the Woman, the Dragon, and the Vials or Plagues). The first eleven chapters deal with historical facts, at times raised to inspirational necessity by the entrance into the history beyond human comprehensibility. To the believer, these eleven chapters come to a satisfactory close of God's justifiable purpose of His creation (Ephesians 3:8–12). The second portion is also equally plain: the recapitulation of God's infinite patience and love in "these last days" is seen in chapters 12 to 22 (Exodus 34:6).

The book of Revelation is the key from the "known (chaps. 1 through 11) to the unknown" (chaps. 12 through 20). The *consummation* of all things is found in chapters 21 and 22.

A. THE THREE-FOLD KEY

In searching the Scriptures and especially in the study of *Revelation*, we seemed led of the Lord to note THREE distinct lines of study which run throughout the whole Bible. The book of Revelation gave us the clue: chapters 2 through 11 follow an historical pattern and it is possible to recognize that much of history is God's dealing with nations from the beginning. It is therefore easy to think of HISTORY as HIS STORY. It was once said by Arthur W. Pink that "History, in fragments, denies God; but history as a whole is seen to be His Story."

The second line of thought was introduced beginning at chapter 12 and continuing through the 20th chapter when the Lord begins to speak in signs and to deal with things which are a MYSTERY. Since chapter 12 goes back to the very beginning of God's revelation and deals with things which have been kept secret from the foundation of the world (Matthew 13:35), we see that the Mystery revealed to the saints (I Corinthians 2:7) might be called the Lord's MY STORY.

The third line is also picked up in the 12th chapter when Satan, the great red dragon, appears and we see him contending against God and the people of God. Here begins a parallel revelation of the continuous history of Satan's rebellion. It is the ages-long account of SATAN'S STORY.

Revelation chapters 2 through 11 outlines History (HIS STORY); these include the historical events on the earth which lie as an open book even of the church, and God appears to the seekers after Him (Isaiah 53:1). HIS STORY is the dealing of God with the nations down through the ages. It is the history of the human race from Adam to Magog in language and historic events of all national records. HIS STORY is discernible in the movement of nations, governments and peoples, even to those who know not God (Romans 1:18—20).

There remains the revelation of the Mystery (MY STORY), the purpose of the Creator. HIS STORY has been a record of observable events; the time has come for the entrance of Deity into the affairs of men: MY STORY is the revelation which is seen only by those who desire to discern the spiritual things (I Corinthians 2:10, 13). Beginning with chapter 12, vs. 1 through chapter 20, is MY STORY. Here John sees from Alpha to Omega and to him is unveiled the signs. He has been told that he must prophesy *again*. The three signs of the Woman, the Dragon and the Vials of Wrath, produce *the Revelation* of all revelations of Jehovah. He sees the Lamb ordained *before* and having been slain *from* the foundation of the world, and alive forevermore, coming in great power to take vengeance, to fulfill Daniel 9:24, "to bring in everlasting righteousness," to answer the prayers of "Thy Kingdom come," "that God may be all and in all."

The story of Satan's place before the fall, his present work and his future judgment are all revealed in the book as SATAN'S STORY, ("the whole world lieth in the evil one," I John 5:19). Satan, the old Devil, was cast down and the iniquity that was in him has been spread as a veil over this part of the kingdom of God. Satan as a *person* does not appear in the *Revelation* until chapter 12:3; his *influence* is seen in chapters 2 and 3 which show the decline of the Church during the church age.

Thus we see that:

HIS STORY is shown from Revelation 2 through chapter 11

MY STORY and SATAN'S STORY are seen from Revelation 12 through chapter 20

And the CONSUMMATION of all things is seen in Revelation chapters 21 and 22.

As we pick up these *three lines* of thought from the book of Revelation and then apply them to the study of the *whole* Book, the Bible, we find that they encompass the *whole* purpose and the *whole* revelation of God.

The following brief outline illustrates the simple analysis by which we can use the book of Revelation as the key to unlock the hidden things of the whole of God's Word.

B. ANALYSIS of BOOK of REVELATION

Chapter 1   INTRODUCTION

a) The subject matter; the parties involved; where located; their meeting; the key to understanding; and the command to "Write!"

Chapters 2 through 11   HIS STORY (History)

a) Chapters 2 and 3, The history of the Church and its decline
b) Chapter 4, A view of Heaven's Divine History
c) Chapter 5, The history of the transfer of the Word of God
d) Chapter 6, The Nations (Babylon, Medo-Persia, Greece, Rome and others) approach judgment (vss. 12—17)
e) Chapter 7, The sealing of the Jews (parenthetical)
f) Chapters 8 and 9, The trumpets and woes sound forth the judgments on nations
g) Chapter 10, The rapture of the Church and the Commission of John to prophesy *again*
h) Chapter 11, The history of nations comes to its conclusion; Israel is found at her restored worship; and "the kingdoms of this world become the kingdoms of our Lord and of His Christ."

Chapters 12 through 20

    MY STORY (Mystery) and SATAN'S STORY (The Destroyer)

God's whole purpose from Alpha to Omega is unveiled through these three signs (wonders).

    a) Chapter 12:1, The first sign: The Woman (Genesis 3:15)

    b) Chapter 12:3, The second sign: The Dragon, Satan, (Gen. 3:1, 15)

    c) Chapter 15:1, The third sign, The Vials of Wrath:

        The Vials reveal the storing up of the wrath of the long-suffering God who in patience withholds His righteous judgment that all might come to repentance. Their out-pouring in the Day of the Lord concludes the mystery of God's long-suffering

    d) Chapters 12 through 20 show us in the unveiling of these three signs, the whole purpose of God in the mystery, and the ages-long effort of Satan to defeat God's purpose. With the end of the 20th chapter, we find Satan, the Destroyer, himself destroyed and the Son of God, the Victor, ready to turn over all things to the Father.

Chapters 21 and 22   The

Chapters 21 and 22   The CONSUMMATION

    a) The consummation of all things is laid bare before our eyes in Revelation 21 and 22

    b) The word "Blessed" is pronounced upon all who enter this book

Proverbs 25:2:

    "It is the glory of God to conceal a thing: but the honor of kings (all men) is to search out a matter."

        May the hidden truths of this book
        Serve
        As the Cryptic Lenses
        Through which
        God's Purpose is unveiled to our eyes.

Having "studied" and been "approved," we are prepared to receive
"The Revelation of God."

THE SEVEN SECTIONS

of

THE WORD OF GOD

"The secret things belong unto The Lord our God:
but those things which are revealed belong unto
us and to our children for ever, that we may do
all the words of this law."

Deuteronomy 29:29

140

A SEVEN FOLD CHART — THE SEVEN SECTIONS OF THE AGES OF THE WORD OF GOD — GOD'S PROTHESIS

Section ONE:
ALPHA

Revelation 1:8

"The Preparation"

Section TWO:
PERFECTION to KATABOLE

Genesis 1:1–2a

Section THREE:
RESTORATION to TERAH

Genesis 1:2b–11:26

Section FOUR:
ABRAHAM to CHRIST'S SPIRITUAL BODY

Genesis 11:27–John 20:22

Section FIVE:
The CHURCH

John 20:22–I Thess. 4:16

Section SIX:
THE KINGDOM AGE

II Thessalonians 1:7–10–Revelation 20:15

Section SEVEN:
OMEGA

Revelation 1:8

Revelation 21:1–Revelation 22:5
"The Consummation"

THE WORD OF GOD — John 17:24; I Peter 1:19–20

JEHOVAH — THE LORD JESUS CHRIST

THE KING OF KINGS

THE LAMB Revelation 13:8

THE SEVENTIETH WEEK OF DANIEL 9:24 70

THE TRIBULATION — THE COVENANT WEEK OF DANIEL 9:27

ARMAGEDDON

"GOD ALL in ALL" Psalm 90:1–2

Perfection Isaiah 45:8

Katabole II Peter 3:4–6; Jeremiah 4:23

Restoration Psalm 104:30

The Times of The Gentiles

			476 A.D.
		30 B.C. A.D.	The Feet and Toes
	168 B.C.		Kingdoms
331 B.C.		Rome	
538 B.C.	Greece		
606 B.C.	Medo-Persia		
	Babylon		

7 & 62
69 Weeks

70 Weeks are and upon

ABRAHAM'S VISION —John 8:56

"THE LORD'S DAY" Revelation 1:10

"GOD ALL IN ALL" I Corinthians 15:28

decreed upon Thy People Thy Holy City — includes All up to —

The City of God Hebrews 11:8–16
The New Jerusalem Revelation 21:2

(For Sectional developments of this Seven-Fold Chart, see the respective sectional divisions in this book)

𝕿 HE SCRIPTURES are the Holy Spirit's His-Story (history) of the Traffickers in *Dust*[1] and *Divinity*[2] and are comprised of the events between Alpha and Omega which are revealed "to those having eyes to see" in these events—within the Section of the Kingdom of God that "became vanity" at the foundation (the *throwing down*, Gr. *Katabole*) of the world"; and these are marked off from God's Kingdom by time-measurements. Though apparently this is "Man's Day," yet in reality, the purpose of God is in control, moving all things to His intended goal (Gr. *Telos*, end) "when God hath made the pile complete." The seven sections into which the events of the Bible divide, are the necessary adjustments which are required in the working out of that purpose:

Section ONE   : ALPHA
Section TWO   : PERFECTION to "KATABALLEIN"
                                    (a throwing down)
Section THREE: RESTORATION to TERAH
                                    (father of Abraham)
Section FOUR : ABRAHAM to CHRIST'S SPIRITUAL BODY
                                    (The Church)
Section FIVE : THE CHURCH
Section SIX   : THE KINGDOM
Section SEVEN: OMEGA

The accompanying chart, analysis and outlines have been tested, and they have proved to be illuminating and wholesomely helpful. The attempt of the charts, the divisions and the texts of this volume is not to alter, to re-arrange, nor in any way to inject opinion into the Scriptures, for the Spirit has demonstrated His ability to *reduce* to our own level His revelation. This analysis is taking "soundings" at each division to make sure that we are within His purpose on the way from Alpha to Omega, and in no place does violence to the text nor disturbs nor relocates the accepted canonical arrangement of our Authorized Version of the Bible. The division between books and the groupings of books so made, have focussed attention upon the group which at the time, is to the fore in the *Purpose of God*. This is not to say that the people so indicated are those set apart exclusively, for God is not the God of the Jews only (Romans 4:29). Just as the Gospels illustrate the divine method, so the sixteen written prophets divided into four groups[3] make easier reading and clearer understanding of the Word.

---

[1] "Dust," i.e. the Gentiles (Genesis 28:14; Isaiah 23:8; Ezekiel 28:5, 18)

[2] "Divinity," i.e. Saints of all ages (Genesis 22:17)

[3] See SEALED DIVISION, I, *Isaiah to Malachi*, p. 31

Those undertaking to rightly divide the Scriptures, must keep their eyes on the far goal, i.e. OMEGA. Only thus will they be able to "rightly discern":

> "But solid food belongeth to them that are of full age,
> even those who by reason of use have their senses
> exercised to discern both good and evil."
>
> Hebrews 5:14 N.

The chart's purpose is to direct attention to the time-sections and the portion of the Writings that apply, and thus to aid in the "rightly dividing of the Word." I invite you to put this to the proof.

As we study the Word of God, Rightly Dividing according to the Seven Sections of the Chart, we are to keep in mind the three-fold key which was given to us through the book of Revelation:

HIS STORY, *MY* STORY, *SATAN'S* STORY

This three-fold key runs from Alpha to Omega and is discernible in each of the Sections up to the Consummation, Omega. *His Story, My Story, Satan's Story* are each a continuing narrative which runs up to the Great White Throne Judgment. They show the unity of and the oneness of the Bible, and give the complete picture of the purpose of God throughout the whole Book. Each vertical section of the chart outlines the events taking place under that section. Horizontally, is given *His* Story, the record of God and His historical dealings with the nations; next, *My* Story, the record of God's approach to spiritual men; and finally, *Satan's* Story, the record of Satan's rebellion and his continuing attempt to counteract the purpose of God.

When we see the complete record of God's dealings with men of the nations (*His* Story); and His provision for salvation and redemption for the rebellion of Satan (*Satan's* Story) at the Consummation of all things, —then will we have the complete picture of the perfect revelation which is set forth in this Book, God's Word.

> Let any who will walk in Psalm One—
> And be diligent in II Timothy 2:15,
> Put his hand to the plow,
> Take up The Cross,
> And follow Him.

For,
"Every good gift and every perfect gift is from above,
And cometh down from the Father of lights,
With Whom is no variableness,
Neither shadow of turning."
And, at beautiful "evening time, it shall be light."

Section ONE: ALPHA—"GOD ALL IN ALL"

"Lord, Thou hast been our dwelling place in all generations.
 Before the mountains were brought forth,
 Or ever Thou hadst formed the earth and the world,
 Even from everlasting to everlasting,
 THOU art God."

Psalm 90:1—2

"'I am the Alpha and the Omega, beginning and ending',
 Saith the Lord,
 'Which is, and which was, and which is to come,
 THE   ALMIGHTY'."

Revelation 1:8N.*

*See page *xiii*

TABLE of CONTENTS

Section ONE: ALPHA

Page

Chart No. 1
Section ONE

A L P H A
Revelation 1:8

"I am The Alpha and The Omega"

1. THE TIME of ALPHA

"Before the world was"   (John 17:5; I Corinthians 2:7; II Timothy 1:9; Titus 1:2)

2. THE PURPOSE of ALPHA

"The Preparation" for, and beginning of, God's Redemption Program, where Christ is prepared for
and revealed as:

a) Prophet: Matthew 13:35 (Things kept secret FROM, therefore known to God and Christ,
BEFORE The Katabole—a casting down)

b) Priest: I Peter 1:19–20;   The Church (Ephesians 1:4) chosen in Him

c) King: Psalm 103:19

3. THE GOD of ALPHA

The Father; Psalm 90:1–2

The Word; John 1:1; John 17:24; Colossians 1:17

The Holy Spirit; Genesis 1:1; God-Elohim (Hebrew plural: three)

4. THE BEGINNING OF THE HIGHWAY OF HOLINESS — Isaiah 35:8

5. DISTINGUISHING THE THINGS THAT DIFFER

In noting the things that occur BEFORE (Gr. PRO) and FROM (Gr. APO) the Katabole
(the casting down) of the world, these occur BEFORE, and therefore DURING ALPHA

John 17:24 — Christ loved of God — before

Ephesians 1:4 — The Church chosen in Christ — before
(cp. Ephesians 3:9; Romans 16:25)

I Peter 1:20 — The Lamb foreknown — before

(for references on "apo" see Chart No. 2, p. 160)

HIS STORY: GOD DEALING WITH NATIONS

I. THE HEAVENLY SPLENDOR OF GOD

Wrapped up in the glorious robe of His seraphic vision, comes ONE Whom no other pen has so described, Whose Presence fits the vast dimensions. No Taj Mahal, no Mosque, not even a Temple of Solomon could contain Him (I Kings 8:27, 30; Acts 17:24). The created heaven is the realm of God (Isaiah 6:1; 55:8—9; 57:15; Revelation 20:11), wherein is life and its every satisfaction. Here in this heaven, dwelleth a civilization and a creation. The sublimest of life dwells within this creation, garrisoned by the cherubim whose Lord dwells in Light unapproachable (I Timothy 6: 16), guarded by the unsleeping seraphim around the Throne. Such heavenly splendor intensifies loneliness and gives understanding to the character of God. From this, our world has been cast down and "lieth in the evil one" (I John 5:19). He is the God of every and all the impossibles, the One of Whom it is written "before the mountains were brought forth or ever Thou hadst formed the earth and the world, even from everlasting to everlasting, Thou art God." A defeated God is unthinkable; the ageless heavens with their timeless accuracy bear witness to the glory of the eternal God of Power.

The Bible opens with God being all in all and the glory of God all around His eternal residence. One claiming divinity must be in a setting commensurate with such a claim. "In beginning God created the heavens and the earth," (Genesis 1:1)—back of this sublime sentence, the mind of man has never satisfactorily penetrated. God's workshop has been well swept and no chips litter the floor of the Infinite. The pristine heavens still continue their stately procession around the Throne of God (Psalm 19:1—6). The Universe comes into view fresh from its dedication with the reverberation of the music of the morning stars and the shouting of the Sons of God (Job 38:1—7).

This is not God's last word: for "it hath not entered into the heart of man, the things which God hath prepared for those that love Him" (Isaiah 64:4; I Corinthians 2:9). In the expectancy reflected in this Scripture, with unsandalled feet, let us ask to think God's thoughts over after Him. When the Bible is once believingly entered upon, then the glories of God's glorious kingdom, emerge to the Christian (Isaiah 52:7—10).

Psalm 24:7—10

"Lift up your heads, O ye gates; And be ye lift up, ye
everlasting doors; And the King of glory shall come in.
Who is this King of glory?
The Lord strong and mighty,
The Lord mighty in battle.

"Lift up your heads, O ye gates; Even lift them up, ye
everlasting doors; And the King of glory shall come in.
Who is this King of glory?
The Lord of hosts,
He is the King of glory.

Selah."

II. GOD'S HISTORICAL DEALINGS WITH MEN

Through the Bible runs a golden thread of the whole story of God and
man. Here from Alpha to Omega God records His message to all people.
Throughout the whole Book we find the record of God and His historical
dealings with men. These are things which are discernible to the human
eye and which should bring thinking men to a recognition of God's existence and power (Romans 1:18—20).

Paul on Mars Hill said to the Athenians, "in Him we live and move
and have our being" (Acts 17:22—31). The record of creation is written
for all mankind to read and understand, and the scientist today is drawn
to the inevitable conclusion that only a creating God could have brought
forth this earth and the universe. His dealing with the nation of Israel
is evident to students of history down through the centuries and the record
of Daniel indicates that God moves through the nations directing their
destinies.

H. Grattan Grimness once said:

"The Bible is the chart of all history; and it gives us, not events
only, but their moral character tracing the *motives* that influenced
the various actors in the drama, as well as the *results* of their action.
Events are shown in connection with their *causes* and their *effects*,
and the *judgment* of God as to their *character* is revealed. Without the
Bible, history would be a spectacle of 'rivers flowing from unknown
sources to unknown seas,' but, under its guidance, we can trace the
complex currents to their springs, and see the end from the beginning
.... The true plan of history can therefore be found, only in the Bible."

God is the Father of all those who have accepted His Son as their
Savior. The Bible is *His Story* told to His children at the Table of Communion, putting into our speech all of His creation (Psalm 19); and entering, we begin to "think God's thoughts over after Him." Only such can
come "near to the heart of God." In such a spirit may we profitably "search
the Scriptures" and be able to "rightly divide" and to render to each "their
due portion" so that the great statements of the Word of God become significant and the greater forces contending within become meaningful. Be
not deceived that it falls short of inspiration because of its use of our
speech; we need frequent excursions up into its majestic periods (Job,
Isaiah, Paul and John) to keep reminded that His thoughts are not our
thoughts.

Each segment of *His Story* pushes the veil farther back and leaves luminous the steps of Him "Who was, Who is, and Who is coming," to which the sermon of Jesus (Matthew 24 and Luke 21) gives added and accurate direction. These are historic events, world phases.

His Story is from Alpha to Omega. It is in the third Person; He is the Unknown God. *His Story* is Pre-History, is accurate and there are no omissions. God often *seems* to be defeated but He is ever present in a continuous contest. At times in each period, man seemed to be in the ascendancy but never was it completely so.

> Careless seems the great Avenger;
>   history's pages but record
> One death-grapple in the darkness 'twixt
>   old systems and the Word;
> Truth forever on the scaffold,
>   Wrong forever on the throne, —
> Yet that scaffold sways the future, and,
>   behind the dim unknown,
> Standeth God within the shadow,
>   keeping watch above his own. [1]

III. CREATION

The world's very great need is reverence, for we are standing beneath the same Heavens that David in whispered awe breathed, "when I survey" (Psalm 8:3)—and we too, must recapture that same reverence. Through the thoughtful love of an understanding congregation, I have looked upon many of the glories of God's great out-of-doors. There is beauty everywhere. But wonder rises upon wonder when all is reduced into "little drops of water, little grains of sand!" What an artist our Father is! With these He rises to majesty in mountains, sublimity of the seas, and the "Heavens declare His glory." But to one who has traveled the "Highway of Holiness" these are but a passing show! Man does not understand the elements of creation, the very atoms of his life, if he does not understand them as coming out from the love of God which He applied in the development of demonstration of His love and His perfection unto the end that God may be all in all.

There are but two explanations to creation:

A direct creation
Or,
"A fortuitous concourse of atoms" (Evolution)

Matter is either created or eternal. The universe is either a Thought or an Evolution. If it is a Thought, then there must be a Thinker, or at

---

[1] James Russell Lowell, *The Present Crisis*, st. 8

each station we would find the miracle of the lesser producing the greater which is an unbelievable absurdity. If it is a Thought, then why the slowness of evolution? The Bible's statements are most plausible, rational and satisfying. They have stood the test of time, survived all attacks and speak with sureness and assuredness upon the signs and events of these present times. The Creator who could call into existence and number and name the stars, (Isaiah 40:26—28, Psalm 147:4) surely could go one step farther and put to His purpose: "I change not" (Ephesians 3:9; Revelation 24:6; Malachi 3:6; Hebrews 12:22—23; James 1:17; Psalm 138:2; 119:89; I Peter 1:25).

Sir Arthur Eddington in *New Pathways in Science,* under the heading *Thermodynamic Equilibrium,* says, "The chance against evolution if written out in figures, would produce enough zeros to fill every book of a large city library." We are told that the circumference of the Universe is forty septillion miles and that galaxies are expanding at the rate of 24,000 per second. Dr. Eddington furnishes the following scale of sizes:

> "In the Astrophysical Journal, Drs. Otto Struve, G. P. Kuiper, and B. Stromgren of the Yerkes Observatory, Chicago, calmly described the largest star ever found . . . . The new star revolves around Epsilon Aurigae, about eighteen billion million miles away. Because it gives off invisible infra-red rays, no one has seen it through telescopes or on photographic plates. But every twenty-seven years it eclipses the Epsilon Auriagae. So, by studying the visible companion star's orbital irregularities, the Yerkes astronomers could compute the dimensions of the invisible giant—the 'I-Star' of Epsilon Aurigae. Its diameter is three thousand times that of our sun, and, said Dr. Struve, if it were plopped in the middle of our solar system, it would fill all the space out to Uranus, 1,782,800,000 miles from the sun." [1]

Kant said, "Two things awe me: the starry heavens above and the moral law within." As we consider the vastness of the Universe and these starry heavens, there is but one sentence that written across them would shine with a splendor undimmed:

"In Beginning God Created."

---

[1] Sir Arthur Eddington, copied from Bro. Kindred's sermon notes of January 30, 1938

MY STORY: GOD'S APPROACH TO SPIRITUAL MEN

I. THE LOVE TRAVAIL OF THE HEAVENLY FATHER

Would you get a word picture, a pen portrait of God? Then read I Corinthians 13. Love is the mightiest force in the Universe; before It (Him), everything must give way and be dissolved. There is no approach to the understanding of the great Jehovah-God except through the emotion of love. It is written in the sun, moon and stars; it is embedded in the Hebrew and Greek revelation given by Divine inspiration. It is incarnated in the Son of the Living God—"He that hath seen Me hath seen the Father"(John 14:9).

The Bible says "God is Love," but never does it say "Love is God." "GOD IS LOVE" and only love sacrifices and is sleepless. The Cross was necessary to demonstrate that love; loneliness is part of His Insomnia. As the Psalmist wrote: "Behold, He that keepeth Israel shall neither slumber nor sleep" (Psalm 121:4). This eternal insomnolence which God manifested toward Israel is but an example of His sleepless watchfulness that is manifested over His people in every dispensation. We understand more fully the Lord's words as we read again this text when He said, "Lo, I am with you alway (N. all the days), even unto the end of the world" (N. completion of the age) Amen (Matthew 28:20 b).

> Oh, Love, that wilt not let me go,
> I rest my weary soul in Thee;
> I lay in dust life's glory dead—
> And from the ground there blossoms red
> Life, that shall eternal be.
>
> George Matheson

Love is the essence of every manifestation, the motive of any or all exertions of power or authority (Psalm 8; Colossians 1:17). Love is the Presence (Shekinah) Cloud forth out of which God emerged as Creator (Psalm 90:2, 16—17), and creation grew out of a love that hungered for an understanding love.

Such love could not be denied, and so this bit of the Universe was chosen for the seed-bed, a kindergarten if you please, for the children of His "Image." The Universe was used as His demonstration; the Earth as His hieroglyphics; the Alphabet as His introduction and revelation of His last and greatest unveiling of Himself (John 14:9).

The Universe itself is a floating island drifting within love; its nearly one hundred elements are the storehouses of potential combinations intended for the glory of God, but prostituted as the servants of man's caprice whose combinations may be the cause of holocausts and cataclysms and destructive convulsions of nature.

The Almighty, Dynamic Love whose prismatic colors are seen in the creative elements revealed in the universe, is set forth within the pages of this Book. Language contains the thought bulbs through which loving Omniscience reveals to those seeking facts of the universe and the mysteries of life, the answer to their searching. In this volume are references to a world beyond our ken which is peopled by vast multitudes of seraphim, cherubim, and angels.

What can you say and be positive concerning the Creator of the Universe, but just that "God is Love." Love is ever self-less and seeks not its own. Love such as God's love, cannot be understood until a soul has long meditated upon that word and until one has also experienced what love has wrought in the changing of:

Selfishness	into	Service
Avoiding	into	Seeking
Obligation	into	Privilege

Only then can one appreciate the whole writings of John; and the apostrophe of Paul upon I Corinthians 13: "And the greatest of these is love"; and the panegyric of Romans 16. To me it seems that this is just another instance of drawing a little water from the wells of inexhaustible fulness. Our study of the Word of God reveals that:

Love is
(Creative — Genesis 1:1 — (Job 38:1; 40:2)
(Sacrificial — John 3:16 — (Romans 11:33—36)
(Victorious — Psalm 110:1 — (I Corinthians 15:28)

Love
(Fitted up the house (the Universe)
(Made man in His own image
(Came to seek and to save the lost ones
(Rejoices that: that which was lost has been found.

The moment that self comes first, then love ceases, for:

("God *so* loved that He gave"
("Not *My* will but Thine"
("*Thy* Kingdom come _
(*Thy* will be done."

The vindication of God's love is revealed in His Word (Ephesians 3: 9—11). If He had dealt summarily with Satan, He might have been criticized; but Satan is given one thousand years (Revelation 20) in which to meditate[1] and then still is given an opportunity to come back. The purpose of God as revealed in Psalm 19 was sufficient to compensate for His suffering. As sensitive as love is, there must be an immeasurable compensation to endure so much of suffering (Isaiah 53:11).

---

[1] See *The Kingdom Age*, III. The Day of the Lord. D. Satan Bound for One Thousand Years, p. 560.

The Universe was conceived out of the loneliness of God, and born through the love travail of the Heavenly Father. God's agony at the Cross was the greatest display of that love: when He forsook His Beloved Son that He might reach in death, unto the very last one, and that one lost and degraded unto "the uttermost." It is this One whose Autobiography is the purpose of this marvelous Book, the Holy Bible. Its every energy is love-driven: "God is love"; His text is John 3:16.

The Love of God

The love of God is greater far
Than tongue or pen can ever tell;
It goes beyond the highest star,
And reaches to the lowest hell;
. . .
Could we with ink the ocean fill,
And were the skies of parchment made;
Were ev'ry stalk on earth a quill,
And ev'ry man a scribe by trade;
To write the love of God above
Would drain the ocean dry;
Nor could the scroll contain the whole,
Tho' stretched from sky to sky.
. . .
Oh, love of God, how rich and pure!
How measureless and strong!
It shall forevermore endure
The saints' and angels' song.[1]

II. JEHOVAH'S REDEMPTION MISSION

The Mystery or MY STORY, is the story of the suffering God. His sufferings are not discernible to the man of the world but can only be understood by those who are seeking to know the mind of Christ and to fill up His sufferings in the Church.

Out from love beyond our measure from the great high God, came forth Jehovah upon His redemption-mission (John 1:14). Love alone could be trusted with such power upon such a mission, and the story of that mission is the theme of the Sacred Writings. Within this love, Elohim (plural: The Father, Word and Holy Spirit) set forth the Cross (Revelation 13:8; Ephesians 1:4; John 1:29). The Scriptures are one long, continuous outpouring of an Almighty God and Father's inexhaustible love, a love that paid the price before the plan was launched (I Peter 1:18—20), and was set forth in victory *before Alpha*. The working out of that plan from Conception to Consummation, is the motif of the Bible.

---

[1] F.M. Lehman, *The Love of God,* (Copyright renewed 1945. Assigned to Nazarene Publishing House, Kansas City, Mo.)

Paul says in Ephesians 3:9 and 1:4 that the fellowship of the mystery from the beginning of the world had been hid in God Who created all things by Jesus Christ, and that the Church had been chosen by God in Him *before* the *Kataballein* (the casting down of the world). Not only was the Cross prepared and established in God's program from the beginning, but the Church, the Body of Christ, was set forth in the purpose of God during Alpha, while Perfection reigned over a perfect universe. This mystery, the Joint Body or the Church, remained hidden through the ages until it was revealed under the preaching of the apostles and especially that of Paul (Ephesians 3:3—5).

My Story concerns the called-out of every age or dispensation. It is a continuous process. Each dispensation reveals to "those having eyes to see":

1. That Jehovah is their God
2. That He is a rewarder of those who diligently seek Him
3. That they "must believe that God is"
4. That He is "the same yesterday, today and forever."

In this Alpha section Jehovah, while dwelling in glory in heavenly splendor (John 17:5), prepares for a great redemption mission which will call out spiritual people to the salvation which He will accomplish. *My Story* is spiritual and can only be seen by those who desire to discern spiritual things (I Corinthians 2:13). In Section FOUR of the chart, we note that Jehovah manifests Himself in appearances to His saints and these theophanies will be noted as they occur in the events of the Bible.

In Exodus 6:3 we find the Name *Jehovah* being used of God Almighty as He speaks unto Moses. It is this Name which becomes significant in its use in *My Story* as contrasted with Elohim in *His Story* (Proverbs 30:4).

My Story covers the three-fold work of Christ as Prophet, Priest and King. His *prophetic* work begins in Alpha; His *priestly* work began at the Cross; and He enters into His *kingly* work with His return to this earth to establish His Kingdom during the Day of the Lord. [1] During His *prophetic work*, He is known as Jehovah; His *priestly life* began at His birth in Bethlehem as the seed of woman; and His *kingly reign* will be the fulfillment of the type set forth in Melchisedek, King of Salem:

> *To Moses:*
>
> Was given the pattern of the Tabernacle (which is still basic) in which to house the Law that God gave to him
>
> *To whom Solomon:*
>
> The wisest of men prayer: "hear Thou in Heaven, Thy dwelling

---

[1] See Section SIX, *The Kingdom Age.* III. *The Day of the Lord.* E. The Reign of Righteousness and Peace. 1. The Church, the Body of Christ, Reigns with Him. p. 561

place," at the dedication of the most magnificent Temple ever erected

To whom Job:

The most tried and tested of his time, resisted under the most severe temptation, came forth "tested as by fire" confessing, "I know that my Redeemer liveth"

And archaeologists of today are bringing forth out of a long ante-Bible past, buried civilizations out of all continents, the productions of science and skill that challenge the achievements of our greatest.

As the intellect of today seeks and is challenged by "them of olden times," so also the meditative spiritual minds are "striving to enter into" "the fellowship with the God and Father of our Lord Jesus Christ,"—"Whom to know aright is Life Everlasting." To Him be Glory and Honor and Praise and Power forevermore, Amen!

III. THE HIGHWAY OF HOLINESS

"And an highway shall be there,
And a way,
And it shall be called 'The way of holiness';
The unclean shall not pass over it;
But *it* shall be for those:
The wayfaring men, though fools,
    shall not err therein."

Isaiah 35:8

The Highway of Holiness is the path over which God moves from the beginning in carrying out His purpose for supervising the campaign that is going on until He arrives at the end of the journey from Alpha to Omega. There is an un-soiled-ness about the holiness of the highway that runs from end to end in the purpose of God (Daniel 12:19; Hosea 14:9). It is one continued story that runs throughout the whole Bible and renders futile any attempt to divide this Book into Old and New Testaments. God has ONE purpose and people are called to study this Highway of Holiness to see how God is working out that purpose and having His way. The Highway is a way of mystery, *My Story,* and is only for those who are spiritual; the unclean, the man of the world, cannot enter upon it but the child of God finds unrestricted entrance.

SATAN'S STORY

> "Thus saith the Lord Jehovah:
> Thou sealest up the sum (measure), full of wisdom, and
> perfect in beauty. Thou hast been in Eden, the garden
> of God; Every precious stone was thy covering, The
> sardius, topaz, and the diamond, The beryl, the onyx, and
> the jasper, The sapphire, the emerald, and the carbuncle,
> and gold: The Workmanship of thy tabrets and of thy pipes
> was prepared in thee in the day that thou wast created.
> Thou art the anointed cherub that covereth; and I have
> set thee so: Thou wast upon the holy mountain of God;
> Thou hast walked up and down in the midst of the stones
> of fire. Thou wast perfect in thy ways from the day that
> thou wast created,
>
> *Till iniquity was found in thee."*
>
> Ezekiel 28:12*b*—15

The Scriptures reveal that Satan[1] was created as an angel of God, perfect in every way, dwelling in the midst of the cherubim and seraphim and the hosts of the Armies of God partaking of the Glory of God (Psalm 19; Ezekiel 28:13—15).

Satan, the destroyer, was a part of God's original creation which was perfect until iniquity was found in him (Ezekiel 28:15). He was cast out of heaven into the earth which was his dominion. In the beginning Satan was the covering cherub who was permitted to have fellowship with all the Sons of God in all the Universe. The fall of Satan and the consequences of the fall will be considered in the second section of the chart.

Concerning Satan:

1. He is living and is as real as Gabriel, Michael, or other of the angelic hosts
2. He has no imagination or vision but is a Creature of habit, but he does believe what God says
3. "We are not ignorant of his devices" (II Corinthians 2:21*b*)
4. This solar system was once his as the covering cherub and this was the chiefest province of the "Sons of God" (Job 1:7).

Eden, earth's capital and Satan's abode, was the only point in the Universe from which all of the revelation of the glory of God could be seen (Psalm 19) (See also Matthew 4:8—10).

---

[1] See Appendix D. *Satan, The Serpent in Genesis 3,* p. 603 ff.

Section TWO: PERFECTION to KATABOLE
(the throwing down)

"In a beginning God created the heavens and the earth.
And the earth was (became) without form, and void;
And darkness was upon the face of the deep."

Genesis 1:1—2 a N.*

"The heavens declare the glory of God;
And the firmament showeth His handywork.
Day unto day uttereth speech,
And night unto night showeth knowledge.
There is no speech nor words,
Without their voice being heard."

Psalm 19:1—3 N.*

*See page *xiii*

TABLE of CONTENTS

Section TWO: PERFECTION to *KATABOLE*
(the throwing down)

PERFECTION to KATABOLE (The Throwing Down)
HIS STORY

THE GLORY and HANDYWORK of GOD

"He hangeth the earth upon nothing.

. . .

Lo, these are parts of His ways:
But how little a portion (what a whisper) is heard of Him?
But the thunder of His power who can understand?"

Job 26:7*b*, 14 N.

In the beginning God created the heavens and the earth and the heavens declare the glory of God and the firmament showeth His handywork. Here are two different things:

One is,
"The glory of God" which is *perfection*
The other,
"The firmament showeth His handywork" which refers
to the *restoring* of the earth's surface following its
having been wrecked through the work of Satan.

The Bible *assumes* creation (Genesis 1:1, Psalm 19), making no attempt to defend or justify this assumption. God is all and in all, and in Creation, He has water-marked the Universe with His Glory and His Handywork (Colossians 1:12—17). Within *this* Creation all "live and move and have their being" (Acts 17:22—31). Beyond this, all is speculation, an hypothesis or guesswork.

"For thus saith Jehovah the Creator of the heavens;
God Himself the Former of the earth and the Maker of it;
He hath established it,
He created it not in *vain*, (waste and void; for nought)
He formed it to be inhabited:
I am Jehovah;
And there is none else."

Isaiah 45:18

Here we are told that the earth was not created "without form and void" but rather that it was "formed to be inhabited." God the perfect Creator (Matthew 5:48) could not produce less than the perfect creation (Deuteronomy 32:4). In Jeremiah 4:23 we read, "I beheld the earth, and lo, it was without form and void; and the heavens, and they had no man, and all the birds of the heavens were fled." This reveals the judgment which followed Genesis 1:1 because of Satan's rebellion.

The heavens are static while the firmament is volatile; the earth has suffered violent catastrophe at the hands of ambitious pride (Ezekiel 28; Luke 4; Revelation 13:4 and chap. 12). The rising up of pride in Satan,

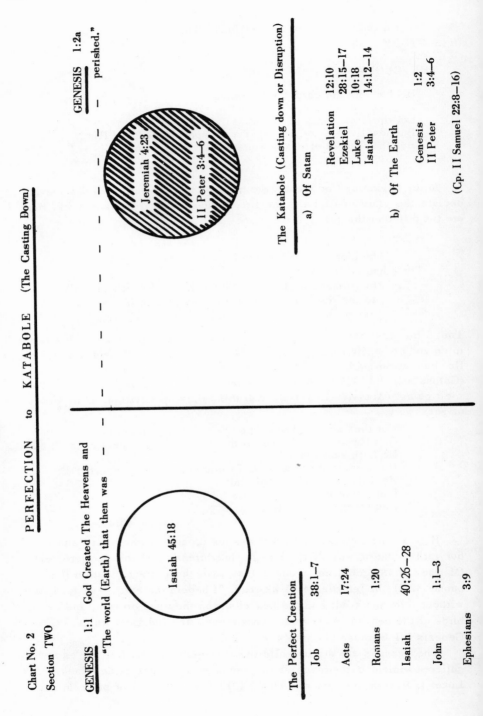

160

Chart No. 2
Section TWO

PERFECTION to KATABOLE (The Casting Down)

GENESIS 1:1 God Created The Heavens and
"The world (Earth) that then was

GENESIS 1:2a
perished."

Jeremiah 4:23
II Peter 3:4—6

Isaiah 45:18

The Perfect Creation

Job	38:1—7
Acts	17:24
Ronams	1:20
Isaiah	40:26—28
John	1:1—3
Ephesians	3:9

The Katabole (Casting down or Disruption)

a) Of Satan

Revelation	12:10
Ezekiel	28:15—17
Luke	10:18
Isaiah	14:12—14

b) Of The Earth

| Genesis | 1:2 |
| II Peter | 3:4—6 |

(Cp. II Samuel 22:8—16)

conceived and brought forth sin and sin produced the chaos (*Katabole*) in Genesis 1:2; but these have never been able to add to, or take from, "The heavens declare the glory of God." When the *Kataballein* took place, all paroxysms were effects. What scientists compute into billions of years, to God were as seconds. Creation includes all which God wrought in heaven and earth (Genesis 1:1); the agony displayed in the rocks was produced after this (Genesis 1:2). The heavens undefiled and unsoiled by efforts of angels or man, await their dismissal after services.

Inasmuch as hypotheses have been offered, should faith rising from the soil of God's Word be denied a place especially as it would seem to be more in line with some modern findings, the immeasurable power resident within the atom would be more than sufficient to destroy creation.[1]

According to the accepted dictum, what is evolved must first be involved out of nothing. Especially as the Bible asserts Genesis 1:1, Psalm 19:1—6, Psalm 90, et al. Its statements also are taken as a fact, as is also the one perfect Man Who spake as never man spake. Is it therefore presumptuous to offer an hypothesis in harmony with these known facts?

There was an abundance of atoms to create the Universe and to produce the power to wrench the earth into an agony of contortions in the *Kataballein* that would simulate the ages of time other guessers predicate. In I Corinthians 15:51 "Behold I show you a mystery . . . but we shall all be changed, in a moment, in the twinkling of an eye . . .," faith accepts the existence of such power and is made perfect, not void.

The foundation of the Universe (II Timothy 2:19) rests upon atoms, and these are the love blocks of God (I John 4:8); and all response is always instantaneous in creation or judgment. "And the earth was (became) without form, and void; and darkness was upon the face of the deep"— here begins His Handywork, prophetic of His redemption.

Like these rock formations at the *Katabole*, people today are often aged in a day. What is the sense in aging or insisting on long ages to explain the rock formations and to accommodate our senses? Would that lessen the wonder? Rather the wonder is increased. Consider Romans 1:20 and Hebrews 11:3, for, "the things which are seen were NOT MADE of things which do appear. Modern science has illustrated conclusively that the unseen properties of atoms, electricity, and personality are vital to every part of life and material things (II Corinthians 4:18).

Scientists agree that several ice ages have taken place on this earth and that the evidence of their effects are seen in many parts over the face

---

[1] There are scoffers today who say, "where is the promise of His coming"; not realizing that recent developments in atomic energy give us full proof, that there is more than enough power within the elements of the earth to destroy all creation (II Peter 3:2—12).

of the globe. [1]One of the evidences that it was something which took place quickly, instantaneously, is found in the discovery of the frozen body of a mastodon in Siberia. The flesh of this great prehistoric animal was so perfectly preserved by the freezing that it could be eaten, [2]and further investigation disclosed that the freezing took place so suddenly that the grass which the animal was feeding upon was found undigested[3] (II Peter 3:3—7). This event pictured by this illustration could not be confused with the flood of Noah's day for there the water rose gradually and there is no mention of freezing nor of geological convulsions (Genesis 7:11, 17; 8:13). It is evident that this ice age was a judgment of God, caused by the withdrawing of the sun's rays between Genesis 1:1 and 1:2.[4] Here the earth was cast down because of Satan's rebellion and the restoration that took place with verse 3. God's actions are instantaneous like the Lord's healing of the bodies of men.

We realize as we enter into this study, that the shadowless God is a purpose*ful* God (John 3:16; Revelation 5:6; 13:8). The Bible reveals God's (Elohim's[5]) unfolding of His Purpose to the intelligence of the Universe (Ephesians 1:3—23; 3:8—13; 1:1—8). He is the ever-living, the replenishing and the Almighty God.

God deals in facts; men deal in hypotheses; the Fiat and Finish are two sides of God's work. In man, the head forces and cracks the atom; but in man, also the heart believes, and then seeks Him of the Nucleus.

> The night has a thousand eyes,
>   And the day but one;
> Yet the light of the bright world dies,
>   With the dying sun.
> The mind has a thousand eyes,
>   And the heart but one,
> Yet the light of a whole life dies,
>   When love is done.[6]

---

[1] Report of Smithsonian Institution 1952, *The Ice Age in the North American*, p. 243: "Artic North America in common with the rest of the world, is now emerging from the latest of a series of glacial ages which as a group have characterized the last million or more of geological time. During the glacial ages, each of which was 100,000 years or more in length, the mean temperature at the earth's surfaces were markedly lower than today . . . ."

[2] See illustration p. 156: *The Banquet of the Ages* (Herald Examiner, April 15, 1934).

[3] See Appendix B. 2. *Frozen Mammoth in Siberia* (Smithsonian Institution, 1904, p. 611); and Appendix B. 3. *Mammoth Is Found in Ice*, (N.Y. Times, Mar. 4, 1935, p. 8), p. 597 ff.

[4] See Appendix, B. *Ice Ages*, 1. *Bible and Modern Science*,p. 593 ff. (Lt. Col. L. Merson Davies, M.A., F.R.S.E., F.R.A.I., F.G.S. Lieut. Col. late of Royal Artillery, Pickering and Inglis, London, 1935, Third Ed., pp. 100—103, 108, 113, 117, and Davies App. p. 190, Note 7).

[5] *Elohim*: Genesis 1:1; Exodus 6:1—3; Psalm 2:2; I Corinthians 2:8; Daniel 3:15; Isaiah 36:20; Daniel 8:10—11; Acts 17:2; Revelation 13:6—7; 19:18—20.

[6] Frances William Bourdillon

MY STORY

The character of God, Christ and The Holy Spirit as set forth in *Alpha*, continues unchanging during this age and those that follow. The next Section (THREE) of the outline, *RESTORATION to TERAH,* introduces the *Restoration* of the Earth, the *Creation* of man, and the first *Promise* of the Redeemer (Genesis 3:15).

> "In the beginning was the Word,
> And the Word was with God,
> And the Word was God.
> The same was in beginning with God.
> All things were made through Him;
> And without Him was not one thing
>   made that was made.
> In Him was life;
> And the life was the light of men.
> And the light shineth in darkness;
> And the darkness comprehended it not."

John 1:1—5 N.

> "God who in many parts and in divers manners spake in time past unto the fathers by the prophets, hath in these last days spoken unto us by Son, whom He appointed heir of all things through whom also He made the worlds; Who being the brightness of His glory, and the express image of His person (exact expression of His subsistence), and upholding all things by the word of His power, when He had through Himself purged our sins, sat down on the right hand of the Majesty in the heights;"

Hebrews 1:1—3 N.

> "But unto the Son He saith,
> 'Thy Throne, O God, is for ever and ever;
> A sceptre of righteousness (equity) is the sceptre of Thy Kingdom.
> Thou hast loved righteousness and hated lawlessness;
> therefore God, Thy God, anointed thee with oil of gladness above
>   thy companions.'
> And Thou Lord, at the beginning hast laid the foundation of the earth;
> And the heavens are works of Thine hands:
> They shall perish; But Thou remainest;
> And they all shall wax old as a garment;
> And as a vesture shalt Thou fold them up, and they shall be changed;
> but Thou art the same, and Thy years shall not fail."

Hebrews 1:8—12 N.

Jehovah God, the Christ of the New Testament, continues in His prophetic office and God's redemption plan prepared in *Alpha* is held in abeyance during this period as the perfect God removes the rebel Satan and casts him down and also the earth which is his abode.

SATAN'S STORY

I. THE TRAGEDY of DEFECTION

"How art thou fallen from heaven,
O Lucifer, son of the morning!
How art thou cut down to the ground,
which didst weaken the nations!

"For thou hast said in thine heart,
'*I will* ascend into the heavens,
I will exalt my throne above the stars of God:
I will sit also upon the mount of the congregation,
In the sides of the north:
I will ascend above the heights of the clouds;
I will be like the Most High.'

"Yet thou shalt be brought down to hell,
To the sides of the pit."

Isaiah 14:12—15

The Bible has been called the record of the tragedy of defection for in it are recorded those who sin having missed the mark. The defection begins with Satan[1] and all mankind follows in his steps. It is stated in I John 5:19 that, "the whole world lieth in the evil one." What happened? The old devil was cast down and the iniquity that was in him has been spread as a veil over this part of the kingdom of God. Sin always calls forth investigation and correction:

"Thou wast perfect in thy ways
from the day that thou wast created,
Till iniquity was found in thee."

Ezekiel 28:15

This original perfection of Satan came from the hand of Christ Himself (John 1:3; Colossians 1:13—17; I Timothy 1:17 and 3:16). Satan was not tested of God to determine the attitude of his heart, but rather he was a wilful prodigal. That there be no mistake concerning Satan's prodigal spirit, he is to be bound a thousand years (Revelation 20:2) before his final judgment takes place (Revelation 20:10).

The first eleven chapters of Genesis are the prologue to the whole hegira of sin. The Story must begin with The Traffickers of The Dust and The Divine, a struggle that continues throughout this "throwing-down"

---

[1] E. W. Bullinger, D. D., A. K. C., F. R. G. S., *The Companion Bible*, (London, Oxford University Press, Lamp Press), *The Serpent of Genesis 3*, (App. 19, pp. 24—25). See our Appendix D. p. 603 ff.

(*Katabole*) period. It begins with rebellion in Heaven (Isaiah 14:12 ff. and Ezekiel 28:14 ff.), and it ends before the Great White Throne of Judgment and the Restoration of sin-freed earth to its former glory where God is All in All (I Corinthians 15:28). The Bible records the whole story of the battle of the Universe fought between Satan and God. Satan, the subtle adversary (Genesis 3:1; I Peter 5:8) is also a spiritual adversary (Ephesians 6:11—12; 4:14); the battle is between *Spiritual* forces and begins before man was created and will only end at the Great White Throne Judgment when God becomes All in All once more. The forces contending in the battle are made up of those groups that are set forth in The Scriptures: Israel and the Church are on God's side; and Satan, his angels and "the whole world that lieth in the wicked one" are on the other side. Therefore, the *Bible* can be called "the battle-ground of the Universe." When Satan, the Deceiver, was found out and iniquity was found in him, he was cast out of heaven into the earth and his angels were cast out with him (Luke 10:18). God is still in the place that He occupied when Creation began. And God is love, known and revered by the principalities and powers in the heavens, but by the rebel Satan, God was despised; and Satan was cast out with his following (Revelation 12:9).

II. THE PROVINCE OF SATAN

This earth was the province that had been assigned to Satan. This planet is the only place in the whole universe where can be seen all the points of the universe in every direction. Earth was the only planet from which could be shown signs, seasons, days, years and set times (Revelation 12:10). It is Satan's province and from here *pride* could survey the universe (Isaiah 14:13; Revelation 12:9—10). Satan is called the god of this world, or age, the prince of darkness; and the prince of the powers of the air; and "the whole world lieth in the wicked one" and he is in control.

III. THE HARMONY OF THE UNIVERSE

God is a lover of music and harmony and the creation of God was perfect and was made up of temples, peoples, cherubim and seraphim. We read, "When the morning stars sang together, And all the sons of God shouted for joy?" (Job 38:7). There is music; there is harmony in the universe. In *The Merchant of Venice*,[1] Shakespeare has Lorenzo say to Jessica:

> Sit, Jessica, Look, how the floor of Heaven
> Is thick inlaid with patines of bright gold:
> There's not the smallest orb which thou behold'st
> But in his motion like an angel sings,

[1] Shakespeare, *The Merchant of Venice*, Rev. Henry N. Hudson, LLD. (Boston, Ginn and Company, 1894), Act v; sc. 1, p. 185

Still quiring* to the young-eyed cherubins,—
Such harmony is immortal souls;
But whilst this muddy vesture of decay
Doth grossly close it in, we cannot hear it.

**Quoted footnote:* QUIRING (choiring): "A continually sound-ing an accompaniment—of course everybody has heard of 'music of the Spheres,'—an ancient mystery which taught that the heavenly bodies in their revolutions sing together in a concert so loud, various and sweet, as to exceed all proportion to the human ear, and the greatest souls from Plato to Wordsworth, have been lifted above themselves, with the idea that the uni-verse was knit together by a principle of which musical harmony is the aptest and clearest expression. Milton touches it with surpassing sweetness in the Morning Hymn of Adam and Eve, *Paradise Lost,* verse 177."

(While assembling the notes for this book,)
(apropo above quote,—an interesting and timely)
(article[1] was discovered from which we quote:)

". . . Stars I can understand. I lie awake in awe beneath them. But the Milky Way is almost too much; it is more than man can even hope to grasp or comprehend. A star is a definite point of light; the Milky Way is a hazy symbol of inscrutability. Thought expands to the Infinite in its very contemplation.**

**. . . Yet not quite all of the night sky is black. On any clear moonless night, we see a great arch of faint, pearly light, spanning the sky from horizon to horizon. We cannot see what happens to it below the horizon, unless we travel around the world. We then find that its two ends join up in the southern sky—a belt of light encircling the world. In nearly all languages it has the same name—the Milky Way. (James Jeans, *Stars in Their Courses, The Milky Way,* p. 99).

"I spoke of Jupiter as a silent friend. Being a planet, it may in-deed be silent. But the stars which surround it are not. Lying on my back on the moonless night under Arizona skies, *I had a sen-sation of music in the stars.* I analyzed it thus.

"After having separated each sound of the night which I knew—and classified it as best I could into bird call, or wind, or breath of trees—there was still a constant undertone of singing vibration, low but distinct, which filled the air.

"Perhaps it was an accumulation of tiny unnamed noises—the breath of a million insects, the disintegration of a million rocks, the tag ends of a million pulses from the other side of the earth. At all events, that undertone of constant singing was there. Abso-lute stillness in the world, I discovered, did not exist. *I have since learned that definite sound vibrations can be picked up from the*

[1] Francis Raymond Line, *Arizona Highways,* "Sheep, Stars and Solitude," April 1955

stars by delicate instruments. At all events, that singing of the
night (for such it was) which I heard along the sheep trail, in my
mind easily became associated with the stars, which were a luminous reality at midnight, much greater to the eye and the consciousness than insects or rocks or the far side of an unseen earth . . . ."

And the song of the poet sums it thus:

> 'Tis not in the high stars alone,
> Nor in the cups of budding flowers,
> Nor in the redbreast's mellow tone,
> But in the mud and scum of things
> There alway, alway something sings.[1]

Within this perfect creation, Satan dwelt in harmony with God until
he said, "I WILL." And from this time Satan and his province were "cast
down." His rebellion violated the harmony of the universe and the violence
of the disruption is written in the rocks and soil of the earth's surfaces
today. The Bible reveals his domain—(I John 5:19); and also his destiny—
(Matthew 25:41; II Corinthians 2:11, 5:11; Revelation 20:1—10).

Satan was called "the covering cherub" and remained such until iniquity was found in him; he might be called the "Old Testament" prodigal
son. God's appeals and handywork (restoration) were to demonstrate the
futility of sin to this "Old Testament" prodigal son!

The character of Satan is developing in this section. As we go through
the different sections of the chart, we will see him acting in the various
ways in which he is described: in heaven he was known as the accuser
of his brethren (Revelation 12:10); he was God's policeman, a discipli-
narian. He was a creature of method and was not creative, and is now
"fallen." Today he has the power of death, (Hebrews 2:14; see *Job*); he
has the power to destroy the body only. And we are urged to fear Him (God)
Who judges all men, but Who "snatches away *before* death" the Christian
(Luke 12:4—5; Matthew 10:28; John 8:52; 11:26). Satan's fallen angels
are listed in Genesis 6:1—4, I Peter 3:19, II Peter 2:4—6 and Jude verses
6—7. Demons can only become incarnate in man, but Jesus and the angels
have bodies of their own (Hebrews 10:5).

IV. THE NAMES OF SATAN

> I send you here a sort of allegory,
> (For you will understand it) of a soul,
> A spacious garden full of flowering weeds,
> *A glorious Devil,* large in heart and brain,
> *That did love Beauty only,* (Beauty seen
> In all varieties of mould and mind)

---

[1] Ralph Waldo Emerson, *Fragments on The Poet and The Poetic Gift,* Part V.

And *Knowledge for its beauty*; or if Good,
Good only for its beauty, seeing not
That Beauty, Good, and Knowledge, are three sisters
That dote upon each other, friends to man,
Living together under the same roof,
And never can be sunder'd without tears. 1

The following is a brief and limited resume of Scriptural names characteristic of Satan which show the extent to which he had fallen:

1. He was called SATAN: I Chronicles 21:1; Job 1 through chapter 2 and on; Zechariah 3:1—2
2. The ADVERSARY: I Peter 5:8; I Timothy 5:14
3. The ACCUSER (Gr. *Diabolus*): Revelation 12:10; he might also be called the "Old Testament" prodigal's brother, Luke 15:29—30
4. And often and pointedly he is called the DEVIL: Matthew 4: 1—11; 25:41; Luke 4:2—13; John 8:44; Ephesians 4:27; 6:11; I Timothy 3:6—7; Hebrews 2:14; James 4:7; I John 3:8—10; Revelation 2:10; 12:9, 12 and 20:2, 10
5. We find him called DECEIVER: Revelation 12:9 and 20:3, 8, 10
6. And the name DESTROYER: Psalm 17:4; I Corinthians 10:10
7. Also a TEMPTER: I Thessalonians 3:5; Matthew 4:3
8. And even a SERPENT: Revelation 12:9 and 20:2
9. He was known also as (PRINCE of this WORLD (age): John (12:31; 13:30; 16:11
   (PRINCE of the power of the AIR: (Ephesians 2:2
10. And the GOD of THIS AGE: II Corinthians 4:4
11. Once he is called LUCIFER: Isaiah 14:12
12. The Lord calls him a LIAR and a MURDERER from the beginning: John 8:44; Hebrews 2:14—15
13. And originally, the devil was the ANOINTED CHERUB that covers: Ezekiel 28:14, 16
14. And Revelation 12:9 lists him as the GREAT DRAGON.

These are the out-working of Satan's rebellion as verified to us in John 8:44 and Job 1:6—7; I Peter 5:8 and Revelation 12:7, from the story of his rebellion in Isaiah 14:12—15.

V. THE *KATABOLE*

The phrase "foundation of the world" when literally translated from the Greek *Kataboles Kosmou* should read "the casting down of the world."

---

1 Alfred Lord Tennyson, *Poetical Works of*, (N.Y., Thomas Y. Crowell & Co.),"To———, With The Following Poem," p. 48

This term "cast down" is used to describe God's judgment on:

1. Satan who was "cast down" from heaven
2. The original perfect earth into which Satan was cast; and this casting down produced the condition described in Genesis 1:2, and the resulting Ice Ages which we have described on page 162. This "cast down" earth was refurbished in Genesis 1; and in Genesis 1 and 2, man and other living creatures were placed upon it and it remained *perfect* until Satan once more entered.
3. The earth (ground).

   Man was led into sin by Satan and fell from his perfection and the earth (ground) was "cast down" once again by the curse in Genesis 3. This "cast down" *Kosmos* with its curse continues until the new heavens and new earth of Revelation 21 appears.

Since this phrase "foundation of the world," ("casting down of the *kosmos*")[1] is used a number of times in the New Testament, we must "rightly divide" and "distinguish the things that differ" in order to properly locate the events related to this term.

A. BEFORE THE *KATABOLE* (i.e. In Heaven)

1. Jesus Christ:

   a) John 17:24: ". . . Thou lovest me *before* the foundation of the world"[1]

   b) I Peter 1:20, "Who verily was foreordained *before* the foundation of the world"

2. The Church:

   a) Ephesians 1:4, "According as He hath chosen us in Him *before* the foundation of the world"

---

[1] "Foundation of the world," (Gr. *katabole kosmou*) literally translated is, "casting down of the world." No definite articles are used before either of these two words where they are used *together* in the New Testament. As seen in II Corinthians 4:9 "cast down but not destroyed," we note that this word does not include the idea of destruction. The "casting down" of Satan and the world (*kosmos*) did not mean their destruction. This destruction will occur at the end of the ages in fiery judgment (II Peter 3:7–13).

B. THE KATABOLE
  1. Satan cast down (Revelation 12:10; Ezekiel 28:16b–17

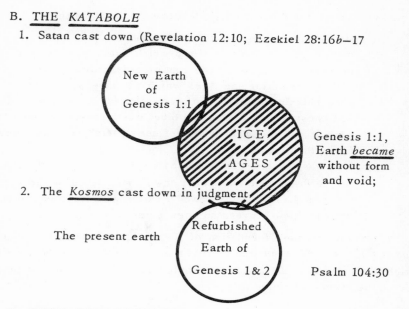

  2. The Kosmos cast down in judgment

The present earth

C. SINCE THE KATABOLE

    Jesus Christ now becomes:

    1. "The Lamb slain from the foundation of the world"
        (Revelation 13:8)
    2. The One Sacrifice "since the foundation of the world"
        (Hebrews 9:26)

This present "cast down kosmos" remains until the New Heavens and
and the New Earth.

RESTORATION to TERAH (father of Abraham)

"Thou hidest Thy face, they are troubled;
Thou takest away their breath, they die,
And return to their dust.

Thou sendest forth Thy Spirit, they are created:
And Thou renewest the face of the earth.

The glory of Jehovah shall endure for ever:
Jehovah shall rejoice in His works.
He looketh on the earth, and it trembleth:
He toucheth the hills, and they smoke.

I will sing unto Jehovah as long as I live:
I will sing praise to my God while I have my being.
My meditation upon Him shall be sweet:
I will be glad in Jehovah.

Let sinners be consumed out of the earth,
And let the wicked be no more.

Bless Thou Jehovah, O my soul.
    Praise ye the Lord."

                              Psalm 104:29—35

TABLE of CONTENTS

Section THREE: RESTORATION to TERAH
(father of Abraham)

RESTORATION to TERAH (Father of Abraham)

HIS STORY

I. GOD, THE WORKMAN

"And the earth became without form and void;
And the Spirit of God (Elohim) moved (fluttering)"

Genesis 1:2*b* N.

Here the "handywork" of God began to be manifest (Genesis 1:2 to 2:6). That God is a workman is established by the words of Jesus:

"My Father worketh hitherto, and I work."

John 5:17

The Psalmist David testifies:

"When I consider Thy heavens,
the *work of Thy fingers,*
The moon and the stars,
which Thou hast ordained;

. . .

Thou madest him to have dominion
over the *works of Thy hands;*
Psalm 8:3, 6
(cp. Psalm 19:1—2 and 90:2)

The unchanging, un-turning God directs those who walk upon the Highway of Holiness (James 1:17). "Who can bring a clean thing out of an unclean?" (Job 14:4) From chaos to the creation of man His Handywork is demonstrated upon the wrecked (frozen) earth, Satan's domain. The work of God in restoring begins with Genesis 1:2*b* and the earth in its present restored form is the result of the work of God's hands. The process of restoration produces its first results in Genesis 1:3 with the restoring of light and the division of light from darkness:

"And there was evening and there was morning, the first day."[1]

Genesis 1:5*b* N.

The introduction of light would also begin the melting of the ice formed over the earth during the judgment period (Genesis 1:6); and the withdrawing of the sun's rays produced the ice age of judgment of Genesis 1:2.[2]

Introducing the second step of restoration is the expanse which is

---

[1] "'Day' (Heb. *yom*) approximates the meaning of the English word 'day'; a period of light; 24 hours; a lifetime; an age. The days of Genesis 1 were evidently long periods, the events of which were revealed to Moses in six 24-hour days. Cf. Exodus 24:12—18 for the probable occasion. Hence the use of 'evening and morning,' a term used only when a vision is given (Dan. 8:26)"—B. W. Carrier, Hammond, Indiana. *O. T. Lesson 2*, page 8.

[2] See Appendix B. 1. *The Bible and Modern Science*, (London, Pickering and Inglis, 1935), Article by Lt. Col. Merson Davies, pp. 593-597.

Chart No. 3

Section THREE   R E S T O R A T I O N   T O   T E R A H

From Genesis 1:2b — — — — — — — — — — — — — — — — — — — To Genesis 11:26

H I S   STORY

Genesis 1:2b—31; 2:4—25 (The Six "Days" (Heb. Yom of Re-storation and Re-Creation	2:1—3 Seventh Day God's rest	3:1—7 Sin Enters Man and Eden	3:8—24	4:1 Traffickers of Dust

3:8—24: Man is judged; the ground is cursed and the Katabole is completed.

These seven passages use the phrase: "from (Gr. apo) the Katabole (casting down(, and must therefore occur after the final act of the ground following Adam's and Eve's sin: Matt. 13:35; 25:34; Luke 11:50; Heb. 4:3; 9:26; and Revelation 13:8; 17:8.

4:1 Traffickers of Dust: Cain   The Flood   Nimrod Babel   11:26

The Refurbished Earth Psalm 104:30

THE HIGHWAY OF HOLINESS — M Y   STORY

Adam Genesis 1:26—31 2:7—25

The Way of the Tree of Life is established with a "Tabernacle" at the East of the Garden.

Genesis 3:15, The First Promise of "The Seed"—Christ; Genesis 3:21, the first sacrifice for sin.

Traffickers of Divinity: Abel, Seth, Enoch, Noah, Shem, Terah

The Everlasting Gospel is revealed in the Stars—The Zodiac, Genesis 1:14—18; Job 38:32.

SATAN'S   STORY

(II Corinthians 4:4; I John 5:19 Satan has access to heaven (Job 1) but his abode is the earth into which he was cast (Ezekiel 28:15—17) after "iniquity was found in him."

Genesis 3: 1—5 Satan speaks "The Lie" John 8:44

Genesis 6:1—7 Satan corrupts all families except Noah's Fallen Angels (Sons of God) reserved in Everlasting chains under Darkness (Jude 5—6 made between the waters separating the clouds above from the waters on the earth; and evidently a mist existed in this expanse which obscured the sun (Genesis 2:6; II Peter 2:17).

Genesis 1:9 reveals God's work of gathering the waters into seas and the dry land is made to appear (Psalm 95:5, 7). On this same day God said, "Let the earth bring forth grass" showing that the earth already contained the seeds from the original creation which had been preserved in the freezing judgment which the earth had suffered. [1]

In Genesis 1:14 the next step of restoration is set forth where God said:

> "Let there be lights in the firmament of heaven
> to divide the day from the night;
> And let them be for signs, and for seasons,
> and for days, and years."

In this and the following verses, we are told that the sun, moon and stars are made to appear and the Hebrew word *Asah* indicates that this was not an act of *creation* but rather of *restoring* the host of heaven by *making* them serve their original purpose. The phrase "signs, seasons, days and years," reveals that the orderliness and the purpose of the Zodiac[2] was set forth at this time in preparation for the man whom God was soon to *create* (Psalm 102:25; Isaiah 45:11*b*—12; Isaiah 48:13). In chapter 1:20—23 sentient or animal life is *created* since no such life could survive the judgment that had preceded.

God's final act of restoration is set forth in the 26th and 27th verses when He created man in His own image, into whose nostrils He breathed the breath of lives (Hebrew *pl.* Genesis 2:7). Only the breath of God can apprehend love—and only love can overcome:

> And he that shuts Love out, in turn shall be
> Shut out from Love, and on her threshold lie
> Howling in outer darkness. Not for this
> Was *common clay ta'en from the common earth*
> Moulded by God, and *temper'd with the tears*
> Of angels to the perfect shape of man.[3]

God endued this man-creation of His with power and with authority:

> "And God said, 'Let us make man (Hebrew *ahdahm*—red earth)
> in our image, after our likeness: and let them have dominion
> over the fish of the sea, and over the fowl of the air, and over
> the cattle, and over all the earth, and over every creeping

---

[1] *Ibid.* Appendix "B" p. 595 ff. The Extinction of Life.

[2] *Ibid.* Appendix "B" p. 596 para. 3. "Bacteria and seeds . . ."

[3] Tennyson, *Ibid*; for foregoing portion of poem, see Section TWO, *Perfection to Katabole*, SATAN'S STORY, p. 164

thing that creepeth upon the earth'."

Genesis 1:26

And though man was given dominion over all animals, yet for his suste-nance, he was given a vegetarian diet (Genesis 1:29).

Edwin Markham in his great poem, *Lincoln, the Man of the People,* affirms man's earthy origin (I Corinthians 15:47) as he eulogizes the great President:

> When the Norn Mother saw the Whirlwind Hour
> Greatening and darkening as it hurried on,
> She left the Heaven of Heroes and came down
> To make a man to meet the mortal need.
> *She took the tried clay of the common road—*
> *Clay warm yet with the genial heat of earth,*
> . . .
> *The color of the ground was in him, the red earth;*
> The smack and tang of elemental things: . . . .[1]

And in his poem *Man-Test*, Mr. Markham emphasizes the freedom of choice which God gave to this man whom He had created in His own image:

> When in the dim beginning of the years
> God mixed in man the raptures and the tears
> And scattered through his brain the starry stuff,
> He said, "Behold! Yet this is not enough,
> For I must test his spirit to make sure
> That he can dare the Vision and endure.
>
> I will withdraw my Face,
> Veil Me in shadow for a certain space,
> Leaving behind Me only a broken clue—
> A crevice where the glory glimmers through,
> Some whisper from the sky,
> Some footprint in the road to track Me by.
>
> I will leave man to make the fateful guess,
> Will leave him torn between the No and Yes,
> Leave him unresting till he rests in Me,
> Drawn upward by the choice that makes him free—
> Leave him in tragic loneliness to choose,
> With all in life to win or all to lose.[2]

Genesis 1:31 brings us to the conclusion of this *restoration,* and we read:

> "God saw everything that He had made,
> and, behold, it was very good . . . ."

---

[1] From *Poems of Edwin Markham*, ed. by Charles L. Wallis, (Harper & Brothers, 1950, By Permission).

[2] *Ibid, Shoes of Happiness*

Having taken man from the dust of the earth, and having given to him the breath of lives," making him far above the animals, then:

> "Jehovah God took the man, and put him into the
> garden of Eden to cultivate it and to keep it."
>
> Genesis 2:15

Into this *restored* earth God placed the man whom He had *created*.

From this earth come up the nearly one hundred elements that were used in creation and which have since occupied the mental powers of man. Creation supplies us with a vast storehouse of elements and potentials. When God made man, forming him from the dust, He included in man's body many of the chemical components of which the earth is made.[1] Some of these elements are named when referring to the four rivers flowing out from the Garden (Genesis 2:10—14). The use of such minerals as gold, silver or other metal alloys in the body today, illustrates its harmony with chemical matters. The Universe is like the spider's web, and the one hundred laws in the Universe are the invisible web on which Creation is woven. When we consider all of these things, then we come to the end of it: *God is Love.*

II. EDEN, GOD'S WORKSHOP

One of the great efforts of men today in the study of history has been to search out the location of the earliest life upon this earth. Such efforts are still continuing. The Bible tells us that man was placed by God after his creation in "a garden eastward in Eden." The location of Eden has long been a source of speculation and research. Is it not possible that the answer to all the searching can be found within the pages of this Living Word? The following may give light and direction to those seeking the place where the first man once stood:

> "And Jehovah God planted a garden (Paradise)
> eastward in Eden (Pleasure or Delight)."
>
> Genesis 2:8 N.

A. THE HOLY LAND

In Exodus 3:5 God said to Moses from the burning bush:

> "Draw not nigh hither; put off thy shoes from off thy feet,
> for the place whereon thou standest *it is* holy ground."
>
> (cf. also Acts 7:30—33)

---

[1] Henry C. Sherman, *Chemistry of Food and Nutrition* (N.Y.Macmillan, 1937); Harrow and Sherwin, *Textbook of Biochemistry,* (Philadelphia, Saunders & Co., 1935); *World Almanac and Book of Facts,* (N.Y. World Telegram & The Sun).

This statement by God would indicate that the land had been holy before Moses arrived there. Commenting on this statement in Exodus 3:5, Park H. Netting, (Owosso, Michigan) states the following:

"In regard to the last portion of Exodus 3:5, a very literal (much more so than necessary) translation even to Hebrew word order follows: '. . . for the place which you standing upon him, holy ground he.' In Hebrew there is no neuter personal pronoun, but both the feminine and the masculine are used on occasion where English would use the neuter; hence, the masculine pronouns in the above passage may be translated 'upon which' and 'it' respectively. (The 'which' in the literal translation is a relative particle and in translation may be combined with the personal pronoun, hence 'upon which'). 'Standing' is not a finite verb but rather the active participle and therefore may be translated as present tense 'are standing.' The very last phrase has no verb of any kind. Because of the sense of the passage 'is' (present tense) understood, is justifiable. Hence a readable and at the same time justifiable translation would be:
'. . . for the place upon which you are standing, it is holy ground'."

Therefore, this was God's appointed place—but what made it holy? What had occurred here on the land or on this portion of the earth that would set it apart as *holy*?

    a) In Genesis 15:18 we read:

        "In the same day, Jehovah made a covenant with Abram, saying, 'Unto thy seed have I given this land, from *the river of Egypt* (Nile) unto *the great river*, the river Euphrates"

    b) Referring also to Exodus 23:31:

        "And I will set thy bound from *the Red Sea* even unto the *sea of the Philistines*, (Mediterranean), and from *the desert* unto *the rivers:*"

Here we find these same boundaries stated which encompass all the land promised unto Abraham and his seed from the Red Sea whose western branch touches the Delta of the Nile to the Euphrates on the north.

    c) Turning also to Deuteronomy 1:2—10, we find Israel at Mt. Horeb in the southern part of the Sinaitic peninsula, and in the 7th and 8th verses God said unto them:

        "Turn you, and take your journey, and go to the mount of the Amorites, and unto all nigh thereunto, in the plain, in the hills, and in the vale, and in the south, and by the sea side, to the land of the Canaanites, and unto Lebanon, unto the great river, the river Euphrates.

        "Behold, I have set the land before you: go in and possess the land which Jehovah Lord sware unto your fathers, Abraham, Isaac, and Jacob, to give unto them and to their seed after them."

This establishes that the land they were to occupy included all of the territory from the southern part of the Sinaitic peninsula to the Great River Euphrates.

    d) In Deuteronomy 11:24 and in Joshua 1:3—4, the Lord states that every place upon which the soles of the feet of the children of Israel shall tread from the wilderness to the River Euphrates, is to be theirs. This then of necessity includes that portion below and around Mount Sinai to the south and all of the country to the north up to the River Euphrates. This is the Holy Land which God promised to Abraham and his seed.

B. ISRAEL'S PROMISED LAND

The Jews were God's chosen people. Would He choose a people and not also choose a land for that people? "This land"[1] was chosen *before* Abraham and it was ready for him when God called him. And because this land is Holy Ground, explains why it is absolutely essential for God to bring Israel back to the land to complete the promise that He made to them.[2] There would be little point in it if He had not made those promises concerning this *specific portion of ground*. God led the children of Israel out of Egypt to this land; His Presence was manifested to them in the pillar of cloud by day and of fire by night. As they approached this land of Holy Ground in crossing the Red Sea, the pillar of cloud cast darkness over the pursuing Egyptians but radiated a glorious light toward the Israelites as they moved into the Promised Land, Eden. After setting their feet upon this "Holy Ground," God revealed Himself to Moses on Mt. Sinai and gave to the children of Israel the Tabernacle which was set up *within the land*. It was within this Tabernacle between the cherubim above the Mercy Seat where the Shekinah Glory Cloud came to rest, as God manifested through the Cloud His Presence with Israel (Exodus 40:38; and II Samuel 6:2).

Although this whole land from the Red Sea to the Euphrates River was promised to Abraham, yet the children of Israel occupied only the center portion of it. It was this portion which Moses was permitted to see but was prevented from entering upon (Deuteronomy 32:49—52; 34:1—4). The largest occupation of the land by the children of Israel occurred during the reign of David and his son Solomon. It yet remains for the children of

---

[1] In respect to "this land" as noted in the reference Genesis 12:7, the Newberry Bible, p. viii, states that the two Hebrew articles (definite and objective) are used preceding these particular two words: "Here the word 'this' is rendered more emphatic by *ha* being prefixed before it, and 'land' is made doubly emphatic by *eth ha*, two articles being inserted in the original."

[2] See Sec. SIX, *The Kingdom Age*, E. *The Millennium Age*, 2. Israel is Restored, p. 562

Israel to completely occupy the Holy Land which God promised to Abraham and to his seed. One might conclude from reading Deuteronomy 34:4 and other references which are similar that the land *occupied* by Israel was all that had been promised unto Abraham, Isaac and Jacob. The Lord said unto Moses:

> "This is the land which I sware unto Abraham, Isaac and Jacob saying I will give it unto thy seed: I have caused thee to see with thine eyes but thou shalt not go over thither."

God did not say that this was the *whole land* which He promised unto Abraham, but that the land which Moses *saw* was land promised to Abraham even though only a part of the original promise. By way of illustrating this, we might note that the Church is referred to as the "Kingdom of God" (Acts 8:12) and some have concluded that the Church is the *whole* kingdom of God. Rather we should recognize that God's kingdom is "from Everlasting to Everlasting" and that the Church is but *one portion* of the *whole* kingdom of God. It yet remains for the complete revelation of God's kingdom to be realized after "the kingdoms of this world become the kingdom of our Lord Jesus Christ." So also Israel shall some day occupy the *whole* land promised to Abraham (Hebrews 4:6; Isaiah 11:10—16).

This land is significant as "Holy Ground" not only because it is the "Promised Land" but the Scriptures give clear evidence that this land was EDEN.

C. GOD'S WORKSHOP

The thirty-first chapter of Ezekiel is a prophecy against Pharoah, using Assyria as a warning. The symbol of trees is used in the prophecy and in verses 8—9, 16, these trees are referred to as "Cedars in the garden of God"; "any tree in the garden of God"; "all the trees of Eden that were in the garden of God"; and "all the trees of Eden, the choice and best of *Lebanon.*" These references would indicate that the garden of God and the trees of Eden were located in close relationship to Lebanon which is almost in the center of the land promised to Abraham and his seed. Other references which might be used in locating Eden are: Genesis 4:16; 13:10; Isaiah 51:3; Ezekiel 28:13; 36:35, and Joel 2:3.

Why was this portion of earth set aside by God? God must have had a place to rest His feet (Isaiah 60:13*b*) and take His Handywork (Isaiah 60:21*b*); it had to be somewhere on the earth; is there any more probable place than Palestine? God needed a place on this earth where He could approach people and express Himself to them. The Holy Land is the piece of earth which God has kept for Himself and chosen for His Workshop in which He demonstrates Himself to man.

This land is "Holy Ground" not because it was promised to Abraham but because God had long before(John 8:58) produced His Handywork here. In the beginning of God's Handywork described in the first two chapters of Genesis, the restoring of the earth from its chaotic condition caused by the wreckage of Satan, was begun in Eden. Out of all the earth God chose this land of Eden on the shores of the Mediterranean Sea as the spawning ground from which life went out to all parts of the earth. Life within the Sea went out into the Atlantic Ocean and from there it was picked up by currents and was taken everywhere. Here God stooped down into the dust of the earth and made a man; but did not pronounce him as finished until He breathed into his nostrils the breath of lives (Gen. 2:7).

D. GOD'S SACRED GROUND

Of significance also are the relationships between God and man as set forth within the confines of this Promised Land:

a) It was here that the cherubim with a flame like a sword, located — and where Abel brought his offerings (Genesis 3:24; 4:4; Hebrews 11:4). The Presence of the Lord was here, from which Cain went out after his offering had been rejected and his brother slain (Genesis 4:16). It was from this "Holy Ground" that the blood of Abel cried out (Genesis 4:10).

b) It was upon Mt. Sinai where Moses was given the law (Exodus 19:20)

c) To this same region of Horeb, Elijah went in discouragement (I Kings 19:8) and God spoke to him in "a still small voice"

d) Within the borders of this land the ministry of Jesus took place (Matthew 10:5—6; 15:24; Romans 15:8), during which demonstrations of resurrection were given such as the widow's son of Nain (Luke 7:11); Lazarus (John 11:43; 12:17) and others; including His own resurrection which gave evidence of the life-producing power which God has manifested in this remarkable land, His Workshop.

The Transfiguration of Jesus took place on "an high mountain apart" (Matthew 17:1) somewhere in Galilee. It was at Jerusalem that He was crucified, buried and raised again and from the Mount of Olives (Acts 1:6) He ascended; and to this same Celestial Airport, He will one day come again (Zechariah 14:4)

e) Here in God's Workshop, His revelation is set forth for all men to see. The Author of the whole Book, the Holy Spirit, was here given to men. At Jerusalem and Caesarea, the baptism of the Holy Spirit occurred, empowering the apostles to set forth the revelation which God gave to them.

    f) It was to Mt. Sinai in Arabia that Paul went to receive the reve-
lation from Jesus Christ (Galatians 1:17; 4:25).

    g) Jerusalem was the Cradle of the Church, and from this "Holy
Ground," the Gospel has gone to all parts of the globe (Acts
2 and 8:4).

The Promised Land[1] or "Holy Land" is the navel of the whole earth
(Ezekiel 5:5). Daniel's prophecy calls it "the pleasant land" (Daniel 8:9);
"the glorious land" (Daniel 11:17, 41). For centuries the great currents
of travel traversed this land[2] as men and armies came from different continents over this highway which God has said, "IS HOLY GROUND."

CONCLUSION

From the foregoing, sufficient evidence should be apparent to conclude that Eden and the Land promised to Abraham and his seed, were one
and the same, by recognizing:

    a) The dimensions of the land from the Red Sea on the South, to
the Euphrates on the north

    b) The statement to Moses, "the place whereon thou standest, it
is Holy Ground"

    c) The unusual events which occurred to the nation of Israel with-
the land

    d) The Scripture references which bring the land of Eden in con-
junction with Lebanon

    e) The location of Palestine with regard to the other continents
and the seas making it a logical place from which to start,
to fulfill the command: "multiply and replenish the earth"

    f) The significance which God attached to the Promised Land in
His revelation of Himself throughout the Bible

All of these together should help to draw the conclusion that this
"Holy Ground," the Promised Land, was Eden—God's Workshop.

III. GOD'S HANDYWORK: TRAFFICKERS of DUST (Isaiah 23:8)

Beginning with Adam in this land of Eden, out from this Holy Ground,
go Traffickers of Dust and Divinity. All men though dust formed, are God-
breathed-upon at birth (John 1:9), but the inevitable choice of "Dust or
Divinity" must always be made; and there are those who, responding to
the appeal of God, traffick the road of Divinity, the Highway of Holiness.

---

[1] See *The Rape of Palestine* by William B. Ziff, (N. Y., Longmans, Green and Co. 1938)

[2] An interesting article on Palestine and the Bible is found in the *Reader's Digest*
for March 1954 by Blake Clark, (pp. 26—30), which emphasizes the remarkable qualities
of this land; I commend it to your careful reading. —C. G. K.

This section will call attention to those Traffickers of Dust who went out from the Presence of the Lord and produced the present world system. Following man's creation we read in Genesis 2:15—17:

> "And Jehovah God took the man, and put him into the garden of Eden to cultivate it and to keep it. And Jehovah God commanded the man, saying, 'Of every tree of the garden thou mayest freely eat; But of the tree of the knowledge of good and evil, thou shalt not eat of it: for in the day that thou eatest thereof thou shalt surely die!"

God's Handywork is seen from Genesis 1:2 to 2:25 and we see man in his innocency, naked and unashamed, dwelling in the Garden where was the Tree of Life, and where God was his teacher. In Genesis 1:14—18 God spoke through the heavens[1] and then gave to man speech (Genesis 2:19—20) that he might name the animals and every living thing of God's creation. God caused every beast of the field and every fowl of the air to go before Adam, and "whatsoever Adam called every living creature, that was the name thereof"; and having named all of them—"there was not one to be a help meet for him." From Adam's side God took a rib and made woman and brought her unto the man and they became one flesh. The record of man's fall through sin will be discussed in this section under *Satan's Story*, p.195 ff.

In Genesis 3:20 we read: "And Adam called his wife's name Eve because she was the mother of all living." God has always made available to man a way of approach to Himself and having taken Adam and Eve from the garden of Eden, He *placed* (made to tabernacle) at the East of the garden, cherubim and the "flame of a sword which turned every way" to keep the way of the tree of life (lives). Cherubim[2] in the Bible are always associated with a place of sacrifice and with the Presence of the Lord (Exodus 25:17—22; Leviticus 16:13—16; Hebrews 9:5). When the Tabernacle was built and ready for service, the fire on the brazen altar was kindled by heavenly fire (Leviticus 9:24) indicating God's approval and acceptance of the Tabernacle and of the burnt offering upon the altar. Evidently God used this same method signifying His acceptance of Abel's

---

[1] See Appendix E, *Zodiac*, p.608 ff.

[2] ". . . At one time Layard conjectured that Ezekiel having seen these Assyrian figures might from them describe the figures of his visions. But Ezekiel says of them, 'I *knew* they were the Cherubim,' and as a Jewish priest, he must have been well acquainted with these forms, which had recently been in the temple of Solomon, and long before in the tabernacle of Moses. Ancient Jewish writers say that they were 'in the tabernacle from the beginning,' and so known to Noah, Abraham, and the children of Israel before they went into Egypt. Many modern commentators are of the same opinion. 'They were held to be the same figures with those at the gate of Eden'." (Frances Rolleston, *Mazzaroth*, Note on Cherubic Forms, p. 127)

offering at this place of sacrifice where the cherubim with a "flame like a sword" were located, and by the same token rejecting Cain's offering (Hebrews 11:4). Thus, the "flame like a sword" foreshadowed the revelation of the Word of God which is pictured in Hebrews 4:12:

> "For the word of God is living, and effectual, and sharper than any twoedged sword, also piercing even to dividing asunder both of soul and spirit, and of joints and marrows, and is a discerner of thoughts and intents of the heart."

God first walked with Adam (Genesis 3:8) and visited him (Psalm 8:4) but following the coming of sin and man's departure from the garden, some of the descendants of Adam went out from the Presence (countenance) of the Lord into atheism (A-Theos) (Ephesians 2:12c; Romans 1:21—24). The man of the world is subnormal for he has fallen from the origin intended by God (John 1:9); he begins on the Highway of Holiness but he descends because of his sin.

The flaming sword at the East of the Garden was a discerner between that which was acceptable to God and that which was to be rejected. God rejected Cain's offering, and shortly thereafter Cain murdered his brother, and his reason is set forth in I John 3:11—12. The earth was cursed to him that it should not henceforth yield her strength. He was to be a fugitive and a vagabond in the earth and in Genesis 4:16, we read, "Cain went out from the Presence of Jehovah and dwelt in the land of Nod, on the east of Eden," thus becoming the first atheist. At this time, the line of mankind divides into two groups:

> Traffickers with the earth — world, "dust"
> Traffickers with the sky — heaven, "divinity"

Cain leads the way for these traffickers of earth and his first act is to build a city calling it after the name of his son Enoch (Genesis 4:17). Cain builded this city after the description which was brought down from heaven by Satan which later Abraham having seen in a vision, chose to live in a tent ("for he *waited* for *the* City which hath *the* foundations," Hebrews 11:9—10). Cain's children were gifted inventors[1] (Ecclesiastes

---

[1] "The first civilization, that which perished in the judgment of the Flood, was Cainitic in origin, character, and destiny. Every element of material civilization is mentioned in verses 16—22, city and pastoral life, and the development of arts and manufactures. Enoch, after whom the first city was named, means 'teacher.' The *el* termination of the names of Enoch's son and grandson shows that for a time the knowledge of Elohim was preserved, but this soon disappears (Romans 1:21—23). *Adah* means 'pleasure,' or 'adomment'; Zillah, to 'hide'; Lamech, 'conqueror,' or 'wild man.' (cf. Romans 1:21—25; see Genesis 6:4). The Cainitic civilization may have been as splendid as that of Greece or Rome, but the divine judgment is according to the *moral* state, not the *material* (Genesis 6:5—7)" (Scofield *Bible*; Oxford University Press, p. 11 note on Genesis 4:17).

7:29; Psalm 106:29), but they were "without God in the world" (Ephesians 2:12). Those who followed the line of Cain produced a civilization centered in city building that flourished in the arts, but also in lust. The origin of mythology and decrees arose out of this background, and today after these and later-built wrecked cities are uncovered, each is still a "magnificent ruins." [1] This is the pathway of the nations of the world. The great nations coming into view upon history's stage before the audience of the Universe and Nature, have a star-spangled sky which is not merely a "Milky Way" but a sky spelling out the revelation in Solar and Lunar Zodiacs of hours, days, weeks, months, years and cycles whose accuracy remains arbitrary unto this day. The Grand Cycle of these is beyond the reach of man to take from or add to.

From here men of violence have seized the kingdom of God and by their theories and traditions "have made the Word of God of none effect" until this day (Mark 7:13). Man must choose between the two ways: the way of Holiness (James 1:17), or the way of the ungodly (Psalm 1). Out from the thinking of "all those who forgot God" came all the myths of gods, goddesses and half divine men, giants whose survival is to be found in "the divine right of kings." These "Traffickers in the Dust" brought forth in their "own image after their likeness" abnormal deities in stature and passions and left behind huge monuments and structures. Herod's temple had been made "a den of thieves" (robbers) by the religious leaders of Jesus' day whom He called "the generation of vipers" (Luke 3:7) which was as near to the return to the divine as Satan could approach.

The complete depravity of men in Noah's day is set forth in Genesis 6:5 and this became the basis for the judgment of God which brought forth the flood of Genesis 6:6—13 N.:

> "And it repented Jehovah that He had made man on the earth, and
> it grieved Him at His heart. And Jehovah said, 'I will wipe-off
> man whom I created from the face of the ground; both man, and
> beast, and creeping thing, and the fowls of the air; for it repenteth

---

[1] For references *in re* "Magnificent Ruins," *Birs-i-Nimrood, Tower of Babel,* see:

   a) George Rawlinson, *The Five Great Monarchies of the Ancient Eastern World,* (Dodd Mead and Co.) Vol. II. *Birs-i-Nimrud,* p. 544

   b) Rev. William G. Blaikie, D.D., LLD., *A Manual of Bible History,* (Thomas Nelson and Sons) *The Tower of Babel and Confusion of Tongues,* pp. 44—46

   c) Ira Maurice Price, Ph.D., *The Monuments and the Old Testament,* (Christian Culture Press, Chicago, 1905), Vol. I. *The Great Sargon,* pp. 46—47

   d) Flavius Josephus, *Josephus,* (International Press, Winston Co.), *Concerning The Tower of Babylon,* p. 39

   e) Charles J. Thynne and Jarvis, *The Student's Commentary on The Scriptures,* (London) *Re: Genesis XI:1—9,* p. 15

   f) Appendix E, *Zodiac,* 11. *The Witness of the Stars,* p. 637

   g) Appendix E, *Zodiac,* 1. *Mazzaroth,* p. 611

Me that I made them.' But Noah found grace in the eyes of Jehovah.

"These are the generations of Noah: Noah was a just man, perfect in his generations, and Noah walked with God. Noah begat three sons, Shem, Ham, and Japheth.

"The earth also was corrupt before God, and the earth was filled with violence. And God looked upon the earth, and behold, it was corrupt; for all flesh had corrupted his way upon the earth.

"And God said unto Noah, 'The end of all flesh is come before Me; for the earth is filled with violence through them; and, behold, I will destroy them with the earth . . .'."

Noah's salvation by God was the result of his being "a just man and perfect in his generations"; Noah's ancestors had not shared in the corrupt dealings which are reported in Genesis 6:1–4.[1] With this one man and his wife and three sons and their wives, God began anew His purpose to fulfill Genesis 3:15. Satan had succeeded in corrupting all other families on the face of the earth with the exception of Noah's family. Only the removal of all corrupt flesh could make possible the carrying out of the promise of Genesis 3:15. Following the flood, (Hebrews 11:7; Genesis 6:14—8:19), we find in Genesis 8:20 that Noah built an altar unto the Lord and offered sacrifice. God at this time made a covenant with Noah which is found in Genesis 8:21 through 9:17. The three sons of Noah (Shem, Ham and Japheth) have become progenitors of every nation under heaven today; and we read in Genesis 9:19, "these are the three sons of Noah and of them was the whole earth overspread."

Noah's moral and spiritual lapse soon followed (Genesis 9:20–21), but the blessing and promise of God was not hindered for it was carried forward in the line of Shem. The beginning of *nations* through the generations of Shem, Ham and Japheth is recorded in Genesis 10:1–32; and the beginning *kingdoms* is found with Nimrod who established Babel, Nineveh and other cities and kingdoms. In the kingdom of Nimrod in the land of Shinar (Chaldea), the descendants of Noah's sons found a plain and dwelt there, and decided to build a city and a tower.[2] Genesis 11:4 describes this tower "whose top with (signs of the) heavens."

There has been much speculation concerning the Tower of Babel both as to its purpose[2] and its location. A vast mound called Birs-Nimrood was once thought to be the remains of the Tower of Babel. While this does not seem to be likely, the following paragraph from Blaikie's *A Manual of Bible History*[2] (p. 46), throws some light on this subject:

---

[1] See this Section THREE, *SATAN'S* STORY, V. "Satan Corrupts . . ." p. 199

[2] *loc. cit.* Footnote 1, *"Magnificent Ruins,"* p. 186

"Birs-Nimrood is a huge brick mound, oblong in form, measuring about seven hundred yards around, and rising to the height of from one hundred and fifty to two hundred feet. From an inscription deciphered by Sir Henry Rawlinson, it appears that Birs Nimrood was situated, not in Babylon, but at Borsippa, and that its name was 'The Stages of the Seven Spheres.' It is not unlikely that the tower of Babel was an erection of the same kind. It consisted of seven stages or stories, coloured so as to represent 'the seven planets,' according to the tints which the Sabaeans considered appropriate to each."

The eleventh chapter of Genesis tells of this effort to build a city and a tower, the purpose of which was: "let us make us a name lest we be scattered abroad upon the face of the whole earth." The building of the tower was to preserve their knowledge of astronomy and the Zodiac, which was given to the Antediluvians as being the revelation of "The Everlasting Gospel." God's covenant had been: "be fruitful and multiply and replenish the earth" (Genesis 9:1). This attempt to build a *city* was in direct disobedience to God. As God could see that the purpose of these men was to disobey His commandment, He confounded their language, scattering them abroad upon the face of all the earth, and forcing man to do that which he should have done willingly.

Beginning with Genesis 11:10, the story of man then centers in the generations of Shem. From this man have descended Abraham, the nation of Israel and Jesus Christ Himself through Mary. This portion of the outline section concludes with Terah, the father of Abraham. Joshua 24:2 states:

"'Thus saith Jehovah God of Israel,
Your fathers dwelt on the other side of the river in old time,
even Terah, the father of Abraham, and the father of Nachor:
and they served other gods'."

(cf. vss. 14—25)

Terah, the father of Abraham, was an idolator and tradition tells us that he was a maker of idols. From this background God called one young man, Abram, who was to be known as "The father of the faithful."

RESTORATION to TERAH (Father of Abraham)

MY STORY

I. GOD'S HANDYWORK: TRAFFICKERS of DIVINITY

"Surely, The Sovereign Lord Jehovah (Heb. *Adonahy*)
will do nothing,
But He revealeth His secret-counsel unto His servants
the prophets."

Amos 3:7 N.

The Universe is the product of a designed plan of a Master Mind's Purpose whose object is for it to be peopled with like-minded folks as Himself. This Universe is a scaffolding necessary for God to approach unto man; when all things are perfected, it shall be taken away as are all impediments (Matthew 34:35). What God does, He purposed from the beginning; He left nothing to chance or post-tragedy. The phrase "in the beginning" is used twice in the Word of God with special significance: In Genesis 1:1 "In the beginning God"; the Hebrew plural *Elohim* is used here, and the significant meaning is centered on God Himself (see Deuteronomy 33:27; Psalm 90:1–2; Hebrews 9:14; Malachi 3:6a; James 1:17). Through the Bible this unchanging God is telling *His Story* of His dealings with men and nations. This is the Almighty Who said:

"'I AM the Alpha and the Omega,
the beginning and the ending,' saith the Lord,
'which is, and which was, and which is to come,
the Almighty'."

Revelation 1:8

The second phrase is in John 1:1, "In the beginning was the Word," and as the fourteenth verse indicates, this applies to Jesus Who said, "before Abraham was, I AM" (John 8:58). Through this Word is revealed "MY Story" of God's revelation. To Adam, Seth, Enoch, and others of their day, was given the first revelation of the *mystery*. The Word of God is filled with the names of those who were added to the line of those who share in the mystery (*My Story*) through the ages. God is able to reveal Himself to those only who are *believers* (John 1:12). Jesus Christ builds His Church upon faith in Himself as the Son of God (Matthew 16:18); and through His apostles like Paul (II Corinthians 12), and John (Revelation 1:10), He reveals those things which are yet future and which deal with the consummation of all things (I Corinthians 15:28). To Peter He said, "I will give unto thee the keys of the kingdom of heaven"; in Luke 24:44–45, we find the Master opening the understanding of the disciples that they might understand the Scriptures contained in the law of Moses and the Prophets and the *Psalms* which concerned Him. The understanding of the Prophets (Luke 1:70) become the keys of the kingdom of heaven to those who are men of faith and who "believe on His Name."

> "But apart from faith it is impossible to please Him: for he that cometh to God must believe that He is, and that He becometh a rewarder of them that diligently seek Him."
>
> Hebrews 11:6 N.

Abel, a prophet, was of this company of believers (Hebrews 11:4); Enoch, a prophet, "walked *with* God" (Genesis 5:24); "Noah, a prophet, was a just man perfect in his generations, and Noah walked *with* God" (Genesis 6:9); and Abraham, a prophet, was asked by God to "walk *before* Me" (Genesis 17:1; 24:40). These were the first in a great line of prophets who spoke of things yet future and whose prophecies unlock the door to the mysteries of the kingdom.

II. THE EVERLASTING GOSPEL

God as Teacher and Historian is revealed from *Genesis* to *The Song of Solomon*. For more than twenty-five hundred years, longer than any other dispensation, He was revealing Himself (for "God is love"), fixing in man His Image through astronomy, agriculture, archaeology and Himself,—"himself from God he could not free."

The callings of Adam and his sons or descendants vary: Adam dealt with biology (Genesis 1:28); Seth with astronomy[1]; and Enoch with prophecy (Jude 14). Cain sought to build a city; Abraham sought one that was already builded. In the dawn of history, this age was an age of scholars.[2] God's school of prophets began with Adam, Abel, Seth, Enoch and was co-educational for it included Eve in the prophecy of Genesis 3:15 which begins with Eve and includes those women in the line of Abraham, Israel and David; and finds its fulfillment in the virgin Mary through whom the Christ was born (Isaiah 7:14; Matthew 1:23; Isaiah 9:6—7; Luke 2:11). During the age of the Antediluvians, this first division of divine revelation, God would not be silent: He talked with Adam and Eve, with Seth, Enoch and others in the language of Psalm 19. The Unknown God reveals Himself to those who are spiritually-minded in every age. God invites to participation every soul of like desire in every generation and dispensation. To these above named men, He gave His revelation through the Zodiac and by direct contact (Genesis 5:22; Hebrews 11:4 ff.), that through these prophets, He might reveal Himself to all of the descendants of Adam. The Scriptures are replete with incidents and statements of a heavenly realm and its occupants.[3] While ancient writings and myths grew up inspired by

---

[1] See Appendix "E" *Zodiac*, p. 630, para. 6: "If indeed Seth and his family were the inventors of these emblems . . . ."; and p. 635 (middle), "Seth in whose time . . ."

[2] *Ibid*, p. 609 ff.; and *Inevitable Inference*, p. 625

[3] See Section ONE, *Alpha*, p. 143 ff.

similar incidents and statements handed down by tradition, would it not be strange if the Bible were silent, especially as we read that "male and female" were created in the likeness of God Who dwelt in the heavenly realm? Man was given dominion over the things of earth at his creation and remained in the image and likeness of God until sin entered and he was found naked. The heavens declare God's glory *before* the *Kataballein* and the Scriptures declare His Handywork *afterward* as manifested in the restoration of the face of the earth. As people forgot God's teaching, mythologies arose as men added or substituted. This habit still persists in hypotheses, religions and creeds.

The *heavens* reveal God's *immortality* from Alpha to Omega, the Highway of Holiness where:

> "My thoughts are not your thoughts—
> neither My ways your ways."
>
> Isaiah 55:8

The *earth* reveals *man's mortality* in the rise and fall of nations. And the Latins, Greeks, and Egyptians join with Josephus, the Jewish historian, in ascribing the appearance of government, culture and the sciences in the East from Babylon, Chaldea, Arabia and the Chinese:

> "Josephus hands down to us what he gives as the traditions of his own nation, corroborated by his reference to eight of the ancient Gentile authorities whose works are lost. He says that they all assert that 'God gave the antediluvians such a long life that they might perfect those things which they had invented in astronomy'." [1]

These are all from a common stock of one tongue or speech (Genesis 11:1). The antediluvians "taught of God" became adepts in astronomy (Psalm 19: 1–6). Later their sons were tutored in Psalm 19:7–8. Out from these came our calendar days, months, years, and the "Grand Year 600," [2] whose near completion and beginning recurrence prepared thoughtful observers to give weight to Genesis 3:15, the hope and the expectation of His Star and His second return (Matthew 25:31). [3] Ours is the only planet amid "the stars also" from whose surface its occupants could possibly appropriate all the revelations of God (Isaiah 55:7–8; 9:6).

---

[1] E. W. Bullinger, *The Witness of The Stars*, (The Lamp Press), Ltd. London, pp. 9–10

[2] *Star of Bethlehem Lecture*, Adler Planetarium, Chicago

[3] See Appendix "E", *Mazzaroth*, 8. The Star Pictures of the Zodiac, p. 617 ff.· and 2. The Star p. 612; and 12. Principal Truths, p. 629. para. 5 ff.

"And I saw another angel fly in the midst of heaven, having
the EVERLASTING GOSPEL to preach (N. declare unto
them as good tidings) unto them that dwell on the earth,
and to every nation, kindred, and tongue, and people."

Revelation 14:6

For twenty-five hundred years man was upon the earth before the sacred
writings of Moses. God must have convened and communicated His Gospel
to them else Romans 1:20 is a mis-statement. What was God doing the
twenty-five hundred years before the beginning of revelation? God alone
was man's teacher and the heavens were His school room with the Zodiac
as His blackboard. He was teaching the antediluvians the revelation of
His *Prothesis* in the stars and demonstrating His power to make good by
His Handywork in restoring and re-creating in Genesis 1. Later, He was
teaching and demonstrating to Satan and to the world His power in His
redeeming love for Job, and in His dealings with Israel. God wrote "The
Everlasting Gospel" in the stars beyond the reach of man and archangels,
before the fall of Lucifer (Satan). It was first told to the antediluvians
in the Almanac. The Zodiac, the heavenly story of the Everlasting Gospel
which is recorded in the stars, was a part of the creation described in
Genesis 1:1. The sun, moon and stars were all brought into being as a
part of "the heavens" at that time. In Genesis 1:14 through 18 which follows the fall of Lucifer and which is included as a part of the story of
God's handywork, we find set forth the *purpose*[1] of these luminaries (the
Zodiac). In Section TWO of the Chart, the Zodiac was *created* (Genesis
1:1), but in this section *Restoration to Terah* the Zodiac (heavenly bodies)
is given meaning and purpose (Genesis 1:14—18). The traditions of the
ancients, the Chinese, Arabians, Coptics and the Egyptians were the offspring of the Hebrew proto-type, the Zodiac, and were derived from God's
ETERNAL GOSPEL. The stars and heavenly bodies are frequently referred to in the Bible: Genesis 1:14—18; Isaiah 13:10; Ezekiel 32:7; Job
38:42 (*Mazzaroth*, the signs of the Zodiac); Jeremiah 31:35; II Kings 23:5;
Matthew 2:1—11 (His Star).[2]

That "the groves were God's first temples" is more poetry than fact
and we have seen that the Scriptures are replete with references to the
heavens (Matthew 6:9; I Kings 8:27). Rather it was the siderial heavens
where God was at the blackboard placing the sun, moon and stars as his
hieroglyphics (priestly writings); "their voice is not heard" (Psalm 19:3).
His scholars wrote books, studied the sciences and knew the names of the
stars and creatures before the flood. By these they measured time with

[1] See Appendix E, *Zodiac*, 10. What are the real meanings . . . p. 626

[2] *Ibid, His Star*, p. 612

seven days of the week, twenty-eight days of the moon, and the solar year. The ancient solar zodiac with its twelve signs introduces each with suffering though each ends in victory—LOVE IS TRIUMPHANT. The Zodiac begins with Virgo foretelling the virgin birth of the Savior and it closes with Leo, the Lion, foretelling the triumphant reign of the King.[1] Enoch prophesied of the time yet future (Jude 14—15). This prophet of God, the seventh from Adam, demonstrated immortality to the Gentiles by his translation, foreshadowing the rapture of the Church, and called a Nation into a living hope which is vividly foretold in Ezekiel 37. God's message of His sacrificing, redeeming love was written upon the constellations before the casting down (Gr. *Kataballein*) of the world (Gr. *Kosmos*), and was the living hope which is vividly foretold in Ezekiel 37. God's message of His sacrificing, redeeming love was written upon the constellations before the casting down (Gr. *Kataballein*) of the world (Gr. *Kosmos*), and was the first gospel preached from (Gr. *apo*) before the fall of man (Genesis 3:15). And this Everlasting, Eternal Gospel came from the heart of God, John 3:16. The myths, traditions and human failures are not able to reach to defile what first was written in the stars and then later revealed unto Israel by holy men of God as they spake (were borne along) of the Holy Spirit (II Peter 1:21).

Let *us* then, be slow to boast our superiority; for as research expands, our boasting loses volume; man and nations have descended.

Frances Rolleston in her book *Mazzaroth* [2] says:

"If there (in the Zodiac) we find recorded some hope, some promise given to the first parents of mankind, to support them under the loss of innocence and of Eden, will not that memorial be equally precious even now, shining like the stars that bear it, with undiminished lustre, on us their remote descendants? So read, the 'poetry of heaven' will become its Scripture, and its line once more go out to the ends of the earth, declaring the glory of God to every nation."

The inspired Psalmist's picture of the Universe and all within it, is found in Psalm 19 and its Creator and Sustainer is Love.

	(Initiated
	(Inspired
Every approach of God is Love:	(Motivated
	(Controlled
	(Carried on and Completed.

His every movement is toward a divine event, from Alpha to Omega.

---

[1] *Ibid* (Bullinger), The Star Pictures of the Zodiac, p. 617

[2] See Appendix "E" Rolleston, Part I. *Mazzaroth*, p. 636, para. 4

III. NOAH and THE FLOOD

> "By faith, Noah, being warned of God of things not seen as
> yet, moved with godly-fear, prepared an ark to the saving
> of his house: through which he condemned the world, and
> became heir of the righteousness which is according to faith."
>
> Hebrews 11:7 N.
(cf. Genesis 6:13——7:16)

The flood of Noah's day is not only an historical fact attested to by
archaeological findings but is clearly stated as a fact in all parts of the
Word of God and is used as a warning example to all men everywhere:
first of all as a demonstration of God's judgment (Matthew 24:36—39; Luke
17:22—27); and secondly, as an example of His faithfulness in that He
has kept His promise that He would never again bring a universal flood
while the present earth remains (Genesis 8:21—22; Isaiah 54:9).

In II Peter 3:18—21, we find reference to the "spirits in prison which
sometime were disobedient when once the long-suffering of God waited in
the days of Noah while the ark was a preparing." Who these spirits are,
is not indicated here but other references in this study[1] help us to conclude that they were the fallen angels who corrupted all flesh in Noah's
day. The ark in this same passage of Scripture is used as a type of the
Christian baptism: "the like figure whereunto even baptism doth now also
save us by the resurrection of Jesus Christ.' The covenant applied to all
of the descendants of Noah from whom came all of the nations of the earth.
This covenant is to be the basis of God's relationship with the nations
while the present earth remains. While no law of capital punishment had
been given before this time, it is included in this covenant, thus becoming
the first law against murder. The first record in history that life is in the
blood is stated here in verse 4.

It is this covenant which man once knew but rejected, and then departed from God into atheism after the flood (Romans 1:21—32).

---

[1] See this Section THREE, *Satan's Story*, V. *Satan corrupts all flesh*, p. 199

SATAN'S STORY

I. SATAN'S LIE

Jesus said,
"*Ye* are of your father the devil, and the lusts of your
father ye are willing to do. *He* was a murderer from
the beginning, and hath not stood in the truth, because
there is no truth in him. When he speaketh a lie, he
speaketh of his own: for he is a liar, and the father of it."

John 8:44N.

Satan's rebellion which began in heaven through his pride and ambition,
and caused him to be cast out into the earth (Revelation 12:7—13), did
not cease with his being exiled from heaven. The third chapter of Genesis
finds man in his innocency in the garden of Eden and Satan, the rebel a-
gainst God, is at work. God placed Adam in a garden Eastward in Eden
and clothed him in His Own Image and likeness. Satan manifest himself
in the garden of Eden to Eve introducing sin into God's perfect family,
and through his lie, Satan stripped Adam and Eve and left them naked for
God again to clothe, this time with the skins of animals. Satan's presence
in the Garden of Eden reveals that Eden was his capital, his headquarters
on earth (Ezekiel 28:13). The whole earth has been given to him as his
realm (Luke 4:5—6; I John 5:19; II Corinthians 4:4). He is called by the
Lord a *liar* and a *murderer* from the beginning,[1] and the record of Genesis 3
vindicates this judgment of the Lord (Romans 1:25).

The event in Eden centers not around the word "serpent" but around
its more accurate translation "the shining one," and not around the commonly accepted "apple" but rather the "fruit of the tree of knowledge of good
and evil." "The shining one[2] was more subtle (cunning) than any living
creature which the Lord God had made," and he said unto the woman, "Yea,
hath God said ye shall not eat of every tree of the garden?" This was a
taunt which omitted the name "Jehovah" even as Judas in the Upper Room,
omitted calling Jesus "Lord" and instead called Him "Rabbi" (Matthew
26:25). This was not Satan's first conversation with Eve but it was the
last fatal one.

Vice is a monster of so frightful mien,
As, to be hated, needs but to be seen;
Yet seen too oft, familiar with her face,
We first endure, then pity, then embrace.[3]

[1] See Section TWO, *Satan's* Story, *Names of Satan,* p. 167

[2] See Appendix D, *The Serpent of Genesis 3,* p. 603

[3] Alexander Pope, *The Complete Poetical Works of Pope, Essay on Man,* (N.Y. Leavitt
& Allen Bros., Vol. I), Epistle V, p. 29, line 217 ff.

Eve temporized and lost as all such must do. *She* said, "neither shall ye *touch*[1] it"; and Revelation 22:18 warns against, "if any man shall add to these things, God shall add to him the plagues that are written in this book." So this gave him his chance to "touch" unbelief.

The success of his lie is recorded in this second chapter of Genesis where we find the first woman believing his lie and entering into sin, her husband joining with her, thereby coming under the judgment of God:

> "But the tree of the knowledge of good and evil, thou shalt
> *not* eat of it: for in the day that thou eatest thereof thou shalt
> *surely* die."
>
> Genesis 2:17

I Timothy 2:14 tells us that it was not Adam who was deceived but Eve. A little later Cain murdered his brother and "went out from the presence of the Lord."

The Bible is a record of Satan's successes and failures with men to whom he repeats again and again the lie "ye shall *not surely* die." Usually he was successful but the record of his failures gives us courage. The book of Job records Satan's attempt upon a faithful servant of God: Job, "a perfect and upright man, one that feareth God, and escheweth evil" (Job 1:8). Satan was permitted to test him in all things but not to take his life; and through all of his testings Job remained faithful to God; the story concludes with God saying, "My servant Job shall pray for you and him will I accept" (Job 42:8).

Satan failed in his attempt on Nebuchadnezzar after nearly succeeding and the story in *Daniel,* chapters 1 through 4, give the account of the great struggle, but the conclusion is reached in 4:37 as we read:

> "Now I Nebuchadnezzar praise and extol and honour the King
> of heaven, all whose works are truth, and His ways judgment:
> and those that walk in pride He is able to abase."

Satan endeavored to defeat God's purpose for Abraham (Genesis 12:10—20; 16:2; 20:1—18), but Abraham, the father of the faithful, "believed God and it was reckoned unto him for righteousness" (James 2:21—23).[2]

The Bible records not only that Satan was victor over men as individuals, but that he also won empires. The rise and fall of Babylon, Medo-Persia, Greece and Rome give historical evidence of his remarkable power of devastation.

---

[1] See Appendix D, *The Serpent in Genesis 3,* p. 603

[2] See Section FOUR, *Abraham to Christ's Spiritual Body,* SATAN'S Story, p. 314

II. THE COVERING DARKNESS

"The whole world lieth in the wicked one" (I John 5:19) and throughout the Scriptures the life of the men of the world is pictured as in darkness, in contrast to "the light of the glorious gospel" (Acts 26:28). Satan is called the anointed cherub that covers (Ezekiel 28:14) and this was his position and his work in heaven. In his work of "covering," could it not have been that he used the Shekinah Glory Cloud with which God shields Himself from the view of men today (Acts 1:9)? It is this obscuring veil, or covering, which still produces spiritual darkness in men's hearts and minds today (Acts 9:18).

III. SATAN'S REPERTOIRE

Here in the Garden, Satan the Serpent,[1] is placed at the beginning even as Adam and Eve for God's redemption to make its most effective appeal as man chooses between the lie of Satan and the truth of God. Thus the scene in Genesis 3 opens with the adversary in the ascendancy. Satan, though himself a "cast out" has persuaded into a like fate, the first occupants of Eden. Four thousand years later, he is seen in his same role with the same bag of tricks. There is nothing new in the struggles and the attempts upon all the peoples in between; but over believers, he has no influence for we are Scripture-armored (Ephesians 6:21 ff.), proving to those of open minds that in the day in which he was "created," there was omitted the inventive mind. Satan is but a creature of sight and void of initiative; the only difference being that Eve fell for the first temptation (Genesis 3:6); but the Lord triumphed over Satan's whole repertoire (Matthew 4:1—11; I John 2:16).

Satan's devices which he used in the garden of Eden are the same which he uses today. I John 2:16 says:

"For everything that is in the world, the lust of the flesh,
and the lust of the eyes, and the pride (vain glory) of life,
is not of the Father, but is of the world."

The Scripture outlines the appeal of Satan to mankind in each age: pride or lust of the eye is first recorded in Genesis 3:6:

"And when the woman saw that the tree was good for food,
and that it was *pleasant to the eyes,* and a tree to be desired to make one wise, she took of the fruit thereof, and did eat, and gave also unto her husband with her; and he did eat."

The "lust" of life is shown in her belief of the lie of Satan, "Ye shall *not* surely *die,*" and the vain glory of life is indicated in her acceptance

---

[1] See Appendix E,*Zodiac,* Decan "Serpens and Draco," p. 613 para. 2, and p. 620.

of the promise of Satan:

> "For God doth know that in the day ye eat thereof, then your eyes shall be opened, and ye shall *be as gods*, knowing good and evil."

The temptation of Christ by Ṣatan as recorded in Matthew 4 and Luke 4, follows this same old pattern; nothing new had been added, nothing had been left out. It was this love of "vain glory" which caused the rebel Cain to go out from the presence of the Lord and enter into the building of great cities, subduing the earth, introducing culture and murder (Jude 11)! And this same "vain glory" is seen as a controlling factor in Nimrod who built Babylon, Nineveh and other cities. Here in Genesis 10:10—11 we are looking at a fallen section of the kingdom of God, and its god is controlling his own subjects (II Corinthians 4:4; Ephesians 2:2). Satan, who has the power of death (Hebrews 2:14*b*), leads men upon the highway into "the valley of the shadow of death" with the same methods he has used from the beginning, James 1:15:

> "Then when lust hath conceived, it bringeth forth sin;
> And sin, when it is finished, bringeth forth death."

Satan begins with lust as he draws men after him and this brings forth sin and the completion of sin brings forth death (Romans 5:12—21).

The book of Genesis opens in the first chapter with the chaos wrought by Satan when he was cast out of heaven, and the concluding words of the book, "a coffin in Egypt," are found at the close of the fiftieth chapter (Genesis 3:19*b*, "for dust thou art, and unto dust shalt thou return"). This is the influence of Satan in every age. Those who were Satan-deceived in this age included Eve, Cain, Nimrod, and all those who were corrupted in their genealogies before the Flood; and myths and theories are attempts by such men to escape God (Romans 1:18).

IV. THE BRUISING OF SATAN

> "And Jehovah God said unto the serpent, . . .
> 'And I will put enmity between thee and between the woman,
> and between thy seed and between her seed;
> he shall *bruise* thy head,
> and
> thou shalt *bruise* His heel'."
>
> Genesis 3:15 N.

The idea of *bruising* as introduced in this passage of Scripture goes clear through the Bible. The seed of the woman is to *bruise* the head of the serpent, and the serpent is to *bruise* His heel. Sin bruises men in every age (Luke 14:18; Matthew 10:20), but those who are bruised of Satan can find comfort and help in the Lord. In Luke 9:39 we find the bruising power of the demon who was cast out of the man; and Isaiah 53:5 and 10 point out to us the bruising of Christ on the Cross; also the place of the Church in the bruising of Satan is presented in Romans 16:20*a*:

> "And the God of peace shall *bruise*
> Satan under your feet shortly . . ."

This will occur when the Lord returns and Satan shall be *bruised* under the feet of the saints of God as they are caught up to be with the Lord and the bondage of death has ceased. You will note prophecy says that the serpent's *head* is to be *bruised* and this occurs when the Church is raptured. Satan is not destroyed at that time for this will take place later, following his being bound for one thousand years, and then released (Revelation 20:10).

V. SATAN CORRUPTS ALL FLESH

Genesis 6:1—4 describes a condition which developed upon the earth corrupting all mankind with the exception of the family of Noah. This was the attempt of Satan to defeat the promise of God made at Genesis 3:15 by corrupting the seed of woman. His influence is manifested continually through the pages of God's Word in his attempt to counteract this prophecy. The phrase "sons of God" is only used in the Scriptures before the birth of Christ to apply to angels and the result of this un-natural union between angels and the daughters of men, produced giants in the earth in those days and also "after that" in the days referred to in Joshua 11:18—23. These giants in physical stature were also giants in sin. The size of the ancient cities, monuments and the stone writings of men of that day reveal that these things arose in a world of behemoths. This was a "pride world" which was seeking a name but it was blind to spiritual things.

These Scriptures, I Peter 3:19—20; II Peter 2:4—6; Jude 6—7, indicate that these fallen angels did sin and "kept not their first estate" but left their own habitation and went after strange flesh; these were the "sons of God" who are mentioned in Genesis 6:1—4 who were disobedient "when once the long suffering of God waited in the days of Noah while the Ark was preparing." A later recurrence of this same type of corruption occurred in Caanan, producing the Anakim giants which caused the children of Israel to doubt that they could take the land; and undoubtedly Goliath was one of this race of giants; God's judgment did not fall on this group because of His promise in Genesis 9:11—16. Satan's influence here and later in the Caananite nation shows his unending effort to defeat the purpose of God; and this effort of Satan begins with the antediluvians and their progeny and runs through to the end referred to in Zechariah 14:21:

"Yea, every pot in Jerusalem and in Judah shall be holiness
unto Jehovah of hosts; And all they that sacrifice shall come
and take of them, and seethe therein; and in that day there
shall be no more the Canaanite in the house of Jehovah of
hosts."

Section FOUR:

ABRAHAM to CHRIST'S SPIRITUAL BODY

Jesus said:
"Your father Abraham rejoiced that he might see My day:
and he saw it and was glad."

John 8:56 N.*

*See page *xiii*

201

Section FOUR: ABRAHAM to CHRIST'S SPIRITUAL BODY

Continued on page 203

ABRAHAM to CHRIST'S SPIRITUAL BODY

HIS STORY

> "When the most High (*Eleyohn*) divided to the nations
>   their inheritance,
> When He separated the sons of Adam,
> He set the bounds of peoples according to the number
>   of the sons of Israel."
>
> Deuteronomy 32:8N.

> "And made of one blood all nations of men for to dwell on
> all the face of the earth, having determined the times be-
> fore appointed, and the bounds of their habitation;"
>
> Acts 17:26N.
>
> (Cp. Genesis 10:32 and 11:8)

I. DIVIDING *THE* NATION from THE NATIONS

In Section THREE, *His* Story, we saw the beginning of the nations who make up "the kingdoms of this world" and we noted that these were men who went out from the presence of the Lord. God dealt with these nations directly, personally, and on an equal basis from Adam through Terah (the father of Abraham). In this Section FOUR beginning with Abraham,[1] God makes a new approach to the nations. Abraham is called out from the nations to begin the race that shall be later known as Israel or the Jews. This nation is to be an example to all other nations.

To Abraham was given this three-fold promise concerning his descendants who were to be as:

a) The dust of the earth   (Genesis 13:16)   — Nations
b) The stars of the heavens (Genesis 22:17*a*) — Church
c) The sand of the seashore (Genesis 22:17*b*) — Israel

This three-fold division of mankind continues through the rest of the Scriptures and is indicated in I Corinthians 10:32. It is interesting to note that two of the lines of Abraham's descendants are by nature earthly: the *dust* and *sand*, and have only earthly promises; the third line, the *stars*, is by nature heavenly and has heavenly promises. In this section FOUR, we are concerned with God's attitude toward these dust descendants of Abraham, the nations. God said to Abraham:

> "And I will make thy seed as the dust of the earth;
> so that if a man can number the dust of the earth,
> then shall thy seed also be numbered."
>
> Genesis 13:16

---

[1] See this Section FOUR: *MY* Story, Abraham, the Forerunner, p. 217

Chart No. 4

Section FOUR

A B R A H A M   T O   C H R I S T ' S   S P I R I T U A L   B O D Y

HIS STORY
God's dealing with Nations and men of the world

From Genesis 21:27

THE TIMES OF THE GENTILES

| Beginning 606 B.C. Nebuchadnezzar | THE 538 B.C. Darius | TIMES 331 B.C. Alexander | GENTILES 168 B.C. Caesars | | 30 A.D. |

Babylon — Gold — Lion — White

Medo-Persia — Silver — Bear — Red
I Abomination Daniel 5:30

Greece — Brass — Leopard — Black
II Abomination Temple polluted by Bagoses, Persian General

Rome — Iron — Non-descript Beast — Pale
III Abomination Daniel 11:4

IV Abomination yet to come Matthew 24:15

Daniel 2 (Image)
Daniel 7 (Beasts)
Revelation 6 (Horses)

Genesis 13:16 "DUST" Descendants: Nations

To John 20:22

MY STORY
God's dealing with Spiritual people: ISRAEL and CHURCH

John 8:56
ABRAHAM
Genesis 12:1
Hebrews 11:8-10
Genesis 22:17a "SAND" Descendants: ISRAEL
Genesis 22:17b "STARS" Descendants: CHURCH

Moses
Deut. 18:15

David
II Samuel 7:8
Psalm 78:70-72

Daniel
Daniel 10:12

Sixty-Nine Weeks
"Seventy" Weeks are decreed upon Thy people" (Daniel 9:24)

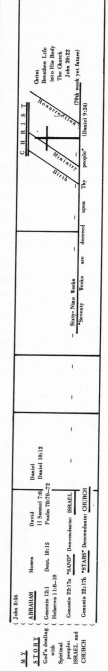

C H R I S T
Birth — Ministry — Resurrection
Christ Breathes Life into His Body The Church John 20:22
(70th week yet future)

SATAN'S STORY
Satan attempts to corrupt "The Seed," The Nation, and The Lord,

The Temptation Matthew 4 and Luke 4
The Lord's disciples are tempted by Satan Luke 22:31-32

Hagar Genesis 16
Abimelech Genesis 20:1-6

"Dust" in the Scriptures is continually associated with the things of earth (Genesis 2:7; 3:14, 19, *et al*), and those who are called "dust" receive an earthly destiny rather than a heavenly one. The word "dust" is used once as a simile of judgment which came upon the nation of Israel in their disobedience (Isaiah 29:4—5).

These "dust" descendants of Abraham are men of faith arising out of the nations, and they are *neither* a part of the *Church* nor are they *Israel*. In Matthew 25:31—40 at the appearing of the Lord in Glory for the judgment upon the nations, these "dust" descendants of Abraham, the sheep, will be separated from the rest of the nations, the goats, and will be given their inheritance as was promised to Abraham. These righteous nations will have no heavenly promise for they, like dust, are doomed to earth with only an earthly reward: The Kingdom (Matthew 6:10). The basis of the judgment to which these are submitted, is found in verse 40:

> "Verily I say unto you, Inasmuch as ye have done it unto one of the least of these My brethren, ye have done it unto Me."

And the principles on which this is based, are set forth in Matthew chapters 5 through 7, "The Sermon on the Mount." Thus Romans 2:14—15 N:

> ". . . For when the Gentiles, which have not law, do by nature the things contained in the law, these, having not law, are a law unto themselves: which shew the work of the law written in their hearts, their conscience also bearing witness, and their reasonings between themselves, accusing or else excusing one another;"

This text shows that these Gentiles distinguish themselves in doing by nature the things contained in the law. Looking to the day when Abraham's "dust" descendants will be identified, we read:

> "And I will shake all nations, and the desire of all nations shall come: and I will fill this house with glory, saith the Lord of hosts."
>
> Haggai 2:7

> "I saw in the night visions, and behold, one like the son of man came with the clouds of heaven, and came to the Ancient of days, and they brought Him near before Him. And there was given Him dominion, and glory, and a kingdom, that all people, nations, and languages, should serve Him, His dominion is an everlasting dominion, which shall not pass away, and His kingdom that which shall not be destroyed."
>
> Daniel 7:13—14

II. MOULDING THE NATIONS FOR HIS PURPOSE

During the events of this portion of the Bible, from ABRAHAM to

CHRIST'S SPIRITUAL BODY, some of God's dealings with the nations were in Person or direct; some were through prophets, but *all* were for the purpose of moulding these nations *for His Purpose* in accomplishing the redemption of lost mankind:

1. In Genesis 20:3 God came to Abimelech in a dream, to prevent the corruption of *the seed* of the woman
2. And in Genesis 41:1—7, 25, He speaks to Pharaoh through a dream, making provision for the protection of the descendants of Abraham
3. In Exodus 5:1ff, God speaks to Pharaoh ("who knew not Joseph") through His prophet Moses; and out of the persecution of Egypt God was able to bring forth the nation of Israel to the land promised to Abraham, Isaac and Jacob.

In an article *The Bible Explains Course of World Empires,* [1] John Meredith says:

"A correlation of world history and the Bible reveals many things concerning the great nations and empires that have arisen upon the earth.

"Genesis 12:1—3 tells of God establishing great nations through descendants of one man, Abraham. One of these nations was spoken of as the 'covenant' nation. This was to be the nation descended from Abraham, Isaac and Jacob. These are Jews.

"In Deuteronomy 32:8 we read:

> 'When the Most High divided to the nations their inheritance, when he separated the sons of Adam, he set the bounds of the people according to the number of the children of Israel (Jacob).'

"This Scripture is a pivot about which the history of every nation and empire of nations revolves. God's purpose in bringing this nation into being was to accomplish His own purposes in the entire world. The world, to be governed by His Son Jesus the Christ, is being put into shape, as it always has, by the hand of God to this end.

"Babylon, Assyria, Egypt, Greece, Rome, all grew into mighty nations and empires that they might serve God's purpose with His covenant people. When each had served His purpose, it fell into decay. Every nation which has persecuted these people, has felt the heavy hand of God.

"Babylon, Assyria, and Egypt were used to develop, train, punish these people for their own infractions of God's commands. Greece was used to develop a culture, a language that should spread over the nations as a language of commerce. This in preparation for the coming of Christ, the long-promised Messiah.

1

John Meredith, *The Bible and The News* (Chicago, March 29, 1947)

"Rome was used to establish a peace over the same world, road-ways of travel by land and sea. Rome was brought into being to be powerful enough to issue the momentous decree of Augustus, and to affect the life of every individual in the entire Roman Empire. That decree sent Joseph and Mary to Bethlehem in Judea to arrive there on the day and hour that Jesus should be brought into the world.

"The Roman Empire was being gradually built up for eight hundred years before it accomplished its God-appointed task. That task was to see to it that Mary, the mother of Jesus Christ arrived at Bethlehem in Judea in time to deliver her child there and nowhere else."

III. WORLD RULERS ORDAINED OF GOD

That God not only divides to the nations an inheritance of this earth and set boundaries upon them, but that He also has given governmental authority and rulers over these nations, is revealed in Daniel 5:18 through verse 21 N. (cp. Ezra 1:2):

"O thou king, the Most high God (Heb. *Elahah*) gave Nebuchadnezzar thy grandfather a kingdom, and majesty, glory and honour: And for the majesty that He gave him, all peoples, nations, and languages, trembled and feared before him: whom he would he slew; and whom he would he kept alive; and whom he would he set up; and whom he would he put down.

"But when his heart was lifted up, and his spirit hardened in pride, he was deposed from his kingly throne, and they took his glory from him; And he was driven from the sons of men; and his heart was made like the beasts, and his dwelling was with the wild asses; they fed him with grass like oxen, and his body was wet with the dew of heaven; till he knew that the Most high God (Heb. *Elahah*) ruled in the kingdom of men, and that He appointeth over it whomsoever He will."

Nebuchadnezzar[1] was the mightiest of world rulers over the first universal empire. He was the "king David" of the Gentiles' world. His was the first world mind that felt the weight and responsibility to posterity which drove him into insanity from whence God restored him.

That this same God-given authority continues to abide in the nations through the Scriptures is seen in the statement of Jesus to Pilate:

"Thou couldest have no authority against Me,
except it were given thee from above: . . . ."

John 19:11

Paul in Romans 13:1–4 states that "the powers that be,"—these governmental rulers—are ordained of God. God-given moral order and governmental authority reside in these dust descendant nations until

---

[1] See *Sealed Division:* A. 4. b) *Daniel and Nebuchadnezzar—The Two Strong Men,* p. 40

Christ returns. The present world system which is controlled by Satan, the god of this world, often seems to have supremacy over this God-given authority; that both have existed in every age is evident from the record of history.

In the parable of the tares, Jesus explains that the good seed and the tares are to grow together until the harvest (Matthew 13:36), which is the time of the separation between the children of the kingdom and those of the wicked one. This separation is found in Matthew 25:31ff., and this judgment distinguishes between the nations, the sheep, that have followed the moral order and laws which are God-given, from those, the goats, who have followed the god of this world.

IV. THE FOUR GREAT EMPIRES

We have already stated that to Pharoah, the friend of Joseph in Egypt, was given the dream which prophesied the years of plenty and the years of famine. More than one thousand years later, to Nebuchadnezzar,[1] king of Babylon, was given a dream concerning the image of the Times of the Gentiles:[2]

> "And in the second year of the reign of Nebuchadnezzar, Nebuchadnezzar dreamed dreams, wherewith his spirit was troubled, and his sleep brake from him" (Daniel 2:1 N.)

> . . .

> "Then was the secret revealed unto Daniel in a night vision. Then Daniel blessed the God of heaven" (Daniel 2:19 N.)

> . . .

> "Daniel answered in the presence of the king, and said, 'The secret which the king hath demanded, cannot the wise men, the enchanters, the magicians, the soothsayers, shew unto the king; But there is a God in heaven that revealeth secrets, and maketh known to the King Nebuchadnezzar what shall be in the latter days. Thy dream, and the visions of thy head upon thy bed, are these'." (Daniel 2:27, 38 N.)

> . . .

> "THOU, O king, was seeing, and behold a great image. This great image whose brightness was excellent, stood before thee; and the appearance thereof was terrible" (Daniel 2:31 N.)

---

[1] The character and quality of Nebuchadnezzar are set forth in II Chronicles 36:13 and Jeremiah 25:9

[2] "Times of the Gentiles": II Kings 24:11–16; Luke 21:24

V. THE PROPHECY

THE PROPHECY   THE IMAGE

A. GOLD   HEAD

Daniel 2:32a:

"This image's head was of fine gold, . . "

The Interpretation:

a) THE FIRST WORLD EMPIRE: BABYLON under
Nebuchadnezzar

(cf. Daniel 7:4 — — — LION)

Daniel 2:37—38:

"Thou, O king, art a king of kings: for the God of heaven hath
given thee a kingdom, power and strength, and glory. And
wheresoever the sons of men dwell, the beasts of the field
and the fowls of the heaven hath He given into thine hand,
and hath made thee ruler over them all. Thou art this head
of gold."

This World Empire, BABYLON, began in 606 B.C.

B. SILVER   BREAST

Daniel 2:32b: and

"his breast and his arms of silver . . ."
                                                                 ARMS
The Interpretation:

b) THE SECOND WORLD EMPIRE: MEDIA—PERSIA

(cf. Daniel 7:5 — — — BEAR)

Daniel 2:39a:

"And after thee shall arise another kingdom
inferior to thee,"
                (see Daniel 5:30—31; 8:20)

This World Empire, MEDIA—PERSIA, began in 538 B.C.

C. BRASS   BELLY

Daniel 2:33a: and

"his belly and his thighs of brass,"   and

The Interpretation: THIGHS

c) THE THIRD WORLD EMPIRE: GREECE

(cf. Daniel 7:6 — — — LEOPARD)

Daniel 2:39*b*:

"And another third kingdom of brass, which shall
bear rule over all the earth" (see Daniel 8:21).

D. IRON   LEGS

1. Daniel 2:33*a*:   *"His legs of iron*   and

2. Daniel 2:33*b*:   *"His feet part of iron and part of clay"*   FEET

The Interpretation:

d) THE FOURTH WORLD EMPIRE: ROME

(cf. Daniel 7:7 — — — NON-DESCRIPT)

1. Daniel 2:40:

"And the fourth kingdom shall be strong as iron; forasmuch as
iron breaketh in pieces and subdueth all things: and as iron
that breaketh all these, shall it break in pieces and bruise."
(see Daniel 9:26).

THE TEN KINGDOMS ARISING FROM THE ROMAN EMPIRE

2. Daniel 2:41—43 N.:

"And whereas thou sawest the feet and toes, part of potters'
clay, and part of iron, the kingdom shall be divided; but there
shall be in it of the strength of the iron, forasmuch as thou
sawest iron mixed with miry clay. And as the toes of the feet
were part of iron, and part of clay, they shall mingle themselves with the seed of men: but they shall not cleave one to
another, even as iron is not mixed with clay."

This World Empire, ROME, began in 168 B.C.

E. CONCLUSION OF THE PROPHECY: THE STONE

Daniel 2:34—35:

"Thou sawest till that a stone was cut out without hands, which
smote the image upon his feet that were of iron and clay, and
brake them to pieces.
"Then was the iron, the clay, the brass, the silver, and the gold,
broken to pieces together, and became like the chaff of the summer threshingfloors; and the wind carried them away, that no
place was found for them: and the stone that smote the image
became a great mountain, and filled the whole earth."

The Interpretation: The Coming Kingdom

Daniel 2:44—45 N.:

"And in the days of these kings[1] shall the God of heaven set up a kingdom, which shall never be destroyed: and the kingdom shall not be left to other people, but it shall break in pieces and consume all these kingdoms, and it shall stand for ever.

"Forasmuch as thou sawest that the stone was cut out of the mountain without hands, and that it brake in pieces the iron, the brass, the clay, the silver and the gold; the great God hath made known to the king what shall come to pass hereafter; and the dream is certain, and the interpretation thereof sure."

As the dream of the image was revealed to Daniel, setting forth these Four World Empires, so also to John, in Revelation 6, is given a like revelation but using different figures:

These same Four Empires are summoned, are seen of John, and are described. Here John hears the noise as of thunder as the Lamb opens one of the seals and he hears one of the four living creatures saying: "Come," and he sees four horses with riders, representing the Four World Empires, for each one exercises his authority over the earth in his time of reign:

The First: The white horse (Daniel 5:19) and his rider, represent the First World Empire of Babylon under Nebuchadnezzar

The Second:
   The red horse and rider are Cyrus,[2] and the Kingdom of Media-Persia

The Third: On the black horse is Alexander, The Great Empire of Greece

---

[1] The phrase "in the days of these kings" refers to the ten toes of the feet of the image which The Stone smites and which arises after the days of the Roman Empire. That this prophecy cannot refer to the coming of the Holy Spirit and the establishment of the Church on Pentecost can be easily seen in that Pentecost occurred in A.D. 30 in the days of the iron legs of the image and the fall of Rome did not occur until 476 A.D. We are now living in the days of the "toes" of the image and though there have been nineteen hundred years of the preaching of the gospel, kings and nations still continue and will continue until after the Church is raptured and Christ "The Stone" returns in power to judge the nations and smite the image upon its feet, and then, "in the days of these kings" shall the God of heaven set up a kingdom.

[2] In Isaiah 44:28 through 45:4, Isaiah writes the prophecy of the Lord that Cyrus is to build Jerusalem. This prophecy was given almost two hundred years before the decree of Cyrus (Ezra 1:1–2). Cyrus must certainly have been impressed and stirred in his heart to hear his name read from the writings of Isaiah, the prophet. That his heart was stirred is shown by the proclamation which he made the first year of his reign throughout all of his kingdom, concerning his being charged by God to build a house at Jerusalem.

The Fourth:

The pale horse and rider, The Roman Empire and its rulers.

Here the Great Voices of the Four Living Creatures reach down into all the past and call forth these Empires: The Babylonian, the Medo-Persian, the Grecian, and then the Roman. And all must fall before Him who is King of Kings and Lord of Lords (Revelation 6:15—17).

CONCLUSION to HIS STORY, Section FOUR

In this Fourth Section, "ABRAHAM to CHRIST'S SPIRITUAL BODY —HIS STORY, we have seen the rise of world dominions, with authority from God. These Empires are used of God for His Purpose which He is demonstrating to all the Universe through the nation of Israel. As this section closes, we find God using the Fourth Great Empire, Rome, bringing to pass the events surrounding the birth, ministry, death, burial and the resurrection of our Lord. And God continues to use this great Empire through the beginnings of the Church as we shall see in Section FIVE.

From all of these nations of men and their successors, the Lord will call forth His Church through the Gospel. Peter recognizes the universal application of the Gospel when he says:

"Then Peter opened his mouth, and said,
'Of a truth I perceive that God is no respecter of persons:
But in every nation he that feareth Him, and worketh
righteousness, is accepted with Him . . .'."

Acts 10:34—35

ABRAHAM to CHRIST'S SPIRITUAL BODY

MY STORY

I. PROPHETS BEGINNING WITH ABRAHAM

The Bible is the only consistent, progressive and constructive literature known to man. The immortal characters of the Bible from *Genesis* on, are fixed on far goals; this is not so of other authors, historians and empire planners. There are galaxies of immortals, like star clusters grouped at Athens, Paris, Boston; but they have no connection nor articulation of thought, plan or purpose amongst themselves. This makes intensely significant the Master's groupings of *all* revelations of His purpose into ONE Book; and such inference could be nothing less than timeless. Of Its Author alone can it be written "the eternal God." It is a *sure* Word: the One book surviving the wrecks of time, the erosion of the ages and the lethal attempts of critics. This Book outrides changes and all who enter into It are carried into the Beyond—the Omega which is the Ark of the reborn. The Bible is the record of the Divine Anabasis, the Fall, the Theophanies, the message of the Prophets, The Incarnation, and the Rapture of the Redeemed. Having dealt with the Fall in Section THREE, we come in this Section FOUR to the Theophanies, the Prophets, and the Incarnation. The Rapture of the Redeemed will be set forth in Section FIVE.

A. THE THEOPHANIES

God had councils with men through all the Book. In times of great emergencies He met with men Himself, and then went up from them. The Theophanies were really an accommodation of Deity to our sight (Exodus 43:20; Isaiah 6:5; I Timothy 6:16). In several portions of the Bible, we find recorded the appearances of the Lord to some of His prophets; these are here listed in the order of their occurrences in the Scriptures and under the names of the men to whom He appeared:

1. To Abraham
   a) Genesis 11:31 (Acts 7:2); The Call
   b) Genesis 12:1–3; The promise to go through to the consummation
   c) Genesis 12:7; "The Lord appeared"; Perpetual Covenant and everlasting possession
   d) Genesis 18:1ff.; "The Lord appeared"; Perpetual Blessings would come through the promise of a son
2. To Isaac:
   a) Genesis 26:2, 24; "The Lord appeared"; Perpetual Covenant, blessing and multiplying

3. To Jacob:
   a) Genesis 35:9; "God appeared"; Perpetual Covenant; changed name to *Israel*
   b) Exodus 6:3; "And I appeared unto Abraham, unto Isaac, and unto Jacob, by the name of God Almighty (Heb. *El Shaddai*), but by My name Jehovah (*El*, singular) was I not known to them."

4. To Ezekiel:
   a) Ezekiel 40:3; Appearance of a man, like brass, "with a line of flax in his hand and a measuring reed"; vision of the fulfillment of Perpetual Covenant to Israel.

5. To Daniel:
   a) Daniel 8:15; Appearance of man; Perpetual Purpose of God, the nations, the time of the end, the vision, and judgment on the nations (Revelation 1:19)

6. To Paul:
   a) Acts 9:3—6; "heard a voice saying unto him"
   b) Acts 26:13—20; "I have appeared"; "I will appear unto thee"
   c) II Corinthians 12:1—4; "I will come to visions and revelations of the Lord"

7. To John:
   a) Revelation 1:9—19; "And I turned to see"; "one like unto the Son of man."

B. THE PROPHETS[1]

The Bible is not a book of rare specimens but a window in God's laboratory or workshop where the approval of the Master is put upon the process of taking men up into Himself; a process operative from Alpha to Omega. The "like-passioned," "falling-short" humanness of its Saints prove them to be men not set apart, but to be "flesh of our flesh"; and therefore, their God and our God is not only "He Who was," but He Who IS, for the elements of Him are still potent today. Man as a prophet is concerned with the fixed and the mutable; he is a restless surveyor and a conqueror of far horizons; he is "heir of all the ages"—and an epitome of all the ages. Even though it was not until Jesus came "in the fulness of the times" that the "Word was made flesh" (John 1:14), yet through the prophets from the very beginning (Adam), God was putting His Word into flesh that all mankind might know His purpose. In each dispensation no provision was made for there was no need for them as long as men were in normal relationships with God; but when they fell below this level, then God raised up prophets. Where the prophets speak in the Word of God, they bring a message from

---

[1] See Appendix C, p. 602 *PROPHECY*, C. G. Kindred

MY Story

God to a people who could have experienced the reality of God's Presence at this same time had there been no lapse. *My Story* (The Mystery) delineates what He purposes to reveal and His method in the use of the prophets (Amos 3:7) permits a pre-supposition for the last revelation.

The story of the starry heavens provides an illustration for us in this procession of the Equinox (Hebrews 11:3): what is this ceaseless procession of "choiring giants"[1] but the witnessing to those "having eyes to see" that all space and all time is filled with God (Acts 17:26,[2] Psalm 139:7—8):

> But such a tide as moving *seems* asleep,
>   Too full for sound and foam,
> When that which drew from out the boundless deep
>   Turns again home.[3]

So every nook and cranny and the whole are crammed with the divine resources and personalities of it:

> "Wherefore *we* also are compassed about with
>   so great a *cloud of testimony-bearers* . . . ."
>
> Hebrews 12:1*a*N.

This "cloud of testimony-bearers" is growing as we turn the pages of God's Word. Already we have met Adam, Abel, Seth, Enoch and Noah; and now into the effulgence of this cloud steps Abraham.

C. ABRAHAM, THE FORERUNNER[4]

Of all the immortals, there was none like unto Abraham, this God-intoxicated pilgrim who moved always so apart from motives that drive greatness. The great problem of life is salvation; that comes by faith. As in all other lines of achievement, we study their great masters, so Abraham in faith. We read, "he went out *not knowing*," and he "dwelt in

---

[1]
See Appendix E, *Zodiac*, p. 609; also, see Section TWO, *Perfection to Katabole*, *SATAN'S* Story, "Quoted footnote", p. 166

[2]
Paul's quotation here is from a poem by Aratas, a native of Paul's own province. Aratas, a Greek Stoic philosopher, lived about 300 B.C.; he was author also of an astronomical epic "Prognostics of the Weather" which was translated by Cicero. The portion of his poem "Phaenomena" quoted by Paul, follows:

> "From Zeus being: and never let us leave His name unloved.
> With Him, with Zeus, zre filled all paths we tread and all marts of men;
> Filled, too, the sea and every creek and bay;
> And all, in all things, need we help of Zeus;
> For we, ɔo, are his offspring."

[3] Tennyson, *Crossing The Bar*, St. 2

[4]
Abraham "walked *before* God," (Genesis 17:1)

M Y Story

tents." Definiteness is the fetish of our times, but the mystic moves before veiled angels and the forces that urge him are from without the known factors of earth. Dante was not so mysterious a figure in the streets of Ravenna; neither was Abraham on the Highway of Holiness, and it was possibly a contemplation of him that caused Matthew Arnold to write, "there is a power not ourselves"; or that gave point to Shakespeare's:

> "There's a divinity that shapes our ends,
> Rough-hew them how we will."
>
> *Hamlet,* Acts v.sc 2, 1.10

To look intently upon this man Abraham who proved the reality of God, will confirm our own faith and will open vistas into the eternal which are not elsewhere revealed. Across all fields of great achievement, some apocalyptic figure moves:

a) Franklin was the heroic figure of the electric world, and Edison made possible its use for the common man with many revolutionizing projects to follow.

b) The Wright Brothers, the Winged-Mercurys of aviation, foresaw man's opportunities of making an highway in the heavens; like as Tennyson foresaw in his poem:

> ". . . For I dipt into the future, far as human eye could see,
> Saw the Vision of the world, and all the wonder that would be;
> Saw the heavens fill with commerce, argosies of magic sails,
> Pilots of the purple twilight, dropping down with costly bales;
> Heard the heavens fill with shouting, and there rain'd a ghastly dew
> From the nations' airy navies grappling in the central blue . . ."[1]

But prior to the fruition of all of their labors, the lightnings had flashed their secrets across the heavens; and the flight of the bird had challenged man's thought of conquering the firmament above. So Abraham brought within our grasp the practical workableness of faith and proved the reality of God.

The greatest text upon faith (Romans 5:1) is the direct product of Abraham's life in *Romans*, chapter 4. We must be familiar with the incidents of his life for faith is itself the child of facts. We must study of where he met God—this hypothesis-zone of Theos-life. In no other way can we account for Abraham, the tenting-nomad pilgrim, and for his spiritual nobility that moves out from comfort and prosperity. Ambition drives, but dreams allure. Driven by a strange tidal power that enters a life, to rise up to burst into a glorious bloom, the vital current flows from soil through vegetal seed; flows up to man, spinal into brain;—so yet one other

---

[1] Tennyson, *Locksley Hall*

MY Story

zone—and *in that one*, move those whom Abraham saw rising toward "the city that hath the foundations." Herein is Life Sublime and Life Awe-full,— a life rising up into great epochs before our eyes. It is a most mysterious and emotion-creating event of earth: a man steps forth,—and Institutions, Sciences, and Languages group around him. Such a man's effect on his generation is illustrated in the poem of George Washington Goethals, the American Engineer and builder of the Panama Canal:

> A man went down to Panama,
> Where many a man had died,
> To slit the sliding mountain
> And lift the eternal tide.
> A man stood up in Panama
> And the mountain stood aside. [1]

Let that man cease his sky-striving, and civilization decays. Institutions, Sciences and Languages are but creatures or servants, and when centered in God, they are like spotlights to praise Him. Geike wrote "Abraham's tent, like the Ark of Noah, preserved the Hope of the World in a wild ocean of religious and moral degeneracy."

1. The Call of Abraham

a) Epoch I: His Call

> "Now Jehovah *had* said unto Abram, [2]
> 'Get thee out of thy country, and from thy
> kindred and from thy father's house, untó
> a land that I will show thee: . . .'."

Genesis 12:1

No description is given concerning his call, but definite hints are gathered from similar calls such as those given Moses (Exodus 25:40), or Paul (Acts 9:12). These with Abraham saw real things and real persons. Abraham endured as seeing the invisible. To such and upon such only, can God reveal and build His eternal purpose (Hebrews 11:1). God's call of Abraham *had occurred* previous to this time—while he dwelt in Ur of the Chaldees with his brothers Nahor and Haran, in the house of his father Terah. Abraham was the youngest son in his family, as also were Shem, David, Abel, Jacob, and Moses in their families. As at Samuel's call, Eli interpreted the heavenly call, so must Terah have helped Abraham (Genesis 11:31). The background from which he arose is briefly described in Joshua 24:2, 14 N.:

---

[1] Percy Mackaye, *The Present Hour*, (N.Y. The Macmillan Company, 1914), *Goethals*, St. 1, p. 68

[2] Abram—Abraham: "before and after" Genesis 17:5

> "And Joshua said unto all the people, 'Thus saith Jehovah God of Israel, Your fathers dwelt on the other side of the river in old time, even Terah, the father of Abraham, and the father of Nahor: and they served other gods . . .'
>
> "'Now therefore fear Jehovah Lord, and serve Him in sincerity and in truth; and put away the gods which your fathers served on the other side of the flood (river), and in Egypt; and serve ye Jehovah God'."

The idolatrous practices of the family from which Abraham came, are mentioned here. It was from these pagan gods and from a family that worshiped such gods that Abraham was called out by the Lord.

b) Epoch II: His Response

Abraham's call was shortly followed by his response; his obedience to this call and his purpose are set forth in Hebrews 11:8—10 N.:

> "By faith Abraham, when he was called to go out into a strange country, dwelling in tabernacles with Isaac and Jacob, the heirs with him of the same promise. For he looked (*waited*) for *the* city which hath *the* foundations, whose builder and architect is God."

Also, Acts 7:5 N.:

> "And He gave him none inheritance in it, not so much as to set his foot on: yet He promised that He would give it to him for a possession, and to his seed after him, when as yet he had no child."

Abraham was a man of culture, a gentle man, living in a nomadic existence; a man of culture living apart from that culture. What was the separating force? The ancestors of Abraham were *nomads* but they sought to *stay* and to *build Babylon*. Abraham was the *first nomad* with objectives for he sought *the City*, and he rejoiced to see, and he saw it and was glad. He lived in his visions, and as he sat at his tent-door, he was quick to discern angels (Genesis 18:1), for this was more to his manner of life than his neighbors. "The sons of God" brought to the earth tales of *the City*, and they sought to build its rival in Nineveh; Abraham escaped their corruption and became a pilgrim in a land not his own, dwelling in tents (Hebrews 11:8—16). His quick response:

(1) Wrote the conviction of God into the consciousness of man
(2) Blazed the trail for the "Wise Men of the East" who traveled the way which he had pioneered
(3) Drew up out of the bosom of humanity its most glorious race
    —the Jews.

Rising up out of the turgid stream of humanity, there blossoms forth those who were gropers and seekers after God (Acts 17:27; Proverbs 25:2).

Man's sky-striving comes to a describable expression at the call of Abraham. The history of man records:

> Heaven-aspiring souls
> Traffickers in Divine
> The Upward Strivers
> Those who rose up as lilies from the scum of a mud pond
> Those who became mighty teachers as Confucius, Buddha
>   and others
> Blind Samsons groping at the pillars of the City of God.

True enough there were sporadic, isolated, non-copyable experiences "from the beginning," yet "The Highway of Holiness" was not opened up to the "Whosoever-wills" until Abraham "departed to go into Canaan." Mankind was an inchoate mass—religiously and politically (Genesis 11:9)—but with the coming of Abraham and later Nebuchadnezzar, the race became Israel and Babylon. From the time of Abraham the will of man determined his destiny and this is seen through every dispensation, especially:

a) In the Church Age of Grace, clear up until the "spewed out" ones of the *Church* of Revelation 3:16

b) In the Kingdom Age until the "cast down" of the *State* (Revelation 20:15).

Then God cleanses and restores the Universe wherein dwelleth Righteousness and Peace—even the Redeemed of the Lord.

Abraham's call included also God's promise of Genesis 12:2–3N.:

> ". . . 'And I will make of thee a great nation, and I will bless thee, and make thy name great; and be thou a blessing'." (N. Imperative Mode)   ". . . 'And I will bless them that bless thee, and curse him that curseth thee; and in thee shall all families of the ground be blessed'."

This promise of blessing and curse has remained through to this present day as it refers to the seed of Abraham and the nations of the world.[1]

---

[1] Apropo God's promise of blessing and cursing of Israel:

a)   The Emperor Titus who destroyed Jerusalem A.D. 70 said, "God was against the Jews, else I never could have conquered."

b)   Disraeli: "I can afford to be called a Jew; when *your* fathers walked as naked savages in forests of Germany, *my* fathers worshiped God in a Golden Temple in Jerusalem."

c)   A. B. Simpson, *Israel and the Nations; Israel, Past, Present and Future,* (Harrisburg, Pa., Christian Publications), p. 28:

"It has been well said that long before Socrates taught philosophy, and Herodotus wrote history, the Jews were living sublimest philosophy and making immortal history. Long before the Greeks captured Troy, Joshua led his hosts to

(Continued on page 222)

The incomplete obedience of Abraham to the Lord's call is seen as he tarries in Haran until his father's death and then continues his journey to the land of promise. Those who entered the land with him were Sarai, his wife, and Lot his brother's son, "and all their substance and souls which they had gotten in Haran" (Genesis 12:4—5). And while Abraham tarried at Haran, Lot became *tainted by city life*; always cities have been the cess pools of "A-Theos." The result of their delay in obeying the command of the Lord is recorded in Genesis 12:6 where we read, "And the Canaanite was then in the land." Abraham saw through the walls of the material world and cleft a crevice through into the spiritual. As the woman who touched Jesus (Matthew 9:21) was made whole, so Abraham touched God, and God's life flowed down into man's being; this was not just an act, but it was purpose-inspired.

D. ABRAHAM THE VISIONER

". . . Slowly comes a hungry people, as a lion creeping nigher,
Glares at one that nods and winks behind a slowly-dying fire.
. . .
Yet I doubt not thro' the ages one increasing purpose runs,
And the thoughts of men are widen'd with the process of the suns."

As Tennyson beheld his vision of the world and firmly believed God's "one increasing purpose" would bring it to pass, so Abraham was given a perfect vision by God of His complete purpose for man.

We have noted that Enoch walked *with* God, but we find that Abraham walked *before* God (Genesis 17:1; 24:40; 48:15). To this God-empowered man of faith was given this "far look" (Genesis 15:7—21), and being a prophet, he received the revelation which came not from man but from the Lord Himself (Genesis 17:22; 18:33; 35:13). There was no vision before Abraham but as the friend of God, he was the first to be given visions which were later revealed to Daniel, Paul, Peter, John and others.

(Conclusion of footnote 1, page 221)

the conquest of Canaan. Long before Greek and Roman literature, the Jews had a splendid civilization. When Homer wrote the *Iliad*, David had already written his *Psalms*. Long before Nebuchadnezzar, Cyrus, or Alexander conquered the world, Solomon sat on an ivory throne and swayed a scepter of a world dominion. Long before the Parthenon rose at Athens, or the Pantheon at Rome, there rose on Mount Moriah the most magnificent edifice the world ever saw, built at a greater cost than all the churches of the world combined. Compared with the hoary past of Israel,—Marathon, Salamis and Thermopylae are modern names and memories. Israel has been Egypt, Nineveh, Babylon, Persia, Greece, and Rome rise and fall; and when Macaulay's inquiring stranger shall stand on London Bridge searching for the ruins of London, Jerusalem will still be the center of the world's dominion, and Israel the Queen of Nations."

"After these things the word of Jehovah came unto Abram
in a *vision*, saying, 'Fear not, Abram, I am thy shield,
And thy exceeding great reward'."

Genesis 15:1

This promise of God's presence with Abraham came to him after Genesis 14:18 when Melchizedek, king of Salem, brought forth bread and wine
to Abraham and blessed him. Those with whom God shares His purpose
have "meat to eat that the world knows not of" (John 4:32) because they
are vision-sustained; if there is no vision, there is no partnership (II Corinthians 12:1). A vision requires two: a See-er and a producer. Abraham
and others heard speech, saw visions and became acquainted with persons
in a super world. God's intention was, "let us make man in *our* image and
in *our* likeness" that he might share in this super world. Man lost this
through sin, but, like the nobles of Israel (Exodus 24:11), Abraham and
others of the prophets were given an entrance into the realm of God through
visions. The importance of visions to the people of God is recorded in
Proverbs 29:18, I Samuel 3:1, and Amos 8:11—12, for through the visions
came the Word of the Lord to the prophets and in turn to the people of
Israel. God told Abimelech, king of Gerar, that Abraham was a prophet
(Genesis 20:7), and that Abraham's prayer for him would bring blessing
in Abimelech's obedience. Thus to Abraham, the prophet, was given the
vision of that far off "Day" (John 8:56) and the City which hath foundations, for which, because of the vision, he was willing to wait.

1. The Vision of "My Day"

Abraham was the first to see the day of Christ, John 8:56:

"Your father Abraham *rejoiced* that he might
see *My Day*: and he saw it, and *was glad*."

a) He "*rejoiced*" exultantly, as Simeon to see the Infant Jesus
   (Luke 2:26); or as Paul in II Corinthians 12
b) He "*was glad,*" a calm joy: "My peace I give unto thee";—
   and as Mary "kept these things and pondered them in her
   heart" (Luke 2:19)
c) And as the Wise Men (Matthew 2:10) who were led in another
   direction, but "when they saw the Star, they *rejoiced* with
   exceeding great joy."

The exultant rejoicing and the calm joy of gladness which Abraham
experienced, help us to see that his vision included more than the events
of the crucifixion. Note here that Jesus said, "My Day" and not the "Mine
Hour" of John 14:1. Within this *whole day* there was much more included
than in "*the hour.*" "Sufferings" were the vital part of the "Mine Hour";

and "The glories that should follow" come later; but both are within "My Day" as is seen in I Peter 1:11*b* N.:

> ". . . when He testified beforehand the sufferings pertaining to Christ, and the glories after these things" (that should follow)

This was not revealed even to the prophets (Luke 10:23—24) but unto Abraham, the friend of God. "*My Day*" included:

a) *The Cross:*

Here is a plain statement of what Abraham saw:

(1) The Gospels (The ministry of Jesus), John 1:29
(2) The Gospel (Galatians 3:6—9) as set forth in I Corinthians 15:1—4 N.:

> "Moreover, brethren, I declare unto you *the gospel* which I announced unto you, which also ye received, and wherein ye stand; Through which also ye are saved, if ye hold fast in memory what I preached unto you, unless ye believed in vain. For I delivered unto you first of all that which I also received, how that *Christ died* for our sins according to the Scriptures; And that *He was buried*, and that *He hath been raised* again the third day according to the Scriptures."

Prophetically, Abraham lived through *the crucifixion* even as John *the Revelation*. Next to God he saw the resurrection demonstrated. He was "the friend of God" who could lead understandingly and sympathetically all seekers unto the propitiatory of John 1:29: "Behold, the Lamb of God, the bearer away of the sin of the world." "*My Day*" included the true tabernacle and the "Lamb slain."

A "horror of great darkness" (Genesis 15:12) hung over the Cross and the "flaming torch" (Genesis 15:27; John 1:5) was the blazing announcement of the resurrection. Thus Abraham beheld the propitiatory (Romans 3:25; Revelation 13:8) that taketh away the *death* of the world and he was made sad. But beholding these mighty events, Abraham was also prepared for offering up his only son Isaac, for he had seen Christ's day and his "rising again" and had beheld His glorified Body and therefore believed that Isaac would live again:

> "Accounting that God was able to raise up, even from among dead ones; from whence also he received him back in a figure."

> Hebrews 11:19 N.

b) *The Whole:*

"My Day" referred to by Jesus in John 8:56 begins with his

earthly ministry and continues through the events of the Cross and Resurrection: the Church Age; the Day of Christ; the Day of the Lord; and the Great Day of God Almighty. Abraham saw these events from the Incarnation to the day of triumph when the Lord Christ turns all things over to the Father at Omega[1] (I Corinthians 15:28).

Each phase of "My Day" from the incarnation to "The Great Day of God Almighty" should be studied by searching of the Scriptures. These selected references on "The Day of the Lord" will be helpful toward an understanding of just this one portion of "My Day":

Ezekiel 30:3	Isaiah 2:12	Joel 2:30—31
Amos 5:18	Zephaniah 1:7, 14—18	Zechariah chap. 14
Malachi 4:1—5	Luke 17:24	I Thessalonians 5:2
II Thessalonians 2:2(Day of Christ, Day of Lord, A.S.V.)		
II Peter 3:8—11		Revelation 16:14

Abraham saw the mighty events of the "Times of the Gentiles" and the "Seventy Weeks are determined upon thy people" of Daniel when he saw "The Day of the Lord" (Genesis 15), and he noted the exactness of the phrase "it came to pass," and so reasoned back to a controlling Personality. Upon these two concurrent streams of prophecy are focussed all prophecy and all personality of the Scriptures. Both "rightly dividing" and "steering a straight course" require even as do all divine appointments, a whole sacrifice and a goal; these are not possible except as we take our bearings from these divine locutions.

The Times of the Gentiles are definitely stated in these several Scriptures: Daniel 1:1 to 2:31—35; Luke 21:24; II Kings 24:11—16; and II Chronicles 36:7. The Seventy Weeks have been meticulously fulfilled up through the sixty-ninth; and just as surely as God is God, this last (the seventieth) will as surely "come to pass." Here, at this pronounced beginning of "Separations," the Sensual from the Spiritual (Jude 19), must the "rightly dividing" of the Word take on significance. Their cleavage has been discernible from the very beginning; it now becomes Literature, so that "the man of God" may steer a straight course.

Abraham saw, therefore every believer up to his stature must see these same revelations.

---

[1]
See Section SEVEN, *Omega,* p. 575 ff.

c) The City[1]

> "For he looked (waited) for the city which hath the
> foundations, whose builder and architect is God."

The eventual triumph of "My Day" is seen as The Holy City,
the Bride, comes as a flower bursting forth into bloom out of a
stalk. Revelation chapter 21 describes the city prepared for the
people of God spoken of as "thy people" to Daniel. In this city
they are to dwell, but the nations will bring their glory and honor
into it. The prophets speaking as they were "moved" or "borne
along," saw the grandeur of this prophecy but they did not understand it.

Abraham having seen "The City" in his vision, chose to live
in a tent and wait.

E. THE INDEFECTIBLE PROMISES TO ABRAHAM

In Genesis we find that God visited with Adam; walked with Enoch;
transported Noah; scattered at Babel; and now He finds a friend in Abraham. Out of this man's loins arise the three streams of destiny: "Dust";
"Stars"; "Sand"; (Genesis 13:16; 28:14; 22:17; I Corinthians 10:32).
To these three classes of humanity the compassionate God unconditionally
pledges Himself. Hitherto His agony effort had been exerted and directed
towards a grossly blinded unbelief until He "gave them up," but now He
is at work through agents: man for men. To Abraham was granted "the
vision splendid,"[2] that "far off divine event to which the whole creation
moves."[3] As this progressive program was unrolled: in Egypt a Race
(Sand): was formed; in Babylon, The Gentiles (Dust) were given supremacy;
and in Jerusalem, The Church (Stars) was called out.

Abraham is the prophet of the Prothesis (God's Purpose), looking to
the Lord's Day and Victory; he rejoiced through the crystal of the Church
to see "The Day of the Lord." A book was written by the prophets (Isaiah,
Jeremiah, Ezekiel, Daniel, et al.) all looking to this same event. God's
promise that Abraham's seed should be numerous, was to be fulfilled thro'
Isaac (Genesis 17:4—19; 18:10—15; 21:1—6; 22:1—18; James 2:23). To
Abraham was given the three-fold promise, that his seed should be as:

1. The Dust of the earth
2. The Stars of heaven
3. The Sand by the seashore

---

[1] Ibid, The Holy City, p. 580 ff.

[2] Wordsworth, Ode on Intimations

[3] Alfred Tennyson, Poet Laureate, In Memoriam, st. 131

And each of these three was faith-compelled (Hebrews 11:6), and all are summed up in the statement of John 8:56. The working out of earth's redemption through these three martyr (witnessing) peoples, will be the justification and glory of God (Ephesians 3:9—10; I Corinthians 15:28; Revelation 21:22—24).

1. The *Dust* of the earth (The Nations)
   See this Section FOUR, HIS Story, p. 205 ff.
2. The *Stars* of Heaven[1] (The Church)
   "That in blessing I will bless thee, and in multiplying, I will multiply thy seed as the *stars* of the heaven . . ."

   Genesis 22:17*a*

And,

"I will make thy seed to multiply as *the stars* of the heaven,[1] and will give unto thy seed all these countries; and in the seed shall the nations of the earth bless themselves."

Genesis 26:4 N.

From a few Scriptures (cf. Deuteronomy 1:10; 10:22; I Chronicles 27:23), where reference is made to the "Stars" descendants of Abraham, it would seem that they are associated only with the physical descendants of Abraham, i.e. the nation of Israel. But since Galatians 3:29 definitely calls Christ the Seed of Abraham; and, since Ephesians 1:3; 2:6 and 3:10 state that the Church, the Body of Christ, is "in the heavenlies" in Christ Jesus; then this would indicate that the Church, occupying the *realm* of the stars, is fulfilling the "star" prophecy concerning Abraham's seed in a far greater way than Israel could ever fulfill it.

This "Stars" promise refers to the mystery and the age of grace (Ephesians 3:6—10; Matthew 16:18; I Thessalonians 4:13; Malachi 3:16—18). Today, God's blessing upon the nations is through Abraham's Seed, Christ and His Church (Colossians 1:18), *the stars* of heaven.

> *Spiritual blessings* come to the nations through the preaching of the Gospel and its influence on the life of the nations

> *Earthly blessings* come to the nations through Israel, God's chosen people (Deuteronomy 28:13; 32:8—9; Isaiah 61:6; Numbers 23:9).

The distinctive place of *the Church* in its inheritance in the Kingdom of God is found in I Corinthians 15:50—58.

---

[1] Heaven: Hebrew *dual*

3. The *Sand* Upon the Seashore (Israel)

> "That in blessing I will bless thee, and in multiplying
> I will multiply thy seed as the stars of the heaven, and
> as *the sand* which is upon the sea shore; and thy seed
> shall possess the gate [1] of his enemies;"

Genesis 22:17

The Scriptures up to the coming forth "out of Egypt" is history validated by the Omniscience of Its Author: the history of creation; of the fall; of sin and its working out unto death ("a coffin in Egypt"). The man who at the Call of the Heavens, became God-intoxicated, rose up to forsake all and to follow Him. The large place accorded Abraham comes through the children of his vision ("Dust-Stars-Sand")—that awe-full day of His Gethsemane (Genesis 22:10—18). God's love and respect for Abraham is found in Genesis 26:5, following the confirmation of the covenant with Isaac:

a) "Because that Abraham obeyed My voice"

he understood; he heard intelligently, and he was simple in his obedience to God's voice

b) "Kept My charge"

he kept or hedged about the charge of God as a guard does at a prison

c) "And My commandments"

whether they concerned human relationships or divine orders, Abraham respected both

d) "And My laws"

A law means to point out as if by pointing the finger.

Abraham was faithful in all these things; his children and their children soon departed from such faithfulness and we read, "the law was added because of transgressions" (Galatians 3:19).

The promise of God to Abraham that his seed would be as *the sand,* refers to the nation of Israel. Abraham, Paul,[2] and Daniel saw in visions, the events recorded by Daniel in chapters 9 thro' 12, prophesying that "Seventy Weeks are determined upon thy people" and of the eventual judgment upon the nations at their conclusion. These prophecies point out the likeness of the people of Israel to the indestructible grains of sand [3], and also show us

---

[1] Gate: Matthew 16:18; Revelation 1:18; Hebrews 2:14—16

[2] See II Corinthians 12:1—4; Daniel 12:4, 8—9

[3] See Isaiah 10:22; Hosea 1:10; Romans 9:27

that the "sand" prophecy parallels the visions given to Daniel of the Seventy Weeks, and the Times of the Gentiles.

In Israel, God raised up gifted men ("holy men") to whom He transferred the story of the heavens into human speech, viz. I Samuel 9:9:

> "Before time in Israel, when a man went to inquire of God, thus he spake, 'Come, and let us go to the seer': for he that is now called a Prophet was before time called a Seer'." [1]

Following the flood and the attempt to build Babel, God visited the nations to take out of them a people for His Name whose history is traceable to the present time, becoming more discernible in the events of today to even the unbelieving world. At the birth of Abraham, God began to choose out a peculiar people for His Name's sake through whom He might have a way of approach to *all* nations. They were to be a peculiar people and were given a distinct patrimony of land that has never been completely possessed nor ever withdrawn. The purpose of God through the ages must begin with "to the Jew first," "His chosen people," upon whom as a blackboard, He is working out His Purposes (Isaiah 48:10).

Through Abraham, Palestine and Israel became immortal [2]; and when God fulfills His promise, "the earth shall be full of the knowledge of God as the waters cover the sea," then is God's unceasing love demonstrated to the nation of Israel: Isaiah 65:2; 41:8—9; Romans 10:21; Luke 24:25—44; Acts 3:19—26; Deuteronomy 18:25.

The Jews are proof of God's power to raise the dead; were they not Abraham's seed and was not he "as good as dead" (Hebrews 11:12)? They are as great a demonstration as is the Church today. This is the most satisfying introduction to faith, and Abraham illustrates "the father of the faithful." His blessings are *earthly*, yet future, and not heavenly even though being prepared in heaven (Genesis chaps. 13 and 15; Hebrews 11: 8—16; Romans 4:13; and James 2:23).

In Jeremiah 18:1—10 God gives the basis for His blessings or judgment upon a nation; and here Israel is set forth as that example. The Bible is the record of God's dealings with the nation of Israel:

a) In the past

b) In their present defection as they are set aside during this age (Acts 11:11; Matthew 23:39).

---

[1] *Newberry Bible:* "*Prophet:* one who makes known the mind of God. *Seer:* one who sees visions . . . . A prophet is one who has insight into divine things and speaks for others; to foretell is secondary." P. 223m.

[2] See Section SIX, *The Kingdom Age*, E. The Reign of Righteousness and Peace; or The Millennial Age, 2. Israel Restored; also see Section THREE, *Restoration to Terah*, p. 173 ff.

F. ABRAHAM'S GETHSEMANE

Abraham's Gethsemane is found in Genesis 22:1—18. What was the significance of this time of suffering and testing which he endured?

> "And the angel of the Lord called unto Abraham out of heaven the second time. And said, 'By Myself have I sworn, saith Jehovah Lord, for *because thou hast done this thing, and hast not withheld thy son*, thine only son: That in blessing I will bless thee, and in multiplying I will multiply thy seed as the stars of the heaven, and as the sand which is upon the sea shore; and thy seed shall possess the gate of his enemies; And in thy seed shall all the nations of the earth bless themselves; *because thou hast obeyed My voice*'."
>
> Genesis 22:15—18 N.

Abraham was *willing* to submit to the death test (Hebrews 11:19); and Jesus Christ actually did so (Mark 10:8—9). Isaiah 48:10 says:

> "Behold I have refined thee, but not with silver;
> I have chosen (tried) thee in the furnace of affliction."

Now read in Genesis 15:5—6:

> "And He brought him forth abroad, and said, 'Look now toward the heaven, and tell the stars, if thou be able to number them'; and He said unto him, 'So shall thy seed be.' And he believed in Jehovah Lord; and He *counted* it to him for righteousness."

Comparing "spiritual things with spiritual" we turn to Romans 4:1—3 N.:

> "What shall we say then that Abraham our father, as pertaining to the flesh, hath found?
> "For if Abraham were justified by works, he hath whereof to boast; but not. before God.
> "For what saith the scripture? 'Abraham believed God, and it was *reckoned* unto him unto righteousness'."

And then to Romans 4:19—22 N.:

> "And being not weak in faith, he considered not his own body now dead, when he was about a hundred years old, neither yet the deadness of Sarah's womb;
> "But he staggered not at the promise of God through unbelief; But was strong in faith, giving glory to God;
> "And being fully persuaded that what He had promised, He was able to perform.
> "And therefore it was *reckoned* to him unto righteousness."

In all of these we find that Abraham's faith was *imputed* or *reckoned* unto him for righteousness. But in James 2:21—24 we read:
> "Was not Abraham our father justified *by works, when he had offered Isaac his son upon the altar?*
> "Seest thou that faith wrought with his works, and by works was

made perfect?

"And the scripture was *fulfilled* which saith, 'But Abraham believed God, and it was *reckoned* unto him unto righteousness:' and he was called 'the friend of God.'

"Ye see then how that by works a man is justified, and not by faith only."

Therefore, we conclude that it was not until Abraham's agony on Mt. Moriah that the Scripture was fulfilled which said, "Abraham believed God and it was imputed unto him for righteousness:" and in Hebrews 6:15 we read, ". . . after he had patiently endured, he obtained the promise" (see Hebrews 6:13—18). And then Hebrews 11:17—19 summarizes the events set forth in Genesis 22.

Abraham walked before God, not to save himself but to be where God wanted him to be for new revelations. When he offered his son, and his hand was stayed by the Lord, the ram of sacrifice was found "behind him" because he had not faltered nor loitered in obedience for he always exercised himself to be at the next trysting place. Here Abraham walked on "through the valley of the shadow of death" and became the John the Baptist of the resurrection.

And to conclude we read in Genesis 22:14:

"And Abraham called the name of that place 'Jehovah-Jireh' (Jehovah will provide): as it is said to this day, 'In the mount of Jehovah it shall be seen'."

Since Abraham had seen the vision of Revelation 21:2, it may well be that as a dissolving view, the Holy City arose about him as he stood compassed about on Mt. Moriah (Hebrews 11:10).

CONCLUSION

Abraham "went out not knowing whither he went" but only that he sought a vision. So faith today seeks a vision: "for eye hath not seen"—and "it doth not YET appear." Rather would I die than that the vision fade; my faith is in Christ. There is a breathing from out this Book that calls forth faith from soul-yielding character, as Spring evokes crops, or the little flower of which Tennyson wrote:

"Flower in the crannied wall,
I pluck you our of the crannies,
I hold you here, root and all, in my hand,
Little flower—but IF I could understand,
What you are, root and all, and all in all,
I should know what God and man is."

Abraham is the *plus ultra*; as the palm in the desert by a spring stands forth from its surroundings, so towered this man of God over all other men of faith.

II. THE GROWING CLOUD OF TESTIMONY-BEARERS

The Bible is the purpose-full Book whose longevity and up-to-dateness combined, should cause us to study expectantly. The student of the Word of God should expect "gaps" because of the time covered. Though the Bible was only sixteen hundred years in production, yet it covers at least six thousand years of history. These Scriptures rose quietly like the temple of Solomon (I Kings 6:7), and thus was fitted together the visions and the inspirations which are "An Highway for our God."

> "Concerning which salvation the prophets enquired and searched diligently, who prophesied concerning the grace that should come unto you: Searching into what manner of time the Spirit of Christ which was in them did signify, when He testified beforehand the sufferings pertaining to Christ, and the glories that should follow."

I Peter 1:10—11N.

> "We have also the prophetic word confirmed; whereunto ye do well that ye take heed, as unto a lamp that shineth in a murky place, until the day dawn, and the day star arise in your hearts: Knowing this first, that no prophecy of scripture is its own solution. For the prophecy was not borne at any time by the will of man: but holy men of God spake being borne[1] along by the Holy Spirit."

II Peter 1:19—21N.

Before Him of Whom Isaiah spake, Jeremiah wept a deluge of tears for sinners of all the earth; Ezekiel laid out a temple too large even for the Holy Land; Daniel mapped out the course of Empires ("The Times of the Gentiles") and the ages for Israel; and the Gospels stand apart from all languages and all men: "Behold! The Man." To this end "Holy men spake as they were 'borne along' by the Holy Spirit" to give unto the world (John 3:16) this Book of instruction (II Timothy 3:14—17) — this copy of the things in Heaven. These divine visioners have laid before the eyes of those willing to see the glory of God, their Father, in the Heavenlies.

The era of prophecy is opening; "the seekers after God" are being heard; and heaven's silence is breaking forth into the utterance of hope; "the Desire of all nations" is becoming the concern of the prophetic souls of chosen Israel (Abraham's seed) who began preparing the way of the Lord (Acts 26:22). In all and every emphasis, the *climax* of prophecy is not the *first coming* of Christ, nor the Church, but His *second* and *final* coming at the Day of the Lord. The restoration of Israel in the living generation at the time of the second coming, and the fulfillment of the promises

[1] The late Frank R. Buck of Chicago says: "A careful study of the original text of II Peter 1:20, indicates a probability that Peter's idea was not related to *interpretation* of a prophecy, but to the *source* from which prophecy came. Consider the following literal translation: 'This first understanding, that every prophecy of Scripture occurs not of one's own releasing: for not by will of man was borne along a prophecy at any time, but men being borne along under the Holy Spirit, talked from God'."

M Y Story

made to the nation of Israel through Abraham, will occur *after* the rapture of the Church and at the return of Christ to the earth with the Church when He and His Body shall be united with Israel, His Bride. As our chart indicates, the Day of the Lord lasts one thousand years.

In Hebrews 11:39—40 we are told these "all," (i.e. the saints who are mentioned in Hebrews 11), received not the promise which was given to them through Abraham, and, "God having provided some better thing for us (the Church), that they (the saints) without us should not be made perfect" (complete). Hebrews 12:22—24 introduces again "the City" for which Abraham waited and for which his seed looked with desire (Hebrews 11:10, 16). Following the Day of the Lord, this City comes down from God out of heaven to the new earth and it shall be indwelt by the redeemed of all ages made up of the Church, Israel and the Nations. Here in "the City" shall all the saints (Hebrews 11 *et al*) be made perfect (complete).

God keeps in personal contact with the "Dust-Stars-Sand" descendants of Abraham through the prophets. Through some of these prophets:

  a) He reveals His purpose to the nations
  b) He deals with Israel concerning things of
      immediate importance and also for the future
  c) He speaks to the Church both of things near at hand,
      and of those which are yet future and eternal.

THE PROPHETS OF GOD

In the Scriptures[1] JESUS CHRIST is called PROPHET, PRIEST and KING. The following is a list of *the prophets of God* who are mentioned in the Scriptures (*the false* or *lying prophets* have been omitted). Added to this list could be these *prophetesses*: Miriam (Exodus 15:20); Deborah (Judges 4:4); Huldah (II Kings 22:14); Noadiah (Nehemiah 6:14); Anna (Luke 2:36); and the four daughters of Philip (Acts 21:9).

PROPHET	SCRIPTURE TEXT	Approximate time of Prophecy
Adam	Genesis 3:24; Luke 1:70	4004 B.C.
Abel	Genesis 4:4; Luke 11:50—51	4003
Seth	Genesis 4:25—26	3874
Enoch	Genesis 5:24; Jude 14	3382
Noah	Genesis 6:8—9; II Peter 2:5	2353
Abraham	Genesis 20:7	1921[2]

[1] For the discussion of His fulfilling of these offices, see this Section FOUR, C. 4. *Jesus as Prophet, Priest and King,* p. 259 ff.

[2] Note the interim between the flood and the call of Abraham of about 400 years; Noah died three years before Abraham was born.

Isaac	Luke 13:28; Psalm 105:9—15	1800
Jacob	Genesis 28:12—17; Genesis chap. 49	1760
Joseph	Genesis 41:38—39; 50:24—25; Psalms 81:5	1729
Job	James 5:10—11	1520
Moses	Deuteronomy 34:10	1491
Aaron	Exodus 7:1	1491
Eldad	Numbers 11:26	1490
Medad	Numbers 11:26	1490
Balaam	Numbers 24:2	1452
Joshua	Joshua 6:26; 8 Kings 16:34	1451
Unnamed Prophet	Judges 6:8	1256
Samuel	I Samuel 3:20	1165
Saul	I Samuel 10:1—11	1095
David	Matthew 13:35; Acts 2:30	1063
Gad	I Samuel 22:5	1062
Asaph	II Chronicles 29:30; Psalm 78:2; James 5:10	1040
Jeduthun	II Chronicles 35:15	1040
Nathan	I Kings 1:32	1015
Heman	I Chronicles 25:5	1015
Ahijah	I Kings 11:29	980
Shemiah	II Chronicles 12:5	975
Unnamed prophet	I Kings 13:1, 18 (other one false)	975
Azariah	II Chronicles 15:1, 8	941
Oded	II Chronicles 15:8	941
Hanani	II Chronicles 16:7	940
Jehu	I Kings 16:7	930
Elijah	I Kings 18:22 (Malachi 4:5)	910
One Hundred Prophets of the Lord,	I Kings 18:4	910
Micaiah	I Kings 22:7—8	899
Elisha	II Kings 2:14—15; 6:12	896
Unnamed Prophet	II Kings 9:4	892
Jonah	II Kings 14:25; Jonah 1:1; Matthew 12:39	862
Joel	Joel 1:1; Acts 2:16	800—720
Amos	Amos 7:14	787—898
Hosea	Hosea 1:1; Romans 9:25	785
Isaiah	II Kings 20:11; Isaiah 1:1; Matthew 3:3	760—690
Micah	Jeremiah 26:18; Micah 1:1	750
Nahum	Nahum 1:1	713
Zephaniah	Zephaniah 1:1	640—609
Jeremiah	II Chronicles 36:12; Jeremiah 1:5	629
Habakkuk	Habakkuk 1:1	626
Urijah	Jeremiah 26:20	609
Daniel	Daniel 2:19	603

MY Story

Hananiah	Jeremiah 28:10	596
Azur, father of Hananiah, Jeremiah 28:1		596
Ezekiel	Ezekiel 1:3	595
Obadiah	Obadiah 1	587
Haggai	Ezekiel 6:14; Haggai 1:1	520
Zechariah	Zechariah 1:1	520
Iddo	II Chronicles 12:15; 13:22	458
Malachi	Malachi 1:1	397

Another Interim of 400 years

JESUS CHRIST	Matthew 21:11	1 A.D.
Zacharias	Luke 1:67	7
John the Baptist	Luke 7:28	26
Paul	Acts 9:15; 27:10; 13:9	35
Agabus	Acts 11:27—28; 21:10	42
Judas	Acts 15:32	52
Silas	Acts 15:32	52
Peter	II Peter 3:10—13	66
John	Revelation 1:19; 10:11	96
"My two witnesses"	Revelation 11:3	

The above list of 167 prophets of God reaches beyond this section of the outline and includes those who were in the Church, but they are given here for the purpose of showing the complete line of the prophets of God. For comment on the specific books of the Bible, and especially the writings of some of these prophets, see the sections of this book concerning the *Unsealed* Division (*Genesis* to *Song of Solomon*), and the *Sealed* Division of the Bible (*Isaiah* to *Revelation*).

Abraham's exalted place in Holy Writ is almost paralleled by a like responsibility given to several other prophets used by God to call His chosen people back to Him. The succeeding pages give briefly the stature and character of the specific message of these particular prophets: Moses, David, Elijah and Daniel.

III. MOSES—PROPHET AND LAWGIVER

"Jehovah thy God will raise up unto thee a Prophet from the midst of thee, of thy brethren, like unto me; unto him ye shall hearken;"

Deuteronomy 18:15 N.
(cp. Acts 3:22—26)

Moses, born of the priestly tribe of Levi, nurtured by his Godly mother and father, was brought to the Court of Pharoah's daughter (Exodus 2) where he was educated in the learning and culture of the Egyptians. Here the astronomical knowledge of the day was part of the required education in the court of Pharoah; [1] and "when Moses was grown," God led him thro' the slaying of the Egyptian, out into the land of Midian. What was this Moses doing with his knowledge as "he kept the flock of Jethro his father-in-law" in the Midian wilderness beneath the starry skies with which he was familiar? This was the one place to study and carry on in his knowledge of the stars. Later this learning enabled him to be used of God in establishing a new calendar for the Jewish nation, and in giving to each of the twelve tribes an ensign for each tribal standard[2] out of the twelve signs of the Zodiac. In Exodus 3:1—5, the angel of the Lord spoke unto Moses from the unconsumed burning bush and informed him that the place whereon he stood "IS holy ground,"[3] and that now he must become the readied servant of Jehovah's flock, leading forth the children of Israel out of the hand of Pharoah's bondage. Through this great prophet of the Lord, Israel is called from out the furnace of Egypt (Deuteronomy 4:20; Jeremiah 11:4), into the desert wilderness where God seeks to woo and to win them unto Himself,—"in what a forge, and in what a heat!" Idolatry leads His chosen "wife" aside repeatedly (Acts 7:37—44), but always there is God's merciful promise of restoration again (Hosea 2:14—23).

Because of Abraham's faith,[4] God was able to say, "Out of Egypt have I called My Son"; first, concerning the nation of Israel (Hosea 11:1); and secondly, concerning His Only Begotten Son when He raised Him "from among the dead ones" (Romans 1:4; Matthew 2:15; Acts 13:33); and this Son broke the bars of death and "brought life and immortality to light through the Gospel" (II Timothy 1:10).

Abraham was the father of that nation born out of the Egyptian womb, "a nation born in a day" (Isaiah 66:8 A.S.V.). The book of Genesis which began with the words "In the beginning" closes with the words "a coffin in Egypt." Israel went down into Egypt and died there as a family, but was reborn as a nation. And God calls His son Israel out of Egypt (Hosea 11:1). Later when Jesus was a child (like Israel), He too was called out of Egypt (Matthew 2:15), but the Scriptures are clear in indicating that it was after He came out of the "Egypt" of the grave (Psalm 2:7; Acts 13:33; Hebrews 1:5), that God said, "Thou art my son, this day have I begotten thee."

How great was the love of Moses for his beloved people is revealed

---

[1] See Appendix, *Zodiac*, (Dr. Seyfarth, p.614); (p.612—617, 625 ff.)

[2] *Ibid.*, p. 633—634

[3] See Section THREE, HIS Story, II. *Eden, God's Workshop*, p. 177 ff.

[4] This Section, E. *Abraham's Gethsemane*, p. 230

in the heart-ache of Exodus 32:31—32:

> "And Moses returned unto Jehovah, and said, 'Oh, this people
> have sinned a great sin, and have made them gods of gold.
> Yet now, If Thou wilt forgive their sin—;[1] and if not, blot
> me, I pray Thee, out of Thy book which Thou hast written'."

And we are reminded of another who loved his brethren according to the
flesh, even the apostle Paul when he said:

> "For I could wish that I myself were accursed from Christ
> for my brethren, my kinsmen, according to the flesh:"

> Romans 9:3

The love for Israel reflected in the lives of these men, helps us to understand God's great love for these same people.

The loneliness of Moses is seen in his great desire to see the *way*
and the *glory* of God (Exodus 33:13—18), and following his forty days and
forty nights in the Mount with the Lord, the glory of that experience shone
from his face so that upon descending from the Mount, he placed a veil
over his face that the children of Israel might approach him.

Moses asserts and raises the expectancy of the Coming One; in Hebrews 11:27 we read that Moses "endured as seeing Him Who is invisible,"
and for his endurance, he is permitted to appear with Elijah in the presence
of Christ Himself (Luke 9:28—31). Though not permitted to set foot in the
land of promise while in his flesh, yet now, clothed in the splendor of
God's glory, he stands within that land at the Transfiguration;—and a bit
more is revealed unto us of how great a place Moses holds in the purpose
of God.

The earthly history of this "Sand" nation makes incidental reference
to the nations that touched them as in *Exodus, Chronicles* and elsewhere.
The children of Abraham went down into Egypt which is a symbol of death,
but they came forth a nation welded into an united nation and life.

The Bible is replete with the record of God's continual efforts to
redeem Israel and all men from the grasp of Satan (Ezekiel 18:24; 33:11;
Job 1:5—6 and 22; Job 42:9; James 5:10—11). And so this Israel, God's
example on earth, stands over all political groups at the head of his class
for all men to see: *a)* He is close-sealed

                         b) The Bible is his Book

                         c) And Israel's Promised Land is God's Workshop
                              (Ezekiel 28:13) wherein He led, warned, loved
                              and promised them through His prophets.

---

[1] Note here that this sentence in Scripture, is one of the very few incomplete sentences
of the Bible. Moses, so full of emtoion and concern for his people and their forgiveness,
could only implore that the memory of him might otherwise just be blotted out; "O love,
that wilt not let me go."

A portion of this continual effort for Israel's redemption, is seen in David:

<pre>
                        (THE SWEET SINGER
IV. DAVID, THE PROPHET (IN ISRAEL
                        (THE SHEPHERD—KING
</pre>

As the Gospel was preached before unto Abraham, in like manner was the death, burial and resurrection of the Lord revealed to David. There is a redundancy of prophetic expression for Israel and the Church in this God-breathed volume—*The Psalms*.[1] God's promise to Moses had been that He would raise up a Prophet like unto him; but unto David, God covenants to make his kingdom an everlasting kingdom. Through Nathan the prophet, He speaks to David saying:

> ". . . Thus saith Jehovah of hosts, I took thee from the sheep-fold, from following the sheep, to be ruler over My people, over Israel:"

> II Samuel 7:8N.
> (Cp. Psalm 78:70—72)

And concerning David's seed, He said in verses 12 through 16:

> ". . . I will establish his kingdom. He shall build a house for My name, and I will stablish the throne of his kingdom to Me for a son. If he commit iniquity, I will chasten him with the rod of men, and with the stripes of the children of men: But My loving-kindness shall not depart away from him, as I took it from Saul, whom I put away before thee. And thine house and thy kingdom shall be established for ever."

In Psalm 89:20—37 the immutability of the covenant with God unto David is again stated. Though Israel forsakes God's laws, judgments, statutes and commandments, and He punishes them, yet He will not allow His "faithfulness to fail" in keeping the covenant which He had made with David:

> *a)* In Luke 1:30—33 the renewal of this covenant is given to Mary, a descendant of David
>
> *b)* In the first gospel sermon preached, David is quoted as a prophet

---

[1] Note these:

Psalm 2:1–2, 6–12	Psalm 8:2–6	Psalm 16:8–11	Psalm 18:4–6
18:4–6,	22:1, 6–8, 12–18, 22–23, 27–31	27:12	23
24:7–10	27:12	30:3	31:5
34:20	35:7, 11–12, 15, 21	40:6–8	41:5,9,10
45:6–7, 11	50:3–6	56:5	68:18
69:8–9, 21	71:10	78:2	89:4
89:26–29, 36, 45	90:1–2	102:2–4, 25	110:1–7
117:1	11F 19, 22–23, 25	132:12	

of God foretelling the resurrection
(Acts 2:25—31; Romans 1:3—4; II Timothy 2:8)

c) In Acts 13:22—40, Paul in proclaiming the gospel refers to:

". . . the promise which was made unto the fathers, God hath
fulfilled the same unto us, their children, in that He raised up
Jesus: as it is also written in the second psalm, 'Thou art My
Son, this day have I begotten Thee.' And as concerning that
He raised Him up from among the dead ones, no more to return
to corruption, He said on this wise, 'I will give you the sure
mercies (kindnesses) of David'." (Acts 13:32—34; Revelation
1:18; Isaiah 22:22)

These Scriptures show us that "the sure mercies of David" *included*
the promise of the resurrection of Christ. The fulfillment of the covenant
to David was not *completed* at the resurrection or the ascension of Jesus,
for in Acts 2:33 we read that He is exalted at the *right hand of God* and
in Revelation 3:21, He is seated on *His Father's (God's) throne.* It yet
remains for Him to occupy the throne of *His father David* (Luke 1:32) and
establish His Kingdom (Jeremiah 23:5; Ezekiel 34:23—24; Hosea 3:4—5).
The *fulfillment* of God's promise to David is seen in the return of Christ
to the earth when He establishes His Kingdom in Jerusalem and reigns
over all the earth (II Peter 1:1; Revelation 11:15*b* and 19:16; Zechariah
14:4, 9, 16; and I Corinthians 15:24—28).

V. ELIJAH, THE TISHBITE

"The grandest and most romantic character
that Israel ever produced."

Robert Young, LL.D.
Analytical Concordance

The ministry of Elijah the prophet to the nation of Israel, was a most
effective and dramatic ministry; he dealt with the great need for righteousness in God's holy people, the Israelitish nation of that day. Like Enoch
of old, Elijah did not see death but was translated (II Kings 2:11) and on
the wings of a whirlwind took flight into heaven. Elijah's next appearance
in the Word is on the Mount of Transfiguration, in the company of Moses,
and in the Presence of Jesus. Both Moses and Elijah conversed with Him
about His forthcoming departure "which He was about to accomplish at
Jerusalem" (Luke 9:31).

Then we have in Malachi 4:5—6, the definite, future commission of
Elijah which was carried out for the first time by John the Baptist who
came "in the spirit and power of Elijah" (Luke 1:17), but who was rejected
by Israel (Matthew 11:10—14). Because of this rejection, Elijah himself
shall yet come again before the *great* and *dreadful* day (Malachi 4:5*b*)—

or *notable* day (Gr. *Epiphanes*, Acts 2:20)—of the Lord. The orthodox Jew of today, reserves an empty chair for Elijah at the Passover Feast which he celebrates each year. Because of the language used in Revelation 11:3—6, one of the two witnesses described here, may be Elijah fulfilling the prophecy of Malachi 4:5.

VI. DANIEL—PROPHET[1] and STATESMAN

> ". . . Fear not, Daniel: for from the first day that thou didst set thine heart to understand, and to humble thyself before thy God, thy words were heard, and I am come for thy words."
>
> Daniel 10:12N.

Daniel is the most human of personalities in the Old Testament. Other prophets uttered their messages (Ezekiel 8:27; 10:2—3, 8—9, 17), but with no agony of prayers, confession of sins, or sleepless nights. Whatever he writes will be of great importance; it is both sane and beyond question. No other prophet was a statesman; "another king arose that knew not Joseph," but this is never said of Daniel. Even Joseph and Isaiah were but advisors to kings, but "in the fulness of the times" when there arose a world empire with a devout king, then: "there was a man sent from God whose name was Daniel" and within the framework of his book of prophecy, is contained the unfolding of "The Divine Plan of the Ages."

Daniel's character demonstrates the background and homelife from which he had come. The first chapter, verse 8, relates that Daniel "purposed in his heart that he would not defile himself . . . ." And this lad so nurtured with these homely virtues, reflecting the mother's face, stood unabashed before the face of the king. Nebuchadnezzar's specification for these young men who were to serve him, drafted the very best that motherhood could provide (as Cornelia provided for the training of her sons, The Gracchi[1]), and the face of this young man Daniel, mirrored

---

[1] See also *Sealed Division*, I. Isaiah to Malachi, A. 4. The Prophecy of Daniel, p. 37.

[2] Cornelia, the famous mother of Tiberius and Gaius Gracchus, was one of the many influential Roman women who helped to make Roman history so different from Greek; she was the daughter of the ruler Scipio Africanus. Since her sons' father died at an early age, it was Cornelia's ambition to make her two "Jewels" worthy of her glorious name. Accordingly she employed the most eminent of Greek tutors for them; training them in Greek oratory to declaim in praise of liberty and tyrannicides; and in Greek history and political science, to divine constitutions up into monarchies, aristocracies and democracies; and to believe that in the latter, all power belongs to the people. From this background of training, these men grew to be determined opponents of the capitalists and the unjust, merciless aristocracy of Rome in that day. Both Tiberius and Gaius became tribunes in Rome and both championed the cause of the common people and the agrarian law. These two great Roman reformers fell victims to foul play and were each brutally murdered in the Roman forum. The policy of Gaius Gracchus, was eventually adopted by Rome after a century of unceasing bloodshed.

something of the Divine.

Consider how great was this Daniel who for seventy years, walked unafraid amid kings, bending them to his will: he was chaplain to Nebuchadnezzar; a rebuker to Belshazzar; a Prime Minister to Darius; and an exegete to King Cyrus. The Wise Men of the East who came following the birth of Jesus were from the School of Astronomy founded by Daniel (Daniel 1:19—20; 5:11—12).

From interpreter of dreams to kings, this Daniel becomes the redactor of God for inspired Prophets (9:23—24). As Paul revealed the Mystery in the church epistles, so Daniel held his spirit steadily up before the Triune God, and the plan of God for the "Seventy Weeks determined upon *thy people* and upon *thy holy city*," is unraveled and is laid upon chapter 9. Just as a prism imperiously saws a beam of sunlight and spreads it over a spectrum, Daniel's Seventy Weeks' prophecy becomes the spectrum whereon all prophecy unerringly "goes to its own place." Daniel saw no sign of slightest desire in the people of the captivity for the hardship of return to their homeland, and so gave himself to prayer and supplication before God, to move heaven for His people; and for this similitude of Gethsemane in Daniel's life, his prayer of confession (Daniel 9:3—19) before God, that: "to us belongeth confusion of faces, to our kings, to our princes, and to our fathers, because we have sinned against Thee,"—for this imploring solicitation of God's mercy for "Thy City" and "Thy people,"— whilst yet praying, he was confronted by the angel Gabriel (Daniel 9:20— 21). Daniel's transition was from men to angels; his soul's anabasis went from ancient Babylon to the New Jerusalem. Visited by the angels both Michael and Gabriel (8:13), this man was the only one to whom it was told:

> "But go thou thy way till the end: for thou shalt
> rest, and stand in thy lot at the end of the days."

Daniel 12:13 N.

Following the close of *Malachi*, there are four hundred years when no prophet's voice is heard but with the coming of Zacharias (Luke 1:76), we are brought to Him of Whom the prophets wrote, and who Himself said:

> "Search the scriptures;
> for in them *ye* think ye have eternal life:
> and *they* are they which testify concerning Me.'

John 5:39 N.

VII. THE LORD JESUS CHRIST

"What should we say if we were to be asked to review the biography of a public man and were to discover that less than half of the book was devoted to his active career, and more than half of it, to the circumstances of his birth, his death, and his funeral? We should be driven

to one of two conclusions: either that the author had been guilty of a
deplorable failure in a sense of proportion or that there was something
wholly exceptional in the very being of the man—a something in what
he was and what he suffered,—that was greater even than what he said
or did. *That is precisely the impression created by the record of Christ.*

"If we take an ordinary copy of the Bible, we find that the four Gospels cover about one hundred sixty columns of print. Of this space, a
rough calculation indicates that about fifteen columns are devoted to
the earliest period, ending with the Baptism and Temptation; thirty-
two columns to a few weeks between the Transfiguration and the Entry
into Jerusalem; and fifty-five columns or more than a third of the entire
record, to the Death, Resurrection and Ascension. Out of one hundred
sixty columns, *this leaves only sixty or less than half the total narrative for the whole of the Thousand Days.*

"The upbringing of our Lord, and even His ministry, though full of
profound significance, were no more, therefore, than an intermediate
scene in the drama that began with His birth, and reached its climax
on Calvary. This life, so full of fascinating word and deed, was a
prelude to something more wonderful, if that be possible, than itself.
The life was wholly love. But as Jesus Himself taught us, the greatest
love is life laid down. The three and thirty busy years, spent chiefly
in Galilee, were a preparation for the Three Hours on the Cross and
the Three Days in the Tomb."[1]

> "Let this mind be in you, which was also in Christ Jesus: Who,
> being in the form of God, thought it not a thing to be grasped at,
> to be equal with God: but emptied Himself, took the form of a bond
> servant, and was made in the likeness of men: And being found
> in fashion as a man, He humbled Himself, and became obedient
> unto death, even the death of the cross. Wherefore God also hath
> highly exalted Him, and gave Him a name which is above every
> name: that at the name of Jesus every knee should bow, of things
> in heaven, and things on earth, and things under the earth; And
> that every tongue should confess, that Jesus Christ is Lord, to
> the glory of the Father."
>
> Philippians 2:5—11 N.

A. THE PRE-EXISTENCE and DEITY of THE LORD

JESUS CHRIST

> If Jesus Christ is a Man—
> And only a Man—I say
> That of All Mankind I cleave to Him
> And to Him, will I cleave alway.
>
> ————————
>
> If Jesus Christ is a God—
> And the only God—I swear

---

[1]
See Philip Whitesell Wilson, *"Is Christ Possible"* (Revell 1932) pp. 80—81

I will follow Him through Heaven and Hell,
The Earth, the Sea, the Air. [1]

Mount Shasta rises up like the Old Testament and as we look upon it, we are told to "Behold! Him of whom Moses and the prophets did write." Browning's Pearl Diver [2] plunges into the sea, a pauper, and emerges a Prince;—so even I plunge into the Scriptures and arise, speaking with Thomas, the apostle, "My Lord and My God," and I possess the Pearl of Great Price.

Jesus Christ is the Son of Man and the Son of God. He said, "the works that I do, bear witness." Tennyson used words as garments of thought which others had not seen, and for this he was knighted; that is, he was taken up among the elect. The ceremony of the king and his court did not make, but rather revealed his genius. So the Lord's use of nature revealed His Deity and they said, "What manner of man is this that even the wind and the sea obey Him." Language and genius are common to all civilized nations, yet it remained for four obscure men to produce The Lord's biography; and even with this as copy to follow, none attained unto His stature. His oratory (John 7:46), His works (John 5:36), and His pre-vision (Luke 2:52), classify Him as Divine. All of my ministry I have preached Him and He has met my every need; "Lo, I come to do Thy will," and to set the standard, the copy, and to complete and to restore—wherein we come short.

"For as the Father hath life in Himself; so hath He
given also to the Son to have life in Himself."

John 5:26 N.

Christ is God-extended. God is visible in Christ (Hebrews 1:2; John 24:9). The effulgence of His Glory was veiled except at the Transfiguration; just as Moses' face shone when descending from the Mount, and was then veiled; and in Christ we see the "exact expression," the stamp, seal or writing of God upon flesh. There are rare moments when a veil is lifted for an instant; so God in the Bible at times, lifts the veil and we catch a glimpse of His glory. Jesus said, "no man hath seen God at any time"— for an instant; so God in the Bible, at times lifts the veil and we catch a glimpse of His Glory. Jesus said, "no man hath seen God at any time"— only My Body hath he seen.

MAN has a :

	Nature	Person	and	Personality
GOD is a :	Father	Son	and	Holy Spirit

---

[1] Richard Watson Gilder, *"The Song of The Heathen,"* (Boston, Houghton Mifflin Co.)

[2] Robert Browning, *Paracelus,* (N.Y. Thomas Y. Crowell & Company, 1835). Part I, *Paracelus Aspires,* line 827 ff.

BOTH God ·and Man are :

    a Nature   a Person   and   a Personality

The

CENTRES of Being are :

    Father   Son   and   Holy Spirit

Where did the New Testament writers get this so far in advance? "Not from, by, nor through man" but from God! (I Thessalonians 5:24; Galatians 1:11—12). The very nature of the Universe is at its heart; there is a Triune God, else man is not in His image. Christ is the key or door to all in both worlds; you may go anywhere and apply Him, and the secret unfolds.

Christ is the divine parable (Hebrews 1:1—8; John 1:1—14; 14:9, 12, 20); and Mark 4:30 is the test, as this "I AM";

    This Parable of God
      This Source of the new creation
        This Frame (form) of the Universe—
        ALL transfer the glory of God (Psalm) 19).

Is there a moral equivalent to fit into that frame? or an occupant to adorn the setting? (II John 1—3 cp. with Genesis 2:7 *formed* and *breathed;* cp. Ezekiel 37:7—8, 10 *breath;* John 14:1—2; John 3:7; II Corinthians 5:7). We are looking for new heavens and a new earth (II Peter 3:13). All this is "in Christ" (Hebrews 2:10; Ephesians 1:23). Colossians 1:17—19 shows that Christ is Jehovah of the God and in Him all "the fulness" dwells. In I Corinthians 15:28 Christ turns over all things to the Father "that God may be all in all." His part and power in the God-head is also seen in Hebrews 1:3

    "Let any name be uttered, whatever it is,
        Christ is above it;
    He is more exalted than that which the
        name affirms."
                Meyer

In Philippians 2:9—11 we see the prominence given to the name of Jesus. Before and after the "*Katabole*" time and during Psalm 138:2; John 6:44—45; Matthew 28:19—20; Acts 9:6. Through all we see the exalted place of Him, the Word of God. God as the Father *begets;* God as the Son *redeems*; and God as Spirit *comforts, seals*; the result is a Spiritual Body through the Church.

When Pilate said, "Behold the man!" the mob cried out, "Crucify Him"; but when God says, "Behold!"—then "the inhabitants of Jerusalem shall mourn for Him" (Zechariah 12:10). He is the Wonder-Man; He is the only wholly natural Man who is redeeming this sordid segment of an otherwise clean universe. He fits into the frame of the original as "The Stone which the builders rejected which is become the head of the corner." He Himself alone is perfect and restores the lost horizon. Time blots out lesser and seeming important ones who but the more immortalize Him. Only He fits into the God-man and also into "The God Man," and fills out Ephesians 4:1—16 and Colossians 1:17. Those who "debunk" Him, have not touched Him. Other characters are dimmed by time, but He "grows brighter"; more majestic; more sublime; and more radiant. The Great High, Mighty God in Him makes rational to us the afore-mentioned prophecies, beginnings and hopes. It is upon this Jesus as God that we focus our attention. He is the *pro* ("before," John 1:3), and He is the One *apo* ("from above," Colossians 1:18), and He is "The Beloved in the three great Personalities of Father, Son and Holy Spirit."

B. THE INCARNATION OF JESUS CHRIST

"Behold, the virgin shall conceive,
and bear a son, and shall call his
name Immanuel" (God with us).

Isaiah 7:14

Though our *Isaiah* text calls the Savior "Immanuel," the Gospels record His name as Jesus; *Jesus* is His sacred and saving name, and *Christ* is His official title.

The Incarnation put the Savior on our side, for "it behooved Him to be conformed unto His brethren," and, He "was found in fashion as a man," and "clothed Himself with man." The Incarnation was to make love visible and vocal (I John 4:16). The "other Scriptures" are thought-incarnations where God is speaking and doing; they are not topical but deistical; God is constant and omnipresent (James 1:17).

The Four Gospels each peculiarly set forth His Incarnation:

In *Matthew*:
(He is born *King of the Jews*; Isaiah 40:9;
(Matthew 2:1—2; John 1:11; Matthew 23:39
(He is the prophecy of John 1:45
(His prophecy (John 1:14) yields to Personality
(as seen in Haggai 2:7; Matthew 2:2; 3:17;
(John 19:5

In *Mark*:
(He is the *Servant* of God (Isaiah 53:1—3)
(He is called "My Servant" of Isaiah 42:1
(There is no genealogy given concerning Him,
(but He is a Wonder Worker

In *Luke*:
(He is the *Great Physician* (Luke 4:16—23)
(He is a Son given (loaned) in Isaiah 9:6
(and John 3:13

(He is *"The Way, The Truth, and The Life"*
(Here is set forth the Age of Grace
(Isaiah 40:9, John 1:29—36
In *John*:
(This seems to cover also Paul's ministry
(as suggested in Acts 9:15, 15:7 and 28:28
(The Word became flesh; this is the key to the
(Scriptures of John 1:14; Psalm 19:1 and John 5:39

His Incarnation fits each promise, prophecy and description of the Old Testament, and each one opens, just like a Yale lock, so that we are enabled to see God (John 14:9 and 19:5; Matthew 27:54 and John 20:28). *Believers* by faith saw, and they still see; *Unbelievers* will be forced to acknowledge Him (Revelation 1:7 and Matthew 23:39).

Here is a reverent suggestion as to the Incarnation of the Christ Child: the barrier between God and man arose out of "the desire of the flesh," and still the curse and penalty inhere within; the only way to remove the barrier is to redeem man.

The journey of Jesus' ministry was from the manger to the Cross, and like the river Jordan which ends apparently in the Dead Sea, so the Cross of death apparently ends all; this shakes even the apostles in its apparent culmination; but just as scientists today reveal to us that the mineral wealth of Palestine was being removed by the Jordan River without observation and is continuously deposited into the Dead Sea;—just so today, Christians are being called out without observation into the Body of Christ; and that which seems to culminate in death upon the Cross—instead rises up and brings wealth untold!

The word "seed" used in Galatians 3 is masculine, and not neuter. "The Law" was the seed-bin in which the seed was carried till the "fulness of the time." Israel was but the productive shield about the sperm; the roots were in Abraham and the stem in Israel. How else can we understand these significant words of John 1:14:

"And the Word:

to Abraham and to all the prophets;

"Became:

of its own will;

"Flesh:

The Everlasting Gospel brooding over chaos of inchoate humanity, in "fulness of time," arrived at the place of incarnation;

"And dwelt among us, and we:
> who could not grasp the fulness of the words
> of prophecy "for our eyes were holden";

"Beheld His glory."

This "Word"—this genealogy of "The Seed,"—stirs our emotions and moves us to emulation; it compels aspirings, for "it doth not yet appear."

1. The Incarnation: "A Child is Born; A Son is Given"

The Incarnation just had to be; for God and man were in alienation and each was hungering for the other. The heathen-pagan rites were propitiatory and the Tabernacle sacrifices were vicarious. This separation of the divine and the human is only healed by a perfect agent, a Person. Therefore, of all plans, the virgin birth alone could have met the requirement and produced such a life.

> "For unto us a child is born,
> Unto us a son is given;
> And the government shall be upon His shoulder;
> And His name shall be called Wonderful, Counsellor,
> The Mighty God, The Father of eternity,
> The Prince of Peace."

> Isaiah 9:6 N.

"Unto us a child is born"—"born king of the Jews" (Matthew 2:2—but He is rejected by the Nation and is still rejected by them; but He will yet be received by them, fulfilling Matthew 23:39, Acts 3:21, and Acts 28:28. A child came to give to Israel. He was the king of the Jews and they killed Him for they would "not have this man to reign over" them. They killed Him and the kingdom is put in abeyance but God took Him back into heaven. This phrase "a child is born" is used with reference to Jesus and His earthly ministry. The next phrase "unto us a son is given" ("loaned"), refers to His saving power as the Son of God, and refers to the coming of Jesus as the Head of the Church. He is the Son loaned because His stay on earth was temporary and He was taken back at His ascension to be with the Father.

> "A child is born"—and they rejected the child;
> "A son is given"—and the Son is taken back.

As the child of Mary, His earthly parent, He was rejected; and as the Son of God, His heavenly parent, He is taken back, and is glorified again. In John 1:1 the Greek for "word" is "*logos*." It is a one-way word which goes out. It was not idle writing which caused John to change from the

248

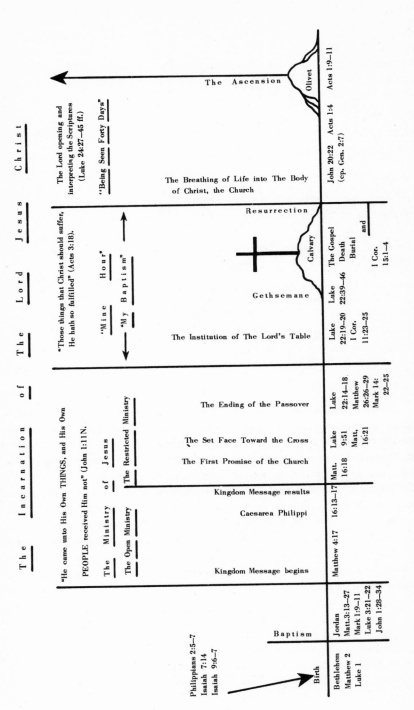

The Incarnation of The Lord Jesus Christ

The Ascension
Olivet
Acts 1:9–11

The Lord opening and interpreting the Scriptures (Luke 24:27–45 ff.)

"Being Seen Forty Days"

The Breathing of Life into The Body of Christ, the Church

John 20:22 Acts 1:4
(cp. Gen. 2:7)

Resurrection

"Those things that Christ should suffer, He hath so fulfilled" (Acts 3:18).

Calvary

The Gospel
Death Burial and

I Cor.
15:1–4

Luke
22:39–46

"Mine Hour"

"My Baptism"

Gethsemane

The Institution of The Lord's Table

Luke
22:19–20
I Cor.
11:23–25

The Ministry of Jesus

The Restricted Ministry

"He came unto His Own THINGS, and His Own PEOPLE received Him not" (John 1:11N.

The Ending of the Passover

Luke
22:14–18.
Matthew
26:26–29
Mark 14:
22–25

The Set Face Toward the Cross

Luke
9:51
Matt,
16:21

The First Promise of the Church

Matt.
16:18

Kingdom Message results

Matt. 16:13–17

Caesarea Philippi

The Open Ministry

Kingdom Message begins

Matthew 4:17

Baptism

Jordan
Matt.3:13–27
Mark 1:9–11
Luke 3:21–22
John 1:28–34

Birth

Bethlehem
Matthew 2
Luke 1

Philippians 2:5–7
Isaiah 7:14
Isaiah 9:6–7

word *logos* in the first chapter to "son" in the latter part; (from John 1:14 to the change in John 1:18, 34, 49, 51); for the *logos* goes out *from* the Father and the Son goes back *to* the Father, thus making the complete circuit. The Universe has a goal; not like science which is empty and frozen without a goal. "The goal" is *back* to the Father (Romans 8); and John 1:14 *logos* was going out *from* the Father; and John 1:14—15, 17, is the picture of the Son who carries creation *back* to the Father.

2. The Incarnation: Emmanuel

The enormous condescension of the Almighty God in "The Word became flesh and dwelt among us and we beheld His glory"—"that which we have seen with our eyes and our hands have handled"—has so god-ized the very soil of Palestine that it remains "holy land" demonstrating "My thoughts are not your thoughts nor My ways your ways" (Isaiah 55:8—9).

The word "Emmanuel" of John 3:16, II Peter 1:21, and I Peter 1:10—12: "The Word was *made* flesh" (Matthew 16:17; John 6:44); and "the Word *became* flesh" for a purpose greater than within the power of words. This is Emmanuel even the Word that *took on* flesh and dwelt among us, even the Christ who said, "he that hath seen Me hath seen My Father"; also, "I and the Father are one." The elements of the Scriptures are so mixed in Him that the Bible might stand up and say, "This is THE Man of whom Moses and all the prophets did write" (Luke 24; Hebrews 2 and Acts 3:24).

3. The Incarnation: The Virgin Birth

In the Incarnation Genesis 3:15 and John 3:16 come together in the "seed of the woman"; prophesied also by Isaiah concerning the virgin (Isaiah 7:14), the mother of Emmanuel. Micah wrote of His birth place Bethlehem. He was begotten of God, but "born of a woman"; and as the suffering servant, He is revealed in Isaiah 53.

The Scriptural record of the virgin birth gives meticulous and minute proof of its divine origin:

    a) in its *biological* accuracy

    b) in the *textual dexterity,* avoiding errors and inconsistencies

    c) in the *nobility* of language

    d) in the *chasteness* of recital

    e) in the *elevated emotion* of re-action

    f) and in the *exquisite spiritual* beauty.

All of these, "and how much more," combine in such consistent evidence as to make doubt a moral bias rather than a mental attitude. Some there be who would say that there is no need whatever for a "virgin" birth,[1]

---

[1] See Revised Standard Version, *"maiden"* Isaiah 7:14, or use of *"descendant"* for "seed" (Galatians 3:16), "and to thy *the* seed (Christ).

because of their implicit belief in "The Brotherhood of Man"; unto all such the sense of sin and the need for a new birth are absent; rather, man in his thoughtful and self-inspecting mood, would have invented some supernatural, climactic event in order to account for Him;—"but God," whose ways are not our ways, fulfilled prophecy in the *virgin* birth, for, in the words of Theodore Parker, "It takes a God to forge a God."

There are two comings of the virgin born Son of God, set forth with meticulous detail in the Scriptures (Revelation 9:12—21, 11:7—19, Matthew 24:15, Daniel 9!27):

At the first coming:
(He is the Messiah of Israel of Isaiah 53
(He is the seed of the woman
(He is the descendant of Abraham, Isaac
(and Jacob
(He is born in Bethlehem; grown to man-
(hood in Nazareth
(His Messiahship fulfills to the letter the
(prophecies made concerning Him.

At His second coming:
(He is the Savior of all that believe.
(He is set forth with like vividness of detail
(as that of His first coming, especially in
(the book of Revelation

Spanning the second interim of four hundred years[1] when "no prophet's voice was heard" from the voice of Malachi to the voice of Zechariah heard in Luke 1:67 ff., comes the fulfilling of prophecy in the birth of Jesus (the loaning of a Son), born of a virgin, and cared for as an infant.

Mary's child was the "seed of the woman" that bruised the head of the serpent. The Wise Men came saying, "where is He that is *born* King of the Jews for we have seen His Star." And that child is the Messiah, Son of David, *born of a woman* in Bethlehem of Judea.

> "Sacrifice and offering Thou wouldest not,
> But a *body* hast Thou prepared Me:"
> Hebrews 10:5*b*

Mary did not prepare that *Body*; she gave birth to a child, a king; but in *Isaiah* we read, "unto us a child is born, a *son is given*." These are two different words and we should read "a son is loaned" for He was taken back. The only place that "a body" could be prepared for *Christ's spiritual body* was in the *life of Christ*. And, in the "council at Jerusalem" in the Upper Room following His resurrection, "He breathed on them and

---

[1] See list of prophets this Section pp. 233—235

saith . . . 'receive ye Holy Spirit, whose soever sins ye remit, they have already been remitted . . .'." (John 20:22—24 N.)

4. The Incarnation and The Gospel

"The Gospel" is in flesh.[1] If there is no Incarnation, there can be no Gospel. In the flesh is wrought out "The Lamb slain from" (John 1:1—2 and Revelation 13:8); and Psalm 90:1—2 reveals to us the existence and the everlasting need of God. In Genesis 1:26 in the phrase "let us make man," we see the Presence of God, Christ and the Holy Spirit at work in the creation of man. In Isaiah 55:8 through 11, we find the description of the contrast between the nature of God and of man. When Jesus came, He left His glory behind in the realm of God, but He brought to earth God's nature in the flesh (Philippians 2:5—11). In John 1:14 is set forth this same truth; Jesus said, "search the Scriptures . . . they testify of Me" (John 1:1; Acts 7:38; Revelation 13:8; I John 4:12; Revelation 2:13, 20).

The good Father in His divine wisdom, opened and closed this Word of His Grace Salvation in words of our language:

"In a beginning was the Word, and the Word was with God . . .
"Without Him was not anything created . . .
"And this Word became flesh and dwelt among us,
and *we* beheld His Glory . . .
"And He that hath seen Me, hath seen the Father."

John 1:1 ff.

And Jesus Himself said, "I came that (Gr. *hina*) they may have life, and have abundance" (John 10:10 A.S.V.). By precept and example, He continued by the enduement of the Holy Spirit who had been upon Him, and upon those He had chosen and trained, God's revelation was continued unto the purposed end. His last word was "The Book of the Revelation of Jesus Christ which God gave unto Him to show unto His servants," which He sent through the one most like unto Himself, even John the Beloved, and accompanied the same by many signs.

5. The Soul of Two Cities: Bethlehem and Jerusalem

The abundance of life which Jesus came to give, prefaces our daily choices in life; and the contrast is more easily seen in the soul of two cities of Palestine: Bethlehem and Jerusalem. David longingly said, "Oh that one would give me drink of the water of the well of Bethlehem . . ."

---

[1] *Gospel* (Gr. *Euaggelion*). The word *euaggelion* is used by the Septuagint for the Hebrew word *besorah*, from Hebrew *basar*, "flesh" as representing some good thing in *bodily* reality, and so very descriptive of the good tidings of Emmanuel, God manifest in the flesh (I Timothy 3:16). (Chr. Wordsworth, D.D. *The Introduction and Notes on the New Testament* (London, Rivingtons, MDCCCLXXXIL, Vol. I, p. 1

(I Chronicles 11:17); and the Lord cried out in respect of the Eternal City:

> "O Jerusalem, Jerusalem, thou that killest the prophets, and stonest them which are sent unto thee, how often would I have gathered thy children together, even as a hen gathereth her chickens under her wings, and ye would not!"

> Matthew 23:37

BETHLEHEM	JERUSALEM
a) Kept the Passover Lambs	a) Kept the Law
b) The shepherds worshiped at the birth of Jesus	b) The King knew not of the birth of Jesus though he was a steward of Messiah's throne
c) Appeals to the heart	c) Appeals to the intellect
d) Above this city shone the Star which the Wise Men found again after leaving the city of Jerusalem	d) Above this city the Star eclipsed; where the Wise Men became as the man of Bethsaida who was told: "go *not* into the city" after he had been given a second treatment for his blindness.

The contrast of the souls of these two cities is seen in the simplicity and faith of Bethlehem, and the ambitious aspirings for noble standing and and political gain in Jerusalem.

> Howe'er it be, it seems to me,
> 'Tis only noble to be good.
> Kind hearts are more than coronets,
> And simple faith than Norman blood.[1]

So each makes a choice: going either through Bethlehem or via Jerusalem.

6. The Light of The World

Jehovah is the un-obligated God who took upon Himself the flesh encased Deity. By His Name *Jehovah* He was not known even to Abraham (Exodus 6:3), but Jesus "beginning at Moses showed them all things in the Book concerning Himself" (Luke 24:44, Revelation 5:1). He said, "Before Abraham was, I AM" (Proverbs 30:4; Revelation 19:12, 13:8)— "and shall call His Name Immanuel" (Isaiah 7:14). When the great "I AM" was incarnated in the Lord Jesus Christ and entered into our life, did He come as "A Man Without a Country?" Or did He come to mock our deepest aspirations? Instead the Incarnation of Jesus Christ was the incandescence

---

[1] Tennyson, *"Lady Clara Vere De Vere,"* st. 7

of nature; as Arcturus' rays lighted up "A Century of Progress,"[1] so also He much more has lighted up the world; for He said, "As long as I am in the world, I am the light of the world" (John 9:5).

C. THE DISTINCTIVE MINISTRY OF JESUS CHRIST

To the Lost Sheep of the House of Israel (Matthew 15:24)
Jesus Christ is *The* Man of *All* Men (John 18:33—19:15;
John 8:23: ". . . I am not of this world."

1. The Place: The Holy Land

There are two great phenomena: A Book and A Race; and these are apart from all books and all races and are within a land—The Holy Land. Each of these is beyond dispute:

a) Sir Walter Scott said, "There is but ONE BOOK."
b) Ernest Renan said, "Whatever the surprises of the future, Palestine remains the tattered remnants of a Fifth Gospel, torn but still legible."
c) Lew Wallace studied the New Testament seeking to discredit it, but instead upon completing the reading of it, wrote *Ben Hur.*

Out of the soil of Palestine and the solidarity of Israel, and out from the prophetic ecstasy of the Book, there emerged one: The Man of men who gathers up into Himself, all the transfiguration glory; men from every avenue of life—authors, thinkers, painters—all cluster about Him. As the exploring mind, questing, always reaches earth at the end of the trail and stands facing illimitable heavens,—so love's emotional avenues converge at their best "in HIM."

These "Alls" (Land, Race and Book) "agree in one," having a common "Power, not of themselves" which urges toward that "far off divine event." The parable of the vineyard (Mark 12) brings this into clear relief and also the tragedy of defeat, but somewhere, there must be a satisfactory reason for the Universe that is not discernible in ANY of the uses or attainments up until now. No Race, Continent or Creation, or their total, has equalled the effort required to produce the raw material; this is proven by the words of Jesus when He said, "I go to prepare a place for you." The Book and Race are super-human but the "Book" is a catalogue of failures; and the "Race" bulks majestically, but its individuals disappoint. Then, as the eyes become adjusted to the limned stature of Him "of Whom Moses and all the prophets spake," He appears in the midst of His brethren, and the eyes of all in "The Book" are fastened upon Him. This "Coming One" is glorious and compelling, and is the focal point of All.

---

[1] Chicago, Illinois, May 1933

2. His Mission

Christ's understanding of His mission is stated in John 10:10; and of the way in which it was to be achieved, He also was aware, and He also stated it in Mark 10:45. The "Mine Hour" was the time set apart to accomplish the "decease" (*exodus*) of Luke 9:31. All else that He was or did was the by-product or effect of this one thing. Character and speech were external to, and were transitory elements to, the Cross; and were inevitable to such a Life. The language and life, the dialect and deposit of the Holy Spirit were working upon such a place. To stress His Character and teaching at the expense of His Cross is to deny His *deity* and His *power* to save. Character can be copied, and teaching when mastered, makes the disciple as his teacher, but He Himself said:

> "It is the Spirit that quickeneth; the flesh profiteth nothing: the words that I speak unto you, are spirit and are life."

John 6:63 N.

Read that chapter, and especially verse 40:

> "And this is the will of Him that sent Me, that every one which seeth the Son and believeth into (Gr. *eis*) Him, may have everlasting life; and *I* will raise him up at the last day."

Also, "no man *can* serve two masters":

a) If Jesus is a *Teacher* only; then a pupil can eventually achieve unto his "master's degree." This is evolution.

b) If Jesus is a *Savior*, then He must give salvation (John 10:10 and I John 5:12).

This is the meaning of John 3:1—5. Nicodemus said, "We know Thou art come from God . . ."; but the Lord said, "*Ye* (THE Teacher of Israel) *must be born again.*" We are faced by the same tragedy as Israel (John 5:39): we are searching for life from the Scriptures but they only witness to Him who "is *The Life.*"

Three great *events* witness:

First, hear those who saw and wrote:

a) Of His baptism (*Mark, Matthew, Luke John*)

Second, His Transfiguration:

a) "They spake of His *exodus*"—not of His *discourses*

b) Moses and Elijah talked, but God said, "Hear ye Him"— that which He had to "teach" (see Mark 9:8—31); here they are: The Table and the baptistry which testify, for "He left Himself not without witness."

Third, The Last Supper:—a covenant, a *new* testament; then all before this is old covenant. The New did not begin and men were not saved, until *after that.*

God's purpose for Israel was rejected but He so loved the world, He would not give up. God is love and love is the essence of every manifestation, the motive of any or all exertion of power or authority. "He came unto His own things, but His own people received Him not,"—but to as many as did, He gave eternal life." The Great Commission was to preach the Gospel (I Corinthians 15:1—4); to make disciples and *then* to "teach." How long? "Till He come"; has He come? Not the second time. Then keep on until He does come again.

Three great tests prove His Deity:

First, He is the *Image Revealer* who dissects *out* of the race the crafty and hypocritical, revealing their true purposes (Luke 20:23). He Himself "came to seek and save the lost"; and this ministry was like a bath of regeneration in which He washed the nation of Israel and revealed the true and the false worshipers of God. As a photographer's film is developed, it must go through a bath or a washing in order for the pictures to be developed; so the ministry of Jesus "develops" the true character of the nation of Israel. As the X-Ray shadowgraph reveals the hidden designs behind the outer paint of masterpieces, [1] so Jesus' ministry also penetrated through the false surface of the religious rulers and He laid bare the true desire of the people of Israel. A microscope like a telescope, ignores objects that are near and obvious, but reveals the essences behind the surface. The earth is crammed with mystery and fame is ever knighting the conquestors of the new and unusual. God is a Master of Mystery, and He makes intelligible and lovable the Universe. He makes visible the unseen, and the laws and vitalities upon which the "seen" floats.

Second, He is a *Life-bringer,* not simply a pulmotor who restores, but one who brings abundant life and such life is too great for this present world to contain (John 14:2); and man has not yet attained to this spiritual realm in this earthly life.

---

[1]
"Trade secrets of the Old Masters, including the fact that some of their work was 'ghost-painted,' were revealed yesterday at the Art Institute by Edward W. Forbes, director of Harvard's Fogg Art Museum. Designs hidden for centuries behind the outer paint of masterpieces have been disclosed by the X-Ray Shadowgraph recently developed by Dr. Alan Burroughs, also of the Fogg Museum. In some cases, as shown by shadowgraphs brought to Chicago by Forbes, the work under the top layer of paint is superior and far different from its present form. One of the best examples of this is shown in the shadowgraphs of 'Christ Crowned' attributed to Tintoretto, Italian master. While it is a superior painting, experts have been puzzled by the lack of genius shown in the delineation of Christ and those mocking him. Shadowgraphs show why. Underneath these figures are other heads, boldly drawn and far superior to those on the surface. It is assumed that the original was painted over by a meddling student after the master died." (Chicago Tribune, June 1933)

Third, He is a Love-applier—for the application of love produces "changed eyes." To some, baptism is a "church rite," but to one who loves, baptism "is *into* Him" as a marriage scene. To pour lavish love upon pain causes it to become impearled; upon a mother, it produces a Madonna; and lavish love poured upon the earth (John 3:16) makes man glorified. Josh Billings wrote "love is blind," but never forget that "No man can say Jesus is Lord, but by The Holy Spirit" (I Corinthians 12:3). Not until the imagination has seen and has "swept and garnished the house," can "The King of Glory come in."

Confirming these tests about the Deity of Christ, the editors of Saint Martin's Review[1] have this to say about the wisdom of Jesus:

"'The wisdom of Jesus is not sanity or common sense; it is wisdom.' Murry quotes familiar passages about losing one's soul to find it, or about 'to him that hath,' or about loving enemies, and says that it is only with advancing age that he has found in them 'the key to the great riddle of life,' but a key which is beyond sanity and sense. For either of these excellent qualities, (of sanity and sense) says Mr. Murry, he goes to Montaigne, to Machiavelli, to Voltaire, to Hume and to Gibbon. They have a contribution to make to his thinking which he fully acknowledges. But from them he returns to find in the words of Jesus 'the mystery of the kingdom of God.' He says that Jesus used the term 'mystery' not in the sense of something unfathomable, but as 'a secret that could be understood by anyone who would be humble enough to receive it.'

"To Mr. Murry, the supreme example of this 'mystery' as the heart of the teaching of Jesus is found in the parable of the prodigal son. Both sense and justice, he declares, are on the side of the elder son. But, after listening to the answer of the old man to the indignant son, 'something happens in our hearts.' In them as well a mystery is accomplished. We see visions, and we dream dreams; we glimpse what love was once in one man's experience of God, and because it was, it *is*; it is born again in us, and our souls are born to receive it. But 'there's a mystery in it'; the mystery of a wisdom before which both both sanity and common sense must hide their heads."

Jesus escapes analysis, cataloging and classification; when others are coralled, He is at large:

a) He was called a *prophet* and prophets performed miracles; and searching Andrew said, "but what are these among so many" as he wondered at the feeding of the five thousand (John 6:9)

b) He was called *teacher* and one who "spake as never man spake"; and baffled Peter said, "Lord, to whom shall we go? Thou hast the sayings of eternal life" (John 6:68N.)

---

[1] J. Middleton Murry in *St. Martin's Review,* London, 1933

c) But to classify or catalogue Jesus as only prophet and teacher
would be to fall into the same error as those of Matthew 16:24
If we are to understand Jesus and His place in our relationship
to God, we must stand with *believing* Thomas, who, overcome
at the indisputable Presence of Jesus, said, "My Lord and my
God." But no man can say this until he has seen a *crucified*
and a *living* Christ. When once so seen, He fills, He glorifies,
and He satisfies; and following Him becomes one continuous
song. May not this explain the "apartness" of Bible writers?

It is this "something" that set Him apart uniquely. His access to
limitless resources, power sources and fellowship with the Father; this
response of His which changed men and events; these were the fixing
elements that universal judgment acclaims "PERFECT." Three years with
this Lord made "unlearned men" proclaimers of an unalterable and unfail-
ing Gospel; these same men broke through provincialism and created an
immortal literature and erected an amaranthine Body (and this not by their
own power of Godliness but in the Power of the Spirit which came through
prayer) by a requisitioning of God, as, "My God shall supply your every
need."

The ease of His contacts make Him at one with others, and the Master
of every situation:

He is Master
(of all classes of people
(of every situation
(of circumstances whether they are
(terrestrial, celestial, human or divine.

He is the true cosmopolitan and He is so native to all and every thing,
that even the wild beasts were gentle. Yet, *humans* dared to crucify Him.

The upthrust of Deity in this Son of God and Son of Man is seen in
His:

a) *Character:* "which of you convicteth Me of sin?" (John 8:36)
The moral ascendancy of this Son of Man amazes all peoples,
as we consider that out from this Human Unit should emerge
and persist so perennial a Leadership

b) *Words:* in one syllable words, they said of Him, "Never man so
spake like this man" (John 7:46)

c) *Works:* "Believe Me that I am in the Father, and the Father is in
Me; or else believe Me for the very works' sake" (John 14:11)

The Lord was not a great Personality; He made a small impression
upon the rulers of His age (I Corinthians 2:8); all of them examined Him
(Isaiah 53). He had no magnetism; no large following; and the following

which He did have, diminished as He drew nearer the Cross. The important thing is not a Life, but the Post-Mortem results: "An institution is the lengthened shadow of a man"—Emerson.

He came "in the fulness of time"—this "God-sent One" and God said, "This is My Son," but they received Him not. BUT, and this was the first offer of life by which those accepting Him enter into a spiritual world,— "to as many as received Him, gave He authority (Gr. *exousia*). This is the life abundant of which He spoke in John 10:10, and which is experienced by the Church in this Age of Grace. Here is the first dividing between the "quick and the dead" (I John 5:12).

3. His Disciples

The Twelve imprisoned in their limitations, went blindly on in loyalty to Him. Thomas said, "let us go and die with Him." Evidently this would be better than life apart from the Master. This same Thomas will yet see the Father even though through crucified wounds as he says, "My Lord and my God." They were not able to grasp *His words*, but they did believe *in Him* and, wonder beyond wonder, in "The Upper Room," with Him dead, this was still "Upper!" How could they? Today's life is the incarnation of yesterday's thinking: "as ye sow, so shall ye also reap." "Were a star quenched on high . . . ." They had been with Jesus and in the momentum of that, it carried them through the three days. Their endurance was from the enduement of Matthew 16:15 "but whom say YE that I am? So also will "seeing Him" carry you through conflicts mental and spiritual. "No man hath seen God," yet, "he that hath seen Me, hath seen the Father"; as God creates, He provides; as the Father redeems, He forgives and loves. As the God of His Workshop, I'll never see Him, nor do I even want to, for as such, He is beyond man; but as the Father of Home, I want to be near Him. What child does not want to be near a real father? Moses said, "If Thy presence go not with me, carry us not up hence . . ." (Exodus 33:15*b*); and as Barak said unto Deborah, the prophetess, "If thou wilt go with me, then I will go; but if thou wilt not go with me, then I will not go" (Judges 4:8). So men of every age have felt a need of the Presence of God. This is the cry of a child for its father and were the Universe an Aeolian harp, that would be the note that it would utter.

> Oh, restless, troubled brain, cease thy search for God,
> And with thy heart, arise and go unto the Father and say unto Him,
> "Father, I have sinned against heaven and against thee,
> And am no more worthy to be called thy son . . . ."
> Luke 15:18

Jesus said, "If any desire to come after Me, let him deny himself, and take up his cross daily, and follow Me" (Luke 9:23). Of His disciples it was later said, "they took knowledge of them that they had been with Jesus" (Acts 4:13). These men had counted the taking up of a cross a privilege and would not consider themselves as martyrs nor yet as holier than others. Jesus had taught that those who fasted, were not to display themselves, but rather to act as though not seeming to fast, and He Himself demonstrated the same.

"He took captivity captive and gave gifts unto" them. He outbuilded the builders. Looking back:

a) Ralph Emerson said, "I am a part of all that I have met"

b) William Baxter said, "There but for the grace of God lies William Baxter,—a Judas Iscariot."

c) And in Victor Hugo's chapter on "Conscience" in *Les Miserables,* Jean Val Jean meditates morbidly on "Poor" Judas, and vascillating Pilate.

But "thanks be unto God" *He* emerged from Gethsemane, to heal the servant Malchus, to restore Peter, to bring forgiveness even upon the Cross. And still He governs the Ages; for only such an One is worthy, the Lion of the Tribe of Judah, the Root of David (Revelation 5:5); and praise be unto Him!

4. Jesus as: PROPHET, PRIEST and KING

"And from Jesus Christ, the faithful witness, the first begotten from among the dead ones, and the prince of the kings of the earth. Unto Him that loved us, and washed us from our sins in His own blood,"

Revelation 1:5 N.

This text sets forth Jesus Christ in His three-fold work of Prophet, Priest and King.

a) He is called:
   (1) "the faithful witness"—Prophet
   (2) "the Prince of Kings of the earth"—King
   (3) "Him that loved us and washed us from our sins in His own blood"—Priest
   (4) Added to these three He is called:
       "The first begotten from among the dead ones" by which He is declared the "Son of God with power" (Romans 1:4).

b) The Lord was:
   A Prophet—like unto Moses (Deuteronomy 18:15—22; Acts 3:20—26) (Acts 3:20—26)

   A Priest—like unto Aaron

   A King—like unto David, from whom He descended through Mary

c) As a Prophet, He was the Jehovah of the Old Covenant
As a Priest, He came as the seed of a woman
As a King (Priest-King), He is after the order of Melchizedek

d) As a Prophet, He speaks in Genesis 3:15
As a Priest, He comes — John 1:11—12
As a King, He reigns one thousand years (Revelation 20)

e) He is:
The Prophet of John 1:1—14 and Genesis 1: "God said"
The Priest of John 14:6 and John 3:16
The King on the Throne: "Sit Thou at my right hand."

f) Christ is:
Prophetic — Hebrews 1:1
Priestly — Hebrews 1:2—3
Kingly — Hebrews 1:8

g) As a Prophet, He uses "The Word" Genesis 1:1; John 1:1
As a Priest, He uses "The Gospel"; He is in heaven;
His Body is here participating
As a King, He will use His "Sceptre" (Acts 1:11; Hebrews 1:8)

h) He *was* Prophet
He *is* Priest
He is *the Coming* King.

i) As Prophet He was the faithful witness
As Priest He was the first born from among the dead ones
As King He is ruler over kings.

5. Christ, The High Priest

Christ is our High Priest; and the Bible is His High-priestly robe;
and His Breastplate consists of Paul's letters. As a robe is symbolic,[1]
so is a word (John 18:20; Acts 26:26; Ephesians 1:1; Galatians 1:15;
Acts 9:15; Hebrews 10:1—25). The High Priest's robes (Psalm 138:2;

---

[1] "Aaron and his priestly garments and his sacrifices form a beauteous picture of the
Person, the graces, and the ministries of the Great High Priest who has passed into the
heavens . . . . The ephod was essentially the priestly garment. It was worn by Aaron the
priest, Samuel the prophet, and David the king. Christ combines all three offices. It was
made of the same as the veil, but with threads of gold and no cherubim . . . . In the pocket
of the breast-plate were placed the mysterious stones, known as Urim and Thummim by
means of which the Divine judgment of a matter was made known to Israel. Thus robed
Aaron bore the judgment of the congregation before the Lord, and communicated the judgment of the Lord to the congregation. The precious stones upon the shoulders and upon the
heart of Aaron were so securely bound to the ephod that they could not be detached from
it. 'Who shall separate us from the love of Christ'?" (*The Student's Commentary on The
Holy Scriptures*, published by Chas. J. Thynne and Jarvis, Ltd. London) pp. 58—59.

Isaiah 9:6, Exodus 28:6—30) are the most royal of robes, for each item is of significance. He is a type of Christ and his clothes are a type of the Lord's work. They are God's Urim (lights) and Thummim (perfection); the breastplate was folded and contained the twelve stones; the Urim and Thummim were within the folds on the heart and when passed behind, the stones were lighted. So God's spotlight focused upon the point of emphasis or activity. He opened the Scriptures (Luke 24:32), and the seven ages or dispensations are seen infolded within God's one purpose.

6. Jesus and Prayer[1]

In Luke 11:1 ". . . a certain one of His disciples said unto Him, 'Lord, teach us to pray' (not *how* to pray) . . . ." This was the first step; that which was most important was not the method but the necessity. How well they were prepared for this teaching is stated in the conclusion of the verse "according as John also taught his disciples." The first language a little child is taught to say is "father"; so Jesus taught His disciples the first speech for God's children when He said, "say, 'Our Father'."

The prayer habit of the Master is impressed upon us at His baptism (Luke 3:21) and at the Cross (Luke 23:34), but we have not "laid hold upon" this privilege. Our material treasures are not currency in spiritual things, yet we stand at the edge of the Infinite and Its resources which are available to us through prayer. To Adam was given the naming of all creatures and over these he had dominion, but we would rather count as treasures our pride of wealth, our pride of family, and of intelligence (I John 2:16). In the prayer life of our Lord, we find that Jesus placed the highest value upon prayer, even above that of:

a) healing and *teaching:*
When fame drew multitudes to Him,
He retired to pray (Luke 5:15—16)

b) rest:
For, "A great while before day . . . and prayed . . .
(Mark 1:35)

c) miracles:
His statement of prayer for Peter, to shield him, that his faith fail not (Luke 22:32)

d) money and *organization:*
Rather that there be prayer for "labourers into harvest"
(Matthew 9:38)

e) preaching:
"seeing He ever liveth to make intercession for them'
(Hebrews 7:25)

---

[1] See also Section FIVE, *The Church*, VI. "Things, . . ." G. Prayer, p. 469 ff.

For seeking first in prayer the kingdom of God, all these other things would be added. The heavenly Father honors prayer and the intelligent working out of that prayer by the guidance of His Holy Spirit.

The Transfiguration of Jesus was a by-product of prayer (Luke 9:29), yet it occupies the whole of our attention. There was something terrifying in Peter's suggestion:

> ". . . 'Master, it is good for us to be here; and let us make three tabernacles; one for Thee, and one for Moses, and one for Elijah."
>
> Luke 9:33

For, after Jesus had foretold His sufferings, then "for a season" the devil, through Peter, is at it again (see Matthew 16:23, Luke 9:28—36); but as in Luke 4:14, such decisions make destiny and change currents. "It is good for US to be here"; if we know what that means, *yes*; but if our knowledge is half complete as was Peter's, and then we are content, *no*. Beyond are things which "have not entered into the heart of man" (I Corinthians 2:9).

David saw clearer in Psalm 17:15:

> "And where is now my hope?
> As for my hope, who shall see it?"

Peter said:

> "And this voice which was borne from heaven, *we* heard, when we were with Him in the holy mount"
>
> II Peter 1:18N.

John said:

> "Beloved, now are we children of God, and it is not yet manifest what we shall be; but we know that, when we shall be manifested, we shall be like Him; for we shall see Him according as He is." (I John 3:2N.)

The condition of the world and of this age is upon us because we have stopped short in order to build tabernacles; a vision is eclipsing the Cross and all such are foredoomed. We are given panaceas instead of the specific but the world needs the Cross; so we must "go everywhere preaching." Each individual must receive it and no "spade-leaners" can ever take it to this generation; there is chaos everywhere and opportunists are building flimsy and inflammable make-shift tabernacles. Only disciples of "the set face" who see and accept the Cross will ever bring in the abiding, tarrying and uniting Spirit.

D. JESUS AND THE SCRIPTURES

1. Christ and The Bible; or, The Lord Imprisoned Within The Scriptures

All approach to any and all understanding of the Scriptures must begin with the Lord Jesus Christ; in all things and in everything, He has the preeminence (John 1:1—3, Colossians 1:17 ff.); His paramount place is in the Holy Writ:

"For Thou hast magnified Thy Word above all Thy Name (Psalm 138:2*b*)
"Because they are they which testify concerning Me" (John 5:39*b* N.)

The virgin Scriptures are as the virgin mother; the Scriptures give birth to the story of Christ.

In Hebrews 10:5—7 is given the fulfillment of the prophecy of Psalm 40:6—7. The Psalmist said, "in the volume of the book it is written of Me." In Luke 24:24—27, Jesus expounds unto the Emmaus disciples "in all the Scriptures concerning Himself." Moses had written in a book (Deuteronomy 31:24) concerning this One whom he said, would be "a prophet like unto me." It was from this volume of the book that Jesus drew out some of the things concerning Himself.

Christ, the Light, unravels the Bible alphabet as rain drops act as prisms; and the Christian who opens the Bible so adjusted to Christ, is edified, and will not be like Israel who is veiled (II Corinthians 3:16).

In John 17:4 He said:

"I have glorified Thee on the earth;
I have finished the work which Thou gavest me to do."

Try to say that to and of yourself! Yet Jesus could say it, for such is our Savior. And we might say, "Is there a God worthy to be His Father?" Surely, He has earned freedom. Who broke out so many paths as He? Who has so added to the stature of mankind? Hear this Savior pray: "Sanctify them *in* the truth." He is saying, "take them up into the Scriptures." He is asking that we might be taken out and up into green pastures. The Bible as a fold or climate is an invisible "aura," or an impenetrable cloak as that which sheltered the three in the fiery furnace. For us who are "sanctified," it is promotion, for then "to die is gain"; for we are to be received up into the company of the Bible worthies. Within the Bible are the "green pastures" of every unsatisfied longing, but have we measured the text implied inhibitions? Jesus said, "I sanctify Myself." This is restriction not freedom, even as motherhood restricts. No matter how brilliant or how philosophic you may be, you are restricted to the Scriptures in matters of salvation. Jesus said, "for their sakes, I sanctify Myself." This is the language of sacrifice, like that when He said, "I go to prepare a place for you." Once, He was sanctified or incarnated in flesh, and He went not out of the flesh but was subject to its demands (except at the Mount of Transfiguration). So now during this age He is sanctified in the Scriptures and as He once consented to the Cross, now He consents to be limited by the revelation of the Bible. This you must see. For the right focus, *you must adjust yourself to Him and to the Bible's sacredness.* Jesus is saying that He locks up His saving power within the Bible though all authority is His. There are no works or miracles or evidences today save those in the Scriptures and "they are they which testify of Me" (John 5:39*b* and Luke 16:31). Why? So that the lowliest, most hungry-hearted could "arise and go" (Acts 17:27—28). It would have been much easier for Him to save by wonder and fiat, but He could not so reach ALL, and He must not make distinctions! *His restraint emphasizes the Bible's value.* And as the Scriptures "house" or imprison—i.e. sanctify—such a Son, they will be as nearly perfect as the Almighty God can make them. So criticize cautiously for God has a Holy Land and a Holy Book!

Consider in the Old Testament, that for fifteen hundred years there is no fulfillment of the prophetic hope of the Messiah (I Corinthians 10:4); and in the New Testament there is another two thousand year period while the Church waits and watches for His *"appearing."*

> "And all that dwell upon the earth shall worship him, whose names are not written in the book of life of the *Lamb having been slain, from the foundation of the world.*"

> Revelation 13:8 N.

And all this is within the Universe which He helped to create. I see Him wounded at heaven's gate; breathless I watch as He looks within and then back to earth. Which shall it be? Then, Oh Wondrous Lord, we are beholding "the joy set before Him" as He lifts wounded hands and shuts the door.

> "Who, being in the form of God, thought it not a thing to be grasped at, to be equal with God; but emptied Himself of no reputation, and took upon Him the form of a bond-servant, and was made in the likeness of men:"
>
> Philippians 2:6—7N.

This is renunciation (Hebrews 2:8—18), even as our missionaries turn from home and go back to their fields of service. Today, like the prodigal son's father waiting at home, so our Lord waits within the Scriptures:

> "And while the lamp holds out to burn,
> The vilest sinner may return."
>
> Isaac Watts,
> Book I, Hymn 88

The Scriptures are like a place where pottery is made and where we are to enter and be fashioned according to the "Potter's" design. For within the Scriptures, the Spirit and God's skilled workman toil at redemption.

Love's supreme expression is found in the Gospel (John 3:16), and is again told by John in I John 4:8. Our Lord's estimate of the Word of God is found in Matthew 4:4. This Word reflects the eternal gospel found specifically in Isaiah 55:8—11, Genesis 1:14, Revelation 14:6, 22:18, I Corinthians 2:1—16, John 5:39, 10:35, Luke 16:31, John 6:44, Hebrews 11:6.

a) To the lawyer, Jesus said, "How readest thou" (Luke 10:25—28); and upon the lawyer's reply quoting the law, He said, "This do and thou shalt live."

b) To Dives (Gr. for "rich man"), He said, "if they hear not Moses, neither will they believe though one rise from the dead" (Luke 16:19—31).

c) To Israel, He said, "think not that I came to destroy the law, or the prophets; I am not come to unloose, but to fill-up" (Matthew 5:17N.).

d) And His own words on the Cross, "It is finished" is the requiem of Matthew 5:18, for "heaven and earth shall pass away, but My word shall not pass away" (Matthew 24:35).

2. Fulfilling The Scriptures

Let us accept His gracious invitation (Matthew 11:28) and put to the test, not His miracles nor His sayings, but His use of the Scriptures. In His introduction to Israel (Luke 4:18), He says, "Today is this Scripture fulfilled in your ears." This is a literal quotation taken from their own scroll in the synagogue.

As He goes on to Jerusalem, we find Him riding upon an ass in order that (Gr. *hina*) it might be fulfilled (Matthew 21:4). Again, in order that the Scriptures might be fulfilled, on the Cross He said, "I thirst." In other words, He compelled them to fulfill Scripture that, "not one jot or one tittle shall pass from the law till all be fulfilled."

At Satan's tempting of Jesus we see the power and influence of this Adversary. The Lord's proof books were *Jonah* and *Deuteronomy*, and the book of Deuteronomy is first to be fired upon by Satan (Deuteronomy 8:3, 6:16). *Jonah* is set forth in proof of the resurrection (Matthew 12:40, Luke 11:30), and as Jonah became a sign to the Ninevites, so shall the Son of man be to this generation.

After His resurrection He rehearsed in ALL the Scriptures, "the things concerning Himself." The object of the Old Testament is to leave no doubt that the Christ proclaimed at Pentecost was the One limned in the Old Testament "in all the Scriptures" (Luke 24:27). That *must* be established for this is the foundation upon which He accepted the Cross; we are not reading something strung together, but a proof—a printer's proof off the "types,"—set up from copy of "counsels in eternity"; a plan prior to man's creation; a twin conception in the Mind of Deity; just as the seasons and the seeds are fitted together. The Father and the Son collaborated; and when I read the Old Testament Scriptures, I read the record of a plan conceived, thought-out and adjusted to every atom of man and to the smallest fraction of time. If the Scriptures are post-fact records of concatenated events, then am I skeptical, for the outcome would have "just happened" out of a number of possible endings, and so it would have "just happened" out of a number of possible endings, and so it would still be a hazard in the outcome for me! The Scriptures are something like an experimental farm whereon men build up to a standard: a grain or an animal—with this difference, that *there is no experimentation in the Scriptures*. The results in both places are for man's profit. So we expect a a statement such as Galatians 2:20 N.:

> "I have been crucified with Christ; nevertheless I live;
> no longer I, but Christ liveth in me; and that life which
> I now live in the flesh I live in (Gr. *en*) faith of the Son
> of God, who loved me, and gave Himself for me."

HIS faith, not mine, enabled Him to endure the taint of sin, the experience of death, and to return from such an experience, perfect in all ways. Then comes along my faith, rising up out of emotion from One "Who loved me and gave Himself for me." This love enables me to live "in flesh" and yet remain His.

As the coming of Jesus Christ into flesh has produced transformations beyond hopes raised by prophecies, can anyone believe that He is through? Or that He has no further interest in us or plans for us? If so, I could not respect Him! The first coming of the Saviour was made the "hope of Israel" (Acts 28:20) and was earthly; for through Abraham was promised the land, and through David was promised the throne. Christ was the "seed of Abraham" and the "seed of David."

The difficulty of Jeremiah 22:30 is solved by the reading of the record, for following Josiah the good king, the sons Jehoiachim and Coniah never did obtain kingship. Joseph's *legal* son, not his blood heir would be valid in any earthly court, but not in a heavenly one.

The unbreakableness of prophecy completes this Matthew 5:17—18 "till," and Matthew 24:35 "heaven and earth shall pass away, but My word shall NOT." Here are a few listed:

a) Born of a virgin, in Bethlehem
b) Raised in Nazareth
c) Betrayed for thirty pieces of silver
d) The purchase of a potter's field

e) On the Cross—"I thirst"

f) When He was rejected and crucified, the Jews were scattered and will be until they say, "Blessed is He that cometh in the Name of the Lord."

g) Making His grave with the rich.

As there were those who misunderstood Abraham and David, Mary and Joseph; so also, the nation of Israel failed to grasp "the *sufferings* and the *glory*" of the Lord. And this has wrought confusion in the minds of the unwilling. Some have "seen His glory" (John 17:5); and "change" is the demand of ever present attainments of science. A release from inhibition is man's daily struggle; and is not this prophetic? And so "in like manner," in clouds of glory, the dead shall hear His voice; and shall be at Home in the Universe that is measured by "light years."

E. JESUS AND PROPHECY

1. Prophecy of the Building of the Church

"And I say also unto thee, That thou art Peter, (Gr. *petros*, stone), and upon this rock (Gr. *petra*, two distinct words), I will build My church; and the gates of Hades shall not prevail against it. And I will give unto thee the keys of the kingdom of the heavens: and whatsoever thou shalt loose on earth shall have been loosed in the heavens."

Matthew 16:18—19N.

In this text we find the first promise of Jesus concerning His Church. He is in the region of Caesarea Philippi, and John 7:1 says, "He walked in Galilee, for He would not walk in Judea because the Jews sought to kill Him." Judas had decided to betray Him and the Pharisees and the Sadducees came desiring a sign from heaven from Him, and He replied that no sign would be given to them but the sign of the prophet Jonah. He then goes with His disciples to the other side of Galilee and when they realize that they have forgotten to take bread, Jesus tells them to beware of the leaven of the Pharisees and Sadducees, and in Mark 8:15 He says, "Beware of the leaven of the Pharisees and of the leaven of Herod." In Matthew 16:12 they understood that He bade them to beware not of the leaven of the *bread*, but of the *doctrine* of the Pharisees and of the Sadducees. Then follows the healing of the blind man in Bethsaida, healing him through two treatments (Mark 8:22—26); and as He sent the man away to his own house, He said, "neither go in to the town nor tell it to any in the town." Now the hour is come to test His disciples and, as the good Shepherd, to separate them. Their minds were racing at high tension, for they had correctly understood His teaching concerning the leaven, and that it concerned doctrine and not physical bread. If ever His disciples were keyed to perceive, it was now. He said to them then, "Whom do men say that I, the Son of Man, am." In Matthew 16:14, they said, "some say Thou art John the Baptist, some Elijah, and others Jeremiah or one of the prophets." If He had been one of the prophets, there could have been no advance beyond "restore again the kingdom to Israel" (Acts 1:6). And then Jesus speaks directly to His disciples: "but whom say *Ye* that I am." And then is fulfilled Christ's promise (Matthew 13:11, Luke 12:12), and here we find also a fulfillment of Psalm 81:10*b*.

The New Age of Grace is about "to come to pass"; the great moment for which "the ages were framed" burst upon them in this revelation glory. Peter's inspired reply is:

"Thou art The Christ, The Son of The Living God." Matthew 16:16

Jesus replied, "Blessed!" . . . "For flesh and blood hath not revealed it unto thee." Now Matthew 11:25, I Corinthians 2:9—10: "Cans't thou by searching find out God?" (Job 11:7) Peter speaks as though by intuition:

a) Just as a surgeon through an incision sees the condition of a man's body, and immediately knows the recourse

b) Or as the astronomer, almost automatically sees the thread upon which crystal worlds are strung

c) Or as the inventor or genius sees behind the phenomena to the cause.

Just so Peter through the revelation of the Father, received as a flash this "good confession." So it is likely that this is all that we will receive or even could stand (Exodus 33:20—23), but God wants us to be so conscious of Him that we could put forth prayer and touch Him (I Corinthians 10:4). Had Peter grasped and retained the revelation of this moment:

a) He would not have sought to hinder Jesus (Matthew 16:22—23)

b) Nor would he have denied Him (Matthew 26:74)

c) Nor would he have gone to the tomb (Luke 24:12)

d) Nor would he have needed the vision of Acts 10

e) Nor would he have disputed with Paul
(Acts 11:2; Galatians 2:11).

Paul on the other hand, saw clearly and set his faith to pain (II Corinthians 11:30); and whoever catches a view of the Church, at once becomes impervious to pain and he glories in the Cross.

Jesus said, "thou art Pe*tros*." This is a proper noun and is only used in the New Testament. Peter's new name did not in any way suggest that he was superior to the others (Galatians 2:7, II Corinthians 11:5 and 12:11). Then Jesus said, "And upon this Pe*tra*" which thou hast seen, a cliff or a mountain peak, "*I* will build," *of Me* the Church. "All things were made by Him . . ." (John 1:3). This is the genetive indicating the source of "out of Me" and does not refer to Peter. Jesus said, "I am the vine, ye are the branches." The Church was not upon *"petros"* but *"petra."* "One is master and all ye are brethren" (Matthew 23:8). Life is first, and it forms its Body (I Corinthians 15:38). The miracle or mystery is that all are drawn up "into Him" and are "changed"—"like Him" "after His kind" (I Corinthians 1:26, 2:16), "we have the mind of Christ."

"Upon this *Rock* I will build *My* Church"   (Matthew 16:18)
(Ref. Exodus 31:1—11)

In this text we are clearing off, digging deep, to "the rock." To see clearly "this rock" is to accept the inspiration of the prophets, the virgin birth and the physical resurrection of Jesus. The luminous, dominant fact of this text, "this rock," quenched all. Jesus said, "upon *this* (apart from the flesh) rock, I will (go to prepare to) build" for He will be out there when it begins (Acts 2). This text stopped Jewish time until II Thessalonians 2:6, and the presence of Moses and Elijah six days later at the Transfiguration indicates the tremendous significance of these events. Here Moses, the Law-giver, and Elijah, the great prophet, appear with the Son of God in glory as He receives from God the Father honor and glory (II Peter 1:16—18). As the high priest in Exodus 28:2 is clothed with the priestly garments, so Christ is acknowledged as the High Priest who is on His way to the Cross of *suffering* (Matthew 16:21); but also He is journeying to the *glory* which shall follow when He makes His departure at the ascension and enters into the Holy of Holies, heaven itself. Thus the announcement "upon this rock I will build My church" sets in motion the pre-determined series of events which result in the Cross, the Resurrection, the Ascension and the Church. The Law is nailed to the Cross, the prophecies of *suffering* are fulfilled and the prophecies of the *glory* that shall follow, are held in abeyance while the Jewish clock is stopped till the end of the church age and the time of the Tribulation.

The purpose of this revelation (Matthew 16:18) is to get His co-laborers familiar with the site of the Church. He is saying, "here is where I I will build. If others say, 'lo, here or lo, there,' believe them not." His Church is not builded on creeds or men. The Transfiguration (Matthew 17:1—9) followed this time of revelation to free their minds from Judaism, and to show them that Christ alone is the architect and builder of the true tabernacle (Hebrews 9:24). This revelation at Caesarea-Philippi was to reveal the true materials of His Church, the acceptors of His Deity, and to reveal the use of these just as do elements in building (Ephesians 2: 21—22). This revelation also shows the meaning of *"petros"* in the shadow of "*petra*" as Bezalel "In the Shadow of God" (Lamentations 4:20*b*, Exodus 36 and 37, and 39:43).

> "I will build My Church . . .
> and the gates of Hades shall not prevail . . . ."

An institution with such a Founder and mighty enough to overcome death, is interesting to the Geneticist, and to the Pragmatist, and to the Palingenesist (Titus 3:5). "Upon this rock" and *nowhere else, I, and no one else*, will build *My* Church, and *no one else's Church!* This is never used elsewhere; it is the only such creation, so we expect Him to say:

> "For as the Father hath life in Himself; so hath He
> given also to the Son to have life in Himself"
>
> John 5:26 N.

and we expect Peter to add:

> "Ye also as living stones, are built up a spiritual house,
> a holy priesthood, to offer up spiritual sacrifices,
> acceptable to God through Jesus Christ."
>
> I Peter 2:5 N.

And then Matthew 16:21 reads:

> "From that time forth *began* Jesus to show unto His disciples
> how that He must go unto Jerusalem and suffer many things
> of the Elders and chief priests and scribes and be killed and
> be raised again the third day."

Thus *begins* the effort to produce the Church which He builds. I Timothy 3:15 speaks of the pillar and ground of the truth; and the Master Himself said, "I am the truth." So Christians as living stones (Gr. *lithos*) are built upon Him, and this testimony of Peter's has been taken over by us all (John 4:42). And those believing and obeying, are "changed from glory unto glory." Often the missionary unwittingly raises the heathen to the missionary's standard though he purposes only to preach Christ; but Christ changes all into a new man. Christ and His Church are but hypotheses until one accepts them; then they are vital; and the Church, His laboratory, with unmeasurable power of transformation, is what you and I are in this day. Of particular notice are the Greek words:

Petra — Petros — Lithos

"The Rock" was made both foundation and head of the corner (I Peter 2:1—12, Ephesians 2:11—22, I Peter 2:6—7, and Psalm 118:23). My hope is to suggest solutions that confront the disputer whom you may meet later. The Scriptures interpret themselves to those who go to them and abide there. Just now we are seeking light upon some "from the beginning" doctrines. I was led by a group of preachers to look more closely at Matthew

16:18—19, and, undiscerned truth hitherto hidden, stood forth revealed, combining Scripture with Scripture which was satisfying and faith-confirming; it was accidental just as in a laboratory.

At His first coming when Jesus took on the likeness of sinful flesh, He became a part of *Petros* (mankind). At His second coming when He comes as a stone cut out of the Mountain without hands (Daniel 2:44—45), He is *Lithos*. But at all times, He is God and therefore *Petra*.

The Rock (*Petra*) being revealed, now the Christian (*Lithos*) of the Body follows. This can only be spiritually discerned:

a) By the *Begetting*: John 20:22, which was the same as Genesis 2:7. This "breathing" was upon the apostles (ten were present); it was upon the apostolate and not upon persons. So the Church cometh into the world according to prophecy, as did He: "Lo, a Body hast Thou prepared for Me." To a different group He said, "Whose soever sins ye forgive, they are forgiven unto them." (A.S.V.) Men ask "who can forgive sins but God?" This is true but the Church is the Body of Christ. This is not as Matthew 16:19 when He said, "I will give unto thee the keys . . . ." Here is a divine function and therefore it must be a divine institution but He said, "Tarry till endued with power from on high" (Luke 24:49).

b) By the *Birth* (Acts 2:1—4) which was the same as at Bethlehem with heavenly signs attending. The men of Jerusalem asked, "What shall we do?" The answer is Acts 2:38, the Spirit speaking through (Gr. *dia*) them. As in John 5:19, the Son receives from the Father and carries out His will, so in John 16:13—14, the Holy Spirit receives from Christ and reveals it unto His disciples. The result is that the Lord "added" and the Church was "together in one place," (i.e. in Christ) Acts 2:1.

This is *the* beginning of the Gospel of Romans 1:1 where *petros* becomes *lithos*. The reborn are baptized into (Gr. *eis*) Him. Martyrs are the witnesses of the Gospel who have laid down their lives for Christ. The word "gospel" (Gr. *euaggelion*) finds its roots in the Hebrew word *basar*[1] which literally means "flesh." So in Romans 12:1 and Luke 9:23 the followers of Christ are asked to present their *bodies* and to deny self and to take up their cross in following Christ; but until we can meet Him in *baptism* and *The Lord's Supper*, there is no Gospel for us. The Gospel is power *only* when planted in flesh. Then it transforms and carries over into *petra*. Were it anywhere else, it would be dynamite unapplied and as medicine in the bottle, or as a charge in a gun.

---

[1] See this Section, footnote 1, "*basar*" p. 251

In the palin-gensia (Titus 3:5, Matthew 19:28), such regenerated ones can be added (John 3:3). It is for all classes: Nicodemus, Mary, the thief on the cross, the three thousand at Pentecost who were spiritually fed, and who soever stands before *"This Rock"*; and who soever sees the test and passes (Luke 9:23). "This Rock" is unique, for He said, "I am the Way"—"No man cometh unto the Father, but by Me"—"there is none other Name under heaven . . ."; and,

a) He demonstrated Deity (Romans 1:4)
b) He formed His Spiritual Body
c) *He* added to that Body—and He alone
d) He promised the Rapture; for we, the Church as the wild olive tree were grafted onto the natural olive tree.

Peter's revelation was *not* a vision but was as Paul's, and Paul said,

"For I neither received it of man,
neither was I taught it,
but through the revelation of Jesus Christ."

Galatians 1:12N.

And as John's:

"The Revelation of Jesus Christ, which God gave unto Him, to shew unto His bond servants things which must shortly come to pass; and He sent and made it known by signs, through His angel unto His bondservant John."

Revelation 1:1N.

And so Peter spake moved by the Spirit:

"Thou art the Christ, the Son of the Living God."

Matthew 16:16

2. Prophecy of The End Times

Jesus' relationship to prophecy is two-fold:

First, He *fulfills* prophecies as illustrated in His birth, ministry, crucifixion, and resurrection
Second, He *rends* the veil *to rightly divide* the Word of Truth as He speaks concerning the writings of Daniel and Ezekiel.

If there is to be understanding of the Scriptures, we start as one must always—with the Lord (John 5:39). Jesus gives *definite answers* to His disciples *definite questions* which arose out of His *definite* prophecy found in *Matthew, Mark* and *Luke,* in regard to the Temple. He had just gone back to "the blood of righteous Abel" (Matthew 23:35); and now the prophecy leads to "the abomination spoken of by Daniel, the prophet";

and this is followed by a most "awe"-ful word picture of a tragic world
event, unique and separate from all sufferings. Here then, is the suggestion of "Him who made all things,"—for whom they were created; of
whom this Book speaks,—as to how to "rightly divide the Word of Truth."
In these two selections, Matthew 24:15—22 and 23:35, our Lord brings
together *Daniel* and *Revelation*; *Daniel* reveals "the times of the Gentiles"
and *Revelation* reveals the *Telos* (end) of all "the age of the ages," and
sets forth Jesus the Christ as the Alpha and the Omega, the beginning
and the ending; the first and the last.

In these following passages, the Synoptic Gospels have been forced
into a unity which is not a unity; these synoptics are not necessarily
parallel, but they are three answers to the same question and they are
directed to three types of interest (Jew, Gentile and Church, I Corinthians
10:32); they are not of *one* event, but are of *three* events. Of grave importance is the Lord's three-group emphases, and heeding such emphases
will make plainer His purposed plan.

a) The Account of LUKE:

In Luke 21, Jesus is *in the Temple*, as He speaks to those
who may be proselytes and here in cahpter 21, we read,
"*some* spake," and, "*they* asked Him"; these are in distinction from the Jewish leaders or the twelve disciples.

Luke writes to Theophilus, a Greek, and to the (largely) Gentile Church (Luke 1:1—4), concerning the unbelieving Jews
and their judgment: "for there shall be great distress upon
the land and upon *this* people (Luke 21:23*b*). Luke alone
mentions the "Desolation" of 70 A.D. (vss. 20—24) and its
results. *This was not the "Abomination" for Titus did not
defile the Temple.*

Their questions[1] of Luke 21:7 were:

(1) "Master, but when shall these things be? and
(2) "what sign will there be when these things are about to
come to pass?"

[1] The study of *Daniel* illustrates that as a glove fits to the hand, so *Daniel* fits with
Revelation, and seals to us the importance He placed upon these things. This validation
from such an One as the Lord should cause serious consideration ere judgment is passed,
especially upon those whom He singles out for personal mention, such as Jonah (and Nineveh) (Matthew 12:40—41); and Daniel (Matthew 24:15, Ezekiel 14:20, 28:3). A man's life's
work is no stronger than the authorities upon which it rests. The Lord's Deity and all His
claims stand or fall *with His men and His materials*. Added importance arises from close
attention to the Lord's words as He stands midway between these two "beloved" ones,
(Daniel and John) who are the nearest to God in the Old Testament and in the New Testament (Daniel 9:23, John 13:23—24). So we expect much from them for they receive the most
space in the Gospels. Neither the Sermon on the Mount nor the Upper Room surpasses the
space allotted to these two.

His answer is that before 70 A.D., the Jerusalem-centered Christians are to suffer (vss. 12—19).

He continues:

(1) "And when ye shall see Jerusalem compassed with armies then know that the desolation thereof is nigh"

(2) "And there shall be signs in the sun, and in the moon, and in the stars; and upon the earth distress of nations, with perplexity; the sea and the waves roaring"; "men's hearts failing them for fear" (vs. 25).

Remember that they asked for signs when the events were "about to come to pass." Verses 8 through 11 are a general warning to the Church.

b) The Account of MATTHEW:

Matthew writes primarily to the Jew first and reference is often made to Kingdom promises (Matthew 19:28).

In Matthew 24, *as He sat upon the Mount of Olivet;* He is speaking to the twelve. These twelve disciples came unto Him *privately,* and their questions are "tell us":

(1) "When shall these things be?"

The answer is found in verses 15—28 (note vs. 21); the time of the Great Tribulation which leads up to Armageddon

(2) "What shall be the sign of Thy coming, . . ."

The Lord's answer is in vss. 29—34 which will be the beginning of the thousand years' Kingdom reign

(3) "And what . . . sign of the completion of the age?"

The Lord's answer here is in 24:35—51.

The general statement of *Matthew* is found in vss. 4 through 14. Parables of warning are found in chapter 25 to the Jews, to the Church, and to the Gentiles (I Corinthians 10:32).

c) The Account of MARK

In Mark 14 we read:

(1) "As He went forth, *one* of His disciples said unto Him"

(2) "As *He sat upon the Mount of Olives* over against the temple, Peter, James, John and Andrew asked Him *privately*." The *twelve* disciples (Matthew 24(and the *four* dis- (Mark 13) both came *privately* as He *sat,* for this was a place of meditation (John 18:2).

Likewise, their questions were "tell us":

(1) "When shall these things be?"

The answer is in 13:14—23, and describes Armageddon.

(2) "What . . . sign . . . all these things are about to be?"

This is answered in verses 24—27 as the signs of heavenly
phenomena are described.

The general statement in *Mark* is given in verses 5—13.

The exhortation in all of the synoptics is to all to "WATCH" (Luke
21:34—36, Matthew 24:42—44, Mark 13:33—37), for the Roman ensign which
will be ON but not IN the temple.

In *Matthew* chapters 2 through 7, Jesus presents Himself to His own
people as their Messiah; in *Luke*, chapter 21, and in *Matthew*, chapter 24,
He gives the pre-history of the Church and Israel, preparing them for what
was to come. In Luke 24:25—49, we have a simile to the book of Hebrews,
and in verse 27, He interpreted unto them "in all the Scriptures, the things
concerning Himself," thus to prepare Israel to say "Blessed is He that
cometh in the name of the Lord."

Jesus Christ, the Messiah, at His first coming, fulfills *the sufferings*
foretold by Isaiah (Isaiah 53); and at His second coming, He will fulfill
the glory to be unveiled in the revelation (I Peter 1:11). The King was
rejected (John 1:11), but the Savior, the Head of the Church, catches up
His Body (I Thessalonians 4:17), and then God sends Jesus back to the
earth at Israel's call for Him (Matthew 23:39, Acts 3:20), and the King
reigns over His Kingdom.

F. "HE STEADFASTLY SET HIS FACE TO GO TO JERUSALEM"

1. The Set Face

This was the anabasis of the aeons, "that He should be *received up*";
Moses and Elijah appeared in glory on the Mount of Transfiguration and
spoke with Him of His *"exodus"* which He should shortly *accomplish* at
Jerusalem. Like as a woman knowing her hour of travail is upon her, He
set His face toward Jerusalem (Mark 10:32—34, Luke 13:33—34). For this
was the "Saul" of cities (Jerusalem); and He was the "David" of kings.
Whoever would be God's prophet must be proclaimed king in Jerusalem;
so, when "Mine Hour" [1] is come, because He was the Son of God, He could
"at-one" (atone) here for man's sin—or, as King of Kings, He could be the
conqueror of the Holy City. Roman crosses for Hebrew prophets were to be
found only in *Jerusalem*. As a radio is a trap for the voice through ether
vibrations, or a steel mill for metals on the way to skyscrapers—so Jerusalem either broadcasts or de-incarnates Deity. The Cross like the an-
tennae of the radio, traps the message that He may be glorified, and so
"Jesus knowing that the Father had given all things into His hands . . ."

---

[1] John 2:4*b*, 12:23 and 17:1; also see this section under G. "Mine Hour" 1. The Upper
Room, Preparing the Disciples, p. 284 ff.

(John 13:3–4), destiny then starts throwing the shuttle for the good or evil. And at once the thoughts of many hearts are revealed:

a) Peter talked of tabernacles (Luke 9:33)
b) James and John talked of thrones (Mark 10:37)
c) Poor, poor Judas plans to bargain and betray his Master (Matthew 26:14–16).

The tide of His anabasis pounds against all barriers and opposers. Even Jerusalem and the Roman Empire that braced the Cross, were beaten down:

"Lo, all our pomp of yesterday,
Is one with Nineveh and Tyre!" [1]

Those competent to estimate the thought, power and genius revealed in such a revelation as the Cross, will appreciate all that was required to plan:

a) The program of redemption and to make pre-vision for every last detail
b) And to conceive the Life of Christ, the fulfillment of which even while "Wonderful," is not equal to the "Lamb slain from the foundation of the world."

As Nature's children reveal an invisible mold, so Christ reveals the elements of character. The Scriptures are just a spring blanket of potential divinity, and the release and control of such an influence in the world makes all the further prophetic glories believable! The Crucifixion of Jesus makes inescapable demands upon the Creator; there has to be an adequate reason for such wreckage!

2. The Baptism of Self-Renunciation

The setting is on the way up to Jerusalem (Mark 10:38, Romans 5:8, John 12:20–37). This trip is different from the other ones; His looks, tone and attitude are changed. "It was in the air." There is harmony in nature everywhere and we have often witnessed the stillness before a storm, and the silence of a crowd in the presence of some brave deed. The disciples' spirits were awed unknowingly by the nearness of Gethsemane. They said, "we are able." This was the greatest tribute ever paid to Jesus. They had been His intimates for three years and did not measure the burden! He *made it appear easy to be second to Him!* He was fulfilling His own teaching: "appear not unto men to fast" (Matthew 6:18). This is the pattern of every unselfish soul. They had not weighed *all* of His life; they had all over-looked the nights of prayer; the pain of rejections and they had given

---

[1] Rudyard Kipling, *The Five Nations,* Copyright 1903 by Rudyard Kipling, reprinted by by permission of Mrs. George Bambridge and Doubleday & Company, Inc.

answer in kind with others and had forgotten. But not so this "World Lover" for He said, "I will never leave thee nor forsake thee." They saw only His giving out, not the cost of preparation nor the "Mine Hour" of every miracle. They had not seen the end of such a *life* and *momentum* which must eventually collide with selfishness. They asked "that we may sit at Thy right hand." They imagined it already done. There had been a few parables and sermons and miracles, but *no pain*. It was a sort of "spiritual" battle, and then He should sit down in glory. Now *we* know better for them for we have the record of the Master's blood-sweat of Gethsemane; His standing judgment in Pilate's hall; His suffering of death on the Cross and His three days in the grave. We know of the disciples' toil in the Gospel and of their martyrdom for the Faith, and that they received no "kingdom" as they had first expected. But as we read and study, do we know that for ourselves it takes the same today? There seems to be no apparent change in the world after we have given *our* best. The building of the Eternal requires more than that, for the Trinity worked on the eternal Purpose of God. It was not wrought out at a work bench with human hands. Beloveds, we need to sit before this text and study our conceptions of it as shown by our acts. Jesus said, "I am to be baptized 'with'"—the tense was still in the future. There was that perfect Life, and yet still a baptism! *Perfection does not save*. He said, "My blood,"—and this was no martyr spirit (Matthew 26:28). This baptism was one of utter humiliation and self-renunciation, "Thy will, not Mine." He was clothed with God's will; we are "baptized into Christ," and He into God. We sing with the hymnist, "My will be lost in Thine," and as metal is placed in a furnace and becomes steel to be poured into the molds and plans of men, so we with Christ yield our wills to God. After the time of "His baptism," He spoke and said, "All authority hath been given unto Me." Earth's gain ever comes through such renunciation. Real life is a series of self renunciations. It is life's enrichment. If one escapes from it, he suffers as rich men's sons often do. We are shaping an eternity and life needs disciplining. All discontent is a complaint of the selfish; a "dis"-ease of the "do"-less, and these need a baptism.

The transfer of the Cross is from the Head to the Body (Luke 9:23–26, 14:25–39 and Luke 23:26). The meaning of the Cross is found between the Confession and the Transfiguration. Peter rebukes the Lord for the Holy Spirit was not yet given; that no physical cross was in sight, the incident illustrates. No one is fit to live who is not ready to die for someone; no one who is conscious of carrying a cross or of making a sacrifice, is really doing so; such already have their reward. "Appear unto men not to fast," so our Lord preached and so He practised; neither Mary's other children, nor James, nor John discerned this. The occasion calls out the man as Ernest's "The Stone Face." Baptism is the assumption of the Cross, the induction into the *Ek-klesia*. The Lord Himself said, "Sacrifice and offering Thou wouldest not, But a Body hast Thou prepared Me . . . Lo, I come . . . to do Thy will, O God," (Hebrews 10:5, 7). At His baptism the voice from heaven said, "This is My beloved Son in whom I am well pleased"; and so many of us as have been baptized into Christ, have put on Christ. At the resurrection, following His baptism of suffering, the Father fulfilled Psalm 2:7:

> "Thou art My Son; this day have I begotten Thee"
> (cp. Acts 13:33—34, 44).

As Jesus goes stedfastly up to Jerusalem, a predetermined course of action now entered upon the Divine Plan for the Lamb of God (Revelation 5:6 and 13:8). This was no strolling minstrel whose vagrant course was changed by any caprice. "Mine Hour" must be considered in the light of "for the joy set before Him, endured the Cross" (Hebrews 12:2), as just an incident on the way to "He hath sat down." We have allowed the Cross (I Corinthians 2:2) to eclipse, short-vision and crowd out, whereas it should be vice versa. Compare Jacob serving for Rachael (Genesis 29:20); or, Othniel, successful in battle, for the hand of Achsah who was given by her father, Joshua (Joshua 15:16—17); or, Moses who "endured as seeing Him who is invisible"; or, David who said "I beheld the Lord always before my face." In Luke 9:51 note that the more important phrase is that "the time was come that He should be received up," rather than the phrase "He stedfastly set His face to go to Jerusalem." Note also, that the words are *"received up,"* and not "if I be *lifted* up" (John 12:32). The reference in Luke 9:51 is to His *glory* and not to His *suffering*; just as Psalm 27:7 and John 17:4—5 are closely related to Isaiah 53:11—12. "Mine Hour" is the supreme, isolated act consisting of the elements, issues and vitalities of salvation which become the "faith . . . once delivered" (Jude 3). And to complete "Mine Hour" is why He "set His face," for this must be accomplished *before* He could "be received up." When He said, "It is finished," it was the "Un-set-ting" of His face, as He was "laying the armour by." That "Set Face" set standards of right, and changed the face of the world. At the first, He *amazed* His disciples (Mark 10:32); and at the last, He *appalled* Caesar's hardened soldiers (Isaiah 52:24, John 18:6). We can assess "set" (Gr. *starizo*) by comparison. In the following references the word *stayridzo* is translated by various words. A study of these texts will give further light as to the meaning and usage of this word:

a) In Luke 16:36 "there is a great gulf *fixed*";
    "stayridzo" is translated "fixed"
b) In Luke 22:32, re Peter, "when thou art turned again, *establish* the brethren"; here it is also translated

"strengthen" for the same Greek word *"stayridzo"*

 c) In Romans 1:11, "to the end ye may be *established"*
  (Gr. *stayridzo*)

 d) And in Romans 16:25, "*stablish* (Gr. *stayridzo*) you
  according to my gospel."

By comparing "spiritual things with spiritual" (I Corinthians 2:13) we receive a greater understanding of this phrase: "he *stedfastly set* His face."

In the light of this "set face" men's words and plans and lives are weighed. Such weighing happened to His unbelieving brothers, to the adulterers who came before Him, and to those who claimed He wrought miracles by Beelzebub. Around this Peasant of the "set face," we have seen the immortals cluster and the "near" immortals fading away. Even the dirt of Palestine becomes the Sarcophagus of Unbelief: His "set face" "Christ-ized" the very dirt of Palestine as when soil is treated for crops.

 3. In Bethany

  "SIX days before . . ."—John 12:1–8
  "And after TWO days . . ."—Luke 10:38, Mark 14:1–9

Jesus of the "Set Face" arrives at Bethany Friday afternoon. This picturesque suburb, like a bride's corsage or bouquet, rose like a crown-jewel greeting the pilgrim as he approached the Holy City of our God, David's Son's capitol! From its site could be seen the road to Jericho, the Dead Sea, the mountains of Moab, and the silver strand of Jordan as it comes down from Galilee. Jerusalem was walled off by Olivet, and here at Bethany is sanctuary for the city's business man. All of the places where Jesus tarried were "beautiful for situation"; God loves beauty and His children should strive for it. A stranger on a street sees a row of houses; but Jesus, the "set face" traveler, turns in to a *home*, and makes thereby an immortal of the village of Bethany.

A Sabbath of quiet rest follows in order that the "Set Face" might be readjusted in a love atmosphere. On His first journey from Bethany into Jerusalem, there is a triumphal entry ending at the Temple (Mark 11:11), and on Monday and Tuesday, follow the days of bitter hostility, closing Matthew 25:31–46, and with Caiaphas and the chief priests plotting to take Jesus subtly and kill Him (Matthew 26:4, Luke 22:2). But the Lord knew these things and because of His divine acumen, was never taken by surprise (Matthew 26:1–2). Events follow: Judas goes out and joins the betrayers; and this Tuesday evening, which is the Jews' beginning of Wednesday, in His loneliness, Jesus retires to Bethany's friendly circle for the last night of rest under a roof.

These friends of Bethany are one of the most wonderful groups that the Lord ever assembled upon earth. Evidence from surrounding facts point up the probability that Martha was the wife of Simon of Bethany, the leper. Through the eager solicitation of Martha, Simon had gained faith in Jesus and though the Scriptures bear no record of this man's healing from leprosy yet it comes under those of John 21:25; and now in Matthew 26:6 is indicated Simon's return from ostracized leprosy, to his home in Bethany, and there Simon's heart prompted him to feast Jesus—as had also Matthew (Luke 5:29), and Zacchaeus (Luke 19:2). Here in Bethany at this feast, were also Lazarus and Mary; and Martha served. Martha was no servant but here she served in her own home with her husband. Perhaps Simon was like two others of whom the Scriptures record their implicit faith and its reward: You remember that Naaman, "captain of the host of the king of Syria, was a great man with his Lord, and honourable, . . ." yet he was a leper (II Kings 5). Though at first he despised the child-pleading of the little Jewish servant maid that he visit the prophet Elisha in order to be healed of his leprosy, yet faith gave victory. Nathaniel doubted the possibility of Messiah's coming from a filth-stained and despised city like Nazareth, yet through the persuasive faith of Philip, He came, saw, and believed (John 1:45—47), and continued faithful (John 21:2).

At this same feast at Simon's home, Lazarus was there with a price on his head, for his rising from the dead disposed the Jews to believe on the Lord (John 12:10—11). He was completely loyal to Jesus and was continually concerned about Him. Very likely he was the "certain young man having a linen cloth cast about his naked body" who followed Jesus the night of His betrayal (Mark 14:51—52). This was the first night that the Lord had failed to come home to Bethany. Lazarus, concerned for the absence of Jesus, risked capture by the Jews and fled naked when the young men attacked him; for they sought to kill him also in order to remove evidence of his own resurrection.

Martha once *before* had made a feast for Him (Luke 10:38—42) in the *home of Lazarus* when with "set face" He first came, arriving all strained. His disciples had said earlier on that day: "shall we call down fire"; and on another occasion when they returned rejoicing at their successful e-vangelistic campaign, said, ". . . even the devils were subject unto us." No one understood "The Son of Man hath not where to lay His head," for there was no understanding heart into which He could go and confide. At this time Mary had sat at His feet, and after that her understanding made a place of rest for Him. Seeking sanctuary, He had come to Bethany, and Martha, always the practical one, thought it a matter of food; so on this His first day of ease with loved ones, Martha like Peter, got in the way (Matthew 16:23); but Mary, choosing the better part, thirstily quaffed the Cup of Living Water.

During this second visit of Jesus, Mary helped to serve, for the Master needed hospitality, and there was nothing more to be treasured; that she served, the story shows: for "Martha served and Lazarus sat at meat," and Mary was moving about, for she attracted attention only at the shattering of the cruse of ointment; and it was "shivered into pieces' as she *"poured down* upon Him" (Mark 14:3–9, Matthew 26:6, 13, John 12:1–8). This is an unusual expression for an unusual significance: "His head, His feet, His body" were anointed at this time. Here we find a beautiful simile to Queen Esther in devotion to her people; like as these Bethany saints *serving* with Martha, *sharing* with Lazarus, and *worshiping* with Mary.

In answering the criticisms of those who claimed this was a waste of the ointment Jesus said, "Let her alone; why trouble ye her? . . . she hath done what she could: she brought it *beforehand to anoint My body* to the burying" (Mark 14:4–8 N.); and this is fruit from Luke 10:42. Now the Son of Man hath one "place to lay His Head." She understood, and she will not be at the grave. Here in Bethany, first was revealed and received, the great truth of the Resurrection. Simon, the leper, is a type of sin, and "sin bringeth forth death." Lazarus demonstrates the Lord's power over death, and now Mary's anointing is for sleep. A Jewish commentator, writing on The Song of Solomon, chapter 1, verse 12, says that "spikenard was a sack placed about the neck to induce pleasant sleep." Perhaps the tomb where He lay and His Body were still fragrant from this anointing. As a lady buckled on a knight's sword before battle, so Mary anointed Him for battle—"Go forth, O King Eternal!"

4. In Jerusalem

Jesus' entrance into Jerusalem has been called the triumphal entry. There were at least three entries into the city, and the second time of the three, He is in tears (Luke 19:41–44); these are not tears of joy, but of excessive sorrow. The company that went with Him was composed of the multitude which included those who were at the tomb of Lazarus, and augmented by the multitude whom they had told of Lazarus' resurrection (John 12:17–18). They shouted "Hosanna to the Son of David; Blessed is the King of Israel." As Jesus came near, He beheld the city and wept over it (Luke 19:41). From Olivet, the Master could envision the heaven-prepared and adorned New Jerusalem, His Bride, descending from the new heaven to the new earth at the Consummation (Revelation 21:2). At the beginning of His ministry, He had been shown "the kingdoms of the world and the glory of them"; now (Luke 19:42–44), He X-rays the sensualism, decay and rottenness of the grinning skeleton of the spiritually dead and is driven to tears (John 12:36–43).

But as Isaiah 35 looks to the future of joy and gladness "when sorrow and sighing shall flee away,' so our Lord beheld "the far off interest of tears"; and He could "see of the travail of His soul and be satisfied" (Isaiah 53:11). Though the Lord's face was set toward Jerusalem and the Cross, yet the glory vision (Hebrews 12:2) gave Him the goal of victory. As William Harper and Lorado Taft visioned the campus of the University of Chicago and the Midway Plaisance which served as Midway of the World's Fair of 1893 whose climax in sculpture was the Statue of Time,[1] so our Lord Jesus Christ over-looked the city, this Jerusalem of His Gethsemane, the mob, and the Cross, and sees "the world to come." He sees the Glory City, the set stage whereon the regeneration shall occur, and in the new Jerusalem, this golden milestone, are the converging lines:

a) "In bringing many sons into glory" (Hebrews 2:10)

b) Of "the kings of the earth do bring their glory and honour into it" (Revelation 21:24)

c) Of the consummation of "the Age of the Ages" (Ephesians 3:21) into the "Glory" of God.

"Suffering became Him," that is, the humiliating of the flesh, for the way of life to glory is through death. The coming of "the world to come" awaits the removal of the world that now is.

Now Jesus moves on into Jerusalem, and the blind and the lame come to Him in the Temple and "He healed them all" (Matthew 21:14); and the priests saw it done (vs. 15). The children cried in the Temple saying, "Hosanna to the Son of David," fulfilling Psalm 8:2, "out of the mouths of babes and sucklings, Thou hast perfected praise." In His first journey to Jerusalem from Bethany, He only *entered* the temple, and "when He had looked round about upon all things," He returned to Bethany (Mark 11:11). The next morning He was again before the doctors of the law in the temple. And their business was to examine and credential a new Rabbi; the Lad who once faced them (Luke 2:46)—now, twenty-two years later faces them once again. Because He had been proclaimed the Messiah yesterday, they asked Him, "By what authority doest Thou these things and who gave Thee this authority" (Matthew 21:23); Jesus' reply is found in verses 24—27.

Then follow the three parables: (The two sons (Matthew 21:28—32)
                                     (The vineyard (verses 33—46)
                                     (The wedding garment (22:1—14)

These men then "sought to lay hold on Him" for they "perceived He spake against them."

---

[1] This portrayal in sculpture is known as "The Fountain of Time." In the center is "Time" personified, and before him pass all of mankind, the youth and the aged, in all walks of life, rising up out of birth and passing on. On his masterpiece Mr. Taft placed this inscription: "time goes, you say? Ah, no! Alas, time stays—we go."

And following the parables, come three questions:

First, concerning the tribute to Caesar (Matthew 22:15—22)
Second, concerning the man who had seven wives (vss. 23—33)
Third, concerning the great commandment of the Law (vss. 34—40).

And the Lord's clear answers to all of these questions is found in these texts.

We come next to the Lord's unanswerable question (vss. 41—46). His question was, "what think ye of Christ; whose Son is He?" But His further questioning brings a refusal to answer and this ended their questioning.

Then follows the terrible denunciation of the Scribes and Pharisees in Matthew 23; yet Jesus tells the multitudes and His disciples to "do what they bid you for they are in Moses' seat."

His last public word is found in chapters 24 and 25 of Matthew, and as the disciples call attention to the Temple, they ask questions and He replies with questions, answers and warnings.[1] Chapter 25:31 takes up the great judgment on the nations and then that last *public word,* verse 46. The tender close of Jesus' ministry is taken up in Matthew 26 as He tells His disciples of His own death, verses 1—2; and this is followed by His anointing at Bethany and His last *act* will be the restoring of the servant's ear which Peter cut off.

Why was there this implacable hatred of the Jews toward Jesus? It came through neglect of God's revelation. Here were four million people from the ends of the earth to celebrate The Passover at the time of Jesus' crucifixion; these were the choice spirits of the religious world, and they worshiped in a temple unequalled in lines and furnishings. If we could compute the total of the money and labor loss involved in this one Passover Pilgrimage, the cost would be immense. Yet this observance was so diverted from its original intent that *He was not recognized* (John 1:11), and these were good men! Had they been usurpers or supplanters, we might criticize, but not one of them would have assumed to be "that Prophet!" Here is an institution fully financed, equipped and manned, with every part functioning at the highest efficiency; yet *lost,* as our earth would be, were it adrift in the sky!

The Jews were given an *institution,* (The Temple), a *day* (The Sabbath) and a *place* (The Holy Land); the values of each arising out of a Person (God); and the institution was to keep real God's Person, Power and His Presence until "The Lamb of God" should come. These all became e-clipsed in "Activities":

    a) The day was to be a time to meditate upon God, His work, and
        His rest, and their rest to come

_____

[1] See this Section, 2. *Prophecy of The End Times,* p. 272

b) *The Place* (Palestine) was to preserve a unity of Tribes until David's Great Son should "come unto His own"

c) And when *Personality* departed, *the institution* became the usurper. It was no longer a house of prayer, but had become a den of thieves.

So, in this defiled, fallen city with the muck of decadence as the silt of sin, all of the animosities of all time were mobilized for His blood. Upon the Cross are centered all the prophets, and from it radiate all of God's ways with man. To *understand* the Cross is to understand all.

G. "MINE HOUR"

"Mine hour is not yet come."

John 2:4*b*

"The hour is come, that the Son of man should be glorified."

John 12:23*b*

"Mine Hour" is the supreme, isolated act consisting of the elements, issues and vitalities of salvation which become "the faith once for all delivered" (Jude 3).

Jesus Christ towers as the "fairest among ten thousand, and the One altogether lovely" as a Lamb that had been slain. Fronting pride, He took a towel; fronting sin, He took a Cross; and that Cross towers "o'er the wrecks of time!" It rises as man advances and expands as "the thoughts of men are broadened." It "horizons" between One-born and the Twice-born.

1. The Upper Room: Preparing The Disciples

"Jesus knowing all things, took a towel." The God-sent One is indifferent to equipment at hand. Any equipment may be used by the "God-sent"; Peter used a sword in Gethsemane, but He used the Scriptures in the Upper Room (Acts 1). Peter said he would die with Christ, but a thief did die with Him and took Peter's place.

In the Upper Room we witness Jesus cleansing His friends in a crucial battle for His own (Ezekiel 28:11–19, Luke 22:31). The word "crucial" has its roots in the Latin word for "cross"; and out of the testing and trial of "Mine Hour" which included the Cross, we have this word coined for our language today. From the agony of Gethsemane three times He came back to His disciples; and the best that human loyalty could supply, was sleeping; only Judas His betrayer was awake!

He has withdrawn from facing His enemies; each having gone to his own place; they too await the arrival of Judas, and possibly Peter! But

Jesus goes to the Upper Room to prepare the disciples, and then on to Gethsemane.

Let us view again the break that there may be no question of His courage or their wilfull blindness. In Matthew 25:46 in His final warning to the nation, He shows that the choice is between eternal punishment and eternal life. They make the choice: the issue is clearly joined and the choice has now been made: the nation wins Judas, and Jesus wins Joseph and Nicodemus!

In John 13:34 Jesus says, "A new commandment I give unto you, *that* (Gr. *hina*, meaning "in order that") ye love one another." From I John 3:23 we understand that the new commandment is not "love one another" which is really an old commandment stated in the Law: "Love thy neighbor as thyself," but rather the new commandment is stated in John 14:1*b* "believe in God, believe also in Me." Faith in Jesus Christ makes possible our love for one another. Jesus' statement to Peter that He had prayed for him that his *faith* fail not (Luke 22:31—32), shows the need for giving heed to the new commandment which He gave to them following this statement.

Satan had desired all of the disciples that he might sift them as wheat. [1] All of them needed the encouragement of the new commandment that they might remain faithful. This faith must be in Him of whom Isaiah wrote (Isaiah 9:6) and in this One Person, Jesus Christ, is the whole revelation set forth. He is truly the "Wonderful, Counsellor, the Mighty God, the Everlasting Father, the Prince of Peace." And because He is all of these, He can give assurance and strength to His disciples.

Judas has been rebuked (John 12:1—8) and from that moment he had kept brooding over his rebuke till he betrayed his Master. Even His enemies had not thought of a disciple betraying Him for they had not so much as approached any of them, but rather Judas went to the chief priests and asked "what will ye give me and I will deliver Him unto you" (Matthew 26:15).

When the disciples heard Jesus say, "one of you shall betray Me," it is said that they looked one at another doubting of whom He spake, and they each said, "Lord, is it I?" They were a wholesome group and they trusted each other. But Peter was so sure of himself that he said, "though all men shall be offended because of Thee, yet will I never be offended" (Matthew 26:33), to which Jesus replied, "this night before the cock crow, thou shalt deny Me thrice."

In this time in the Upper Room, the Lord is wholly at ease as at no other time in His earth life; now He talks freely and revealingly; in John

---

[1] "Satan sifts to get rid of the corn; God winnows to get rid of the chaff" (Matthew 3:12; I Peter 5:8—9). (Thynne, *Student's Commentary* p. 772.)

13:33 He says, "dear little children, yet a little while I am with you. Ye shall seek Me: . . . whither I go, ye cannot come; . . . ."

> *a)* Peter asked, "Lord, whither goest Thou?"
> Jesus answered, "I go to prepare a place for you" (John 14:1—2)
>
> *b)* Thomas said, "Lord, we know not whither Thou goest, how can we know the way?"
> And to Thomas He gave the diameter of Deity (John 14:6), "*I* am the way, the truth and the life; no man cometh unto the Father except by Me."
>
> *c)* But Philip said unto Him, "Show us the Father"
> And to Philip He said, "Have I been so long time with you and yet hast thou not known Me, Philip? He that hath seen Me hath seen the Father." To what purpose had Philip applied his advantage; of how much better was he than the Jews of John 6:28—31?

Jesus said,

> "If I had not done among them the works which none other man did, they had not had sin; but now have they both seen and hated Me and My Father."
> John 15:24

And Philip had seen every one of the works: he saw the five thousand fed; the Gadarene healed; Jesus walking on the water; the stilling of the wind and also the sea; the boat at land from' the midst of the sea, four miles; the healing of the lepers; the raising of Lazarus; and still he said, "show us the Father, and it sufficeth us." He was like Peter and the other two disciples at the Transfiguration who said, "Let us build three tabernacles"; and as Moses (Exodus 33:18) who said to God, "I beseech Thee, show me Thy glory."

Since Philip's request, we have seen Him on a large stage demonstrate His Sonship to God. It is set forth in His choice of parent (singular); His choice of home and disciples, for He could have founded an aristocracy, but His followers chose to be "pilgrims and strangers" for the marks of the new birth are *humility*. His words blasted empires and unseated dictators as Richter wrote, "wounded hands lifted empires"; and through His institutions: *The Day* and *His Supper*, He has led men to a loyalty where Napoleon said of Him, "millions would die for Him."

Facing Jesus Christ, there is a door open upon Infinity; I become aware of my own potentials; and I am a citizen of The Transcendent. I am beholding telescopian dimensions and unveiled holiness; and I am enfolded by the indissoluble which reaches above the highest, and below the needs of depth, and which are wider than all dimensions; my every out-reach contacts peace. I am drawn out of infinity, yet I am unafraid, for I am not alone (Psalm 23:4). There is a bridge of eyes and ears over which personality is transferred to me (I John 1:1—4, II Peter 1:16—17). Those who are seeing these things are being changed (John 17:3, 21 and II Corinthians 3:18), and are being taken up into God (I John 1:2—4). While others are putting forth hypotheses and gropings, He of them all, speaks as One having authority—"hear ye Him," (John 18:21, 7:17).

The Lord entered His ministry attended by the Father and the Holy Spirit (Matthew 3:16—17). He returns to God also attended by these same Two, "knowing that He came forth from God and goeth unto God" (John 23:3). Every incident is compounded of the Trinity and in these last hours with His disciples, He tells them in John 14, that He is going to prepare a place in the Father's house, but while absent in body, He will send the Comforter (John 14:1, 7, 26). So also in John 14, He says, "I am the vine and My Father is the husbandman"; and as branches of that vine, His disciples would receive the Comforter whom He would send, Who when come, would "testify concerning Me" and they were to bear witness. In John 16 He repeats for the third time, that now He goes, and that It is even expedient for Him to go, for otherwise the Comforter cannot come. After these words of great comfort and assurance, Redemption's hour draws nigh, and now was the time to say, "Arise, let us go hence," for there is a world to save and here is a world-Savior, prepared and obedient "to the uttermost."

2. The Upper Room; The Lord's Table [1]

What happened in "The Mine Hour"? As an *innocent* child He stood in the temple; and even now, this Holy One though "tempted in all points like as we," He eats the Passover and goes to the Cross. The veil of the temple is rent in twain; the clock of the Universe is stopped, and we hear "the silence of God." As the Good Shepherd, He stops a fifteen hundred year old ritual of the sacrifice of the Passover lambs; and their house is left unto them desolate. God, at Joshua's request, stopped the sun; so Jesus, the Son of God, stopped the Passover service "till" Daniel 9:27; and here is where the Communion arises until I Corinthians 11:26. It was not the *outer* veil of the Temple which was rent in twain, but the veil between the Holy and the Most Holy places where the veil was "rent in twain from top to bottom"; and the outer veil which shut out the Jew from the Holy Place remained intact. It was the Holy Place and the Holy of Holies which were now made into one. The Temple once stood as the most wonderful of all buildings, but in its stead now rises "the Table of the Lord," a continuing Presence in every tongue telling of John 3:16 so that men

---

[1] See Section FIVE, THE CHURCH, VI. "Things Most Surely Believed . . ." E. The Lord's Table, p. 441 ff.

everywhere might say, "hear we every man in the tongue wherein we were born"; for now He had removed their sacrifices, their priestly service; and even their very Temple itself; and He replaces it by putting a Table "in their midst" which is done as simply as in the presence of a child. Then He said, "for as often as ye do this . . . keep in memory." He, "having loved His own, . . . loved them unto the end"—yea, and "until I come" again; let us remember this when we observe His Supper. Here indeed, is a tryst made holier than all others. In the chambers of imagery as we reconstruct "Mine Hour," may we see growing out of this time of our Lord's sufferings, the parting of the rent veil through which all men might now pass for salvation. In the midst of these saved men, the Church, we see the Table of Remembrance where we "so partake" discerning the Lord's Body and Blood, and continue His life and share His sufferings, and enter into His glory.

The place of the first occurrence of the Lord's Table was in the house of the man with a pitcher. This humble-spirited "good man of the house" completes the picture of the "lowly Jesus' born in a stable, raised in Nazareth, and buried from the Cross in a borrowed tomb. "Being found by His enemies, He humbled Himself EVEN unto death."

"As they were eating"; the materials essential to the Supper were common to that feast (Romans 10:6), and they rise from there into immortality, even as Bethlehem and Gethsemane. "He took bread" which was ready at hand of God's *pre*-vision; nothing was imported; will there ever be aught imported? If we have not, or if we neglect to prepare, we are passed by. Judas went out seeking, but Moses was asked, "what is that in thy hand?" If we have not, we cannot impart. The God-sent use the things that are at hand.

Note Luke 22:7—20, I Corinthians 10:21, Exodus 25:30. This is Redemption's song of "Mine Hour" where two ages meet and separate; here we have the Passover and the Bread of Faces, which after fifteen hundred years, are replaced by the Cross and the Table of Remembrance. And, as we "Behold, The Man," let us go reverently, slowly and hear fully, as He says with intensest desire:

> ". . . 'With desire[1] I desired to eat this
> passover with you before I suffer':"
>
> Luke 22:15 N.

Did He eat the Passover? Twice the Scriptures say that He did: Luke 22:8 and 11 show His anticipation in preparation for the Passover; see also Matthew 26:26 and Mark 14:22. From the text we understand that He ate

---

[1] Gr. *epithumia*, Philippians 1:23 and I Thessalonians 2:17

of the Passover but He did not partake "after supper" as He established a new covenant; He gave as His reason for eating *this* Passover Luke 22:16, "I will not any more eat thereof until it be fulfilled in the Kingdom of God"; and in Luke 22:18 He says, "I will not drink of the fruit of the vine until the kingdom of God shall come."

3. Gethsemane

"Then cometh Jesus with them unto
a place called Gethsemane . . . ."

Matthew 26:36a

Forth from Gethsemane came a power beyond any of the Universe. There is an articulate, consecutive, increasing ascent out of the natural— up and into the super-natural. Before the Cross was set up, nations, events and achievements were unrelated; Egypt, Babylon and other pagan nations were not related; Rome even with Latin ability to organize, *could not* bind together. Since the Cross, there is consecutiveness as set forth in canvas, cathedral and constitution; the great paintings, buildings and governments of history and today, are based upon the ideals and motives of the Christ. The Lord perhaps is not named; yet HE is there (Psalm 139:7); there is a glory upon all from Him.

"*Then cometh*" a uniting motive to the world. Such a uniting motive is demonstrated in the history of these United States of America:

a) Men went out in 1620; our pilgrim fathers *united to find* freedom of worship

b) Others were invited in 1776 to *unite to defend* the newly found freedon, the Republic

c) These went for others in 1917; our American patriots *united with* other nations *to vindicate* the freedom of men of every nation.

We today are in danger from money and ease and sacrilege, and we need anew these uniting motives. It was a "New Motives' Birth Hour" when Christ came to Gethsemane. That "One-Will" which was here demonstrated (Hebrews 10:7, Psalm 40:8) shows the wonder of a surrendered will. Just as Raphael's *Sistine Madonna* was not understood until it was placed in back of an altar so that the eyes of the principal figures were focused upon the Altar—so all of us must now focus upon Gethsemane.

His last week is the most publicized, as is Daniel's Seventieth Week, for here God vindicates His "This is My Son." Though unworthy, let us company with Him that "this mind may be in us" (Philippians 2:5). We must first tarry at Gethsemane "till endued" and we get control of ourselves for we are to meet men like unto Annas, Herod, and Pilate; even

Jesus dared not venture "until" He had tarried in prayer. If we have "eyes to see," we then have before us a study in mass psychology. These rulers were merely hypnotized puppets, and no one of them was normal; and the entire city was under this same hypnotic spell.

"Then cometh Jesus with them unto a place called Gethsemane . . ." and,

> "Now is My soul troubled; and what shall I say?
> 'Father, save Me from this hour?' but for this
> cause came I unto this hour."
>
> John 12:27

Jesus of the "Set Face" "cometh unto Gethsemane," for He said that for such a time had He come unto this hour. This One of troubled soul had left eight of His disciples just inside the garden; and three others a little nearer; and then He went on alone. In realities, *we* strip the dependables and the essentials. Within which circle of disciples would you or I be dropped? Would we be among the one hundred twenty, the seventy, the eight, or the three?

In Luke 22:41 "He *was with-drawn* (Gr, *apospao*) from them about a stone's cast. Note the use of the passive voice here, for the Messiah is "the *stone* which the builders rejected." Also in the *suffering* portion of Isaiah 53, the passive voice is used. "Upon this *rock*," He said, "I *will* build My Church." It is harder to hold still, to be passive, than to *do*. Here we see His wonderfulness. How terrible it must be when faith is going against one's will. He "was removed"; this reveals His complete submission to the will of His Father; God was carrying out upon the Son, the plan prepared *before* the foundation of the world (I Peter 1:19—29); Jesus' own volition was not evident. Here He was "alone," and "Jehovah hath laid on Him the iniquity of us all." He made Him to be sin in that lonely place for a world's redemption. Within that circle of "prayers and supplications with strong crying and tears" (Hebrews 5:7*a*), He *alone* could go. Our Lord, "holy, harmless, undefiled" came to an infection of sin, and God "made Him to be sin for us," and "laid on Him the iniquity of us all" (Isaiah 53:6). His prayer was *not* that He might escape the Crucifixion (Matthew 26:39, 42, 44) for which He had been prepared *from* the foundation of the world (Revelation 13:8), but *rather He was praying that He might not suffer death until He had reached the Cross* (Matthew 26:38, Luke 22:43—44); "and He was heard by Him who was able to save Him from death" (Hebrews 5:7*b*).

The agony of that hour distorted His features and they were "marred." In Genesis 6:11 is the first use of this word, and it is translated "corrupt" (the Hebrew meaning "gross immorality"), which when God looked upon, He decided to destroy. "Jehovah hath laid upon Him the iniquity of us all," and here it was touching Him. The soldiers and Judas "went backward" and "His visage was so marred more than any man, and His form more than the sons of men" (Isaiah 52:14b). This was fulfilled as they held a lantern to His face. Their going backward recalls Him to His ministry, and so His face became natural again.

In these closing days of His ministry, Jesus is set forth stripped of parables, as the redeeming love-art of God our Father. This phrase, "Then cometh Jesus unto Gethsemane," is a part of the far vision which had been seen by Abraham (John 8:56). The Jews' high regard for the name of *Jehovah* is emphasized by their refusal even to pronounce it, and for it they substituted the word *Adonai*. This should be an example for us to follow in the careful use of the word *Gethsemane*; it should never be used carelessly or ever applied to the finite sufferings of men.

Here in Gethsemane is a parallel of His world work. God's face is not "rouged" or Grecian. The face is a symbol of what one is; of what he has done and will do. Sight gives way to vision for suffering is becoming to Him, and how else can so much power and greatness get hold of us. We fear Him if there is no common point of contact, but pain is the common denominator of life and He took it. Pain is an old door of entrance to life and so pain was the more written on the Cross which is our door to *life*. There is blood on the threshold of all progress and every achievement has its grave yard. The three in the fiery furnace became a symbol, and the king believed (Daniel 3:19—30).

A lofty building is seen to be made of brick and stone, but this does not explain the iron which went through fire in its process of being made, which is hidden and forms the framework of the building. So the Cross of Christ is to the heart of character and mighty ideals.

The Church was in Christ's side as the place of pain. Your agony is a cross, fire-hardened, to bear the weight of the mass who only give assent as bricks. You must "fill up the measure of the sufferings of the Christ." You must be the strength of the frame of the Universe and of Society. The bricks may reflect the beauty, but the "Within" holds it in place. The Cross of Jesus and others is the way of salvation: "The Way of the Cross Leads Home." The Cross stands there "O'er the Wrecks of Time." That distorted face of the Holy Creator and Redeemer is sin's judgment and is my warning!

"Then cometh Jesus unto Gethsemane" (see John 18:2); "Jesus knowing all things . . . and went forth" (John 18:1—9) from *meditation* unto *mediation*. The last long mile of "the way" is to be broken at Pilate's: "Behold, The Man!"—and ended at, "come and see the place where the Lord lay."

4. "Behold, The Man!"

Isaiah 53 contrasts with John 1:

> "All things were made by Him'
> "He was in the world and the world knew Him not"
> "He came unto His own things, and His own people knew Him not"
> They said, "we will not have this man to reign over us"

As The Son of God He was presented:

To the Jews (Matthew 26:63—64N.):

> "And the high priest answered and said unto Him, 'I adjure Thee by the living God, that Thou tell us whether THOU be the Christ, the Son of God.' Jesus saith unto him, 'THOU hast said: nevertheless I say unto you, Henceforth shall ye see the Son of man sitting on the right hand of power, and coming on the clouds of heaven'."

Though there is the absence of the trappings of royalty, there is no mistaking HIM. Never are we so impressed about our Lord's being "every inch a King" as when we read His trial before the Sanhedrin.

To Pilate (John 18:33—36N.):

> ". . . 'Art THOU the King of the Jews?' Jesus answered him, 'Sayest THOU this thing from thyself, or did others tell thee concerning Me?' Pilate answered, 'Am I a Jew? Thine own nation and the chief priests delivered Thee unto me: what hast Thou done?' Jesus answered, 'My kingdom is not of (Gr. *out of*) this world; if My kingdom were of (Gr. *out of*) this world, then would My officers fight, that I should not be delivered to the Jews: but now is My kingdom not from hence'."

Jesus came out wearing a crown and a robe, and Pilate said,

"Behold, The Man!"

In His humiliation, still He was *"The Man."*

Pilate then retired and wrote, "Jesus of Nazareth, King of the Jews"; compared to their best, Jesus was still *"The King."*

To His Own (John 14:1—3N.):

> "Let not your heart be troubled; believe in God, believe also in Me. In My Father's house are many abodes: but if it were not so, I would have told you. I go to prepare a place for you. And if I go and prepare a place for you, I come again and will receive you unto Myself: that where I am, YE may be also."

What of this old earth? "But according to His promise, we look for a new heaven and a new earth (II Peter 3:10, 13, John 14:2). In Isaiah 11:11, we read:

"And it shall come to pass in that day, That the Lord shall *set His hand again a second time* to repossess the remnant of His people, which shall be left, from Assyria, Egypt, Pathros, ..."

This is the post-mortem kingdom of the King of Kings. These documents, the Scriptures, rest their validity upon the above affirmations.

5. The Anthology of The Cross
        or
Immortelles [1] in the Most Unlikely Places

The Gospel begotten in the Orient was incarnated in the Occident when "the Word became flesh and dwelt among us." The word *Evangel* or *Gospel* means sacrificial flesh coming from the Hebrew word *"Basar."* The gospel was conceived in love and constructed in sacrifice; and so must it enter each life as a miniature Jerusalem. In this city of Jerusalem, the Orient and the Occident came together; and met at Calvary; here the veil of the temple was rent in twain, opening the Gospel unto all mankind. Here were also the Jews and the Roman soldiers present together. Jerusalem was the cross-roads of commerce for the nations, and the Gospel begotten in the ancestry of the Orient was projected into the Occident beginning at Jerusalem. From this "Cross-roads" city emerged this "Via Dolorosa" anchored in Love's tributes though bordered by deadly nightshade!

"The Cross of Christ was God's Act, NOT Ours:
    'God so loved the world, that He gave
    His only begotten Son.'
"The one thing that *distinguishes* the Gospel of God's grace and *extinguishes* the religions of the world, is that in the religions of the world, the blood is flowing from the devotees to the gods to appease them, but in Christianity the blood is flowing from God to the sinners.
    'See from His head, His hands, His feet,
    Sorrow and love flow mingled down;
    Did e'er such love and sorrow meet,
    Or thorns compose so rich a crown.' [2]

"God Himself meets His own requirements in the Death of Christ. He is not acting apart from Him, therefore His action is God's act." [3]

His name is Emmanuel, God with us; but will man receive Him? Once

---

[1]
    Immortelle: "A flower that retains its form and color for a long time after having been gathered."

[2] Isaac Watts, *When I Survey The Wondrous Cross,* st. 3

[3] Mrs. M. Watts, Fetcham, Surrey, England, Prize Illustration, *Moody Monthly*

more John 3:16 reminds us that God was made lovable in the Cross. The impeccable puissance of Jesus aroused murderous envy and fear (John 11:53, I John 4:18) but the Cross hath broken every barrier down. In John 12:32 Jesus stated He "will draw all men" and those who "are drawn" become the Church (Colossians 1:17, Romans 8:22). There is a power not ourselves within which man and the universe move at ease, frictionless beyond our explaining and which is impossible to duplicate. It is the pull of *Hypostasis "dia"* (through) the Cross:

> Oh, Cross, that liftest up my head,
> I dare not ask to fly from Thee;
> I lay in dust life's glory dead,
> And from the ground there blossoms red
> Life that shall endless be.[1]

The power of the Cross's rays from *"sub-stans"*[2] is like the healing rays from radium and is fore-shadowed in fact (Genesis 1:3) and prophecy:

ALPHA:

> ". . . There shall come a star out of Jacob,
> And a Sceptre shall rise out of Israel . . ."
>
> Numbers 24:17*b*

OMEGA:

> "But unto you that fear My name shall the sun of
> righteousness arise with healing in His wings;"
>
> Malachi 4:2*a*

At ALPHA "a star shall arise" whose course is fixed (Revelation 13:8) from the beginning. At His birth the Father sent Wise Men from the East following a Star until it leads them to Him who is "the bright and morning star" (II Peter 1:19, Revelation 22:16). At OMEGA "The Sun of Righteousness shall arise with healing in its *beams* (i.e. rays). John the Baptist sought to hinder His "fixed course" (Matthew 3:14), but God had ordained:

> "Let the Son ARISE!"
> "Behold, The MAN!"
> "I, if I be lifted up from the earth,
>   will draw all men unto Myself."

He came and needed only to be placed to function and the Cross was the only way. As the *Sun* draws water, so the *Son* draws souls. The stars of prophecy came and stood over where the Cross was, and all else and all others went into eclipse.

---

[1] George Matheson, *O Love That Wilt Not Let Me Go*, st. 4

[2] *"Sub-stans"* hypostasis (Gr. *hupostasis*), See Section FIVE, VI. *"Things Most Surely Believed . . ."* B. *Faith*, 4. The Realm of Faith, p. 397

a) The Place of The Cross

"Wherefore Jesus also, that He might sanctify the people through His own blood, suffered without the gate. Let us go forth therefore unto Him without the camp, bearing His reproach. For here have we no continuing city, but we seek one to come."

Hebrews 13:12—14

They crucified Him *without* the city for the Cross was too great for Jerusalem to contain. The bigotry and spiritual darkness of the city's life forced this Cross of Supreme Love beyond its walls to "the place of a skull." We His believing followers, like the great cloud of witnesses of Hebrews 12:1—2, also go forth without the camp to the Cross bearing His reproach. (John 17:15—16).

The unforgeable accuracy of the Crucifixion narrative puts the Scriptures—the garden wherein this immortelle is found—beyond every controversy, for the Cross has "roots" in its every book "for they testify of Me." The incidents, persons and speeches are unforgeably natural, for no author could have blended them by his imagination. These all fit and bring to fruition their intended purposes:

b) Bearing The Cross

Tradition tells us that Jesus manifested weakness in carrying His Cross; that He stumbled under its weight, and that therefore, one Simon of Cyrene (Luke 23:26) was compelled to bear it *after* Him. No indication in the Scriptures is given that Jesus manifested weakness nor that He was unable to bear His own Cross. His clean life had been kept strong by hard labor. Was He a weakling that another must be required to carry His Cross? Others were condemned but Jesus had been scourged prior to crucifixion. This torture had been added in His case that Jesus, "wounded . . . bruised . . . and chastised . . . for by His stripes we are healed," might become the fulfillment of the prophecy of Isaiah 53:5. Pilate had thought that by scourging Him, His enemies might be appeased and he might let Him go, and thus he had tried to save Jesus. Rather than the tradition of weakness it is far more feasible to think that the Roman soldiers, seeing His marred visage, the crown of thorns, and the lacerated back, that *they* doubted His strength to carry the Cross and to complete the journey to Golgotha. Paul, the Lord's greatest disciple, sought to get minute information about this Golgotha pilgrimage.[1]

---

[1] This Simon was the father of the two sons Alexander and Rufus (Mark 15:21). Paul, in writing his postscript of love in Romans 16:13, gives greeting to this Rufus. And from the wife of Simon, the mother of Rufus, Paul must certainly have time and again thrilled and burned to hear first hand, these episodes of Jesus' life. Thus also, in the latter part of the same verse, is the tender greeting to "his mother and mine."

c) The Seamless Robe

Consider also the accuracy of the account of the seamless robe of the Master's. What woman had so wrought beauty into this robe, seamless throughout for her Lord, that uncultured soldiers could not rend—thus fulfilling prophecy? (Psalm 22:18, John 19:24).

d) The Accuracy of the Record

(1) *Concerning the Rulers*

The unforgeable accuracy of the record of activities of the rulers, chief priests, scribes and elders, can be seen by all who will read the text. No man could have imagined the details which are reported by Holy Spirit-inspired men. In Matthew 27:62—63, the chief priests and Pharisees came to Pilate saying, "Sir, we remember that that deceiver said while He was yet alive, that 'after three days I will arise again'." Evidently something occurred which refreshed their memory! And the answer to it must be in Matthew 27:51 when we read, "the veil of the temple was rent in twain from the top to the bottom."

Edersheim says:

> "As we compute, it may just have been the time, when at the Evening-Sacrifice, the officiating Priesthood entered the Holy Place, either to burn incense or to do other sacred service there . . . ."[1]

As we see this priest standing before the great curtain, we might say, "O, Priest, behold the rending of the curtain; there is yet time to undo thy infamy!" We see him rushing out, and we say: "Ah, he is gone to rectify his evil deeds; or as Judas, to take his own life." But no! Rather he has chosen to go out to ask Pilate for a guard for the tomb, and three days later they bribe the soldier witnesses! No wonder his race has suffered ignominy!

Fifty days later the apostle Peter on the day of Pentecost reminded the nation of Israel that God had approved Jesus among them by miracles, wonders and signs, as they themselves also knew (Acts 2:22). The rending of the veil certainly was one miracle, wonder or sign which the temple priests themselves had beheld. This was much like the miracle of the healing of the man at the Gate Beautiful of the Temple (Acts 3:.—11, 4:14 —16) for the rulers of the Jews saw this miracle also, and could not deny it, and yet they would deny the One who made possible the miracle. Thus John 1:11 was fulfilled: "He came unto His own *things* but His own *people* received Him not." At the Cross these rulers, scribes, priests and elders,

---

[1] Alfred Edersheim, M.A. Oxon., D.D., Ph.D., *Life and Times of Jesus The Messiah* (N.Y. Longman's, Green, and Co., 1910) Vol. II. p. 611.

with hateful audacity and sarcasm, put forth their lie: "He saved others, Himself He cannot save" (Matthew 27:42).

(2) *Concerning the Malefactors*

In the account of the malefactors who were crucified, the one who railed against Jesus was true to form, but a forger of the account would never have converted either of them!

(3) *Concerning Christ's Endurance*

A forged account of His Crucifixion would very likely have shown Him to be strong at the beginning of His suffering, and very weak at the end. But the Scriptures show Him coming bruised and beaten from the scourging hands of Pilate's soldiers, having quietly endured their torment, the journey to Golgotha, and the nails of the Cross for six hours; and the Crucifixion account closes with the words:

"And Jesus crying with a loud voice, said 'Father,
into Thy hands I commend (commit) up the Spirit."
Luke 23:46 A.S.V.

Only an inspired account would have Him cry with a *loud* voice just before death! This is not the cry of a weakling, but rather it is one of richness. Jesus is saying, "I have finished the work which Thou gavest Me to do, now I commit (deposit) My Spirit with You." The snyoptic writers are all very definite in their record of this occasion:

(*a*) "When He had cried again with a *loud* voice . . ."
Matthew 27:50

(*b*) "Jesus cried with a *loud* voice . . ."
Mark 15:37

(*c*) "And when Jesus had cried with a *loud* voice . . ."
Luke 23:46

And this was the same intensity of voice which we find that the Master used when He called forth Lazarus from the tomb (John 11:43) "He cried with a *loud* voice . . . ."

e) The Seven Words From The Cross

Let us unsandalled approach the Cross and watch it put forth and bloom as Aaron's rod that budded (Numbers 17:1–13). These Seven Words on the Cross are as the Seven-Branched Candlestick (Exodus 25:31). The stamen of this immortelle is found in these seven words, and they are set forth in three groups in which are found the Alpha and Omega of the Cross:

(1) *While it was light* (9 a.m. to 12 noon):

First Word: "Father, forgive them, for they know not what they do   (Luke 23:34)

Second Word: "To-day shalt thou be with me in Paradise" (Luke 23:43)

Third Word: "Woman, behold thy son" (John 19:26b)

(2) *Darkness* (12 noon to 3 p.m.):

Fourth Word: "My God, My God, why didst Thou forsake Me?" (Matthew 27:46N., Mark 15:34N.)

(3) *While it was again light* (after 3 p.m.):

Fifth Word: "I thirst"—"that the Scripture might be fulfilled" (John 19:28)

Sixth Word: "It is finished" (John 29:30)

Seventh Word: "Father, into Thy hands, I commend My Spirit" (Luke 23:46)

FIRST WORD

During the three hours of light from 9 a.m. to noon, His first word was "Father, forgive them, for they know not what they do," His enemies had cried, "Crucify Him" and said, "His blood be on us and on our children," and they passed by the Cross, reviling Him, wagging their heads (Matthew 27:39 and Mark 15:29). It is hardly believable that they could do these things for I Corinthians 2:8 says:

> "which none of the princes of this age knew:
> for had they known, they would not have
> crucified the Lord of glory."

If one could see the outcome of one's indulgence, surely he would never begin. We all enter into the darkness of sin which is contrary to the light of God.

SECOND WORD

The second word on the Cross was, "Today shalt thou be with Me in Paradise." This was not heaven but Abraham's bosom, for He was a Jew with a *kingdom* hope (Luke 23:42). Why did Jesus say "today"? Crucified men do not often die this quickly. He Himself hung on the Cross less than six hours, but He died of a broken heart. How did He know that it would be "today"? He was the Son of God! He was ushered into this world by way of a stable, and "homed" in Nazareth. He was ushered out by way of a felon's cross and squired by a thief. He was a Divine *Don Quixote*! No wonder He was challenged in such company!

"Lift up your heads, O ye gates;
And be ye lift up, ye entrances of eternity;
And the King of glory shall come in.

"Who is this king of glory?
The Lord strong and mighty,
. . .

"He is the King of Glory."

Psalm 24:7—8, 10N.

No wonder He has admonished unto all:

"For ye see your calling, brethren, how that not many wise ones
after flesh, not many mighty, not many noble: But God hath chosen
the foolish things of the world to put to shame the wise ones;
and God hath chosen the weak things of the world to confound
the things which are mighty; And base things of the world, and
things which are despised, hath God chosen, and things which
are not, to bring to nought the things which are: That no flesh
should glory in His presence."

I Corinthians 1:26—29N.

THIRD WORD

In this time of light, He also said to His mother, "Woman, behold thy
son." Here on the Cross, Jesus gave away His own mother to John: and
took a thief on the Cross beside Him! Here also, He demonstrates that
there are ties stronger than blood, confirming His earlier teaching found
in Matthew 12:46—50.

It is written in Daniel 9:26 that following the seven weeks and the
sixty-two weeks "shall Messiah be cut off, but not for Himself"; literally,
"there shall be none belonging to Him" (A.S.V.); and this fulfillment is
seen when the Lord speaks this Third Word. There is a tender illustration
of this same phrase "shall be cut off" in the Christian wedding ceremony
of today: the father representing the family gives up his daughter, though
she has not yet been wed-locked to her husband, and for brief moments,
she is physically dis-owned by everyone; she stands alone. Thus we see
something of the complete loneliness and poverty of Christ on the Cross;
but in that hour, God comes to Him in the cloud (John 16:32, Isaiah 43:2,
Psalm 27, esp. vs. 10).

FOURTH WORD

Christ and the Father were one even when darkness surrounded the
Cross and He was not forsaken by the Father in the cloud of darkness
until He went in to the hour of death. The hours of darkness (Matthew
27:45—46) were from 12 noon to 3 p.m. At this time of the month it was
full moon and therefore this was not an eclipse. This was a time of silence

and infolded in this silence and the Shekinah, the Son was with His Father with the sustaining comfort of:

"When Thou passest through the waters" (Isaiah 43:2)

He leadeth me beside the still waters" (Psalm 23)

On the Mount of Transfiguration in the darkness (Luke 9:32, 37) Moses and Elijah "appeared to Jesus and spoke of His *departure* which He should shortly accomplish at Jerusalem." Here He entered in to the "joy set before Him" (Psalm 23:5). Such fructifying darkness is necessary that life may be brought forth out of darkness (John 12:24). On the Cross during the first three hours:

   a) He prayed for His enemies' forgiveness
   b) He placed His mother into the protection and care of John
   c) And to the thief, He gave assurance:
        "To-day thou shalt be with Me in Paradise."

Then came the darkness and silence to be followed by His exit as He accomplished the atonement for our sins. In Egypt a thick darkness plagued the Egyptians for three days (Exodus 10:22); and in the exit of the Israelites from Egypt, the Shekinah cloud became darkness to the Egyptians but light toward Israel; and we are reminded that a same darkness was upon the faces of the deep in Genesis 1:2. Out of chaos came creation, including man; so also out of the Cross came spiritual beauty and glory over this Holy ground.

   As at the Transfiguration when a bright cloud over-shadowed them;
   Or, when in John 12:28—29 the people heard God's Voice and said
      it thundered;
   Or, at the Ascension when a cloud hid Jesus from the sight of His
      disciples;—

So now, a cloud descends over the Cross and darkness falls over all the land.

At the Transfiguration Peter was within the cloud; but now that Peter has denied his Lord, a thief shares the inner brightness of the cloud with the Master! As the Father spoke to the Son at the Transfiguration, why is it incredible to believe that He spoke to His Son here? After the inner glory of the cloud passed and the Father with-drew, the utter loneliness wrenched His soul. This brings us to His only word out of the darkness: "My God, My God, why hast Thou forsaken Me" (Matt. 27:46, Mark 15:34).

FIFTH WORD

As He returned to humanity, coming out of the darkness into light, we find the first of His words after the darkness is taken away, "I thirst." For this had been forgotten in the cloud as in John 4:32, and He spoke this in order that the Scriptures might be fulfilled.

They offered Him wine but He received it not (Matthew 27:33—34), for He would not stupefy Himself. He said, "the cup which My Father hath given Me, shall I not drink it?" (John 18:11). He had much to say and therefore must be clear in mind. But in order that the Scriptures might be fulfilled, in John 19:28 we read, "He said, 'I thirst'." The importance of the fulfillment of Scripture is demonstrated here for He could have gone on into death without asking for something with which to quench His thirst. Further fulfillment of Scripture is seen in John 19:31—36 when they did not break His legs (Psalm 34:20, Exodus 12:46, Numbers 9:12). The railing and abuse He endured on the Cross is found in Mark 15:29—31 and Luke 23:36—39.

SIXTH WORD

His sixth Word, "It is finished" reveals that the purpose of His coming is ended and it is *"Telos."* He said, "I go to prepare a place." It is an even much greater creation than this present one. This is as a repetition of II Kings 2:12 and the "Song has NOT ceased when scarce begun." But what "It" is this which is finished?

It is *Not*
(His life which is finished (Hebrews 7:16, John 17:4,13)
(The Gospel, for He was not yet risen (I Cor. 15:1—4)
(Redemption; for the Spirit had not yet been given
(His work (John 14:2, Hebrews 2:8)

But there are a few of "lower finishes," and the foremost of them is His humiliation (Acts 8:33, Philippians 2:5—11), when He took "the form of a servant" and was treated as one; His "judgment was taken away from Him"; and as well from those living with Him:

a) Of His parents it is said, "and He was subject unto them"
b) The failure of His very apostles is seen in "here is a sword"
c) The people rejected Him for we read, "He came . . . own *things,* . . . own *people* received Him not"
d) The Sanhedrin said, "we will not have this man to reign over us"
e) And all "kings of earth" :

"The kings of earth set themselves,
And rulers take counsel together,
Against Jehovah,
And against His Messiah . . . ."

Psalm 2:2N.

These humiliations are now finished as He speaks this Sixth Word. And He said to Israel:

> "Henceforth, ye shall see Me no more until ye shall say,
> 'Blessed is He that cometh in the Name of the Lord';"

Not until then could He say, "It is finished."

But the *supreme* "It" is LAW. In a death grapple, law and love went to the Cross and *Law* remains nailed to the Cross, even though man still quotes:

> Sovereign law, That State's collected will,
> O'er thrones and globes elate,
> Sits empress, crowning good, repressing ill. [1]

Such Law is incarnate in Society and Governments; and men are of less value apparently than institutions, yet He has spoken, "IT is finished." Those "having eyes to see" can observe the passing from "Reign of Law" to the Sovereignty of Personality. No modern rich young ruler is able to say, "I have lived in all good conscience unto this day"; for the Lord stands in the door of a tomb as the scientist in a laboratory, and the past (i.e. law) is dead! And God is no more a statesman with a Constitution, but is the living Father, a-tremble with passionate Personality, throbbing with love.

SEVENTH WORD

And these were His last words: "Father, into Thy Hands I commend My Spirit." And this word "commend" has three meanings:

   a) To set before as food
   b) To deposit
   c) To bring forward as evidence

It is very likely the meaning here is the second one given, "to deposit" for in I Peter 4:19, it says:

> "Wherefore also let them that suffer according to
> the will of God commit the keeping of their souls
> to Him in well doing, as unto a faithful Creator."

In this Seventh Word we have evidence of return from His bearing the sin of the world, into His former place of close fellowship with the Father.

The life of Jesus was always within His control (John 10:18). As we come to the Cross, we are experiencing a very great event which is more wonderful because of its freedom from coercion, save that of love (Luke 19:10). As we shrive our own souls anew in the fires of these impassioned utterances, then what we were, we never shall be again. The events of the Cross open and close upon the word "Father." All problems raised by this event are quieted in the alembic of that last Word: "Father." This word interprets the Cross and as we hear it, we know that all is well. As

---

[1] Sir William Jones, *What Constitutes A State?*

He died, He cried with a loud voice as at the grave of Lazarus which is concerned with the same condition and manner. This was the shout of a conqueror and graves were opened. "The loud voice" of the last utterance, lifts above others with the one exception when He cried, "My God, My God." These are twin peaks of emotion that are the cry of the *Lamb of God* and that of the *Son of God*.

The manger and the tomb where "there they laid Him" are only eight miles apart. He came not from Nazareth nor from Egypt, but Bethlehem where were raised the sacrificial lambs (Leviticus 3:2), and He traveled from Bethlehem to the Tomb—from man's hands to God's hands—and the Lamb was nearest to God when He was between man and God—when "devoted"; and the Lord was within the cloud. As He was visible on the Cross to man, there were three hours of light, but when the three hours of darkness descended upon the land, He was with God (John 16:32, Psalm 97:2). Here it was true:

> "Standeth God within the shadow,
> Keeping watch above His own."

And at the going of the cloud, He was saying, "Why leave Me behind?" (Hebrews 13:5b); and later He said to Mary (John 10:17), "touch Me not for I am not yet ascended to My Father"; and He was saying, "I have been left behind." And now He says on the Cross, "into Thy Hands, I commend My Spirit." He dismissed His Spirit (Gr. *pneuma*), and sent it away. Read Habakkuk 3:4, "He had *rays* coming forth from His Hands and there was the hiding of His Power" (Acts 2:34–35, Hebrews 1:13). Into the Almighty sustaining Hands of the Father, Jesus commits His Spirit (Psalm 8:3, Luke 11:20, John 10:29). These all-competent, mothering Hands of God have been empty since creation but are now being readied for the Church, His Body.

The last word from the Cross could be said to be that of the dying thief, and the centurion when he saw that *He so* cried out and gave up the Spirit, said, "truly this was the Son of God." And here with a thief and a soldier, and I trust with you also, I take my stand.

Having thus committed His soul to the Father in well-doing, did He at this time, "go, preach" of I Peter 3:18 and 4:6 N.?:

> "For Christ also once for all suffered for sins,
> a just for unjust ones, that He might bring us
> to God, being put to death indeed in flesh, but
> quickened by the Spirit:
>
> "For, for this cause was the gospel preached
> also to the dead ones, that they might be
> judged indeed according to men in the flesh,
> but live according to God in Spirit."

6. Cross Notes

The Roman Empire had crosses stacked up at the doors of every Roman Court of Justice. There were at least three that day that had significance:

> a) An "A-Theos" (apart from God)
> b) One who was repentant
> c) One who was a forgiver

ALL that our Lord touches, He glorifies!

*   *   *   *   *

The two colossal events of His last week were both catastrophic and benevolent:

> a) The Veil of the Temple, this sanctuary of Law;
>   The rending of the Temple curtain was atomic
>   in its blow to the Jew
> b) The Veil of His flesh, this sanctuary of Love;
>   The riven tomb became the anastasis of Hope
>   to sinners

With so simple a phrase, "It is finished," the Lord uttered a colossal revelation, for by the rent curtain of His flesh He made the Holy Place and the Holy of Holies ONE! Truth is that eternal stuff which in itself is invisible; out of its invisibility rises the visible—and upon its invisibility rests the visible. "It is finished," so the Lord said on the Cross; so also Handel may have stretched his wearied body when he finished The Messiah score. The "finished" of the actuality of the Cross and the score of The Messiah looked very much alike. Christ is only One of several men crucified with Him; but pour over each of the crosses your needs and see which responds! Musical symmetry stems from middle C(ross); so The Messiah looks like any other book of music, but pour one thousand voices through its pages, and a King George will rise in its honor. The crosses within The Messiah score were flooded by Deity in Handel's genius; for "the great High God doth enter and make it beautiful." And, on down the years, love goes resistlessly on its way: Saul becomes Paul; and Massillon lifts Louis, the Magnificent, and his court to their feet as he preaches upon The Great Assize. Yes, and we too this day can move out from here and quicken the very dead, and bring our city as Florence to its knees, if the chords of our heart are harmonized to the Cross.

*   *   *   *   *

The Cross was an incident in the life of the Lord (Hebrews 12:2, Luke 9:51), "Who for the joy set before Him" endured its suffering (Psalm 2:8,

Isaiah 53:11, John 3:16); and this joy was the joy of setting souls free
and leading them back Home (Psalm 24:7).

*   *   *   *   *

The Cross is the Blood guarantee; you trifle with it at your own peril
(Hebrews 10:20); and Christ is the "Blood Bank" of John 6. He said, "My
Blood," therefore no other shares with Him. He contains the serums and
the vitamins needed. Those who have been blood donors can throw light
on the text for they leave their life in the blood and yet they come away
undiminished.

*   *   *   *   *

God's agony at the Cross was the greatest display of Love. He forsook His Beloved Son that He might reach in Death to the last lost and
degraded one reaching even to the uttermost. It is this One whose "Auto-
Biography" is the Purpose of this marvelous Book, The Holy Bible.

H. "THE LORD IS RISEN INDEED!" (Luke 24:34)

The resurrection of Christ is the most attention-absorbing event of
human experience occurring within history. Here is an offer of immortality
with a demonstration of it for each and every life coming in to the world.
God's purpose has now been manifested by (Gr. *dia*) the appearing of
"Christ who abolished death and brought life and immortality to light
through (Gr. *dia*) the Gospel" (II Timothy 1:10).

This open tomb is the laboratory which is the baptistry of the new
creation; and His last week is a strange concatenation of friends and
enemies whose apparently unplanned movements take on a definite pattern;
here indeed is a strange alignment of unbelievers:

1. There were His enemies, the Priests and the Pharisees
2. There were His friends, the counsellors (Nicodemus, and
   Joseph of Arimathea); the apostles; and the women.

Three groups brought spices and ointments, so proving their skepticism:

1. Joseph and Nicodemus (John 19:38—42)
2. Mary Magdalene (Mark 16:1)
3. The women of Galilee (Luke 23:55)

The testimony of these who were skeptical at the first but who later believed, forms a vital part of the evidence of the resurrection,

In the oldest book in the Bible, God said, "Where wast thou when I
laid the foundation of earth? . . . when the morning stars sang together
and all the sons of God shouted for joy" (Job 38:4, 7). None were there
to help or hinder, but at the resurrection, the laying "of the corner stone"

of the "new creation," about five hundred fallibles were on the stage with but two who saw clearly: Mary the mother of Jesus and Mary of Bethany. Timid, uncoached and unlearned witnesses were used, whose undesigned actions wove a seamless robe about the events over that Passover, in a pattern over which they were not aware, which no "disputer of this world" (I Corinthians 1:20) has been able to rend.

At the *burial* two groups watched:

1. Mary Magdalene (Matthew 27:61) and "the other Mary" were sitting (Mark 15:47)
2. The women of Galilee ALSO prepared spices (Luke 23:55)

Note that one group *sat* after the burial; the others went to buy ointment, and then these rested on the Sabbath day according to the commandment (Luke 23:56).

Then consider the events around the *Resurrection* of that first day, so lovingly prefaced by the anointings at Bethany:

1. In Matthew 28, we read "in the end of the Sabbath*s* as it began to dawn toward the first day of the week, came Mary Magdalene and the other Mary to *see* the sepulchre." This occurred *before* 6 p.m. on the Sabbath and they did not plan to anoint the body until sun-up. The phrase "as it began to dawn" is the same as used in Luke 23:54 "the Sabbath *drew on*," and note Luke 24:1; therefore the phrase "as it began to dawn" literally means it was getting dusk
2. *At* 6 p.m. the Lord arose; completing three days and three nights in the heart of the earth. Matthew tells of the great earthquake (the second, cp. Matthew 27:51 and Matthew 28:2), "and the Angel of the Lord descended from heaven and rolled back the and sat upon it" revealing that the Lord had risen

There are fourteen appearances of Christ after His Resurrection from the dead. The events given in the order of their occurrences make the testimony of these witnesses unimpeachable:

He Appeared:

1. To Mary Magdalene (John 20:14—18, Mark 16:9—11). He said, "touch Me not." This is His Passover body (Isaiah 53:6, 52:14, II Corinthians 5:21, Hebrews 9:24—28). "Him who knew no sin, He made Him to be sin for us," and He was "not yet ascended." Until that time, He was "a body of death" and not to be handled; so He must not be fondled nor held on to (Philippians 2:6). Later, He said, "handle Me and see" (Luke 24:39, I John 1:1). This was:

2. To Mary the mother of James and Joseph; the wife of Cleopas; Salome, Joanna; and other women (Matthew 27:56, John 19:25, Matthew 28:5—10, Mark 16:1, Luke 23:55, Luke 24:9). These came at sunrise and talked "among themselves" (Mark 16:2—3); they saw the tomb and heard the angels say, ". . . the Lord is risen," and ". . . He goeth before you into Galilee and there shall ye see Him according as He said unto you" (Mark 16:4—8) As they were returning from the tomb at sunrise they saw the Lord and since there were no mists, in the harsh daylight He was most real to them. These women gathered the five hundred brethren of I Corinthians 15:6

3. To Peter in the afternoon, verifying His resurrection (I Corinthians 15:5, Luke 24:34)

4. To two disciples in the evening on the way to Emmaus (Luke 24:14—31). These Emmaus disciples, one of whom was named Cleopas and the other who may have been Mark, were told by Jesus: "ought not Christ to have suffered these things and to enter into His glory? And beginning at Moses and all the prophets, He expounded unto them in all the Scriptures the things concerning Himself" (Luke 24:26—27).

   After He had been made known to them in the breaking of bread, these disciples returned to Jerusalem in the same hour after He had left them and they found the eleven gathered together saying, "The Lord is risen indeed and hath appeared to Simon." If Thomas did not believe under the witness of the ten disciples who claimed the Lord appeared to all of them at one time, why would none of these eleven have doubted that the Lord had appeared to Peter?

5. To the apostles, the same evening, Thomas being absent (Luke 24:36—43, John 20:19—23)

6. To the apostles again, eight days later, Thomas being present, (John 20:24—29). It was here that Thomas said unto Him, "My Lord and My God" when he saw the glorious Body of his Lord, the promised resurrected One who had said also, "destroy this temple and in three days I will build it again" (John 2:19)

7. To the seven disciples on the seashore by the Lake of Tiberias (Galilee) (John 21:1—13)

8. To the eleven disciples and five hundred brethren on a mountain in Galilee (Matthew 28:16—17). "Some doubted" would indicate the presence of more than the eleven disciples (I Corinthians 15:6)

9. To James later (I Corinthians 15:7), who might have been His half-brother
10. At His Ascension from the Mount of Olives near Bethany (Acts 1:9—12, Luke 24:50—51)
11. To Stephen outside of Jerusalem (Acts 7:55)
12. To Paul near Damascus (Acts 9:3—6)
13. To Paul in the Temple (Acts 22:17—21)
14. To John on the Isle of Patmos (Revelation 1:10—19).

One of the qualifications for an apostle was to have seen the Lord after His resurrection (I Corinthians 9:1, Acts 1:21—23); and this "Great Cloud of Witnesses"—of women, apostles, "above five hundred brethren at once," James, Paul and others—these did not know how great a part was theirs in this greatest of dramas as they witnessed the experience of God's full power (Ephesians 1:15—23).

Paul's "Fifth Gospel" account of the Resurrection evidences is found in I Corinthians 15:1—8. This, the mightiest of the Gospelers, roots and rests *his* great immortality argument in this chapter upon the reports of these "Night Roamers" of John 20:1 and I Corinthians 1:26—30. The Five Gospel accounts (*Matthew, Mark, Luke, John* and Paul) do not harmonize but they do agree.

Did the Lord appear to His mother? Though none of these books record the incident, it is logical and in character with the Lord, that after He arose from the dead, He first went to Mary, His mother, and to His half-brothers who had not accepted Him before, but would now be compelled to know that He had risen from the dead. The next we hear of His earthly family is that they are continuing with Mary and the rest of the disciples in the Upper Room in prayer.

It is hard for us to evaluate the mental explosion which the Lord's death produced upon His disciples. It tore their world into fragments and only two out-rode this terrible blast: Mary His mother, and Mary of Bethany who sat at His feet.

Mary Magdalene said, "they have taken away my Lord" and her words to the disciples "appeared as idle talk"
But *Peter* arose and ran to the tomb and departed wondering
The *Emmaus disciples* on the road from Jerusalem, declared, "we were hoping that He should redeem Israel." These had some insight concerning these events because Jesus began at Moses and all the prophets and declared the Scriptures unto them.
Thomas said, "except I shall see in His hands the print of the nails and put my finger into the print of the nails and thrust my hand into His side, I will not believe."

To the *Eleven* Jesus appeared "as they sat at meat and He up-
braided them because they believed not them which had seen Him
after He was risen."

Though nature accepted Him, yet His own people did not (John 1:11)
for the Jews rejected Him and they still do; but the apostles "believed
not for joy." Prior to the crucifixion, they had all forsaken Him and fled;
they were cowering behind locked doors. Yet out of this most unpromising
material (I Corinthians 1:26—29), Jesus said,

> ". . . I will build my Church, and the gates
> of Hades shall not prevail against it."

Here out of these, and nowhere else, came forth this mightiest of institutions. "An institution is the lengthened shadow of a man" (Emerson);
but the Church of Jesus Christ, is the extended Body of

"The Man, Christ Jesus."

I. REFLECTIONS ON THE RESURRECTION

At the Lord's death, the curtain of the Temple was rent from top to
bottom; and at His resurrection, the graves were opened. That which was
obverse became that which was observable and more, so that all of the
Infinite was visible in Him as He was to Peter in Matthew 16:16. There
is speculation and theorizing upon immortality, except at this one place
of the Resurrection. Men discuss what happened to Enoch, Elijah and
Lazarus, but in these men are seen as adumbrations of that which is fully
revealed in Christ; and the record of Scripture from the beginning concerning the history of man is "and they (all) died." But He arose and in three
days He was "riding herd" upon His scattering disciples even as He must
be doing today.

*   *   *   *   *

Before the Cross was set up, or "in the garden a new tomb' fashioned,
for four millenniums the time of nature's resurrection had been "preparing'
man to "receive" the Gospel of hope. There is no more noble confession
in literature of the immortal persistence of personality than in this line
from Tennyson's *Crossing The Bar*:

> "When THAT which came from out the boundless deep
> TURNS again HOME."

Tennyson's poetic insight was more spiritual and more true to the facts
than Michelangelo's "Creation of Adam" over which he toiled for months
locked in from even the Pope. He pictures life as a spark from Deity's
finger to Adam which was a creative act (Psalm 8:3), while life-imparting

is from "spirit unto spirit." Moses wrote in Genesis 2:7 that breath "comes from without the boundless deep."

*   *   *   *   *

Because of Abraham's faith, God was able to say, "Out of Egypt have I called My Son":

> *First,* He could say this concerning the nation of Israel (Hos. 11:1)
> *Secondly,* He could say this concerning His Only Begotten Son, when He raised Him "from among the dead ones" (Romans 1:4, Matthew 2:15, Acts 13:33); and this Son broke the bars of death and "brought life and immortality to light through the Gospel" (II Timothy 2:10).

*   *   *   *   *

The Lord took up where Adam (man) left off; what man cast away, Christ salvaged. Compare these: Romans 5:12—21... "so death passed upon all men . . ." (Genesis 2:17, Luke 12:4); but in Ezekiel 18:4b and Luke 12:20, sin was not imputed; nevertheless, death reigned. The ability to commit sin is *im*-plicit (UN-expressed); and transgression itself is *ex*-plicit (plainly expressed).

> Through Adam—in one act—"all died"; Romans 5:12
> Through Christ—in one act—"all have been made alive"
> > I Corinthians 15:22

Forth from the grave (and Baptism) came the miracle of Romans 4:25 and 6:5 N.:

> "Who was delivered for the sake of our offences, and was raised again for the sake of our justification."

> "For if we have been planted together in the likeness of His death, we shall be also of His resurrection."

VIII. THE BEGETTING OF THE SPIRITUAL BODY OF CHRIST

> "Jesus therefore said to them again, 'Peace be unto you; as the Father hath sent me, even so send I you.' And when He had said this, He *breathed* on them, and saith unto them, '*Receive* ye the Holy Spirit; whose soever sins ye *forgive*, they are *forgiven* unto them; whose soever sins ye *retain*, they are *retained.*'

> > John 20:21—23 A.S.V.

> "It is the Spirit that giveth life; the flesh profiteth nothing; the words that I have spoken unto you are spirit, and are life."

> > John 6:63 A.S.V.

'It is the Spirit that giveth life; the flesh profiteth nothing; the words that I have spoken unto you are spirit, and are life."

John 6:63 A.S.V.

"Jesus answered and said unto him, 'Amen, Amen I say unto thee, Except one be born from above, he cannot see the kingdom of God'."

John 3:3N.

In the begetting of the Church, the Body of Christ, there are items of vast importance in this "Forty-Days-Plus Ten-Days Foundationing" period between Resurrection and Pentecost. Here we find the Resurrection of Christ, the begetting of the Church, the commissioned-disciples and Pentecost. To get a wrong conception of any one of these items will confuse our thinking and gender divisions. If we are confused, we must go back to Christ. As we consider the begetting of the Church, we note that it was "not done in a corner" but where three civilizations mingled in the tensest moment of the most luminous Life of all Time. The Church was by His fiat and He declared it to be His Body. This was after He had re-collected them and convinced them of His Resurrection.

The Church (Gr. *ek-klesia*) is a most common term which may be used of any called meeting. Indeed the language and the life of the spiritual are rooted in the Old Testament and are of divine purpose. I Corinthians 15:45 tells of the two Adams and as we read the account of the first Adam (Genesis 2:7), where "The Lord God *formed* man of the dust of the ground and *breathed* into his nostrils the breath of lives and man became a "living soul"—so this same process is applied to the Church, the Body of the Second Adam. This event is the holiest act of love, *the begetting of The Church* (John 20:22) and took place in "The Upper Room" the evening of the Day of His resurrection as "He breathed upon them." This "breathing" upon them was *not* the empowering of them (that came at Pentecost), but was the *begetting* as in Genesis 2:7 and John 3:6. "He breathed upon them and said, 'receive ye Holy Spirit'" and then at once He said, "As the Father hath sent Me, so send I you" (cp. Revelation 5:6); but He also said for them to tarry at Jerusalem even as He had at Nazareth (Luke 2:51).

The Forty Days are as the begetting and birth of an unborn child whose eyes are yet in darkness, whose ears are in silence, whose hands and mouth are incapacitated. Suppose the unborn child were to try to lecture upon the uses of eyes, ears, hands and mouth, or to try to explain the world into which it was soon to be ushered. So the Lord's mission depended on these men's *tarrying* for Power; for, if these should fail, all would be futile; but "they went everywhere preaching the Word," and "The Lord was with them." This breathing must have imparted The Will; now they awaited The Empowering. Who is included in "breathed upon them?" All would need it (John 7:39, 3:1—5, Acts 19:2). Keep in mind that the Gospel is a democratic movement to every creature (I Corinthians 1:27, Mark 12:37). As aforesaid, this "breathed" is the same word as in Genesis 2:7 (Septuagint) and for the same identical purpose; that is, the receiving of the image of the "Breather." God "breathed" upon Adam and said, "have dominion over the fish . . . fowl . . . cattle . . . creeping things"; and Christ "breathed" upon His disciples and said, "As the Father sent Me, so send I you." This was the imparting of quality to their own lives; to Adam, the ability to rule; to the disciples, the willingness to die. This was the Spirit of Himself and was not the baptism of Holy Spirit for Jesus had re-assumed His own place (John 16:5). He was above the Spirit [1] and this was imparting-"breathing" just as a priming coat for paint. To illustrate: they were to "Tarry till clothed upon" just as the Spirit of the Lord came upon Gideon (Judges 6:35). As the Rugby atmosphere was Arnold's spirit, even if he were absent, yet when Arnold was with them in person, it was electrifying. So was Pentecost the breaking over barriers and flooding into the earth; and in that moving spirit-flood is faith's new Paraclete, the Holy Spirit. So likewise does Catholicism create its spirit-world in which members in rebellion wither and die even though that member be the Pope; likewise the spirit-world which rises at Pentecost bears upon its fructifying bosom, the personalities and the Church of the First Born.

Here within these Forty Days, "behold the Christ stands" and is facing both of these Scriptures, Luke 24:27 and Acts 1:2*b*—3. He said, "While I was *yet* with you." *Now* He is in the heavenlies as He told Pilate: "not of this (i.e. that) world." And to His disciple He said, "Thou shalt come after a while." Thus:

      a) He quieted their fears
      b) He showed His wounds
      c) "He did eat before them."

These disciples needed:

      a) Life—and "He breathed upon them" (John 20:22)
      b) Prayer, "open Thou mine eyes that I may see"
      c) Opened eyes to know Him and to witness His daily miracles; "and their eyes were opened" (Luke 24:31)
      d) Opened minds to understanding the Scriptures; "then opened He their minds" (Luke 24:45, Revelation 5:1—5)
      e) The baptism of the Holy Spirit, for "as yet there were no Scriptures" to direct them (Acts 2:4, II Peter 1:21, II Timothy 3:16)

---

[1] Note: *"moved"* Genesis 1:2; Acts 2:4; II Peter 1:21.

When such as these "breathed-upon" men speak, it will be with authority and finality, having the seal of the Father and of the Son upon their
word. Christ said, "they testify of Me" and the sermon of Acts 2 was of
what they had seen and heard which was "made more sure by the Word
of Prophecy." Thus the Spiritual Body of Christ was *begotten* in "The
Upper Room" (John 20:22); and was *born* fifty days later, the Day of
Pentecost (Acts 2:1, 4, 7).

> . . . "But first I mean
> To exercise him in the wilderness;
> There he shall first lay down the rudiments
> Of his great warfare, ere I send him forth
> To conquer Sin and Death, the two grand foes,
>
> By humiliation and strong sufferance:
> His weakness shall o'ercome Satanic strength,
> And all the world, and mass of sinful flesh;
> That all the angels and ethereal powers,
> They now, and men hereafter, may discern,
> From what consummate virtue I have chose
> This perfect man, by merit called my Son,
> To earn salvation for the sons of men."
>
> So spake the eternal Father, and all Heaven
> Admiring stood a space; and then into hymns
> Burst forth, and in celestial measures moved,
> Circling the throne and singing, while the hand
> Sung with the voice; and this the argument:
>
> "Victory and triumph to the Son of God
> Now entering his great duel, not of arms,
> But to vanquish by wisdom hellish wiles.
> The Father knows the Son; therefore secure
> Ventures his filial virtue, though untried,
> Against whate'er may tempt, whate'er seduce,
> Allure, or terrify, or undermine.
> Be frustrate, all ye stratagems of Hell,
> And devilish machinations come to nought."
>
> Hail! Son of the Most High, heir of both worlds,
> Queller of Satan, on thy glorious work
> Now enter, and begin to save mankind. [1]

---

[1] John Milton, *Paradise Regained,* The Poetical Works of John Milton, Vol. 8,(Philadelphia, Porter & Coates), Bk. I, lines 155–181 and Bk. IV, lines 633–635.

ABRAHAM TO CHRIST'S SPIRITUAL BODY

SATAN'S STORY

> "And the great dragon was cast out,
> That old serpent, (Diabolus, the Accuser),
> And Satan, (i.e. Adversary),
> Which deceiveth the whole habitable world;
> He was cast into the earth,
> And His angels were cast with him."

Revelation 12:9 N.

I. SATAN'S SEDUCTIVE ATTEMPTS

The Satanic assaults[1] to corrupt the *Kosmos* make one continued battle. Every age is offered in proof of this; and in each age, he uses the same technique, "ye shall be as gods."

Only three examples are needed: THE RACE, THE SEED THE GOSPEL:

- A. His first attempt upon Adam was against THE RACE;
  Adam was banished from Eden but repented and survived.
- B. His second attempt was to corrupt the genealogical line, THE SEED.

  In Genesis 6 we find that Satan sees that he cannot destroy The Race, so he *corrupts* The Race in order to destroy The Seed; and the result is "There were giants (lit. "fallen ones") in the earth in those days . . ." which God removed through the flood.[2]
- C. And now the third attempt of corruption is against THE GOSPEL as he assaults Christ Jesus Himself.

The Assault Upon the Genealogical Line

The Abrahamic covenant was given in Genesis 12:3 N.:

> ". . . and in thee shall all families of the ground be blessed."

Note that it is first stated "in thee," i.e. in *Abraham*, and not in his seed, that *all families* of the earth (ground) shall be blessed. And in Genesis 13:12:

> "I will make *thy seed* as the dust of the earth."

Then He followed it in 22:18 N.:

> "And in *thy seed* shall *all nations* of the earth bless themselves."

But in 28:14*b* the Lord says to *Jacob*:

---

[1] See Appendix, *The Serpent in Genesis 3*, p.603 ff.

[2] See Section THREE, *MY Story*, The Flood, p.194; and Satan Corrupts, p.199

"In *thee* and in *thy seed* shall all the families of the ground be blessed."
Then in Galatians 3:16 we read:

"Now to *Abraham* and his *seed* were the promises made,
He saith not, 'And to seeds,' as unto many; but as unto
ONE, 'And to *thy seed*,' which is CHRIST."

At the time God gave this covenant to Abraham, Satan's assault began anew upon the genealogical line: Satan incites Sarah to give Hagar her handmaid to Abraham, and the whole story of Sarah's, Rebekah's and Rachel's barrenness, is the result of Satan's attempt to defeat the promise of God in Genesis 3:15.

The Extent of Satan's Attempt

All along these assaults by Satan have increased in intensity:

> First, in the *garden*
> Then, over the whole *earth*
> Also, upon *Deity*, Christ Himself
> And finally, in the heavenlies upon the *Church*,
> the Body of Christ.

These are heaven-shaking assaults which attack heaven as they attempt to ascend into the Presence of God (Job 1:7) and rail at Dignities (Jude 8, Glories).

All of the above attempts were aimed at the Lord; and the succeeding ones show Satan's cleverness:

> First, we read of Jesus that "He was a root out of dry ground"
> Secondly, there was a stigma attached to Him because of His place of residence, Nazareth
> Thirdly, men denied His credentials:
> *a*) His works (Luke 11:15 and John 12:37)
> *b*) His Deity (Matthew 13:55)
> Fourthly, Satan led the rulers of the Jews to choose Barabbas, (Matthew 27:20)
> Fifthly, he instigated perjury and subornation "to this day."

II. SATAN A HEAVENLY BEING

Satan is as living and as real as Gabriel, Michael or other heavenly beings. This Solar System was once his when he was "the covering cherub" (Ezekiel 28), and it was the chiefest province of "the sons of God" (Job 1:7). Eden, Satan's capital on earth, was the only point from which all of this Solar System could be viewed. This earth is the place of decision, the testing ground, or battle ground, of Christ and Satan.

III. THE TEMPTATIONS OF JESUS

The Temptations of Jesus lasted forty days in the wilderness (Luke 4:1—13, Mark 1:12—13).

A. THE THREE-FOLD TEMPTATION

A three-fold temptation by Satan was placed before Jesus continually through this forty day period. These are the same three temptations which he used in the Garden of Eden [1] (cp. Genesis 3:6 and I John 2:16):

1. "And when the woman saw that the tree was *good for food*, . . ."
   i.e. "the lust of the flesh"
2. "And that it was pleasant to the eyes,"
   i.e. "the lust of the *eyes*"
3. "And a tree to be desired to make one *wise*,"
   i.e. "the pride of life" (*ostentation of living—N.*)

B. LUKE'S RECORD of the TEMPTATION versus MATTHEW'S

The temptations in *Luke* preceded those in *Matthew* for at the end of the temptation in *Luke*, it says that "the devil departed from Him for a *season*" (Luke 4:13). The temptation in *Matthew* was the final one and in Matthew 4:11 it reads:

"Then the devil leaveth Him, and, behold
angels came and ministered unto Him."

The pattern of the temptations in *Luke* follow those set forth in Genesis 3:6 and 2:16:

1. The Temptation of the *lust* of the *flesh* (hunger) was in Luke 4:3:

   "If Thou be the Son of God,
   command this stone that it be made bread."

   The Lord's answer from the Word of God Itself (*Deuteronomy*) was sufficient to rebuke the tempter:

   ". . . that He might make thee know that man doth not live on bread only, but on every word that proceedeth out of the mouth of Jehovah doth man live."

2. The second Temptation *"the lust of the eyes"* is found in Luke 4:5—6N. From a high mountain, the devil *shows* Jesus all the kingdoms of the world in a moment of time and says unto Him:

   "All this authority will I give Thee and the glory of them: for to me it hath been delivered; and to whomsoever *I will* I give it.

   "If Thou therefore will worship before me, all shall be Thine."

---

[1] See Section THREE, *RESTORATION TO TERAH*, III. Satan's Repertoire, p. 197.

The answer of Jesus to this temptation again appeals to the Word of God:

"Thou shalt worship Jehovah Thy God,
And Him only shalt thou religiously serve."

Deuteronomy 10:29N.

3. The third temptation, the *Pride of Life* (to become a spectacle), is found in Luke 4:9—11. Satan suggests that He cast Himself down from the wing of the outer Temple, with this expectation:

"For it is written: 'He shall give His angels charge concerning Thee: . . . they shall bear Thee up with hands, Lest Thou dash thy foot against a stone'."

Psalm 91:11—12

Jesus answers the third time, drawing again upon God's Word:

"It is said, 'Thou shalt not tempt Jehovah Thy God'."

Deuteronomy 10:20N.

Forty days of such temptation and of the appeal of Jesus to the authority of the Word of God finally ended with the devil leaving Him and angels coming and ministering unto our victorious Lord.

> So struck with dread and anguish fell the fiend,
> And to his crew that sat consulting, brought
> (Joyless triumphals of his hop'd success,)
> Ruin, and desperation, and dismay,
> Who durst so proudly tempt the Son of God.
> So Satan fell; and straight a fiery globe
> Of angels on full sail of wing flew nigh,
> Who on their plumy vans receiv'd him soft
> From his uneasy station, and upbore
> As on a floating couch through the blithe air;
> Then in a flowery valley set him down
> On a green bank, and set before him spread
> A table of celestial food, divine,
> Ambrosial fruits, fetch'd from the tree of life,
> And from the fount of life ambrosial drink,
> That soon refresh'd him wearied, and repair'd
> What hunger, if aught hunger had impair'd,
> Or thirst; and, as he fed, angelic quires
> Sung heavenly anthems of his victory
> Over the temptation and the tempter proud. [1]

---

[1] *Ibid,* John Milton's *Paradise Regained.* Following the Forty Days of Satan's offers and temptations to Jesus, Satan then leaving Him on the precarious "highest pinnacle" of the Temple, dejected at his own failure, consults with his cohorts of the "joyless triumphals"; while Jesus is removed from the pinnacle and ministered to by "angels on full sail." pp. 147—148, lines 576—595.

IV. SATAN TEMPTS THE DISCIPLES

Since Satan could not touch the Son of God Himself and bring Him into subjection, he next tried to reach the Lord's disciples. Goethe in his *Faust* pictures Satan in the person of Mephistopheles, and in Gounod's opera of the drama, the great basso Chaliapin portrayed Mephistopheles as a very sinister character "going to and fro" amongst the merry-makers at the ball. Suddenly a chill startles them as the Tempter touches and persuades his desired victim Faust, to follow him. What an accurate portrayal of:

> ". . . your adversary the devil, as a roaring lion,
> walketh about, seeking whom he may swallow up."
>
> I Peter 5:8N.

Of Satan it was said, "thou wast in Eden," (Ezekiel 28:13—14), but also we might say, "thou wast in the Upper Room and in my heart." Peter and others[1] were approached by Satan, but Judas succumbs to his temptation and "goes out" (John 13:30). The serpent of Eden, of the Upper Room, and of my heart, are leaving a slimy trail everywhere. Of Judas' yieldedness to Satan, it was written, *"And it was night";* but this was not said of Peter in his denial, for he "went out and wept bitterly" (Luke 22:61—62). "It was night" is an arresting statement to searchers, for this is no idle phrase. Here in the Upper Room we recall the blackness of Egypt (Exodus 10:22—23), and the darkness of the Crucifixion hours. Was this the Shekinah glory cloud, black and impenetrable to His enemies, but glorious and bright now to Jesus (John 13:31—32)? For later at Gethsemane (John 18:6, cf. Isaiah 52:14), as He steps outside of the Shekinah His enemies "went backward and fell to the ground." Of Moses, we read that His face shone as he returned from the Presence of God on the top of the mountain, but here Christ's visage was marred by the touch of sin which He was to bear for mankind.

V. SATAN'S KNOWLEDGE OF GOD'S PLANS

Satan, the Adversary, cannot *fore-read* God's Mind, but he does seem to know of God's plans as soon as they are revealed in heaven. Satan *can* know man's mind; and he nearly destroyed Israel several times.

The Serpent in Eden knew God's plan of Redemption and had seen the heavenly Jerusalem. Using his usual tricks, He was the one who incited Cain and his descendants to build cities; and he has used these same methods on short-visioned flesh in every age. But Satan failed when he used them at the Lord's temptation. Satan today continues his effort

---

[1] Note in Luke 22:31 the Greek word for *you* is plural.

to mind earthly things and to shut out the vision of I Corinthians 2:9:

> "But as it is written, (Isaiah 64:4)
> 'Things which eye hath not seen,
> Nor ear heard,
> Neither have entered into the heart of man,
> The things which God hath prepared for them that love Him'."

Isaiah in his vision was told:

> "And He said, 'Go, and tell this people,
> Hear ye indeed, but understand not;
> And see ye indeed, but perceive not.
> Make the heart of this people fat,
> And make their ears heavy,
> And shut their eyes; lest they see with their eyes,
> And hear with their ears,
> And understand with their heart,
> And convert (turn), and be healed'."
>
> Isaiah 6:9—10

So Satan today continues to deceive men; there are two separate lines through the Scriptures: that which is *earthly* and that which is *heavenly*. All through the Scriptures Satan is trying to counteract God's program. From Genesis 3:15 on, the Serpent is trying to work against the Seed of the woman, and we are warned against his increasing activity.

> "Woe to the inhabiters of the earth and of the sea;
> For the Accuser is come down unto you, having great wrath,
> Because he knoweth that *he hath a short time*."

Satan, a blind Samson, is himself moving toward a crashing down of nations, peoples, and kings into an eternal lake of fire where they will taunt him forever:

> "Art thou become as one of us?"

The Englewood Church of Christ
Stewart Avenue at 66th Place,
Chicago, Illinois.

Section FIVE:

THE CHURCH

A FULL-LENGTH PORTRAIT
OF
CHRIST'S SPIRITUAL BODY

"That Christ may dwell in your hearts through faith;
that ye, being rooted and grounded in love,
May be fully able to comprehend with all saints
what is the breadth, and length, and depth, and height;
And to know the love of Christ, which surpasseth knowledge,
that ye might be filled into all the fulness of God."

Ephesians 3:17—19 N.*

"Till we all arrive at the unity of the faith,
and of the full knowledge of the Son of God,
unto a perfect man, unto the measure of the stature
of the fulness of Christ."

Ephesians 4:13 N.*

*See page *xiii*

322

Prelude to Section FIVE:

THE LIVING CHURCH

Prelude to Section FIVE:

THE LIVING CHURCH

a) "The Servant In The House" [1]

". . . You must understand, this is no dead pile of stones
and un-meaning timber. *It is a living thing.* When you enter it,
you hear a sound—a .sound as of some mighty poem chanted.
Listen long enough, and you will learn that it is made up of the
beating of human hearts, of the nameless music of men's souls—
that is, if you have ears. If you have eyes, you will presently
see the church itself—a looming mystery of many shapes and
shadows, leaping sheer from floor to dome. The work of no ordinary builder! On the security of one man's name! The pillars of
it go up like the brawny trunks of heroes: the sweet human flesh
of men and women is moulded about its bulwarks, strong, and
impregnable: the faces of little children laugh out from every
corner-stone: the terrible spans and arches of it are the joined
hands of comrades; and up in the heights and spaces there are
inscribed the numberless musings of all of the dreamers of the
world. It is yet building-building and built upon. Sometimes the
work goes forward in deep darkness: sometimes in blinding light:
now beneath the burden of unutterable anguish: now to the tune
of a great laughter and heroic shoutings like the cry of thunder.
Sometimes, in the silence of the night-time, one may hear the
hammerings of the comrades at work up in the dome—the comrades
that have climbed ahead."

---

[1] Copyright, 1908, by Charles Rann Kennedy; Copyright, 1935 (in Renewal)
by Charles Rann Kennedy; Reprinted by permission of the Copyright Owners
and Samuel French, Inc.; *The Servant in The House*; Act II, pp. 67–69.

Prelude to Section FIVE:

THE LIVING CHURCH

b) "What Jesus Means To Me" [1]

What Jesus Christ means to me is beyond putting into words. My regret is my own unworthy response to Him. He is my interpretation of life; my standard of measurements; the color that glorifies my environment; the lens that brings God down to my apprehension. I love Him for He satisfies every longing of my life.

Since the days I turned from infidelity under a convicting sermon upon Psalm 77:3, "I remembered God and was troubled"—after a night of torture between yielding and resisting, I entered into the perfect peace of an untroubled faith that, until this day, has proven adequate and satisfying and inspiring. He has cleansed my sins, inspired my living, eased my mind into an undisturbed calm, and has cast out every care and anxiety from my heart. No, I'm not a saint; I'm just telling, "What Jesus Means to Me." Not what I have attained, but what He has done.

With a child's trust I accepted, and began reading the Bible; I was led by the Holy Spirit to study the writings of Paul; and was led through these, past the "Salvation" of *Romans*, into a dwelling place "in the heavenlies" in *Ephesians* from which I looked forth through the windows of *Thessalonians* into "the glory that shall be revealed" unto me, "and not to me only, but unto all those who love His appearing." Bless His Name forever and for ever!

There is not a question, problem, choice or experience that the light of His face does not give solution and victory unto. There is nothing that does not yield to His Presence; and to be still before Him, to await His conscious leading, is the sure path of victory.

May I be very definite about this. Most of my life has been spent in serving the Englewood Church in the great, but wicked city of Chicago. The Englewood Church many times has been conscious of the helpful interference of the Holy Spirit in hindering our plans; but a blessing has ever followed great frustration. It was a matter of just pride, we thought, to be in a new building in which to welcome visitors during the 1933 Century of Progress Exposition. Our plans and the financial response to appeals were most encouraging; twice the amount of cash anticipated had been paid into the treasury, and then, without friction or any one's being offended, matters came to a standstill; it was just impossible to make further progress. Right when we would have been midway in our building program,

---

1

C. G. Kindred, *What Jesus Means to Me* (Cincinnati, Ohio, *The Christian Standard*, January 6, 1934)

the financial collapse opened our eyes to where we could understand. Had we gone forward, we would have been in a new building, but with an obligation around seventy-five to one hundred thousand dollars which would have swept our property from our hands and left us a homeless congregation. As it is, our vacant lot has been beautified; the church and club house and educational plant redecorated; everything is in good condition, and we owe no one anything but to love; while others are having their mortgage worries, we, by the intervention of the good Father, are freed from that embarrassment. There is no explanation but that God gave us the right leadership when we ourselves were unable to see clearly ahead.

I have not always been obedient unto the heavenly vision, but as I look back, it is where I have at least partially tried to be that He has made good His every promise. This is so unfailingly true that I marvel at the many times I failed to act upon it; the heart certainly is deceitful, above all things, and desperately wicked—at least mine is. In the finer moments of my life, my desire is to wait constantly upon Him—"but I find a law in my members, that when I would do good, evil is present with me"—yet I rejoice in the increasing territory in my life which, under His grace, is being brought more continuously under His control.

And thus He means to me:

    a) Salvation achieved
    b) Comradeship in the present,
       and
    c) Rapturous, glorious victory in the future.

Hitherto hath the Lord blessed me; and now,

> "I beseech you, . . . brethren, for the Lord Jesus Christ's sake, and for the love of the Spirit, that ye strive together with me, in your prayers to God . . . ."

For,

> "in due season we shall reap if we faint not."

Section FIVE: THE CHURCH

TABLE of CONTENTS

HIS Story
MY Story
SATAN'S Story

Table of Contents—*Continued*   Page

Table of Contents—*Concluded*

Chart No. 5
Section FIVE

THE TRIBULATION — THE COVENANT WEEK
II Thessalonians 2:2—7; Matthew 24:21; II Corinthians 3:13—15; Daniel 9:27

THE RAPTURE

To I Thessalonians 4:16

From John 20:22

THE CHURCH
THE AGE OF GRACE

HIS STORY

(THE TIMES OF THE GENTILES

ROME: The LEGS OF The IMAGE OF DANIEL 2, Ending at 476 A.D., Followed By The FEET and TOES KINGDOMS Continued

God's dealing with Nations, and men of the world.

ROMANS 13

Romans chapters 2 and 3: Both Jew and Gentile is happened in part to Israel until the fulness of the Gentiles be come in"

("Blindness in part is happened) (Romans 11:7—11, 25)

WORLD RULERS

MY STORY

(The Resurrection of Christ
(Christ breathes on His disciples
(giving them Life
John 20:22

Christ's Ascension

FORTY DAYS PLUS TEN DAYS

Holy Spirit descends, endures Church with Authority at Pentecost A.D. 30

A "THE MYSTERY"

God's dealing with Spiritual People Israel and The Church

Acts 1:3
Luke 24:27—49

Acts 2
Luke 24:49
The Birth of The Church

The Joint Body of (Jew (and (Gentile)
Ephesians 3:1—9

"In the heavenlies"

I Thessalonians 4:13—18
Philippians 3:20—21
I Corinthians 15:51—53

(THE UNBORN BODY OF CHRIST) (THE BIRTH OF THE CHURCH) (THE GROWTH OF THE BODY) YET TO COME — —

ISRAEL'S SEVENTIETH WEEK LAST STAND as "AN ANGEL OF LIGHT"

SATAN'S (II Corinthians 4:3-4 THE ADVERSARY'S (II Corinthians 11:3—14)

Ephesians 6:10—12
II Thessalonians 2:3—9
I Peter 5:8

STORY

During this present age Satan attacks:

a) The UNITY of the Church (John 17: I Corinthians 1:10)
b) The HOPE of the Church (Philippians 3:11)
c) The SCRIPTURES of the Church (II Peter 2:1—2, II Timothy 2:15)

THE CHURCH

HIS STORY

> ". . . We also are men of like feelings with you, and bring glad tidings unto you that ye should turn from these vanities unto the living God, which made the heaven, and the earth, and the sea, and all things that are therein: Who in generations past suffered all nations to walk in their own ways. Nevertheless He left not Himself without witness, in that He did good, and gave us rain from heaven and fruitful seasons, filling our hearts with food and gladness."

Acts 14:15—17N.
(cp. Acts 17:22—31)

I. UNSTABLE ADUMBRATIONS OF GOD'S PATTERNS

𝕿HE PERVERSITY of the human will is vividly seen in this book. The Jewish race, the greatest ever, is the living proof that produced, perpetuated and protected the God-chosen witness of its own judgment— the Bible. This nation was in continuous rebellion against His purpose. The record of six thousand years of God's revealed purpose is set forth in the Bible, a sixteen hundred year production of One-Mind-Unity, from everlasting to everlasting; for "I doubt not through the ages, one unceasing purpose runs." Where did Tennyson get that idea? Or whence came the Elysian fields of the Greek poets; or the lost Atlantis (The New) of Lord Bacon or Utopia (nowhere) of Sir Thomas More. Bunyan's *Pilgrim's Progress* was not wholly "of such stuff as dreams are made of"; and was not Abraham, "the father of us all," seeking THE City? The human mind which is God's Image, is set to such music. There must be a reality back of all this for all dream. So also diviners, dictators, and Satan are driven by the like urge, for all copy God's patterns.[1] There's an angel in the sun and that is why we are so easily deceived for expectancy is our heritage. These myths, dreams, Utopias, rebellions, are unstable adumbrations of God's patterns and are not the pre-creation plasm of *kosmos*. I have stood where the Lord "lifted with His pierced Hand Empires off their hinges"[2] and all of these have pyramided and must needs say, "we are from beneath, ye are from above."

II. THE HISTORICAL CERTAINTY OF THE CHURCH

At the conclusion of HIS Story in Section FOUR, we noted that the

---

[1] See Section TWO, *Perfection to Katabole*, pp. 157—170; and Section THREE, *Restoration to Terah*, Satan's Story, p. 195

[2] Jean Paul Richter: "The life of Christ concerns Him who, being the holiest among the mighty and the mightiest among the holy, lifted with His pierced hand empires off their hinges, and turned the stream of centuries out of its channel, and still governs the ages."

events surrounding the birth, ministry, death, burial and resurrection of our Lord, came to pass in the days of Rome, the Fourth Great Empire of Daniel's vision (Daniel 2:34—45). In HIS Story of this Section FIVE, we note that the Church likewise came in to being during the days of the Fourth Great Empire. The beginning of the Church was not the *fulfillment* of Daniel's prophecy concerning the destruction of the world empires for Rome, the legs of iron of the vision, continued until 476 A.D.; and then the feet of mixed iron and clay began and this continues to this day.

The Gospel was commanded to be preached in all nations beginning at Jerusalem; and the effect of that gospel upon the nations is clearly recorded in history. The Church came in to being well within the period of historical certainty; its protagonists were examined by able, pitiless and scornful historical characters of note of the first century who are not only mentioned in the Scriptures but are specifically marked by them:

a) The four *able* Herods
(Herod The Great—Matthew 2
(Herod Antipas—Matthew 14
(Herod Agrippa I—Acts 12
(Herod Agrippa II—Acts 25 and 26

b) The *pitiless* Pontius Pilate, the Roman Governor; Matthew 27:2; John 19:10

c) The careless, indifferent and *scornful* Gallio, the Roman proconsul, deputy of Achaia, of Acts 18:12, 17; this is the same Gallio who was brother to the philosopher Seneca, teacher of Nero, and uncle of the poet Lucan.

III. THE HISTORICAL INFLUENCE OF THE CHURCH

The Church was soon so well established and its influence had so penetrated lives, that the Roman Emperor Nero, known for his merciless cruelty, could accuse the Church of causing the troubles afflicting the Roman Empire. The great councils over the doctrines of the Church which arose out of the text of the New Testament, were presided over by one Flaverius V. Constantine, an unbaptized pagan yet known as the first Christian Emperor of Rome.

Some satisfactory explanation must be found for the rise of the Christian Church; for the lives it produced; and for the holdings of art depicted on walls; and for the propagation of culture. The Church's doctrines, its buildings and art treasures were but markers along "The Way" as each period of history is but a workshop set up "by the Side of the Road." Each produced strength over the truest, purest and noblest of characters.

Peter instructs the first century Christians to:

"Submit yourselves therefore to every ordinance of man for the Lord's sake: whether it be to the king, as supreme; Or unto governors, as unto them that are sent by Him for the punishment indeed of evil-doers, but for the praise of them that do well. For so is the will of God, that with well doing ye may put to silence the ignorance of foolish men."

I Peter 2:13—15 N.

This effect of Christianity upon world history and nations has been recognized by men of note, and history's philosophers affirm:

a) William Ewart Gladstone: [1]

> "Remember that He who has united you as human beings in the same flesh and blood, has bound you by the law of mutual love; that that mutual love is not limited by the shores of this Island (England), is not limited by the boundaries of Christian civilization; that it passes over the whole surface of the earth and embraces the meanest along with the greatest in its un-measured scope."

b) William Shakespeare:

> "There's a divinity that shapes our ends,
> Rough-hew them how we will, . . ." (Hamlet, Act 1. Sc. 3)

c) Edwin Arnold:

> "There is a force (power) not ourselves
> which makes for righteousness."

d) Alfred Lord Tennyson:

> "For I doubt not through the ages,
> One unceasing purpose runs . . . ." (Locksley Hall)

e) And Rudyard Kipling lifts his voice in petition to the Lord God who is God of all the nations:

> God of our fathers, known of old—
> Lord of our far-flung battle line—
> Beneath whose awful hand we hold
> Dominion over palm and pine—
> Lord God of Hosts, be with us yet,
> Lest we forget — lest we forget!
>
> The tumult and the shouting dies—
> The Captains and the Kings depart—
> Still stands Thine ancient sacrifice,
> An humble and a contrite heart.
> Lord God of Hosts, be with us yet,
> Lest we forget — lest we forget!
>
> Far-called, our navies melt away—
> On dune and headland sinks the fire—

---

[1] D. C. Somervell, *Disraeli and Gladstone,* (N. Y., Doran) pp. 178, 222.

Lo, all our pomp of yesterday
Is one with Nineveh and Tyre!
Judge of the Nations, spare us yet,
Lest we forget — lest we forget!

If, drunk with sight of power, we loose
Wild tongues that have not Thee in awe—
Such boasting as the Gentiles use,
Or lesser breeds without the Law—
Lord God of Hosts, be with us yet,
Lest we forget — lest we forget!

For heathen heart that puts her trust
In reeking tube and iron shard—
All valiant dust that builds on dust,
And guarding, calls not Thee to guard,
For frantic boast and foolish word,
Thy Mercy on Thy People, Lord! Amen![1]

During this church age the Roman Empire has been succeeded by the Ten Toes' Kingdoms of Daniel's image. The Gospel is still being preached to the nations while everywhere we await the rapture of the Church. When the Age of Grace has ended, the long suffering of God will also come to an end and God will deal with these world empires by sending His Son (the Stone) to smite the image, to establish His kingdom and to bring to an end "the kingdoms of this world."

---

[1] From: THE FIVE NATIONS, by Rudyard Kipling. Copyright 1903 by Rudyard Kipling, reprinted by permission of Mrs. George Bambridge and Doubleday & Company, Inc.

THE CHURCH

MY STORY

I. THE DEVELOPMENT OF THE UNBORN SPIRITUAL BODY

OF THE LORD

"And beginning from Moses and from all the prophets
He expounded unto them in all the Scriptures the
things concerning Himself."

Luke 24:27N.

". . . He through the Holy Ghost had given commandments unto the
apostles whom He had chosen: to whom also He presented Himself
alive after His suffering by many infallible proofs, being seen of
them during forty days, and speaking of the things pertaining to
the kingdom of God."

Acts 1:2*b*–3N.

INTRODUCTION

This is the biography of the once-dead and twice-born Son of God;
from *life* to *death* to LIFE. The wonder and splendor of this period in the
Four Gospels grows upon me as I muse upon:

    a) His unique glory
    b) Time's change from B. C. to A.D.
    c) The transfer from Literature to *Personality*
    d) The change in apostles, men, things and events.

God is at work in His laboratory, producing the Mystery Body of the Second
Adam. As privileged onlookers, let us consider His last sermon (Luke 24:
27, 44–45), and the commandment "tarry." Prayer alone was compatible
to such exegesis and so there was a need for the command to tarry. We
might note the process which He used:

    a) He *gave* them the Scriptures
    b) He *opened* their minds to understand
    c) He *set* them aside to "tarry"
    d) They *began* to take on Christ in prayer
        and the choosing of the apostles
    e) So they were *ready* for Acts 2:1
    f) The Lord *"added"* (Acts 2:47)
    g) Years later, He *"taught"* (Galatians 1:11–12);
        "Named and *gave"* Barnabas and Saul (Acts 13:2);
        and *"Sent"* (vss. 3–4) them forth by the Holy Spirit.

We are to consider how the Old Testament is to be clarified and per-
sonalized upon reflection (Malachi 3:16); but before they reached "The
Upper Room" (Acts 1:13), their need for such reflection is revealed by
two events:

a) Their question in Acts 1:6, "Lord, wilt Thou at this time restore the kingdom to Israel?"

b) And their "looking" in verses 9—11 (cf. Matthew 17:8).

A. THE LORD "RIGHTLY DIVIDING" THE SCRIPTURES
THROUGH THE FORTY DAYS

The book of Hebrews is the syllabus of the Lord's "speaking concerning the Kingdom of God" (John 16:12—14, Acts 1:3), as He faced three fronts in those forty days of speaking:

a) "Concerning Me" (Luke 24:44, John 5:39); "The Messiah" of "yesterday"

b) The Church (Mystery) (Luke 24:44—49, Acts 1:4—5, 7—8 and 2:1—4; "The Savior" of "today"

c) "Concerning the Kingdom of God" (Acts 1:3); "The King" of "forever."

Here Christ is seen in the Assembly Room of the "Purpose of the Ages," as He is fitting together, i.e. "framing the ages" (Hebrews 11:3). He is "the same yesterday, today and forever," and to the one who observes intently: "ye shall not walk in darkness but have the light of THE Life" (John 8:12).

> ". . . being seen of them during forty days and speaking the things pertaining to the kingdom of God: . . . When they therefore were come together, they asked of Him, saying, 'Lord, wilt Thou at (in) this time restore the kingdom to Israel?' And He said unto them, 'It is not for you to know times or seasons (Daniel 2:21) which the Father put in His own authority'."
>
> Acts 1:3, 6—7N.

The need for rightly dividing is the reason for this emphasis upon these forty days. Here the Lord is rightly dividing between the kingdom of heaven and the kingdom of God. Paul in Philippians 1:10 asks us to "approve the things that are excellent" (A.S.V. *m*.: 'distinguish the things that differ'), and this we must do. The "kingdom of the heavens" is first, in importance, for John (Matthew 3:2) and Jesus (Matthew 4:17) came preaching the kingdom of heaven necessarily to Jews only. This is not the rule *by men* but *of God* (I Samuel 8:1—7); "The son of David *is* Deity! When He came as king, He came to restore the autocracy of God (Acts 1:6). Upon their rejection of Him, *viz*. "we will not have this man to reign over us," we hear at once His teaching on "the Kingdom of God" (Acts 1:1—11, 3:18—26, Matthew 11:12). To rightly divide we must have correct definitions:

a) The Kingdom of The Heavens:

(1) The entering of this kingdom is through man (Matthew 1), and only those who were descendants of Abraham participate (Matthew 9:11, Luke 13:28—29), and only a descendant of David can reign over it (Luke 1:21—33). Those who share in this genealogy are to participate in the Kingdom of the Heavens and are to see the Shekinah Glory which is to return (Ezekiel 43:1—2).

(2) The Kingdom of the Heavens continued up to Samuel (I Samuel 8:7). There is no Kingdom of the Heavens in effect from the beginning of the reign of Saul until Messiah's return when it shall be re-established after the rapture of the Church (Matthew 25:31ff., Revelation 5:5—14, Luke 19:11—27).

b) The Kingdom of God:

(1) This is an all-inclusive term which covers God's reign from Alpha to Omega. Sometimes the Kingdom of the Heavens is referred to as the Kingdom of God, but the context will give indication as to which is meant; the two terms are NOT synonomous. Matthew is the only one who uses "Kingdom of Heaven," but five times he uses "Kingdom of God," making a distinction between the two terms. The other Gospel writers use only "Kingdom of God."

(2) The Kingdom of God is advancing, conquering from above (Gr. *anothen*, Matthew 6:9, Luke 11:2), and is putting down the *rebellion of Satan*. There are three stages to this rebellion:

(*a*) It began in heaven (Isaiah 14:14, Ezekiel 28:14, Revelation 12:7)[1]

(*b*) At Armageddon it is manifested on earth

(*c*) Its earthly conclusion is at Gog and Magog, previous to which the Messiah is on His Throne on earth. He comes at Armageddon as the stone of Daniel 2:44 and reigns over His Kingdom which fills the whole earth. In the parable of the wicked husbandmen (Matthew 21:33—45), a further promise concerning the establishment of the kingdom by Messiah, the Stone, is set forth.

c) The Church:

(1) The Church was *not* an after-thought in the mind of God, but was planned from eternity:

---

[1] See Section TWO, *Perfection to Katabole*, Satan's Story, pp.164—170

"According as He hath chosen (Gr. aorist *chooses*) us in Him before the foundation of the world, that we should be holy and without blemish before Him" (Ephesians 1:4N.).

(2) This body is "in the heavenlies" (Ephesians 1:22–23, 2:6).

(3) It is the Shekinah—God's Presence Cloud for today—the extension of the Kingdom of God upon earth (John 2:13, 27:11–19, and Acts 4:13). This Body is God's present concern.

The rightly dividing between "The Kingdom of the Heavens," "The Kingdom of God," and the Church, and the understanding of their relationship one to another, makes possible the understanding of the whole purpose of God through the Bible. *This was the purpose of Jesus in spending Forty Days speaking to them concerning the Kingdom of God.*

Thus we see that "to distinguish the things that differ" refers to our discerning the dispensations, for this instruction is to:

a) Teachers: (Jewish (Romans 2:17–21*b*)
(and
(Christian (Philippians 1:9–10)

and

b) Preachers: (II Timothy 2:15) "holding a straight course in the Word of truth."

Especially is this "distinguishing" necessary through the two parentheses: the *Jewish* "fold" (*Romans* chaps. 9 through 11), and the *Christian* "flock" (John 10:16). The "fold" is "contripetal" or exclusive; while the "flock" is "centrifugal" or dynamic, as a game of "Touch and Go." The two olive branches (Romans 11:22–23)—the Jewish fold and the Christian flock—are as "life from the dead"; so, while the Jew thus stands on the edge of the Holy Land, *we* stand on the brink of the broken tombs, and in sight of our Holy Land—"for what shall the receiving of them be but *life* from the dead."

Note their question in Acts 1:6: "Wilt Thou at (Gr. *en*, in) this time restore the kingdom to Israel?" Many commentators have said that the disciples of Jesus were earthly-minded and did not understand that His kingdom was a spiritual one. Isn't is unusual that the Son of God, alive from the dead, could spend forty days speaking of these things, and yet at the end of this time, His disciples upon whom He had breathed the Holy Spirit could still misunderstand His purpose? Note that He did not rebuke them for asking the question. He did not say that they had misunderstood Him, but He answered their questions saying: "It is not for you to know the *times* or the *seasons* which the Father hath put in His own power." When we note later in the chapter that they had been standing on the Mount of Olives as they asked this question, we can understand their concern for they knew the prophecy of Zechariah 14:4. Their question was not of *what* the Lord was going to do, but rather of the time in which He would do it. Therefore this "Forty Days" was:

a) A *Demonstration* of immortality
b) The *Opening* of the Scripture and the opening of their eyes concerning Himself
c) The *Teaching* them concerning the Kingdom of God
d) The *Syllabus* of His sermons which appear later in *Hebrews*
e) The *Preparation* for Pentecost at which time the functioning of the Holy Spirit demonstrated that the Plan of Redemption was of God:
    "But if it be of God, ye cannot overthrow it;
    lest haply ye be found even fighters against God"

Acts 5:39 N.

B. THE TRANSFER OF LEADERSHIP TO THE HOLY SPIRIT

The transfer of leadership to "Another Comforter." is the inter-regnum from the Passover to Pentecost (John 15:22, 16:14). He said, "While I was *yet* with you"; and then, "Lo, I *am* with you" (Luke 24:44, Matthew 28:29). The transferring from *Him* to the *Church*, of the Word of Salvation, is the most critical of His mission:

"As the Father hath sent Me, so send I you."

	("shall take of Mine, and shall announce unto you"
	((John 16:15N.)
	("and bring all things to your remembrance, whatsoever
The Comforter	(I said unto you" (John 14:26*b*N.)
	("will guide you into all truth" (John 16:13*a*)
	("will announce to you things to come"
	((John 16:13*b*N.)

The Holy Spirit's (the Comforter's) control was, and is, absolute; too much depends upon His control to allow an optional: "The words which I speak unto you, they are spirit and life" (John 6:63). The book of Acts indicates both the *direct* and the *indirect* control of the Holy Spirit. These verses from Acts 2:4, 5:3, 11:28, 13:2, 4, and 15:28 specify some of those who are under the *direct* control of the Holy Spirit. Of these, Acts 5:3 deals with Ananias, showing the penalty suffered by one who tried to lie to the Holy Spirit, to Whom he was *directly* responsible if he had received the "laying on of hands." Others were *indirectly* responsible to Him, and resisted the Holy Spirit by resisting His Word of revelation (Acts 28:55 ff.). We are *indirectly* responsible to the Holy Spirit and can resist Him today

338 Section FIVE: THE CHURCH—MY STORY

by rejecting the Word of His revelation, and refusing to welcome His indwelling Presence. The *direct* control of the Holy Spirit was promised to the apostles, and was evidently given to those also on whom the apostles laid their hands (Matthew 10:18—20; John 14:26; 15:26—27; 16:13—14; Acts 6:10; 8:29; 10:19 and 12:12); such power was not transferrable (Acts 8:14—18). The apostles were told that they would be brought before kings and rulers and that they were not to be concerned as to what they should say, for the Holy Spirit would give them the words which they needed. These words and other instructions are what is meant by *direct* control. Later, Paul wrote to Timothy (II Timothy 2:15 N.):

> "*Study* to show thyself approved unto God,
> a workman not ashamed,
> rightly dividing the word of truth."

And the importance of the written word in seeking the Mind of the Spirit is there manifested.

The *direct* control of the Holy Spirit furnished the power for miracles, and special knowledge and tongues; and this *direct* control passed away when the last one on whom the apostles laid their hands, had died. All those who had *not* received the laying on of the hands of the apostles for the miraculous power of the Holy Spirit, were under the *indirect* control of the Holy Spirit through the Word. The *Acts of the Apostles* is the Auditor's (Spirit's) Report of this transitional period. A reader of this Book is aware of the brooding, creative Presence Who is near, and Who was and is responsive to those who are spiritually minded. His work is to direct aright; to fix the form and names; and to speak of "things to come." Because these assertions are of fact, then *Acts* is the source and authority section of the New Testament and seekers do well who consult and obey this Word.

C. THE GREAT COMMISSION

In the Upper Room Jesus said:

> ". . . 'Peace unto you: as the Father hath sent Me, even so send I you.' And when He had said this, He *breathed into* them (see Genesis 2:7), and saith unto them, 'Receive ye Holy Spirit: Whose soever sins ye remit, they are remitted unto them; whose soever ye retain, they are retained'."

John 20:21—23 N.

Following this, near the close of the forty days, Jesus gives further commands:

1. John 21:15—17 (to Peter):
   a) Feed my lambs
   b) Tend or shepherd (guide, guard, fold) My sheep

c) Feed My sheep (cf. Luke 12:42)

This is the threshold challenge; the trifler, the irreverent, and traditionalist, are all warned to beware and to repent. The Book of Acts is Holy ground; it is the Church's "Lying-In" room.

2. The content of the Great Commission in *Matthew* is:
   a) "All authority hath been given" (Matthew 28:18)
   b) "Make disciples of all nations" (Matthew 28:19)
   (1) By baptizing them (cp. Acts 14:21 "having disciples many")
   (2) "Into (Gr. *eis*) the Name"—thus: the accuracy
3. Mark gives the commission which emphasizes the conversion of the individual (Mark 16:15—16)
4. Luke tells:
   a) of the Emmaus sermon (Luke 24:27, 32).
      How can teachers, preachers and editors who question the text of the Scriptures, prepare converting lessons?
   b) of the day of ascension (Luke 24:44—49);
   (1) "All things written MUST be fulfilled"
   (2) He opened their minds;
   (3) That repentance and remission of sins should be preached
   (4) But they are to tarry till clothed with power from on high
   (5) And then, "He led them out over against Bethany, and He lifted up His hands and blessed them"; "He was parted from them and carried up into heaven"; "they worshiped Him and returned to Jerusalem with great joy," into the Upper Room where the twelve and Mary, the mother, and about one hundred twenty disciples tarried as commanded, and they prayed.

The events following and the preaching and the commands, will be the Holy Spirit's taking the things of Christ and declaring unto them and applying the same unto us, and they must be infallible. The Book of Acts is the Workshop of the Holy Spirit where the Lord's plan to propagate and perpetuate the Gospel of His Salvation is to be worked up into the Church. The Lord's plan is divinely implemented with *the Name* which indicates the resources of enabling power available; with *Baptism* and the *Lord's Supper*, and with *the Person*, the Holy Spirit, for "He shall take of Mine" and "not speak of Himself." Through Him is promised the *guidance*—"He will guide you"—also the *language*—"in words which the Holy Spirit teacheth."

Therefore, this period beginning at Acts 2:1 would become the time of the assumption of leadership by The Great Invisible—the "Another Comforter" of John 14:16—17 and 17:21—23. Consider the condition of the world:

the people of Israel were as "sheep without a shepherd"; and they said, "what shall we do?" That the end had come, they knew, and that the curtain in the temple had been rent they also knew, signifying that the way into the Holiest of all was now made manifest. His disciples had heard Him say, "when I was yet with you," and they listened through the forty days as He spoke concerning the Kingdom of God, and so they said, "Wilt thou in this time restore the kingdom to Israel?" He had explained to them the coming of the Golden Age: the Kingdom of God. But *when* would Israel come into its place in the Kingdom of God? And so He said, "It is not for you . . . (the Church) to know such times and seasons—but ye shall receive *power* to be my witnesses, only beginning from Jerusalem to the uttermost part of the earth" (Acts 1:6–8, 3:17–26, 28:23–31).

The map of the world bears witness to the above assertions. The earth was builded about a strip of land. Other capitols gain recognitions by sheer force, but Jerusalem by a fore-ordained, inescapable contour, for Palestine was located for "Influ(flow)ence." No other strip is like it in earth's hemisphere, nor is "so beautiful for situation . . . ." (Psalm 48). "If I forget thee, O Jerusalem, let my right hand forget her cunning" (Psalm 137:5); it is rhapsodic; roadways because of deserts and mountains, detour through this land; and,

> The Universe was planned just for Palestine
> And Palestine was planned for The Cross and for The Throne
> And Jerusalem in Palestine was prepared for the Cradle of the
> Church.

For, as "the heavens declare the glory of God," so also, Palestine is created for the worship of God. Every nation has its glamor, its traditions and its heroes; but this Holy City of Palestine, and this Son of Palestine, out-ranks them all in satisfying solution of Life, Income and Worship. And here, Jerusalem, its Throne City, sits as a gem in an engagement ring, flashing its glory story through the Universe, and nations and continents grouped about her, find her accessible and desirable. Her pride was as justified as the young Irish soldier decked out in his regalia and marching in line, thought to himself: "wish I might stand on the sidelines an' watch me-self go by!"

Thus the Church's exceeding high calling is witnessed by two unimpeachables: the geography and the Gospel locale; and here hopefully yet nearly despairingly, His choice followers like "a child with no language but a cry" uttered Acts 1:6, "wilt Thou at *this* time restore again the kingdom to Israel? For here in Palestine the Church was born to greatness and the Scriptures were centered; and this word "restore" from this passage is concerned with fragmented harmony, but never the *status quo*; every ascent even of the Transfiguration makes *restore* more important (see (Hebrews 11:15).

D. THE ASCENSION; PALESTINE THE CELESTIAL AIRPORT

"And when He had spoken these things, while they beheld,
He was taken up;
and a cloud bore Him from out of their sight."

Acts 1:9 N.

Pentecost and the two super-phenomenal events—the Resurrection and the Ascension—made of Palestine a Celestial Airport (Luke 34:44—53, Acts 1:1—11, Ephesians 4:8, Matthew 27:51—53). Out from this marvelous fifty day period has arisen an institution of such inherent and wondrous grandeur and hope as to conqueringly challenge every contender, and so occupy man's moral sense of right, that he, "himself being the judge," refuses to entertain a rival. These two unique elements of this fifty day period, (the Resurrection and the Ascension), are wholly apart from even the Christian's experience, yet these are so firmly held by many as to make martyrs.

This whole book of Acts is one of "Descendings" and "Ascendings"; the former is wholly for the latter. What are the creations of genius but the cloud "around about the Throne" of the "Ascendeds." Such genius is as the Cherubim guarding the way to the Tree of Life from all that is sensual and "of the earth, earthy." It was this which separated Cain from Abel, and Barabbas from Jesus. The Gospels each declare what John 13:3 so calmly asserts as the reason that Jesus could wash their feet. He was *in* the earth but not *of* the earth. The Second Adam was not after all of earth earthy (I Corinthians 15:47).

These Gospels all bear witness to the heavenly nature of Christians as they tell of the annunciation and birth of Jesus, His transfiguration, and the events at the tomb and the ascension. The Communion proclaims a living "Ascended" and "Coming Again" Lord (John 6:48—63). The homely fare of which genius eats, rises up into apocalyptics. He is risen; we also are risen. Our felicity of virtuous refinements is contrasted with Japanese Shintoism and Mohammed's Moslems whose appeal is to the sensual and the gross. During the Fifty Days, the Lord was re-forming and forming anew, His nascent Body, the Church.

E. THE TEN DAYS – THE UPPER ROOM INTERIM FROM ASCENSION TO PENTECOST

1. Unity

The Upper Room was a meeting place for Jesus and His disciples

(Mark 14:13–15), and in Acts 1:4 we read, "And being assembled together with them (Gr. *sunalizomenos*: "eating with them" A.S.V.), commanded them that they should not depart from Jerusalem but "tarry till endued with the Spirit." The emotions of this place are evident as we read the text of the book of Acts. Beginning at John 20:22 in this Upper Room and on, Peter and John are at one; there are no divisive bickerings now (Matthew 20:21–24), for they are "of one accord"; they "continued stedfastly"; they were "in prayer"; and "all together in one place."

2. The Upper Room Group

A familiarizing study of this group who met in the Upper Room is "like a handful of corn upon the mountain" (Psalm 72:16). It will be most profitable, for we the Church are the extension of them, the unsung and unknown of them. Joseph Justus called Barsabas, was not elected to the place of an apostle, yet he "carried on." These forgotten martyrs planted churches everywhere. Still more revealing is the phrase "with Mary, [1] the mother of Jesus, and with His brethren" (Acts 1:14). This reminds us of the angel's message to the women at the tomb: "go tell His disciples *and* Peter" (Mark 16:1).

3. Prayers and Supplication

All of these in the Upper Room "continued with one accord in prayer and supplication," realizing their need for tarrying, even as must you and I.

After such preaching by the Master (Acts 1:3, Luke 24:27, 44–45), and prayer (Acts 1:14),—now, what next?

---

[1]
It is well to note that although Mary the mother of Jesus is mentioned, that she is accorded no special place of honor or authority in this group of The Upper Room. The exaltation of Mary to a place equal with or above the Father, Son and Holy Spirit arose out of Roman Catholic traditions.

In an article on *The Worship of Mary* quoted from *The Churchman's Magazine*, (London, The Paternoster Press, March 1954, DAWN, p. 94), it is stated:

". . . To Mary is ascribed equally with Christ the work of Redemption. She is said to be 'The Life of the sinner, since she obtains for him the pardon of his sins.' (*The Glories of Mary*, by Liguori, pp. 63–64). 'The hope of all the children of Adam' (pp. 86–87). 'She is the patroness and protectress of the Church in every great calamity, to destroy heresies and to be the entire ground of hope to sinners.' ('Encyclical of Gregory XVI' 15th of August, 1832).

". . . She is omnipotent in power and infinite in mercy according to Liguori: 'Jesus has rendered Mary Omnipotent and obliged himself to grant all the desires and requests of His Mother . . she is as rich in mercy as in power.'" (*The Glories of Mary* pp. 138–139) Again on page 121 he wrote:

"No grace, nor pardon, emanates from the throne of the King of kings, without passing through the hands of Mary . . . no one enters heaven without passing through her."

"Rome has gradually built up the worship of the pagan Goddess until she replaces God Himself . . . ."

4. The Lord Chooses Matthias

Peter stood up to speak. We must listen now for this is the most momentous speech ever spoken in a prayermeeting. Take note that they have been with Jesus and it sounds as though it is His Master's Voice which speaks (Acts 1:16), "it was needful that the Scriptures be fulfilled" (Luke 24:4, John 19:28). In Acts 1:16 through 22, he points to the need for the fulfillment of Psalms 41:9 for *one* must replace Judas in "The Twelve," and this Scripture is another like John 19:28 ("I thirst"). That "the Scriptures cannot be broken" is my conviction; I prefer to face God with "thus it is written."

His "breathing into them" and His Great Commission had infected them so that:

a) Peter quoted the Scriptures (Psalm 109:8)
b) And he adopted the Scripture method of casting the lot (Lev. 16:8)

I am persuaded that a Pentecost experience is impossible to a Scripture-*slighting* ministry! The Spirit of Pentecost was *Word* loyalty; the disciples had received the Holy Spirit and should have been able to choose an apostle especially as they knew the qualifications; yet they "cast lots" "that all things must needs be fulfilled"; even as at the Cross, we saw it demonstrated: "they gave Him vinegar to drink . . ." and Peter takes up this *sine quo non* of meticulous obedience; Pentecost must mean this to all believers!

The fate of Judas shocked even hardened Jerusalem, and the field which *he* had purchased with the reward of iniquity, *money stolen from the disciples' treasury* (John 12:6), evidently was the place where he took his own life, and was called by Jerusalem *Aceldama,* the field of blood. As tragedies occurred in the ranks of the Jewish rulers, the field of blood grew even more gruesome, especially with the events surrounding A.D. 70, and the destruction of the city by Titus (Matthew 27:25).

Peter said in Acts 1:21—22:

"Wherefore, of these men who have companied with us . . .
must one be ordained to be witness of His resurrection;"

and they put forth or made to stand up two, Joseph and Matthias. Why was there so much fuss? Either one would have been alright for both were qualified—but such is not the Lord's way in the Church. We read of their actions "and they put forward . . . prayed . . . and said, '*Thou* Lord, who knowest the hearts of all, show whether of these two *Thou* hast chosen'." In Matthew 16:23 Peter had gotten *in* the way of the Lord, but now having learned one lesson, he gets *out* of the way and asks the Lord to choose! And the result of the giving forth of lots, showed that Matthias had been chosen by the Lord, and he was numbered with the eleven apostles (see Acts 6:2).

II. THE BIRTH OF THE LORD'S SPIRITUAL BODY—PENTECOST[1]

The converging of so much of the Bible in Christ, certainly gives weight to His commission and raises Pentecost to importance unrivaled. Section FIVE of this seven-fold outline of the Word of God began with the development of the *unborn* Spiritual Body of Christ, His Church. The *birth* of this Spiritual Body took place on the day of Pentecost, A.D. 30, and this portion of the outline continues to the catching up of this Body at our Lord's second coming.

> Then the Master,
> With a gesture of command,
> Waved his hand;
> And at the word,
> Loud and sudden there was heard,
> All around them and below,
> The sound of hammers, blow on blow,
> Knocking away the shores and spurs,
> And see! she stirs!
> She starts—she moves—she seems to feel
> The thrill of life along her keel,
> And, spurring with her foot the ground,
> With one exulting, joyous bound,
> She leaps into the ocean's arms![2]

The Church "started to move" in the resurrection of Jesus Christ and as disciples were added to it day by day, impetus became more manifest, and finally got to where the Lord went back and preached to the spirits in prison; He could not have done that before!

A. PREPARATION FOR PENTECOST

The place and preparation for Pentecost should cause a reverent fear to be upon anyone approaching it. Pentecost is as the Niagara Falls and the Rapids. There at Buffalo four mighty lakes are condensed as they rush to open out into a fifth. Just so at Pentecost the Four Gospels are condensed to open out into *The Acts*. This period of the transfer of leadership with the continuance of the Power repays reverent survey.

There is first the preparation of the *Presence*. Jesus said, "I go away," and again He said, "The Father . . . shall give you another Comforter." In the Upper Room He told them, "Now is the Son of Man glorified" (John 13:31) as He was with the eleven disciples (Matthew 28:16, Acts 1:26,

---

[1] See this Section FIVE, VI. "The Things . . . Fully Established Among Us," D. *The Holy Spirit*, 4. *Tarrying*, pp. 436–437.

[2] Henry Wadsworth Longfellow, *The Building of The Ship*, (N.Y., Houghton, Mifflin and Company), st. 1.

I Corinthians 15:5, Acts 1:21—22). After hearing Jesus speak in the Upper Room, the disciples said, "Now . . . we believe that Thou comest forth from God" (John 16:30); and these same apostles:

> ". . . began to speak with other tongues as the Spirit
> gave them to utter" (in short weighty sentences).

Next comes the continuance of the *Power*. In Mark 16:20 we read, "The Lord working with them and confirming the word with signs following"; and shortly after Pentecost, the Jews "took knowledge (recognized) of them, that they had been with Jesus,"—and confessed, "that indeed a notable miracle hath been done . . ." (Acts 4:13*b*), 16*a*). These same empowered disciples were described by these "Jews who believed in," as having "turned the world upside down" (Acts 17:6). The apostle Paul maintained that he had obtained help of God (Acts 26:22). This power was harmonious with the life which they had received in the Upper Room (John 20:22—23).

Watch Love's supreme expression in these Gospels, for just as The Great Lakes flow together, so also do these:

> MATTHEW: "Going, make disciples . . . and lo, I am with you"
> LUKE: "Tarry till endued"
> MARK: "They went, the Lord working with them"
> JOHN: "And many other signs truly did Jesus . . . which
> are not written . . . ."

> MARK: "Going into the world (Gr. *Kosmos*) and preaching"
> i.e. broadcasting
> MATTHEW: "discipling" nations, i.e. Christianizing the nations;
> "teaching them to observe all things which I have
> commanded"; i.e. beginning from John's baptism
> LUKE: "He opened their minds that they might understand
> the Scriptures; that "Christ should suffer," and
> that "repentance and remission of sins should be
> preached" "Ye are My witnesses, . . . but tarry
> till endued with power from on high."

The *need* for this tarrying is shown in Acts 1:6. Their question concerns the restoring of the kingdom to Israel, but only the *time* of restoration is in doubt. From the teachings of Jesus during His earthly ministry, we see that the time can be:

a) Astronomically discerned (Matthew 24:29, Luke 21:25, Acts 2:19*a*—20)

b) Geologically discerned (Matthew 24:7, Luke 21:11, Acts 2:19*b*)

c) And will be also spiritually discerned by them if they "tarry till endued with power from on high."

It is well also to refer to Acts 3:21 and *Romans*, chapters 9 through 12. In Acts 1:3 we read:

> "To whom also He presented Himself alive after His suffering by many infallible proofs (John 20:30), being seen of them during forty days, and speaking the things pertaining to the kingdom of God."

His disciples were obsessed by Israel's place today. How tremendous was the issue; and how inadequate were the workmen; and how necessary is prayer; "stand still and see the glory." The Holy Spirit who had indwelt Jesus, now takes up His abode in the Body. Clothed in the rags of the prodigal, self-righteous Church, He is going to begin a work of glory. The Holy Spirit is a pioneer of holiness whose work is to eventuate in a "new heavens and a new earth."

B. THE VALLEY OF DECISION

Now comes "The Valley of Decision" (Acts 2:1—4, vss. 12—36, Joel 3:14): "And when the day of Pentecost was being fulfilled." Here is the first (fundamental) apologetic of Christianity. The Book of Acts is the transfer from the theocracy of Israel to the Christocracy of the Church. There must needs be overlappings that confuse the careless as in truths for Israel and for the Christian. The disciples were commanded to go to to the Jew first. If there had been an abrupt break, it would have been easily discerned, but a compound fracture (parallel fracture) is more difficult to see; for the appeal to Israel continued to the very end of the book of Acts. And there at the end of the appeal to anointed "opened" eyes, arose the Church in *Romans* as the Twentieth Century U.S.A. before the Pilgrims of Plymouth. *Acts* is the appeal of God, "be ye reconciled to God." "All day long have I stretched out my hands to an untoward and gainsaying nation." Our attempt is to unravel the elements native to each, as the scribe referred to in Matthew 13:51—52, "things (of) new and old" Testaments, so that children may not stumble and the wayfarer may not err. Here in *Acts* is the emergence from crude materials into the refined products inherent in each.

Here at Pentecost a rejected King risen from the dead proposes "My Church" which is absolutely *heteros* (different) from "the kingdom" presented in the Gospels, replacing NOW, but NOT forever the Romans 11:26—29. Israel and the Church are never one but are contemporary; they are two peoples, twin wonders. The one is a *kingdom* and an organization; and the other is a *Body*, an organism; the laws, names and place of each are also *heteros*:

1. Israel, an organization, a Kingdom:
   a) Calls upon The King
   b) Has her place prepared in Palestine, for the very boundaries

        are fixed[1] but the people are not

2. The Church, a Body, an organism:

    a) Is Called out (Gr. *Ek-klesia*)

    b) Where the people are prepared—but the place is not (John 14:2)

Thoughtful folk are challenged by a "cutting off" of Israel and a "grafting in" of the Church. They see a valley of dry bones—these are dead but are to be resurrected (Ezekiel 27:11—28). And these who have been apart from God (Gr. *A-Theos*), sensual minded, are to be sainted, or set apart.

Two solemn points should be noted at Pentecost:

1. These apostles were not making an extemporaneous speech; they had been with Jesus for forty days after His resurrection; following this they had been ten days in prayer, and now in Acts 2:4N., "they are all filled with the Holy Spirit and began to speak as the Spirit gave them to utter (in short weighty sentences)."

2. The sermon and materials were Spirit-selected and Spirit-directed. These facts were considered sufficient by the Omniscient God. Anyone should be slow to contradict this, for it is God's most sacred moment of revelation (Ephesians 3:9).

This then, is the junction of the two ages, dispensations and institutions, and God the Father has put His best—yea, His All into it. Selah.

Then there is a further reason for emphasis: Peter says, "give ear unto my words." These words of caution are as solemn as could be spoken. It is used only here in the New Testament, and puts the obligation upon the hearer. He is asked to "give ear," to take into his ear and make division between the thoughts (Luke 8:18). "Unto my words" (Gr. *hremata*), i.e. "the joining together of words in a sentence";—could any wording be clearer! Peter then quotes from Joel 2:28—32, and the 28th verse says:

> "And it shall come to pass *afterward*, that I will pour out of my Spirit upon all flesh, and your sons and your daughters shall prophesy, your old men shall dream dreams, your young men shall see visions."

To understand this word "afterward," we must look back to the 27th verse where God says, "ye shall know that I am in the midst of Israel, that I am the Lord your God and none else, and my people shall never be ashamed." The pouring out of God's Spirit upon all flesh indicated that this was taking place *after* the Lord had been in the midst of Israel and the nation had rejected Him. This is the argument of Peter, especially in Acts 2:22 thro' 25, and his conclusion from this argument and that of the prophecies of David, is found in verse 36:

---

[1] See Section THREE, *Restoration to Terah*, Eden, p. 177 ff.

"Therefore let all the house of Israel know assuredly, that God
hath made Him whom ye have crucified, both Lord and Christ."

The coming of the Holy Spirit was to show that the Lord *had* been in
the midst of Israel, but that at the close of the Church age there *will be*
wonders in heaven above, signs in the earth beneath (Acts 2:19–20), and
these are to come *"before* the great and notable day of the Lord." One
portion of Joel's prophecy is concerned with events which *follow His first
coming*, and the other portion with those events which *precede His Second
Appearing*. Peter makes distinction between "Ye men of Judea," and "Ye
men of Israel," and then "all the house of Israel" (vs. 36). To ignore these
distinctions would be fatal to clearness. These "last days" of Joel began
at the crucifixion as there was darkness and the rocks were rent (Matthew
27:52). We see the events of the Cross and then 70 A.D., the destruction
of Jerusalem, and since that time the Jews have been the people who have
been "trodden down."

At Pentecost the Gospel was preached to Israel only, and the Book
of Acts is to Israel first: "Ye men of Judea; Ye men of Israel"; then "to
the Crucifixion; and now they are told to "save yourselves from this untoward generation" (vs. 40). Here the Jews' clock stopped and time ceased,
as one who is asleep notes not the passage of time—and so will they be
until they return to the land.

Pentecost is the most important event to man within the Universe (Leviticus 23:9–21). It was a very great day when the angel said, "there is
born to you this day in the city of David, a Savior who is Christ, the Lord"—
yet there was another day greater when the angel said, "He is not here,
He is risen." The birth of Jesus (Emmanuel) was the tabernacling of God
among men and the resurrection was the Christ-conquering death, but these
while proving to be an interest in man, were yet apart from us. Then comes
Pentecost and Peter's arraignment of the nation of Israel for their unbelief
and the murder of Jesus. They cried out "what shall we do" and Peter said,
"Repent and be baptized," and they that gladly received his Word were baptized, and the Lord added to Himself (*unity*, Acts 2:47). Here first and only
as we are related to Pentecost does it become so today. Here and here only
is John 10:10 become a reality. Here is where we can examine ourselves
(II Corinthians 13:5) and here is the way to test I John 5:12. Here alone
man is begotten into the divine (life) image and become a partaker of divine
nature (II Peter 1:4, Luke 20:24, Romans 8:29, I Corinthians 15:49, Galatians 1:1).

The Lord's prayer is recorded in John 17, but at Pentecost and nowhere
else are the elements of this prayer exclusively to be found. There is no
other *beginning* for Acts 11:15 to refer to than at Pentecost. Here is, no
more or no less, than the revelation of God (Deuteronomy 4:2, Revelation

22:18). Another even more wonderful mystery is that there are fixed meanings of other feasts (Leviticus 23), but not so of Pentecost. Then there were two leavening loaves but no explanation is given. These *two loaves* represent the Jews and the Gentiles (Romans 21:32) and leaven is a type of sin which now comes to light (I Corinthians 5:7). Acts 2:38 promises the remission of sins but who can remit sins? "Behold the Lamb of God who taketh away the sin of the world." This is the one unleavened loaf (Revelation 5:5). Pentecost was not calculated from the Passover which was a fixed date but from the wave sheaf from the feast of first fruits. The Passover could occur on any day of the week but Pentecost on the first day of the week only.

We cannot offer leaven before God. There must be a mediator (I Timothy 2:5), so, wonder beyond wonders, above raising and rising from the dead, the Lord is taking two living, dead bodies, and making of the twain ONE— His Own Body (Ephesians 2:15). Whoever makes division between Pentecost and the Rapture is assuming an exceedingly hazardous role.

The reverent mind unsandals in approaching the events of Pentecost which is the converging of prophetic fulfillments. This is the crown of the Old Testament and the Gospels. The life and transcendant events of our Lord are as preparatory to Pentecost, and they are removed before Pentecost is possible.

Even though these phenomena incite us to great haste, as they did Peter and John (John 20:4), yet we "tarry" as did John (John 20:5, 8) for reverence stands at the edge. I boldly assert that a *like approach* will obtain and restore *like faith*. The pilgrimage to Pentecost is "the way" made holy by its pilgrims and made glorious from their creations. We hear the songs, we see the temples and we listen to the bells as though we walk a great cathedral aisle with a ritual nineteen hundred years long "where congregations never break and sabbaths never end." Past these redemptive commands and ordinances, we are to enter her fellowship in order to know the power energizing the Church and to receive and reproduce her doctrines, fruits and life, for this Pentecostal group is the norm or sample or first fruits and is the Lord's standard of measurement.

The events of Pentecost are the most stupendous of all time. The very least of its parts are of infinite import as are a stratosphere baloon gondola and its contents. The change in Peter defies psychology, for he is as a lion, though timid and impulsive before and after (Acts 10:23, 11:12). The spiritual and intellectual elevation of the ten days of prayer had lifted all of the disciples to one accord with God. Peter's sermon transcends all homiletics for it is unique, complete and perfect. There is nothing like it before and after. Compare it with the Lord's in Luke 24; and Paul's sermon in Acts 17. The by-products of Pentecost, the church buildings, psalmody, and civilizations are seen everywhere. But consider now the spiritual elevation of the converts at Pentecost as a further crowning proof. Let us catch and analyze the tears at the loss of loved ones (I Thessalonians 4:13). The Christian has "a rainbow in the rain." Who dares the attempt to reduce this "plus" into our symbols of value? Note also the momentary courage for occasions (Luke 21:15); know when they saw . . . the boldness . . . they took knowledge of them that they had been with Jesus"—and He was with them! Finally note the readjustment of values (Luke 18:29). "We have left ALL." Desire, wealth and peace are reborn, passing from body to soul. All of the above and very much more arises from the events of Pentecost.

III. THE GROWTH OF THE SPIRITUAL BODY—THE CHURCH

INTRODUCTION

The only demonstration that the Church can give as the children of God is motion. In Acts 2:47 we read:

"And the Lord added together day by day
those that were being saved" (A.S.V.)

It does not say that they added "to the Church." These who *obeyed* the Gospel were the ones that were being saved. That was the Church, the prepared Body that the Holy Spirit was taking up and the Father was calling out from the world. As food is added to the physical body, so the Lord was adding to that Church, and that was the increase of the Body of Christ. This was the increase of power and they were growing.

Then came the organizing of the organism, for the poor must be cared for, and for the cause of the poor, the first deacons were appointed; and Church polity followed. After this organizing "when the number of the disciples was multiplied," then was "The Word of God increased, and the number of the disciples multiplied in Jerusalem greatly" (Acts 6). Immediately upon the birth and establishing of the Church, persecution arose; Herod Agrippa the First killed James, and intended also to kill Peter (Acts 12:1–3). Still the Word of God grew; and not only grew, but prevailed (Acts 19:20); the Church was here to stay! Not even the magicians of Ephesus, with "the whole city in an uproar" could resist this "embryo" Church in its preaching, "so mightily grew the Word and prevailed!"[1] In other words, it won every contest the Adversary promoted! And this is the way back to power today!

---

[1] "'The Ancient Fathers' recorded the growth of the early church and stated: 'The gospel had better claims than any furnished by equivocal miracles; and, though it still encountered opposition, it moved forward in a triumphant career. In some districts it produced such an impression that it threatened the speedy extinction of the established worship. In Bithynia, early in the second century, the temples of the gods were well-nigh deserted, and

What if the Church in the potency of being the real Body of Christ had gone into the campaign battle of evangelism and carried it out? The task of the Church is to evangelize, recruit and outfit saints for the Rapture; and its duty is to agonize and to function both as sacrifice and priest. This we have not done. We have failed to evangelize the earth. We have failed to convert the world and to point out where the kingdom of God is going to come in its wonderful power after the real, separated Body of Jesus Christ has gone on. The Church has never fully evangelized any generation. When the Lord comes again, He will accomplish this task.

A. THE CHURCH'S EXCEEDING HIGH CALLING—EVANGELISM

The silent Church is un-apostolic (Acts 8:4) and is a departure from Pentecost (Acts 2:6), for "Let the redeemed of the Lord say so . . ." (Psalm 107:2).

The Church—every last one of the Church—must live a great life and speak as one having authority, for he knows not what great soul is or may be before him. Live greatly and you will bring forth after you; a student takes on the words and thought forms of an attractive instructor; clear ideas make vivid the ideal. The Church must know her calling; only "if thine eye be single (clear), thy whole body shall be full of light."

The Church is a one hundred-gated Thebes with access to all callings; whose members "go out and in and find pasture." The Church is an homogeneous Society of gregarious spirits, indwelt by transforming Power, and that, "not of ourselves" (II Corinthians 3:18). The Church is the sole repository of all saving truth and the literature thereof. Its patent copywriting is exclusive and age-lasting. This is not to say that the Church has all truth but all that it does have, is saving. This being a fact, there rests down upon her such an obligation which once sensed, will make her members Pauline in that they will say, "Woe is me if I preach not the Gospel" (I Corinthians 9:16), and this being our obligation, we need to pray, "Lord, increase our faith."

Amplius-Cecil Rhodes entombed in the solid rock of a mountain, had engraved on his tomb stone, "so much to do, so little time in which to do it." A man doesn't think in minimums in regard to his love, his business,

---

(*footnote 1 concluded from page 350*) the sacrificial victims found very few purchasers" (Pliny). "The pagan priest took the alarm; the power of the magistrate interposed to prevent the spread of the new doctrine; and spies were found willing to dog the steps of the converts to discover their meeting-places. Many quailed before the prospect of death, and purchased immunity from persecution by again repairing to the altars of idolatry. But, notwithstanding all the arts of intimidation and chicanery, the good cause continued to prosper. In Rome, in Antioch, in Alexandria, and in other great cities, the truth steadily gained ground; and, towards the end of the second century, it had acquired such strength even in Carthage— a place far removed from the scene of its original proclamation—that, according to the statement of one of its advocates its adherents amounted to a tenth of the inhabitants" (Tertullian).

nor his patriotism. To ask him, "are you a minimum patriot" would be an insult! How much more of a Christian! So also a quickened mind can look *up* from Olivet, like as the students of history say, "Beyond the Alps lies Italy," and from its height, see a new heaven and a new earth. Just so all reforms seek a paradise. How much more then for a Christian? His literature is aflame with maximums of ever-expanding horizons. The Minor Prophets close by opening out "in the face of" Apocalyptic Visions; they sit on great heights, wrapt away into silence; for all of the Scriptures are opening up into Glory. Should we then use the term *Minor* Prophets because some of the prophets arrived the sooner at the place of vision?

> Back of the beating hammer
> By which the steel is wrought,
> Back of the workshop's clamor
> The seeker may find the Thought—
> The Thought that is ever master
> Of iron and steam and steel,
> That rises above disaster
> And tramples it under heel!
>
> The drudge may fret and tinker
> Or labor with lusty blows,
> But back of him stands the Thinker,
> The clear-eyed man who knows;
> . . . . [1]

Isaiah took longer to arrive, for he was worse entangled (sown among thorns) in courts and customs. The vision commission of Isaiah 6:1 shows him as a leper who rushes forth and as he went, he was cleansed (Luke 17:24). Amos in the mountains had a better start. Then Isaiah in chapter 53, sees the Lord, and he too ends as do the Minor Prophets. Ezekiel also, in chapter 43, came to see before the glory returns. These all were eclipsed —why? "These all" were on the verge of the Babylonian captivity and that because of the desecrated Sabbaths (Jeremiah 29:10, Leviticus 26:34, and II Chronicles 36:21), and those at the close were "God-robbers":

> "Even from the days of your fathers ye are gone away from Mine ordinances, and have not kept them. Return to Me, and I will return unto you . . . . Ye are cursed with a curse for ye have robbed Me, this whole nation. Bring ye all the tithes into the storehouse . . . . And prove Me . . . ."

Malachi 3:7—10

And until such a time as the Church rises up, even as Israel rose up to bring back David and the Ark (II Samuel 5 and 6), there is naught but defeat and shame-facedness. Christians! Measure up to your setting! For

---

[1] Berton Braley, *The Thinker*, (from *The Best Loved Poems of the American People*, selected by Hazel Felleman, Garden City Publishing Company, N. 6), sts. 1, 2, p. 109.

now it is not the Sabbath breaking nor the tithe with-holding, so much as it is the condition of Spirit-prompting. We are like unto the intractable child breaking school rules. God and a teacher are not primarily concerned about rules and laws, but rather about life. The keeping of the *day* brings its privileges of fellowship with God, and the bringing of the *tithe* is the expression through its fealty of our fidelity to God. Let us therefore arise to the challenge of Malachi 3:10.

Then some will say, "what then about Micah 6:7; isn't that all that the Lord requireth?" This text must be applied as the Sermon on the Mount and to this we would say, "Yes, split that text open and within you will find the kernel," for *The Faith* is trust where *The Facts* are beyond the verification:

> "He hath shewed thee, O man, what is good;
> And what doth Jehovah require of thee,
> But to do justly, (see Malachi 3:8),
> And to love kindness, and to walk humbly
> with thy God?" (Amos 3:3; Luke 6:46;
> Matthew 8:21)
>
> Micah 6:8 N.

And again, "Be ye also enlarged"; "Arise to your heights; "set your affection on things above"; and then join Jonah 2:9bN.:

". . . I will pay that that I have vowed. Salvation to Jehovah."

The Church is a repository of sealed (Eph. 4:30) souls; a Customs House without which there would be no traffic in matters of divine life. There is no place else to secure these things, and the pulpit if it be prostituted, shrivels souls. Think of the pulpit of the Lord Jesus Christ denying the Divine! Some one says, "Oh, there would still be Bibles"—but for how long? The few mentions of the Church (Matthew 16:18; Ephesians 1:22; Hebrews 12:23; I Timothy 3:15) aside from the incidental, carries the imagination out into tremorless, spaceless and timeless immensity.

Christ and His Church are but hypotheses until one accepts them. Then they are vital and the Church, His laboratory, with unmeasurable power of transformation, is what you and I share in. The *visible* Church is that against which the gates of Hades cannot prevail. Acts 6:4 tells of seven men being appointed over "this business" of the visible Church in the feeding and care of the widows; but the *invisible* Body of Christ is that of Colossians 1:17:

"And He is before all things, and by Him all things consist."

The Church became the means of applying the Blood of the Lamb to the work of Satan. The Christian is encircled by His *saving* and *keeping* Blood (Ephesians 2:13) and the all-pervading Presence and Knowing of

Jehovah is enjoined in Psalms 121 and 139:12. Now the Hebrews were *behind* the Passover blood which was on the door lintel and sides, but the Christian is *encircled* by the Blood of the sinless Lamb of God. The *"encircled"*[1] is the inference of the Greek preposition *en* (vs. 13), that is, *at rest within*, and not *dia* meaning *through* the Blood of Christ. This is for the Christian to realize that he therefore has a "Peace that knows no ending, and a joy that knows no measure"; this is the satisfying portion of "those who put their trust in (Gr. *en*) Him"; and this becomes the Christian's "City of Refuge" which is ever accessible and is never closed to "those who to Jesus for refuge have fled."

The purpose of God, this Highway of Holiness (Isaiah 35:8) transverses all time as "My Story." The entrance and cleansing upon this Highway of Holiness today are exclusively through Christ, the new birth and the new creation. The Word is the Seed of new birth, the revelation to those seeking; its virgin purity must be accepted.

B. THE GROWING INDIVISIBLE CHURCH OF CHRIST

The Church had to be completed at Pentecost and it is revealed in its completeness through its doctrine, ordinances and life. Out from that Church goes the division between Peter to the Jews and Paul to the Gentiles. The completed Church was apparent when it began even though for seven years, no one but Jews had access to the Gospel. The early Church had the impact of the message but they were still preaching to Jews only. They were at fault because they did not think it was for anyone but the Jews. They had neglected to recognize the fact that the Jews had refused Him as King and they could not have Him as Messiah. They were good Jews and were waiting for the Messiah but, "He came unto His own things and His own people received Him not" (John 1:11N.). This they do unto this day and we are not to fault them. Jesus said, "Father, forgive them, they know not what they do." Go to where the Church is *One* in the book of Acts, and though even here it has the elements of dissension and discord in it, it has also the indivisible Church of Christ. Christian Unity is an *effect* and never a *cause*, for Unity is not manufactured, but it is grown. One cause of division in the Church stemmed from the seventeenth chapter of John and the prophecies of Jesus in the 14th, 15th, and 16th chapters; and the other division stems from human nature. The human nature portion begins with good-hearted Barnabas (Acts 4); and from here we go on to Ananias and Sapphira (Acts 5); and from that to where "our widows are neglected" (Acts 6). This development is just gradually coming on and it grows. Good people are being sloughed off as you go along this path. From the 8th chapter of Acts on, we see the scatterment, and Peter is called

---

[1] *Newberry Bible*, "Graphic Scheme of the Greek Prepositions" p. x.

to go to the unclean Cornelius.

Others of the Jerusalem Christians were scattered *abroad* and went everywhere, but preaching only to Jews. Some of them went as far as to Antioch and preached to the Gentiles also. The hand of the Lord was on these folks and He blessed them. Barnabas went down there, and being a spiritual man, he saw that the Lord's hand was there. He knew of only one man who could handle it, Saul of Tarsus, and so he brought him to Antioch and they were there quite a while.

1. "Human Nature" Separations Arise Within The Indivisible Body Of Christ

a) Paul, Rufus and Alexander

In Acts 11:20 there were men of Cyprus and Cyrene at Antioch also. Rufus, one of the sons of Simon of Cyrene could have been among these (Mark 15:21—Mark was at Antioch). In the last chapter of Romans (Romans 16:13), Paul refers to Rufus and "his mother and mine." At the time Paul wrote *Romans*, Rufus was in Rome which indicates that he had gone on from Antioch where he had evidently waited. These folk are getting to where they are converging into a bigger job than what they had so far experienced. In Romans 16 Paul does not mention Alexander, the brother of Rufus; he had given him trouble. Alexander was a maker of idols and he opposed Paul, yet this Alexander was the other son of the man who carried the Lord's Cross, and was also the son of a good mother whom Paul calls "his mother and mine."

b) Peter and The Gentile Christians

The Scriptures indicate that Peter came to Antioch in the early days of the Church and associated with Gentiles there until "certain came from James" (Galatians 2:12). According to Acts 11:22, it was Barnabas who was sent by the Jerusalem Church to Antioch, and at this time, James was the recognized leader of the Church at Jerusalem. Evidently upon the arrival of Barnabas, Peter withdrew from the Gentile brethren fearing criticism of the Jewish group and even Barnabas was carried away with their dissimulation (Galatians 2:12—13). Later Barnabas brought Paul to Antioch and when Peter returned to Antioch, Paul withstood him to the face and rebuked Peter before the whole Church (Galatians 2:14—21). From this time Peter seems to limit his preaching to the Jews and Paul goes to the Gentiles.

c) Paul and his Jewish Brethren

The book of Hebrews was written out of a great love such as that of Moses and Jonah. We endeavor here to tell *Why, How, When and Where* Paul wrote *Hebrews*.

Paul starts out to the Gentiles, and he is always ready to go to them, but Paul himself had to be rebuked by the Holy Spirit because he wanted to tarry at Jerusalem. Jesus told him: they will not hear you here; get up and get out! And Paul said: why? they know that I have persecuted the Church; they know these things about me. But the Lord said: they will not stand for you. — So Paul must never try to win those decent Jews because they won't hear him. Therefore, he later wrote *Hebrews* to those Jews to whom he was not permitted to preach at Jerusalem and he also wrote it to some of their descendants.

Paul and Barnabas separated over Mark, and I believe Peter was the father of Mark. When he was in prison in Jerusalem, the disciples were praying for Peter and when he was released, he went to the house of Barnabas' sister, the mother of Mark. Why did he go to her house? The Church was in prayer there, but why did they go to her house? She was an influential woman for Rhoda was a housemaid and this indicated an influential home. Remember the time that Peter's wife's mother lay sick with a fever? They were in Capernaum which was a health resort by the seashore. Now if her mother was sick and needed to go to that resort, they could afford to do so if they were well to do. It is likely that at Capernaum she met Peter who was an impetuous and fascinating fellow. Peter became acquainted with them while he was at Capernaum and they were married and went there to live; but there was nothing hindering having a house at Jerusalem. John also had a home in Jerusalem. All of this fits together, and, even though it is not in the record, it does not deny the record. Now then, Barnabas was related to Mark (Colossians 4:10) and liked him, but when Paul would not have him go along the second time, Barnabas could not stand to hurt Mark, so he took him and went back home to Cyprus. Where do we find Peter when he wrote his epistle? Peter, the most Israelitish of any of them, was at Babylon, and the young man Mark was with him (I Peter 5:13). Who else was there? The letter of I Peter was written by Sylvanus which is another name for Silas. Why was he in Babylon? Peter had Mark, his son, with him, and Paul said to Timothy, "Bring *Mark*, for he is profitable to me." Silas and Mark were associated together, so Paul could now write to his Jewish brethren that which the Lord had not at first permitted him to speak because they would not hear him. Paul knows that the Church is going to be taken away, and we must have the Jews' place established, and so when he was to write the Hebrew letter, he told Timothy:—Bring Mark because he can say things. I can write these things through him so that the Jews will not recognize my style but they will get the message that I want to say.—The commentators have tried to say that Apollos or Silas wrote it, or this one or that one. Its authorship is covered up by the Holy Spirit, for He is able to do that.

Paul was at Ephesus for three years, disputing daily in a school of Tyrannus for two of those years. Why did he do it? He himself did not know why, but in this brief time, we read that they evangelized the whole of Asia Minor. When Paul left Ephesus to go to Corinth and on to Rome, he left Timothy there. Paul was travelling light and he left some things because he was figuring on coming back. Then comes a change for Paul before his return from Corinth. A plot was laid to kill him and he sent his associates across where he couldn't go, and where also they would not be jeopardized, but he himself went around the Philippian way. That took more time than he had figured on and he was in a hurry to get back to Jerusalem for Pentecost. He called the Elders down from Ephesus to come to Miletus, and in Acts 20:31, we note that his ministry to them had been for the space of three years. This is longer than he spent at any other place as far as the record of the New Testament shows. In II Peter 2:15—16, Peter refers to Paul as "our beloved brother Paul" which shows that they had been reconciled after Galatians 2:11—14; and the reconciliation very likely took place here in Ephesus. In II Timothy when he sends for the parchments on which he is to write the book of Hebrews, it is evident that he has received permission before this time to write the book. Upon further searching of the Scriptures, we can conclude that the permission of the Lord to write *Hebrews*, was given to Paul during his three year stay in Ephesus.

d) Grievous Wolves at Ephesus

What was the condition of the Ephesian Church? Revelation 2 tells us something about it: they had left their first love. But here in Acts 20:38 we find the Elders were "sorrowing most of all for the words which he spake that they should see his face no more." Paul had warned them of the "grievous wolves" that would enter in among them not sparing the flock, and he had warned them also, that from their *own selves,* men would arise, speaking perverse things to draw away disciples after them. When their sorrow should have been centered on needs and conditions of the Church, they were sorrowing rather in the loss of their preacher. We often give more weight to the visible rather than to the invisible which occurs to us later.

e) Ecumenicity

In reading the first chapter of Ephesians, I was disturbed by those honest and intelligent friends of mine who have gone in to "Ecumenicity." As I read through *Ephesians* I began to see that this attempt toward unity was short-circuited. Their idea of ecumenicity would be to have the denominations go together in a Federation and in that Federation have some one, similar to the President of the United States, a man head up the whole group. Now no man can head up this. It would not be ecumenicity if that should happen. When should we anticipate true ecumenicity?

It can come only when the Lord takes up His Church, taking His Body unto Himself at the Rapture. That is the Ecumenical Church and that is the only place where it can come.

The Church is off "The Way" and has built its own way in creeds, away from the life-nourishing truth of the New Testament. It is under-nourished and sick. Creeds are expedients; they are confessions that the key to the Scriptures is lost. Creeds arise because the New Testament has not been rightly divided and therefore it is hard to understand, when the Lord meant for it to be easy. What makes the situation all the more appalling is that these lost Sects are within sight of each other, be-calmed and indifferent.

2. Human Error Deviates from the Indivisible of Christ

Today the Christian world is repeating the Jews' *"A-Theos"* blunder. The Church, Christ-centered and Christ-controlled, has lost its "Head" to "leaders" (Matthew 23:8); "My Church" is now "The Church of the Disciples"; the "First day of the week" is now a rest day for dissipation; "My Baptism" is now "the door into the Church"; and "My Body and Blood" are now "sacraments." It was a sorry day when the Church became so intrusive and obvious with her incense forms and influence that the Lord was pushed aside—and thus, "they have taken away my Lord." Our Plea, "The Restoration of the Primitive Order," included Christ as Lord and Master and the Head of His Church with the doctrines and practices revealed in the Scriptures.

"WE would (and must) see Jesus"—"THEY saw no man save Jesus only" (Matthew 17:8).

"The true Christian stands upon the authority of the Word of God. He knows that the "church" (which is the company of the saved, gathered out of the world by the gospel) did not originate the Word, but, as all things were created by the word cf God (He spake and it was done) the church itself also is the creature of the Word. And the Word is not subject to the church—as though she had the right to pass on it, to modify it, to alter it (Galatians 1:8—9)—but the church is subject to the Word of God.* The Christian has for his only and final authority the Bible—endorsed to him and given to him by his Lord and Savior Jesus Christ. 'For the husband is the head of the wife, as Christ also is the head of the church, being himself the savior of the body. But as the church is subject to Christ, so let the wives also be to their husbands in everything'." (Ephesians 5:23—24).[1]

*The Church is the creature of the gospel, incomparably inferior to the gospel. 'The church cannot give more authority or force to a book than the book has in itself. A council cannot make that to be Scripture which, in its own nature, is not Scripture.' (Luther to Eck.)

---

[1] Robert H. Boll, ed. *The Word and Work* (Louisville, Ky., Vol. XLII, May 1948), p. 97

3. The Christian's Exceeding High Calling

"For we are His workmanship (or His "Poem"),
created in Christ Jesus unto good works, . . "

Ephesians 2:10*a*

A Living Sermon

I'd rather see a sermon, than hear one any day;
I'd rather one would walk with me than merely tell the way;
The eye's a better pupil, and more willing, than the ear;
Fine counsel is confusing, but example's always clear.
The best of all the preachers are the men that live their creed,
For to see good put in action is what everybody needs.

I soon can learn to do it if you'll let me see it done;
I can watch your hands in action, but your tongue too fast may run;
The lectures you deliver may be very wise and true,
But I'd rather get my lesson by observing what you do.
I may not understand the high advice that you may give,
But there's no misunderstanding how you act and how you live!

(Author Unknown)

a) The Gospel is Global

Though the Church is a living, vital organism, born from above, yet the Gospel requires a cosmopolitan organization. The command of "going into all the world, TEACH, DISCIPLE" cannot however become a reality unless the admonition be heeded: "how can they preach except they be sent." Here then, in this outward appearance of this inward organism, the Church, is our starting point. How great is the scope of this organism? Empire builders work on but a fraction of a whole continent, but the Church, Christ's own living Body, must work on a *whole* Globe and whoever slights this wide scope of her calling, is both blind and shallow. Now then, if you want something really *big*, here it is and this globe-building scope challenges the greatest of minds, abilities and talents of any Christian, or of one desiring to become a Christian. The giving of one's self to a noble cause is man's glory; it is his chief distinction from animals. But the Church's mission is to put John 3:16 into *actual-practical circulation*:

"A man has not begun to live until—
He has espoused a cause for which he is willing to die."

Hobson

b) The Christian is Challenged

A man coming into the Church desires to be saved; he acknowledges his own lack and sincerely seeks to find *The Way*; this one is to be commended. But if, once he has entered, he then sinks back into a satisfied living, and stops at that, that one is reprehensible; he has come with his sins, has received forgiveness into a new life, but he has stopped short, for he has taken with him his opinions and "these are they" which have acquired his sins! How then shall he truly become free? He is in need of a new set of opinions, even the truth of the Lord, for in salvation-obedience he has become a new creation; he now becomes "partaker of a divine nature" and must acquire the conviction that "old things have passed away; behold,[1] all things are become new" (II Corinthians 5:17).

Jesus said if He had not done among them the works which none other man did, they had not had sin, "but now have they both seen and hated both Me and My Father" (John 15:24). And Philip had seen every one of the works: he saw the five thousand fed; the Gadarene healed; Jesus walking on the water; the stilling of the wind and also the sea; the boat at land from the midst of the sea, four miles; the healing of the lepers; the raising of Lazarus; and *still* he said, "show us the Father, and it sufficeth us." He was like Peter and the other two disciples at the Transfiguration who said, "Let us build three tabernacles," and also like Moses (Exodus 33:18) to God, "I beseech Thee, show me Thy glory."

Since Philip's request (John 14:8) we have seen Him on a large stage demonstrate His Sonship to God. It is set forth in His choice of parent (singular); His choice of home and disciples, for He could have founded an aristocracy, but His followers chose to be "pilgrims and strangers";— the mark of the new birth is *humility*. His words blasted empires and unseated dictators as Richter wrote, "wounded hands lifted empires"; and through His institutions: The *Day* and His *Supper*, He has led men to a loyalty where Napoleon said of Him, "millions would die for Him."

The Church, His Body, thus becomes a re-cruiting station. But in this free process of conversion, is it a thing of stagnancy or degeneration? If stagnant, men become slaves; if free, they become willing soldiers and promotion for them is Paul's admonition, "be thou a good soldier of Jesus Christ." This my friend, is the only escape from disgrace!

> "God had One Son without sin,
> but none without suffering and sorrow."
>
> Gabelein

c) Devotion versus Ambition

"Faithful is the word:

---

[1] The Greek uses the word *idou* which is the Imperative Aorist Middle of *eidon* and this latter word implies not the mere act of looking, but the actual perception of the object, thus differing from the Gr. *bleppo* meaning to use the eyes; the use of the word *idou* in this passage means "See! Behold!" calling attention to something external to one's self (*The Companion Bible*, App. p. 163).

if a man desire overseership, he desireth a good work."

I Timothy 3:1 N.

Desiring a definite place of work in the Church according to his own ability is "a good work." In I Timothy 6:10 we find that not *making* money was evil, but the *love* of money is found to be the *root* of all evil things. Just so the emphasis of *devotion* and not *ambition* is the Bible method of "seeking" for the Eldership which is the highest place of service in the Church. Peter, the Pentecostal orator and the Holy Spirit's mouthpiece, was a "fellow-elder" (I Peter 5:1). The Eldership is the ideal goal. The Elder has been "aged" not *because* of his years, but he *becomes* (fits) his his age when he reaches this required stature. It is the upward expanding of Life; just as Jesus *increased* from youth up into wisdom and knowledge and favor with God and man, not of necessity as the Son of God, but having become in our body of flesh, human as we, but sin apart; so His followers must increase. *Everyone* who has grown normally, has moved toward the Eldership. This growth comes out of I Timothy 3:13 where deacons were instructed, and the deacon's place becomes a testing-ground where all are "first proved" and the result becomes "great boldness in the faith which is in Christ Jesus." Only such may rightfully purchase to themselves the authority to "rule" and to "teach." Only thus by growth, does the Church become as the unit of an orchestra. If the members are not present, there is no orchestra; if its members are present but are not functioning, then the orchestra is crippled—so also is the Church with its separate units (Ephesians 4:15—16):

"God hath not given us the spirit of timidity; but of
power, and of love, and of a sound mind . . . ."

II Timothy 2:7 N.

d) The Christian's Abiding Place

A Christian who is rightly nurtured "sees the invisible"; and this vision is the natural sight of the "born again"; and this "seeing" is the most humble Christian's birthright. How far we have wandered from the Father's house!—"Here, O my Lord, I see Thee face to face,"—for in some such ecstasy God's child "beholds" (see Paul's *beholding* in I Corinthians 2:9—10 and Philippians 3:8). And after seeing, the Christian's abiding place is in the book of Ephesians. Here is the place of THE "In the heaven-lies"; this is "The Garden Eastward," and no matter how far or how often you go in and out of the other Scriptures, here in *Ephesians* is the abiding place of the Christian.

The consecration vow of a real novitiate is "I will see" and "Whoso looketh" (i.e. stoops to look in to, or having stooped looks into fixedly) for "if any man willeth, he shall know." But the "I see" is the creed of a Christian. It took high concentration power for Abraham to "see," but like Moses he "endured as one seeing the Invisible" One. The face of Abraham Lincoln was a pictorial history of the Civil War; and any mother's heart contains the story of her child's life; our Lord said, "for the joy set before Him" He endured the Cross;—and every longing soul knows periods of its own rapture!

e) The Two-Leaved Gates (Isaiah 45:1*b*)— A Double-Door Entrance

One who is purposely prepared for approaching the double-leaved doors of *grace* and *peace*, is received as saints in the Old Testament of the faithful in the New Testament, and receives the benison "grace" to the Gentile or "peace" to Israel. Through this double-door entrance of Grace and Peace we are ushered into an atmosphere that challenges our best by "A New Commandment," where none but the self-coerced can abide; and only then as you compel yourself to *love*, can you be of Christian usefulness. This is illustrated in the Lord's preparation of Peter (John 21:15—17) when He said, "lovest thou Me," using the two Greek words for love: *"agapao"* and *"phileo."* A new commandment (John 13:34) given by *"phileo"* is not subject to the will, but *"agapas"* is always subject to the will and is under control and this is why it is commanded, and failure to show such love is condemned. Peter was grieved, not that Jesus had asked him the third time, but that he used the weaker word at the third asking, and he was grieved also that he had failed to measure up. Peter never reached the *"agapao"* in practice, but Paul could say, "the *love* (*"agape"*) of Christ constraineth us."

f) Reform versus Restore [1]

Two determinative words often in our speech are these: "Reform" and "Restore"; and these are frequently used interchangeably. But they ought not be, for they are descriptive of two states:

> *Reform* is political, and is repressive—from the outside
> *Restore* is ecclesiastical, and is expansive, vital [2]

The two words share common ground but the distinction is nevertheless significant. To "swear off,"—to "take the pledge,"—describes the moral phase of the first; while "Repent"—"Be born again" is typical of the other. As a citizen, I am obligated to reforms,—but as a Christian, my duty is to restore. The soul is the battle-ground (cf. Galatians 5:17), and the battle is for the soul; the soul suffers scars and needs restoration (Psalm 23:3).

---

[1] Also used in EtCEtera (Chicago, Englewood Christian Endeavor Publication, 1947)

[2] See this Section FIVE, *The God-Conscious Leaders of the Restoration Movement*, p.488

Moses was a Reformer, encompassing the people within Law. The Lord is a Restorer, fitting the fallen-away, back again into a vital relation with Himself. Reforms become effective through organizations—such as the Protestant Reformation that sought to correct Romanism; but Restoration is the brushing aside of all between, and going back to Christ, the Body of which He is the Living Head. A Reform is a group movement; while Restoration is individual. Here is the real value of the Church. Each unit within the Church is related to Christ, even as the branch is to the vine; while there is congregational fellowship and group action, yet the real life is one's own abiding in Him.

So, while we are concerned with conditions about us and feel the obligation of our citizenship, the Christian is aware that all such activity is of political significance, and is void of vitality. Nations and movements rise, flourish and fall, but the Church of Jesus Christ "hid in God" lives on. The Reformer is busy with others first; the Restorer starts upon himself; considering himself, he is less critical of others; he is easy to live with. Do you belong to a Society or to a Person! Are you out to reform—or to restore? The test is easy to apply: The Reformer is critical—the Restorer is sympathetic and meditates on: "Consider thyself, lest thou also be tempted."

IV. THE PURPOSE AND ACTIVITY OF THE CHURCH

A. PURPOSE

The stated Purpose of the Church in the world to those who will acknowledge themselves to be "dead in sins," was stated by its Head, even Jesus, in John 10:10b N.: "*I* am come that they might have life, and in order that (Gr. *hina*) they might have life in abundance."

B. INSTRUMENT

The life-giving *Instrument* by which this would be made possible, was stated by His foremost Apostle, Paul, in Romans 1:16, "for it (the Gospel) is the power of God unto salvation, to every one that believeth; . . . ."

C. METHOD

The *Method* by which the Church accomplished its beginning and continues growth today, is to "preach," i.e. "witness" (martyr); the Holy Spirit "Helper," giving them understanding to these things.

D. PRODUCT

The *Product* of the Church was foretold by Jesus when He said, "Ye are the light of the world—the salt of the earth" and He said also, "Blessed are the peacemakers."

E. GROWTH

The *Growth* of the Church is produced by the function and membership of the Church until by such unity in Christ, "all fitly joined together through that which every joint supplieth, maketh increase of the body . . . ." (Ephesians 4:16), that we "might attain unto the out-resurrection from among the dead ones" (Philippians 3:11N.).

1. The Church—The Age of Personality

When Peter made his great confession, "Thou art the Christ, the Son of the living God," Jesus said:

> "Blessed art thou, Simon-Bar-jona: for flesh and blood
> hath not revealed it unto thee, but My Father which
> is in heaven."
>   Matthew 16:16—17

From the time of this statement by Jesus, institutions gave way before Personality (Luke 16:16). The Law reached its glory in the temple of Solomon which was a mausoleum for a dead-letter-law. The age of Personality had come. Jesus said, "Upon" this rock, that is, upon Personality, "I will build My Church"; and this is the changeless, tremorless "sub-stans"[1] of any and all phenomena.

> "Knowing that He which raised up the Lord Jesus
> shall raise up us also through Jesus, and shall
> present us with you."
>   II Corinthians 4:18N.

So God was channeled down to the Christian through Christ:

> "If then we were raised with Christ, seek things which
> are above where Christ is seated on the right hand
> of God."
>   Colossians 3:1N.

Up from this and out of it, arises all creations. We do not think of ascribing buried cities to chance, and it is equally sure that nature with all of her inflexible laws and habits (as the spectrum and elements) does not operate by chance. This then is the significance of this occasion (Matthew 16:16), for here were caught the tones of the Eternal in that hour. Jesus said, "My Church"; His Divine Personality is expressed in the word "I AM" which acknowledges that He was before all things (Col. 1:17).

---

[1] The Century Dictionary defines *Hupostasis*:
   a) "That which underlies something else.
   b) "In Theology a *Person* of the Trinity; one of the three real and distinct Subsistencies; in the one undivided Substance or essence of God
   c) "A real Personal Subsistence or Substance. In this sense the Word could be used of God either as The Trinity, or each Person of The Trinity."

The way back to power is to go back to the Church which stands upon the firm foundation of the Rock which is Christ, and be taken up into Him as living stones (Gr. *lithos*) which "groweth into an holy temple of the Lord." We are baptized into the life of Him, that is, we are planted and so nourished that we grow up into His Image. And as living *Stones*, we are built up into a spiritual house "not made with hands" into *the Stone* cut out without hands, "until we attain unto the stature of the fulness of Christ." We read in Acts 2:47, "The Lord added"; to what? Not just to the visible Church nor solely to a human congregation, but He adds to "His Body" which is spiritual. They were "divinely called Christians first at Antioch" for they had matured enough to be named, i.e. "write upon them My Name." These had a new quality not seen before (Ephesians 3:6, 4:11—16 and 3:18). And they are spiritually discerned, not having spot or wrinkle (Ephesians 5:27); the life of Christ unhindered, will fill out the perfection, the entire capacity of man's personality. *Here* at Antioch Paul sees its *"telos"* (end) as Abraham (John 8:56) saw "The City" for he "endured as seeing the invisible."

2. The Church—The Mystery

This "My Church" "which has been kept in silence through times e-ternal" (Romans 16:25), is also called the "Way," the "Mystery," and the "Body" by Paul; for he sought to join himself to those who were in "The Way"; he was caught up into "The Mystery"; and he visioned "The New Man" in Christ. This Church of the New Testament though *heaven*-born had *land*-marks easy to follow; it was demonstrated in Acts 2:37 to the bewildered "devout men, Jews, from out of every nation under heaven," who, upon hearing Peter preach on the Day of Pentecost, received definite instructions including easily practiced ordinances which imparted a quick sense of security to anyone seeking refuge. The Ethiopian convert-example given to us in the book of Acts, "went on his way rejoicing," and it is even so today. While this "Mystery" was hid in God, its plans had been carefully formed. Today we speak of heredity and environment; and accord-ingly a mother has a *plan* formed above the life she is about to bring forth; God must surely be as fore-thoughted as a mother! An architect's plans always precede the building; his plans must first be approved and accepted and then rigidly adhered to. The Church has both Father and Husbandman, for it is "planted" in the book of Romans, and "watered" by husbandmen in the books of Corinthians, unto the "rightly dividing" of II Timothy 2:15 to a development which is "full grown" (II Timothy 3:17).

3. The Church—The Body of Christ

The Church is a benevolent autocracy, the highest form of absolute perfection; especially so, since Christ our autocrat, is all-wise, all-seeking, all-powerful, and all-compassionate. The Church is not first an organization, but it is first a life-organism made to include an organization in order to implement human ability (Ephesians 2:10) and to receive divine life (Ephesians 4:11, 15, 16 and II Peter 1:4).

This Church composed of *"Dramatis Personai,"* is the Body of our Lord Jesus Christ. It is not a school of ethics and institutionalized society nor is it a production factory, but it is a "Born Again Body" (I Timothy 3:15). Its earth-time is from Pentecost to the Rapture (Ephesians 1:15–23). The Church is the called-out (Gr. *Ek-klesia*) from above (Gr. *Anothen*) or from heaven (Gr. *ouranos*, Philippians 3:20) for the Up-Calling (Gr. *anokleseos*) of Philippians 3:14. Christ as the Head of this Church is seated in these heavenlies (Ephesians 1:20), where the Father in Ephesians 1:22–23, gives us His Son's position:

> "And hath put all things under His feet,
>   and gave Him to be the head over all things to the Church,
> Which is His body, the fulness of Him that filleth all in all.'

As Nebuchadnezzar saw a political figure filling the whole world—a world government, and as Daniel saw the calendar of the ages (Seventy Weeks)—just so the "Mystery" of "My Gospel," the Body, is discernible to those whose eyes are opened.

The Church, this Spiritual Body of His Son, is a taken-out people for His Name, composed of "as many as received Him," the Son. This group, "these saved by Grace" were not revealed, for the Church remained a mystery throughout the Scriptures, "hid in God" (Ephesians 3:9)—to be caught up before Isaiah 11:11 when God "shall set His Hand a second time" to recover the remnant of His people, the chosen of Israel, which shall be left. The parable of the old and the new wine thus fits the picture of the Epistles to the Church (*Romans* through *Philemon*); and when "He shall set His Hand a second time . . ." then the books of *Hebrews* through *Jude* will have their greatest significance.

Facing Jesus Christ there is a door open upon Infinity; I become aware of my own potentials; and I am a citizen of the Transcendant. I am beholding telescopian dimensions and unveiled holiness; and am enfolded by the indissoluble which reaches above the highest and below the needs of depth and which are wider than all dimensions; my every out-reach contacts peace. I am drawn out of infinity yet I am unafraid for I am not alone (Psalm 23:4). There is a bridge of eyes and ears over which personality is transferred to me (I John 1:1–4, II Peter 1:16–17). Those who are seeing these things are being changed (John 17:3, 21, II Corinthians 3:18), and are being taken up into God (I John 1:2–4).

John 1:12 introduces "the heavenlies"—those who received authority to become sons of God and walk the highway of holiness (Isaiah 35:8, I Corinthians 15:45). In John 20:22 we find the beginning of the spiritual body of Jesus Christ as He breathed into His disciples and said, "receive ye the Holy Spirit." To enter in to the heavenlies, is to contact life (Hosea 11:11, 12:13, Deuteronomy 26:5), and so man becomes immortal.

In preparation for these above events, this Church of Pentecost is being refined into the Temple of God (Ephesians 2:22), where it is being set forth as a glorious Church in the Heavenlies (Ephesians 1:3, 14, 22—24, 4:11—16 and 5:27). And this is the same Pentecost Church at which Peter officiated at birth; and which Paul saw in II Corinthians 12 and which in Ephesians 3:9, 14, he prays for them "to make all men SEE." Paul makes mention of the weaker Church as a group of people to be treated as in illness; but the stronger Church as His Body of spiritual elements if Holy and Divine, and is not to be lightly esteemed.

> Hear, O Church of Christ!
> This promise and pledge of God (Ephesians 3:20—21, Jude 24—25).
> And, disciple of the fainting heart,
> Lift up "the eyes of your heart" to the far horizons—
> Behold "the City coming down out of heaven from God" (Habakkuk 2:3, Revelation 21:2).
> For our Lord God works also in the night;
> The stars are lamps in His Workshop:
> "He that keepeth Israel shall neither slumber nor sleep" (Psalm 121:4);
> No one of us knows what a day bringeth forth.
> The Lord commanded His own to "WATCH"—and said:
> "Blessed are those bond-servants whom the lord when he cometh shall find watching" (Luke 12:37N.).
>> I would rather be laughed at now,
>> Than be condemned at "His Coming."

4. Membership in the Church

Membership in this Church is through (Gr. *dia*) death, burial and resurrection; and such "fellowship" is with Christ (Philippians 3:10, I John 1:3); but this is God's "norm" and is still less than our subnormal for the gospel "reaches down to the depths of shame."

There are three classes of membership spoken of in Revelation 2 and 3:

  a) Membership to *Him* (Ephesians 4)
  b) Membership to the *Church* (I Corinthians 12)
  c) Membership to *Self*; and these are the floaters, the drifters, and the critics.

Concerning this first group of "Membership to Christ," we see Him in the midst (Revelation 2:1, and see Matthew 18:20). Here He is the ever-present Lord:

"Speak to Him thou for He hears, and Spirit with Spirit can meet—
Closer is He than breathing, and nearer than hands and feet." [1]

This group are those who will be raptured (Ephesians 1:21).

The second group are those who are members of the Church, but are *"Ex-Cathedra."* They are dependable folks and their favorite Scripture is James 2:14—26. They say, "we build" and "The Twenty Centuries look down upon us." These are those who go through The Great Tribulation and are like those of Abraham's bosom (Luke 16:23).

The third group are those who are members to self, and are best described in Revelation 3, as "neither hot nor cold"; these are easily offended and drift away to another. These are to be "spewed out," and are like those in torment (Luke 16:23).

Switzerland's days of prayer and Bible study and its many churches, make it easier for the traveler to distinguish it from surrounding countries. Anyone crossing her boundaries is made aware of the change in their surroundings. There is a Switzerland within the Church—a little flock who rests secure in the Father's Hand and has "meat to eat that the world knows not of" (John 10:28—29).

"I know not where his islands lift
Their fronded palms in air;
I only know I cannot drift
Beyond His love and care." [2]

5. The Literature of The Church

This Church also possesses a cultural, vital literature,[3] i.e. Paul's letters which are as a three-sectioned telescope; and in them we have:
ROMANS,
        I and II Corinthians, Galatians
        These are concerned with *Salvation*
EPHESIANS,
        Philippians and Colossians
        These are concerned with *Sanctification*
THESSALONIANS,
        First and Second, and these two letters
        are concerned with *Glorification*

---

[1] Alfred Lord Tennyson, *Poetical Works of; "The Higher Pantheism";* (N.Y., Crowell), coup. 6, p. 188

[2] John Greenleaf Whittier, *Poetical Works of, "The Eternal Goodness"* (Houghton, Mifflin and Company, Boston, Mass., 1892), p. 319, st. 20

[3] See Sealed Division, *Paul's Church Epistles,* p. 95 ff.

To these should be added John's REVELATION, especially chapters 2 and 3. All other Scriptures are profitable for every Christian going in and out and finding pasture (John 10:9).

The Mystic Mystery of the Church catches even speech up into wonder heights of silence (Ephesians 3:18). Within the writings of Paul, revelations attain unto Apotheosis. Salvaged out from sin in *Romans*; set apart in and with Him in the heavenlies of *Ephesians*; facing the prospect of the Great Hope (Colossians 3:1–3), "The Church His Body," has entered into life. There remains the fulfillment of the promise unto Abraham which John in *Revelation* sets forth and the present times proclaim. To any who tarry long within its pages, there is revealed the urge of resistless movement; it is a vital, living voice of the Lord God, the Almighty *Prothesis* (Purpose).

6. The First Love of the Church

There was cleavage at Ephesus and there was separation at Sardis; all have sins which are common to all. And were not the Bible the Book of all books, we would be the most miserable of all men. In the book of Ephesians we see the first and greatest sin, and also the last call to repentance. We see here her virtues (Revelation 2:1–7)—yet, "one thing thou lackest" (Luke 18:22): the life that is hid with Christ in God.

> "I have been crucified with Christ, nevertheless I live; yet no longer I, but Christ liveth in me; and that which I now live in flesh I live I live in faith, that of the Son of God, who loved me, and gave Himself up for me."
>
> Galatians 2:20 N.

To count oneself as *dead* is to be love-mastered (I Corinthians 13 and John 21:15–17); and only so comes fellowship with Him which produces this abundant entrance (II Peter 1:1–11).

> The night hath a thousand eyes,
> And the day but one;
> Yet the light of the bright world dies,
> With the dying sun.
>
> The mind has a thousand eyes,
> And the heart but one,
> Yet the light of a whole life dies,
> When love is done. [1]

7. The Elect

There is but one effect that we can have upon the purpose of God—

---

[1] Francis William Bourdillon, *The Night Hath a Thousand Eyes* (MACMILLAN, 1927) Golden Treasury of Modern Lyrics, selected and arranged by Laurence Binyon, p. 253

to hasten it (see Matthew 24:20—22, 24; II Peter 3:15). "The Elect" is a plural word and would include those of both the Old and New Covenants. The prayers of these "Elect Ones" turn Omnipotence to serving (Esther 4:15—17; Daniel 9:3; and Jesus, Hebrews 6:17—20). Tennyson wrote in *The Passing of Arthur*[1] when the dying King exhorted "bold Sir Bedivere":

> "Pray for my soul. More things are wrought by prayer
> Than this world dreams of. Wherefore, let thy voice
> Rise like a fountain for me night and day."

Who are these "elect" for whom the days are shortened? They are the "called of God" who respond and are "sainted," that is, they are put in their "own place." These "workers together with God" are upon God's *prothesis* in *every* age. God's Purpose was first revealed in a man, Abraham;[2] and then in a nation, Israel; and today, in a people, the Church. This Church Age will be followed by the regeneration at the conclusion of which "God will be all and in all." These above are the "called," "elected," and "sainted" unto "good works." God is building for Himself a temple, an habitation (Ephesians 2:22); and the ages or dispensations are as the stories of a house. The Bible is His advertising in which is contained His "call" for workers. Those responding are elected, sainted and fitted. God calls, that is, He advertises in the Bible; man responds, he comes and replies and he is put to work; he is "sainted" (Mark 8:34 and John 6:37). And these God's advertisers, or broadcasters, His messengers are "in all the world." Thus "The Purpose of God" moves sublimely on to its grand Consummation; its elect workers together with God coming on and passing from the foundation, as the priests in the Jewish temple came and went in their courses.

Let us look into this word "elect" which comes from two words—*ek* and *lego*. *Ek* denotes the origin or the point from where the motion or the action proceeds. *Lego* is usually used of a systematic or set discourse in the Bible and means "to relate in words"; for it is written that "they shall all be taught of God" (John 6:45); "Whosoever cometh" (Luke 6:47); "The ages were framed by the Word of God" (Hebrews 11:3) which indicates

---

[1] Tennyson, Op. cit., *The Passing of Arthur*, p. 377

[2] "Abraham believed God and it was accounted unto him for righteousness"; here we have an intimacy and a comradeship which produced faith; and "they of faith are the Sons of God." "The Scriptures foreseeing" Abraham's faith could say of him "In thee" (in thy life and faith as Franklin did with his kite)—"in thee shall all nations of the earth be blessed." Those who believe are blessed with Abraham but all others are under the curse (the irritation) of the law; for "the righteous shall live by faith"; and so "Christ redeemed us" in order that "upon the Gentiles might come the blessing of Abraham." Again, in order that we "might receive the promise of the Spirit through THE FAITH."

that they were each a part from the other and did not come from the pre-ceding one. As a spark leaps from point to point, so each age is peculiar to itself. They are not composite as the Four Empires of Daniel seen in the image of Nebuchadnezzar; but each age has its "elect" saints. Our fathers of the Restoration Movement were not far from a great discovery when they outlined the ages as the "Starlight, Moonlight, and Sunlight Ages";—as God passed through each age, He called and blessed those that "rose up." Who are these "elected candidates" called of God and blessed by Him?

> a) *Israel*—Deuteronomy 7:6, I Corinthians 10:11 and 11:19
> > (1) Cyrus[1]—Isaiah 45:1–4, A gentile is called "His Anointed" by the Lord
> b) *The Church*—Romans 8:28
> > The messages to the Churches of Revelation 2 and 3 are in the Lord's own words

It is important to note the two "Elects" through the Scriptures:

> > a) The Remnant, Israel
> > b) The Body, the Church

And these two "Elects" are to be identified by their names:

> a) Israel is to become "Hephzibah"
> ("My delight is in her") (Isaiah 62:2–4)
> b) The Church is given veiled reference in Isaiah 65:15b
> and the members of the Church, disciples, are given their distinctive name "Christian" in Acts 11:26b.

Therefore, let us recognize the distinctions between these "Elects" which continue even into our day. Israel and the Church exist side by side and are both to be dealt with by the Lord.

"When earth's last picture is painted, and the tubes are twisted and dried,
When the oldest colors have faded, and the youngest critic has died,
We shall rest, and faith, we shall need it—lie down for an aeon or two,
Till the Master of All Good Workmen shall set us to work anew . . . ."[2]

V. RIGHTLY DIVIDING BETWEEN THE CHURCH AND ISRAEL

INTRODUCTION

The Church's standing before the God of Israel is conditioned upon

---

[1] See Scofield Bible *footnote* on Isaiah 45:1, p. 753.

[2] From *The Seven Seas* by Rudyard Kipling, reprinted by permission of Mrs. George Bambridge and Doubleday & Company, Inc.

our attitude toward Israel. In our failure to "rightly divide" we are as the Jews, for by our traditions we "have made the Word of God of none effect" (Matthew 15:6). We go to Sunday School, yet we do not *know* the Word of God. This surface knowledge is the fertile soil of faddists. Psalm 107:20 reads:

> "He sent His Word and healed them, and
> delivered them from their destructions."

A *surface* knowledge of this Word does not bring deliverance but rather it prepares minds and hearts for wild theories to grow and flourish (Matthew 13:19—22).

At the very beginning of *Romans* in the doctrinal theology of Paul is set forth explicitly the foundational facts of God's TWO PURPOSE GROUPS (Israel and the Church) with their relation being clearly stated. Jesus' statement in Matthew 16:18 marks the definite break between the preaching of the Kingdom of Heaven and the Church which is established in *Acts*. If this section is thought through, it will save anyone from the labyrinthian confusion of the "Dispensationalists" who have muddied the waters of God's Salvation-S; for that there is a designed purpose which provides for *All*, is discernible to the least informed. Some have erred by making two *church* groups: Acts 2 the *Jewish* Church (or works); and then Acts 28, the *Gentile* Church (of Grace). Others have erred in recognizing only one group and have cast off Israel. But the terms "remnant" and "little flock," and the record of the prophets, *et al*, set forth in speech of simple words, these *two destinies*, so presenting insuperable problems unless these two groups are reckoned with. The *Gospel* is for the Church. The *Blessings* coming to Israel are for the fathers' sakes (Romans 11:28). Israel has been "shut up together" into (Gr. *eis*) disobedience in order that (Gr. *hina*) God might show mercy. When Israel is restored, and the Church reigns with Christ—then comes the final and apocalyptic adoration!

Thus the Purpose (Gr. *Prothesis*) of God is even as His Word tells: Psalm 33, Romans 8:28, 9:11 and Hebrews 11. He is the Alpha and the Omega God, the non-changing, non-swerving, non-turning One. And to make more sure our understanding of this God, He uses the astronomical figures to describe Himself (James 1:17) in contrast to mankind who beholds:

> "Change and decay in all around I see;
> O Thou who changest not, abide with me!"

> *Abide With Me*, H.F.Lyte

A. DISTINGUISHING BETWEEN THE PEOPLES Who Are Different

And

DISTINGUISHING BETWEEN THE LITERATURE Which Is Different

"So that ye may distinguish the things that differ."

Philippians 1:10*a* A.S.V.m.
(cp. Romans 2:18 A.S.V.m.)

With the birth of the Church at Pentecost, there are now closed the two divisions between the nations and the Jews. A separation once existed with impassable barrier. They spoke of each other as "Dog of a Jew" or "Unclean Gentile." With Christ, the Messiah crucified, the Adversary apparently triumphed and "the kings of the earth rejoiced together"; and the infernal regions "shouted for joy"; it was truly "A Roman Holiday."

When Lo, Behold! "HE IS RISEN"—then the Church is born! and Paul is called; and an age "with energy sublime, burst full-blossomed on the thorny stem of Time." A Seed, Spirit-driven, fell upon that "middle wall of partition" (Ephesians 2:11—18), and struck *dis*integrating roots *downward*, and *int*egrating affection *upwards* (II Kings 19:30, Isaiah 37:31); and from His tomb came forth the Church (Matthew 16:18). From *here on*, there is reckoned a third group: not only Jew and Greek (nations), but THE JOINT BODY (Ephesians 3:6) which is ushered in and accompanied by such supernal phenomena as to acclaim it Divine. To rightly divide we must distinguish the *peoples* that differ (I Corinthians 10:32):

Israel   (Sand) —Romans 11:25
The Church   (Stars) —Ephesians 3:10 .
The Nations (Dust) —Matthew 25:31—32

Beyond the book of Acts rise the Epistles (II Timothy 2:15). The book of Acts alone of the Bible's sixty-six books contains the vital elements of the new birth. Here in *Acts* and here alone, we see men risen to walk in new life, and to them the Epistles become the Tree of Life. The mountains begin to lift unto the heavens and just as in the physical realm, it is necessary to know your way around or become lost. Today, a second "tower of Babel" has arisen with a confusion of tongues through the lack of following our text of II Timothy 2:15. To those whose custom it is "to go to Church," these Epistles will be of little interest; but to those seeking to know the mind of Christ, there is a richness which is thirst-quenching and soul-nourishing when the Word of God is rightly divided.[1]

The Bible is cumulative (Isaiah 28:10); it adds one dispensation upon

---

[1] See this Section FIVE: *THE CHURCH, MY* Story, IV. The Purpose . . . Activity, E. Growth, 5. The Literature of the Church, p. 368.

another ("come ye out from among them"). This, our age of Grace, is not the last one; the Church is to be raptured, but there will still be people left. What of these? There must be *A* Gospel for them, but it is not *THE* Gospel which belongs to the Church. So a message must be made available to the Jew after the Church is removed (see *Romans* chaps. 9 through 11 and Matthew 23:39). The church letters do not meet the situation. Are there any that do? Yes: *Hebrews* to *Revelation*. The books of Hebrews through Revelation were directed primarily to the Hebrew people and the message concerning Christ was for the most part, ignored or rejected. [1]Because of their Jewish wording, these books will become meaningful to Israel *after* the Church has been raptured and these will prepare Israel for the coming of Christ in His Kingdom. The book of Hebrews is a book of symbols and fits into or joins the Gospels as Abraham joins with Melchizedek. Its heroes are of the Old Testament (Hebrews 11):

> "God having of old time spoken unto the fathers . . .
> hath at the END of these DAYS spoken unto us in Son."

Hebrews was dictated by Paul and written by Mark (Romans 9:1, II Timothy 4:11); and see Acts 22:18 as the reason for this anonimity. All the way through, there are words, symbols, and a motif familiar to the Israelite, but these are not primarily the literature for Gentile conversion.

The book of James is written to the dispersion and they are called a kind of first fruits (1:18), and reference is made to the perfect law (1:25). These were Jewish Christians (Acts 21:17—26), and a study of them confirms these conclusions.

Then the Epistles of Peter are written to the Elect Dispersion (II Corinthians 12:4, Acts 16:6), and they are pointed to "an inheritance incorruptible and undefiled that fadeth not away, reserved in the heavens for you" (Revelations 21:1—2). In II Peter 3:8—18, Peter points to the new heaven and the new earth which is a Post-Rapture promise which will be fulfilled *after* the thousand year reign of Christ (Revelation 20:4——21:1). And then he mentions Paul's writings which could only refer to *Hebrews* since this book alone was written to the same group and was concerned with Peter's portion.

To John is given The Revelation:
> a) Containing things which "must shortly come to pass"
> b) Including the statement, "the time is at hand"
> c) Which closes with the unveiling of The Holy City (Revelation 21:1—15). This Holy City hath the foundations which Abraham sought (Hebrews 11:10) and which John describes as coming down to the new earth after the Great White Throne Judgment,

---

[1] See *Sealed Division VI*. Epistles of *Hebrews* through *Jude*, p. 122ff.

and closing of the Seventieth Week of Daniel.

Daniel and John were co-laborers in this revelation.

An analysis of these books will increase the conviction and cause us to exclaim:

> "O the depth of the riches both of the wisdom and knowledge of God! how unsearchable are His judgments, and His ways past finding out!
> For
> 'Who hath known the mind of Jehovah?
> Or who hath been His counsellor?'
> Or who hath first given to Him, and it shall be recompensed unto him?
> For of Him, and through Him, and unto Him, are all things: to Him be glory unto the Ages. Amen."

Romans 11:33—36 N.

B. DISTINGUISHING BETWEEN THE AGES THAT DIFFER

Some oft-recurring topics of the day are:

a) The Church—Its Rapture
b) The Israel—Her Restoration
c) The New Heavens and The New Earth

The unprecendented events of any age dispose most minds toward these things, and always remain very much up to date; so much so that some of us discern an intentional guidance. We are approaching The Age of The Ages which is the end (Gr. *telos*) of The Ages (Gr. *aionon*). To set forth the teaching and the distinction of their beginnings and endings is our purpose here.

1. The Pattern of The Ages

The pattern of the ages can alone be seen by the Church because it is in the heavenlies. The Church alone can "shorten the time" as it is "henceforth expecting" the return of the Lord; and we hasten the coming of "The Day of the Lord" by building up the Body of Christ. This pattern is seen from Alpha to Omega. God's dealing with *men* began with Theocracy; then Theophany and Law; next Emmanuel and Grace; and finally, Emmanuel and God over all and in all:

a) *Theocracy* begins with Adam
b) *Theophany* begins with Abraham
c) *Law* begins with Moses
d) *Emmanuel* (God with us) begins at Bethlehem
e) The period of *Grace* begins at Pentecost

f) Following the Church Age, Emmanuel comes again
at the *Kingdom of Christ*

g) Finally, at the end of the Kingdom reign,
God is all and in all at the New Heavens and
a new earth, God is at home in His Universe

Like the sections of the Outer Drive Bridge in Chicago, so the Seven
Sections from Alpha to Omega accurately fit together for they comprise
God's Book of The Ages. Note the distinct breaks ("same day") between
God's Ages which are mentioned in Exodus 12:41, Genesis 7:11 and Luke
17:27.

2. The Church Age of Grace

First in *importance* must come the Church because it *is* first and is
most precious both to God (Ephesians 3:10) and to man (II Timothy 1:8—14).
The Church, this Pearl of Great Price, was begotten in the Upper Room
(John 20:22), born at Pentecost, and is to be raptured. God was making
the Church, His Son's Body; and this explains why Paul is so insistent
upon his apostleship and revelation. At the Church's beginning, Israel was
set aside "until" the rapture; following that, Israel will be restored. The
Church Age of Grace is in the heavenlies (Ephesians 2:6, 1:23), and His
Body is therefore "A Colony of Heaven" dwelling on earth. The Church is
a sphere of "in'flow'ence" where the Sphere and Rule of heaven prevail.
It is "IN but not OF the world" (John 17:15). This "Age" is our responsibility; and we should be about the Father's business as He is beseeching
us and others to worship, "not forsaking the assembling of ourselves together as the manner of some is." We are to examine ourselves as we partake of the Table; and present our possessions, our time and income, as
a living sacrifice (Romans 12:1). If we are "His Body" (and such we are),
then we will be sensitive to Him and will respond to His leadings (Romans
8:14).

3. Israel's Rejection and Restoration

Israel's *rejection* is set forth in Matthew 23:29, and her restoration[1]
is set forth in Romans 11:26. When we the Church are removed at the rapture, then Israel will be restored at the Lord's appearing after The Tribulation. There are TWO immortals in the Scriptures: The Church and Israel.
Of these twin wonders, this Mystical Body of Christ which is the Church,
is heavenly, and Israel is earthly, becoming immortal in the earth through
the Promised Land. Some have attempted to rob Israel of her rights by
applying to the Church the Old Testament promises given to Israel. These

---

[1] See Section SIX, *The Kingdom Age*, E. The Reign of Righteousness and Peace
2. Israel is Restored, p. 562 ff.

folks fail to distinguish between the prophecies concerning the Lord's "sufferings" and those of His "glory" (I Peter 1:11, Isaiah 53 "suffering"; and Isaiah 60 "glory"). Our language must not trespass on these distinctions by confusing the "Kingdom" and the "Church." There are two parts here to each of them:

a) The Church:
> Composes the called-out ones; and all of these are "seated in the *heavenlies*"

b) Israel:
> Is called out of the *Nations*; and these are seated in *The Land*.

A CONTEMPORARY PORTRAIT OF ST. PAUL
Courtesy "Illustrated London News" (1921?)

This and other remarkable frescoes, probably the oldest
Christian paintings in Rome, were found on the walls of
an immense underground building recently uncovered by workmen digging the foundations of a taxicab garage. Subterranean halls
and crypts were built by the early Christians for secret worship and

VI. "THE THINGS WHICH HAVE BEEN FULLY ESTABLISHED
AMONG US" (Luke 1:1 A.S.V.m)—THE VITAL DOCTRINES
OF SALVATION

INTRODUCTION

This is a re-statement of "The things which have been fully established among us" (Luke 1:1 A.S.V.m.) which should:

1. Challenge our indifference
2. Give objectives to teaching and preaching
3. Stir up the gifts of each congregation into zeal
4. Bring clearer convictions as to the victorious
   supremacy of the Bible in every battle field.

The Book "having done all" still "stands." What other text book of
any decade so authoritatively survives. Other books die in the midst of
their own friends, but the Bible, bleeding at every chapter from wounds
of its enemies, *lives*. Let us "ask for the old paths," i.e. the doctrines
of this immortal, this "well by Bethlehem's gate," and drink and be restored and refreshed.

The Bible is most definite. And one can dispute but not misunderstand.
In the fundamentals, no vital doctrine of salvation is obscure. The Bible
is the Text-Book upon the Gospel. It contains prophetic utterances and
dramatic fulfillments, illustrative incidents, miraculous events and the
Church (more wonderful than all wonders). The Jew and the Church are
twin wonders. I think that there is discernible an increase of emphasis as
these elements of salvation are approached. The slogans of our fathers
are illuminated signs to "The Old Path,"—and they said:

"The Gospel consists of:
   a) *Facts to be believed*"—which are fulfilled prophecy
   b) *Commands to be obeyed*"—which were demonstrated
      at Pentecost
   c) *Promises to be enjoyed*"—now and in the future

Our fathers of the Restoration Movement also said:
      "Where the Scriptures speak, we speak,
      Where the Scriptures are silent, we are silent."

These are the *Facts* of the Gospel to be believed: the death, burial
and resurrection of Jesus and all other fulfilled prophecies concerning
Him. This must be preached first. Then, to those who have received these
Facts are given the *Commandments* to be obeyed. And when they have been
obeyed, they are ready to receive the *Promises* to be enjoyed. Therefore,
this portion of Section FIVE, will deal with the unique doctrines (teachings) of the Apostles, concerning the *Commands* to be obeyed.

Section FIVE: THE CHURCH—MY STORY (Continued)

VI. "THE THINGS WHICH HAVE BEEN FULLY ESTABLISHED

AMONG US" (Luke 1:1 A.S.V.m*)

THE VITAL DOCTRINES OF SALVATION

Page

A. REPENTANCE

* *Marginal reference*

A. REPENTANCE

1. Repentance: Its Place

> "Testifying both to Jews, and also to Greeks,
> repentance toward God, and faith toward our
> Lord Jesus Christ."
>
> Acts 20:21 (cf. Mark 1:15)

REPENT is the first word of salvation (Acts 26:19—22, Romans 2:4, Acts 2:38). We have rightly divided the Scriptures but we have also over-emphasized *a Part* (The New Testament) versus *the Whole*. My college advice was "get the essentials" which meant the plan of salvation and the pattern of the Church. There are seven branches or divisions in the Scriptures with Light evenly spread over all:

> *a*) Law—Prophets—Psalms
> *b*) Gospel
> *c*) History—Doctrine—Hope

These are all "essentials." The Unity of the Divine is stressed in every section. To differentiate between the God of the Old Testament and the God of the New Testament, or to enter *this* side of *Genesis*, is to find oneself in danger of John 10:1N.:

> "Verily, verily, I say unto you, He that entereth not through the door into the sheepfold, but climbeth up some other way, the same is a thief and a robber."

The Bible is "ONE *Book*" revealing to us God, Christ and the Holy Spirit:

> *a*) God is set forth in Genesis 1:1
> *b*) Christ is set forth in John 1:1
> *c*) The Holy Spirit is set forth in Acts 11:15

Or, this "ONE *Book*" reveals that:

> *a*) Jehovah   )   (Authority
> *b*) Jesus Christ   ) is the God of (Persuasion
> *c*) The Holy Spirit)   ("All Comfort"

And that:

> *a*) "The fear of Jehovah is the beginning of wisdom"
> (Psalm 111:10)
> *b*) "The long suffering of our Lord IS Salvation"
> (II Peter 3:15)
> *c*) "There is ONE that restraineth"
> (II Thessalonians 2:7)

So, "all things are yours" (I Corinthians 3:22—24). These must be taken as a whole—a "seamless robe" of salvation.

> "No one can come to Me, except the Father which hath sent Me draw him; and I will raise him up at the last day . . . 'And they shall be all taught of God'."
>
> John 6:44–45 N.

It is not possible to accept the Christ of the New Testament while rejecting the God of the Old Testament (John 5:39). We begin with Repentance toward *God*, followed by Faith toward our *Lord Jesus Christ*; and then receive the Gift of the *Holy Spirit*. Hear for yourselves:

> *a*) The Lord in Mark 1:15
> *b*) The Spirit in Acts 2:38
> *c*) and Paul in Acts 20:21

John the Baptist, the Lord, and Paul came saying, "Repent" and the Lord made it *sine qua non* (Luke 13:3) and He and Paul both make it *pre-faith*.

> "For John came unto you in the way of righteousness, and ye believed him not but the tax-gatherers and the harlots believed him: and ye, when ye had seen it repented not afterward, that ye might believe him."
>
> Matthew 21:32

> "Testifying both to Jews, and also to Greeks,
> repentance toward God,
> and faith toward our Lord Jesus Christ."
>
> Acts 20:21

First, man must "get right with God." One fronts God as the first step at school, in the Law, the Prophets and the Psalms; the repentant ones said of Jesus, "we have found Him of whom Moses and the prophets did write." Therefore, the word "Repent" is a threshold challenge. It is the Voice of God in the conscience of an aroused soul; one who has "come to himself." Others might say, "it thundered," but to the aroused one, God has become definitely personal; even as to Saul of Tarsus, and to such an one *repentance* is a coveted joy (Hebrews 6:1). Jesus gave His parables to the multitudes but He explained them only to His disciples; the multitudes were unrepentant toward God and therefore could not believe on Him as the Son of God. And this same thing is true in Romans 10:16–21. Isaiah said, "they have not believed our report"; — "all day long have I stretched out my hands to a disobedient (unrepentant) and gain-saying people." In Revelation 3:18–22 we are admonished, "be zealous therefore and repent; behold I stand at the door and knock, if any man hear my voice . . . ." "These having eyes to see and ears to hear" refers to those who have repented "to the acknowledging of the truth" (II Timothy 2:25).

The elements of repentance are found in Luke 24:44–53, Acts 2:37–41 and 20:21. "The Bible is the only book in existence that can close itself to the reader; and He who wrote it can alone open it."[1] It is a super-natural control, one that is ever present just as life is in nature itself.

Repentance comes first in every age and is "toward God," and it opens to our understanding "in a beginning—GOD"; and, "ye believe in God . . ." (John 6:44). In repentance the face turns from the clod toward God and we read in Luke 24:45, "Then opened He their understanding that they might understand the Scriptures"; and in John 20:22, "He breathed on (into) them and said unto them, 'receive ye Holy Spirit'"; but even then, they were not ready for He told them to "tarry ye in the city of Jerusalem until ye be endued with power from on High." This then would enable them to apply their understanding and to "teach all nations." These men were to "fix" the *norm* of the New Testament, therefore they must be error-less; they must be "filled with the Spirit" (Acts 2:4). Their work was to begin at Jerusalem, the chief city of sinners (Luke 13:33—34), for if Jerusalem and the sinners in it can be saved, then may *any* sinner have hope.

"Repentance and remission" were to be preached at Pentecost and repentance was FIRST toward *God*. That order has never been revised. Our first need is to "get right with God" and all other things will be added to us.

2. Repentance: Its Source—Heaven

> Jesus said,
>
> ". . . but, except ye repent,
> ye shall all likewise perish."

Luke 13:3

"And the times indeed of ignorance God having over-
looked; now chargeth all men everywhere to repent;"

Acts 17:30N.
(cp. also II Corinthians 7:5—10, Luke 13:3—4)

So long as men are saved through Christ, so also the conditions must be Christ-ordained and tested. "Forever, O Jehovah, Thy Word is *settled* in heaven" (Psalm 119:89).

> "For My thoughts are not your thoughts,
> Neither are your ways My ways, saith Jehovah.
> For as the heavens are higher than the earth,
> So are My ways higher than your ways,
> And My thoughts than your thoughts . . . ."

Isaiah 55:8 . . . 11N.

So—"Seek ye the Lord," (in very great assurance) . . ." (Isaiah 55:6—9).

---

[1] Charles J. Thynne, *"Students' Commentary,"* p. 775

These elements of John 3:16 must have been first in heaven, "close to the heart of God," forged and tempered in the heat of a great love, then brought down by one thoroughly tested (Matthew 4:6)—"in all points as we."

Repentance seems incongruous if it is from heaven. This is only because it has been so long dis-associated from heaven and has taken on "of the earth, earthy." Debased practices have debased language. That which is illicit is not allowed. In Acts 27:30 we read, "but now commandeth all men everywhere to repent." The phrase "all men everywhere" means that not one is excluded, excepted nor exempted, but justice must fit each from the holiest saint to the vilest sinner.

Let us *know* this Word which is both divine, heavenly and also human, earthly. Just as we read in Galatians 2:20, "by faith *of* the Son of God," so also, we are saved by *His* repentance! Please keep in mind that Repentance may not always include *sin* but it always requires *sacrifice*, and "here is wisdom" if we have "ears to hear."

Repentance may be illustrated by several parables. A student goes to school until he comes to the time of "commencement." He has been "educated" and this word comes from the Latin *educare* which is allied to the Latin *educere* to bring out or to draw out; and thus it is concerned with the making of a choice. As a student comes to the place of commencement, a spectrum of callings seek to win him to a life's work and in his choice, he "repents," that is, he is educated—drawn out and chooses:

a) Thus, he turns from the many to the one. The diploma which He receives, grants liberty and then the *call* is clearer, and he can say, "here am I."

b) Another illustration is in the call to the service of our country. A lad is changed into uniform, and his habits and all other ways of life have "repented." This is not the Biblical repentance, but it is as externally radical, and "all (U.S.A.) men everywhere" have repented with him; each of us has shifted the emphasis.

Now, unsandal before "the holiest among the mighty and the mightiest among the holy." Let no word detract from His holiness but may we follow Him as He *turns* in Luke 9:51 when "He steadfastly *set* His face to go to Jerusalem!" The disciples let these words sink into them and they were amazed (Mark 10:32). The Lord was as Paul when he said, "This one thing I do . . . ." Israel's leaders had vowed to destroy Him (Exodus 32:8) and He said, "Ye shall see me no more till . . . ." He set His face toward Gethsemane, Golgotha and the loneliness of the Cross when He said, "My God, My God, why hast Thou forsaken Me." But this was not His destination for we read that, "when the time was come that He *should be received up*, He steadfastly set His face." And this was looking to Acts 3:21

into "the heavenlies." The nation of Israel turned aside, so His Father set the Church before His face. We read, "He became flesh" and "The Lord laid on Him the iniquity of us all" (Isaiah 53:11). "He made Him to be sin . . ." (II Corinthians 5:21) "in order that we might become the righteousness of God." He set the current of flesh back toward God, and, ". . . that from out of the boundless deep, turns again home." He ceased His Messianic work and the Church "entered" to "provoke Israel." The elements of salvation must come from a pure source or else they are unable to make pure (II Corinthians 5:21, Luke 9:23, John 12:26).

Now He commandeth all men everywhere, the purest and the best, the worst and the vilest, to "set their minds on things above where Christ is" that He might transport and translate them just as thought is translated from one language into another (Colossians 1:13) and thus men become "a colony of Heaven."

3. Repentance: In The Original Greek

Two Greek words are translated "Repent" in the New Testament:

George Ricker Berry Ph.D. [1] says:

"*Metanoeo* to change one's views and purpose, to repent; as Matthew 3:2, Acts 8:22. *Metamelomai* to change one's mind, feel sorrow for, regret; *Metanoeo* is the nobler word, the regular expression for thorough repentance; *Metamelomai* is more loosely used, generally expressing sorrow, regret or remorse."

Thomas Sheldon Green, M.A. [2] says:

"*Metamelomai* to change one's judgment on past points of conduct; to change one's mind and purpose . . . . *Metaneo* to undergo a change in frame of mind and feeling, to repent; to make a change of principle and practice, to reform; *Metanoia* a change of mode of thought and feeling, repentance; practical reformation, reversal of the past . . . ."

Joseph Henry Thayer, D.D. [3] writes:

"*Metamelomai, metanoeo*: The distinctions so often laid down between these words, to the effect that *the former* expresses a merely emotional change; *the latter* a change of choice; *the former* has reference to particulars, *the latter* to the entire life; *the former* signifies nothing but regret even though amounting to remorse, *the latter* that reversal of moral purpose known as repentance—*seem*

---

[1] George Ricker Berry, Ph.D., University of Chicago and Colgate University, *A New Greek English Lexicon to the New Testament*—supplement to *Interlinear Literal Translation of the Greek New Testament,* (Chicago, Handy Book Company, 1897), p. 64.

[2] From *A Critical Greek and English Concordance of the New Testament* prepared by Charles F. Hudson with *A Greek—English Lexicon to The New Testament Revised and Enlarged* by Thomas Sheldon Green, M.A, (Boston, H.L. Hastings, 1881), p. 117.

[3] Joseph Henry Thayer, D.D., *Greek-English Lexicon of the New Testament,* (N. Y. Harper, 1887), p. 405.

hardly to be sustained by usage. But that *Metanoeo* is the fuller and nobler term, expressive of moral action and issues, is indicated not only by its derivation, but by the greater frequency of its use, by the fact that it is often employed in the imperative (*Metamelomai* is never so used), and by its construction with *apo, ek* (cf. *he eis theon metanoia*) (Acts 20:21)."

4. Importance of Repentance

Repentance is the one most needed of the emotions, but it is the most nearly withered for many are "being past feeling" (Ephesians 4:19).

John the Baptist, and Jesus the Saviour, are symbols of the Prodigal Earth and the Merciful Heaven:

a) John said, "Repent ye"
   (1) Jesus said, "I have compassion"
b) John was a "voice crying in the wilderness" as Israel wandered
   They were to prepare and to make ready for the wedding feast
   (1) Christ is to become the Robe for the garmentless.

John, the "greatest born of woman" came preaching repentance which must be of incalculable importance, especially as we read Acts 20:21 and John 6:44. Without repentance:

a) One cannot approach God (Acts 20:21)
b) Nor understand the Scriptures (II Timothy 2:25)
c) Nor be baptized into Christ (Acts 2:38)

In Luke 1 we find Gabriel's estimate concerning John the Baptist; his *estimate* is in verse 15; his *influence* is stated in verse 16; and his *work* in verse 17. He was to turn the hearts of the fathers to the children (Ezekiel 18:2, Romans 1:32). The father gives thought to his effect upon his child. He was to turn the disobedient to the "wisdom of the just." To change, "repent," will draw the disobedient child to "just" (righteous) acts. We can have a revival in any week when we will "arise and go unto the Father" and truly say, "make me as one of thy hired servants," i.e. put me to work. He was to "make a people prepared for the Lord" (like II Timothy 2:20—21). This is an invitation accepted by "fathers" and "children" to the King's feast.

"Repentance" is the mark of real greatness. It takes a real man to say it meaningfully. When this occurs it cleanses the eye to see much which was not before noticed and it quickens the conscience to re-called wrongs; and you will find a cess pool where once you thought there was a crystal spring!

5. The Purpose of Repentance

"And (Jesus) said unto them, 'Thus it is written, and thus it behooved Christ to suffer, and to rise from among the dead ones the third day: And that repentance and remission of sins should be proclaimed on His name unto all nations beginning from Jerusalem."

Luke 24:46—47N.

Pentecost is birth's first movement. The inalienable essence of a noble mind is repentance (Luke 15:11—32, Acts 2:38). Repentance is the Great Common Denominator—the solvent of every advantage, inequality or pride. Someone has said, "six feet of earth makes us all of one size." And so repentance is the great leveler or commonizer for we are all standing in the need of prayer. Faith and baptism are not equal: "one has faith to eat"—"have it to thyself." Baptism has a richer experience, and there are degrees of significance. But repentance is basic, a levelling down into the "burial into Christ" wherein age and youth and class and mass are all swallowed up as each feels, "I am the chief of sinners." This is real repentance. If even now you can look around you and think of any honest soul and feel superior, you need to "repent." Repentance is "the sweet sorrow." We live in a world of half truths and in the twilight zones of faulty speech and vision where "to err is human." For we, being so circumstanced, instrumented and facultied, must misjudge and injure when least intending to do so. A real man is conscious of this and is willing rather to suffer injuries. And when one discovers this quality in themselves, they should thank God and take a day off to rejoice as when one might find oil on a farm, or stocks in an old trunk; or as the "lost coin" or "sheep" owner. Nothing equals the value which is in the construction of a Christ-acceptable life.

John the Baptist, Jesus, Peter and Paul preached "Repent." What is the meaning? It is "to undergo a change" (reconstruction) in the frame of your mind. To illustrate:

During the last War an industrialist could reconstruct from the manufacture of tractors to tanks; from automobiles to planes; the same management, buildings and machinery could be readjusted. Someone asks how can one be "reconstructed" when he is old. We must call in a contractor; for with God all things are possible (e.g. Nicodemus). The Pharisees and lawyers (Luke 7:30) refused to be "reconstructed" and we see the result. The same material (Gospel) was fed to all. One resists unto Death; the other accepts unto Life. "Repent!" This is an imperative command and is urgent for the danger is extreme. The warning is meant to be even more urgent than a fire siren or an air raid warning for "night cometh when no man can work."

Concerning the nation of Israel, we read that they "repented NOT." They heard the witness of John the Baptist and of the Lord and of the Apostles, plus Paul; still "the veil lieth upon their hearts" (II Corinthians 3:15). Romans 11 refers to them as a "broken off olive branch." Such a rejection is as though a factory plant were besieged by our President and the Members of Congress and our Army; and in spite of all of these, yet the owner refuses to reconstruct his plant to serve his country. So Israel was still impenitent and the Lord said:

> "Ye shall see me no more till ye shall say,
> 'Blessed is He that cometh in the Name of the Lord'."

The great re-framing of Israel is yet to be and soon:

> "Even so come Lord Jesus—quickly."

6. Repentance of the Unbeliever: Toward God

The word "repent" does violence to the text; it is a Vulgate device for bondage from which the Romanist phrase "do penance" is derived. The Greek *Metanoeo* as before explained means to change the frame of mind as a "Dr. Jekyl and Mr. Hyde." It could be further illustrated by the changing of a factory from the manufacturing of over-alls to that of manufacturing shoes. The man born blind said, "whereas I was blind, now I see." And Paul said, "the things I once loved, now I hate" even though he practiced them at times. It is NOT going back to the fork in the road. Paul said "forgetting those things which are behind"; these are not to be brooded over. Romans 12:1 suggests the transfer or to transform (Gr. *meta*) at once (see Acts 2:38). "Repent" means to *change* the frame of mind *toward God* and this is to be by your own will (John 7:17). Then when you are baptized into Christ, it "fixes" you so that no relapse can take place. Christ alone can do this for He is the Master-Worker.

Repentance is toward God for only those who have taken this step can take up the evidence that leads to Christ. *Repent* toward God (Gr. "Petra," the basic rock); *believe* in Christ (Gr. "*lithos*," a stone); and man (Gr. "*petros*," a small boulder[1]) is to be baptized *into* Christ. When the mind is once re-set, then all that passes through it, carries God, and "sees God in everything."

"Except ye repent ye shall all likewise perish." Not just "turn around," for *direction* is not the important thing here. Pentecost illumines its meaning. The Jews had persecuted and crucified their Messiah in the zone of half truth; they were prejudiced. Now the resurrection had re-manded, or opened up the case for a new hearing. Pentecost sets Gethsemane, the Cross, the Tomb, and Olivet "in the midst" of man's faculties and man is hearing and answering and inquiring, not only "what then will I do *with*," but "what have I already done *to* Him."

Concerning the Scriptures Christ said, "they testify of Me" and the sermon of Peter's in Acts 2 was of what the disciples had seen and heard "made more sure by the Word of prophecy." That it was ordained, blessed

---

[1]   For further reference, see Section FOUR, E. *Jesus and Prophecy*, p. 267 ff.

and used of God was abundantly shown by the immediate results and the events following. The copy proof contained their cry, "what shall we do?" and the apostles' reply, "Repent." This has never been changed or abrogated. Under this commission the church began and continued to evangelize men. This Pentecost message by the same apostle was a few days later proclaimed to the Sanhedrin (Acts 5:29—32). He said:

    a) We ought to obey God rather than men
    b) God raised up Jesus
    c) Whom ye slew,

He concluded by saying, "God exalted Him to be a Prince and a Saviour, and to give *repentance* to Israel, and we are witnesses and so also is the Holy Spirit." Later in Acts 11:18, the Church was made to see that "God also to the Gentiles granted repentance unto life. Still later in Romans 2:4, "The goodness of God leads to repentance." And His goodness is upon all (Matthew 5:45, II Peter 3:9).

Repentance produces a new man in Christ Jesus. This is wrought out within and by Spirit-impregnated "sub-stans" through "the goodness of God." So, Isaiah 1:18 and John 1:7—9; and "Thy love unknown hath broken every barrier down."

7. Repentance of the Believer (Christian) "Away From" Sin

There are three elements of repentance peculiar to the Christian in taking him "away from" sin which are: the "prodigal" within the believer; the "aloneness" of repentance; and finally, the "repeated renewal" of the repentance necessary to the believer:

    a) "The Prodigal" within the believer

> "Repent therefore from (away from) this thy wickedness, and pray God, if perhaps the thought of thine heart may be forgiven thee."
> Acts 8:22N.

"Repent" is not in the church epistles but once (II Corinthians 12:21) and these were like the vile men of I Corinthians 5:2, who, as the prodigal son, were dead; or were as the one lost sheep of the ninety and nine. Here is no renewal but like the Ephesian Church, they are commanded to "repent and do thy first works" (Revelation 2:5). There must be a made-over mind, for the old channels will cause a throw-back into indulgences. There should be "Godly sorrow" for the estrangement from a brother which takes place (see Matthew 18:15—16). And such Godly sorrow is expressed in Psalm 51:4N.:

> "Against Thee, Thee only I sinned,
> And did evil in Thy sight . . . ."

Sin injures, weakens and defiles souls, and God says, "all souls are Mine." Sin is against God. One who sins, sins against God but one who repents, works repentance unto salvation (II Corinthians 7:10). This one is easy to live with, quick to repent, generous to all. He is a reconstructed man and we take knowledge of him that he has been with Jesus.

Conscience is built in for a definite purpose and when aroused it will leap up and will not be denied. The Bible is a Book of repentance and we read in its pages, "I have sinned"; "to seek and to save the lost"; "except ye repent" (Revelation 7:9—17).

There is a "prodigal" within us all, within one's own soul, a sense of sin and failure. It is the presence of the unclean, unwholesome and unworthy which is awakened and we come to the prodigal's statement, "I am no more worthy." And this, the Lost Chord, becomes ours. I never read of any great agony without saying as did Baxter, "There, but for the Grace of God, lies"—myself.

b) The Aloneness of Repentance

"The sins ye do two by two, you answer for one by one." We are to repent ALONE; even as the Lord was alone in Gethsemane; He was there to accept sin for us (Isaiah 53:6); and we are to repent for that sin which we have committed. Real repentance does not desire companions for it is conscious of its vileness as a pariah, an outcast of society. Peter went out into the night *alone* to weep bitterly (Luke 22:62). The Church at Ephesus is commanded to repent or its candlestick will be removed out of its place (Revelation 2:5); though it is one of seven churches in Asia, yet it must stand *alone* in its time of repentance.

c) The Renewal of Repentance

Repentance should be of daily, hourly occurrence. A ship played upon by wind and waves, currents and tides—even though it is steam-driven, yet it must continuously adjust itself to the fixed stars. So our thoughts, words and acts and every and all sins are cast into life's stream. This sewage contamination, even though we resist, still calls for cleansing.

Both repentance and remission are in the Bread of the Communion and in the Cup. Not only were repentance and remission of sins to be preached in the Name of Christ beginning at Jerusalem, but we find these two upon the first day of every week, renewed in the Communion Table: *Repentance* is renewed in the Bread:

"Or despisest thou the riches of His goodness and forbearance and long-suffering; not knowing that *the goodness of God* leadeth thee to repentance?"

Romans 2:4

And *Remission* of sins is remembered in the Cup:

"But if we walk in the light, as He is in the light, we have fellowship one with another and the blood of Jesus Christ His Son cleanseth us from all sin."

I John 1:7

Section FIVE: THE CHURCH—MY STORY (Continued)

VI. "THE THINGS WHICH HAVE BEEN FULLY ESTABLISHED

AMONG US" (Luke 1:1 A.S.V.m*)

THE VITAL DOCTRINES OF SALVATION

Page

B. FAITH

* *Marginal reference*

VI. "THE THINGS WHICH HAVE BEEN FULLY ESTABLISHED
AMONG US" (Luke 1:1 A.S.V.m)—THE VITAL DOCTRINES
OF SALVATION

B. FAITH

> ". . . Believe on the Lord Jesus Christ, and thou shalt be saved, thou and thy house."
>
> Acts 16:31 N.

> "So then faith cometh by hearing, and hearing through the spoken word of God."
>
> Romans 10:17 N.

> "Now faith is the confidence of things hoped for, the evidence of things not seen."
>
> Hebrews 11:1 N.

1. Faith Defined

Tremendous issues are dependent upon faith for faith contacts that which begets life (Mark 16:16, Hebrews 11:6). Baptism is the delivery of the begotten into a new world. We must have an understanding as to just what faith is so that we may recognize it:

Faith is a universal faculty, for salvation is dependent upon it and whosoever will can be saved. This is the inalienable sesame to possession "Ask and ye shall receive," but "let him ask in faith, nothing doubting" (James 1:6a); and Philippians 4:6—7 N.:

> "Be anxious for nothing; but in everything by prayer and supplication with thanksgiving let your requests be made known unto God. And the peace of God, which surpasseth all understanding, shall keep (as with a garrison) your hearts and minds in Christ Jesus."

And neglecting to use faith, brings impoverishment.

Faith is the soul's will; our wills manipulate our bodies, souls and spirits. So faith moved Enoch's feet; Joseph and his brethren; and Daniel's "Prayers." As the organist specializes in the organ, yet does much else, so faith specializes (Hebrews 11:1); that is, man sees at the tomb of Lazarus decay and death, but the soul envisions at this same tomb rejuvenation and life's return. The angels of power are awaiting faith's order.

Faith visualizes "things that are not as though they were." Faith *"walked* with God"; *"endured* as seeing"; *"sought* the city"; *saw* a "ladder up to heaven"; *"for Joy* set before . . . *endured";* *"foresaw* the Lord always before me." Abraham (John 8:56) and John (Revelation 4:1—2) illustrate such faith. Wherefore Hebrews 12:1 N.:

> "Wherefore seeing we also are compassed about with so great a cloud of testimony-bearers, let us lay aside every weight, and

the sin which doth so easily beset us, and let us run with endurance the race that is set before us."

Faith is the "giving substance" to the things hoped for; a test of things
not seen about us which makes the Church much like a laboratory (Hebrews 10:39). Faith is concerned with the un-arrived at goals; the in-
tangible assets at hand. Much that was faith is now become fact (Luke
18:8). Today is bounded by the facts of yesterday and the faith of tomorrow
and so "today" feeds upon the hidden manna (see John 4:32) for, "I have
meat to eat that ye know not of."

Faith is the appropriating faculty by which man is transformed, and
by which man abides continuously within the Scriptures: ". . . and in His
law doth he meditate day and night" (Psalm 1:2*b*), and thus man is "changed
as by the Spirit of the Lord.'

Faith is the atmosphere of every action; it is so much a part of our life
that one is not able to analyze the same.

Faith is beginning to see. We begin to see through faith that "God is
for us" and the things which we experience, help to establish this conclusion. If this be so, what does it matter who is against us? (Romans
8:31—39). In Romans 8:38—39N., the Christian reaches the climax of a
gloating faith:

> "I am persuaded, that neither death, nor life, nor angels, nor princi-
> palities, nor powers, nor things present, nor things to come, neither
> height, nor depth, nor any other creation shall be able to separate
> us from the love of God, which is in Christ Jesus our Lord."

Faith is the "prevailing and all-pervasive element of spiritual enter-
prise and achievement," and the book of Romans is pre-eminently the book
of Faith (Romans 1:16).

2. The Source of Faith

The faith of the Lord Jesus Christ was the original and creative faith
(Galatians 2:20); and thus the Scriptures are the writings between Him
and me. Faith is short and connects only two, God and you. Faith does not
come down through generations of the faithful to anyone. This is *tradition*
and it is the mother of sects. The Church is not a chain of faith from Pentecost to the last convert for that would be weaker than apostolic succession!
But it is as a seed in the grip of the sun, each individual Christian receiving the warmth of the faith of the Son of God into his life. If faith came
through others, it would be as a chain and then the weakest link would
determine the strength of it. Church-ianity comes through such a chain of
tradition, but Christianity comes through direct contact with a Person.
If faith came through one living person on earth, it would "ground out" or
"short circuit," and would debase. This faith is not consecutive but is

directly from Him to each individual. "I AM the vine, Ye are the branches" —there is no church or hierarchy nor priest between. Life is like a ship which leaves no path as it passes through the water but every new ship must pioneer. Each one is linked to Christ; from faith unto faith and His alone is the saving faith (John 15:6—7).

> "Therefore being *justified* 'out of' faith, we have peace with God through our Lord Jesus Christ."
>
> Romans 5:1N.

Something has been done for us which we are unable to do for ourselves; but the guilty justify themselves (Luke 10:29). We are covered (stained or colored) by Another and we are taken over into His account and life. The phrase "out of" bears out a debtor's shortage which is covered out of bank funds, so justification covers me and, unlike Achilles' heel, there is no vulnerable part exposed (John 10:28). So Christ's faith covers me:

> "I have been crucified with Christ; nevertheless I live; no longer I, but Christ liveth in me: and that which I now live in flesh I live through faith of the Son of God, who loved me, and gave Himself for me."
>
> Galatians 2:20N.

> "For therein is the righteousness of God revealed from faith unto faith according as it is written, 'But the just shall live by faith'."
>
> Romans 1:17N.

This is the Faith that went to the front and down into the valley of death and sought and won and returned and gave unto us His victory and peace (Romans 14:8—9).

As a saw mill which is set up in a forest proves the owner's ability and faith and the destinies of the wood of trees; so the Cross demonstrates God's willingness and ability to save, and sets forth the faith of Christ and the destiny of lost men, and thus the Cross becomes our propitiatory and through it we see our redemption. "We have peace with God"—Oh, what blessed relief, for the Christian is at peace with God.

> "They fought from heaven; the stars in their courses fought against Sisera."
>
> Judges 5:20

Therefore, the Faith which the Just live by in *Romans* is seen to be not ours, but HIS in *Galatians*. This glorifies baptism (Romans 6:3, I Corinthians 12:13, Galatians 3:27); and this assures our present protection and eventual salvation (II Corinthians 5:17, Galatians 6:15, John 10:28, Psalm 23:6).

Just so much as Christ's faith fills us wherever that goes in a life, that part becomes as its Lord (Galatians 2:20, cp. Habakkuk 2:4). The text is "The just shall live by faith," but this is "The Just out of faith shall live"; as a fountain that is life-giving is opened (Zechariah 13:1)—so was Calvary such a fountain. Our life is *ek*, out of Faith, and *eis*, into Faith that He is the Vine. It was no accident that Luther's favorite book in the Scriptures was the book of Galatians. Paul wrote, "the (Christian) life I now live by the faith of the Son of God who loved me and gave Himself up for me" (Galatians 2:20, cp. John 3:16). This is in the dative case (Romans 3:22, Galatians 2:16—20 and 3:22—26, Ephesians 3:12—16, Philippians 3:9). "Of" refers to HIS faith and not ours; so must it be for us all. Our creative thinking is by faith.

The Faith of the Son of God is like the faith of a designer of a Rocket to the moon. The vessel and its designer must demonstrate their usefulness and abilities. This was the purpose of the forty days of Acts 1:3 during which the Master gave the Port from which the visible (Church) would be launched; the schedule of its departure (Pentecost); and the rates (Matthew 16:24) "Let him deny himself." In Romans 1:17 we read, "from faith unto faith," (cp. Habakkuk 2:4). The Lord said, "I am the Vine, ye are the branches . . ." (John 15:5); and Paul said, ". . . the gospel is not according to man for I neither received it of man . . . but through revelation of Jesus Christ" (Galatians 1:11—12).

3. Faith's Accomplishment

This is the joy of the Faith-Justified, that "through Him we have access into this grace wherein we stand." Faith is the college or university faculty for each mind. As each professor goes before his class and leads out and into the unvisited, so the mind sends out its faculties under faith and upon their returning with celestial forage, the mind's capacity is enlarged. Just as the mind (intellect) makes one a citizen of this world ("able to stand"), so the faith faculty is spiritual and by it "we live, and move and have our being" in a spiritual world. And not only so, but we rejoice in tribulation (Colossians 1:24, Philippians 2:17). One must really vision the faith world to understand this. To the Christian this is the language of heaven.

> "For if, when we were enemies, we were reconciled to God
> through the death of His Son, much more, reconciled, we
> shall be saved by His life."
>
> Romans 5:10N.

Note the order: first is death and second is life. The life that saves is "Post" death and not "Ante" death. The life that saves us comes after He has died. Anything that Christ taught before His death is not necessarily a part of "the life" that saves. This is rightly dividing the doctrine of salvation.

"This is the victory that overcometh the world, even our faith" (I John 5:4 and Romans 5:17). If death reigned through sin, *much more* shall they that receive grace reign in life through Christ, Hallelujah!

4. The Realm of Faith—God

Now Faith *is Substance* and this "Substance" (Gr. *Hupostasis*) is God (Hebrews 11:1). The Century Dictionary defines *Hupostasis*[1]:

a) "That which underlies something else"

b) "In Theology a *Person* of the Trinity; one of the Three real and distinct Subsistencies in the one undivided Substance or essence of God"

c) "*A Real Personal Subsistence* or Substance. In this sense the word could be used of God either as The Trinity, or each Person of the Trinity."

Since it is used of God, it could not be used of any other persons. God is at the center of all; He is Light (I Timothy 6:46); Spirit (I John 4:8); and Love (I John 4:8). Dr. I. I. Rabi[2] says: "Every atom in the universe emits waves like those that make radios possible." The *"Hupostasis"* is God-Light (Genesis 1:3)—"Let there be light and light was." "The Spirit brooded over (prepared) and light entered." Longinus[3] said, "This (Genesis 1:3) is the sublimest sentence in human speech." God IS Substance and Substance is Personality (not material) and dwelleth in light and sends forth beams—for every man "hath a spark of divinity within him" (John 1:9, Hebrews 11:6); Christ is God-extended (John 5:26).

Faith is *hupostasis*—that is, God-Divine substance—the germ plasm of the reborn. "By it the Elders (and those of today) obtained . . ."—that is, they laid hold upon God (there is no other way); and God "flowed" over into them (Philippians 3:12). In the Universe there is not a someTHING at work, a resident *Force*, but there is the SomeONE whose transforming essence pervades His Universe (John 5:21). For "in Him we live and move and have our being." A great merchant or industrialist takes men into his organization and *drains off* from them for riches for himself. But not so God, for "God so loved the world that He GAVE." Had we the eyes to see: we drain Him (Matthew 9:21) as by a blood transfusion. He gave Himself

---

[1] *Ibid*, p. 362 *Reform versus Restore*

[2] Prof. Isidor Isaac Rabi, PH.D., Christmas Conference $1,000 prize essay, (Macmillan, 100th Yr. of Annual Issue 1948), member National Academy of Sciences, Prof. of Physics Columbia Univ., Am. Asn. Adv. Science 1939, Nobel Prize in Physics for 1955.

[3] Dionysius Longinus, a Greek Platonic philosopher, a rhetorician of Athens

(Galatians 2:20), that is, He takes me up into Himself. In the realm of the spiritual, "Faith is Substance"—God-stuff, as in the realm of the material—bread is substance-foodstuff. Therefore, we are being justified by indwelling "God-stuff" (Romans 5:1) which enters (John 14:23) and begins transformation. What then is this God-stuff? It is a Title-Deed, i.e. Government stuff to your property. If you could carry your farm as you do your watch or money, you would not need the title deed unless a robber met you (II Corinthians 4:18). The title deed is a "scrap of paper" which goes back to its author. So when I have found it (faith), I must search the Scriptures (John 5:39), back to Pentecost and the evidence storms my intelligence while His Love storms my heart; and so our fathers preached "let us go back—let us RESTORE," They found fragments in creeds (broken lights) along the way which were signs or proofs, and as archaeologists, they arrived at Pentecost and saw men being transformed, who asked "what must I do?" and they were told "believe . . ." and they "spake the Word of the Lord unto him." Why? "Faith comes by (Gr. *ek*, out of) hearing" and "hearing by (Gr. *dia*, through) the Word." Faith and belief come from the same root word. The first, Faith, is concerned with personal contact; and the second, Belief, with a series of evidences from witnesses (John 16:30). Though this may not be exact as a definition, still it gives a working idea. Faith is the noun form; belief is the verb form. Where Christ comes *unto us*, we enter *into* Him. The brain "faith-izes" and personalizes all facts, theories, etc. The heart emotionalizes and sacrifices. The Bible is the bank of heaven where "bank runners," prophets and apostles, bring the deposits. Paul speaks of Timothy's and his own deposits (II Timothy 1:14) and in much the same way, a dictionary becomes the depository of intelligence.

The Bible is not a system of facts nor congeries of doctrines, but it is the biography of the Great Lover besieging our intelligence that He might capture our hearts, and make all things new, just as lover ever does. So facts and ordinances are dissolved into a temple for God.

Our faith is not common (Acts 10:15); it is the same faculty as is in every account of faith but the *quality* of what is contacted transforms. Faith is the enveloping atmosphere of the mental world. In faith we are handling dynamic thoughts and these are not pigmy men nor themes. Faith is the substantial conviction of the NOT seen. Abraham was looking for *the City*; and Moses endured as seeing Him Who is Invisible (Hebrews 11:27); and just so the Holy Spirit sustains the spiritual world, for He stands under *all* things. Abraham's wife turned the heads of kings; and Paul's reasoning made rulers to tremble. Here is a "substance" from whose foot-hills you can see the Eternal City of God. If it is neglected, then man's (soul) life is bound for the shallows.

The Church (His Body) is as Isaiah who saw Solomon's spacious temple dissolved into the domain of God's splendor which eclipsed the Jewish Apocalyptic Millennium set forth so gloriously by her prophets. So also the seeking Christian sees that which is pictured in Ephesians 3:18 wherein the Lord promises to "supply your every need"—"to do exceeding above that which ye ask or think,"—"and present you faultless before the Throne of God" (see I John 3:1—2). Can human imagination go higher? Abraham and Paul saw Him who wrought this most mighty transformation of the Most High God, and they alone of all men saw:

a) Christ crucified and raised (John 8:56)

b) The glories which were to follow (II Corinthians 12:4)

And they as the Cherubim of *Romans*, chapters 4 through 7, were privileged with unveiled face to see His (the Lord's) saving faith (Galatians 2:20), and that His Father could (and did) raise Him out from the dead ones, and, "because I live, ye shall live also." It is significant that Abraham and Paul both came from the most cultured cities of their day: Ur of the Chaldees and Tarsus of Cilicia; and they yielded their all unto Him. The call must have been clear and the proof must have been ample; and they were convinced to put their all upon it. Donald Hanky said, "Faith is betting your life that God is true." Both Abraham and Paul were kept from under the power of men; no one helped them but God (Genesis 14:23, Galatians 1:1, *et al.*); and they worked with their own hands. Faith and the trust it begets is between just TWO. It was so with them, and it is so now with you. This is why prayer is of value. This must be believed for only the Scriptures are between us and God; you are on one side and God is on the other (John 5:39).

"Faith *assumes* to be *true* that which it *expects* to become *fact*" (A. E. K.). A member of the Englewood Church (Chicago), "Auntie Dean" as we called her, received a letter in which her sister offered her a home in California. Auntie Dean believed this, and transferred from Chicago to the coastal city. Her faith was *the* moving cause. The letter was not the fact but only a statement of the fact that a home awaited her in California. She, "moved by a thing not seen," went forth unto California. Therefore, faith *assuming*, transferred Auntie Dean unto *fact* and into a home in California.

What is Faith? It is the substance of the hoped for; and is the capacity to achieve. *Where* is Faith found? Jesus is the Author, the beginning; and the Perfecter of faith, the ending.

Faith is the substance of Hope (Hebrews 12:1—2). *Hebrews* is the only book in which this text would fit. Note that it is not just faith but THE faith as we would say, "The Bible, The Christ, The Spirit." *Hebrews* is the book of the definite article. Here is the faith amid towering achievements of man. Will the over-shadowing Shekinah of Christ stand apart in transfiguring glory? Without faith it is impossible to arrive at God and if we have no God, then no Christ (John 6:44—45). Man at his best is not functioning.

Faith is THE substance of Hope in every transaction. Every advance is in the realm of hope to the as yet un-achieved. Each is executed outside of the present facts but with known materials and ability; otherwise, they are experimenting, or pioneering or adventuring into the unknown, just as did Columbus. The Brooklyn Bridge was designed by John Augustus Roebling who drew up the plans; and the construction was supervised by his son Col. Washington A. Roebling from a wheel chair. At the completion of the great undertaking, he remarked that it looked just like he and his father had visioned it. He had authorized the specified materials for supporting the structure and the tensile strength of these materials, but in carrying it out, each act was as though it had been automatic, yet it was based upon a thought-out precedent[1] and had been carefully gone over:

> ". . . During these ceremonies[2] a lonely man—paralyzed, crippled, and racked with pain—sat at an upper window of his home on Columbia Heights, viewing the scene from afar. He saw the crowds surrounding the bridge approach, and the host of more privileged citizens pouring into the reserved space. Through his field glasses he saw the distinguished procession coming over the bridge—the President of the United States, the Governor of the State, and all the other notables, together with the glittering military escort. His gaze was riveted on the scene. The breeze carried the cheers of the crowd and the strains of the band, but he could not hear the glowing tributes of the orators.
>
> "His throat was choked, and he could hardly keep back the tears; for this was the great moment of his life. Through long and weary years he had been enduring paid and fighting on for this consummation. This day gave meaning to his life, and to his father's before him. For this was his father's Bridge—and his Bridge. The father had dreamed the dream, the son had wrought the dream. Both had lived, and battled, and sacrificed, that this Bridge might be built, and both had given their last supreme effort to this achievement.
>
> ". . . Beside the crippled man at the window stood his wife, who had been his ministering angel through the years of pain and struggle.

---

[1] D.B.Stinman, *The Builders of the Bridge,—The Story of John Roebling and his Son,* (N.Y., Harcourt, Brace and Co., 1945), p. 305; "Only twenty-three years before, John Roebling had pleaded for a chance to build his first suspension structure, with spans of only 162 feet. Now he had become the world's foremost authority on suspension bridges and was entrusted with the responsibility of planning and building the world's greatest bridge, with an epoch-making span length close to 1,600 feet . . . The stage was set for the greatest drama in the history of bridgebuilding, the drama of the building of the Brooklyn Bridge."

[2] *Ibid.* "The Bridge is Dedicated," (Ceremonies May 24, 1883), pp. 412—413.

She had been his eyes, his hands, his feet—recording his notes, and carrying his instructions to the job, and bringing back reports of its progress. When others had tried to displace him just as the work was drawing to completion, she had eloquently presented his plea to stop the injustice. Brave and loyal and tender, she had given her strength to carry her husband through his soul-straining ordeal.'

So each act of faith *seems* as though it were automatic in its fulfillment, but faith is actually based upon a Thought-out Precedent, even God.

Faith is defined as the Substance of the hoped for (Romans 8:24, Hebrews 6:18–19), and Faith lives in *tomorrows* the greatest facts of *today*; it endures as seeing the invisibles (Hebrews 12:2). Such faith is revealed by others, that is by speculation (mental gymnastics) wherever there is no precedent, so it is called "The Faith," the Lord being its Author and Finisher. Faith compels "that *tomorrow*" to put on the clothes of *today*, taking "the form of a servant" as do public utilities, so that the life that we now live, we live "by the faith of" the creators of our public utilities. Thus by parables, we are led up to Jesus Christ who died, rose and was raptured, and He said, "they (the Scriptures) testify of Me."

5. Faith Confessed

Confession is not in the great commission; it is included only by implication, but such a revolution as Conversion must ever be accompanied by an outward and observable phenomena as speech. Confession is of the Lord (Matthew 10:32, Luke 12:8) and so it is a universal requirement.

Paul "Christ-izes" the Lord (Acts 9:5) which is the equivalent of Jehovah, i.e. God, and thereafter he writes:

"I give thee charge in the sight of God, who quickeneth
all things, and before Christ Jesus, who before Pontius
Pilate witnessed the good confession."

I Timothy 6:13N.

"Wherefore I give you to understand that no-one speaking
by the Spirit of God calleth Jesus anathema: and no-one
can say Jesus is Lord but by the Holy Spirit."

I Corinthians 12:3N.

"That if thou shalt confess with thy mouth the Lord Jesus,
and shalt believe in thine heart that God raised Him from
among dead ones, thou shalt be saved."

Romans 10:9N.

The Christian must "confess Jesus as Lord"; he must be as the Psalmist wrote in Psalm 84:2:

"My soul longeth, yea, even fainteth for the courts of Jehovah;
My heart and my flesh crieth out for the living God."

As alcohol is to the drinker; fame to the ambitious; and schools to the talented; so, and much more also, is Christ to the benevolent, the compassionate and the idealist. See the violinist with every atom of his being vibrating with his music; or witness the surgeon steeled to stillness save his trained hands. These with every corpuscle in the trained body are at-one with their calling. They are "possessed" and so also must be the Christian. We cannot think of a doctor or a musician who would not expect to practice; nor could we imagine a skilled doctor near sickness who would never help those who needed his treatment. So the confession is a profession and we should be ashamed if we do not practice. For, "he that winneth souls is wise" (Proverbs 11:30 and see Psalm 111:10).

Note Romans 10:1–17, Jeremiah 23:1–8, and I Corinthians 1:26–31. The perfection of the Scriptures is revealed in that Christ is *Telos* (the end) to everyone; for at the end of the (every) way, of every thought, of every person, and of all time—is "Come unto Me." The requirement of confession declares God—that the God of the Universe is a Person; and He speaks to the Jew through Law, and to the Gentile through nature (Acts 14:17––17:28, and Psalm 19). And though we be as "children crying in the night," He hears and comes:

> "Call unto Me, and I will answer thee,
> And shew thee great and hidden (inaccessible)
> things which thou knowest not."

Jeremiah 33:3N.

He hears and answers (Isaiah 65:24) and there is no straining, just trust and peace; "Say not in thine heart, who shall ascend"—the Jew ascends to the Temple while the Gentile descends to build *"Kosmos"* from chaos by his own efforts.

These elements of confession are not separate nor final but as the piano keyboard, they blend and carry through to unity; they are the "homo-*lego*" (speak) as a meeting of minds, or a symphony of sympathy (Matthew 26:57–58, I Timothy 6:11–16, Matthew 10:32–33, I John 4:2, II John 7). Confession is the nearest of at-one-ment with Him of any of the parts of conversion. It is a place where divine hunger comes to expression (Isaiah 55:1–13).

The confession is pictured in Hebrews 11:13–16 as a colony—a celestial caravan—of those who have heard the call and are stepping out on the promises. Confession is not so much acknowledging the extraordinary personality of this Foreigner from Heaven, as it is the "laying hold upon" Him for salvation, just as did Peter in the waves, walking on the waters. As a transformer in transit steps up the current of electricity, so we are "stepped up" and are "changed from glory unto glory" (I John 3:1–3 and Colossians 3:1–4).

To confess means to speak the same thing or hold the same language (I Corinthians 1:10). As God said, "This IS My Son" when He sent Him from His Home to us foreigners; and so we confess Him as God's Son (or speak the same thing). This confession, just as are the other elements of the plan of salvation, is rooted in heaven (Hebrews 11:6) for this confession was first made by God (Matthew 3:17) and Gabriel (Luke 1:32), *et al.* (Matthew 1:21–22).

> ". . . 'The spoken word is nigh thee, even in thy mouth, and in thy heart': that is, the spoken word of faith, which we proclaim as heralds; That if thou shalt confess with thy heart that God hath raised Him from among the dead ones, thou shalt be saved."
>
> <div align="right">Romans 10:8<i>b</i>–10N.</div>

Section FIVE: THE CHURCH—MY STORY (Continued)

VI. "THE THINGS WHICH HAVE BEEN FULLY ESTABLISHED

AMONG US" (Luke 1:1 A.S.V.m*)

* *Marginal reference*

VI. "THE THINGS WHICH HAVE BEEN FULLY ESTABLISHED AMONG US" (Luke 1:1 A.S.V.m)—THE VITAL DOCTRINES OF SALVATION

C. BAPTISM

> "He that believeth and is baptized shall be saved; but he that believeth not, shall be condemned."
>
> Mark 16:16 N.

1. Restoring Reverence Toward Baptism

(I Peter 3:17—22

Texts: (Romans 8:18—30

(Acts 2:38

The Great Commission commands "be baptized upon (Gr. *epi*) the Name." This is to all men everywhere. Surface and shallow thinking, indolence and flippancy have all but banished the rights and reverence of baptism. The result is seen in present day *communism* and *divorce*. We regard symbols too lightly. A title deed assures the individual of his property rights and the marriage contract assures faith in the relationship between husband and wife. These symbols are our *Hupostasis*. They are records of prior facts and future intentions. We have reduced baptism to a form which is emasculated and meaningless.

Baptism is a myriad-symbol ordinance (Acts 2:38, Romans 6:3—8). It is:

a) A birth
b) The washing (or regeneration) away of sin
c) The answer of a good conscience
d) A planting
e) A death
f) A burial
g) A resurrection

This discourse on baptism is an effort to restore unto its pristine purity and power this birth ordinance under the conviction that Christ is our contemporary. The Bible contains living oracles and baptism is one of the universal immortals.

2. Rightly Dividing Between Baptisms

Some of the overlooked connotations in the use of baptism are:

a) The baptism of water unto repentance (Matthew 3:11)
b) The baptism of the spiritual unto enduement (Luke 24:49)
c) The baptism of fire (Acts 1:8) unto everlasting judgment

While all three of these baptisms were always associated with The Great, yet,

>   *d*) Christian baptism stands apart, for it unites us with Him.

3. Baptism and the Scriptures

"Baptism . . . is it from heaven or man?' This is the Lord's own question to the rulers of the Jews who were connecting baptism with The Messiah, for the priests and Levites from Jerusalem asked John the Baptist "if you are not the Christ or Elijah, why baptizeth thou?" (John 1:25).

Baptism must be of exceeding importance, for baptism is always associated with The Great:

>   *a*) With Great Men
>   (1) John's baptism with John the Baptist
>   (2) Christian baptism with the Lord and with Paul
>   *b*) With Great Events:
>   (1) The manifestation at Pentecost
>   (2) The household of Cornelius
>   (3) The Great White Throne Judgment
>   At Pentecost and also at the household of Cornelius, we see both the baptism in Holy Spirit and in water; at the Great White Throne Judgment will come the baptism in fire
>   *c*) With Great Doctrines
>   (1) The New Birth
>   (2) Remission of sins
>   (3) Gift of the Spirit
>   (4) A good conscience
>   *d*) With a great book of conversions (*Acts*) and in this book baptism is *never* omitted from any of the detailed accounts of conversion
>   (1) Chapter 2—Pentecost, Acts 2:41
>   (2) Chapter 8—The Samaritans, vs. 12; the eunuch, vs. 36
>   (3) Chapter 9—Saul, vs. 18
>   (4) Chapter 10—Cornelius, vs. 47
>   (5) Chapter 16—Lydia, vss. 14—15; the jailer, vs. 33
>   (6) Chapter 18—Crispus and other Corinthians, vs. 8
>   (7) Chapter 19—at Ephesus, vss. 1—5; and these were re-baptized for they had been baptized only unto *John's baptism.* And consider then the import and divineness of *Christian baptism* in contrast.

Baptism is also associated (either by reference or inference) with all the epistles of "our beloved brother Paul"—"according to the wisdom given unto him, in all his epistles, speaking of things . . .":

a) In *Romans*, things which are foundational, fundamental and sal-
vational; imbedded within "that *form of doctrine* (baptism)
whereunto ye were delivered" (Romans 6:17)

b) In *Corinthians*, he writes "they were all baptized unto Moses
in the cloud and in the sea" (I Corinthians 10:2, 11 and 1:13)

c) In *Galatians*, "for as many of you as were baptized into Christ
did put on Christ" (Galatians 3:27)

d) In *Ephesians*, Paul goes beyond salvation into sanctification;
and in 5:26 he writes concerning Christ and the Church, "having
cleansed it (the Body) by *the* washing of *the* water in the Word."
This is in a book which is not in the salvation group

e) In *Philippians*, Paul had baptized most of them (Philippians
2:12–16, Acts 16:27–34)

f) In *Colossians*, he writes "having been buried with Him in baptism" (Colossians 2:12, cf. 3:1–4)

g) In *Thessalonians* as he commends their following or imitating
the Apostles' teaching, and also that of the Lord (I Thessalonians 1:5–6). This of necessity includes baptism

h) In the pastoral epistles, Paul writes:
 I Timothy:
  1:19 "holding faith and a good conscience"
  6:20–21N.:
  "O Timothy, guard that which is *committed to thy trust*,
  avoiding profane and vain babblings, and oppositions of
  knowledge falsely so called; Which some professing have
  missed the mark concerning the faith . . ."
 II Timothy:
  1:13 "hold the *pattern*"
  2:15–16 "handling aright the Word of Truth, but shun profane
  babblings"
  4:2 "preach *the* Word"
 Titus:
  3:5 "He saved us through the washing of regeneration and
  renewing of the Holy Spirit"

i) In *Hebrews* (6:1–2): the call here is to go on to perfection

Baptism is likewise associated with Peter's writings:
In Peter's epistles the magnitude and glory of baptism is strikingly set
forth to those "having eyes to see" (cp. I Peter 2:17–22 with Romans 8:18
–30). The ark was a type of Christ: "In Him all things consist." Man
entered the ark willingly, the animals entered compelled; but both were
saved. So, "baptism doth now also save us"—as the ark saved them through
water, "not the washing away of the filth of the flesh, but the appeal of

a good conscience." Our sin has outraged (cursed) all; conscience smites us. *Paul* crowns this longed-for event of salvation with the Apocalyptic Romans 8:18—39.

First century evangelism resulted in universal acceptance of Christ through faith and baptism.

Paul's *first missionary journey* emphasized faith; and the baptism of believers must have occurred though it is not mentioned. So this first missionary journey *fixed* the necessity of *faith*. On his *second journey*, *baptism* is stressed and along with faith, baptism is specifically mentioned, so baptism also was *fixed*. This spiritual anabasis is today's business. Peter began in Acts 2:38 with the Jews and then took the Gospel to the Gentiles in Acts 10:48. Paul carried on this ministry to the Jews, speaking in their tongue (Acts 26:23, 21:40, 22:2, .26:14, Romans 11:1, Philippians 3:5). Neither Peter nor Paul baptized many with their own hands (Acts 10:48, I Corinthians 1:15—17, cp. John 4:2).

The Roman Church has perverted baptism. Fisher[1] says:

> "Inasmuch as, in the Catholic theology, baptism cleanses the soul of guilt, Justification is rather by baptism than by *Faith*. 'For all sins committed after baptism, the offender must himself make satisfaction'."

In Acts 16:9 a vision appeared to Paul in the night:

> "There stood a 'certain' man of Macedonia and prayed
> him saying, 'come over into Macedonia and help us'."

The fulfillment of this vision seems to take place at Philippi; and note that the Greek text specifies that it was a "certain" man of Macedonia. A few verses later (vs. 14), we find a "certain" woman; and then three chapters on (Acts 19:1), we find "certain" disciples at Ephesus. Each of these "certain" were baptized.

First to be baptized was Lydia "whose heart the Lord opened" (Acts 16:14). This word "opened" is a medical term used at the birth of a first born child as in Luke 2:23. The same term is used in Luke 24:31 and 45 as Jesus "opened" the eyes of the Emmaus disciples; and then it is used of all of the disciples, so that they understood the Scriptures. Thus, we read that Lydia's heart is "opened" and that "she attended unto the things which were spoken of by Paul"; "and when she was baptized . . ." she extended hospitality to these who brought the Gospel. Baptism was a natural conclusion to receiving the Gospel.

The "certain" man of Macedonia must have been the jailer of Philippi. Like the Jews in Jerusalem (Acts 2:37), and like Saul of Tarsus (Acts

---

[1] George Park Fisher, D.D., LL.D., *History of The Christian Church* (N.Y., Charles Scribner's Sons, 1928)

9:6), so the jailer asks the all-important question "what must I do to be saved? *Believers* did not ask this question but rather asked for baptism (Acts 8:36). *The Jews at Pentecost had not repented, neither did they believe, and therefore they asked "men and brethren, what must we do?"* In a sense they were as far from the truth and from God as this pagan jailer. When he had heard the word of the Lord, and had believed on Jesus Christ, he "was baptized, he and all his, straightway" (Acts 16:33); and this "certain" man of Macedonia became a part of the Church at Philippi.

We follow Paul on to Thessalonica where we find that he is:

> "Opening and alleging 'that Christ must needs have suffered and suffered and risen again from among the dead ones and that this Jesus whom I preach unto you is Christ'."
>
> Acts 17:3 N.

In John 5:39 Jesus said, "these are they that testify of Me." And at Thessalonica Paul opens the Scriptures and places them alongside of Christ even as the doctor places the new-born child alongside of its mother. As Paul "opens" these Scriptures, Christ emerges and commands.

Moving on from Thessalonica to Athens, Paul preaches on Mars Hill:

> "And when they heard of the resurrection of the dead ones, some indeed mocked . . . howbeit, certain men *clave* unto him and believed."
>
> Acts 17:32, 34N.

This word "clave" is the same as is used in Matthew 19:5, "a man . . . *cleave* to his wife; and they twain shall become one flesh"; and as in I Corinthians 6:17 "he that is *joined* unto the Lord is one spirit." Baptism is a symbol of the resurrection and when these certain men heard of the resurrection, they *clave* unto Paul and therefore they must have been baptized.

At Corinth Paul baptized Crispus (Acts 18:8, I Corinthians 1:14) and mention is made of Sosthenes, the chief ruler of the synagogue. Five years later, Paul calls Sosthenes "the brother" (I Corinthians 1:1). Truly, many of the Corinthians hearing, believed and were baptized.

From Corinth we follow Paul to Ephesus where he finds "certain" disciples. He asks these men "into what then were ye baptized" and they said, "into John's baptism." Paul's reply was:

> ". . . John verily baptized with the baptism of repentance, saying unto the people, that they should believe in Him which should come after him, that is in Christ Jesus. When they heard this, they were baptized into the name of the Lord Jesus."
>
> Acts 19:4–5N.

Following this Paul laid his hands upon them and the Holy Spirit came upon them. This was the same laying on of apostolic hands as when Peter and John laid their hands on the disciples at Samaria in Acts 8:14. The laying on of the apostles' hands through which came the receiving of the Holy Spirit for special gifts, always *followed* Christian baptism and never preceded it.

4. The Context of Baptism

The saving and cleansing import of the context of baptism is added to the fact that it never appears alone (Ephesians 4:1—16, Titus 3:5); but baptism is included in every recorded conversion, and we are admonished to study:

a) Does a reverent scholar inquire concerning Jesus?

Yes, and Nicodemus was told "except a man be *born* again . . . born of *water* and the Spirit, he cannot enter into the kingdom of God" (John 3:1—5).

b) Do irreverent scholars quibble concerning the authority of Jesus?

Yes, and the chief priests and elders are answered by the question, "The *baptism* of John, whence was it, from heaven or of man?" (Matthew 21:23—25).

c) Do murderers cry out at the hearing of the Gospel?

Yes, and at Pentecost, the multitude heard the command of the Holy Spirit through Peter, "Repent and be *baptized* every one of you in the Name of Jesus Christ for the remission of sins."

d) And what does a member of the Sanhedrin hear after he has personally talked to the Lord and been blinded by the event? The Lord's disciple says to him: "Now why tarriest thou, arise and be *baptized*, washing away thy sins' (Acts 22:16).

There is a wonder and a power in baptism that one who reads here and meditates on, will never cavil, for in baptism are transcending miracle elements. It is a rebirth and it de-racializes (II Corinthians 3:18, I John 3:2). Baptism dissolves races, classes and sex. We do not say that it will, but that it has and does. There is nothing else known to me nor is there any other word uttered by Him by which we can "put on the Lord Jesus Christ and make not provision for the flesh."

When the Holy Spirit would close the Salvation Canon, the Consummation Unity of Ephesians 4 included "one baptism." Can baptism be the way of escape (I Corinthians 10:13) from "the presence of mine enemies?" It is the ever present way of the Cross (Luke 9:23) which gives baptism its context and meaning. Because this seems to me the answer, I invite you to consider some of these significant contexts:

a) When Jesus said, "My baptism," He was not referring to the baptism of John. Jesus alone could have said unto us, "ye have not resisted unto blood" (Hebrews 12:1–4). To John He said, "thus it becometh us to fulfill all righteousness." Until that was accomplished, His baptism could not be completed. The "My baptism" of Jesus included:

"He set His Face"
"This is My Body"
"He sweat blood"
The Cross, Death and the Resurrection

And when we participate in *His* baptism in the Church, we share in these things. If we are baptized into Christ's baptism, we are "dipped"—"dyed"—"colored" by the elements into which we are baptized. So Galatians 3:27 is the same as Matthew 22:11 and I Corinthians 15:53. Therefore, the *baptized* one enters Him (Christ, His realm), and the Spirit-life of Him spreads over and through; it colors and dyes each life till others can "take knowledge that we have been with Jesus." To such the Lord can say, "as the Father hath sent Me, even so send I you";—"for me to live IS Christ" (Galatians 2:20).

b) We are baptized upon (Gr. *epi*) the "My Name," and into (Gr. *eis*) the Father, Son, Spirit. The phrase "In My Name" reminds us that a man's name binds the man; his signature is binding and stands in court (Psalm 138:2). "Heaven and earth shall pass away but *My Word* shall not." We have grown careless of the Scriptures (Luke 16:31). We are baptized into "The Name" and God has "magnified His Word above all His Name" and therefore our baptism is our acceptance of the authority of the Scriptures. This brings true repentance to fulfillment (II Timothy 2:25).

c) He that disbelieves (Mark 16:16) could be immersed but could not be baptized (Luke 12:50). "My baptism" is into death; and here is the significance of Romans 6:3–4; we were baptized into His death. We are buried with Christ in order to be raised "out from among the dead ones" (Gr. *ek necrone*). So we, in "newness of life walk," "if we have been planted together, (literally, "closely entwined") in the likeness of His death, we shall be also of the resurrection" (Romans 6:5 N.). In baptism we are "born again," buried, planted, cleansed with the washing of water, the bath of regeneration, and it washes away. Is any figure omitted which is necessary to complete the union? Not only is baptism a burial and a planting but also a sleeping. Theologically, these all mean the same thing, and the character of those "obedient to" are the most Christ-like of men. Our induction into Christ is as a miniature Gethsemane where the cross awaits. As a man leaving prison doffs stripes and dons citizen's clothing, so also our old man or "dead body" must be put away, even as that which is infectuous.

d) There is *One* baptism. This is a plain statement of fact, not possible to be misunderstood. There are four baptisms mentioned in the New Testament: Water baptism, Spirit baptism, Fire baptism, and "My baptism." Two of these, "Spirit" and "My" baptism are in this Age of Grace. One of these has ceased (Ephesians 4:5), but the question is, which one? And this is serious matter. The purpose of baptism will determine which one continues:

(1) One is a birth, or to put us into Christ; this is "My baptism" (Galatians 3:27) and it makes Christians

(2) The other is to bring proof to man; and this is "Spirit" baptism, and it made the Scriptures! Spirit baptism's purpose was accomplished when the revelation was perfected and the Gospel message was completed, and thus "that which is in part shall be done away" (I Corinthians 14:10). "My baptism"—Christian baptism—continues until the Lord returns.

Baptism is called: a planting (Romans 6:5), a burial-resurrection, and a birth. And you arrive at the meanings of it by studying the figures used:

a) Just what is a planting?

It is John 12:24 "except it fall and die"; "He that loveth life (Gr. *psuchen* and Gr. *zoen*). It spreads into "others"; so do the baptized lives. In seeds, the outer shell rots and the inner responds to another pull

b) What is a burial-resurrection?

It is a change (I Corinthians 15:51) of the old for the new of my will for Thy will. Change occurs to the living and the dead and it is conditioned upon acceptance of Christ (John 11:25—26)

c) What is the birth of a child?

This is the Lord's own figure (John 3:3) and it is familiar to all. Where were you *born*? Not begotten but born?

A man may be begotten in Italy but born in the U.S.A. When we say: "I first saw the light of day . . ." we are not speaking of where life began, but rather of where we were born, for this is the important event, and age is dated from birth.

And so Jesus told Nicodemus: "except a man is born of water and of Spirit . . . ." Thus each must be begotten of Spirit and born of water, and the two are parts of one whole act.

Baptism is individual: "be baptized *every one* of you" (Acts 2:38*a*). The gift of the Holy Spirit is collective: "*ye* shall receive the gift of the Holy Spirit" (Acts 2:38*b*). Jesus said, "Are ye able to be baptized with My baptism?" And, "I have a baptism" (Luke 12:50); "He shall see of the travail of soul and be satisfied." It is as birth or marriage—it is a lifetime investment. No one living has ever been wholly baptized (cf. John 19:30; and note Revelation 10:7 and Ephesians 3:9). It is an unworthy, shallow and superficial view that one act could give eternal life apart from any other consideration of conformity.

Baptism is the Divine accommodation to our zone (John 3:3) "born again" (Gr. *anothen*, from above). This is the planting of the Word (seed) of God within a surrendered human desire. It produces, as seed ever does, according as the receiving life yields, a spiritually controlled individuality. The soil determines the crop (Matthew 13:3 ff.). The producing of a life is ever out of death as the seed disintegrates to free the vital element. So it is everywhere in our experience. This naturally prepares expectation for like effect in re-generating ordinance (Luke 13:20). With such expectancy based upon His method, let us take up baptism and set our minds at ease. The validity of baptism is not dependent alone upon "much water" (John 3:23). But the unity of His Church, upon which depends a vastly more important issue, does depend upon the validity of this regenerating ordinance. The custom of the Jews has no bearing upon it, just as the Egyptians have none on the Law even though they should use the same words and forms, yet their meanings would lie worlds apart. Even if they could (and did) produce every word from a Jewish source, yet Christian baptism is not the same. Christ chose baptism and *His* use of it determines its meaning. And the Holy Spirit-controlled apostles (*Acts*) will change or augment baptism while Paul will carry it to the highest expression and and significance.

Baptism is a biblical fact and not a church ordinance. We are baptized into (Gr. *eis*) Christ—never into the Church. This error, that is, when men are compelled to submit to baptism in order to "join the church," has much to do with the light regard placed upon membership. Optional baptism substitutes the opinion of an unsurrendered person for the "thus saith" of a crucified and risen God, and the tradition of His Church. There is no "mode" of baptism. Such language limits baptism to water only. But the Spirit-filled more accurately see John the Baptist baptizing "IN" water "INTO" repentance. While the candidate is "IN WATER" something occurs. Paul writes that we are baptized INTO Christ (Galatians 3:27). *Water* is the surrounding element at the time we are baptized INTO Christ. The *place* of your immersion decides your citizenship and responsibility.

For one who believes in Jesus Christ, baptism is inevitable. This is the Great Commission: to make disciples, baptizing them, teaching them. "He that believeth and is baptized . . ." that is, born, delivered, brought forth from Moses (Jews) or the world (Gentiles), "shall be saved." See these examples:

   a) At Pentecost (Acts 2:41N.): "Then they indeed that gladly received (*conceived*, I Peter 2:23) His Word, were baptized."
   b) Titus 3:5N.: ". . . He saved us, through the laver-washing (bath) of regeneration . . ."
   c) I Peter 3:21N.: ". . . baptism doth also now save us . . . through the resurrection of Jesus Christ"

All of these are predicated upon personality needing salvation. "Baptism saves"; it does not create, but it saves and delivers that which is already created. "That form of doctrine by (Gr. *eis*, into) which we were delivered" (Romans 6:17, Gr. Interlinear) is not a mould of repression but is "into Christ" "growing up into Him." The Spirit within is educating or drawing out all that is best and holiest. This gives light and responsibility and confidence and hope (Proverbs 22:6, Isaiah 55:10—11). The ingrafted, begetting Word may long lie dormant, but it is ready at the touch of a tear.

Jesus speaks of "My baptism" as that unto which He had been delivered by His begetting. He said, "for this cause came I into the world." Baptism is inevitable once one believes or else one dies. It is a necessary consequence of a past incident. The facts storm and master a mind (belief) and the will is now responsible (be baptized).

Concerning Christ's personal use of baptism, we find that John would have hindered Him but Jesus said, "it becometh us to fulfill all righteousness" and God Himself said that He was well-pleased. Jesus went sixty miles to receive baptism. His soliloquy and decision of John 12:23 is meaningful here. "Except a grain of wheat fall into the ground and die, it remains alone." (But for this cause, every Christian was buried in baptism). A newly anointed Being emerged from Jordan for from that grave He touched the power of God (II Kings 13:31).

Concerning this incident, Dr. C. Geikie[1] wrote:

> "Holy and pure before sinking under the waters, He must yet have risen from them with the light of a higher glory in His countenance. His past life was closed; a new era had opened . . . . He entered them as Jesus, the Son of Man; He rose from them, The Christ of God."

As a bulb's life comes to ascendancy, so the God-life within Him there took precedence and later He said to Mary, "Woman, what have I to do with

---

[1] Cunningham Geikie, D.D., *The Life and Words of Christ*, (N.Y., D. Appleton and Company, 1890), pp. 413—414.

thee?" Christ's doctrinal use of baptism is found in the text, "Ye must be born *from above*" which explains Mark 16:16 as being more than the dipping. "My Baptism" and "Mine Hour" refer to the same thing. We are "baptized into His death" Paul says. Christ was dipped at the Jordan and buried at Jerusalem, but Jordan made Jerusalem inevitable. Acts 2:38 promises "the remission of sins" and Acts 22:16 says, "wash away thy sins." We find that the phrases, "born again" and "buried in," are as the bulb when buried, rots from around the living center (seed). So runs the parallel. Christ's baptism was from the Jordan to Olivet (Luke 12:50) and is reproduced in Paul's teaching:

a) The *Romans* (Jordan) period (chapter 6:3—6) is like Jesus breaking the home ties (John 2:4). The evangelistic appeal and the emphasis of preaching is "repent" which calls men to a change of mind, away from "home ties" and toward God. God's glory is reflected upon the result as men come in massed-togetherness around Jesus Christ. Their enthusiasm, testimony and unity make possible "that the world might believe."

b) The *Ephesians* (Olivet) period (John 3:13, Philippians 3:20) is God-intoxicated-enduring "as seeing Him who is invisible" (Hebrews 11:27) and this is the culture (personal) emphasis (II Peter 2:18, Philippians 3:13). Paul said, "I count not myself to have apprehended . . . that I may know Him." The object of all planting is that it may attain unto harvest as grain pushes up past clods into a larger life. The persistence of identity and powers, inherent in personality, produces knowledge. Our transfiguration and translation period are as the flower straining to lift soil to seed, and it bursts into bloom in the struggle; so the spirit of man enters into the "apocalypse of the soul." Can you imagine the "stay-at-homes" saying, "you're a fool for sacrificing your life for a future?" Love always is foolish. The roots of this resurrection strike down into His wounds and this is why its fruit is so glorious.

Baptism is the only thing in the whole Bible commanded in the combined Name of the Father, Son and Holy Spirit and all three are present in His baptism. No other requirement is so variously viewed. The Holy Spirit anticipated the confusion and made a way of escape for all seekers. The commands of the Lord are to be obeyed. A command demands action inspired by knowledge. The understanding was to be sought elsewhere. "In (Gr. *epi*, dative) the Name of Jesus Christ" (Acts 2:38) "implies actual super-position, as one thing resting upon another"; hence it is used of the moving principle or motive suggesting the purpose or object *viz.* Ephesians 2:10. In Matthew 28:19 the Greek *eis* (into) is used, meaning *within* the

Name of the Father, Son, and Spirit. There is no Triune baptism here. It is one act into ONE Name, involving all the elements necessary to the plan of salvation. Triune baptism separates the Father from the Son, the Son from the Spirit, and disturbs the unity over which our Lord spoke of Himself and Father, and hinders the unity for which He prayed in John 17 for His disciples. A visitor or a bystander is often at a loss to understand these things, but those who are participating are not. Our slogan was struck off out of this event and the response was intelligent and Scriptural, so that we said, "Where the Scriptures speak, we speak; where they are silent, we are silent." The language is accurate, the occasion is extra-ordinary, and the elements must be essential. Where there are like conditions, we will see like results: "they that gladly received His Word, were baptized." "Repent ye" is plural (see Acts 17:30), and "be baptized each one of you" (Gr. Acts 2:38) is singular. As, "the sins ye do by two and two, ye must answer for one by one." Each one must take *his* place in the silent hall of death (to self). Here "repent" was national (Matthew 3:1—12; Acts 20:21, John 6:44) and it was "toward God." And their sin was against God whose agent was Christ (Psalm 51:4; I Samuel 8:7).

Confession and baptism are the closest elements in the plan of salvation, and yet they are the Zenith and the Nadir. Confession ascends to Deity; and baptism descends to Death (Romans 6:4; Ephesians 2:5—6). Of the elements of the plan of salvation, confession and baptism are the most public. Jesus said, "he that confesses Me before men . . ."; and Paul said, "so many of us as were baptized into Jesus Christ, were baptized into His death" and were "crucified with Christ." Confession "before men" and "crucified with Christ" are basically public. Death attracts numbers; always there is a crowd at a funeral. This is the public or immersion side of baptism. The Lord's figure (John 12:24) "except a corn of wheat fall into the ground *and die*, it abideth alone, but if it die, it bringeth forth much fruit." And from I Corinthians 15:37—38, we know that the fruit brought forth is not the same body that is planted. The invisible part of the seed becomes visible in the plant and the visible part of the seed is lost in the earth. The real dying and rising occurs in the real baptism. Jesus said to Martha:

> "I am the resurrection, and the life; he that believeth in Me,
> though he were dead, yet shall he live: and everyone that
> liveth and believeth in Me shall never die . . . ."

John 11:25—26 N.

Baptism is personal; death is not to be forced; it is only for volunteers. So we read, "they that *gladly* . . . were buried with Him" (Acts 2:41, 21:17). The background of baptism can best be set out by figures:

> *Initiate*: present your qualifications
>
> *Impress*: "fix" by process

In neither of these is a child able. Baptism is not a church ordinance nor is it the entrance into the Church, but rather it is *into* or *with* Him. This must be understood. And the apologist for baptism must be more than formula right; he must be aflame with light from off the Face of Christ.

In baptism we are planted, buried and thus contact life (Gr. *zoe*). There is only one reason for burial and that is death; if we were doubtful about death, we would never inter a body. Baptism is to "wash away sins." But someone says, "this is too easy; it is repugnant to a sense of right;" then how else are sins washed away? Only "in His blood" can sin be cleansed; that fluid cleanses prodigals of every nature.

Each of these references indicates a radical break with the past, while nature parables suggest a "life more abundant" (John 12:24*b*). Baptism, myriad-symboled, is also uncompleted on earth (Romans 6). We are baptized into Christ and into His death (Colossians 1:24; Ephesians 4:13). Baptism is the continued life of the Lord. When you are baptized, you put on Christ to carry on to *telos* (end).

The reasonableness of baptism marks this ordinance as one of peculiar significance. Though the Lord was without sin, yet *He* Himself said, "thus it becometh us to fulfill all righteousness" (Matthew 3:15). *Our* responsibility for being baptized and in teaching others its meaning, is clearly seen as we study the Scriptures:

a) The Lord was baptized

If the Lord felt the compulsion, how can we escape?

b) The Holy Spirit was promised

If the Holy Spirit conditioned His gifts upon Acts 2:38, how can we neglect?

c) The Bible is replete with examples

If it is never omitted from an account of Bible conversion, can we now omit?

d) The Holy Spirit is needed to make it valid

Re-immersion was necessary at Ephesus for the Holy Spirit had not been present to make valid the baptism of the "certain disciples" (Acts 19:3).

Can anyone today then lightly immerse in the presence of the Holy Spirit?

5. The Action of Baptism

Concerning baptism, our fathers of the Restoration Movement said, "Baptism requires water" (Acts 10:47); "much water" (John 3:23); "going to water" (Acts 16:33); "going down into water" (Acts 8:38); and "coming up out of water" (Matthew 3:16).

Baptism is a birth (John 3:5); a burial (Romans 6:4); and through our baptism we are planted (Romans 6:5); and we receive "the bath of regeneration" (Titus 3:5). Only immersion answers all of these requirements.

Baptism requires two elements (or more):

a) Water   — Spirit (John 3:5)
   (Sea   — Shekinah) (I Corinthians 10:1—2)
b) Immersion — Emerging (Acts 8:38—39)
c) Planting — Rising (Romans 6:5)
d) Death   — Life (Romans 6:3—4)
e) Burial   — Resurrection (Romans 6:4—5)
f) Begetting — Birth (John 3:5—6)

6. The Candidates for Baptism

Eventually, everyone faces the question: "What then shall I do?"

The character of those seeking baptism proves that no one is exempted from Acts 2:38 and Jesus is foremost (Matthew 3:15). It was the devout and Godly men and women who were first to recognize the importance of and the need for Christian baptism:

a) Nicodemus: "There was a man of the Pharisees, named Nicodemus, a ruler of the Jews: . . . 'Rabbi, we know that Thou art a teacher come from God . . .'" (John 3:1—2); Jesus said, "except one be born of water and of spirit . . ." (John 3:5)

b) "A man of Ethiopia, an eunuch . . . had come to Jerusalem for to worship . . . . Then Philip opened his mouth and preached unto him Jesus . . . and the eunuch said, 'see, here is water: what doth hinder me to be baptized'?" (Acts 8:28—36)

c) Saul of Tarsus said, "I have lived in all good conscience before God . . ." (Acts 23:1); yet, Acts 22:16, "And now why tarriest thou? arise, be baptized . . ."

d) Lydia's conversion, "And a certain woman named Lydia . . . which worshipped God, ... And when she was baptized . . ." (Acts 16:14—15)

e) Crispus: "And Crispus, the chief ruler of the synagogue, . . . believed . . . and was baptized" (Acts 18:8, cp. I Corinthians 1:14)

f) Cornelius: Peter "commanded them to be baptized into the Name of the Lord" (Acts 10:48). And this man Cornelius was "A devout man who feared God and all his household; and gave much alms to the people, and prayed to God always"(Acts 10:2). I would be before this man as John the Baptist was before Jesus (Mark 1:17)!

If these devout ones needed it, how much more the ungodly. This act of acceptance is a demand more than a command (Acts 8:36). It is the demand of the *believer* who sees its importance. If we so preach Christ as Peter, Philip and Paul, then our hearers will *demand* baptism.

7. The Psychology of Baptism

Baptism is an emotional consequence and not a logical cause (Acts 22:16).

Faith and baptism are "of one piece" with the Cross of Christ. Faith excludes infant baptism! The "My faith, My blood, My baptism" are but parts of ONE whole.

The text Mark 16:16 is a noon-time text and not a "twilight-zone." The statement contains no obscurities. Upon quoting this text, there remained the lexical task of determining the meaning of "faith" and "baptism"—and a Greek lexicon was the only requirement:

Faith is the conviction at the conclusion of sifting and weighing of the evidences. *Baptism* is the passive yielding of one's self to an action (to be "dipped"). The secondary meaning of *bapto* is to "dye, stain"; and Shakespeare wrote, "The mind, like the dyer's hand, is colored by that in which it works."

This interpretation of *bapto* was brushed aside though it contained both of the significations: to *dye* is to cover; to *stain* is to color and this is, the color of the element. So we are baptized "into Christ." If one were to change into the uniform of the United States Army, that would be just a change of clothes, unless there were a true enlistment in the Armed Forces. An act's *moral* value is assessed by the *emotion* which prompts it. In the matter of a crime, the court's part is to determine not the facts of the crime, these are not secret, but rather to determine the psychological factors entering into the act. A man may be *fact*ually right and *emotion*ally wrong. This accounts for a lack of zeal or for the indulgence of bad habits, and one who is emotionally wrong is apt to allow bad exegesis. One of these perverts character and the other perverts the Scriptures. Many have accepted *the text* but have ignored the *Con*-text. We read in Matthew 15 "preach the Gospel" (cp. I Corinthians 15:1–4); also, we see today by Acts 16, that the sects like to choose verse 31, "believe on the Lord Jesus Christ" as the sole necessity, whereas we like to choose verse 33, "he took them . . . and was baptized." But we must note especially verse 32, "and they spake unto him the Word of the Lord and to all that were in his house."

Baptism is a stored up treasure, even as the Dead Sea has enfolded and rapt up within it the mineral wealth of the Jordan Valley into which we may plunge as Naaman and be healed. This is the birth of regeneration with which we are dyed and emotionalized until we say, "Here am I, send me" (Isaiah 6:8; James 1:22–25; II Corinthians 3:18).

I now invite your attention to the psychology of baptism, the emotional background of obeying the Gospel:

a) The preaching of John the Baptist, "as the people were in expectation" (Luke 3:15). Consider their emotional state. In Matthew 3:2 they were told to "repent," and in verse 6, we read that they were confessing their sins. Who reading this could be conscious of the swollen forces of this emotion. Here was the pent-up hope of a thousand years!

b) The Lord's unhurried laboratory dictum (John 3:3, 5), "born of water and of Spirit" (Gr. *anothen*, from above) is as Genesis 1:2 and John 1:29—34. John also "brooded" over the waters (of baptism) from which he was continually looking for The Son of God who baptizes with Holy Spirit. But the emotional content of John 3:5 is our present concern, so the figure of "birth" arrests our attention. Consider the event of birth in a home and the emotional preparation which is necessary (I Samuel 1:9—11).

c) Further light on the emotional background of baptism is found at Pentecost (Acts 2). The explanation of what was occurring is in verses 14—22; their crime; the sin of Israel is stated in verses 22—23; these things are driven into their consciences. Their reaction is in verse 37 and to them is given the comfort of verses 38—39. Their acceptance of such comfort in salvation is found in verse 41. These men were changed from murderers to martyrs, and no "ordinance" apart from emotion could ever beget such a transformation!

d) The eunuch (Acts 8:28) was reading Isaiah 53:7—8, and "Philip beginning at this same Scripture, preached unto him Jesus." When they arrived at water, the eunuch insisted upon baptism. Baptism is always a consequent and is never a cause.

e) The Philippian jailer (Acts 16:31ff.) was told to believe on the Lord, and they spake the Word of the Lord, and he, the jailer, took them and washed their stripes and he was baptized. Here we find the emotion which arises out of the preaching of the Gospel.

Romans 6:3—11 is the most abrupt cataclysm of all the Bible. Baptism is the projection of the Cross into two diametric and antagonistic simultaneous experiences of humanity: that of defeat and death; and that of victory and life; and that is, from the Nadir to the Zenith. The more vividly that this is seen, the fuller is the emotion of a last hour reprieve.

When Victor Hugo wrote *Les Miserables*, he had Jean Val Jean say:

> "My brother, you no longer belong to evil but to good. I have bought your soul of you; I withdraw it from black thoughts and the spirit of perdition and give it unto God."

Divine Love with the surgeon's knife (Hebrews 4:12—13) cuts out sin. Redeemed Love, emotion-moved lets go; and baptism washes it away and cleanses.

422

Section FIVE: THE CHURCH—MY STORY (Continued)

VI. "THE THINGS WHICH HAVE BEEN FULLY ESTABLISHED

AMONG US" (Luke 1:1 A.S.V.m*)

THE VITAL DOCTRINES OF SALVATION

Page

D. THE HOLY SPIRIT

* Marginal reference

VI. "THE THINGS WHICH HAVE BEEN FULLY ESTABLISHED AMONG US" (Luke 1:1 A.S.V.m) — THE VITAL DOCTRINES OF SALVATION

D. THE HOLY SPIRIT

"I used to believe that a few men had a monopoly on the Holy Spirit;
Now I know that the Holy Spirit has a monopoly on a few men."

James H. McConkey

1. The Person of The Holy Spirit

(". . . God is ONE"
Texts: (Galatians 3:20*b*
(I Corinthians 15:20—28

"In a beginning God created the heavens and the earth"(Genesis 1:1N.) The Hebrew word for "God" in this verse is a plural noun "Elohim." The Hebrew language has two plurals, a dual and a trinal. Surely Deity's first gesture would not be a vulgar or loose expression but rather from II Corinthians 12:4, we would conclude that God would use super-grammatic words fused into higher combinations. Here in this verse, Elohim, "God," is trinal; "created" is singular, and "heavens" is dual. This word "Elohim" is a strange craft, as when Columbus sailed his ship into the harbor of San Salvadore and the natives saw on deck these men of another world. These visitors are from the "Mystery" or unvisited dwelling-places of Deity (I Timothy 6:16, Exodus 33:20, Isaiah 6:5). These all—"Jehovah," "Son," "Spirit"—came forth not once, but many times and return into "Elohim" (John 13:3, I Corinthians 15:28). "Elohim" is the combined energies and counsel (Genesis 1:1——2:3). And these unrolled the universe as a tapestry for their royal feet (Psalm 19) and this first work is Thought's vindication and Thought is only from a Thinker! So our approach to the Person of the Holy Spirit is through "Elohim" (Jehovah-Jesus), and if *One* is a Person or a Thinker, so must All be, for all are joined in Elohim and what God hath joined together, man cannot put asunder. Hear the Scriptures:

a) "Jehovah-God" *joined* Himself to a man, Adam, and to a race, the Jews. Moses *talked* to Jehovah; Abraham *walked* with Jehovah; Isaiah *saw* Jehovah; and He is *known* as the "I AM" —"The God (Elohim) of Abraham, Isaac and Jacob.

b) Jesus "God" joined Himself to the flesh and was seen of men; the disciples said, "what manner of man." Pilate said, "Behold the Man." Judas said, "I have betrayed innocent blood." And Nicodemus said, "Thou art a teacher sent from God." The Gospel story is a biographical phenomena. Jehovah is

God-revealed; Jesus is God also, out-from Elohim. But Elohim is *trinal*-plural and so there is at least another. Who is it? It is the Spirit.

c) Spirit-"God." The Holy Spirit joined Himself to a bedraggled Church and carries on the unfinished task of the plural-trinal (I Corinthians 2:11). If Elijah said, "Jehovah before whom I stand"; and the centurion said, "Surely this was Son of God"; and Thomas said, "My Lord, and my God"; even so a "greater than these," Paul, said, "I know Him in whom I have believed." How? Through the writings of the Spirit. Paul also said, "no man can say Jesus is Lord but by the Spirit." Did not Jehovah say, "All day long have I stretched forth My hands to an untoward and gainsaying nation"; and, "Turn ye, for why will ye die"; and, "like as a Father pitieth His children, so doth Jehovah . . . ." Did not the Son "come unto His own things and His own people received Him not"; and say, "Father, forgive them, for they know not what they do"; and, "He gave His life a ransom for many"?

Even so, the Spirit abides with you always, and experiences groanings that cannot be uttered. When the Lord talked to the Father, "He was transfigured," but when the Spirit makes intercession, He is shamed as He "groans" while "clothed" in the Church as in filthy rags, as was Joshua, the High Priest, in Zechariah 3:3.

Does not Jehovah promise victory to "the seed"; and does not the Son promise peace to His own? Even so the Spirit sets men tugging at earth's anchors: "to die is gain"; "when He shall appear"; "changed into the same image from glory to glory." Does Jehovah put a trumpet to the lips of defeated Man? Does Christ set before man an open door? Even so the Spirit broods over and builds a house of worship and meditation, a temple of God, and immortals are created within it.

Thus Elohim's anabasis is:

    (1) "Thy seed shall bruise"

    (2) "The God of peace shall bruise Satan"

    (3) "So they went forth, the Holy Spirit working with them"

> "And I John saw the holy city, new Jerusalem,
> coming down from God out of heaven,
> prepared as a bride adorned for her husband.
>
> "And the Spirit and the bride say, 'Come.'
> And let him that heareth say, 'Come!'
> And let him that is athirst come.

> And whosoever will,
>> let him take the water of life freely."

Revelation 21:2, 22:17N.

In the beginning is Elohim: Father, Son, Holy Spirit; so also are they in the ending, "And the Spirit and the bride say, 'Come'," and in I Corinthians 15:28N.:

> "And when all things shall have been subdued unto Him,
> Then shall the Son also Himself be subject unto Him
> that put all things under Him that God may be all in all."

And did not God Himself say that the Son of God made the heavens and the Spirit of God made "all the hosts thereof" (Psalm 33:6). "God is a Spirit."

> "As it was in the beginning,
> Is now and ever shall be,
> World without end,—Amen."

The Jehovah-God, *A Person*, wrote and Moses destroyed the tablets. Jesus, *A Person*, wrote upon the ground. The Spirit, *A Person*, authored the Book (II Timothy 3:16, II Peter 1:21, Acts 2:4), and this third writing is eternal. What if such a book were found (II Chronicles 34:18); we would conclude that there had been an author, a thinker. To fabricate four gospels would be a greater achievement than to live one life; and this Book, the Bible, reaches so infinitely high (Psalm 19) and so infinitely low (Romans 8:26), that it is outside the range of human speech. The Holy Spirit is a brooding, invisible Wonder-Worker in the midst of the Church making it holy even as Christ did Palestine. "There is a power not ourselves" and so to the Christian there is The Holy Spirit to which we can relate ourselves and He automatically works unless inhibited by *us* (Philippians 2:13); that is, He operates above our intelligence under a Higher One that is native to and inherent in God's creation. It is an attempt to make us aware of a Spiritual world and of Spiritual Personalities and Spiritual agencies which are ready to hand for such times as these. He is the open door, the way of escape and the present help. Men who wrote the Scriptures stated truths which were beyond them (I Peter 1:10). Was it intelligent? Ask civilization, for it is still beyond us. Why? The Author is God.

We preach a Book. Do we find and know its Author? And do we appreciate the opportunity to know His facts? This, His Book, is His laboratory notebook, or chips from His workshop. This Wonder-Worker of chaos, of speech and Gospels, the Holy Spirit, is here at our request, yesterday and today. Just as there were external and heavenly agencies about the Jewish people, and about Jesus Christ, so are they about the Church today and are manifest to this later generation.

2. The Work of The Holy Spirit

    a) The Holy Spirit's Work in *Redemption*:

    (1) The work of the Holy Spirit can be outlined in three phases:
        (*a*) He brooded over chaos (Genesis 1:2)
        (*b*) He organized speech into the revelation of God, and the plan of salvation
        (*c*) He revealed Christ as Lord (I Corinthians 12:3). Jesus said, "He shall take of mine and reveal them unto you." Through the Holy Spirit we are given these intimate revealings of Christ.
    (2) Now consider the materials with which He had to work:
        (*a*) First, the Holy Spirit's agony is expressed over a wrecked world[1] (Isaiah 45:18, Genesis 1:2); and geology shows that this earth has been patched up
        (*b*) Then, the Holy Spirit's agony over the *degenerated speech* of confusion after Babel, is demonstrated at Pentecost (Acts 2:4)
        (*c*) And finally, the Holy Spirit's agony is expressed toward a *corrupted humanity*. These almost two thousand years have been the Holy Spirit's Gethsemane as He is groaning on behalf of the Church. His is the salvation of God's undone materials which are in such condition that they are not able to know what spirit they are of! There is schism here and they grieve the Holy Spirit. He is like a chemist in a divine, degraded material—salvaging the wonders out of these materials and yet, 'Behold what God (The Holy Spirit) hath wrought."
    (3) The results of the Holy Spirit's work with these materials are amazing:
        (*a*) Out of chaos is brought forth the *kosmos* with its prairies and silvery streams; its fields and mountains covered with flowers, fruits and fauna and the song of birds. This change we behold around about us; it is also prophetic of the New Heavens and the New Earth
        (*b*) And into literature, the Holy Spirit has wrought His Story which the historian has recorded and through all literature and oratory, there is that which is classic and divine. Music is like heaven's prelude; so in speech, there is the same beauty and the English version of the Bible has become the norm of our speech.

---

[1] See Section TWO, *Perfection . . . HIS Story,* "The Glory and Handywork" pp. 159—162

(c) And behold also the Church, as the lily above the mud of the pond (Romans 1 to Ephesians 4:16). So rises up His Body, garmented with architecture, art and love as her priestly robe. The Church is washed and cleansed, without blemish or wrinkle, adorned as an High Priest, a glorious Church. From pig iron are builded cathedrals; from pigments are painted immortals; and philanderers become saints. This Holy Spirit is the maximum-izer of the salvaged elements of the de-flowered universe.

(4) Though there is much to be done and much to be desired—yet:

> Stand off, look, marvel,
> Turn aside and unsandal—
> For you are on Holy Ground in the Spirit's Workshop!
> Look around you—
> And behold the Holy Land of Humanity!

Thus Elohim unsheathed an Excalibur,[1] even the Holy Spirit, liberating it from The Stone, and drew the Church up through the wound of The Rock that is The Foundation even Christ. And about the world there ever goes on the silent fashioning forth of His Temple, the Body, as was Solomon's Temple:

(a) The elements of the *kosmos* speak the universal laboratory language

(b) His Story's great words are easily translatable into all languages

(c) And His saints are the ideal, the norm of every people.

Those who are observing a group or congregation, or part of a group, are not conscious of what is occurring before their eyes, and so the Holy Spirit works: wordless, nameless and praiseles—until the Rapture of the Church.

Let us note with extreme care the creation of the *kosmos* through the *logos* (John 1:3) and the palin-genesis or regeneration by the *Spirit* (Genesis 1:1 and 1:2, and note the word "not" in Isaiah 45:18). The Holy Spirit is "hid in God" with every quality of God; His work was to restore the waste and formless vacuity of Genesis 1:2. The two recorded terrifying events of II Peter 3:5—7 cause some men to ask 'where is the promise of His coming"; and these wilfully forget that the heavens and the earth once perished by water, and are

---

1
    Excalibur, the legendary sword which King Arthur drew from the stone. *The Poetical Works of Alfred Lord Tennyson*, (N.Y., Crowell), pp. 203, 318, 372–375

now stored up with fire against the day of judgment. Water washes and dissolves. Out of invisible moulds comes the beauty of Isaiah 45:18, but out of fire comes the stones of emptiness (Isaiah 34:11). The Holy Spirit's work here is to maintain the invisible form of Genesis 1:1; to "brood" over and to "bring forth" anew as He does in Ezekiel 37.

(5) The Spirit's work is equally mysterious and more so at the birth and baptism of Jesus Christ and His Church:

  (*a*) Jesus was:

  Begotten of the Holy Spirit (Luke 1:35)
  Born in Bethlehem (Luke 2:11)
  Baptized with the Holy Spirit (Luke 3:22)

  (*b*) So the Church was:

  Begotten in the Upper Room of the Holy Spirit (John 20:22)
  Born upon the day of Pentecost (Acts 2)
  Baptized with the Holy Spirit that day (Acts 2:4)

b) The Holy Spirit's Work as COMFORTER and GUIDE

  (John 14:15—18, 25—27
  (John 16:7—15
Texts: (John 7:39
  (Romans 8:26—28
  (Acts 16:6—8

"And I will pray the Father,
and He shall give you another Comforter, [1]
that He may abide with you unto the age."

John 14:16 N.

With the taking away of the First Comforter (Christ), there is need for another Comforter to manifest God in this age of silence "to those having eyes to see." There is needed "another" like unto Christ in substance, obedience and purpose, and so we should expect to find parallels for He must take over or change the plan. The parallels prove that He took over, and so He is Christ's successor. Both Christ and the Holy Spirit:

  (1) were given:
    (*a*) Christ — John 3:16 and 10:10
    (*b*) Spirit — Acts 2:38, II Thessalonians 2:7

---

[1] Comforter: Gr. *Paraclete*, one alongside. Newberry (p. 92 N.T.): "Paraclete, one sent on behalf of another, or acting for another . . . ." This word is also used of Christ as our advocate (I John 2:1).

(2) came forth from God:
  (a) Christ — John 13:3
  (b) Spirit — II Thessalonians 2:7
(3) were full and "in the power of":
    both: Luke 4:1, John 20:22, Acts 2:4
(4) were not to "speak of Himself":
    both: John 12:49, John 16:13—14
(5) "gave gifts unto men":
    both: Ephesians 4:8, I Corinthians 12:7
(6) sent out disciples:
  (a) Christ, the Twelve (Matthew 10:5);
    and the Seventy (Luke 10:1)
  (b) Spirit, at Antioch (Acts 13:4);
    at Jerusalem (Acts 15:28);
    and at Ephesus (Acts 20:28)

The Holy Spirit "grooved" the Church as definitely and as accurately as the siderial bodies (Psalm 19). The book of Acts is the workshop of the Holy Spirit where the Lord's plan to propagate and perpetuate the Gospel of His Salvation is to be worked up into the Church. The Lord's plan is divinely implemented with *the Name*, which indicates the resources of enabling power available; with *Baptism* and *the Lord's Supper*, and with *the Person*, (the Holy Spirit) for "He shall take of Mine" and "not speak of Himself." Through Him is promised the *guidance*—"He will guide you"— and also the *language*—"in words which the Holy Spirit teacheth."

Consider the Holy Spirit's guidance of the Church (John 16:7—15), especially note verses 12—13:
  (1) In Acts 2, He controlled the speakers
  (2) In Acts 11, He names the disciples calling them Christians
  (3) In Acts 13, He calls missionaries
  (4) In Acts 15, He guides in decisions (vs. 28)
  (5) In Acts 16, He "bids" and "forbids"
  (6) In Romans 8:26—28, "He helpeth our infirmities"

In Paul's letter to the Galatians (2:15—21) is set forth to those "having eyes to see," the Church "atmosphered" by the Holy Spirit. It is "a house not made with hands" set down in the very center of man's incurable hunger for immortality (cf. *Revelation* chaps. 7—9). As the temple sat at the center of Jewry, and Daniel and others prayed toward it, so the Church is the center of all things today. To become disturbingly aware of this forever unsettles the self-satisfied and even if dimly discerned, the Galahad in us fares forth. At Pentecost there were men from everywhere. Then the Gospel united them into the Church and just as the Temple had been assembled without sound of hammer, so rose the Church: majestic, mysterious and transforming, a pearl from His open tomb. So quietly and silently was the Church formed that none of the early disciples realized that for which they were being prepared. The Holy Spirit makes the Church a wholly divine institution, divinely designed and divine in ownership, for Jesus called it "My Church." It is divine in composition, "My Body," and it is divine in its dimensions (Ephesians 3:18), even as are the earth (Isaiah 40:12), Noah's Ark and the Tabernacle.

The Holy Spirit is at His holiest best as we read Romans 8:26 concerning His work of grace; and you and I, aye, "the whole creation" are sharers in, and so debtors to, Him (I Corinthians 2:13). This bit of the universe is seemingly still out of harmony and step with the purpose of God, and yet prospering; but the spiritual framework under it is invisible and has often emerged, breaking through into literature, government and redemption. The writers of the Gospel and its converts are above the great of the earth.

The Holy Spirit is the controlling production in the Old and the New Testaments. He is not just arbitrarily laying hold here and there, but He chooses the "willing" and then directs and augments their power. Isaiah prays for help, and is seized and used; "holy (willing) men spake as they were borne along." Christ also was Spirit-directed. It is as though the Master went down in a diver's suit into the danger zone below, while the Holy Spirit is on deck directing, sounding the diving bell for the flesh's limitations, for "He humbled Himself" (Philippians 2:8).

The Holy Spirit is not responsible for character or virtue, *et al.* But whereas in Christ, the ministry was external, raising the dead, . . . the Spirit dwelt in the Church and is within—and so these spiritually dead are raised spiritually.

c) The Work of the Holy Spirit as

AUTHOR OF THE SCRIPTURES

(Isaiah 41:21—24
Texts: (I Corinthians 2:1—16
(Acts 10:19

We are trying to show the Author of this Book and that He planned and produced it and each part was perfect for its purpose. The Bible emerges unscathed from eighteen centuries of attack. As its central Factor stood silent before Pilate, so this Book waits, aye, invites such testing Isaiah 41:21—24).

Not one retreat has been sounded; not a battle has been lost; not one of a Company (its books) has been liquidated. It is consistent, sustained and surviving, and there is not one weakling writer of its sixty-six books.

All were used as reporters and their Supervisor is the Holy Spirit. Hear Peter and Paul say:

> "For the prophecy was borne not at any time by the will of man: but holy men of God spake borne along by the Holy Spirit."
>
> II Peter 1:21N.

> "All Scripture is God-inspired (or God-breathed), and is profitable for doctrine, for conviction, for correction, for discipline in righteousness:"
>
> II Timothy 3:16N.

And what was the purpose? "To know God and to enjoy Him forever"— "The joy of Thy salvation."

The Bible is an orchestrated composition upon such an exalted theme so chastely expressed in Psalm 19. The Holy Spirit is the conductor and author of this composition, the Word of God. In this Book there are spiritual wrestlings against invisible world rulers (Gr. *kosmokratos*).

Why, if given Christ and the Church, should not the Holy Spirit be inevitable?

> The Bible made inevitable Christ
> Christ made inevitable the Church
> The Church made inevitable the Comforter.

And the Scriptures are the Comforter's Book of:

> revelation (I Corinthians 2:10)
> instruction (II Timothy 3:16)
> guidance (John 16:13)

while the Holy Spirit Himself is the Oversee-er, the Sustainer and the Restrainer (II Thessalonians 2:7). The Author of the four Gospels, the Holy Spirit, has left us without excuse. That there is design, intelligence and development in them cannot be disputed nor quibbled; nor is there room for any confusion at this greatest of all transitions, that is, from Moses to Christ, from Law to Grace (Ephesians 2:8—10).

God is not the Author of confusion and He never has two concurrent plans. Especially is this so at the meeting of earth and the heavenlies in the Church. The two age-abiding peoples are Israel and the Church. The Lord's curse was upon Israel: "Your house is left unto you desolate"; and the blessing to the Church is promised in "in My Father's house are many mansions." John 1:11—12 identifies those receiving or rejecting Him. And in between these two "houses" He said, "It is finished." But to what was He referring? The law! (Colossians 2:14). Then Grace came in (Romans 8:34, Galatians 3:25—29). In John 20:22 the Church was "begotten" as was the Lord by the same Spirit. This Church was His Body to be born at Pentecost and it was at once taken over by the Holy Spirit and from this moment until the Rapture of the Church, the Holy Spirit is to have complete control (Galatians 1:8—9).

My personal conviction is that the Bible is the inspired revelation of God's Purpose and Plan in words, in persons, and in souls, and that within the Bible, the Holy Spirit has embodied all saving truth and through (up out of) such saving truth, there is a power which is efficient and sufficient for us to attain unto the end (Gr. *telos*, Isaiah 55:11). This conviction has "horizoned" my ministry. Paul wrote "preach the Word . . . fully carry out thy service." I am responsible unto God for the souls of those accepting the Word and must "exhort with all long-suffering and teaching" (II Timothy 4:2—5).

The "God-imposed burden" of I Corinthians 2:13 of "comparing spiritual things with spiritual" pre-supposes that God's revelation is accessible and easy to understand if rightly divided. Therefore a good minister of Christ Jesus must give attention to reading and prayer, thus "seeking the mind of Christ" and the indwelling of the Holy Spirit. Our fathers did this for their age as Moses did for his. And every age has its ministers of truth and that truth will fit the man of that age. It will not be for just a few or for a certain class but for all men who are willing to receive it (Acts 8:4). "The common people" have always "heard gladly," that is, understandingly.

3. The Gift and Presence of The Holy Spirit

Texts: (John 15:26—27
(John 16:7—15
(Acts 2:1—12, 16, 38

"Reverence is the atmosphere exhaled by a man
who is aware of the Presence of God. "

George W. Petter, "Yale Lecture"

The Gospel consists of (Facts to be believed
(Commands to be obeyed
(Promises to be enjoyed

All of these are present in the above texts: (The Facts of the resurrection
(The Commands to be baptized
(The Promise of the Holy Spirit

With the emphasis upon *The Promises*, this beyond-wonder offer is often eclipsed by the proximity of *The Command*. So much "sound and fury" is put forth upon the birth of a soul in baptism, that the still small voice is not discerned, but the newly born is God's concern and is most subject to the perversion of "incompetent" or "resisting" teachers. This is the place of the right start and of fixed ideals. This is the battle ground (Hebrews 2:1, Colossians 2:8). If ever any age was in need of such admonition that age is this present one where materialism is almost religion.

The Church is the tabernacle of the Holy Spirit whose every part is Christ-companioned (Matthew 28:20) and Spirit-"gifted" (Acts 2:38). If a Christian is not aware of this, then he needs Acts 19:2 N.:

> ". . . 'Did ye receive the Holy Spirit when ye believed?'
> And they said unto him, 'We have not so much as heard
> whether the Holy Spirit be come'."

There is a very great need to stir up the gift of the Holy Spirit.

The coming and abiding One is promised in Acts 1:4—5. The disciples were not to depart from Jerusalem but to wait for the promise of the Father. And they were told, "Ye shall be *baptized* in the Holy Spirit." The coming of the Holy Spirit took place in Acts 2:1—4 and His work of enduement is seen as "the disciples began to speak with other tongues as the Spirit gave them utterance." Then the *gift* of the Holy Spirit is promised in Acts 2:38. Here are three mentions of the Holy Spirit:

a) The first is when the disciples "receive" the Holy Spirit as Jesus breathes into them (John 20:22)

b) The second is the promise of the baptism of the Holy Spirit (Acts 1:5) which occurs in Acts 2:1—4 and Acts 10:44

c) And the third is the Gift of the Holy Spirit promised in Acts 2:38

To make these three clear and profitable to those seeking is the preacher's calling:

a) In John 20:22 there is given a new creation for a divine commission[1]

b) In Acts 2:4 and 10:44 were events like that of the baptism of Jesus when it was said to John the Baptist, "Upon whom thou shalt see the spirit descending and remaining on Him, the same is He which baptizeth with the Holy Spirit" (John 1:33), and, "the Holy Spirit descendeth in a bodily shape like a dove upon Him" (Luke 3:22). Both of these descendings of the Holy Spirit at the baptism of Jesus and in Acts 2 and 10 were *temporary* signs. The abiding and permanent presence of the Holy Spirit is declared in John 3:34

c) Now we come up to the text of Acts 2:38. Note the words "every one of you" (individuals); and "*ye* (the collective group, the corporate body) shall receive . . ." John 20:22 was for the

---

[1] See Section FOUR, *Abraham to Christ's Spiritual Body*, MY Story, VIII. The Begetting of the Spiritual Body of Christ, pp. 310—313

Twelve; Acts 2:4 and 10:44 was upon the whole Body; and Acts 2:38 is for each individual and would include those who are "the least" or the ones who are the "are nots" of I Corinthians 1:26. Each individual requires and receives personal adjustment by the Holy Spirit.

Spiritual insight is the most essential of all, and it is the least cultivated. The works of the flesh are as at death, the work of unravelling, dissolving, centrifugal. While life pushes up through nature and covers tree and man with beauty, "take knowledge" for the fruit of the Spirit is manifest at blossom time. When we see the bloom we scarcely notice the trees; so also man loses his identity when the fruit of the Spirit blossoms forth; and they that are of Christ have crucified the flesh for it is fertilizer of the spiritual. "If we live by the Spirit, let us also walk by the (same) Spirit," and not "become vain-glorious so provoking, envying one another."

Do we appreciate what occurs at baptism (Galatians 3:27—28)? Baptism is into one Body (Ephesians 4:4—5) and that Body is Christ (I Corinthians 12:13). Here we are buried and resurrected, becoming conformed to His Image as we receive the Gift of the Holy Spirit. The Spirit indwells the whole body, blessing and empowering each member and thus the newly born Church in *Acts* became the Spirit's Tabernacle. When Christ ascended He gave gifts perfecting His Body. No thoughtful mind could consider the Church or compare it with any other institution without being impressed by its Leadership. Such a Body, so diverse in elements must be motivated by an heavenly Guest (Ghost) in order to function acceptably. The Holy Spirit has the "pattern," "authority," and the "wisdom" and He needs our cooperation and yielding.

I Corinthians 12 is devoted to Him and this chapter outlines His work of Omnipotence as He "divided to everyone severally even as He will":

a) Verses 1—3, "no man can say that Jesus is Lord but by the Holy Spirit"

b) Verses 4—6, the Spirit gives, the Lord adjusts the workers, and God supplies the energy

c) Verses 7—10, there are three classes:

  (1) verse 8, the Word of wisdom and knowledge

  (2) verses 9—10a, there is faith, gifts of healing; working of miracles, prophecy and the discerning of spirits (I Corinthians 14:32)

  (3) verse 19b, there are tongues and interpretations (I Corinthians 14:5, 27—28)

Gift: A careful distinction should be made between the *Gift* or the personal Presence of the Holy Spirit to each Christian, and the

Gifts of the Holy Spirit which are related to miracles, prophecy, speaking with tongues, healings and other manifestations. Gifts were given to confirm the Word (Mark 16:20); these Gifts were given originally to the apostles when they were "endued" with the Holy Spirit; then they in turn could transfer these gifts to those on whom they laid their hands (Acts 8:17—18); but these on whom *they* laid their hands were unable to transfer the gifts to others. When the last one on whom the apostles had laid their hands and to whom they had given these special gifts had died, then these gifts passed away (I Corinthians 13:8—10).

d) The Church as a Body is set forth in verse 12

e) And that we are baptized into One Body is seen in verses 13—18

f) "God hath set the members . . . every one of them in the Body as it hath pleased Him" verse 28 ff.: apostles, prophets, and teachers, miracles, gifts of healings, helps, governments, and tongues. In Ephesians 4 they are set forth as apostles, prophets, evangelists and teachers.

The contrast between the desire for spiritual gifts and the more perfect way, the way of transcendance which is love (John 3:16) is seen in John's Gospel, chapters 12, 13? 14; and love leads us to I Corinthians 14:4N.:

> "He that speaketh in an unknown tongue edifieth himself; but he that prophesieth edifieth the church."

And so today there is such an One who continues as an energizing, informing spirit; "The Gift of the Holy Spirit!" What riches of grace in Christ Jesus! Our analysis of this gift enhances it:

a) "The Gift" posits personality for we can only give one's self in part or wholly. All you possess is acquired through taste, so the Body was made a gift of God (John 4:10) and a gift of the Spirit. As a father gives his daughter away, so God gave first His Son, and then the Holy Spirit. Think of what God has "denied" Himself!

b) "The Holy Spirit" on Pentecost changed residence even as the Lord had done thirty years before, "Lo, a Body hast Thou prepared for Me." And,

(1) He indwells the Church as man does his body, though much diseased and even though there are dead parts in it.
   "The fruit of the spirit is love" (Galatians 5:22); and contains joy, peace, *et al.* Just as the fruit of Spring is life; and life contains grace, flowers, crops (see 1 Corinthians 13)

(2) The sorrows of God for Israel, the Cross and Christians are expressed by the Holy Spirit "with groanings which cannot

be uttered." This sorrow is too deep for words; and "there is no speech without their voice being heard" (Psalm 19); and in these groanings is expressed the eloquence of God. Think of the Spirit's and the Lord's "emptying" for these nineteen hundred years!

(3) What is the purpose of this "en-ek-klesia-zation"—this entrance of a higher or better informed, into our physical nature? The purpose is really to draw out the Church and to present it perfect (Ephesians 5:27). He indwells and so contacts every member. He informs, that is edifies or forms within; and He takes the latent, sleeping ones and breathes into them and builds or erects a temple (Ephesians 2:22).

Note: As an executive pervades every compartment of his plant; so, "in Him we live, and move and have our being."

Each several part partakes of the total as heat would reduce brick, but in the diffusion each receives his portion and supplies every need "till we all attain unto the stature of the fulness of Christ."

Thus the Spirit's growing ministry to the Church is the fulfilling of the Lord's last request:

a) "That they all may be one . . . that the world
may believe . . . and know"

b) "That they may behold My Glory"
(cp. I John 3:1—3; and II Thessalonians 1:10)

> May these His last requests to which
> The Holy Spirit is committed,
> Stir our evangelistic fervor,
> And become our consuming desire.

4. The Price of Power: Tarrying.

("Tarry till . . . clothed with power . . ." (Luke 24:49)
Texts: ("Wait for the Promise of the Father . . ." (Acts 1:4)
("These all continued . . . in prayer . . ." (Acts 1:14).

This group of disciples were waiting for Power, some of which was to be revealed at Pentecost and some at the Lord's return in Glory and they were as "a handful of corn upon the mountains" (Psalm 72:16); and these were the prologue of the Church. In them is set forth the end "to be," a glimpse of heaven. They are samples in the small of what the millennium is to be. Then the whole earth will be an "Upper Room." When those of any age shall go up to these, there another Pentecost will come and the New Jerusalem shall descend for we shall draw it down.

A biologist studies a germ and this group is the "germ" of the heavenly things to be revealed in the last times. They were men of like passions and would not always live up to Pentecost, but they did, and therefore it is still possible. And so the command is to tarry. A biologist's character is not necessarily a part of his equipment, but a Christian's character *is* a part of *his* equipment, for souls are material and the attitude of the soul determines the results.

These Pentecostans were Scripture-grounded for they had been three years with Jesus, so we too must be grounded. After Pentecost's enduement, they ceased "tarrying." We must tarry until we get in step with God. All who are neglectful of "tarrying" are not satisfied, for God and the "tarried" soul are at one and they become a part of the timeless mind "forgetting those things which are behind." They were to "tarry" until they forgot and were rid of the past with its tyranny of sin, traditions and law:

> Build thee more stately mansions, O my soul,
>   As the swift seasons roll!
>   Leave thy low-faulted past!
> Let each new temple, nobler than the last,
> Shut thee from heaven with a dome more vast,
>   Till thou at length art free,
> Leaving thine outgrown shell by life's unresting sea! [1]

Mark the prize, "tarry till." We are rushing into shallowness; we have time for novels, the daily paper and dissipation, but little or no time for the deeper things.

Paul paid the price; he "tarried" three years in Arabia which may seem like a waste of time, but see the result of his tarrying—*Mastery*. The poverty of the Church today is caused by the absence of "tarrying." The endued, those who have "tarried," are known by name in heaven. To the tarrying apostle, the Lord says, "Rise, *Peter*, kill and eat" (Acts 10:13). And Ananias is told to "go . . . inquire . . . for one called *Saul* of Tarsus, for behold, he prayeth" (Acts 9:11).

Jesus stopped when a woman touched the hem of His garment and it is even so now when we touch heaven. Those who stood sky-gazing were rebuked by the angel, "Why stand ye here gazing up into heaven?" But those who are sky-touching, tarrying, are blessed though not seeing but believing (John 20:29).

5. The Holy Spirit and Pentecost [2]

Texts:
(Acts 1:6—11
(Acts 2:1—4

---

[1] Oliver Wendell Holmes, *The Chambered Nautilus*, (Cambridge, Mass., Houghton, Mifflin and Company, Riverside Press), Vol. I, stanza 5

[2] See this Section FIVE: II, The Birth of the Lord's Spiritual Body, Pentecost, p.344 ff.

Having arrived at Pentecost, the devout mind "can give attention" only to the phenomena accompanying the induction of the Holy Spirit into the Vice-gerency. His commands are imperative and final and take precedence over all others, for they annul and abbrogate all others and they include the orders of the Christ who finished the Law. Christ appointed the Spirit and He, the Holy Spirit, is an additional force; yet our first concern is to fully "lay hold" upon this transfer of leadership so that every appeal from now on will not be "back to Christ," but "back to Pentecost." Whatever the world's explanation might be, there is a dominant body of spiritual influences that cannot be ignored whose rise was at *this* Pentecost:

> *a*) Because a resurrected, reigning Lord was proclaimed at Pentecost, our calendar dates have been set to a new meaning: B.C. versus A.D. [1]
>
> *b*) Racial lines are obliterated as illustrated by the Ethiopian, Cornelius and Saul
>
> *c*) And the days of the week are re-assigned in importance as the day of Worship is moved from the *seventh* day of the week, to the *first* day of the week, Sunday. [2]

Besides all of these, there is given a new *object* of worship, a new Law of salvation and a new *method* of forgiveness, and there is access to the Presence of the Almighty God. One who has intelligently evaluated *this* Pentecost, can in truth say, "I have seen strange things this day."

The day of Pentecost, "the great day of history" is impressive because of the events recorded concerning it. In the City of Jerusalem and its environs, there were assembled at least four million worshippers, and in "The Upper Room" there was assembled a "little flock." Each of these two groups were expectant of the morrow, Pentecost, for it was an High Day. Then is heard the sound of "a rushing mighty wind" and the vacant streets of the city begin to fill. The "little flock" witness the descent of "red" tongues as of fire, and the *multitudes* are distinguished by "red" hands from the shedding of His blood (Acts 5:28).

The two explanations of events of Pentecost (the "little flock" and the "multitudes") are so true of today that they must be a true transcript of the events of that day. The multitude said concerning the "little flock": "these men are full of new wine." They are like the multitude of today who:

---

[1] See Philip Mauro, *The Chronology of the Bible,* "The Christian Era," (N.Y. Doubleday and Co., Inc. 1922), p. 103

[2] For source of the name "Sunday" and other names of days, see App. "E" *Zodiac, 6. The Sabbatic Week and the Stars . . .* p. 615

> "Drunk with the sight of power,
> Loose wild tongues that have not Thee in awe."

> Kipling

But Peter, the gospel preacher of the "little flock," said, "these men are not drunk as ye suppose but this is that which was spoken of by the prophet Joel" (Joel 2:28–32) and through His servant, God has:

> "Loosed the fateful lightning of His terrible swift sword"

and the "loosed sword" of that day overcame the "loosed tongues" of three thousand who received the Word and were baptized.

Pentecost was a day of Wave Loaves (Leviticus 23:9–21). The feast of "first fruits" came near the time of the Passover and from the grain offered at the feast of first fruits, loaves were made at Pentecost. At the Passover there was no leaven and so "Christ our Passover," the "first fruits of them that slept" is unleavened. But this feast, Pentecost, there is leaven in the two loaves which are offered, for these are typical of the Church and the two loaves represent the Jew and the Gentile. Man can put leaven *into* bread but only God can *remove* it, and so man can put sin into himself but only God can remove it, and the two leavened loaves at Pentecost become one unleavened bread in the Church:

> "Purge out therefore the old leaven, that ye may be a new lump, according as ye are unleavened. For even Christ our passover was sacrificed for us: Therefore let us keep the feast, not with old leaven, neither with the leaven of malice and wickedness; but with the unleavened bread of sincerity and truth."

> I Corinthians 5:6–8N.

> "Now all these things happened unto them for types: and they are written for our admonition, upon whom the ends of the ages arrived."

> I Corinthians 10:11N.

And this unleavened body, the Church, will be the first fruits of the grave at the Lord's return (I Corinthians 15:3, I Thessalonians 4:16–17, Revelation 20:5).

That night at the close of this eventful day of Pentecost, the Christ was "in heaven clothed upon with His house from heaven," while on earth the Holy Spirit tabernacled in the infant Church, His Body, and so began the long struggle.

As we consider the events of Pentecost, we realize anew that the purpose and plans of God are measured and as accurate as the stars (James 1:17). The awesomeness of God's inevitableness is set forth in all of the Scriptures (Ecclesiastes 12:1, 14, Galatians 6:7, Job 5:26b, Luke 9:51). Even Jesus felt this as He "set His face to go up to Jerusalem." There is not a chance of retard or speeding up, to add to or to take from, God's purpose. All the events of God are measured (metered). "Even the hairs of your head are numbered"; and the Lord Himself said "I must"—the "night cometh"—and "Mine hour is come." For there was no un-needed minute in His ministry.

And to Christians is measured out the waiting for the Lord's return (I Thessalonians 4:14). Thus "when the day of Pentecost was being fulfilled," there rose up into finishedness, the ordained events of God's own purpose.

> May that brooding Presence of Genesis 1:2,
> This Gift Distributor of The Mystery of God,
> Be the Holy Guest of every welcoming heart;
> And may He become consciously present in our lives.

Section FIVE: THE CHURCH—MY STORY

VI. "THE THINGS WHICH HAVE BEEN FULLY ESTABLISHED

AMONG US" (Luke 1:1 A.S.V.m*)

THE VITAL DOCTRINES OF SALVATION

Page

E. THE LORD'S TABLE

* *Marginal reference*

VI. "THE THINGS WHICH HAVE BEEN FULLY ESTABLISHED

AMONG US" (Luke 1:1 A.S.V.m) — THE VITAL DOCTRINES

OF SALVATION

E. THE LORD'S TABLE

> Perhaps at first they talked of little things
> At supper-time that evening in the spring—
> The upper room was dim with candle-shine
> As Jesus sat with twelve remembering.
> Then quietly He said, "There is one here
> Whose kiss will bring betrayal by and by."
> They did not look at Judas curiously
> But each man murmured, "Master, is it I?"
>
> Each one looked inward, frightened lest he find
> A shoddy place where he had dreamed of steel.
> None placed the guilt on any other guest
> Who had partaken of that gracious meal . . .
> When there are hungry on my little street,
> When I see tears or hear a heart's hurt cry
> Because some one has failed to keep high faith,
> May I, too, murmur, "Master, is it I?"[1]

Text: I Corinthians 11:23—26

The marvel of this event is so wonderful that it numbs the imagination. Here in a borrowed Upper Room ordinary men with a "Son of Man" begin a book of martyrs, and a church of "common people" is launched in an Empire which is mistress of the world. Imperial Rome faded, but the spires of the church circle the whole earth.

The great laws of God are anchored in eternity woven upon the loom of the Universe. Here first, we are at "The breaking of the bread" and we contact the basic *kratos* (Power) that makes for righteousness which is unveiled upon the Cross (John 3:16). Here we see the Saviour, the Sustainer (Colossians 1:17), and here His Blood is first seen. This is God's greatest and last supreme bid for our hearts. This, the Table of Memory, is linked to the Fourth Commandment. In each (the Table and the Sabbath), there is need for the proper preparation, observance and perpetuation (Luke 9:23), for we are "no longer children tossed to and fro" (Ephesians 4:14), but we are:

> "Not forsaking the assembling of ourselves together, even as
> the manner of some is; but exhorting one another and so much
> the more, as ye see the day approaching."
>
> Hebrews 10:25 N.

---

[1] Helen Welshimer, *Singing Drums*, "The Last Supper" (N.Y. E.P. Dutton and Co., Inc.)

1. The Lord's Table in Type and Shadow

   a) At Eden

Always there has been a Presence Table (I Corinthians 10:4, John 6:33). God's people have never been without it. It was this right which each felt "to appear before God in Zion" (Psalm 84:7) that gave significance to the Presence Bread. This is well known but even more significant and less known is the first place of worship in Genesis 3:24. Here we read that "God placed" (Hebrew *shaken*, caused to tabernacle) at the East Gate of the Garden of Eden, cherubim and a flaming sword . . ." and this was the Shekinah glory which tabernacled upon or covered the altar; for the altar was a place of worship where the worshippers appeared "before" the face of the Lord (Genesis 4:16). Here is where Cain and Abel brought their offerings. Here also Rebecca (Genesis 25:22), Abraham and others were to inquire before the Lord, that is, to worship, for here was a Table, a Presence [1] (Bread) of the Lord.

There were three rejections of God by man: one at Eden, the second at Sinai; and the third at Golgotha. God said, "They will reverence My Son," but the nation of Israel refused "to have this man to reign over us." And these things bring into solemn review the consequences that followed—for Eve, it was the curse; for Israel, it was the yoke of bondage; and to the nation of Israel at the Cross, it was, "His blood be upon us and upon our children."

In Eden Jehovah Elohim created man naked knowing only good and being "not ashamed," until the more subtle brazen serpent (Philippians 3:20) promised him that he would live forever as Satan does. So He drove out the man and He "placed" (Genesis 3:24) "in a tent of meeting" cherubim over an altar. This was a meeting house, "a house of prayer for all of the nations"; and Adam could say, "Here, O my Lord, I see Thee face to face." Later we read:

> "God shall enlarge Japheth, and he shall dwell in
> the *tents* of Shem; and Canaan shall be his servant."

This is the plural of Majesty: Japheth reared empires and hypothesized his religions but the God of Shem, David's Son, "built Him an house"; but first He dwelt in the tent (tabernacle) of Shem.

   b) In The Passover and Other Feasts

The Passover Feast was accepted by Israel in Egypt and their baptism in the Red Sea followed (I Corinthians 10:1). But the true Passover, Christ, was rejected by Israel and they were cast out (Acts 3:21).

---

[1] "Presence," Heb. *panim*, "face or countenance"; also "showbread," Numbers 4:7.

The Passover Feast in the closing chapters of the Gospel was the occasion of the multitudes filling Jerusalem and as the milling throng passed in the street outside, they were unaware that in the "Upper Room" the breaking of a bit of unleavened bread and the passing of the last cup was taking place, ending forever a ritual of fifteen hundred years. And these multitudes were tolerated by the Master for His "little flock" in the Upper Room, for it was His "Mine Hour."

Concerning the Passover, the Lord commanded that the blood was to be on the lintels and all the family were to be in the house, and this was voluntary and of free will. So Christ, our Passover, and the Cross are the door to the Church and it is still voluntary (Ephesians 3:18).

The Passover and John 3:16 were complimentary for they contain a world outlook. The Lord's Passover for Israel protected the first born of man and beast that came out of Egypt the night of their deliverance, and this looks in expectation to the hour when "Christ our Passover is sacrificed for us." Here we see in its fulness "God so *loved* the world" and *this* Passover is for all who are born anew and it extends into all the world. Now "Mine Hour is come" and the Master says, "*this* (bread—not *that* lamb), is *My Body*."

The Passover Lamb brought remembrance year by year of that one night of the Lord's deliverance out of Egypt for the nation of Israel, and now the Communion Table becomes a place of remembrance for the deliverance of all men which was purchased by the Lord "one day upon the Cross." At the Passover and the feast of first fruits, only that which was *unleavened*, could be offered, but at Pentecost two *leavened* loaves were offered. At the Last Supper we see the transfer from the Lamb to the Loaf; and then at once *after* supper, the New Covenant is instituted. Here, to those who are discerning, it becomes *raison d'etere*, or "reason for coming together" (Acts 20:7); and if we discern not the Body, "we eat and drink condemnation to ourselves." These things give significance to Paul's strong words: "Let a man prove himself"; and, "for this cause many are weak and sickly among you and not a few sleep" (I Corinthians 11:28, 30 A.S.V.). There is life in the Communion but not always in the preaching.

A study of Leviticus 23 introduces us to "the feasts of Jehovah" which later become "the feast of the Jews." The following days and events of the worship of Israel are found in this chapter:

(1) The Sabbath, verse 3, is for every people.
   God's laws are not just arbitrary but are beneficial, fitted to the soul, the body and the spirit

(2) The Passover, verses 4—5.
   This is "The Lord's" versus "The Jews'" (John 2:13 and 11:55)

(3) The feast of "Unleavened bread," verses 6—8.

Note that the Passover and the feast of "Unleavened Bread" take place in the spring; and these are separate from the latter feasts

(4) The Feast of First Fruits, verses 9—14.

No calendar date is attached to this feast or the next one.

(5) The Feast of Pentecost, verses 15—21.

Here two leavened wave loaves were offered

(6) The Feast of Trumpets, verses 23—25.

These point to the Rapture

(7) The Day of Atonement, verses 26—32.

This day has its fulfillment at Armageddon

(8) The Feast of Tabernacles, verses 33—36.

"Holiness unto the Lord of hosts"; "and punishment unto all nations that come not up to keep the feast of tabernacles." These seven Jewish feasts from Passover to the Feast of Tabernacles (see Exodus 23:14—17, Leviticus 23) have been eclipsed. Christ, "the first fruits of them that slept," nailed the law to His Cross but hidden away within these feasts was the Lord's Supper. In I Corinthians 10:6—11, and especially in 11:23, is Paul's basis of understanding the Mystery. If we are apprehending this Mystery, we are now ready to appreciate the importance of the Lord's Supper which was so long over-shadowed and was so intimately related to the spiritual.

In his book "The Gospel of the Glory," Dr. Massee of Tremont Temple (Boston) says of Psalm 19:1: "There Christ was sacrificed; there is the true tabernacle. There is the Table!" Here is the heavenly proof or the suggestion: Jesus said, "This Passover." Joshua's long day took the calendar off one day (Psalm 19:1). The Jews neglected to give God the glory and so lost step with Him. Jesus ate at the exact time. So must we if we participate (commune) with the Lamb. There has been controversy over "this" Passover, but spiritual sensitivity will show that the shadow was displaced by substance; and that which was observed at the time of Jesus' sacrifice was "the Jews' Passover" (John 2:13, 11:55) and was part of the Jews' religion (Galatians 1:13—14, see Matthew 22:29, Jude 13). The Passover Feast contained unleavened bread whereas at Pentecost two leavened loaves were offered. Christ, our Passover, who was without sin —unleavened—said, "This is My Body which is given for you." At Pentecost, the Church began and the Lord "added" both Jew and Gentile, two *leavened* loaves, together into ONE Joint Body and they became ONE UNleavened bread. These leavened loaves, sinful men, were cleansed by the Blood of the Cross, and so the many became ONE Bread and ONE Body (I Corinthians 10:17, Ephesians 4:4, 1:23, Galatians 3:27). And today, through the Communion of the Body of Christ (I Corinthians 10:16), there is participation of that Body and this dissolves races and sects into the One Body as we eat in memory.

The Lord gave to the Communion Table a high and transcendent purpose when He instituted it (Ephesians 3:12, II Timothy 1:9); and to Paul it was a Holy Home-sickness (Philippians 1:23—26). We cannot too often tarry in remembrance at the Table. If the Lord had "desire" and if Paul took time for it, and both were under stress (the Lord with His set face, and Paul hastening, Acts 20:13—16, 22—23 "by land"), then should we also be faithful. The Savior said, "This IS My Body" (cf. Exodus 12:12, 41). Thus we read, "the self same day" and both must be ready on time. This is a New Testament in blood and that blood sprinkled door is Cherubim-guarded. The Body is vicarious; the blood is vitalizing; as grapes when pressed out, the juice is life-sustaining. Thus, a testator dies but his estate keeps his heirs. First came the Lamb in Egypt and then later the Law at Sinai. The Lord said, "I will pass through the land of Egypt this night" and at once, irrevocably, He passed over. In the Upper Room, He said, "This is My Body" and His Body is laid upon the Altar of His Deity (Matthew 23:19, I Corinthians 9:13, Hebrews 13:10, I Timothy 6:13); and we read that three days later in this same Upper Room, "He breathed upon (into) *them* (John 20:22, cf. margin Genesis 2:7), that is *His Body* so "they were added to the Lord" (Acts 2:41—47, 5:14, 11:24). Thus the Lamb of God came first; then the Law; later at Pentecost "The New Testament in My Blood" was added, that is, stored up, made safe and was applied on the lintels (the Cross) of the Church. These things above, develop the place and importance of the Lord's Table and so make clear the Savior's concern. We can also see how it is of like importance to Paul through his Epistles.

c) In The Tabernacle

A type of the Church is seen in the Holy Place of the tabernacle and here within the holy place is found:

> (1) The seven-branched lampstand—a type of the Scriptures
> (2) The altar of incense—a type of prayer
> (3) The table of showbread—a type of communion

This Holy Place was like an insert or a parenthesis for it was of no significance to the Mosiac religion, and the High Priest passed through the Holy Place unconscious of its real significance (Hebrews 11:40); and prophets and angels tried to look in to its meaning (I Peter 1:10—12). The raptured Church leaves the order of the temple worship unmarred as it is taken away (Revelation 11:1). The showbread of the tabernacle was literally the Bread of the Faces; and so here at the Communion Table, we renew this "face to face fellowship" through the breaking of the Bread.

The Church and its ordinances are central. In the holy place of the tabernacle were the Table, the Lampstand and the Altar of Incense; and within the Church is the Communion Table, the Bible and prayer. Jesus said, "No one cometh unto the Father but *through* Me," just as no one could approach the Holy of Holies but *through* the holy place in the tabernacle. In Hebrews 10:20 we are shown that Christ through His flesh made a way open which in a new and living way and through this "way," His flesh, the Church has entered into the heavenlies; but this veil of flesh remains a veil before the nation of Israel yet today, for they accept Him only as a man and not as The Son of God. Our obligation is to pray for Israel and thus we may remove the veil that is between us and them (II Corinthians 3:12–18).

Baptism opens the way for God to enter. Faith is born out of Deity bearing about His dead body but the Table transcends all of these. It is set at the center of the tabernacle; here Ephesians 4:4 is itself as secret as Romans 8:28. We eat and drink in our Father's House with Him, seated in Christ. The Table is set at the center of the heaven of heavens with a "Lamb slain from the foundation" as the sacrifice (Hebrews 9:23–24). As the Table was central in shadow or type, so must it be in the substance. It has been moved out of its place from the heavenly to the earthly by our ideas of it, by our failure to take heed to The Word. Here is the beginning of tradition and apostasy.

> "For as often as ye eat this bread,
> and drink this cup,
> ye do proclaim the Lord's death till He come."

I Corinthians 11:23N.

"Be still and know that I am God: . . ."

Psalm 46:10a

This is the hour of self examination. There are two outlooks from the Communion Table: Alpha, backward, "in remembrance of Me"; and Omega, forward, proclaiming the Lord's death till He come. The Table is central in time, for we are *remembering backward* almost two thousand years; and we are *looking forward* till those two thousand years are ended. The Table was in the Tabernacle in the Holy Place; to the East was the Court and to the West was the Most Holy Place; and the Table sat upon the side of the North in the Holy Place. In Exodus 40 in describing the tabernacle contents, there is first the Ark of the Testimony, and then the Table and the Bread upon it before the Lampstand and the Altar of Incense. It seems like the Table should have come last. Human wisdom would have taken in the lampstand first. May it not be that here Moses became a bit careless, and because of his "unworthy manner" God stopped and rebuked him?

> "According as Moses was admonished of God when he was about to complete the tabernacle; for, 'See!' saith He, 'thou make all things according to the pattern showed thee in the mount!'"

This same divine oversight was manifest toward both the tabernacle and the Church. The Table is the *prothesis* (The Bread of Faces). How long God had looked upon this Table! Zangwill's phrase "The eternal insomnia of God" (Psalm 121:3–4) so fitly expresses God's vigilance. God's earth outlook is through the Table, the Cross, and the Church, and He cannot touch us without The Son. Only "Worthies" can really sit at the Table and partake; "let each one examine himself and so let him eat."

Abraham saw the Lord's first coming (John 8:56) and Paul wrote, "I received" His second coming. We also sit before Him if garmented in the glory of His Resurrection Day and we as Thomas see Deity through wounds. Poor Pilate saw only "the man," but blessed Thomas said, "My Lord and my God!" To us today, He says, "What came YE forth to see!"

2. The Lord's Table Established in The Upper Room [1]

a) The Preparation for the Passover

The Lord's Supper is a "Communion of the Blood and Body of Christ." If we are to be edified there is a need for definiteness when "searching the Scriptures." The set feasts of the Bible with their time and element are all clearly set forth in Leviticus 23.

These are the events surrounding the preparation for the observance of this last Passover:

> (1) It was on the day when the Passover must be killed (Luke 22:7)
> (2) The disciples spoke of it first (Matthew 26:17, Mark 14:12, Luke 22:8) for they were formalists and they were concerned about observing the Jewish law
> (3) He sent Peter and John saying "Go and prepare us the Passover that (Gr. *hina*) we may eat." They were directed to a man with a pitcher who would show them a guest chamber where Jesus said, "I shall eat the Passover."

b) The Ending of the Passover

This annual feast of the Jews commemorating the deliverance of the first born of Israel in Egypt, was brought to a conclusion by the One fulfilling the type of the Passover Lamb (I Corinthians 5:7). We read, "The hour was come and He sat down with His disciples and said, 'With desire

---

[1] See Section FOUR, *Abraham to Christ's Spiritual Body*, MY Story, G. "Mine Hour" 1. The Upper Room, and 2. The Lord's Table, pp. 284–289

have I desired to eat *this* Passover' . . . ." Note that He said *this* Passover, not the Communion. In Luke 22:14—16 and in Matthew 26:26, we read "As *they* were eating . . . ." This would include the Lord, and therefore, He observed, that is, partook of and participated in the Passover in the evening at the beginning of the day; and at its close, the next afternoon, He Himself became "our Passover" (Hebrews 9:26).

In Matthew 26:26—30, Mark 14:22—26, and Luke 22:14—18, the ending of the old Passover Feast takes place. Jesus said, "I will not drink henceforth of this fruit of the vine until that day when I drink it NEW with you in my Father's Kingdom." [1] This will be fulfilled when Luke 22:29—30 has been brought to pass. Today Israel has been cast off but is to return and the Passover as a memorial of their national life will always be necessary even as our July Fourth. Note that in these above passages, the Lord says, "This is My Body and this is My Blood," but He makes no mention of continuing to do this "in remembrance of" Him. This is the ending of the old Passover and now He is ready to establish His Table of Remembrance.

c) The Institution of the Table of Remembrance

The Supper is instituted at the end of the Passover and at once He took bread—not the lamb—and He said, "Take, eat, this is My Body which is given for you." "This do in remembrance of Me." It was a finished fact which was past. The Bread is for ALL and so Judas partook of the bread (John 13:26 and vs. 2); and Judas was the first to "remember" (Matthew 27:3—4). May this not be why Luke records the announcement by Jesus of His betrayal? (Luke 22:21). Judas goes out after taking "the sop" and Jesus says, "Now is the Son of Man glorified" (John 13:31). He washes their feet and to Peter He said, "if I wash thee not, thou hast no part with Me" (Acts 1:17).

"Likewise also the Cup after supper, saying, 'This cup is the New Testament, (or New Covenant) in My blood which is shed for you'" (Luke 22:20). These events of the establishing of the Table of Remembrance are found in Luke 22:19—20 and I Corinthians 11:23—26. The Passover Lamb was to "show forth" till Jesus, our Passover, came. Now the Lord's Supper will show forth till He come.

Unless a distinction is made between the events recorded in Matthew 26:26—30, Mark 14:22—26, and Luke 22:14—18, and the event recorded in Luke 22:19—20 and I Corinthians 11:23—26, there is confusion as to what actually took place. One distinction to be made in "discerning the things

---

[1] See Section SIX, *The Kingdom Age*, E. The Reign of Righteousness and Peace, Millennial Age, 3. The New Covenant with the House of Israel, p. 564

that differ" is to note: when the *old feast* was being ended, He BLESSED the bread, and GAVE THANKS for the cup. But now as He establishes *His* Table of Remembrance, *after* supper, He GIVES THANKS for the Bread, and it is evident that He BLESSES the Cup (I Corinthians 10:26). The Greek word *eulogesas* means to ask God's blessing upon; and the Greek word *eucharisteasas* means to give thanksgiving for. Here are two entirely different phrases, or else the Lord would not have so separated them. In Mark 6:41 at the feeding of the five thousand, the loaves and fishes were blessed at one time.

This Table is to be in the midst of His Church and is to be continued until He comes again. We must study the Lord's teaching in regard to the significance of the Supper to get closely what He intended; then "as often as ye eat this *Bread* and drink this *Cup*, ye do show the Lord's death till He come":

> (1) The loaf (Bread) is vicarious for He replaces the lamb: holy, harmless, undefiled. He tasted death (Hebrews 2:9) and drew the poison out of Pentecost's leavened loaves; this we should "remember."
>
> (2) The Cup of the New Testament is "as often as ye do this . . . ye do show forth till He come."

To Israel He said, "I will not any more eat thereof . . . I will not drink of the fruit of the vine until the Kingdom of God shall come." To the Church He said, "*you* do show forth the Lord's death till He come." Mark especially that it is "you." He said, "with desire have I desired . . . before I suffer"; and we read, "Who for the joy that was set before Him, endured . . ."; and He prayed, "restore unto Me the glory . . ."; and Peter wrote, "the suffering and glory to follow." So we, "if any come after Me" are at the Table before our week of testimony to the joy that is here set before us.

Baptism and Communion are both personal, for they concern the Lord and you alone. A slighted Table is a hurt to Him for "could ye not watch one hour?" Israel is blind and helpless and waits, wholly dependent upon us, as does also the Lord's coming which is contingent upon our zeal; the "falling away" delays His coming. The only Scriptural reason for our being here, is found in Acts 20:7. We are *ek-klesia-ed* (called out) to "break bread" and then "sent forth" to evangelize.

An army advances upon its stomach and the supply line is the lifeline and must be kept open whatever the hazard (John 5:58). This Table is that nourishment of which He spoke and when it is broken, life declines. Here we find the most definite details of time, place and purpose of any of our Lord's commands.

(1) By WHOM was it given?

> By the Lord (I Corinthians 11:23). Those who were apostles had to meet the conditions of Acts 1:22 and so there is no possibility of error in the record of these inspired men.

(2) WHEN was it given?

> (*a*) "In the night in which He was betrayed"; and the Table was not in force until Israel rejected Him, and the curtain was rent, and John 29:22 had taken place; for God's covenant laws are *consecutive*, never *concurrent*.
>
> (*b*) The Passover, the most patriotic of Jewish feasts, was brought to fulfillment in the Upper Room, but is to be restored (Matthew 26:29). "After Supper," i.e. the ending of the Passover, the Table is instituted.
>
> (*c*) "The Bread" (Hebrews 9:23, 36) is back to the Cross and is the "Once-for-all" sacrifice (I Corinthians 2:2), but we must remember Hebrews 13:8 and that what He once did, He would do again. The Bread is as far as many get. "The Cup" is the life (see John 15, cf. Ephesians 2:6), and the Cup looks forward.

The Bread is back to the Cross and the Cup is forward to the Rapture. This is the only divinely instituted feast for this Age; and it is a memorial to His absence. This Table continues up to the Rapture in II Thessalonians 2:1 and is only for baptized believers, awaiting the Lord from heaven.

3. The Lord's Table in the Book of Acts

Pentecost gives us the story of the erection of the Church and the first furnishing of the "Table of the Lord." In Acts 2:42 "the disciples continued steadfastly in the breaking of the bread" which is to be distinguished from that of the 26th verse when they broke bread at home, indicating that this was the eating of daily food.

And we read, "upon the first day of the week when the disciples came together to break bread"—indicating that this was the primary motive and purpose bringing them together.

To a home and loved family, the evening meal is the most tender event of home. Here work has been left behind; love reigns and confidences are exchanged. So it is with the Christian's evening meal, the Lord's Supper. The Lord Himself said, "with desire, I have desired to eat *this* Passover with you" (Luke 22:15) and the Lord's "Table Talk" is recorded in *John*, chapters 12 through 17. We would expect to read concerning the disciples that they gladly received His Word and continued steadfastly in "breaking of bread" before the Lord speaks of "added to them."

when the disciples came together to break bread . . . ."
Acts 20:7a

This text shows us the hold which the Lord's Table had over the infant Church, indicating that this was the primary motive and purpose which brought them together; and it also shows us that the time of its observance was the FIRST day of EVERY week, and the place of this Remembrance was before the sermon. It was fixed by the Jews who became the first Christians and they had been temple-trained.

As we read this twentieth chapter of Acts, can anyone fail to note the high tension recorded here? Now if ever, the "Set Face" will remember and will lay hold upon adequate and satisfying resources. David wrote, "Thou preparest a Table"; and the Lord said, "I have meat to eat ye know not of." To follow in the footsteps of Paul when he "turns again home" will reveal to us what he relies upon and this will "supply our every need" for this our day. Paul's return starts in Acts 20:3, and we note that from Philippi he sailed away after the "days of unleavened bread" and came to Troas in five days. The items of this return gather importance in the goal before him, for he must be in Jerusalem by Pentecost, and he continues steadfastly "with desire," "hastening"—yet he remains at Troas, the place of his vision in Acts 16:9. His tarrying for seven days at Troas must have been to be present with the disciples there for the Lord's Table. Though he was hastening, yet his desire to be at the Table caused him to wait one full week. He walked from Troas to Assos; Samos and Trogyllium were both nearer to Ephesus than Miletus, but he was making time; he said, "ye shall see my face no more," but they had in their weekly remembrance, "the bread of faces."

In Acts 21:1 following "a straight course," he journeys on and then in the second verse, having found a ship ready and a fair wind blowing, they set forth, finally landing at Tyre, where we read in verse 4, "finding disciples, we tarried for seven days. Why tarry seven days? Perhaps it was for the same purpose as his seven days of tarrying at Troas: the celebration of the Lord's Supper. These disciples said to Paul through the Spirit, that he should not set foot in Jerusalem. "And as they departed, they kneeled down on the seashore and prayed." This journey took him to Jerusalem and the brethren there received him gladly. In leaving these journeys of Paul, we would note again, the emphasis upon FAITH during the first journey; BAPTISM during the second journey; and THE LORD'S SUPPER on this third journey. This is the orderly progress of a mighty mind moved by the Spirit of the Lord.

4. **The Purpose of The Lord's Table as Set Forth in Paul's Epistles**
   a) The Significance of "Prothesis" (Purpose)

My great disappointment as I passed from *Acts* to *Romans*, from Peter to Paul, from the Jewish revivals to the Church Epistles, was to not find the Lord's Table; especially since the commentators made little of the Communion. All of the essentials of salvation were present in *Romans—faith* in chapter 5, *baptism* in chapter 6, and *the Holy Spirit* in chapter 8—but not *the Communion*. And then came one memorable study time and Romans 8:28 N.:

> "And we know that all things work together for good to them that love God, to them who are the called according to purpose." [1]

I had known that it must be there somewhere and when I found this text, I experienced something of the elation of the reformers. There I read, "to them who are called according to purpose." That word "Purpose" has as its meaning, "a setting forth" or "to set before," something that is vivid. God set before Himself a Table in the Old Testament (Exodus 25:30); a Cross in the Gospels (Romans 3:25); and a Church in the Epistles (Romans 8:28); and He permits no variations without divine sanction (Hebrews 8:5; cf. I Corinthians 11:23, 15:3 and also 11:30). In the Old Testament the Greek word *prothesis* is used in the same way (Matthew 12:4, Luke 6:4, Mark 2:26), for the word "*Show* bread" or *Presence* bread which was eaten by David in the Tabernacle. *Prothesis* is also used of the Church or rather of God's Purpose in the Church in the passage above quoted and in Ephesians 3:8—13 and II Timothy 1:9. The Church is to be "set forth before Him" as "Exhibit A" in His controversy (Ephesians 3:10, II Thessalonians 1:10).

The Church is as the rainbow (Genesis 9:14—15) which God set before the whole world, or we might better say, as the Son was before Him so is now the Church before Him (John 16:32, 20:21). In John 21 as the disciples drew the net full of fishes ashore, so here on Redemption's shore in *Romans*, there is drawn up for inspection the great words of Salvation (Romans 8:28—30): *Purpose, Foreknew, Predestinate, Called, Justified, Glorified.*

There are two memorials in the Church: *Baptism* is at the entrance; and to those passing through this door of fulfilling all righteousness, there is loving and loyal access to the Table and only such can partake. Here

---

[1] Joseph Henry Thayer, D.D., *A Greek-English Lexicon of the N. T.* (N.Y. Harpers 1887), p. 539: Greek *Prothesis* 1. "The setting forth of a thing, placing of it in view; Gr. *"hoi artoi tes protheseos,"* the showbread, used in Septuagint Exod. 35:14; 39:18; 38:36; I Kings 7:48; I Chron. 9:32; 23:29. Twelve loaves of wheaten bread corresponding to the number of the tribes of Israel which loaves were offered to God every Sabbath, and, separated into two rows, lay for seven days upon a table placed in the sanctuary or anterior portion of the tabernacle, and afterwards of the temple. Matt. 12:4; Mark 2:26; Luke 6:4 *"hoi artoi tou prosopou."* 2. "A Purpose" Acts 27:13; Rom. 8:28; 9:11; Eph. 1:11; 3:11; II Tim. 1:9 and 3:10.

at baptism, God's love is presented to the world. And the second memorial is the Communion Table within the familiar circle where the Father reveals His Mind which is secret, the mystery. A memory storehouse contains mementos, letters, poems. Here is the Bread of Faces, a Presence Face, and by it we proclaim (evangelize). The observance of the Lord's Table sets forth the Lord's death of His "My Baptism." The Supper was in secret, so it is only "spiritually discerned"—'In the Secret of His Presence." This spiritual discernment has been necessary in every age: Judges 13:18, Deuteronomy 29:29, Psalms 25:14, Amos 3:7, and I Corinthians 2:6.

The Communion "Purpose" is discerning the Lord's Body (I Corinthians 11:29) which is that Spiritual, united Body, awaiting Romans 8:23, the return of Its Head. This is why we break bread. He was known to the Emmaus disciples in the breaking of bread. Does this not imply that He will be made known to us in the same act? On the first day of the week, we are to be breaking bread in memory of Him. At what more propitious time could our hearts be better "made ready"?

The text "Purpose" means "A deliverate plan" and it is as deliberated and as "ordained" (Psalm 8:3) as nature or the tabernacle (Exodus 25:40). It is used of the *position* of the twelve loaves of showbread in the Tabernacle referred to in the Old and New Testaments and in the latter it is replaced by the Church; as a student "purposes" the "Ph. D." as his goal, so also the Christian *purposes* to be in the Lord's Presence (Acts 2:25); and much more so, God the Almighty "purposes" in Christ's Church. "Purpose" is the most fitting word as the Table is swallowed up in the spiritual. As Christ was raised and appeared and disappeared at will, so "purpose" becomes clear in the manner and place of its usage.

By translating *prothesis* "before the face of" and applying this to the Bread of the Tabernacle and also to the Church, we can understand better its real significance. It is that which one sets before his mind or that which comes first as "the apple of Thine eye." Adam was created in the image of God but he failed (James 1:17), so Christ is making His Body as His image today and we are "set before His face." "As He was so are we" and we are of His purpose. What is so gripping as this vision of our part? It is this which holds us to Him and it with-holds us from sin. Truly, we have "A Table in the presence of enemies" and "meat to eat that the world knows not of."

b) The Location of *"Prothesis"* in *Romans*

The Communion Table in *Romans* is just where it ought to be and where we would expect to find it. As astronomers can locate a new planet by its effect on other related planets, so we find this Table of the Lord in Romans 8:28 on the shore of the sea of the dead (Romans 1:18 through 8:27), from whence we have just escaped. The Psalmist wrote:

> "Thou preparest (settest in order) a table before
> me in the presence of mine enemies; . . . ."

> Psalm 23:5*a*N.

And in a home where death had entered, we read of the Lord:

> "And He took the damsel by the hand, and said unto her,
> '*Talitha cumi*'; which is; being interpreted, 'Damsel I
> say unto thee, arise.' And straightway the damsel arose
> and walked; . . . . And he charged them straitly . . . and
> commanded that something should be given her to eat."

> Mark 5:41—43

Jesus having raised the damsel from the dead, commanded food for her physical body; and just so He has prepared a Table for us who have been made alive and have received the Holy Spirit (Romans 8:11).

It is of special interest to note the place where *prothesis* is used in *Romans*; it is at the shore of escape. This food of the Table is prophetic of the abundance available when once we are in the house. On the banks of the Jordan River, Joshua was commanded to erect a pile of stones, and these would serve to awaken the children of Israel concerning the Lord's deliverance. So at this Communion Table, this Table of Memory, we find food, friendship and victory both now and evermore, and this is the beginning of our prophetic hope of "our Plea."

On the far shore of this sea of the dead stands the Risen One, the soon-to-be glorified Christ (Romans 1:4, John 21:12); and on this shore (Romans 8:28—30) stand the redeemed; a sorry but saved lot. Now it is not "Christ and Him crucified" and we with Him—not a crucified, defeated Jesus—but a Risen, Victorious and Glorified Christ, and we as joint heirs with Him, are at His Table, "in the heavenlies." This is the Christians' Upper Room. When we sit there "in a worthy manner" like a Thomas, we see with him, "My Lord and my God" through interstices of the broken Bread, or, as assembled parts of a map. Christ risen and glorified, spans this sea of Romans 1:18—8:27 from shore to shore. And He says, "Lo, I am with you," back there in the flesh, and down there in the propitiatory. Here in fellowship, it is the mystical Presence that refreshes. So we pass at once from Romans 8 to the Ephesian "heavenlies" into "The Interpreter's House" where we "sit with Him" and commune or eat with Him. Here this mystical Presence joins us for the Homeward Journey.

This Table is a secret or mystery and only those who are "saved" in *Romans* can be seated in *Ephesians*. Jesus said in Revelation 3:20:

> "If any man hear My voice and open the door,
> I will come in to him, and will sup with Him,
> and he with Me."

This kind of "eating" is not understood by the world (John 4:32, Judges 13:18). The Communion Table has on it a broken Body which gives us a backward look and a view of the Lord's Day. Here is theology! Contemplate what has occurred and then "set your face" at the future. The Restoration Movement could here learn.

We today often visit battle fields to remember what was done, but we live today in the government which that battle saved. We read, "they shall look on Him whom they pierced," and that "they shall call for the rocks to fall upon them." If He were still wounded (Revelation 6:15—17) they would not be afraid, but because He is glorious, they are afrighted (Revelation 1:17).

Romans is the book of Salvation and is the exclusive work of Deity. There is no fellowship in salvation between the Christian and the sinner for we are to raise the dead and then give them to eat. And while sitting in heavenly places (Ephesians 2:6) and eating, we have Communion. When a child is born into the home, it is first a care and then it becomes a companion. And lest this appear straining at words consider the word "mystery" of Romans 11:25 and 16:25 which becomes clear to "Ephesians" Christians only (cp. I Corinthians 2:2 and Ephesians 3:9). Remember that in the Upper Room at the disciples' first arriving, Jesus washed their feet, and then afterward, He sat down and talked with them. So here on this Upper Bank, indwelt by the Holy Spirit in Romans 8, the text in 1:16 sends its light across to us and in it we sit at the Table (Psalm 27:13).

c) The New Meaning Given to The Table by Paul

The apostle Paul wrote, "For I received from the Lord": the Gospel (I Corinthians 15:1); Baptism (Galatians 3:27); and the Lord's Table (I Corinthians 11:23). He had received something not before revealed, and to these he brings a richer, fuller teaching. What is it that Paul has "added":

(1) That we are baptized into Him (Galatians 3:27)
Paul reveals a deeper significance in baptism; it is a continuing of the resurrection (Galatians 1:1, Gr. *egeirontos,* rouses)

(2) He relates the Lord's Table to His return
In all of his epistles, Paul uses the word "unworthily" (Gr. *anaxios*) only twice (I Corinthians 11:27, 29), and "as often" is also used only twice (I Corinthians 25—26).

Paul went to Arabia, very likely to Sinai where the "unworthy" in Israel fell (I Corinthians 10:7). In the Church at Corinth there were those who were worthy and discerning though many were sick. The Lord's Table sets forth the Lord who was slain from the wrecking of the world (Revelation 5:6, 13:8). God prepares these things before He creates Adam and the "place" of John 14. If anything is of God, it is prepared before man has the need.

At the Lord's Table each week, we enter in to commune with Him (I Corinthians 10:16—17), and we are one bread, one Body. Here in the Church, the many are one and though there are divisions of the Body (I Corinthians 11:17), yet there are no variations except through divine warning (cf. Hebrews 8:5 m.).

Jesus said, "This do in remembrance of Me," and Paul adds "till He come." There is mystery as to show-bread. Men are confused in their statements of its meaning. The Passover and circumcision are plain. The showbread and the candlestick of the tabernacle were beyond the symbolism of the Jews but the showbread was not a memorial like the Passover. Each tribe was represented in the bread as being in the Presence of God and they had a common hope, that of Acts 26:6—7. Now the Church is before Him and it has a similar concern in this His Table (I Corinthians 11:26) as it looks to His coming again. Note especially, "Ye do show (proclaim) the Lord's death," that is, you are a "setter-forth," a "proclaimer" (cf. Gr. of Acts 17:28). The twelve loaves in the tabernacle proclaimed their prophetic expectancy of the Messiah and the one loaf is also prophetic to us, for "Ye do show forth . . . till He come." Aside from these hopes there was and is no meaning. Whoever sits at the Lord's Table meaningly and intelligently, is a pre-millennarian! Should you decide otherwise, then in what is your attitude different from the Romanist with a crucifix, i.e. a dead Christ. This is the hope "set before us" (Hebrews 6:18—20), the golden thread which is prophetic of the Rapture (Acts 1:11, Philippians 3:20, I Thessalonians 4:16, II Thessalonians 1:7, Titus 2:13, *et al*).

In studying the Communion in Paul's epistles, the following should be of interest:

"In this passage of I Corinthians 10:13—23 three communions are mentioned. First, is the *'koinoi tou somatos tou Christou,'* the communion of the body of Christ. The second is, verse 18, the communion of the Jewish altar of which the Jews were the communicants, *'koinonoi tou thusiasterious.'* The third, is the communion of the cup of devils of which the pagans were the *'koinonoi.'* In the Authorized Version this threefold occurrence of the word *'koinonia,'* communion, is disguised by synonymns—communion, partakers, and fellowship (in vss. 16, 18, 20). Paul was no unity faddist. He had too strong a sense of reality. The three communions of Christians, of Jews, and of a demon-worshipping heathenism, excluded each other and could not be combined or assimilated." [1]

---

[1] Ernest Gordon, *Notes From A Layman's Greek Testament,* (Copyright by The Sunday School Times Company and used by permission) pp. 222—223.

Close your New Testament and think of yourself as though you were one of those of the first century to whom Paul was writing, like the Gentiles in Acts 13:42—44, who had not known the Scriptures, and had no promises like those of the nation of Israel (Romans 9:4—5). We would be like those Gentiles: hopeless, atheists. But in Ephesians 2:13ff. we read: "Now IN Christ Jesus ye who once were far off, are made nigh IN the blood of Christ. For He is our peace who made both one," and the enmity is annulled thereby; in order that by the *two* He might *create* in Himself into (Gr. *eis*) *one* new man—the Church! And thus He brings together of the household of God that He might reconcile in one Body to God through the "having slain the enmity IN it." The Communion is a legacy of love, a test of loyalty. And what is its significance?—"When the Son of Man cometh, will He find *the* faith?" All other items will be fulfilled. Here is the conviction of His Deity; the declaration of our faith and the hope and expectancy of our personal immortality.

5. The Lord's Table Properly Observed by the Christian

Modern looseness today in observing the Lord's Table may be "in an unworthy manner," especially as it lacks the canopy of the Resurrection Day."They drank of that spiritual Rock that followed them and the Rock was Christ" (I Corinthians 10:4N.); so we drink of the Cup that follows us. As Israel turned from the worship of God who had delivered them from Egypt and made a golden calf to worship, so today many that assemble at the Communion Table discern not the Body of the Lord, and like many of the nation of Israel, they take no notice of the Lord's Presence; and also like Israel, "with many of them God was not well-pleased." The Holy Spirit's deep concern over our laxness proves His Omniscience.

a) Our Preparation for The Table

What is our preparation for the Communion Table? We read, "let a man examine himself" (I Corinthians 11:28, II Corinthians 13:5), that is, let him take himself apart and look at each item. *God* must do so; should not *you?* Our lives must be examined, taken apart, and compared with I Corinthians 3:10—15, and especially as the day approaches (I Peter 1:7, Revelation 12:2, Zechariah 13:7—9). To neglect this preparation produces those who are weak, sickly and are fallen asleep (I Corinthians 11:30).

On the first of January 1939, the Englewood congregation adopted two slogans: "From the Cradle to the Communion Table," and, "Every Member to be at every service 'unless prevented by some reason which I can conscientiously give to my Savior'." The congregation had decided that if we were to follow Him completely, we must be faithful in both the teaching and the worship-evangelism life of the Church, for, it is "From the Cradle to the Communion Table."

The Communion Table is His Own and His only request. For us to be willingly absent is to deny His request. To forget and neglect this Table is to do "despite" to the Spirit of Grace (Hebrews 10:25). There is no excuse for neglect for it is not fixed after a monument, but it is living and is everywhere present. And always "in the Upper Room" each communicant in the broken Bread sees beyond its wounds, the Christ, even as Thomas saw beyond the wounded hands and side of the Master, a risen Lord and Savior, which caused him to cry out, "My Lord, and my God." Upon this Table is the "Presence Bread" or "Bread of Faces." This is the Church's Shekinah. Jesus said, "Lo, I am with you." And when the Table is within you, it is a memorial, and every thought, act and word must cross that Table to get to you. To those steadfastly beholding, "It doth not yet appear what we shall be" but at the Table, the veil is rent and we are in the Heavenlies at one with Him.

The Lord's Supper is a memorial to the blood of Christ which cleanses (Gr. *katharizei*, I John 1:7); and His blood carries away (Gr. *aphesin*, Matthew 26:28) our sin. The Passover killed those in Israel who were not behind the blood but the blood covered and kept those within. A soap *chemically* cleanses (Gr. *katharizei*), but blood *emotionally* cleanses (Gr. *aphesin*). The Lord's Table is our Sunday morning bath. "Remission" takes away even as the Lord in Luke 4:18 "releases" and "sets at liberty." If we prepare (examine) ourselves, this is occurring in us. What you have let go of, God takes away. This preparation of disciples for worship is another of the works of the Lord during the fifty days of reforming, forming anew and transforming His nascent Body.

The unveiling of "God is love" is so effulgent that it acts as the transfiguration and we see "no man save Jesus only." And then the study of this love reveals to us as a challenge to "unsandal" for we are entering upon holy ground. Let us fix our attention upon our preparation. The Master says, "I gave My life for thee, What hast thou given for Me?"

The Lord's Table is *the* test. Let a man prove himself and no other. The one who does will have enough to keep himself busy and will have no time for being critical of others. And so he partakes as he must for there is no escape. Weigh well these exhortations:

(1) "Not forsaking" our own assembling (Hebrews 10:25 A.S.V.)
(2) "Examine yourself whether ye be in the faith" (II Corinthians 13:5)
(3) "Let a man prove himself" (I Corinthians 11:28 A.S.V.)
(4) "For this cause many are weak and sickly among you," because they discriminate not THE Body" (A.S.V.m I Corinthians 11:29).

Why are these exhortations given? Because they are so important, "so much *the* more as ye see THE day approaching." There is a most definite purpose for observing the Lord's Table; a purpose that is beyond our own good. Here is centered our unity in the one faith, for "as often as ye eat this bread and drink *the* cup, ye proclaim the Lord's death till He come" (I Corinthians 11:26 A.S.V.—John 17). "Till He come"—take that away and the Table becomes a dead thing, an idol which dissolves as do all corpses. For any less purpose, "ye come together not for the better but for the worse" (I Corinthians 11:17). To come together to hear preaching, to "show off" even though not doing this purposely or consciously, still effects our relationship to the Communion Table and the Lord (I Corinthians 11:21—22).

The Lord's Table of Acts 20:7 is in contrast to the statement of Paul in I Corinthians 11:17 for in this he said, "Now in *this* that I declare unto you, I praise you not" and then he lists their divisions (schisms or parties) and factions (heresies or opinions) and it is necessary that these be listed in order that those who are approved in the Corinthian congregation, might be made manifest among them. To meditate upon Him and to long for His coming, dissolves differences and "knits together" (Colossians 2:2, 19; Ephesians 4:15—16).

> *b*) Our Participation In The Table

> ". . . to them who are called ones according to PURPOSE"
> (Romans 8:28*b*)

> "The cup of blessing which we bless, is it not participation of the blood of Christ? The bread which we break, is it not participation of the body of Christ?" (I Corinthians 10:16 N.)
> "But the soulish man receiveth not the things of the Spirit of God; for they are foolishness unto him: neither can he know them, because they are spiritually discerned."
> I Corinthians 2:14 N.

The Christian life of contemplation is not vacuous but is concentrated (Psalms 39:2, 16:8, 1:1 "stand still and see"; and so comes peace, Philippians 4:6—8). The first day of the week is to meditate and the Lord's Supper is to remember. The Comrades of the Cross are those who so contemplate and only as they do so, have they produced men of faith. The first lesson in research is to "forget your body." And the first lesson at the Table is to "lose self and remember" (Psalm 23:5). When Paul was converted he was so active that he was blinded for three days; afterward he went to Arabia, returning to Damascus. There were three years of preparation before the Lord could use him.

The first look upon *Ephesians* is disappointing in contrast to the Gospels, the *Acts*, and *Romans*, for there people have been in motion. The "social gospelers" are all "sermon-on-the-mount-ers." Naturally, we would expect increased motion. But look upon this word "sit." Going from *Acts* to *Ephesians* is moving from the roar of the dynamo to the silence of its light. *Acts* is DOING, while in *Ephesians* it has been done, and we are BEING (2:19—22); we are SEEING (3:18—19); we are ACHIEVING (6:13). This is a mightier work for, "He restoreth my soul"—that is, in this Workshop!

The Table is the symbol of this our Redemption. In the bread, we understand that Christ died for all; there is room for all. And in the blood, we see life which is "shed forth" as the Holy Spirit (Acts 2:33). It is not a dead but a living way (cf. John 14:16), so blood encompasses. Thus, as often as we eat, we show His death; we look back to when we were saved, and we continue till He comes again; we look forward to when we shall be changed. Every Communion Table is a miniature of this. Someone's Life paid for it!

For what purpose was the Table given? It was given to keep in mind the past; that the Cross was for all (John 3:16). And to keep in mind the future through the Cup for Christians. So we *give thanks* for the *Bread*, for He died for all (Romans 2:18), and Judas ate the bread for it was intended for all. Then we *bless* the *Cup* for it is for Christians only (Philippians 1:10). To mix these two is confusion, and there is idolatry when we inject ourselves. God said, "This is My Son." And we read that in the garden of Gethsemane "He was withdrawn (parted) from them about a stone's cast and kneeled down and prayed." So at the Communion Table, *He* must stand apart in our midst and in our prayers, for this is *His* hour. Therefore in our two prayers at the Table, [1] one prayer should always have the *backward* look for the Bread, for what He has done for us, and the other prayer should include the *forward* expectancy in the Cup, for His return for us.

When summer is upon us and we are travelling, the Lord's Supper is most important. It can be observed wherever you chance to be. I would urge you to observe the Table not in a formal manner, but rather to be emotional as you would receive a friend for a week-end visit. Because of its value, I started anew to refresh and prepare my own soul for such a fellowship. That which came out of this, I believe to be profitable.

In Philippians 1:10, we are told to distinguish the things that differ; and there is a difference between "Ye assemble yourselves together," and "when we were gathered together." The disciples assembled on the Mount of Olives, but it was Christ who gathered them together and then He was parted from them. We are to be gathered as though a force not of ourselves which makes for righteousness were bringing us together.

---

[1] During the ministry of Mr. Kindred in the Englewood Christian Church (Chicago), there was no "Table Talk." One Elder read the Communion Scripture, and only these four Scriptures were used consecutively throughout the year: Matthew 26:26—28, Mark 14:22—24, Luke 22:19—20, and I Corinthians 11:23—26. Another Elder gave the prayer of *Thanks* for the Bread, and a third Elder gave the prayer of *Blessing* for the Cup. (N.B.)

This Table is God's solution to the sin problem. Here are spoken the fewest of words and the awesome silence is like that which frightened Pilate and Pompey. One of the methods at Scotland Yards is to place three of their detectives at a table with a criminal and no word breaks the silence until the criminal confesses. This Table is not like the Council Table of Ambassadors where men make great decisions after long discussion and where it often seems:

"Right forever on the scaffold, wrong forever on the throne."

The Table of the Lord is the place where you and I prepare ourselves. The problem for each of us is sin and the solution for this open sore is God's solution. It is the Table of Remembrance wherein we remember His sacrifice for sin; and from whence we look forward to His coming again.

How should we use the Table? Bring your problem; take over into you, strength of food, "meat to eat the world knows not of," for fellowship levels us up in Him, and we will love as "God so loved."

The only way to maintain the unity of the spirit is at the Table "beholding as in a mirror, the glory of the Lord." Unity is an effect, never a cause. Remove the cause and dispersion occurs. "The Hope" unites. Leave it out of the Communion and you have disunity. So I Corinthians 11:28 reads, "Let a man examine himself and so let him eat and drink."

In I Corinthians chapter 10, we read that Israel was baptized into Moses, in the cloud and in the sea, and DRANK of the Rock, and ATE of the manna; and Paul parallels these with Christ at Jordan and Olivet, especially in verse 11 when he says, "these were ensamples." Our baptism is not mentioned but the Table is, and upon this we feed during our pilgrimage as did Israel. Our altar was the *shaken* of Adam, the "Tabernacle" of of Moses, and it is the "Table of" the Church; and through these fragments of bread, as a lattice, we see His Face. It is not the face of a defeated Jesus but of a coming Lord—not a diminishing One, but an Increasing One (Isaiah 9:7). These emblems of His broken body are as scaffolding which when taken away, will reveal the finished structure. As Booth takes the text of Hamlet and through him we see Hamlet live, or as Kreisler takes a sheet of music and brings the composer's work to life; so this Bread and Cup reveal to us Jesus Christ "till the Great High God doth enter and make it beautiful!" These broken fragments recall His broken Body and shed Blood, "the enemy's last final effort," and looking through upon Him, "the devils believe and tremble" for they did their worst and yet He lives! The Table proclaims victory at the darkest hour. "Heaven doth the Mystery explain"—Hallelujah!

c) The Power of The Table

The Mystery is the Power operating through the elements of the Lord's

Supper when rightly used (II Corinthians 3:15—18):

> "Now the Lord is the Spirit; and where the Spirit of the Lord is, there is liberty. But we all, with unveiled face beholding as in a mirror the glory of the Lord, are transformed into the same image from glory to glory, even as from the Lord the Spirit."

> II Corinthians 3:17—18N.

This can only mean the Supper. If we observe rightly, we would behold His glory because we believe John 11:40 and Romans 12:3. Our bodies are presented and our minds are transformed at the Lord's Table. The Table can be wrongly used if one *fails* to prove himself and if he *discerns* not the Lord's Body, the Lord's Blood, for, "for this cause, many among you are weak and sickly, and not a few sleep" (cp. I John 3:1—3 "purifieth himself"). Many come to church not aware of the power resident in the "assembling" (Gr. *ek-klesia*):

> "For where two or three are gathered together unto My name, there am I in the midst of them."

> Matthew 18:20N.

There are always that many present. We have made "common" this House of Prayer for all peoples for it has become a place of pre-occupation and in-attention, and this is most noticeable at the Lord's Table.

"Purge out therefore the old leaven . . . . For even Christ our Passover was sacrificed for us" (I Corinthians 5:7), as the Lamb of God (John 3:16), for the whole world. The Lord's Supper emerged from the Passover and it is for those who accept the Cross. Here we have the Body and shed Blood of the Rejected One. This Bread brings transforming *power* from leavened to unleavened lives (Ephesians 3:6, 18, 20—21, II Corinthians 4:18).

The Cup to the *world* means *weakness*, but to the *saved*, "Christ the *power* of God, for God hath chosen the weak things to confound the mighty." We have been learning that we have been throwing out vitamins, the best part of our food, through our old methods of cooking. Even so the Jews, unknowingly and through unbelief, rejected the suffering Savior, fulfilling "who hath despised the day of small things." Jesus said, "This Cup is the new covenant"; it was not of this earth for it was a demonstration of immortality, of life beyond the grave. The New Covenant is IN or within "My Blood." Life is imprisoned in blood and when released, it "goes unto its own place." Blood is the agent in which life functions upon the elements of this world. As we with "set face" are before the Table, we ask, "what are these wounds?" and "Is any sorrow like unto His sorrow?" And as we realize His betrayal, may we now say, "Lord, is it I?" "Let a man so prove, examine and so partake," and then may we ask, "Does the world see Jesus in me?" "They took knowledge of *them* that they had been with Jesus" at the Communion Table.

Our "clinic membership" percentage is greater than the world's jobless; yet the Church goes blindly on; many do not see or discern. They see only the emblems, not Him, even as Israel: "They sat down to eat and rose up to play." This is idolatry. Power is not to be seized at the Table, "but we all with open face beholding, are changed" for here is the Bread of Faces, and to the spiritual, this is suggestive.

We have been tarrying at the Cross today and we have passed beyond into "the heavenlies" (I Corinthians 10:14—23, 11:23—30, Ephesians 4:4). We are walking a path to the Cross which has been worn by the feet of a man who dared to carry a pitcher. Possibly the Lord used this water with which to wash the disciples' feet. There is no question about the fact that He ate the Passover, and *then* He instituted the Lord's Supper, the Mystery which arose up out of this event as Christ arose out from men. Here arose *The* Mystery as Christ Himself later appeared within the Upper Room's closed doors. There is always power in the presence of The Table.

We see the mystery visions when we "rightly discern." The awesome silence of the Holy Place around Israel's Table should be an example for us at the Lord's Table. For this reason the Englewood Church does not permit the playing of the organ during the Communion service; and all, including the organist, worship together in the silence. As the translators left the phrase "Jesus wept," in solitary splendor, so the Table stands as the mystery of mysteries. Let us ascend up into heights (Exodus 24:1—3) and leave our humanity and priestly robes for here is a greater than tables of stones, feasts and fasts or the tabernacle. As Moses said at Mount Sinai, "I did exceedingly fear and quake" (Hebrews 12:21), so do we, as we suggest the separateness and the sublimity of the Table.

The Lord's Table is as Noah's bow before God: a continuous reminder and challenge wherein we do show forth His death until He comes; and here the most likely emotions are raised to missionary fervor. "Ye were dead but God made us alive . . ." and we are His poem (Ephesians 2:1—10, Ezekiel 37:1—24, Job 14:4, Luke 1:37). The Communion Table is that reassertion of God's Super-Omnipotence, the Remembrancer of Luke 18:27: ". . . The things which are impossible with men are possible with God."

This "Super-Omnipotent" God causes devils to tremble, idols to be broken; and He is the Usherer-in of Revelation 21:1. So long as the Church of Jesus Christ bears the testimony of her faith, so long "the gates of Hades shall not prevail against it." To us He could say, "as often as ye do this, ye do show forth the Lord's death (in great hope) till He come." We are unworthy if we discern not the Body, "the one Body" that is the Church. We are to keep the unity of the faith. We are sharing the suffering and if we discern not these things, then "for this cause, many are weak, sickly and not a few sleep." If we discerned *ourselves*, we should not be so charged. This paragraph of warning is to disturbers.

At the Table we see as He and others saw:

(1) The Lord, "Who for the joy . . ." (Hebrews 12:2)

(2) David who said, "I beheld the Lord . . ." (Psalm 16:8)

(3) Abraham who saw "My Day" (John 8:56), and "The City" (Hebrews 11:10)

(4) Moses "esteeming the reproach of Christ greater riches . . . not fearing the wrath of the king . . . endured as seeing Him who is invisible" (Hebrews 11:26—27)

(5) And "what can I say more, for time would fail me" to speak of that unending caravan that moves resistlessly onwards proclaiming the faith till II Corinthians 4:16—18.

The Lord's Table is your sermon for by it you announce the facts which it presents. We hinder His coming again when we fail to show forth His death till He come, but when we assemble at the Lord's Table, then we are constantly looking for and hastening that day.

> "Till He come:" Oh, let the words
> Linger on the trembling chords;
> Let the little while between
> In their golden light be seen;
> Let us think how heav'n and home
> Lie beyond that— "Till He come."
>
> . . .
>
> See, the feast of love is spread:
> Drink the wine, and break the bread—
> Sweet memorials—till the Lord
> Call us round His heav'nly board—
> Some from earth, from glory some,
> Severed only—"Till He come."
>
> E. H. Bickersteth

Section FIVE: THE CHURCH—MY STORY (Continued)

VI. "THE THINGS WHICH HAVE BEEN FULLY ESTABLISHED

AMONG US" (Luke 1:1 A.S.V.m*)

THE VITAL DOCTRINES OF SALVATION

Page

* *Marginal reference*

VI. "THE THINGS WHICH HAVE BEEN FULLY ESTABLISHED
AMONG US" (Luke 1:1 A.S.V.m)— THE VITAL DOCTRINES
OF SALVATION

F. "THE NAME ABOVE EVERY NAME"

Text:

". . . . . And the disciples were
divinely called Christians first in Antioch."

Acts 11:26*b* N.

The "My Church" promised in Matthew 16:18 was begotten in John
20:22 with the Lord's "breathing into," and had its birth in Acts 2:1–4
as they "began to speak with other tongues." The ones whom the Lord
"added" were Jews and Gentiles, both of whom were "dead in trespasses
and sins" (Ezekiel 37 and Romans 1). Here is THE occasion; these dead
were raised through the operation of the Spirit in baptism becoming "one
new man." In Acts 2 and 10, Peter is the chemist at both of these prepa-
rations of the Church, His Body—still he did *not name* the result. But the
greatest of the Old Testament prophets *did* write:

"And the Gentiles shall see thy righteousness,
And all kings thy glory:
And thou shalt be called by a new name,
Which the mouth of Jehovah shall expressly name."

Isaiah 62:2 N.

"And ye (Israel) shall leave your name for a curse
unto My chosen: For Adonai-Jehovah shall slay thee,
And call His *servants* by another name;"

Isaiah 65:15 N.

Here at the crowning vision of His oracle, God tells of the two names
that His people are to be called eventually. In Isaiah 62, He is speaking
to Israel and He says, "Thou (Israel) shalt be called by a new name which
the mouth of Jehovah shall name." This name is found in Isaiah 62:4 and
it is *Hephzibah* which means "My delight is in her." And the land is to
be called *Beulah*. In Isaiah 65:13–15 we find Israel in rejection and God's
"servants" in favor, and we read, "For the Lord shall call His 'servants'
(the Church) by another name" (Acts 11:26*b*)—"for the Lord shall slay
thee" (Israel). When the veil of the Temple was rent, it was the death
stroke of Israel (Ezekiel 37) "till the times of the Gentiles shall end."

Following His resurrection, at once the mighty power of God, "The
Strong Son of God's Immortal Love," enters upon His great work of salvation through grace:

1. He went to the spirits in prison (I Peter 3:18—19)
2. He released and led captivity captive (Ephesians 4:8)
3. He begat His Body (John 20:22)
4. He sent the Holy Spirit and this One called them CHRISTIAN (in Hebrew, Greek and Latin)

The name "Christian" was never a nickname; whereas the names of "Nazarenes' or "Galileans" were such. The beauty of this name was not compatible with ridicule.

To the Greek it meant they were to be the "anointed peoples," i.e. the kingly or the priestly ones. These were to be patterned after the Lord (Acts 11:26, Romans 6:17—18, II Corinthians 5:11—21). The pattern is fashioned out of His own life and example, for He both conformed to, and then afterwards commanded, that it be made obligatory upon "Whosoever" would come after Him (Luke 14:27). That one who departs from these instructions must assume the personal responsibility (Luke 6:46—48).

"Christian" is the universal name to which the most rabid sectarian clings. It is the name silencing all other names as at the Transfiguration when Moses and Elijah vanished and a Voice was heard saying, "Hear ye Him." And this is the name which was most common to the apostles:

> Luke used it in Acts 11:26
> James used it in James 2:7
> and
> Peter used it in I Peter 4:16

It was also used by King Agrippa who recognized the importance of this name when he said, "almost thou persuadest me to become a CHRISTIAN" (Acts 26:28).

"The Name that is above every name"—that "at the Name of Jesus, every knee should bow"—should drive us to prayer; it should bind us to honor it; it should exalt us to fellowship in the Spirit; and it should transform us to Christ-likeness.

VI. "THE THINGS WHICH HAVE BEEN FULLY ESTABLISHED

AMONG US" (Luke 1:1 A.S.V.m*)

THE VITAL DOCTRINES OF SALVATION

Page

G. PRAYER

THE ESSENTIAL ELEMENTS OF PRAYER

* *Marginal reference*

470

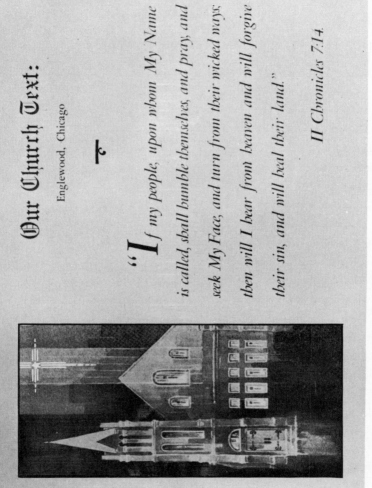

Our Church Text:

Englewood, Chicago

"If my people, upon whom My Name is called, shall humble themselves, and pray, and seek My Face, and turn from their wicked ways; then will I hear from heaven and will forgive their sin, and will heal their land."

II Chronicles 7:14.

This motto hung in many of the church homes and was used as the Scripture text for that year, being very frequently quoted throughout the year (1939?)

VI. "THE THINGS WHICH HAVE BEEN FULLY ESTABLISHED
AMONG US" (Luke 1:1 A.S.V.m) — THE VITAL DOCTRINES
OF SALVATION

G. THE ESSENTIAL ELEMENTS OF PRAYER

Psalm Twenty-Three[1]

"The Lord is my shepherd; I shall not want.
He maketh me to lie down in green pastures:
He leadeth me beside the still waters.
He restoreth my soul:
He leadeth me in the paths of righteousness for His name's sake.
Yea, though I walk through the valley of the shadow of death,
I will fear no evil: For Thou art with me;
Thy rod and Thy staff they comfort me.
Thou preparest a table before me in the presence of mine enemies:
Thou anointest my head with oil;
My cup runneth over.
Surely goodness and mercy shall follow me all the days of my life:
And I will dwell in the house of the Lord for ever."

*   *   *   *   *

More things are wrought by prayer
Than this world dreams of. Wherefore let thy voice
Rise like a fountain for me night and day.
For what are men better than sheep or goats,
That nourish a blind life within the brain,
If, knowing God, they lift not hands of prayer
Both for themselves and those who call them friend.
For so the whole round earth is every way
Bound by gold chains about the feet of God.[2]

The overlooked, neglected and unused resources of prayer
Have marooned us in mud-flats like eagles with clipped wings.
And the lack of exercise of prayer
Often cripples one at the very time of need.

1. The Inner Sanctuary of Every Life

Prayer is native to intellect and becomes the Himalayan heights which are pre-emted, that is, reserved; for "the fear of the Lord IS the beginning (and the ending) of wisdom."

Johannes Kepler wrote, "The great mind at the victory moment is reverent."

---

[1] This Psalm is still used as a prayer of exultation every First Day of the week in the Englewood Christian Church (Chicago).

2 Alfred Lord Tennyson, *The Passing of Arthur* (N.Y. Thomas Y. Crowell & Co.), p. 377.

Lord Bacon stated, "A little philosophy inclineth a man's mind to religion."

And Alexander Pope penned:

> A little learning is a dangerous thing;
> Drink deep, or taste not the Perian spring:
> There shallow drafts intoxicate the brain,
> And drinking largely sobers us again.[1]

The last stage of thought is prayer (meditation):

a) Moses at prayer became a face-transfigured

b) Daniel at prayer was shown vast horizons of history

c) Paul on his first visit to Jerusalem after his conversion (Acts 22:17), while in the temple at prayer, was in a trance, and saw the Lord and heard Him speak; and it must have been at this time that he was caught up into the third heaven, as referred to in II Corinthians 12:2; for Paul in prayer, transfigured the Temple out of Jerusalem into heaven.

d) And our own lives become freed, ennobled and Christ-like in prayer.

There is an inner sanctuary in every life, "enter in to thy closet." This may be defiled as was the temple but it is there (II Kings 22:8, II Chronicles 34:14), for:

> Down in the human heart, Crushed by the tempter,
> Feelings lie buried that grace can restore:
> Touched by a loving heart, Wakened by kindness,
> Chords that were broken will vibrate once more.[2]

"Shut the door"—Jesus said, "I am the door of the sheep; I call My sheep by name and separate them and they shall go in and out and find pasture."

"Alone, alone with Thee, in breathless adoration."

2. From Whence Cometh Prayer?

Prayer—whose idea is it? It is God's. It is the method best fitted as the Incarnation was fitted to the Cross. God is able to answer else prayer would be trifling. How else can God deliver His resources? All of our actions are based upon reason and law. Just where do these end and what is beyond; is there another (Gr. *heteros*) reason and another code of laws? No one will claim infinity for man, but Infinity IS.

The microscope ray can venture as far into the *Little*, as the telescope can venture into the *Large*; and in both ways, the pattern, the design

---

[1] Alexander Pope *"Moral Essays"* Epistle V, "To Mr. Addison" Lines 15 ff.

[2] Fanny J. Crosby, *Rescue The Perishing*, hymn, vs. 3.

and the product are equally larger. This is *Ne plus ultra* for humanity; let us arise and go out there and let us storm our inhibitions and visit with our Father. Can that barrier be crossed?—Only by that One whom He hath chosen. The English tabernacled in India and Ghandi crossed the obstruction through Oxford. So Christ became incarnated and led captivity captive. He has and He does cross it: for He said, "I go" and He said also, "I will come again." The saints that I know, have crossed this barrier, and it is the innate desire of all saints. Prayer life is as the sounds of the Muezzin calling us to prayer, so then:

"Speak to Him thou for He hears, and Spirit with Spirit can meet—
Closer is He than breathing, and nearer than hands and feet."

The storm warnings often hold ships at dock and prepare those at sea. The times are broadcasting to urge all of us that we should pray, but the inner adjustment is that which turns and tunes one's body into an instrument of praise whose every mood and move can be as lights playing over the Urim and Thummim (I Corinthians 3:16—17).

3. The Model Prayer (Matthew 6:9—13; Luke 11:2—4)

In Luke 9:51 we read of the "Set Face" which ended in agony-prayer and blood-sweat (Luke 9:23, Mark 9:29); and which finally said, "It is finished" on the Cross. This was trail-blazing, and those coming after Him must walk "The Way," "and where I am, there shall My servant be also." Is it matter for wonder that they asked, "Teach us to pray?" That is to ask of Him, "make us to be workmen who need not to be ashamed." Sculptors, artisans, and others in the world of comfort and culture need teaching and training, and we as followers of Christ, need much more. They said, "teach us to pray." And He did. He gave us the model for every man to follow. The two vast objectives in God's consummation of the ages are the Kingdom and the Church where are found the definite objectives of prayer; and the Lord's model prayer sums up all items of prayer for man, the nations and the age. As in the Ten Commandments, note the order of importance; the Ten Commandments went from major to minor, so also does this prayer.

The Lord's Prayer must have within its depths the very heart of God. This is not "The Lord's Prayer" of John 17, nor is it a "pattern prayer," but it has the essential elements of any and all prayers.

"If My people, upon whom My name is called, shall humble themselves, and pray, and seek My face, and turn from their wicked ways; then will I hear from heaven, and will forgive their sin, and will heal their land."

II Chronicles 7:14N.[1]

---

[1] See also page 470

The fulfillment of this verse of Scripture will see "Thy kingdom come, Thy will be done."

There is nothing omitted in the model prayer for which any could pray. Here is an exchange of values which are life-transforming, soul-satisfying and heaven-compelling. So we can really experience them and prove the Lord when He said:

> "Ask, and it shall be given you;
> Seek, and ye shall find;
> Knock, and it shall be opened unto you:
> For every one that asketh receiveth;
> And he that seeketh findeth;
> And to him that knocketh it shall be opened."
>
> Matthew 7:7—8

We are limited only by our own limitations (II Kings 13:14—19) and to this extent is our prayer life limited.

In Luke 11:1 the disciples said, "teach us to pray as John taught his disciples to pray." They needed to learn, to study, to prepare themselves; and so to discern their needs and to present their case. Never was prayer to be done *extempore*. See Daniel 9:2—3 and 10:2N.:

> "In the first year of his reign, I Daniel *understood by books* the number of the years, whereof the word of the Lord came to Jeremiah the prophet, that He would accomplish seventy years in the desolation of Jerusalem. And I set my face unto the Lord God, to seek by prayer and supplications, with fasting and sackcloth and ashes;"

> "In those days I Daniel was mourning three weeks of days."

And we note the Lord's example in Mark 1:35N.:

> "And in the morning, rising up a great while before day,
> He went out,
> and departed into a desert place, and there prayed."

This commonly called Lord's Prayer necessitates a place, a preparation, elements, and all of these being present, prayer becomes fellowship:

a) "Enter into thy closet" alone with God—"thinking God's thoughts over after Him." The nearer we get to Him, the more the need of the world presses (John 3:16). "Say"—put words around your need as the Lord required (Mark 10:36)

b) "Our Father"—Here one's language takes on the divine. The closet vision always pluralizes. There can be no prayer until we are able to say "Our Father," for He is a Person (Hebrews 11:6). We must believe that "He *is*" and that He is as real as Jesus (John 14:9) and we must tarry till we realize this. "Like as a father pitieth his children," so our Father gives preference for "Elohim" is *obligated Omnipotence.*

c) "Who art *in* heaven." We are that near: "Speak to Him, thou, for He hears . . ." even as the Spirit is present in our body. There is that intimacy.

> "For My thoughts are not your thoughts,
> Neither are your ways My ways, saith the Lord.
> For as the heavens are higher than the earth,
> So are My ways higher than your ways,
> And My thoughts than your thoughts."

Isaiah 55:8

At the center of all is a Thinker, Creator, Dispenser; and when we are so prepared, we can come boldly (Hebrews 4:16).

d) "Hallowed be Thy Name" (II Chronicles 7:14, Acts 17:28, "In Him we live and move and have our being." No matter what our lapses may be, we still want a good name, and "there is none other name under heaven given among men, whereby we must be saved."

e) "Thy kingdom come." "The times are out of joint" and this is God's chiefest concern for He has put much into the Cross and it is the basis of prayer. Now comes the crowning preparation for the coming Kingdom, for "the effectual, fervent prayer of a righteous man availeth much" (James 5:16, 1:5—8, Romans 8:26, James 4:6—8, Proverbs 9:10). Today, only a Christian can make such a request. During this Age of Grace, the Jew is in unbelief. Before "Thy Kingdom" comes, the Church will be raptured. Only the believer of prophecy can pray this prayer.

f) "Thy will be done, also on earth, as in heaven." This is millennial hunger. The Church enters heaven because it obeyed the Lord. During the Kingdom Age, earth's peoples will do the Lord's will on earth.

g) "Give us this day our needed bread (sustenance and life), and forgive us our debts as we forgive our debtors." That is, "feed us and forgive us." If we knew there were plenty, we would not carry it around; and if I harbor bitterness in place of forgiveness, I am myself lost.

h) "Bring us not into temptation."

> "Keep back Thy servant also from presumptuous sins;
> Let them not have dominion over me:
> Then shall I be upright,
> And I shall be innocent from the great transgression."

Psalm 19:13

"Remove far from me vanity and lies:
Give me neither poverty nor riches;
Feed me with food appointed for me:
Lest I be full, and deny Thee,
And say, 'Who is Jehovah?'
Or lest I be poor, and steal, and
   take the name of my God in vain."

Proverbs 30:8—9N.

i) But if I do fall into sin in spite of all, "deliver me from evil."
"A little learning is a dangerous thing."

j) "For Thine is the kingdom, and the power, and the glory, unto
the ages of the ages. Amen." Herein are the resources with
which all of the above is made possible.

4. The Hypothesis of Believing Prayer

   a) Defined

   The pre-suppositions of believing prayer are defined in Hebrews
   11:13—16 and Psalm 61:2, for:

   (1) There must be One who is listening, able and wanting to
       answer prayer (God).

   (2) There must be another who is intelligently, believingly, and
       unselfishly preferring his request (man).

   There must be a suppliant with a need and a Supplier with a
   supply (Hebrews 11:6). The mental repose of such an effort
   as the above would in itself be therapeutic, a remedial exercise. Such an one would get value out of even an apparent
   refusal (II Corinthians 12:9), and if there be no such sanctuary
   of escape or recess into which one might retire, then life is
   surely "bound in shallows." "We know not how to pray as we
   ought." "How" is not the attitude nor the posture nor even
   what to pray for, for there is no book of forms nor a list of
   our wants.

   b) Demonstrated

   There are three arresting statements in regard to prayer that

   (1) "My house shall be called a house of prayer" (Isaiah 56:7).
       It was not a house primarily to be a house of sacrifice, al-
       though the Sanhedrin, Doctors and Scribes were most con-
       cerned about this, for from the sacrifices, they personally
       profited. It was not to be a house of preaching or of the
       ordinances, but men were concerned about the processionals,
       the liturgy, the *Psalms* and the incense burning. And these
       things had all taken the place of the primary purpose of the
       house of God—the house of prayer. When Solomon had finished

the building of the temple, God said to him:

'I have heard thy prayer and thy supplication,
that thou hast made before Me; I have hallowed
this house, which thou hast built, to put My
name there for ever; and Mine eyes and Mine
heart shall be there perpetually . . . ."

I Kings 9:3

The House of God is like a planetarium where Jobs, Elijahs,
and Daniels are seen operating and lesser lives fulfill their
courses.

If we were to invade a foreign country and build schools,
hospitals, and a radio station, we would recognize these
as outposts of *our* civilization. So every House of God is
one of His outposts and is a receiving and a sending station
and must be an House of Prayer. So the House of God is
a repository of spiritual strength and a consecration for
those who are in fellowship with God.

(2) The second arresting statement is in Romans 8:26, "The Holy
Spirit with groanings which cannot be uttered" intercedes
and as we look upon Moses, Paul, and our Lord in Gethsemane, we witness them enduring the mightiest passion of
life-prayer. Prayer is emotion and emotion is the most unstable element of our life for it needs more discipline and
control. So we expect and find it to be so, that the mightiest
of characters are the mightiest of pray-ers.

(3) And the third arresting statement is found in Revelation 5:8
(cf. 6:10), the Golden Bowls of incense. Incense is incendi-
ary. It is odor released by fire; "a fire in my bones" (Jeremiah
20:9, Lamentations 1:13). Such a burning fire in man's heart
is demonstrated in the prayer of Moses in Exodus 32:32 and
in that of Paul in Romans 9:2. What a few have made heroic,
the many can use in a lesser degree. God's remembrancers,
Habakkuk, Daniel and others, are enough to still our murmur-
ings and to quench our doubts. These harassed and burdened
intercessors won out and we could ill spare them from a spiritual anthology.

c) Proving Our Belief

"Can a man believe in prayer who does not pray? He may think
he believes in it, but does he? Is not his real belief in prayer
measured accurately by the place he gives to prayer in his daily
life? If he says he knows that prayer is the mightiest force in
life, and then gives it less time and exercise in his own life
than almost anything else, does he believe what he says he

believes, or is he deceiving himself? It is interesting to contrast this common attitude with that of General Armstrong of Hampton Institute, Virginia, who not only said, 'Prayer is the greatest thing in the world,' but of whom it has been said that prayer with him was something to be done like other work for God. His daughter has said that it was his meat and drink, and that he spent a tenth of his busiest days at prayer. 'The mystery of it did not appall him.' When we pray in that way, we can really begin to say that we believe in prayer. Until we thus prove our belief, we belie it."

Author Unknown

5. The Rubicon[1] of Prayer

(Hebrews 10:35——11:7
Texts: (Hebrews 4:15
(Luke 6:49

"He that cometh . . ." to seek a favor, that is, to pray to God; must believe that He is, (a Person) even as John "saw an angel in the sun" (Revelation 19:17), whom he had sought to worship (vs. 10) for he could see no higher, so, what one sees at their highest, that is worshipped. "The God of things as they are."

The text: "He IS" and "He is a rewarder of them that seek after *Him*," not *His* (II Corinthians 12:14). Take hold of this as Jacob did (Genesis 32:26). God only has great answers for blood earnestness. The Cross is where seekers find (see Luke 9:23, 14:27). God sees only cross-bearers and it is the key that opens God's treasury. Moses made his choice for "he looked unto the *recompense*." In Egypt the recompense would have been a golden coffin, a museum item; this is in contrast to the appearances at the Transfiguration (II Peter 1:4) where Peter speaks of becoming partakers of the divine (golden) nature. The reward is the inflow of God's life over into ours (II Corinthians 3:18, Galatians 2:20).

Prayer without ceasing, changes things and people. Prayer is limited to them that seek after Him, even as He will *require* for the "blood of Abel" or as Esau *sought* with tears (Hebrews 12:17). So and only so does prevailing prayer prevail.

Launch out—let down; "leave thy low-vaulted past . . .";

Endure hardness; plunge in; ask and expect great things;

Give God what is worthy of His resources;

Make Christ real; not so much to men, but to your own soul:

---

[1] *Rubicon*: "A river in Tuscany; . . . It separated Caesar's province of Gaul from Italy, and by crossing it under arms he committed himself to a war with Pompey; hence, to cross the Rubicon, to be committed definitely to some course of action." (Funk and Wagnalls Standard Universal Dictionary)

> This above all: To thine own self be true;
> And it must follow, as night the day,
> Thou canst not then be false to any man.[1]

6. The Purpose of Prayer

a) The Claiming of God's Promises

As Daniel, the prophet, claimed God's unfulfilled promises (Daniel 9:2—3, 19 and Jeremiah 25:11—12), so Paul's prayers commandeered God. A careful study of Ephesians 1:15—17N. and especially verse 17, will substantiate this:

(1) "That" (Gr. *hina*):

This Greek word *hina* is a "purposive conjunction." Here the meaning is "with emphasis upon the purpose, design and result," or, "in order that." The Holy Spirit permits Paul to use *hina* to commit God! Exegetes seeing such an *implication* in this verse, have weakened it down, but the use of *hina* by Paul is correct. We are in Christ (Ephesians 1:23 and 2:22), and "He is nigh to all them that call upon Him" (Psalm 145:18).

(2) "The God of our Lord Jesus Christ"

To others He is God the Creator, but to us He is the Father of our Lord Jesus Christ who is Alpha and Omega. Him, Paul calls upon to answer his prayer!

(3) "The Father of Glory" (cf. John 1:14, 11:40, Matthew 6:13).

All of this plus the Maker of heaven and earth, is now pledged by that "*hina.*"

(4) "May give unto you the Spirit of wisdom and revelation in the full knowledge of Him": This is the right use of what you know. Through learning and through handling aright of the Scriptures which testify of Christ (John 5:39), we come to fully know (Gr. *epignosei*). We are not promised *wisdom* and *revelation*, but rather we are promised the *Spirit* of wisdom and revelation. One must accept the supernatural for we are to be changed "from glory into glory"; and "it doth not yet appear what we shall be" (I John 3:2; cp. I Corinthians 2:9—10).

Prayer disposes Christians "in order that" God may give, and "in order that" we may accept and put into service.

b) The Preaching of the Gospel

The great purpose of the prayers of Christians is:

---

[1]
Shakespeare, *Hamlet*, (Rev. Henry N. Hudson, LL.D., Ginn and Company, 1894) Act 1, Sc. 3, p. 72.

That the Gospel might be proclaimed

(1) Of the Jerusalem Christians, we read in Acts 4:24, 29—33:
"they lifted up their voice to God with one accord, and said
. . ." "grant unto Thy servants, that with all boldness they
may speak Thy word." "And they spake the word of God with
boldness . . ." and "with great power gave the apostles
witness of the resurrection of the Lord Jesus."

(2) Paul writes in Romans 1:9—16:
"Without ceasing I make mention of you always in my prayers
. . ." "making request, if by any means now at length I might
have a prosperous journey by the will of God to come unto
you" . . . "that I might have some fruit among you also, even
as among other Gentiles." ". . . as much as in me is, I am
ready to preach the gospel to you that are at Rome also."

(3) Romans 15:29—32 (Acts 23:11):
Paul's request to the Roman Christians was (Romans 15:
29—32):
"Now I beseech you, brethren, . . . that ye strive together
with me in your prayers to God for me; . . . that I may come
unto you with joy by the will of God, and may with you be
refreshed."
And the answer to their prayer is found in Acts 23:11: ". . .
for as thou hast testified of Me in Jerusalem, so must thou
bear witness also at Rome."

(4) The purpose of prayer is seen in Paul's request also to the
Ephesians in chapter 6:18—20 where he asks them to be:
"Praying always with all prayer and supplication in the
Spirit . . . that utterance may be given unto me, that I may
open my mouth boldly, to make known the mystery of the
gospel . . . that therein I may speak boldly, as I ought
to speak."

(5) To the Church at Colosse, Paul writes (Colossians 4:2—4):
"Continue in prayer and watch in the same with thanksgiving; withal praying also for us, that God would open
a door of utterance, to speak the mystery of Christ . . .
that I may make it manifest, as I ought to speak."

(6) And to his son in the Gospel, Paul writes, I Timothy 2:1—8:
"I exhort therefore that first of all supplications, prayers,
intercessions, and giving of thanks, be made for all men;
. . . for this is good and acceptable in the sight of God
our Saviour; Who will have all men to be saved, and to
come unto the full knowledge of the truth . . . I will therefore that men pray every where, lifting up holy hands,
without wrath and doubting."

The following suggested daily prayer schedule[1] illustrates something of the purpose of prayer:

Sunday	For blinded Israel—"To the Jew first" (Romans 1:16, 10:1, 11:25)
Monday	For the Church—"the Body of Christ" (Ephesians 1:15—23)
Tuesday	For the Gentiles—neither Jew nor Christian (I Corinthians 10:32)
Wednesday	For "all men"—Jews, Gentiles and Christians (I Timothy 2:1)
Thursday	For revival in the Body of Christ (Revelation 3:20, I Thessalonians 3:12—13, also, Paul's Epistle to the Ephesians)
Friday	For the world-wide preaching of the Gospel (Mark 16:15, Acts 1:8)
Saturday	For the speedy coming of our Lord (Revelation 22:20)

7. The Responsibility of Prayer

   a) Prayer is work
   Our Lord sweat blood in Gethsemane in prayer (Luke 22:44)
   b) Prayer is a sense of burden
   As Paul was facing his supreme hour, the Lord said, "Behold, he prayeth"
   c) Prayer is sin-cleansing; as when Simon the sorcerer was in the gall of bitterness and the bond of iniquity
   d) Prayer is vision-imparting for through it, the heavens are opened
   e) Prayer is God-compelling; the resources of the Omnipotent Father are requisitioned in prayer.

Prayer is never lightly invoked. The Lord never prayed for Himself; He prayed at the choosing of the Twelve and for Lazarus and at the Transfiguration. Paul prayed for the thorn in his flesh to be removed and he was denied the same. *We* must accept the consequence, for he who requisitions the resources of God must use them in His Way! And only then can we sing, "I'll go where *You* want me to go."

What is the intention of your request when you say, "Pray for me?" It must be either the intention of embezzlement, the selfish use of God's blessings secured through prayer for yourself—or, it is the intention of

---

[1] Great Commission Prayer League, *Prayer's Daily Schedule*, (Chicago, "1927 Edition")

crucifying self, being willing to die, to lay down your life for God, whether or no the request is answered. To say, "pray for me" is to make the most awesome request possible. The Creator and Ruler of the Universe is being put to work! We would hesitate to throw the switch at the Niagara Power Plant for great power would be released. So should we approach prayer and our requests for the prayers of others.

8. Preparation for Prayer

Our test for preparation for prayer could be Habakkuk 2:1N.:

> "I will stand upon my watch,
> And set me upon the tower, and will look
>   out to see what He will say unto me,
> And what I shall answer when I am reproved."

And then Psalm 46:10*a*:

> "Be still, and know that I am God: . . . ."

Also Isaiah 6:5:

> ". . . Woe is me! for I am undone: because I am a man
> of unclean lips, and I dwell in the midst of a people
> of unclean lips; for mine eyes have seen the King,
> the Lord of hosts."

Then, and only then, may we "ask what ye will."

Our need is to be sensitive to such wordless, creative utterances as are set forth in Psalm 19, and which encompass all the universe both of heaven and earth. There are two disturbing shocks which come while we search the Scriptures in regard to prayer:

a) First is "the closet"; this is your store-house and God's (Psalm 19, Isaiah 55:9). Jesus said, "When ye pray, enter in to thy closet" and put on words to clothe your needs. This is your storehouse (Deuteronomy 28:8). Here we make requests from "in (within) My name." The Lord is our closet. The man of the world goes to his safety vault and there he sits among his valuables, to become aware of their futility. He has a safety vault but no "store-house." What a striking figure! Here in our closet, storehouse, we sit down and count the cost; this is the best of preparation. We take inventory of our assets and the requirements beyond. Perhaps if we think it through, we will find that we have no need.

b) The second is the word "double-minded" (Gr. *dipsuchos*). This means that a soul is looking both ways. One of the ways must fail, but which one? "Enter in to thy closet and *shut* to thy door." There must be here *one* outlook and it must be "not *my* will but *Thine* be done." And note Peter's statement in John 6:68—69N.:

"Lord, to whom shall we go? Thou hast the sayings of eternal life. And we believe and have known that Thou art the Christ, the Son of the living God."

So must every prayer that moves God be "Thy will"—not mine.

I want to make prayer plausible, practical and profitable; the renewing resources of the "colonized" (Philippians 3:20, "we are a 'colony' of heaven"). The Romans of the first century or the English of today when kept apart from loved ones, were renewed by home ties and through letters kept in touch with custom, language and styles; just as Consuls and other government officials keep in touch today.

The phrase "A Colony"[1] is translated "conversation or citizenship," and it refers to "the life that I now live" which is moated off from *people* in the midst of whom I *now* live. This colony "IS" (Gr. *huparkei*) already set up and is used here denoting *being* which is from the beginning. Vincent says it means "a backward look into an antecedent condition which has been protracted into the present." In Philippians 2:6 this same word (Gr. *huparkon*) is used with reference to Christ "*being* in the form of God."

"From whence *we look*" (wait for) a Savior." This phrase is habitually used in the New Testament with reference to a future manifestation of the Glory of Christ and His people. Christians are admonished to "set your minds on things above" for we will set our minds on something. As "we look," we are actually "the stretched-out-neck" ones, anticipating the Lord's return. Our prayer life is to break through this ceiling into the *Love World*. We are to "ask for the old paths and walk therein." If we are not able to talk, we can listen in (II Corinthians 12:4) as Peter, James and John did at the Transfiguration (Hebrews 12:1). Enoch, Abraham, and Elijah were pray-ers (Hebrews 11:5, John 8:56, James 5:17); yet we do not think of them as such; so surprises break forth from the unsuspected places. Great thinkers become silent and worship at the edge of things. Plate in his *Republic*[2] wrote:

"'. . . you mean that he will be a ruler in the city of which we are the founders, and which exists in idea only; for I do not believe that there is such an one anywhere on earth?' 'In heaven,' I replied, 'there is laid up a pattern of it, methinks, which he who desires may behold, and beholding, may take up his abode there'."

And this the Christian is attempting to do, and according to our stature, we should be "facing UP."

Prayer to many is like "God and the Groceryman"; it is an order sheet

---

[1] "Colony"—Moffat's translation of Philippians 3:20

[2] Plato's *Republic*, Translated into English by B. Jowett, M. A. (London, Oxford, Ed.) No. 592 p. 306, "The City which is in heaven."

where we check off our needs, mostly re-fills, bread, etc., and we conclude with, "deliver all goods in rear" or at the back door.

Great renunciation is prayer's preparation and transfiguring glory. When one has come to surrender, he is "hid with Christ in God." Until we are given over to Him, there is no exultation or victory; this is prevented by secret sins. Until He comes in as Lord, you are in control; you are a mendicant. After He comes in, then "all things are yours."

9. The Near-Omnipotence of Prayer--Ephesians 1:15—23
—John 14:10—21

> "O, what peace we often forfeit,
> O, what needless pain we bear,
> All because we do not carry,
> *Everything* to God, in prayer."

H. Bonar

"In everything by prayer and supplication"
Philippians 4:6

"Prayer changes things." The Lord Himself said so. In Matthew 24:20—22, Jesus says to His disciples concerning the Great Tribulation, "Pray ye, that your flight be not in the *winter*, neither on the Sabbath Day." He was telling them that the God of Mercy so adjusts His plans to the prayer of His saints. And then He said, "except those days should be shortened" which indicates that they take place after the Church has been raptured away for the Grace Age is timeless. God is at work (Genesis 22, Hebrews 4:9—10, John 5:17 "and I work"; I Corinthians 3:9, II Peter 3:11—12). We are God's fellow-laborers looking for and *hastening* the coming of the day of God.

10. First Things in Prayer

There are degrees in prayers as there are items in a business. The first things should come first:

> *a)* "As the Father sent Me, *so* send I you"
> *b)* "He breathed upon them and said, 'Whose soever sins ye remit . . .' ." And then He said,
> *c)* "Give food to My lambs, shepherd and feed My sheep"
> *d)* Then come our own needs. Be importunate (Luke 18:18); be persistent, "this one thing I do, forgetting . . ." and be putting yourself into it.

Prayer is no trivial habit; but rather it is the Christian's calling. Does it mean that I should pray always? We read, "and faint not"; "at all times" "that men pray always." We can "lay off" whenever and wherever we are willing for God to stop answering prayer.

The late S. D. Gordon, known in his writings as "Quiet Hour Gordon," said:

> "The real victory in all service is won in secret beforehand by prayer. Service is gathering up the results of prayer. God does in answer to prayer what He otherwise does not do—not *could* not, but does not.
>
> "The basis of prayer is right relationship with God. The only basis of such relationship to God is Jesus. We have been outlawed by sin. Jesus came. He was God and Man. We get back to God thro' Jesus, and only so.
>
> "The blood of the cross is the basis of all prayer. Through it the relationship is established that underlies all prayer. Only as I come to God through Jesus—the Blood of Jesus cleanseth from all sin—and only as I keep in sympathy with Jesus in the purpose of my life can I pray effectively.
>
> "Let us distinctively understand that we have no standing with God except through Jesus."[1]

11. Definiteness In Prayer

Prayer is precision work. This is today's fetish: manufactured parts are prepared; and vitamins are isolated; but God was first in precision work (Job 38, Isaiah 40, Matthew 5:18).

In the Newberry Edition of the Bible, (between Testaments, p. vi.), the emphasis on the Greek definite and objective articles should be noted:

> "In the Greek language there is but one article, sometimes used like the Hebrew article *eth* as pointing out an object before the mind, or else the object on which an action terminates. At other times it is used like the Hebrew article *ha* as the distinctive or definite article. When used as the objective article it cannot in general be rendered by the English word 'the.'
>
> "The omission of the article either expresses indefiniteness, or else implies that the word without the article is characteristic; that is, it gives a character to that with which it is connected."

In Acts 1:14 "these all continued with one accord in THE prayer" for they were told that they should tarry till endued and they were to do nothing else. In Acts 2:42 "they continued steadfastly in THE prayers," which were "Thy kingdom come," and "Thy will be done" (cp. II Peter 3:9). Our adversary has sown tares and has robbed us of our definiteness and thus our prayers are hindered (I Peter 3:7, James 4:3). Let us return to the definiteness of objectives, and let us pray for "Thy kingdom" to come; "Thy will" to be done. We are not praying for Kingdom *building* but rather for Kingdom *coming*.

---

[1] S. D. Gordon, selected from *God's Prayer Tower Bulletin* by Jas. M. Spencer, minister.

12. Prevailing Prayer

There are two things in prevailing prayer:

a) "Man's extremity is God's opportunity"
Why should we ask God to do that which we can do?
The women going to the Lord's tomb said, "Who shall roll away
the stone?

b) Persistence (Luke 18:8). Prayer is no child's play; and prevailing prayer is never extemporaneous. Prayer is the first speech of New Birth; the alphabet becomes more expressive as we mature.[1]

13. The Fellowship of Experienced Pray-ers; Old and New Testament
Personalities

Prayer is the experience of Jeremiah 33:3 N.:

"Call unto Me, and I will answer thee,
And show thee great and hidden inaccessible things,
which thou knowest not."

and an insight to Revelation 5:8 N.:

"And when He had taken the book, the four living ones and four and twenty elders fell down before the Lamb, having every one of them harps, and golden bowls full of incense, which are the prayers of saints."

Prayer is the experience which is the axiom of all sects, and the satisfying experiences of the majority of their members. Then make a comparison between those using prayer and those not using it, and this will constitute a reasonable certainty that there is an intelligence beyond our horizon which is telescopic and microscopic, where our limitations shut down the *ne plus ultra*. These are not the confines of the lowest order of intelligence but rather the very highest.

1
   Prayer to Brother Kindred was a personal and intimate talk with God; and joined with the congregation's assent, it was a united prayer unto God of praise and petition.
   An incident occurred in the Englewood Church (Chicago) at the dedication of the new pulpit some years back. Brother Kindred, retired from preaching at this time, sat in his accustomed place for the morning worship hour. At the opening of service, Burton Thurston, his successor, called upon Mr. Kindred to make the dedicatory prayer for this new item of furniture from which the Gospel would be proclaimed. With no hesitation and in his usual stentorian tones with clarity and certainty, there poured forth from him for several minutes, such an imploringly earnest dedication of this pulpit, that, in the minds of the majority present, it seemed as though we as a congregation had suddenly been transported on High and there before the Throne of God, Brother Kindred, out in front as spokesman, stood before God, pleading that naught but the truth of the Gospel from The Book of books, and the exaltation of the Lord Christ Jesus, might ever be sounded forth from behind its desk.
   When suddenly his prayer ceased, the vision changed: we were instantly in our places again in the Englewood pews. A silence which could be felt, reigned for several moments afterward—some were wiping tears from their faces—and then the service of the day continued.

a) Prayer in the Veins of History

Prayer as an experience is clearly demonstrated in the life of Abraham (Genesis 12:3, Acts 3:25, John 8:56); and in the life Moses (Exodus 17:15—19, 32:32, Hebrews 11:27); and in Daniel's *Seventy Weeks*. These three foresaw the promise and we have seen the answer. As color injected into veins can be observed by the doctors, thus answers to prayer in the veins of history *may* also be seen; and *are* clearly seen; and all promises given to prayers *are* fulfilled; and we can see Jerusalem being rebuilt (Jeremiah 31, Zechariah 14) in answer to Daniel's prayer.

Another group experienced prayer: Simeon (Luke 2:34—35); and Nathaniel (John 1:48); and Saul (Acts 9:1, 21). Here we find a world transformer, Paul, changed within ten verses of Scriptures. These men "of like passion" changed their times and history, for God is sensitive to prayer.

Another company of prevailing pray-ers is found in the Bible: Elijah (I Kings 17:1, 18:42*b*); Ezekiel (Ezekiel 1:3); Habakkuk (Habakkuk 2:1, Hezekiah (II Kings 19:14—15, 20:1—6); and Hannah (I Samuel 1:10—15).

Still another group in the Scriptures experienced prayer: The Great and The Lowly found listed in Hebrews 11. We find Gideon, Barak, Samson, Jephthah, and David who subdued kingdoms, "wrought righteousness," and obtained promises.

Then we find listed women and others, and these were stoned, sawn asunder, tempted, "of whom the world was not worthy." Who did these great deeds? Oh, just a few "women," "others" and "theys"; and still today God's influencers are the "common people" to whom He listens gladly.

Faith *builds* a life but prayer *exercises* it, for "we are renewed day by day." The incident of the Ethiopian eunuch ought to encourage people (Acts 8:26—39). He was a guest, a proselyte in Jerusalem; he heard the Jews' story of Jesus and He was confused and dis-satisfied and was returning from Jerusalem, reading and praying (Acts 8:27—28). How nearly he came to being overlooked! So may it be with your friend. We have seen and experienced the responses.

b) The Land of Burning Bushes

The Bible is a land of burning bushes wherein men are at wonder worship in the Angelus of libraries.

(1) Moses' face shone after he had said, "blot me out," though before he had been in the mount for forty days

(2) The Lord prayed all night before choosing the twelve, but He was transfigured "as He spoke of His decease"

(3) Paul after Romans 9, came to II Corinthians 12:4 and wrote *Ephesians*, the book of "in the heavenlies"

(4) Stephen prayed, "Lord, lay not this sin to their charge," and his face shone "as it had been the face of an angel"

As Dante rises over evil when an angel guide approached with "face lightened," so there is a life and a language above ours, and those who seek it FIND.

c) The God-Conscious Leaders of The Restoration Movement

The leaders of the Restoration Movement united in a great discovery and many minds seemed to focus on great principles as a new epoch was written into the calendar of events. God is still prayer-hearing and prayer-answering. It is disbelief which says, "prayer is of no avail" and explains man's failure. We have given up God as a factor in living. We have to get back to the "ever present and working God." Faith must sing, "My Father knows . . . and tempers every wind that blows."

This God-conscious group of Restoration leaders was as Emerson writes of Michael Angelo, "himself from God he could not free." These men grew restless, impatient of men's sects and creeds as was to be expected.

Further, if this restless impatience was of submissive conviction and not just a mental irritation, there would be an inner illumination and the Holy Spirit's leading, and that we abundantly find as we study their lives. In the four great leaders of The Restoration Movement (Barton W. Stone, Thomas Campbell, Walter Scott), we find that each was complimentary to the other. These four mighty men "came to one accord" upon:

(1) The All-Sufficiency of the Scriptures
(2) Baptism as being immersion
(3) The Name and Organization of the Church
(4) That the Church of Christ was not, and of right could not be a Sect; that it was "A body distinguished by peculiarities of faith and practice"; and that "Denomination" was a class designation; and they said, "We are peculiar, in that there is nothing peculiar about us."

These four men came to this unity concerning the Scriptures and the Church, through prayerful seeking and study. Arriving at these conclusions individually, upon afterward meeting one another, they found that they were in common agreement. Surely, this is evidence of the inner illumination and the Holy Spirit's leading.

14. The Doxologies of The Scriptures

In the spirit of exultation, Paul has given to the Churches many doxologies, but in the book of Ephesians he gives the prayer for "you" to "apprehend" the dimensions of the high-calling of His Body, the Church, and as a last "capping" towards those heights, he then concludes the description with the doxology:

> "Now unto Him that is able to do exceeding abundantly
> above all that we ask or think, according to the power
> that worketh in us,
> 'Unto Him be glory in the church in Christ Jesus unto
> all the generations of the age of the ages, Amen."

Ephesians 3:20—21N.

The Doxologies of the Scriptures never fail to stir the heart and lift the vision of the one who meditates upon them. As we come to the close of this prayer portion, perhaps we will tarry for a while with these selected, doxologies:

Numbers 6:24—27

Ephesians 3:20—21

I Thessalonians 5:23—24

II Peter 3:17—18

Jude 24—25

Malachi 4:2—3

II Chronicles 7:14

Philippians 4:5—7

II Corinthians 9:8

John 12:21 ". . . 'Sir, *we* would see Jesus'"

14:9*b*—17 and 10:9

Psalms 51:7 and 139:23—24

and Romans 11:36:

> "for of Him, and through Him, and unto Him, are all things;
> to Him be glory unto the ages. Amen."

490

Section FIVE: THE CHURCH—MY STORY (Continued)

VI. "THE THINGS WHICH HAVE BEEN FULLY ESTABLISHED

AMONG US" (Luke 1:1 A.S.V. m*)

THE VITAL DOCTRINES OF SALVATION

Page

H. The TITHE

GOD'S OMNISCIENT FINANCIAL METHOD

* *Marginal reference*

VI. "THE THINGS WHICH HAVE BEEN FULLY ESTABLISHED

AMONG US" (Luke 1:1 A.S.V.m) — THE VITAL DOCTRINES

OF SALVATION

H. GOD'S OMNISCIENT FINANCIAL METHOD

Text:
("Moreover it is required in stewards,
(that one be found faithful."
(I Corinthians 4:2N.

Introduction

This Book, the Bible, is the revelation from God and is His Mind upon affairs both spiritual and moral for the welfare of man, the commonwealth of nations, His Universe, and is final, authoritative, and encyclopedic. The sole mission of a minister is to declare the whole counsel of God, whether it be sweet or bitter (Ezekiel 3:1–3, Revelation 10:10). In this connection we are discussing the financing of the Church. There are just two "hilarious" Christian privileges: first, the giving of money (Romans 12:8*a*), and second, the showing of mercy (Romans 12:8*b*). "Money is THE Acid Test." It is the first if not also the greatest. An *institution* must be financed and one who is able to conceive such an institution would also make "the way" of support and would bless those stewards who were having fellowship "in THIS Grace" (Malachi 3:10, II Corinthians 8:7–9).

1. The Tithe in Scripture

   a) The Origin of the Tithe

"The tithe is the Lord's" (Leviticus 27:30). It is not Jewish in origin but it is found in *Genesis* before the Jewish nation was formed. In Genesis 4:3 we read, "And in the process of time ("And at the end of the days . . .") Cain brought an offering unto Jehovah." Always Jehovah has a place and a time and an ordinance for man to keep. If man failed to keep the Sabbath (a time) certain penalties resulted (II Chronicles 36:14–21, Jeremiah 25:11) and likewise if he failed to bring the tithe (an ordinance) God exacted certain penalties (Malachi 3:8–10). Abraham (Genesis 14) as he traveled from Dan to Salem (Jerusalem) to Sodom. Why did he travel so far out of his way? What prompted him to go to Salem? He was tithe-paying, and he was very sensitive as to how he handled money (Genesis 23:13). Jacob his grandson, was careless but he renewed his vow (Genesis 28:16–22). We wonder to whom he paid his tithes.

It is inconceivable that the God of Genesis 1:26–27 and John 3:16 would leave man uninstructed, and if He would be obscure and vague anywhere, never would it be at the use of a week, or of money, around which center two of the most exacting sciences. This is especially confirmed by physiologists and economists. The keeping of a day and the bringing of the tithe are definitely ordained of God in the Scriptures. It would stagger the imagination to attempt to visualize the Christian wealth that could be tithed for evangelism and especially the accomplishments which would result when these tithes were directed by the Christian intellect.

b) The First Tithers

We all know that tithing was taught, commanded and practiced by the Jews, but we also know that it was a tradition among other nations and was observed by many ancient peoples. It is likely that Abel was a tither (Genesis 4:4, Hebrews 11:4) and it is possible that the traditions of the ancient nations had their foundation here.

Though it is not stated that Abraham was required to pay tithes, yet we read that he paid them (Genesis 14:20); and Jacob his grandson vowed that he would bring the tenth unto God (Genesis 28:22); and the Gentile High Priest, Melchizedek, greater than any of the Aaronic priesthood (Hebrews 7:4—10), received tithes.

c) The Tithe and The Law

It was specifically designated in Mosaism that the tithe be brought into the storehouse:

> "Bring ye all the tithes into the storehouse,
> That there may be meat in Mine house,
> And prove Me now herewith, saith Jehovah of hosts . . ."

Malachi 3:10a

The tithe was to be used for three specified classes:

(1) The Levites
    Numbers 18:20—24, Deuteronomy 14:22—27, Nehemiah 10:37—39
(2) The Priests (Aaronic)
    Numbers 18:25—28
(3) The Levite stranger—fatherless and the widow
    Deuteronomy 14:28—29

The Jews PAID tithes; and GAVE heave offerings (Exodus 25:2, 36:5); and brought also "First Fruits" (Leviticus 23:9—14).

d) Jesus' Teaching on the Tithe
"Woe unto you, scribes and Pharisees, hypocrites! for ye pay tithe tithe of mint and anise and cummin, and have omitted the weightier matters of the law, judgment, and mercy, and faith: these *ought* ye to have done, and not to leave the other undone."

Matthew 23:23

"But woe unto you, Pharisees! for ye tithe mint and rue and all manner of herbs, and pass over judgment and the love of God: these *ought* ye to have done, and not to leave the other undone."

Luke 11:42

The imperial "ought" of conscience in Matthew 23:23 and Luke 11:42 forever stamps the Lord's endorsement upon the tithe.

In the Sermon on the Mount, Jesus said:

"Lay not up for yourselves treasures upon earth, where moth and rust doth corrupt, and where thieves break through and steal: But lay up for yourselves treasures in heaven, where neither moth nor rust doth corrupt, and where thieves do not break through nor steal: For where your treasure is, there will your heart be also."

Matthew 6:19—21

Later, in the parable of the unjust steward, He said:

"He that is faithful in a very little, is faithful also in much: and he that is unjust in a very little, is unjust also in much. If therefore ye have not been faithful in the unrighteous riches, who will commit to your trust the true riches? And if ye have not been faithful in that which is another's, who shall give you that which is your own? No servant can serve as a bond servant two masters: for either he will hate the one, and love the other; or else he will hold to one, and despise the other. Ye cannot serve as a bondservant God and riches."

Luke 16:10—13 N.

2. The Tithe in The Age of Grace

a) New Testament Tithing

"Do you not know that they which minister about holy things live of the things of the temple? and they which wait at the altar are partakers with the altar? Even so hath the Lord ordained that they which preach the gospel should live of the gospel."

I Corinthians 9:13—14

"And here indeed men that die receive tithes; but there he receiveth them of whom it is witnessed that he liveth."

Hebrews 7:8 N.

I have never seen or heard disputed that the tithe was a Jewish obligation and that it was for a certain specific purpose and that it was brought up to the house of the Lord (Malachi 3:1—10). There remains only this question: "Was the tithe incorporated in the *New* Testament?"

(1) That it is mentioned forcibly is conceded (Matthew 23:23,16:21);
(2) Abraham paid tithes to Melchizedek, the lesser paid tithes to

the better, and "another priest should arise after the order of Melchizedek" . . . "after the power of an endless life."

If the tithe is not brought into the New Testament, then we are undone, and this is proven by impoverished congregations; the missionary is left to begging; and money raising devices finance the local church, and we have been wronged. Paul's apology amply illustrates this:

> "For what is it wherein ye were inferior to other churches, except it be that I myself was not burdensome to you? forgive me this wrong."
>
> II Corinthians 12:13

We have just noted that the Lord asserted tithing to be an obligation upon the Jew. The Scriptures of Hebrews 7 declare tithing to be binding upon Christians. This is universal: "The tithe is the Lord's." It is not any more Jewish than "Thou shalt not kill" or "steal . . . ." It is not a religious obligation but it is a tenant tax. If the laws against murder or stealing are done away, it would be because they were replaced with a higher law. The tithe is NOT an investment, but it is a partnership, an incorporated concern of God and you within Christ's Body, the Church. Tithing can be abused (Luke 18:12, I Corinthians 7:31) just like immersion. It is not a cure-all, but it is the Christian's most profitable use of his property. Many a man has been properly born but has gone wrong, and has used his life in an improper way. To tithe is partnership with God but *not* to tithe, is to deny His partnership and to take issue with the Holy Spirit (Leviticus 27:30). This partnership was formed by God ere He decided upon the "business" (Ephesians 1:4). If one tithes solely for gain, then there is no blessing though there may be success in business.

Here is "The Book of the Generations" of the *non*-tithers:

> Wilfulness begat disobedience;
> Disobedience begat sin;
> Sin begat fear;
> And fear begat covetousness.

The objector to the tithe is apt to be one who is in arrears. The tithe PAID transfers all responsibility unto God and leaves unto you peace. The tithe UNpaid leaves the door open to all manner of schemes and catchpenny devices; it degrades the Church and it secularizes the membership. Only fear keeps men from tithing. If you knew that you would be no worse off, wouldn't you be a tither? (Malachi 3:10, I John 5:10). Cowardice and covetousness are inseparables.

The Gospel postulates the *Ek-klesia* and these in turn postulate the expense of worship, propaganda and other local expenses. There is need for a place and the items of worship; the command, "going, *preach*" necessitates the expense involved in obeying this command through the means at our disposal for propaganda; the growth and development of the Church in the community must likewise be provided for. God counts the cost (Luke 14:28) and provides the place (I Corinthians 9:14); and He calls us to provide the expense (Romans 10:14—15). A world-wide campaign calls for a budget to match it and a tithing congregation can underwrite its needs.

The contrast between the Levitical and the Melchizedek priesthood calls for a budget to match it and a tithing congregation can underwrite its needs.

The contrast between the Levitical and the Melchizedek priesthood is revealed in *Hebrews*; and that Christ is now our High Priest, having abolished the Levitical priesthood, is made clear in Hebrews 6:13 to Hebrews 8:6. Here is set forth convincingly the Law of the tithe under God's TWO Immutables.

Hebrews 6:13 to 7:3 reveals:

    (1) The promise to Abraham
    (2) The Two Immutables (The Oath and the Promise)
        to the " Heirs of Promise"
    (3) The "Hope—within the Veil"
    (4) "Jesus (already) entered"
    (5) The High Priest—Melchizedek
        The first immutable was a *Promise* to Abraham himself (Genesis 15:5—6) and the second immutable, the *Oath*, referred to that One who was of "indissoluable life" (Genesis 22:16—18; Revelation 1:18*b*)

Hebrews 7:4—10 tells us:

    (1) Melchizedek was greater than Abraham
    (2) The Levites were lesser than Melchizedek
    (3) Melchizedek blessed Abraham
    (4) Melchizedek received tithes from Abraham

Hebrews 7:11—25 informs us that:

    (1) The Priesthood was changed
    (2) There was necessity to change the law
    (3) There was the "power of an endless life"
    (4) That tithes were paid to Levi; to Melchizedek;
        and to the Lord:

And in Hebrews 8:1—6 we are told:

    (1) That the chief point is, "We have such an High Priest"
    (2) That the True Tabernacle came before Israel's
        Tabernacle (Hebrews 8:5)

(3) "Every High Priest is appointed to offer gifts and sacrifices"

(4) That Christ is now doing this in the heavens.

The New Testament Scriptures make tithing vital to Christian stewardship.

b) The Christian's Obligation

Everyone feels a sense of obligation to his clan, his group or his race. None of us liveth to himself (Romans 14:7), and all of life requires sustenance, so we are obligated to its sustainers. The fair-minded seeks to know, so as to render a return. He says, "what must we do"; or, "Lord, what wilt Thou have me to do." God *never* leaves the answer vague or uncertain. Each dispensation has its Laws of Life and Obligation, no one of which is left for man to ordain. Let us consider the Jew. The Mosiac dispensation is the most detailed and definite of ancient institutions and that also joins to the Church. David fixes the importance of the offering:

> "And king David said, . . . 'Nay; but I will surely buy it of thee at a price; neither will I offer up ascending offerings unto Jehovah my God of that which doth cost me nothing' . . ."
>
> II Samuel 24:24N.

And Moses wrote:

> "And all the tithe of the land, whether of the seed of the land, or of the fruit of the tree, is Jehovah's: it is holy unto Jehovah."
>
> Leviticus 27:30

"The tithe is the Lord's"—not ours. It was not the Jews', nor was it the priests', but the tithe was God's; and the Lord requires from whom He will for any purpose of institution where specifically designated.

Paul wrote, "that there be no collections" when he came (I Corinthians 16:2). The danger of our thinking could be, "the church has plenty," but let us ask, "did I put it there?" The law of the tithe is framed within Grace (Leviticus 27:30). Here is the law (Matthew 23:23) "this *ought* ye to do"; but observe the frame: "Grace," which comes both before and after the law (Romans 4:13—16). Even Levi paid tithes for none are exempt, therefore it is universal. If it were Jewish, it would now be "done away," but we are under Grace (love), and we are responsible for either alimony or a love obligation and the government (law) allows at least twenty per cent. God is the All-Wise Provider for His children and His covenant institutions. He who took detailed care of every least element would not overlook income. He gave detailed instructions concerning tithes and offerings when He instituted the tabernacle, and He said, "Even so" ("in like manner") hath the Lord ordained . . ." when He revealed the Church.

So, at the first appropriate place there is instruction in the church support (I Corinthians 9:6—14):

(1) We are not to muzzle the ox (Deuteronomy 25:4)

(2) "They which minister about holy things" were the Levites who were supported by the tithes of the other eleven tribes and "they which wait at the altar" were the priests, the sons of Aaron, who were supported by the tithes of the Levites. The Greek word *houtos* is translated "even so" or "in like manner"; or "thus" and I Corinthians 9:14 literally means, in the same manner that the Levites and priests were supported in the Old Testament, the Lord has ordained—made a precise arrangement—that the preaching of the Gospel for the Age of Grace is to be supported: by tithing.

A.T. Robertson presents these verses of I Corinthians 9:13 and 14 as follows:

"Just as God gave orders (Law) about priests in the Temple, so did the Lord Jesus give orders for those who preach the Gospel, to live out of the Gospel."

At the times that Jesus said, "It is more blessed to give than to receive," He must have talked about money. Therefore both are of like authority (Malachi 3:1—10, I Corinthians 9:6—14). The Lord's Priesthood is after the order of the Melchizedek Priesthood (Hebrews 7:11 and 8:3). Money is our surplus self; it is our alter-ego; can you withhold it from God and give yourself?

The New Testament which is for this Age of Grace speaks upon the financing of the Church, not the Kingdom. We would not expect the Messiah to mention tithing, for His preaching was to confirmed tithers, and yet note that He said, "this *ought* ye to do"; it was the only time appropriate and He says "ought." At Antioch, Barnabas and Paul and others, labored with the Church, and these came out of Jewish background; there was no need for teaching them.

When Paul went to the Gentiles, he gave instruction concerning a special offering and he writes in I Corinthians 16:1—2N.:

"Now concerning the collection for the saints, as I have given order to the churches of Galatia, even so do ye. Upon the first day of the week let every one of you lay by him in store, whatever he may be prospered in, that there be no collections when I come."

The Greek word *thesaurison* is common to both I Corinthians 16:2 and Malachi 3:10 and is translated "lay by in *store*" and "*store*house."

To Titus Paul gives the instruction mentioned in II Corinthians 8:5—6N.:

"And this they did, not according as we hoped, but first they gave their own selves to the Lord, and unto us through the will of God. Insomuch that we desired Titus, that as he had begun, so he would also finish in you the same grace also."

This "Grace" is further illumined in verse 9 by:

> "For ye know the *grace* of our Lord Jesus Christ, that, though He
> was rich, yet for your sakes He became poor, that ye through His
> poverty might become rich."

And then Paul challenges them in verse 24 to show the proof of their love, for love is abiding and continuing, and their love would be manifest in the bringing of their tithes and offerings.

The contrast in the attitudes of giving are referred to in II Corinthians 9:6—8: the one who sowed sparingly is set in contrast to the "hilarious" giver that God loved; all sufficiency is supplied through Him, and He does not turn down any who go along with Him.

At the Englewood Church we had an $85,000 plant and there was the natural deterioration and salaries of ten paid workers must be kept up. How was this best done? By means of the tithe. Our plan at Englewood was to encourage the members to place into the church treasury sixty-five to seventy-five per cent of their tithes; the balance of their tithes, a twenty-five or thirty-five per cent portion could then be distributed by them in their Bible School classes or in special gifts to missionaries in whom they were personally interested. They were never encouraged to pay any portion of the tithe for such contributions as Red Cross or Community Chest, rather these things should be supported from gifts over and above the tithe, as *offerings*, and the second ten per cent deduction permitted by government. Our slogan was: "Every Member a Tither." When we become Bible tithers, we bring the *whole* tithe for God.[1] God's Word tells us, "Prove Me . . . if

---

[1] Brother Kindred was a firm believer in his coined phrase which so often appeared on our Englewood church calendar on Sunday: *"Tithing develops spirituality."*

Ministers at that time were exempted from deductions by employers, and when his monthly salary check came, the very first deduction taken out, was the Lord's tithe (one-tenth) from his gross income check. A complete bookkeeping account of this tithing amount was kept separate and apart from the household account and the government's additional ten per cent deduction account, making three separate accounts to be kept by the month. A most careful selection of the *tithe* deduction was made: the church's monthly pledge came out first, then Class 43's Bible School regular monthly pledge; after this, the direct missionary offerings. And from the government's *"Extra 10% Account,"* as it was called, were deducted such offerings as Red Cross, Community Chest offerings, special entertainments for Christian and missionary helps; tracts for distribution *et al*. But never was the first ten per cent account, called *"The Tithing Account—Lev. 27:30,"* ever tampered with nor lightly disposed of. Its envelop contents could sometimes have a balance on hand, but such balance must always be disposed of in the right way before the next salary check arrived with a new Lord's tithe. The order of figuring the tithe on other earnings as weddings, funerals, speeches, etc., was also that of love and not law; and here the account was kept entirely apart from other accounts and considered personal spending *after a DOUBLE tithe* had first been taken out for the Lord's use. To Brother Kindred, I Corinthians 14:40 was as important and as sacred a trust in the Lord's tithing accounts as it was in Paul's general instructions to church members:

"Let all things be done decently and in order."

I will not open the windows of heaven.' Ninety cents can go farther than one hundred cents, and this being true, to change would be disastrous.

Someone says, "but how should we figure the tithe?" Let us suggest this: If your employer were to add a tithe to your salary, how would you figure it? If God should multiply by ten your gifts to Him, would it equal your income? The tithe must always be figured BEFORE and not AFTER deductions from our salary; taxes and other deductions are a part of our income, our increase, and are part of God's blessings as well as any other part of our salary. We are a people who believe firmly in the Bible teachings of baptism, but I suppose if it cost us as much as the tithe, there would be a lot of folks who would be denying that there was any Scripture for it!

In Isaiah 44:12—17 we are given the picture of the man who hews down a tree and with a part of the tree he burns for warmth, with a part of it he cooks his food, and with the residue of it, he makes a god (Colossians 3:5, and I Timothy 6:10 should also be read). And as we read this portion of *Isaiah*, we are reminded that that part of the tithe which is withheld, is your god and supplants the OMNI-scient, the OMNI-potent, and the OMNI-present God; and it puts God on your charity list. No wonder He is neither worshipped nor respected. Can we pray to One whom we so treat? Hear the word of Malachi (3:10*b* N.):

> "And prove Me now herewith, saith Jehovah of hosts,
> If I will not open you the windows of heaven,
> And empty you out a blessing, that there shall not
> be room enough to receive it."

Here is a revival ready and prepared, waiting at our door. Beloved, let us put our God to the test.

The right use of our money leads to eternal riches for it is not possible to go bankrupt lending to one's own Father:

> "He that hath pity upon the poor lendeth unto Jehovah;
> And that which he hath given will He pay him again."

Proverbs 19:17

c) God's "Hilarious" Partner

". . . for God loveth a cheerful (hilarious) giver."

II Corinthians 9:7*b*

Are you a TITHER or a TIPPER—which? for you are one or the other; there is no middle ground. Should you GIVE beyond the tithe, even that is only liberal "tipping" for God *ordained* the tithe. It is not of Jew or Gentile but the tithe is of God. We have allowed wrong attitudes to develop in our relation to the heavenly Father. We consider the church service dry and uninteresting; and we think that to be a Christian, one must be a long-faced joy-killer; and to support the Church and missions is a burdensome hardship. All of these are love-provisions and especially the tithe, for it is for the comfort and self-respect of all classes that there be no invidious comparisons, as the one who gave the half-shekel (Exodus 30:13—16). Someone must determine the portion. Who is most able, just and constant? Is it man, this generation, or God? If the portion were determined by man, then there would be fluctations for no two men are alike.

The tithe must be paid from property or possession. Let us ask this question: whose property pays the tithe? The Scriptures tell us that "the earth is the Lord's and the fulness thereof." The tithe is paid from the title-holder's and not the tenant's possession. So we pay to God, the owner of all, one-tenth of His increase which He has placed in our keeping and the tithe that we pay is His, not ours.

I have never met a non-tither who paid more than a tithe; and the mine run of such givers is way below this average. Neither have I met a tither but who was always paid up and happy at the opportunity to give above and beyond the tithe. Again I ask, are you a tither or a tipper? What is God to you, a waiter or a partner? Do you sit down in His Presence and share in His work by your tithe or do you, as in a restaurant, leave a tip under the plate? Are we to treat God as a waiter?

The non-tither or "tipper" might say, there are two objections:

> *One*, "No one is going to tell me how much I should give to the Church!" Now that puts God in *His* place; that is, He is a waiter. The dinner check is your test for no one can tell you the amount of tip which you are to leave, but the law requires you to pay the check.
>
> *Two*, the other objection is, "I'm not a Jew." Then *you* can be very thankful, for *they* brought tithes AND offerings; "offerings" were added to the Jews' tithes.

Even "Uncle Sam" permits us to deduct at least twenty per cent for contributions to religious or benevolent purposes. He allows for more than even God's requirements. Let us concede that the tithe is Jewish though it is NOT. The Jew was under law and the Christian is under Grace; which should be more liberal?

But some one will say, "I can't tithe for I have other obligations." If you are paying these out of the tithe, you are dispensing another's money and if the tithe is doing it, don't *you* take the credit for doing it. The tithe is not Jewish, for Abraham brought tithes before the law, and Christians have tithed after the law.

God and man must meet in worship. And each supplies of self plus: God gave of Himself in His Son and made possible the Cross. Man presents himself and that which he possesses and thus he becomes the means of propagating the Cross. The ideal of Christian giving is therefore found in Malachi 3:10 and II Corinthians 9:6—8, for with it *must* go your life.

> Proof texts inform us (Leviticus 27:30)
> Jesus Christ inspires us (II Corinthians 8:9)
> The early Christians, the Macedonians,
> challenge us (II Corinthians 8:5).
> And still it is up to *you*.

502

Section FIVE: THE CHURCH—MY STORY (Continued)

VI. "THE THINGS WHICH HAVE BEEN FULLY ESTABLISHED

AMONG US" (Luke 1:1 A.S.V.m*)

THE VITAL DOCTRINES OF SALVATION

Page

I. The RAPTURE

* Marginal reference

VI. "THE THINGS WHICH HAVE BEEN FULLY ESTABLISHED AMONG US" (Luke 1:1 A.S.V.m) — THE VITAL DOCTRINES OF SALVATION

I. THE RAPTURE

> "For the grace of God that bringeth salvation appeared to all men, Teaching us that denying ungodliness and worldly lusts, we should live soberly, and righteously, and godly, in this present age; Looking for the blessed hope, and appearing of the glory of the great God and our Saviour Jesus Christ;"
>
> Titus 2:11–13N.

1. Rightly Dividing The Terms of Eschatology

The word *Rapture* has been applied by many different commentators, to the "catching up" of the Church. It is used to describe the event which brings to a conclusion this Age of Grace. The dictionary defines the word as follows:

a) (verb transitive) to enrapture, transport

b) noun: *the state of being rapt or transported; ecstatic joy, ecstasy*

c) An act or expression of excessive delight

d) The violence of that which seizes and carries away

e) A snatching away; violent seizure.

Essentially the word *rapture* is used in a Scriptural sense to describe the transporting of the Church from earth to heaven. There is also an ecstatic joy experienced by those who participate, but this is merely a by-product of that which the act accomplishes.

A careful distinction must be made between THE COMING OF THE LORD for His Church, the Rapture; and the SECOND COMING OF CHRIST which has also been termed "The Revelation" or "The Unveiling of Christ." The differences between the RAPTURE and the REVELATION are quite distinct.

THE RAPTURE	THE SECOND COMING
(The Return for His Church)	(The Revelation or Unveiling)
a) Brings to a conclusion the Church Age of Grace	*a*) Begins the Day of the Lord, or the Kingdom of Christ on earth
b) At this time Christ comes in the air *for* His saints, the Church, who are "caught up" to meet Him in the air	*b*) Is Christ's coming *with* His saints to earth and His feet stand upon the Mount of Olives
c) Is quiet and unseen by those who	*c*) Is the unveiling of Christ before

are "not taken"

d) Is the taking out of the Church; and the Man of Sin is unveiled and the Tribulation begins

e) Fulfills the promise of salvation for His Church

f) Brings to conclusion the preaching of the Gospel of Christ by the Church to all nations.

This Gospel is the New Covenant in His blood (Luke 22:20 and I Corinthians 11:25)

g) Is not revealed in any of the prophets but like the Church itself it was "hid in God" from the beginning of the world.

all the nations when "every eye shall see Him"

d) Is the judgment of the nations; Christ is unveiled; Satan is bound for one thousand years

e) Fulfills His promise to restore Israel and to judge the nations

f) Brings to conclusion the preaching of the Jewish Remnant to both Jew and Gentile during the Tribulation period. The converts here are the Tribulation saints of Revelation 7:14.

The New Covenant with the House of Israel and the House of Jacob begins here and is available to all nations during the Kingdom Age (Zechariah 8:20—23, Isaiah 66:18—19)

g) Is clearly set forth in prophecy and the major emphasis in prophecy is upon the *Second* Coming rather than the First Coming.

With these distinctions being made, let us take up the texts concerning this event of immediate importance to the Church—the Rapture. Our rightly dividing will bring clarity of thinking and understanding as we "distinguish the things that differ."

The longing for immortality is the universal passion of humanity and the hope of immortality was the "substance" of Israel's religion (Acts 26: 6—7, 28:20). This hope of immortality is not peculiar to Mosaism for Job who antedated the time of Moses declared "I know that my Redeemer liveth" (Job 19:25); and the Lord made reference to Moses at the burning bush viz., ". . . when he calleth the Lord, the God of Abraham, and the God of Isaac, and the God of Jacob" (Luke 20:37). The Lord's whole ministry was based upon immortality that "death does not end all." He told His disciples "that He must go unto Jerusalem and suffer many things . . . and be killed and be raised again the third day" (Matthew 16:21, I Peter 1:11). At Nazareth (Luke 4:19) He proclaimed *"the acceptable year of the Lord"* from Isaiah 61:1—2; but He carefully refrained from declaring *"the day of vengeance of our God"* (Revelation 20:4—6) from Isaiah 61:2*b*. It is important that we note the gap here, or the space between "the acceptable year of the Lord" and "the day of vengeance of our God." This space is the Church Age, or The Age of Grace which is concluded with the Rapture.

In noting the difference between "the acceptable year of the Lord" and "the day of vengeance of our God," we must distinguish between the First Coming and the Second Coming of Christ to earth. At His First Coming were fulfilled the *sufferings*, and at His Second Coming, He will fulfill the prophecies concerning *His glory* (I Peter 1:1). The Scriptures are clear in dividing between these two comings to earth, and if we rightly divide, each portion will "go to his own place." We have already noted that the Rapture and the Second Coming are two distinct events and must not be confused; also in each and every emphasis the *climax* of prophecy is not the First Coming nor the Church, but rather it is the Second Coming (Hebrews 11:39—40).

The First Coming	The Second Coming
("The Sufferings of Christ")	("The Glory that should follow")

a) Isaiah 7:14, Matthew 1:18—23, Hebrews 2:14. He was begotten of the Holy Spirit and born of a virgin when He became a partaker of flesh and blood, This virgin-born One is also called: "The Only Begotten of the Father" when He was raised from the grave (Acts 13:33).

b) Genesis 3:15. He was to be the *seed of the woman* and He became such through the lineage of Seth, Abraham, Jacob, and Judah, of the family of Jesse and David. He was born in Bethlehem, lived in Nazareth and died in Jerusalem.

c) Isaiah 9:6a refers to His First Coming, as we read "a child is born" and "He shall be called Wonderful, Counsellor."

d) Isaiah 53:2—10, we find the description of the suffering of the Messiah (cp. Exodus 12:46 and

a) Isaiah 11:10—12, 60:1 ff. In contrast to His First Coming, see the majesty and glory of His Second Coming: "Behold, He cometh with clouds; and every eye shall see Him, and they also which pierced Him: and all kindreds of the earth shall wail because of Him "(Revelation 1:7).

b) The bruising of Satan prophesied in Genesis 3:15 will be fulfilled at the Second Coming (Romans 16:20).

c) Isaiah 9:6b applies to the Second Coming, "A Son is given" and the names applied to Him are "Mighty God, The Everlasting Father, The Prince of Peace."

d) Isaiah 53:11 and 12 look to His Second Coming in glory, "He shall see of the travail of His

Psalm 41:9, 69:2) of the First Coming; and this was fulfilled before the eyes of unbelieving Jews (Acts 3:18)

e) Galatians 4:4 states that the First Coming was in the fulness of time as God sent forth His Son.

The world was at peace and the temple of Janus* was closed.

* Standard Universal Dictionary: Janus, Roman mythology, an ancient Italian divinity, god of beginnings, having two faces, looking east and west; *his temple was closed only in time of peace.*

soul and shall be satisfied . . . therefore will I divide Him a portion with the great and He shall divide the spoil with the strong."

e) II Peter 3:3—4. At the time of the Second Coming, the world will be in turmoil and war, and Peter tells of the scoffers of the last days: "Knowing this first, that there shall come in the last days scoffers, walking after their own lusts, And saying, 'Where is the promise of His coming? for since the fathers fell asleep, all things continue as they were from the beginning of the creation'.' The perilous times of the last days is also described in II Timothy 3:1—9.

Compare the prophecies of our Lord's First and Second ComingS and be scientific; and reason from the known to the unknown. These prophecies were as Josh Billings' story of the gooseberry in the barrel of sugar whose personality was so distinct that when you came to it in going through the sugar, you could recognize it immediately. And so these prophecies and their fulfillment stand apart and distinct in the Scriptures.

The Second Coming is a Palimpsest; it is imposed upon the First Coming. The frugal paucity of God is observable in all His works (Isaiah 28:9—10), as old monks used over and over the parchments in the monasteries, so God wrote over and upon His revelation in such a manner that each is apparent to spiritual minds. The epistles of Paul are imposed upon "the other Scriptures." The proof is seen above in the "ComingS" of the Lord; His *sufferings* and His *glory* which both arise out of the one stem. Though these ComingS are divided into ages, yet they are inextricably woven into one ageless life. Should one believing this be called out of date or unscholarly, then unhesitatingly into His hand goes mine (Matthew 11:25—26), and into my heart comes He; and I go my way in a light divine, a path I had feared to see. I want to be of that group who trustingly believes in an able, willing, loving and redeeming Father-God who "has made known His ways unto Moses; His acts unto the children of men" (Psalm 10:3—7).

Between the First Coming and the Second Coming is the Church Age or the Age of Grace. The Rapture brings to a conclusion this age before the Second Coming to earth takes place. Therefore, isn't it natural that first in human thinking should come the Rapture? This truth is above all other doctrines and when we have stopped thinking upon it, we have given it up as the blessed hope.

2. The Christian's Outpost Observatory

In the epistles of Paul several views of the Rapture are given, but it is from the observatory heights of the *Thessalonians'* outlook's post that we gain our clearest view of "things to come." *Thessalonians* deals with the then non-experienced factors of our religion so that there is no word in this book but which may incandesce with glory light.

a) "Seeing the Invisible"

> "While we look not at the things which are seen,
> but at the things which are not seen; for the
> things which are seen are temporal (temporary);
> but the things which are not seen are eternal."

                    II Corinthians 4:18

The Bible is a level (flat) Book to the indifferent examiner, and such are apt to go to it for a topical study and thus disturb its balanced proportions. Such excursions produce lop-sided fanatics with fantastic theories upon healing or the Second Coming who develop starved souls upon this one value diet and who can see but their own "hobby." To such indifferent readers all of the Bible's authors or writers are considered to be on a par to their hearers. But under such a candle-light the richness and the glory of God's revelation does not glow and scintilate. The result is an aversion to Bible study and an avoidance of church services. Within this Book there are unfoldings and revealings that catch one away from things visible to invisible realities. The disciple who sees not the invisible of his calling has failed. There are heights and depths (Romans 8:38) in the Holy Writ as picturesque as, aye, and more also than in earth. The sole requirement is to rightly divide. There must be a reverent approach, a filial emotion, a self denial, and a cross "taken up."

The "fruits of the spirit" had but intensified Christian love in the hearts of the Thessalonians, and then in an appalling manner came death into the midst of these Christians, and Paul wrote:

> "But I would not have you to be ignorant, brethren,
> concerning them which have fallen asleep, that ye
> sorrow not even as also others which have no hope."

                    I Thessalonians 4:13N.

This verse arose in emphasized importance and was responsible for the then prevalent conception concerning the Lord's coming. Some thought the Lord would come before any Christian fell asleep, but Paul here clarifies the teaching and it is not a strained interpretation, but like Paul himself, was "one born out of due time." Paul is the apostle of the Rapture and his use of words sets this message apart; this "catching up" of the Church is peculiar to St. Paul.

Paul's epistles divide into three groups: *Romans* dealing with *Salvation*; *Ephesians* with *Sanctification*; and *Thessalonians* with *Glorification*. *Romans* is the *closed door* with sin shut out and the saved shut in; and the Cross is between them. *Ephesians* is *within doors* in Him, set apart. It is the "now" of Jude 25, the Holy Spirit's hour. *Thessalonians* is the *open door* upon eternity into immensity; it is the outlook upon "things to come." Paul is "an angel in the sun" (Revelation 19:17) as the New Testament revelation opens up revealing things "hid in God."

This Thessalonian Church, a most perfect congregation, is a sane, intelligent people who were taught and had received the Rapture Hope (cf. II Thessalonians 2:5 and 1:20). This waiting hope breaks forth from every chapter and has a window opened in I Thessalonians 4:13—18 where we may contemplate the personnel and the manner of the reunion at the Rapture:

> *Verse 13*: "I would not have you to be ignorant" (cp. II Corinthians 2:11). This is the cause of all blunders, failures and sins (Luke 23:24). It discredits Jesus Christ, the Head, and stunts one's soul; such disregard is surely by minds not noted for brilliancy.
> *Verse 14*: "For if we believe that Jesus died and rose again . . ." The Thessalonians did believe this and Jesus says, ". . . because I live, ye shall live also" (John 14:19b).
> *Verse 14b*: "them also which sleep through Jesus will God bring with Him." As "they"—these sleeping ones—will come "with Him," so we, the remaining ones, cannot "precede" them; we cannot get between them and the Lord. Jesus died as a sin offering, but the Christian falls asleep through Jesus Christ. He said, "I am the door . . . go in and out . . ." (John 10:9, 11:25—26). "A sleep" is a restful, restorative effect of a temporary nature. It is a word which is used of natural sleep and also of the death of Christians. If there had been no sin, it would have been a natural method of change. It is a goal: *teleois*—"When God hath made the pile complete" and it is used of a workman on a building (Ephesians 2:19, 22); so he awakens Lazarus, the workman, and with David we can say, "I shall dwell in the house of the Lord forever" (II Corinthians 5:1—8).

The above is a statement of a fact. Now we proceed to consider the manner by which it is brought to pass. This is the preface to verse 15, "for this we say unto you by the Word of the Lord"; no human mind could reveal these things (II Corinthians 12:4).

Verse 16: "For the Lord Himself shall descend from Heaven with a shout,[1] with the voice of the archangel, and with the trump of God." He comes not to earth, but into the air as a conqueror pausing before a beleaguered city (cp. Acts 9:7, Job 19:27, Exodus 19:26—27, 20:18—21). Pomp and majesty and the quality of sound are indicated here by the absence of the definite article. This will be the Christian's first sight of Him (I John 3:2).

Verse 16b: "And the dead in Christ shall rise first" (cf. Philippians 3:10—11). This multitude of people God will bring with Christ, so those that are asleep will be like the Shekinah around the Lord at His coming for His Church (Hebrews 12:1, Matthew 17:2—3, Acts 1:9).

Verse 17a: "Then we which are alive and remain shall be caught up together with them in the clouds, to meet the Lord in the air:" We who remain are only fragments to be gathered up or salvaged; i.e., all living Christians at the time of the Rapture are changed from flesh and blood, being "clothed upon with our house which is from heaven" (II Corinthians 5:2b). For these who are living, this is *Rapture,* not *Resurrection,* for the "first fruits" Christians do not die.

> "For I am in a strait betwixt two, having a desire to depart and to be with Christ; which is very far better:"
>
> Philippians 1:23N.

> "Wherefore also we are ambitious, that, whether at home or absent, we may be well-pleasing to Him."
>
> II Corinthians 5:9N.

This is the Christian's exceeding great and precious promise for which our bereaved hearts wait.

Verses 17b and 18N.:

> "And so shall we ever be with the Lord." HALLELUJAH!
> "Wherefore comfort (exhort) one another in these words."

---

[1] This is the only time this word "shout" (Gr. *keleusma*) is used in the Scriptures, and its meaning is "a shout of encouragement" heard *only* by His saints. The distinction is that it is not like the *loud voice* used by Jesus at the tomb of Lazarus which was heard by all present. When the Lord spoke to Paul on the road to Damascus, Paul *alone* "heard." So at the Rapture, only His saints, the Church, will hear the *shout.*

Our being "caught up" (II Corinthians 12:2, Revelation 12:5) will happen "in the twinkling of an eye" (I Corinthians 15:52). The Christian goes "to meet" the Lord in the *air*, expecting to return with Christ to the *earth* for His Kingdom reign. [1]

Is it a matter of wonder that those having caught this vision are "hungering" with Paul (II Timothy 4:6—8), and praying, "Even so, come, Lord Jesus" (Revelation 22:20).

Continuing with Paul's letters on the Rapture, we come to Philippians 3:10—11 (Scofield margin):

"That I may know Him and the power of His resurrection, and the fellowship of His sufferings, being made conformable unto His death: If by any means I might attain unto the out-resurrection from among the dead."

Resurrection is no new truth but the "out-rising" is a *verb* and not a *noun* and this idea or word usage was quite new and strange. Jesus at the

---

[1]
Scofield Reference Bible, (N.T., Oxford University Press) p. 1148:

"The Two Advents-Summary: (1) The O.T. foreview of the coming Messiah is in two aspects—that of rejection and suffering (as, e.g., in Isaiah 53), and that of earthly glory and power (as, e.g., in Isaiah 11; Jeremiah 23; Ezekiel 37). Often these two aspects blend in one passage (e.g., Psalm 2). The prophets themselves were perplexed by this seeming contradiction (I Peter 1:10—11). It was solved by partial fulfillment. In due time the Messiah, born of a virgin according to Isaiah, appeared among men and began His ministry by announcing the predicted kingdom as "at hand" (Mt. 4.17, *note*). The rejection of King and kingdom followed. (2) Thereupon the rejected King announced His approaching crucifixion, resurrection, departure, and return (Mt. 12.38—40; 16.1—4. 21, 27; Lk. 12.35—46; 17.20—36; 18. 31—34; 19.12—27; Mt. 24., 25.). (3) He uttered predictions concerning the course of events between His departure and return (Mt. 13.1—50; 16.18; 24.4—26). (4) This promised return of Christ becomes a prominent theme in the Acts, Epistles, and Revelation.

"Taken together, the N.T. teachings concerning the return of Jesus Christ may be summarized as follows (1) That return is an event, not a process, and is personal and corporeal (Mt. 23.39; 24.30; 25.31; Mk. 14.62; Lk. 27.24; John 14.3; Acts 1.11; Phil. 3.20,21; I Thes. 4.14—17). (2) His coming has a threefold relation: to the church, to Israel, to the nations

(a) To the church the descent of the Lord into the air to raise the sleeping and to change the living saints is set forth as a constant expectation and hope (Mt. 24.36,44,48—51; 25.13; I Cor. 15.51,52; Phil. 3.20; I Thess. 1.10; 4.14—17; I Tim. 6.14; Tit. 2.13; and Rev. 22.20).

(b) To Israel, the return of the Lord is predicted to accomplish the yet unfulfilled prophecies of her national regathering, conversion, and establishment in peace and power under the Davidic Covenant (Acts 15.14—17 with Zech. 14.1—9). See "Kingdom (O.T.)," 2 Sam. 7.8—17; Zech. 13.8, *note*; Lk. 1.31—33; I Cor. 15.24, *note*.

(c) To the Gentile nations the return of Christ predicted to bring the destruction of the present political world-system (Dan. 2.34,35; Rev. 19.11,*note*); the judgment of Mt. 25. 31—46, followed by world-wide Gentile conversion and participation in the blessings of the kingdom (Isa. 2.2—4; 11.10; 60.3; Zech. 8.4, 20,23; 14.16—21).

first spoke of the "rising from the dead ones" (Gr. *ek nekron anaste* Mark 9:9—10). No wonder the disciples were questioning with one another what the "rising from the dead" should mean, for this had never before been known; this was quite beyond them and Martha (John 11:24—25). The Lord by His resurrection prepared us to expect this at His coming (Matthew 16:3, Luke 12:40).

This above text in Philippians is the diapason stop of Paul's letters (I Timothy 3:16). Here—

> The piled-up verbal combinations;
> > The nervous jaggedness of Paul's per-fervid utterances;
> > > His apocalyptic tidal apostrophes;

All of these arrest the attention of the indifferent reader while the earnest-minded are conscious of such ecstasies as those of II Corinthians 12:4. The mighty surge of the Almighty God's Purpose carries the imagination of the immortality-hungered from the realm of troubled hearts into the celestial certainties of II Timothy 4:6—8.

The mystery and aspiration of Philippians 3:10—11 require only cursory attention in order to at once arouse keen interest. Paul's unique wording of the Greek *ek-anastasin ten ek nekron*, the "out-resurrection from among the dead ones," sets in definite terms the glorious hope which is the peculiar possession of the Church, His Body (I Corinthians 15:49—57). He says, "that I may *attain* into (Gr. *eis*) the out-resurrection from among the dead ones," that is, to rise up out, from out, the dead. Were a student to find such an odd phrase, he certainly would turn aside to examine it.

We are prepared to pass once more across this octave of immortality; we are challenged to do so by the arresting goal of the words *attain* and *unto*. The force of a word is revealed in its use and association. This Greek word *kantantao* (attain) is used in Acts 16:1, 26:7, I Corinthians 10:11 and Ephesians 4:13. Does such an hope atrophy or augment our mission? Look upon Paul in his ministry and consider what the completion of Christ's Body meant to him. Here in *attain* is a word with that drive and urge which suggests: the creaking cordage, the drive of overcomers, the distended veins of effort, the sweat of body, the agony of brain, and a heaven-storming faith. Within this word we evoke the inner tones of Paul's spiritual development. The evangelizing of that last soul before the Lord returns definitely augments our mission which the Lord has committed to us. Love by all means, prepares for the beloved!

This brings us to the foothills of victory in *Ephesians*. We are at the *plus ultra*, a song of ascents and degrees; it now is "in the Ephesian heavenlies" where the spiritual process is at work to *attain* (1:10); to "sum up all things in Christ" (2:6—7); to be His show-windows or display (3:10); and His vindication before the whole creation. *Ephesians* is like a granary where the farmer's best seed wheat is stored for future crop raising. Thus does God use the Church which is full-statured and in perfect unity (4:13), without spot or wrinkle (5:27), clothed in heavenly armor, garmented (6:11), and able "to stand" through *ek-anastasis* (out-resurrection) and "upward calling" (Philippians 3:14 *ano kleseos*). The Rapture is the goal of those rising up out of this garden of these church letters. The Rapture of the Church will witness the fulfilling or the completion of this out-resurrection from among the dead ones, and we with Paul labor that we might *attain*. Benjamin Franklin understood this out-resurrection and wrote his own epitaph thus:

> "The body of Benjamin Franklin, printer, (like the cover of an old book, its contents torn out and stripped of its lettering and gilding) lies here, food for worms. Yet the work itself shall not be lost, for it will (as he believes) appear once more in a new and more beautiful edition, corrected and amended by the Author."

Paul's epistle to the Colossians carries on the movement of "the hope" (Colossians 1:5) by which we are "translated" (vs. 13) and which God would "make known" unto us (vs. 27); for this mystery, the Rapture, is "Christ in you the hope of glory." So we are prepared to resist the leaven of "philosophy" in Colossians 2:8, and to "seek things *above*" (3:1) that is *His Coming* (3:4).

A study of *Thessalonians* shows that the Church waiting for the Lord's return is not an effervescing group but rather is a solidly, Scripturally-grounded congregation. To the Thessalonian Church Paul speaks concerning the Lord's coming to be glorified and to glorify His Church, and he was praying that they would be ready. And now he writes to them in II Thessalonians 2:1—2a:

> "Now we beseech you, brethren, by the coming of our Lord
> Jesus Christ, and by our gathering together unto Him, That
> ye be not soon shaken in mind, ..."

Just as a carelessly anchored boat drifts and none is conscious that it is slipping away, so He is beseeching the Church concerning the coming of the Lord and the gathering unto Him. This must refer to the Lord's Supper for it is only used here and in Hebrews 10:25 and each suggests the Communion (Psalm 23:5). Upon every observance "till He come" the Christian renews his loyalty to the Lord even as the soldier swears fealty to his government. As those who are absent from one another refresh their love by means of letters or other communication, so the Lord's Table is our place of refreshing love, and this saves us from "falling away."

Every one of the eight chapters of the two Thessalonian epistles looks out upon the Lookout Nest, the Communion Room (Hebrews 10:25), where we "look for" His coming. *Thessalonians* is the Communion Room of Paul's writings, the "Purpose" place of Romans 8:28. Our progress at the Communion Table is from the weekly observance "till He come" and our participating must be in a "*worthy* manner" or we shall otherwise be guilty of the Body and Blood of the Lord. In the Apocrypha, it is said of Razis (II Maccabees 14:42), that he sought to take his own life, "choosing rather to die manfully, than to come into the hands of the wicked, to be abused otherwise than beseemed his noble birth." This would have been an *unworthy* death for such a worthy man. So, an *unworthy* observance of the Lord's Table is an abuse of our Lord's Body. The Communion is a crucified body indwelt by a death-defying life. A body must be kept for its purpose and the Lord's Body was proof of the resurrection. We who are "crucified with Christ" are irrefutable witnesses to His coming for His Church.

   b) Seeing the Visible

   Since the Rapture is invisible except to those participating in it, so there are no visible signs preceding the Rapture. However, the Second Coming of Christ to the *earth* for "The Day of the Lord" is visible to all, and the Lord announced that certain visible signs could be discerned by those who would watch (Matthew 16:2—3). The Rapture is imminent at all times; "the Day of the Lord" cannot come until the signs have been revealed or have taken place. It is possible that we shall witness some of the signs which precede the Second Coming of the "Day of the Lord," but these signs have no bearing upon the Rapture of the Church.

   What are the visible signs which precede the beginning of the "Day of the Lord"? They seem to fall under the following headings:

   (1) "The Falling Away"
       Paul tells the Thessalonian Christians that they are not to be "quickly shaken" concerning the nearness of "the Day of the Lord," for "a falling away" must come first (II Thessalonians 2:1—12). This proves that Paul was not expecting The Lord's Day immediately but rather that certain signs must be fulfilled first. He said that these things shall not be except first "The Man of Sin" would be sitting in the temple. In their time that was then a long ways off, but the mystery of lawlessness was already at work.
       (*a*) There would come an undermining of the infallibility of the Holy Scriptures
       (*b*) The Lawless One would destroy belief in the miraculous in the Bible
       (*c*) He would deny the physical resurrection of the Lord
       (*d*) This Lawless One would lower Deity to divinity, and raise humanity to divinity

(e) The Jewish Temple would be rebuilt; and until this Temple is rebuilt, the Man of Sin cannot sit within it.

Pulpits and editors today are nearly there. Protestantism is through with the Lord's First Day of the week (the day of worship), and Bible study; while Russia has reached the goal of atheism. The leaven which the woman . . . hidden . . . is working; and soon the whole will be leavened.

> Religion, blushing, veils her sacred fires,
> And unawares Morality expires.
> Nor public flame, nor private dares to shine;
> Nor human spark is left, nor glimpse divine!
> Lo, thy dread empire, Chaos! is restored;
> Light dies before thy uncreating word:
> Thy hand, great Anarch, lets the curtain fall,
> And universal darkness buries all. [1]

"The Day (of vengeance) of the Lord" shall not come except there come a falling away and there is "a revealing of one who opposeth God and exalteth himself above all that is called God and that is worshipped." At that time there will be no kind of religion but only he as god. Paul writes in II Thessalonians 2:5—7 A.S.V.:

> "Remember ye not, that, when I was yet with you, I told you these things? And now ye know that which restraineth, to the end that he may be revealed in his own season. For the mystery of lawlessness doth already work: only there is one that restraineth now, until He be taken out of the way."

In other words, at the time of the Rapture before the Tribulation, there is One who "restrains" up to the point of departure of the "caught away" Church. This "restraining One" is the Holy Spirit who hinders or restrains the work of the Man of Sin during this Church Age and prevents the unleashing of the tides of godlessness in this age (Ephesians 6:12). When He, the Holy Spirit, is taken at the Lord's return, then the things described in II Thessalonians 2:9—10 will come to pass and the Great Tribulation will result. That Lawless One (II Thessalonians 2:8) will be revealed and the Church shall never see him. At the Rapture the Church shall step forth from unfolding lawlessness, even as the Lord from flaming, purifying fire. This veil, the Church, shall be raptured like a curtain being raised, or as when the veil of the temple was rent and then "The Man of Sin" shall be revealed and there shall not be chaos but there shall be the law of the dictator, a man of steel like Stalin, who comes with power and signs and the deceit of unrighteousness. This is in contrast to the Lord in chapter 1:7—12. This Lawless One will deceive with powerful signs and lying

---

[1]
Alexander Pope, Esq., *The Complete Poetical Works of*, (N.Y., Leavitt and Allen Bros., Vol. 1), *The Dunciad*, Bk. IV, 1. 649 ff., p. 374

wonders because "they received not the love of the truth." This is the working of error in order that they might believe "the lie" (John 8:44), and so it explains I Corinthians 11:19 and the division between *pre* and *post* millennialisms. Then with open eyes, some go to martyrdom in the Great Tribulation and cry out for the Deliverer of Acts 3:21. This Lawless One the Lord shall slay with the same power which was creation's instrument (Revelation 19:15, Hebrews 11:3, Genesis 1:1—1)—the Word of God.

(2) The Regathering of Israel to The Holy Land

This is the second visible sign. Israel wandered forty years in the wilderness and finally arrived in the Promised Land. The first return to the land occurred after a captivity of seventy years in Babylon. Today they are again dispersed amongst the nations and the second return is referred to in Jeremiah 23:7—8, Isaiah 43:5—6, and others. Two remarkable comments were made a number of years ago:

(*a*) By E. B. Elliott (1861) who said:

"Some signs are still wanting, especially the non-gathering as yet of the Jews to Palestine."

(*b*) And by H. Grattan Guinness (1879) who wrote:

"When the nations of Europe (whatever their motive) shall conspire to re-instate the Jews . . . *then* the last warning bell will have rung."

(3) The third and final visible sign is that of:

World-Wide Religious ·and Political Distress.

The signs are both religious and political; and today the Church itself has become more worldly and political than religious. The Church is given a definite point to observe: "Till the times (Gr. *kaimoi*—a fixed time) are fulfilled." This is a determined point in time (Gr. *kronos*) and so we know whom and where to watch: the Jew—in Jerusalem.

Preceding or introductory to this "Day of the Lord" (Joel 2:31, Acts 2:20, Luke 21:27), two world conditions will arise: the first will be among nations; and the second, among men:

(*a*) "The distress of nations" (Luke 21:25). This phrase is used elsewhere only in II Corinthians 2:4 and there it is translated "anguish of heart," and it has the meaning of being compressed; i.e., isolated, not knowing with whom to tie up. Within every nation there is:

(i) *The roaring of the sea,* both physical and spiritual (I Corinthians 13:1)

(ii) *The "billows"* (Gr. *salou,* Acts 17:13, root of), a

tossing or a rolling of seas or peoples.

(*b*) *"Men's hearts failing"* (Luke 21:26). In the preceding verse, we are pointed to the distress, that which is compressed. Now note that beyond the distress of nations, is the heart-failure, the breathing out (Gr. *apopsucho*) of men for the "expectation of what is coming" (Hebrews 10:26—31); for all men believe as well as the devils (James 1:19).

The Church is taken up at this time. *Men* are fearful of what is coming to the earth; *Christians* are joyful because of the taking away.

"For the powers of the heavens shall be shaken" (Luke 21:26*b*; disordered, see Isaiah 34:4—5). This is the same as "billows" in verse 25, for there is anarchy on earth and in heaven (see Revelation 12:7—9, "war in heaven," Hebrews 12:26—27).

"When these things begin to come to pass" (Luke 21:28), look up and lift up your head. That these signs have already begun, few will dispute.

"Behold the fig tree" (Luke 21:29). The fig tree is prophetic of Israel; and,

"All the trees" refers to the nations.

"This generation" (Luke 21:32) is the one that sees this beginning of the signs (Matthew 24:24). Satan would deceive the very elect if it were possible.

The *Signs* are for the Church (to see), but the *Events* are for Israel. We spectators are not participants except the foolish (Revelation 7:9).

The Church is an inset, a Parenthesis between Daniel 9:26 *'CUT OFF'* and "CAUGHT UP."

These are sobering prophecies and are not for paralyzing fear, but to cause us "to think on these things." And surely our hope should be heaven high. Nor should acceptance of these prophecies abate our efforts but the rather should accelerate them (II Peter 3:11—12). John Wesley said that if he knew when the Lord was coming, and he looked at his date book, there would be no change in his schedule (he'd be that busy with the work of the Lord).

The Christian today is able to discern the Signs of the Times—see the visible things—which are appearing in daily lives and upon the news fronts of the world. These visible signs indicate the approach of the time of fulfillment of the prophecies concerning "the Day of the Lord." When He comes for His Church at the Rapture, Christ will be invisible to the world, but to us, He will be visible "for we shall see Him as He is." The manifestation of His glory to the Church will occur at the Rapture in the

The Clock in the auditorium of the Englewood Christian Church (Chicago) was a daily reminder of the imminence of the Lord's soon coming for His Church. Brother Kindred designed this clock to relate it to the constant expectancy of the Rapture of the Church.

air, but this will be shielded from the world by the clouds. At His unveiling, His revelation, when He comes to the *earth*, (the second time) then the world shall see Him as He comes in flaming fire-glory.[1]

May we be ready for His glorifying touch upon us
   And so "flame" forth,—
      When the Sun of Righteousness shall arise
         With healing in His wings.

I'M Facing The Dawn

Many have sung of life's sunset
   That comes with the close of the day
That, after the noontide zenith,
   The path slopes down all the way.
Voices have lost their gladness,
   For the forenoon of life is gone.
It may be for them — but I —
   I'm facing the dawn!

One writes of the sails that are folded
   As his ship puts out to sea,
And at night drifts out into darkness
   To be greeted by mystery.
But my Pilot has never failed me;
   I've crowded the canvas on—
And the prow of my ship's pointed straight
   Into the opening dawn!

The Maker of all creation,
   He, who starred the Milky Way,
Wrote in the very beginning,
   "Evening and morning . . . day."
No matter how long the journey,
   No matter how far withdrawn
The goal that still lies before me
   At the end of the way, is DAWN!

                  Bessie Stickell

---

[1]
   See Section SIX, *The Kingdom Age*, III. A. The Lord Appears to Earth . . . p. 556.

Note:

No finer conclusion to this Church Section of the Outline could be found apart from Bro. Kindred's sermon—*Halting at Haran.*[1]

This article sets forth in dramatic and beautiful language the Exceeding High Calling and Heavenly Place of The Church.

R.M.L.

VII. CEASELESS LIFTING OF VISION TIDES, or, "Halting at Haran"[1]

"Arise ye, and depart; for this is not your resting place:"

Micah 2:10

ABRAHAM met God in Ur of the Chaldees. He met Him as "Abram" but after long intimate fellowship became "Abraham." He was called to go out to his country's edge and he obeyed. As the sea follows the moon, so he followed the vision until he lodged at the border city of Haran. Can we not see him at the day's close at the door of his pitched tent looking with longing to the far-off hills of the Promised Land? But, tied with home loyalties, his soul is continuously fretted by the ceaseless lifting of the vision-tides of God. Twenty-five years remain as a memorial of this halting and when he finally yielded, it was to leave behind his only brother who had started so bravely with him but in the long halt had become too firmly anchored to go on.

As our good ship drew near to Glasgow, Commander Hamilton called attention to a canal opposite the skids from which the ship *The Titanic* was launched. The giant proportions of the Titanic required more than the width of the River Clyde in which to maneuver from the yards to the ocean. It wove the impress of its bulk into the traditions of the Scottish builders of "ships that go down into the sea." Doubtless, Abram also remained a tradition in Haran, though no great mystical fact of his faith was experienced while there. All he contributed to Haran was the grave of a father, and a brother "who pitched his tent toward" its attractions.

These two seem like parables of "Our Brotherhood." Called of God to a mighty program of Restoration, our fathers responded and moved most convincingly toward that program for a united church but:—they halted at our theological Haran, Acts 2:38. As they were going, had they and we persistently yielded, the church by now would have been much more sin-conscious of sectarianism and without the excuse of ignorance as to its remedy. The fathers caught the full glory of the mighty, redemptive; unifying gospel of Pentecost but tarried there until the routine over-shadowed

---

[1] C.G.Kindred, *Halting At Haran*, (Abe Corey, *Voices of the Sanctuary*, (St. Louis, Mo., The Bethany Press, Christian Board of Publication, 1930) pp. 102—115.

the mystical. In the minds of the denominational world, we are "the people of Acts 2:38." With the open, though little traveled road before us into the spiritual fellowship of Paul's vision-revealed "mysteries" of the gospel which are consecutively and clearly set forth in *Romans, Ephesians* and *Thessalonians,* we have stood and looked and longed as did Abraham, but anchored to this sure haven, we have feared to launch out.

This text is the widened place of our launching across "the way" leading out into "visions and revelations" whereunto we have failed to arrive. At this beginning of "the way" we have too long halted. A few prophetic souls, as Isaac Errett, have stood and looked and pled. The inward urge of that vision is once more upon us. As Abram, let us not be "disobedient to the heavenly vision." Our fathers are fallen asleep and the creation of their loyalty caught by the tides and currents where seas meet, is threatened with disintegration. And that, too, just as dissatisfied sectarianism was abandoning its party shibboleths in the search for the lost unity of the church. Instead of accepting the leadership within reach, we halted before their instructors and used their literature in preference to our own. And too many are content to have it so!

"Arise ye, and depart!"

Let us go out to the edge of the desert that the spell of "the way," lying across it to the exceeding high mountains—mountains of Beatitudes, Transfigurations, and Ascensions—may call once more that we may take up our pilgrimage as did Abram.

> To every man there openeth
> A Way, and Ways and a Way,
> And the High Soul climbs the High Way,
> And the Low Soul gropes the Low,
> And in between, on the misty flats,
> The rest drift to and fro. [1]

This path is from the gospels to *Romans*—from Acts 2:38 to Acts 11:26— from the Son to the Body—from His perfect physical manhood to His perfect mystical Body—from Christ to Christian. This movement under convoy of the Holy Spirit, is what makes vivid and vital the pageantry of incidents in the book of Acts. Within this book are seen men en-dynamited of God, praying open prison doors, confounding the wise, crashing the gates of empires—"these who have turned the world upside down." O, the beauty of this "way!"

The disciples in this book of Acts are on "the way" from power to authority, from phenomena to parousia, from works to worship, from Acts 2:38 to Acts 11:26. This period is one of intense, unceasing, evangelistic activity. The Master's insistent, quiet voice calling, "Come ye apart and

---

[1] John Oxenham, *The Home Book of Modern Verse,* compiled and arranged by Burton Egbert Stevenson (N.Y., Henry Holt and Co., 1925) *"The Ways"* p. 727

rest awhile,"—"tarry till ye see Heaven opened,"—this Voice is not yet distinguished from other voices—but to those who follow on, it will be! And so the "Upper Room" where we are "seated with Him in the Heavenlies" is not yet experienced. Indeed, a great many have not so much as heard whether there be any "peace," "rest," "heavenlies." "And who knows but we have come for such an hour as this?"

There is set forth here in the book of Acts something in language and tableaux so plain, the marvel is that it has not been written of long ago, but if so I have not seen,—and that is, the passing of the Holy Spirit's ministry from the Christ to the Church and the creation of a body of literature for this new life as unique and adequate as the Gospels were for the preceding ministry of Jesus. The calling of the Apostle Paul, finds fitting explanation in the light of this need, a need no other of the disciples were prepared to supply. Once grasping this explanation, his epistles fit together and supplement one another more discernibly than do the Gospels. This passing *from* the Gospels, is our first call in which there rises The Perfect One of God,—of whom Pilate, the judge of the Roman Empire said, "Behold The Man"—to the new and much more wonderful vision of His Spiritual Body the Church, rising into a glorious heavenly creation out of Paul's epistles, just as gladioli blooms rise into glory from the planted bulbs,—both a new creation:

> "That He might present it to Himself a glorious Church,
> not having spot, or wrinkle, or any such thing; but that
> it should be holy and without blemish."
>
> Ephesians 5:27

Of whom powers greater than Rome, the Principalities of the Heavenlies might say,   "Behold, the vindication of the wisdom
and might and glory of God."
out of Ephesians 3:10

It is seen now by those "having eyes to see," for it is "spiritually discerned" just as was Jesus after His resurrection. This coming to completeness is apprehensible to those who give even slight attention; while those devoutly praying for the hasting toward, have their eyes anointed to see as the architect sees temples rising from stone quarries, or the agriculturist sees spring crops rise out of sowings.

Twice the Saviour spoke of the privileges of this glorious future "Body" in terms that amaze the student—spoken at the very close of His earth life while nearing the foot of the cross, having reached the impeccable splendor of His immortal perfection. These two great prophetic promises are bequeathed to His "little flock":

> "Greater than these shall he (ye) do;
> because I go unto my Father."
>
> John 14:12*b*N.

And,

> "I have yet many things to say unto you, but ye cannot bear
> them now. Howbeit when He, the Spirit of truth, is come,
> He will guide you into all truth . . . and He will announce
> to you things to come."
>
> John 16:12–13 N.

And these beckoning wonders have marked with glory the far-off hills of the promised "heavenlies," tugging at our heart-strings, while like Abram, we have stood halting at our Haran. Before such promises ought we not all cry, "Lord, if there is further word and experience, speak, for thy servant heareth!" Dear Lord, give unto us the yielding trust of Abram as we "strike our tents" and start "unto the place that I will show thee."

The "greater works" is that of raising the spiritually dead—declaring and demonstrating that "the gospel is the power of God unto salvation" to the "dead in trespasses and sins." This is set forth and demonstrated in *Romans*—and nowhere else save in *Romans*. Chapter one is the gate into the cemetery of lost men—the eroded sediment of *a-theos* souls. No viler cesspool was ever uncovered than these thrice God-given-up ones. Dead, Dead, DEAD! And slipping, sliding, slithering into that dead sea of sin is my own soul and every other soul on this sad planet. As mankind resistlessly sinks toward and into this place of the dead, those aroused cry out, "with no language but a cry" and are heard, for the Saviour's compassionate heart is strained to catch the faintest expression of repentance for "He is not willing that any should perish."

As we brood upon that fetid mass, God moves to the center of it and sets down a propitiatory (Romans 3:25)—the Cross, and at once the marvelous work of grace—greater than anything in the Lord's earthly ministry—begins to come to pass before our startled eyes. These spiritually dead arise and walk in newness of the "life more abundant." Faith (chap. 5) and Baptism (chap. 6) are seen as the procuring causes here, just as when Jesus healed the believing blind man when he went and washed; as the star appeared anew to the Wise Men when they left Herod; as must have been Abram's experience when he once more pushed out into "the way." So a rapturous vision salutes the opening eyes of these newly born.

> "Nay, in all these things we are more than conquerors through
> Him that loved us. For I am persuaded, that neither death, nor
> life, nor angels, nor principalities, nor things present, nor
> things to come, nor powers, nor height, nor depth, nor any
> other creation, shall be able to separate us from the love of
> God, which is in Christ Jesus our Lord."
>
> Romans 8:37–39 N.

And this prospect was particularly reserved for us of this age, "that they (of an older dispensation) without us should not be made perfect"—they having seen and greeted from afar, that which is our peculiar possession. Such are the "greater works" peculiar to *Romans*, the authority for which is rooted in Acts 2:38.

There remains however even greater prospect for those of spiritual stature to whom Christ can reveal that which once His disciples were not able to bear. When Jairus' daughter was raised, the command was: "Give her to eat"; and when Lazarus arose, the command was: "Loose him and let him go"—thus passing from the *phenomena* of resurrection at once to the *reason* for it; that they might enter fully into the life into which they had been raised. In *Romans* is the resurrection, but the "food" and the "loosing" of the newly raised must be sought elsewhere. So we must look for a letter of like characteristics to *Romans* if such reason is to be found.

The only other book of Paul's with this essay style of *Romans* is *Ephesians*; and these two books are "treatises rather than letters" (Lightfoot). *Romans* sets forth the "greater works"—the propitiatory's transformation of the dead into "living stones"; *Ephesians* receives these raised ones, and reveals unto them the "many other things" which only those "born from above" are able to receive, and builds them up into the One Body. Such are "in the heavenlies" "in Him," introduced into a new world whose language and privileges are a "mystery" to the un-initiated. In the book of Romans the power of God was being applied and Christians are the manipulators, or appliers of it; while in *Ephesians* they themselves are adjusting themselves to the new life, learning the new language—a speech of the heart—that is fraught with infinite consequences. This is why we find Paul on his face in an intercessory passion of prayer. In *Romans* it was the doxology for victory over death already accomplished; now (in *Ephesians*) it is the blood-sweating agony that these newly raised ones may see and may also appropriate their heritage: first, that "God may give unto you a spirit of wisdom and of revelation" in the things which flesh and blood cannot reveal unto us for they are "spiritually discerned" —such a spirit of wisdom and of revelation in the knowledge of Him:

> "The eyes of your understanding being enlightened; that ye may know what is the hope of His calling, and what the riches of the glory of His inheritance in the saints. And what the exceeding greatness of His power to usward who believe, according to the energy of the strength of His might, Which He wrought in Christ, when He raised Him from among the dead ones, and set Him at His right hand in the heavenlies . . . and raised us up together, and made us sit together in the heavenlies."

Ephesians 1:19—20; 2:6N.

So that we might not be skeptical, Paul once more is driven to prayer (3:14—21), second only to John 17, that we might grasp the spiritual dimensions, not of love this time, but of the Church, Christ's Body. There is a break after the word "depth" (Ephesians 3:18). The greatness of the Church extends beyond the limits of language. Paul's speech breaks down under the stress of the vision. He pleads that we may grow up a spiritual body "by that which every joint supplieth," the result being the vindication of the wisdom of God.

> "To the intent that now unto the principalities and the authorities in the heavenlies might be known through the Church the manifold wisdom of God."
>
> Ephesians 3:10 N.

Those who abide within this mighty purpose are "endued" with "the mind of Christ" and so, "for the joy set before' them, endure . . . despising the shame.

Romans is the book of Evangelism. *Ephesians* is the book of Worship —the book of the deep things of God. Within it is revealed the mind of the Spirit. Here is the "breadth" and "length' and "depth" and "height" within whose spacious atmosphere the soul can rear a statlier mansion with more enduring materials than is possible with the elements of earth. *Romans* is the doctrine of salvation; *Ephesians* is the doctrine of sanctification. They are of two distinct stages in Christian experience and cannot be reversed without confusion—as distinct as two grades in school, and these two books should so be studied.

Is someone wondering as to the books of Corinthians, Galatians, Philippians and Colossians? These are satelites, the former two of *Romans*, and the latter two of *Ephesians*, dealing with the practical and doctrinal problems arising out of departure from these source documents.

And there is yet more, praise His Name! These two have their *plus ultra*. The Salvaged of *Romans* are seated in *Ephesians* but the current sweeps on—and up. The vision invites; the wounded Hand beckons. So *Thessalonians* draws the broken chords of all those who have "loved and lost" into hope's observatory where is revealed unto them the joys that shall be when Jesus brings with Him those once torn from our embrace by the relentless hand of death. That rapturous vision drives us to our knees, as Paul in *Ephesians*,—thus causing us to cry out:

"Even so, come quickly, Lord Jesus."

God's revelations of Himself, His blessings for us, come in threes. In *Romans* is faith; in *Ephesians*, love; in *Thessalonians*, hope. And it remains true as declared in I Corinthians 13, that "the greatest of these is love." For in *Ephesians*—the most profound treatise ever written, the highest experience of fellowship with and in Him,—the solvent for all the ills, schisms and factions that distress Christ's Body are therein to be found gloriously efficacious. In the heavenlies of this section, the Mind of Christ becomes assimilable, and men take knowledge of such that they have been with Him. And the change from glory to glory as by the Lord, the Spirit, is discernible for this is the workshop of God and we are His workmanship (Gr. *His poem*).

To get back to this "Rightly Divided" portion of the church's book of instructions, is to meet and vanquish all the divisive darts of the evil one; is to restore the seamless robe of the church's lost unity; is to make the Scriptures plain, understandable. The least capacity of the lowliest wayfarer will be able to lay hold joyously upon this edifying truth and walk unerringly with glad satisfaction. The proclaiming of this perfect fruitage of Acts 2:38 is our privilege; yea, our duty, for it is the carrying unto perfection of "The Plea" so graciously given unto us.

Perhaps an illustration that helped me will be of service to you. Paul's seven letters are as a western sanitarium where the wasted bodies of the city's defeated are sent for restoration. On the plain is the hospital receiving and ministering to those arriving. On a pleasant plateau from which each cot can be observed, yet with outlook upon the western sky, stands the home of the staff. Here they retire for rest and study and consultation. To the west can be seen the stream of the healed stepping forth in abounding vitality—do you wonder that Christ and all good physicians "for the joy set before them" endure?

> *Romans* is the sanitarium
> *Ephesians* is the home
> *Thessalonians* is the outlook;

> *Romans* is Salvation
> *Ephesians* is Sanctification
> *Thessalonians* is Glorification.

Here is the Church's curriculum:

> "able to make wise unto salvation"
> "to build you up"
> "to receive forgiveness of sins and an inheritance among them which are sanctified by faith that is in Me."

Here are *Faith, Love, Hope;*

Here is God's *Promised Land*, the Mountains of Fellowship.

C. G. Kindred

526

SATAN'S STORY

"But if also our gospel be veiled, it is veiled in them that are lost; in whom the god of this age hath blinded the minds of them which believe not, lest the light of the gospel of the glory of Christ, who is the image of God, should shine unto them."

II Corinthians 4:3—4 N.

"Finally, be strong in the Lord, and in the strength of His might. Put on the whole armor of God, that ye may be able to stand against the wiles of the devil. For our wrestling is not against flesh and blood but against the principalities, against the powers, against the world-rulers of this darkness, against the spiritual hosts of wickedness in the heavenly places."

Ephesians 6:10—12 A.S.V.

INTRODUCTION

ATAN'S STORY of this Section FIVE, is the story of this age; of the efforts of men at millennialism—i.e., the efforts of men to bring in the Golden Age. But the Bible is:

a) The pre-history of God's plan for man's perfection

b) The only Book ever written for the future life before this present age (John 16:33); "for in the world ye shall have tribulation . . ."; and "everyone that hath left . . . all shall inherit eternal life" (II Corinthians 5:5).

A strange, mysterious Power and Wisdom not ourselves, wrote and collected and preserved a scattered collection of writings (Hebrews 1:1) "at sundry times," and "in divers places," yet they are arranged as the colors on a spectrum and no one is able to re-arrange them. We have found that God's three superlatives in man's world are The Book, The Man, and The Church; and strange indeed is it that all have come from beyond man's world through a Divine Invasion, followed by a Satanic Invasion, —and yet man questions the authenticity of God. "There are many adversaries" and the Satanic eruption "in the heavenlies" (the Church) is "the battle of the ages" (I Corinthians 16:9, Ephesians 6:12, II Corinthians 10:3—5, II Timothy 3:1—5, 4:1—8). Those traveling upon "The Way" are strangers and pilgrims (Hebrews 11:13) and for them life is one continued battle.

I. THE BATTLE IN THE HEAVENLIES (THE CHURCH AGE)

". . . your adversary *Diabolos* as a roaring lion, walketh about, seeking whom he may devour."

I Peter 5:8 N.

This is the Adversary's Last Stand as "an angel of light." After this he is seen in II Thessalonians 2:7—8 in his true colors.

This Age is from Pentecost to the Rapture; it is in the heavenlies and the weapons of this age are not carnal. Who can storm the citadel of His Spirit's enemies with weapons which another has forged? None other age was like this; "no, nor ever shall be"; and there follows Hebrews 11:40.

Before the flood, Sinai and the Cross, God used carnal or material weapons, but now from the Cross (The Gospels) to *Hebrews*, there is a great gulf *fixed* which is the Church, indwelt by the Hinderer, the Holy Spirit. He is invisible, but is clearly seen by the discerning Christian (Romans 1:20, I Corinthians 2:9—10). To the world nothing is seen but the visible body of the Church even as water in a glass may seem to have nothing in it, yet when placed under the microscope, it is seen to be peopled. So the Holy Spirit unseen to the world but seen by the Christian, dwells within the Church, "being perceived by things that are made," that is, born again Christians, "even His Everlasting Power and God-head." That gulf is made and occupied by the Church.[1] The Church is as foreign to earth as was Jesus, else it is not His (Matthew 10:24). Yet the insanity of ambition, heated in the fire of jealousy, drives the Adversary to certain destruction (Isaiah 14:12—14) thinking to destroy. Hear the word of comfort: "FEAR not," (though the battle does increase in intensity), for "I have (already) overcome the evil one." This was why the devils could say to Jesus, ". . . art Thou come hither to torment us before time?" (Matthew 8:29). And, ". . . for Diabolos is come down unto you, having great wrath, because he knoweth that he hath a short time" (Revelation 12:12N.).

Consider the awefulness of Hell—populated by salooners, panderers, hypocrites, and the lazy and the indifferent (Psalm 9:17); these are its leading citizens; and it is presided over by a defeated "Mussolini"-Satan, a coward and the most brutal of masters. I do not envy you neglecters. This Age's dominant figure "to those having eyes to see" is the Church, His Body; and it is above "the cloud" "in the heavenlies" where also the Adversary dares to assault, and from whence he is to be hurled (Isaiah 14, Ezekiel 28, Revelation 12:7—12). Forth to this mortal combat, the Lord rode upon "the cloud" (Acts 1:9, Revelation 1:7), and this cloud is the terminii within which the Church is one and indivisible (Ephesians 4:1—6).

---

[1] D.R.Davies, *DAWN* (England, June 1948): "The modern man is hostile to the Gospel. Owing to his changed consciousness, he is less open to the preaching of the Gospel than any of his predecessors. Five hundred years of 'humanism' aided by a secularized conformity, have thickened his soul and intensified his pride of will, and no amount of organized religion can bring him to repentance. He presents the church today with an insoluble problem. In her realization of her impotence lies the hope of the church; for, through it, God will endow the preaching of the church with power."

The Millennium at once follows (Revelation 1:7, I Thessalonians 4:16, Hebrews 9:28); and then all Israel *convicted* by the Rapture and *confounded* by great dangers, will evangelize "the nations," to the reign of the Messiah on earth (note Zech'ariah 12:7). A news commentator once called the Jews "a Race of leaders with no followers," but he had probably never read Deuteronomy 28:1, 13 and 32:8.

Satan's first attempt upon the Church begins in Acts 5:3 with Ananias and Sapphira; and his relentless attack is seen throughout the record of the Church of the first century.

There are three assaults, plus a fourth, upon this Age's Gospel of Grace:

1. *The Out-Resurrection*, Philippians 3:11, has within it inherent belief in immortality. Satan has side-tracked the Church through worldly prestige, endeavoring to cause the Church to forget her preferential calling "out from among the dead ones." This assault is upon *the hope of the Church*.

2. The second assault is upon *the unity of the Church* (John 17, I Corinthians 1:10); and the assault is made through creeds, i.e., opinions; each member has a little creed of his very own. The effectiveness of this assault is evident in the multitude of denominations (Acts 20:29—30).

3. The third assault is upon *the inspiration of the Scriptures*, and many have ceased accepting them as authority. Today, the "autopsiest" (the higher critic who denies the authenticity of the Scriptures), and the "dissectionists" (those writing creeds and causing divisions—II Peter 2:1—2), have run wild.

4. The fourth assault upon this Age of Grace, is *dispensationalism* which is an in-accurate attempt at "distinguishing the things that differ," or rightly dividing.[1]

The external attacks upon "The Way" have spent their force and have fallen back as futile. The internal travail begot great creeds, personalities and bishoprics. One of the first great credal statements concerned the Nature of Christ. Gradually great personalities developed in the Church: Arius and Athansius became known for their differences over the Nature of Christ. Origen, Justin Martyr, and Polycarp are names that stand out as martyrs of the Church. And finally, through great creeds and great personalities came the division of the Bishoprics of Alexandria, Constantinople and Rome. This beginning of creeds has gone to seed in anarchy and is seen in today's sects and missions where every man does right in his own eyes (Judges 17:6N.), and the result is chaos.

---

[1] See RIGHTLY DIVIDING, II. Dividing The Great Lines of God's Intention, pp.11—14.

The insidious infiltration of this traducer, Satan, is seen in his effect upon our age. Former Gov. Herbert H. Lehman of New York said:

> "A sterile and frightening cynicism has replaced faith and hope. Spiritual values have been jettisoned in favor of expedients. Hope has yielded to unconscious nihilism among large numbers of our people."

And Paul Hutchinson, former editor of the *Christian Century*, said that his report of his world tour of observation was not calculated to produce optimism. His fine note in closing was based upon:

> ". . . the power of God to stir to life spiritual forces as yet hidden from our myopic eyes. Christian history is studded with the sudden and mysterious blazing forth of unexpected saving fires . . . ."

Paul, seeing as a General, cites for bravery and only awaits the end of the war to honor and promote; and this sureness once accepted, enriches life now and prepares for yet further suffering at the revelation (the uncovering or unveiling, Matthew 10:26). There is a veil of *matter* over the spiritual world (I John 5:19), and Satan as the god of this world has the ability to veil or cover spiritual things with material surfaces and often the surface matters are instantaneously identified with the spiritual, as in cathedrals, systems of theology, forms of worship and incense burning. Henry Drummond's "Natural Law in the Spiritual World" is as though one end were matter and the other were spiritual. In speaking of the removal of this veil of matter, it is much more exact to use the term "revelation" or "unveiling" which is as a flag draped about a statue; or as the night about the city veils all within it; or as man in his own body is veiled spiritually by his flesh and bones.

The final exhortation of Paul in Ephesians 6:10ff. is "be empowered in the Lord and in the might (Gr. *kratei*) of His strength" (Gr. *ischuos*). "Put on the whole armor of God to be able to stand against the wiles (Gr. *methodeis*) of the devil." Our wrestling is not against blood and flesh but against principalities (Gr. *archas*), powers (Gr. *exousia*), against world rulers (Gr. *kosmokratoras*) of darkness; aye and more,—against spiritual wickedness in the very heavenlies—in the Church itself. Here are found false teachers, false religions, and false standards (cp. Matthew 24:24). Note here the urgency to "put on" (Ephesians 5:11), and "take up" (6:13); and then follows the Greek *hina*, "in order that," in 6:13 "to withstand" and then just "to stand" verse 13*b* (Isaiah 40:39—41). The armor which is to be "put on" is:

a) The girdle of truth (I Peter 1:13)
b) "The breastplate of righteousness"
c) "Feet shod with the preparation of the Gospel of peace"

And then the armor which we are to "take up" is:

a) "The shield of faith" (shield Gr. *thureon* from *thura* door) (cf. Revelation 3:8 and 4:1)

b) Receive the helmet of salvation (John 20:22); for the helmet is our hope (Hebrews 12:2, I Thessalonians 4:8)

c) "The sword of the spirit" which is the Word of God.

All of the armor is to be put on and taken up through all prayer, supplication and watching.

"Andrew Bonar left it on record that he never entered into a session of pure prayer without a fierce battle at the threshold. Satan dreads nothing like prayer. He stands at the portals of the holy of Holies as an 'Angel of Light.' He does not openly attack; he diverts. The one concern of Satan is to keep the saints from prayer. He fears nothing from prayerless studies, prayerless work, prayerless religion. He laughs at our toil, mocks at our wisdom, and trembles when we pray." [1]

Paul requests that prayer be made: "for me *hina*" (in order that):

a) "Utterance may be given unto me"

b) "To make known with boldness"

c) "The mystery for which I am an ambassador in a chain; *hina* (in order that) I may speak boldly as I ought to speak."

Paul concludes this chapter with 6:23—24:

"Peace be to the brethren, and love with faith, from God the Father and the Lord Jesus Christ. Grace be with all them that love our Lord Jesus Christ *in sincerity*. Amen."

The Greek word for sincerity is *aphtharzia*, and literally means incorruptibility; it comes from the Greek word *aphthoria* which is defined by Green in his lexicon as "incapability of decay."

II. MALIGNANT PERSONALITIES, or,

"THE WORLD RULERS OF THIS DARKNESS"

Text: II Thessalonians 2:1—12

The cause of Hope's eclipse is a "Mystery"-sinister presence, and our own intelligence is within impotence. Time (the hypothesis of the evolutionist), and Light Years (the hypothesis of the astronomer), both put intelligence far beyond man's ability. We are surrounded on all sides by Design and Omnipotence, and these dispose us toward belief in a *Super-Realm of Spiritual Intelligence*. Reflection prepares the mind to accept the

---

[1] From "Selected from 'God's Prayer Tower Bulletin' by James M. Spencer, minister."

Bible theophanies and the angelic presences; if such had not been revealed man would have invented them; and mythology which is a corruption of the revelation, proves this statement.

Thus, we are living in the presence of indubitable evidences of super-intelligences; therefore it necessarily follows that we are limited in our understanding.

a) The Man of Sin—II Thessalonians 2:3

The Man of Sin comes to rule, and is an interloper, a rebel, and so has laws that replace God's, even as the laws of the United States of America replace the laws of the Colonies of Great Britain. The Man of Sin is the sum total of ALL rebels and *A-Theos* (apart from God) who has completely surrendered to Satan's will, and who forces the growth of his divine powers. The "I WILL" slogan of Chicago is dangerously near rebellion for "I will" says, "despite circumstances or fate, I will achieve" (James 4:13—16).

The present agitation of the Thessalonian Christians is shown by the words, "be not soon shaken in mind or be troubled" and to this Paul is addressing himself. Some were saying that "the Day of the Lord" (the day of wrath, Isaiah 13:6—11, Zechariah 13:7) was setting in, or was "at hand," but if this was so, the Rapture had not occurred, so Paul was mistaken; and Hope had become eclipsed; so what of their dead ones? Must they go through death also? Paul rushes to their rescue with verses 3—6. He says it will not come *except the falling away come first.* And that had not come, although the "Mystery of Lawlessness doth already work." His very vehemence proves the seriousness of this condition even as when he dealt with the offender in the Corinthian Church (I Corinthians 5). He continues, "remember while I was yet with you, I (repeatedly) told you of these things." This is Paul's estimate of the importance of the Rapture which is followed by the Day of the Lord; and it is the Gospel for Christians. "And now,"— this is an adverb of passage indicating a settled argument, and it is NOT an adverb of the passing of time. Moffatt says, "if this is temporal, it would mean new light, fresh circumstances, BUT—of this there is no hint whatsoever in the text." God needs not to postscript His revelations! "*And now* ye know that (the Holy Spirit) which restraineth to the end that he (the Man of Sin) may be revealed in his own season" (vs. 6). There is a power that restrains. God reigns! As in Gethsemane "this is YOUR *hour*" (but no longer). *Then* it was over the Lord's physical body and *now* it is over the Church, His spiritual body, "until He (the Holy Spirit) be taken out of the midst." Plummer says he could not understand who "he" refers to, but this *must* be at the rapture; Paul does not here say *how* "he" is taken out, but in I Thessalonians 4:13 and I Corinthians 15:51, he gives the answer: "in a moment, in the twinkling of an eye." "And then shall be revealed the lawless one," to be slain at the coming of the (real) Lord; even as the psuedo always dies when in the presence of the real. "Even he whose coming (presence, Gr. *parousia*) is according to the *working of Satan* . . . and . . . the *working of error* that they should believe the lie" (II Thessalonians 2:8—11). Also, Dummelow writes, "those who obstinately refuse the truth become incapable of receiving"; and these had pleasure in unrighteousness. This is seen in the sins of today.

"The Son of Perdition" or the "Man of Sin" is a presence that moves behind incidents of Scriptures:

> "Who opposeth and exalteth himself above all that is called God, or that is worshipped; so that he as God sitteth in the inner temple of God, showing himself that he is God."

II Thessalonians 2:4N.

b) "The Lawless One"—II Thessalonians 2:8—9N.:

> "And then shall that lawless one be revealed; whom the Lord shall consume with the Spirit of His mouth, and shall destroy with the manifestation of His coming: Even him, whose coming is after the working of Satan with all power and signs and lying wonders,"

This one shall be unveiled at the rapture of the Church after the Hinderer (the Holy Spirit) has been taken away.

c) Satan, the Adversary

Satan is the inspirer, the dictator and the manipulator of "the Man of Sin" and "the Lawless One." A sinister presence at times manipulates me and I loathe myself (Romans 7:15—25). Satan literally means *adversary* and is from the same Latin root word as *advert* which means *to turn the mind*. It is similar to the word adverb meaning *modify* or *turn*. Therefore, *adversary* in itself is not inherently bad for it means to move or to direct, and can be used of doctors, preachers, and others. The word *adverse* also comes from the same Latin root and the millionaire, the scholar, or athlete have had to endure ad-versity, for is not all success the offspring of testing, or from "the School of Hard Knocks"? We must beware of this adversary, this sinister presence lest he manipulates us and turns us to his purpose.

Satan has authority over the "world rulers of this darkness"; and it is Christ who delivers us from the power of darkness. The darkness which surrounded Edison in his day did not bring fear but rather he *"gloried"* in the darkness, for the darker it was, the better his electric light shone. So must it be with Christians who are lights in a darkened world today. We are *"in the world but not of the world"* and the light shines in the darkness though oftentimes men in darkness do not lay hold upon it.

The departure from God is set over against two personalities:

(1) *Moses* who established government under the revelation of God

(2) And *Christ* who revealed *the character* which is acceptable
to God.

Satan's purpose is to destroy both government and character, and both
Moses and the Lord worked at revealing a timeless, sinless age (II Peter
3:13) and at pointing the way for men to attain unto. For *us* not to be concerned, is as culpable as Hezekiah in Isaiah 39. The "wise . . . understand," (Daniel 12:10, Matthew 16:3), and the times are pregnant with
"last days'" events, and soon will come the rapture, and "the Man of Sin"
will dissolve into Satan as Faust into Mephistopheles.

The most brilliant descriptive writings with which I am familiar are:
(1) Isaiah's and Ezekiel's delineation of this King of the Ma-
lignants (Isaiah 14:12—15, Ezekiel 28:12—19)

(2) Psalm Nineteen

(3) Job's lyric and terrifying beauty of God's Creation and His
Creatures (Job, chapters 38 through 41)

(4) Isaiah's limned Messiah (Isaiah 53), for Christ was a fact even
then, for He was "slain from the foundation of the world"
—these are they which have become "things seen" by us (Romans 1:20).
The description of Satan by Isaiah and Ezekiel *is not fiction,* but is the
unfolding knowledge of this Adversary. Here is a garment of glory, a Goliath's armour, whose wearer and wielder is regarded as the creation of
an undisciplined religious imagination (II Corinthians 11:3, 13—14). This
garment of glory is of the inhering texture of this blessed Book which is
more nearly seamless than the robe that the hardened soldiers were too
abashed to rend; and despite the superior atmosphere of today, I firmly believe and I dare to proclaim my belief in the Malignant Personalities, or,
the World Rulers of "This Darkness." I am fully aware of the criticism that
such views arouse in practical minds but consider Galileo and Einstein;
the Florentines who mocked Dante, and Britain who outlawed George Washington. Michelson and the Wright Brothers brought into practical use their
findings. I in no sense claim equality with these people except in this:
that they "found a law" that crossed their paths while in pursuit of other
subjects, and this also is true of me. The rapture is victory over death;
and death, Hades and Satan are together. Those who test this will find
a serviceable aid to Christian living.

The Scriptures indicate that my belief in these malignant personalities
places me in good Biblical and mental company. The approaches of E-
phesians 6:12 and II Thessalonians 1:4—14 and 2:2—8, together with *Paul's*
hope (Philippians 3:11 and II Timothy 4:6), make the rapture a "My Peace"
and a *sine quo non* for the *ultima thule* of faith. Insolvable questions start
up from these texts which only faith accepts. This chapter (II Thessalonians 2) is the most baffling of Paul's writings. The key to understanding

(cf. vs. 5), having been withheld, the only thing that we are to show, is a sinister presence whose effluvium breeds fevers of passion and fears of the heart which engender depression, sudden passions and vile thoughts and such. And in these verses there stalks this "roaring lion," this God-defying Goliath, ever intimidating the "weak-in-faith" child of God; but praise His Name, the Lord Jesus shall slay. Hallelujah!

John writes *the Revelation* which is the story of Satan's final struggle and over-throw. "Time would fail to mention" Moses, Job, David, Isaiah, Ezekiel, Daniel and Jude who through inspired writings spake of this enemy of our souls. The Lord said, "I *beheld* Satan fall" (Luke 10:18) and in Luke 22:31, He said, "Simon, Simon, behold, Satan hath desired you that he may sift you as wheat." And in Luke 4:13 we read of the Lord in the temptation at the beginning of His ministry. [1]

"Your adversary, the devil" (I Peter 5:8) is the malignant personality of the Bible. This adversary is a type of mind impatient of any restriction of authority and has aborted man's institutions into dragons preying off of their own children. The battle is against anything that is in the image of God; and it is "self will" resisting all authority." My creed is to "Preach the Word" for Satan has One who will one day judge; and the preaching of this Word will bring fruit for "My Word shall not return unto me void, but shall accomplish that for which it is sent."

The last picture of the Adversary is in *Revelation* when he and his cohorts are cast into the Lake of Fire; for *we* brought forth thorns, fangs, and claws by our rebellion; that which is known ought to prepare us for the unknown. If our disobediences wrought such earth disaster, why shall not the same spiritual disobedience disturb the universe? (Ephesians 2:2).

Whoever reads the Old Testament with these assaults of Satan in mind, will never be far from the war in the heavenlies which attacks "The Way" of the Church today. The re-reading of these events will bring you to your knees in awe and adoration to Him of whom Paul rose to such heights of ecstasy in Romans 11:33—36 N.:

"O the depth of the riches both of the wisdom and knowledge of God!
How unsearchable are His judgments and His ways past finding out!
For 'Who hath known the mind of the Lord?
Or who hath been His counsellor?'
Or who hath first given to Him,
and it shall be recompensed unto him again?
For of Him, and through Him, and unto Him, are all things;
to Him be glory unto the ages. Amen."

---

[1] See Section FOUR, *Abraham to Christ's Spiritual Body,* SATAN'S Story, III. The Temptations of Jesus, pp.316—317

And kneeling beside Paul, you will open your eyes to "behold wondrous things out of all Thy law" (Psalm 119:18). Then His saints, turning to Satan's cohorts will be able to repeat Acts 13:41N. (cf. Habakkuk 1:5):

> "Behold, ye despisers, and wonder, and perish:
> For I work a work in your days,
> A work which ye shall in no wise believe,
> Though a man declare it unto you."

Section SIX: THE KINGDOM AGE

"And in the days of these kings shall Elah (God, singular) of heaven set up a kingdom, which shall never be destroyed: and the kingdom shall not be left to other people, but it shall break in pieces and consume all these kingdoms, and it shall stand for ever."

Daniel 2:44N.*

". . . Thou shalt . . . bring forth a son, and shalt call His name Jesus. He shall be great, and shall be called the Son of the Highest; and Jehovah God shall give unto Him the throne of His father David: And He shall reign over the house of Jacob unto the ages; and of His kingdom there shall be no end."

Luke 1:31b—33N.*

". . . The kingdom of the world (world system) is become the kingdom of our Lord, and of His Christ; and He shall reign unto the ages of the ages."

Revelation 11:15b A.S.V.*

* See page *xiii*

538

Section SIX: THE KINGDOM AGE

TABLE of CONTENTS

Statement

(HIS STORY
THE KINGDOM AGE (MY STORY
(SATAN'S STORY

In the previous Five Sections of the General Outline, we have kept separate:

(HIS Story, God's dealing with the Nations
(of men on earth
(MY Story, God's dealing with spiritual
(peoples: Israel and the Church
(SATAN'S Story, the record of the old
(Dragon's works from the beginning
(to the ending.

In this Kingdom Age, Section SIX, these THREE lines are so inter-mingled in the revelation of these events, that we are presenting them as the ONE final "Story" of God's Purpose:

To the nations of men
To spiritual people
And to Satan

His dealing with each of these is recorded in the order of the events.

INTRODUCTION

SIGNS PRECEDING THE KINGDOM AGE

𝕿 HE LORD'S WORD in regard to the end of the Age so accurately described the events down to 70 A.D. and since 1914 unto this present date, that it seems even a fool could not deny it. This sermon of the Lord's which is found in Matthew 24 and Luke 21, stemmed from the disciples' questions[1] at His statement: "not one stone shall be left standing upon another":

1. In Matthew 24, the Lord's revelation of the course of Israel's history is given.

   In verse 3 the disciples asked:

   a) "When shall these things be?"

   b) "What shall be THE sign of Thy *coming*?" (Gr. *parousia*)

   c) "What shall be THE sign of the *end* (Gr. *sunteleias*, completion or consummation) of the Age?"

Here in Matthew verses 11—14 is the warning of false prophets coming to the Jews, for *there were no Gentile prophets*.

Verse 12 prophesies of the indifference of the Church "when iniquity shall abound and the love of many (N. "the many") shall wax cold."

Here Jesus answers their questions by covering events of history reaching from the first century to "the Day of the Lord"; but the major emphasis is upon the *latter* days.

2. In Luke 21 is found the course of the church's history and as we have seen it come to pass even as He said, up until this very day, how can we doubt the rest of the way?

   In verse 7, "some" asked Him:

   a) "When shall these things be?"

   b) "What THE sign when these things are about to come to pass?" N.

Here in *Luke* the prophecy begins with those days immediately following Pentecost, A.D. 30, and refers especially to the destruction of Jerusalem in A.D. 70 when the Christians in Jerusalem remembered this warning by Jesus and as they saw the prophecies being fulfilled, they fled to the mountains, and we are told by Josephus that "not one perished." In this prophecy the Jewish nation is being scattered and Jerusalem is being trodden down "until the times of the Gentiles be fulfilled." And then the prophecy goes to the signs in the end times (Luke 21:25).

---

[1] See Section FOUR, *Abraham to Christ's Spiritual Body*, MY Story, VII. The Lord Jesus Christ, E. Jesus and Prophecy, 2. Prophecy of the End Times, pp. 267—275.

It is very important in studying these two prophecies by the Lord, to distinguish between that which refers to the Jews and that which refers to the Church. Jesus describes the Great Tribulation (Matthew 24:21) as something that had never occurred since the beginning of the world nor ever shall be; verse 22 says:

> "Except those days should be shortened, there should
> no flesh be saved, but for the elects' sake, these days
> shall be shortened."

This fulfills the prophecy of Daniel 9:27, the Covenant Week which is divided into two parts of three and one-half weeks (years) each. The purpose of the shortening of "those days" is to save Israel from complete destruction during the last three and one-half years. This is the most abominable horror that Israel shall ever pass through. Ezekiel 37 describes Jacob's trouble as do both Deuteronomy 28:64—65 and Jeremiah 30:7. Of these days the Lord distinctly says that the end is not yet, but Luke 19:43—44 and 21:20-- 24 were fulfilled in A.D. 70 at the destruction of Jerusalem.

Sublimely the Lord moves on past Jerusalem's debacle through the heavenly phenomena and earthly terrors, and then cometh the end (Matthew 24:14). And now the Church is also warned of the end times-signs, made doubly sure by the speaker, Jesus; and by the literal fulfillment up to date.

To the disciples' question, "When shall these things be?" Jesus answers, "Watch!" More space is given in the Gospels to the answer to this question than to the Sermon on the Mount (Matthew 24:1—44, Mark 13:1—37, Luke 21:1—36). The *signs* are the fig tree and the ten virgins, and they are for the Church to *see,* but the *events* which the signs foretell, are for Israel to *experience.* [1]

I. RIGHTLY DIVIDING II Timothy 2:15

A. DISTINGUISHING THE TERMS THAT DIFFER
(Philippians 1:10)
1. The Coming (Gr. *Parousia*) of Christ

This word is used 24 times in the New Testament; 22 times it is translated *coming* and two times it is translated *presence.* The usage of the word *presence* is with reference to Paul being present with the Corinthians or the Philippians, but where it is translated *coming,* it is used in at least *four different ways,* or to record *three events* between the ending of the church age and the beginning of the Day of God:

> *a)* It is used of the rapture of the Church when Jesus *comes in the air* to "catch up" His Body (I Thessalonians 2:19, 3:13, 4:15, ———— 5:23, and II Thessalonians 2:1)

[1] See Section FIVE, *THE CHURCH,* MY Story, VI. "Things . . . Established." I. The Rapture, 2. The Christian's Outpost Observatory, *a)* Seeing the Invisible, pp. 507—513

b) In these following passages, it should be noted that these are the books which will be used by the Jewish Remnant AFTER the rapture, and the reference here may have a *double* meaning: they apply *first* to the rapture of the Church, but following the rapture, they have reference *also* to the return of the Lord to earth for the Kingdom Age (James 5:7–8, II Peter 1:16, and I John 2:28).

To illustrate the use of a double application in the Scriptures, see Zechariah 12:10 with John 19:37 and Revelation 1:7.

c) The next usage of the word *parousia* is with reference to the return of the Lord to earth at His coming in glory: Matthew 24:3, 27, 37, 39, II Thessalonians 2:8 and II Peter 3:4.

In I Corinthians 15:23 it is used of this same coming to earth and refers to those Tribulation martyrs and saints that are the Lord's at His coming.

d) The fourth usage of the word *parousia* is in II Peter 3:12 when it refers to the Day of God "by reason of which" the heavens and the earth are to be melted with fervent heat. This occurs at the Consummation of the Age when the new heavens and the new earth are introduced.

In reviewing these "comings" set forth in the preceding references, we conclude that the *parousia* is used to describe three distinct events:

a) First, the rapture in which the Church is "caught up" at the end of the church age

b) Second, the return of Christ to earth about seven years after the rapture

c) Third, the coming of the Day of God "by reason of which" the heavens and the earth are burned with fire.

2. The Appearing (Gr. *epiphaino*) of Christ

Most of the teaching concerning the Lord's coming arises from the Scripture passages which use the words *coming* or *appearing*. As we have noted in the use of the word *parousia* which is translated *coming*, it must be taken in context, for it refers to more than one event; so also the Greek words translated *appear* or *appearing* must also be considered in their usage and context before drawing conclusions as to the order and purpose of events referred to by these words. There are at least three different events recorded by the words *appear* or *appearing*. We take note that there are five Greek words translated *appear* or *appearing* in the New Testament, but we will mention only the differences in the *events* referred to and their order of occurrence as limited by the context in which they are used:

a) The ministry of Christ and His death, burial and resurrection are referred to as His *appearing* in II Timothy 1:10

b) The rapture of the Church is referred to as the *appearing* or as the time when the Lord will appear in Colossians 3:4, I Timothy 6:14, II Timothy 4:8 and Titus 2:13.

In the following references the words are used of the *rapture* which is still future, but after the Church is "caught up," and the Jewish remnant will use these epistles again, then the passages may also refer to the Lord's *second coming to earth* in glory: Hebrews 9:28, I Peter 1:7 and 5:4, I John 2:28 and 3:2. This is another illustration of the double application of prophecy.

c) In II Timothy 4:1 we read "at His *appearing* and His kingdom" which refers to His second coming in glory, and does not include the rapture. The same is also true in II Thessalonians 2:8 which refers to the brightness (manifestation) of His coming when He is revealed to the lawless one at His second coming in glory.

Thus as in the use of the word *coming* (*parousia*), three separate and distinct events are referred to, the same is true in the uses of the word *appear* or *appearing*.

3. The Judgment Seat of Christ

(Romans 14:10 and I Corinthians 3:12—15)

At the rapture the Church appears before the Judgment Seat of Christ (Gr. *bema*) for rewards:

> "We must all appear before the Judgment Seat of Christ for everyone is to give an account of the deeds done in the body, . . ."

> II Corinthians 5:10

This judgment is not for salvation but is for the *place* which the Christian is to occupy in the Body.

B. THE TWO CURRENTS OF BIBLE PROPHECIES

(I Peter 1:10—11)

The Old Testament Scriptures were considered by the nations as a tribal book of religion, but to the Hebrews it was a preview of "The Kingdom of Heaven" wherein "A Prince shall reign in righteousness." It was so vivid that they were blinded to the real values. The prophets limned the King in His *sufferings* (Isaiah 53) and in His *glory* (Isaiah 59:19—— 60:9).

"When the fulness of the time came" (Galatians 4:4) and "as the people were in expectation" (Luke 3:15), "God sent forth His Son," and "He came unto His own, . . ." — but being rejected, He said: "O Jerusalem, Jerusalem, Thou that killest the prophets, And stonest them that are sent unto thee . . . how often . . . ."

Matthew 23:37—39

He came unto His own and the house was desolate because they knew not the time of their visitation. Then is delivered the ultimatum:

> "Ye shall not see Me until ye shall say,
> 'Blessed is He that cometh in the Name of the Lord'."

And *that time* is yet future. All that remains is the sordid story of their sin. Here is the most overlooked and the most significant section of the Scriptures. The Kingdom is in abeyance because it was estopped and the Church is begotten, born, baptized, commissioned and endued. His *sufferings* are fulfilled (Acts 3:18); His *glory* is drawing nigh.

Condensed Order of Events

The TRIBULATION through THE DAY OF THE LORD

For convenience of the reader this outline of events from The Tribulation through The Day of the Lord is given. The references for each part of the outline will be found in the development of the outline on the pages following.

THE TRIBULATION: The Covenant Week of Daniel 9:27; Seven Years

A. The First Three and One-Half Years Include:

1. A Psuedo Peace
2. The Jewish Temple
3. The Remnant evangelizes
4. The Silence in Heaven
   a) The Tribulation Martyrs at Peace
   b) The Trumpeteers
   c) The Raptured Church

B. The Last Three and One-Half Years; The Time of Jacob's Trouble

1. The Temple is defiled by nations
2. Lawlessness becomes rampant
3. The Nations assemble at Armageddon to destroy Israel
4. Israel calls for her Messiah

THE DAY OF THE LORD: (
(THE KINGDOM (AGE) OF CHRIST

(THE MILLENNIAL IRON SCEPTRE
REIGN

A. The Lord Appears to Earth at the Revelation of His Glory;
The Second Coming (Gr. *Parousia*)
B. Armageddon
1. The Rider Upon the White Horse
2. The Kings of the Earth are destroyed at Armageddon
3. The Beast and False Prophet are cast into the Lake of Fire
C. The Judgment from the Throne of His Glory
1. On the Nations, separating the Sheep from the Goats
   a) Sheep
   b) Goats
D. Satan is bound for a Thousand Years
E. The Reign of Righteousness and Peace
1. The Church, the Body of Christ, reigns with Him
2. Israel is restored
   a) Israel is restored to the Land
   b) The King is restored to Israel
   c) The restoration of the Lord's protection over Israel
   d) The Temple (Ezekiel's) is restored
3. A New Covenant is made with the House of Israel
4. Ezekiel's Temple will be built and
   The Lord's Throne will be placed here
5. The Nations come up to Jerusalem to seek favor of Israel
6. Satan is loosed for a little season
7. Satan assembles Gog and Magog to battle
8. Fire from heaven devours Gog and Magog
F. The Seventieth Week
Statement
1. Satan is cast into the Lake of Fire and Brimstone
2. The Land is cleansed
3. The Second Resurrection of *All* the dead in the graves
4. The Great White Throne Judgment
5. The Second Death; The Lake of Fire
6. The Earth cleansed by Fire

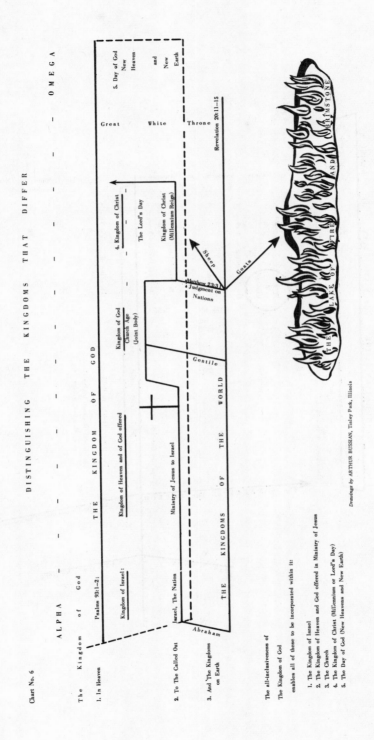

Chart No. 6

DISTINGUISHING THE KINGDOMS THAT DIFFER

ALPHA – – – – – – – – – – – – – – – – – – – OMEGA

The Kingdom of God

THE KINGDOM OF GOD

1. In Heaven

Psalms 93:1-2;

Kingdom of Israel;

Kingdom of Heaven and of God offered

Kingdom of God
Church Age
(Joint Body)

4. Kingdom of Christ

The Lord's Day

Kingdom of Christ
(Millennium Reign)

Great   White   Throne

5. Day of God
New Heaven

and

New Earth

Revelation 20:11-15

Ministry of Jesus to Israel

Matthew 25:31
Judgment on
Nations

Sheep

Goats

2. To The Called Out   Israel, The Nation

3. And The Kingdoms
on Earth

THE KINGDOMS OF THE WORLD

Gentile

Abraham

The all-inclusiveness of

The Kingdom of God

enables all of these to be incorporated within it:

1. The Kingdom of Israel
2. The Kingdom of Heaven and God offered in Ministry of Jesus
3. The Church
4. The Kingdom of Christ (Millennium or Lord's Day)
5. The Day of God (New Heavens and New Earth)

Drawings by ARTHUR BUSSIAN, Tinley Park, Illinois

548

Chart No. 6-a
Section SIX-a: THE KINGDOM AGE

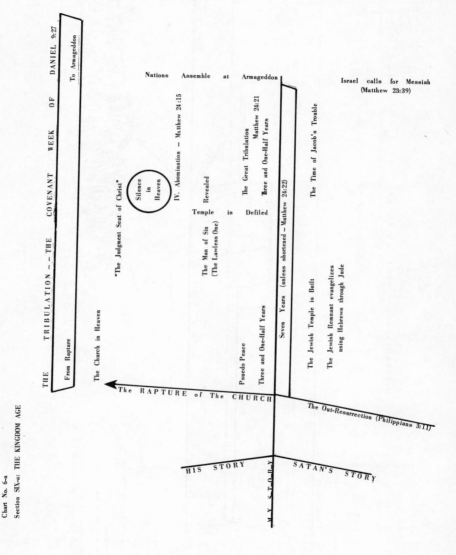

THE TRIBULATION — THE COVENANT WEEK OF DANIEL 9:27

From Rapture

To Armageddon

The Church in Heaven

"The Judgment Seat of Christ"

Silence in Heaven

IV. Abomination — Matthew 24:15

Nations Assemble at Armageddon

Israel calls for Messiah
(Matthew 23:39)

Revealed

Temple is Defiled

The Man of Sin
(The Lawless One)

The Great Tribulation
Matthew 24:21
Three and One-Half Years

The Time of Jacob's Trouble

Psuedo Peace
Three and One-Half Years

Seven Years (unless shortened — Matthew 24:22)

The Jewish Temple is Built

The Jewish Remnant evangelizes
using Hebrews through Jude

The RAPTURE of The CHURCH

The Out-Resurrection (Philippians 3:11)

HIS STORY   SATAN'S STORY

M-Y S-T-O-R-Y

THE DAY OF THE LORD -- THE KINGDOM OF CHRIST

THE MILLENNIAL IRON SCEPTRE REIGN

ISRAEL'S   SEVENTIETH   WEEK   -   DANIEL   9:24

Fire from heaven destroys

GOG and MAGOG

During Which:

The CHURCH reigns with Christ in His Kingdom

ISRAEL is restored and given a New Covenant; and The Temple of Ezekiel's Vision is BUILT during the Kingdom Age, but is anointed in the Seventieth Week.

The NATIONS come up to Jerusalem to worship the Lord

Satan loosed for a little season

ONE THOUSAND YEAR REIGN

Satan is bound

THE ABYSS

THE LAKE OF FIRE AND BRIMSTONE

Sheep

Goats

Beast and False Prophet

The Stone Strikes The Feet of the Image of the World Governments Daniel 2:44-45

Second Coming of Christ to Earth

II Thessalonians 1:7-10

The Rider on White Horse. Revelation 19:11-16

Throne of Glory Judgment on the Nations Matthew 25:31

First Resurrection – The Tribulation Martyrs Revelation 20:4–5; I Corinthians 15:23

KINGS of the EARTH DESTROYED

A R M A G E D D O N

THE TRIBULATION – THE COVENANT WEEK OF DANIEL 9:27

Chart No. 6-b
Section SIX

Drawings by ARTHUR BUSSIAN, Tinley Park, Illinois

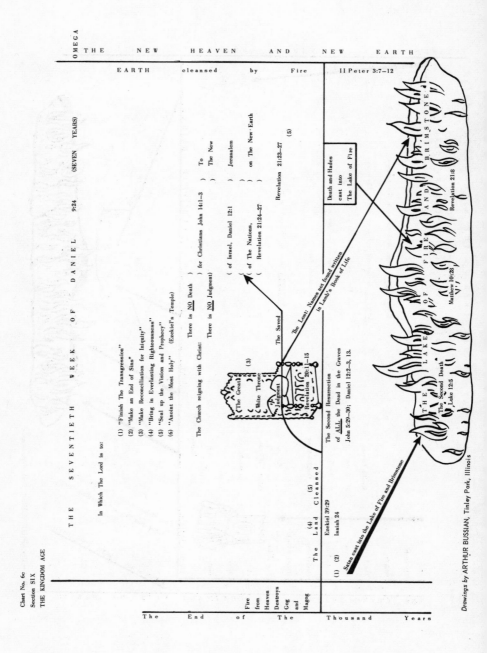

THE SEVENTIETH WEEK OF DANIEL 9:24 (SEVEN YEARS)

In Which The Lord is to:

(1) "Finish The Transgression"
(2) "Make an End of Sins"
(3) "Make Reconciliation for Iniquity"
(4) "Bring in Everlasting Righteousness"
(5) "Seal up the Vision and Prophecy"   (Ezekiel's Temple)
(6) "Anoint the Most Holy"

There is NO Death   ) for Christians John 14:1–3
There is NO Judgment)

(of Israel, Daniel 12:1
(of The Nations,
(Revelation 21:24–27

To
The New
Jerusalem
on The New Earth
Revelation 21:23–27   (5)

The Church reigning with Christ:

The Saved

(3)
(The Grand
White Throne
Judgment
Revelation 20:11–15

The Lost: Names not found written
in Lamb's Book of Life

Death and Hades
cast into
The Lake of Fire
Revelation 21:8

OMEGA   THE NEW HEAVEN AND NEW EARTH

EARTH cleansed by Fire   II Peter 3:7–12

The Second Resurrection
of ALL the Dead in the Graves
John 5:29–30; Daniel 12:2–3, 13.

The Land Cleansed   (4) (5)

Ezekiel 39:29
Isaiah 24
(1) (2)

Satan cast into the Lake of Fire and Brimstone

THE LAKE OF FIRE AND BRIMSTONE
Matthew 10:28
The Second Death
Luke 12:5

Fire
from
Heaven
Destroys
Gog
and
Magog

The End of The Thousand Years

Drawings by ARTHUR BUSSIAN, Tinley Park, Illinois

II. THE TRIBULATION: THE COVENANT WEEK OF DANIEL 9:27[1]

This is NOT the Seventieth Week of Daniel which is God's, but it is a man's mandatory covenant and week. This covenant week is not "determined" beforehand (as is the Seventieth), but here, the one making the covenant comes "in his own name" (John 5:43).

The unbelieving Jews who have returned to Palestine are to be conciliated, but eventually they are to be "framed." The one whom the Jews make a prince is given a mandate to confirm a covenant before "the many" (the League of Nations). This mandatory covenant is not a covenant with the Jews but is with many nations for one week and to these it will have to be submitted. The first problem facing the nations in the covenant week will be the Jew. We note that "in the midst of the week" or after three and one-half years, it is to be broken off and then will come "the abomination of the desolation." Before this time, the Jews will have built their temple and will expect the Messiah at the dedication. The anti-Christ will insist upon eagles or images (the abominations) to be placed upon the temple, but the Jews will resist. It will be easy to fan a mob spirit among the nations inasmuch as they have just ceased fighting and will be quick to stamp out any embers. With their patience exhausted, anti-semitism flares anew and the nations of the League are called in to execute the Jews. This will come as a climax in the Great Tribulation of the latter three and one-half years of the week and is seen in Matthew 24:21. The Tribulation will be concluded and *very likely shortened* by the coming of the Lord (Matthew 24:22). As Israel realizes her coming doom, she calls for the Lord and He comes suddenly at Armageddon as the Rider on the White Horse with an Iron Sceptre to rule and to reign for one thousand years. This will be the Stone striking the Image of world empires. In the Seventy Weeks' Covenant the one week, the Seventieth, is a fragment but it is still a most vital part. Those things which are brought to pass in the Seventieth Week do not in any way compare with these distinctive things of man's covenant week. The outline of the Tribulation or the Covenant Week follows:

A. THE FIRST THREE and ONE-HALF YEARS INCLUDE:

1. A Psuedo Peace:

Pre-Armageddon is a great world war (Matthew 24:6—13); then comes a peace which is questionable (Daniel 11:27 and 8:25) because it is based upon intriguery.

"But concerning the times and the seasons, brethren, ye have

---

[1]
See Sealed Division, *Isaiah* to *Malachi* A. Introduction *Isaiah* to *Daniel* 4. The Prophecy of *Daniel*, *d*) *Daniel* . . . Baseline (2) The Church's Telescopic View, pp. 50—52

no need that I write unto you. For yourselves know perfectly that the day of Jehovah so cometh as a thief in the night. For when they shall say, '*Peace* and safety'; then sudden destruction cometh in upon them, as travail upon a woman with child; and they shall not escape."

I Thessalonians 5:1–3N.

Also compare Isaiah 59:8, Jeremiah 6:14 and 30:5.

2. The Jewish Temple:

The Temple of the Jews must be built; Daniel 9:27 speaks of sacrifice and oblations. The Jews must build the temple for a place in which to offer these sacrifices.

3. The Remnant Evangelizes

When the Rapture of the Church takes place, an horrified earth will be shocked into silence, and then a remnant of the Jews will begin to investigate the absence of those who made up the Church. By reading *Hebrews* through *Jude*[1] and then the rest of the New Testament, they will come to an understanding of the truths which had been taught by the Church. The large majority of Jews will be unbelievers but will be returning to the Holy Land and will build again the Temple. The Remnant (144,009) will go up to an undebatable faith that Jesus was their Messiah and they missed Him and have been brought to a conviction which leads them to evangelize their brethren according to the flesh as well as the Gentile nations (Matthew 24:14). The gospel for this tribulation period will be found in *Hebrews* through *Jude*, and those whom they convert by this preaching are the Tribulation Saints of Revelation 7:14. Some of them will become martyrs and be beheaded for the witness of Jesus and the Testimony of the Word of God (Revelation 20:4).

We should note that it is the remnant, the Bride of Christ, (Isaiah 62:5) who is to evangelize. Nowhere in the Scriptures do we find that a bride bears a cross but the Church does bear one (Matthew 16:24, Galatians 2:20).

The Tribulation saints from the nations (Psalm 2:8) will be made ready for the kingdom of Christ through the evangelistic effort of these Jews who will sow the seeds for another nation to "be born in a day." The remnant will first convert their Jewish brethren, and then all of the converted Jews will go out to bear their testimony to all the world. The result of their witnessing is seen in Revelation 7:9–15.

4. The Silence in Heaven (Revelation 8:1)

"And when He had opened the seventh seal, there was silence in heaven about the space of half an hour."

---

[1] See Sealed Division, VI.*Hebrews—Jude*, D. Israel's New Testament, pp. 127–129.

Compare Zechariah 2:13, 1:11 and Habakkuk 2:20.

Prayer, the highest emotion, is as "the last state of motion is rest." This will be the greatest of all worship services until the final, "Thy Kingdom come, Thy will be done." This is the "Consecration" room; "this is none other than . . . God" (Genesis 28:17).

Every creation is the fruit of the Word "God said." If the keyboard evokes imprisoned notes, then the altar and censer are the keyboard of prayer which contained the stored-up prayers (Luke 1:37). This is to be the greatest of all prayer meetings; consider those who participate:

> *a*) The Tribulation martyrs at prayer (Revelation 6:10); and these join with the Tribulation saints of Revelation 7:10
> *b*) The trumpeteers are "prepared" through prayer
> *c*) The raptured Church is also there.

B. THE LAST THREE and ONE-HALF YEARS of THE TRIBULATION PERIOD; THE TIME of JACOB'S TROUBLE

(Jeremiah 30:4–9, Matthew 24:21, Revelation 7:14)

This Covenant Week will end in the Great Tribulation for Israel. Compare Daniel 7:25, 12:7 with Revelation 11:2, 9, 12:6, 12–19 and 13:5 (forty-two months; twelve hundred sixty days; set time, set times and a half). All of these are within the Great Tribulation of three and one-half years, and these terms are used only here.

> 1. The Temple is defiled by the Nations:
> Daniel 9:27*b* and Matthew 24:25
>
> 2. Lawlessness becomes rampant:[1]
> II Thessalonians 2:1–12, Matthew 24:15–22

The lawless one of II Thessalonians becomes evident in the world when the restraining One, the Holy Spirit, is removed along with the Church at the Rapture.

This Lawless One is more subtle in his actions during the first three and one-half years of the Covenant Week, but his lawlessness becomes rampant during the latter three and one-half years.

> 3. The Nations assemble at Armageddon to destroy Israel
>
> Matthew 24:21, Revelation 16:13–16

This week will end in the Great Tribulation for Israel. The sixteenth

---

[1] See Section FIVE, *THE CHURCH*, MY Story, VI. "Things . . . Established." (The Rapture). 2. The Christian's Outpost Observatory, p. 507 ff.

chapter of Revelation describes the vials which are poured out rapidly up to the twelfth verse which speaks of the "Great River Euphrates," "and the water thereof was dried up that the way of the kings of the East might be prepared" (Cp. I Thessalonians 5:1–9 with Revelation 16:13–16).

These "kings of the sun-rising" are gathered but are not converted. "They repent not and blaspheme God" at the Lord's Second Coming. Revelation 17 and 18 deal with Babylon—Ecclesiastical (Mystery) and Political; both are destroyed with anarchy (Revelation 18:21).

4. Israel calls for her Messiah (Matthew 23:39, Joel 2:18)

This call might shorten the time of the latter one-half of the covenant week (Matthew 24:22). The Lord promises to come to Israel when they say, "Blessed is He that cometh in the name of the Lord" (Matthew 23:39, Revelation 22:12, 20, Isaiah 65:24, Jeremiah 33:3).

The Remnant of Israel, the Bride, joins the hosts of heaven and "all ye His servants" in the model prayer, "Thy Kingdom come, Thy will be done." This is at the end of "A covenant of one week" (Daniel 9:27).

III. THE DAY OF THE LORD: ((THE KINGDOM (AGE) OF CHRIST

((THE MILLENNIAL IRON SCEPTRE REIGN

This is "the day of vengeance of our God" (Isaiah 61:2*b*), when shall appear the Rider upon the White Horse (Revelation 19:11 to 20:6); and Acts 3:20–21 is fulfilled. That portion of Scripture unquoted by Jesus in Luke 4:19*b* (Isaiah 61:2*b*), draws nearer and these things are terrible to contemplate for all those who are not in Christ.

This *day* which lasts one thousand years begins with:

a) The unveiling or manifestation of Christ in Glory (Luke 21:27)
b) The disruption of the heavenly bodies, stars, constellations, sun, moon (Isaiah 13:10, Joel 2:30–32, Acts 2:19–20, Luke 21:25–26)
c) The disruption of nations and men (Isaiah 13:9, 11)

And this same *day* ends with the all-consuming fire of II Peter 3:10–13.

A review of each of the previous "HIS Story" sections through this Seven-Fold Chart will indicate the manner and purpose of God in dealing with the nations from the very beginning to the very ending. In Section FOUR, HIS Story, (pp.205–214) the prophecy of the image given to both Nebuchadnezzar and Daniel is unveiled, showing it to be fulfilled in the Four Great World Empires of Babylon, Medo-Persia, Greece and Rome. Arising out from these Empires are "Ten Toes" Kingdoms which represent the system of world governments which continue until Christ comes to the earth again. The prophecy of Daniel 2:34—35:

> "Thou sawest till that a stone was cut out without hands, which smote the image upon his feet that were of iron and clay, the brass, the silver, and the gold, broken to pieces together, and become like the chaff of the summer threshingfloors; and the wind carried them away, that no place was found for them; and the stone that smote the image became a great mountain, and filled the whole earth.'

The fulfillment of the growth and development of the image has already taken place, but it yet remains for this final prophecy to be fulfilled.

Daniel's interpretation of this prophecy is found in Daniel 2:44—45:

> "And in the days of these kings shall the God of heaven set up a kingdom, which shall never be destroyed: and the kingdom shall not be left to other people, but it shall break in pieces and consume all these kingdoms, and it shall stand for ever. Forasmuch as thou sawest that the stone was cut out of the mountain without hands, and that it brake in pieces the iron, the brass, the clay, the silver, and the gold; the great God hath made known to the king what shall come to pass hereafter; and the dream is certain, and the interpretation thereof sure."

The smiting of the image by the Stone will take place at the Second Coming of Christ to earth. This will be "The Day of the Lord"—a day of wrath and judgment which begins at Armageddon; and the judgment continues until the events of Matthew 25:31—46 have been completed. These judgments upon the nations which take place at this time are revealed in the prophets and the New Testament Scriptures.[1]

We have thought of the image as having been destroyed before this time, but actually that image is to be destroyed when our Lord comes and it is something that exists right in our midst now. It is a *smitten* image, one that has been smitten by sin, but it will be *destroyed* when the kingdom of the world (world system) becomes the kingdom of our Lord and of His Christ.

In I Thessalonians 5:3 and II Thessalonians 1:7—10 are events pertaining to the beginning of the Day of the Lord which occur "suddenly" in the "call" of Israel, the battle of Armageddon, and the judging of the nations (Matthew 25:31). It is here to these that the Lord comes "as a thief in the night." From Pentecost to Armageddon, wickedness flourishes but from Armageddon to Magog, wickedness diminishes. At Armageddon is revealed the One of whom it is written, "This is the Stone" (Psalm 118:22—24, Matthew 21:42—44, Romans 9:32, I Corinthians 1:23, I Peter 2:6—8, Isaiah 28:16). Here Daniel 2:45 (vs. 35) is fulfilled "in the days of these

---

[1] See I Samuel 2:10; Psalm 9:8; 110:6; Isaiah 2:4; Haggai 2:21—23; Matthew 25:31—46

kings." "And the Stone that smote the image became a great mountain (rock) and filled the whole earth." His battle is to smite the whole earth."

A. THE LORD APPEARS TO EARTH AT THE REVELATION OF HIS GLORY (The Second Coming, Gr. *Parousia*) (Revelation 19:11, II Timothy 4:1, Matthew 24:30, Ezekiel 43:2).

At His second coming the Lord will appear in flaming fire (Gr. *phlox*, II Thessalonians 1:7—10). The return of the Lord to earth in His glory is graphically described in this Thessalonian passage and in Matthew 24:30—31. We read, "when the Lord Jesus shall be revealed from heaven with His mighty angels in flaming fire," we are reminded of the description of the Lord in Revelation 1:14, 2:18 and 19:12 as one whose "eyes were as a flame of fire." The Greek word for *flame* (phlox) in both *Thessalonians* and *Revelations* evidently describes His glory which is the Shekinah and which was manifested at the Transfiguration, at the Ascension, and will be manifested when He comes again (Acts 2:11). Out from this Shekinah, He will step as from an aeroplane; Elijah so ascended into the heaven as the Lord will return (II Kings 2:11, Psalm 104:3). This *phlox* fire must not be confused with the Lake of Fire and Brimstone or the destruction of the earth in fire at the end of the Day of the Lord. This flame is the *revelation of His glory* (Acts 7:30, 22:11) which all men will see at His appearing, but it is not the *fire of judgment* which evil men shall experience at the Great White Throne. It is important to note that the words "in flaming fire" in the A.S.V. are included in II Thessalonians 1:7 rather than in the eighth verse as in the A.V. The eighth verse should begin with:

> "Taking vengeance on them that know not God, and that obey not the gospel of our Lord Jesus Christ; who shall be punished with everlasting destruction from the presence of the Lord and from the Glory of His power when He shall come to be glorified in His saints."

This is that "Day of Vengeance" which occurs at the second coming of Christ to earth and which includes His appearing at Armageddon and His judgment on the nations that are living at the time of His coming. Note that there is no mention of a resurrection for judgment here. The Great White Throne Judgment occurs one thousand years later at the time of the second resurrection. The word *vengeance* is humanized in its usage but this is the exact meting out to each of both good and bad of the portion rising up out of justice for those who have persecuted the people of God during the Tribulation.

B. ARMAGEDDON (Revelation 16:13—16)

1. The Rider Upon the White Horse

"And I saw heaven opened, and
    Behold a white horse;
And He that sat upon him was called
    'Faithful and True,'
And in righteousness
    He doth judge and make war.
His eyes were as a flame of fire,
And on His head were many crowns (diadems);
He had a name written,
    That no one knew, but He Himself.
And He was clothed with a vesture
    Dipped in blood:
And His name is called
    'The Word of God.'
And the armies which were in heaven
    Followed Him upon white horses,
    Clothed in fine linen, white and clean.
And out of His mouth goeth a sharp sword,
    That with it He should smite the nations:
And He shall rule them with a rod of iron:
And He treadeth the winepress
    Of the fierceness and wrath of Almighty God.
And He hath on His vesture and on His thigh
    A name written,

'KING OF KINGS, AND LORD OF LORDS'."

Revelation 19:11—16 N.

This Rider with the secret, incomprehensible name is the LORD JESUS CHRIST. He will be wearing many crowns and will carry a sharp two-edged sword which would be the Scriptures (John 5:39, Hebrews 4:12—13). He will use the sword to meet the mouthings of the apostates at Armageddon.

2. The Kings of the Earth are Destroyed at Armageddon

(Isaiah 59:19—20, Revelation 19:17—19)

To vultures come the flesh of kings and the flesh of horses. Here at Armageddon the ambulance corps is ordered out, before the battle begins, to carry away and to keep from pestilences "the kings of the earth" (Revelation 16:12). This will be the Jacob-Ishmael battle for the land, urged by the beast (political) and the false prophet.

This is the drama of all dramas. Here is the oriental splendor of the "Kings of the East" (Isaiah 14 and Ezekiel 28), and the destruction of these kings of the earth at Armageddon might well be likened to that of Sennacherib at Jerusalem:

The Assyrian came down like a wolf on the fold,
And his cohorts were gleaming in purple and gold;
And the sheen of their spears was like stars on the sea,
When the blue wave rolls nightly on deep Galilee.

Like the leaves of the forest when Summer is green,
That host with their banners at sunset were seen:
Like the leaves of the forest when Autumn hath blown,
That host on the morrow lay wither'd and strown.

For the Angel of Death spread his wings on the blast,
And breathed in the face of the foe as he pass'd;
And the eyes of the sleepers wax'd deadly and chill,
And their hearts but once heaved, and forever grew still!

And there lay the steed with his nostril all wide,
And through it there roll'd not the breath of his pride:
And the foam of his gasping lay white on the turf,
And cold as the spray of the rock beating surf.

And there lay the rider distorted and pale,
With the dew on his brow and the rust on his mail;
And the tents were all silent, the banners alone,
The lances unlifted, the trumpet unblown.

And the widows of Ashur are loud in their wail,
And the idols are broke in the temple of Baal;
And the might of the Gentile, unsmote by the sword,
Hath melted like snow in the glance of the Lord![1]

3. The Beast and False Prophet are cast into the Lake of Fire

(Revelation 19:20):

"And the wild beast was seized, and with him the false prophet that
wrought the signs before him, with which he deceived them that
had received the mark of the wild beast, and them that worshipped
his image. The two were cast alive into the lake of fire burning
with brimstone." (Cp. also Revelation 20:10)

These are removed in judgment at the beginning of the thousand year reign.

C. THE JUDGMENT FROM THE THRONE OF HIS GLORY

(Matthew 19:28)

Once to every man and nation comes the moment to decide;
In the strife of Truth with Falsehood, for the good or evil side;
Some great cause, God's new Messiah, offering each the bloom or blight,
Parts the goats upon the left hand and the sheep upon the right,
And the choice goes by forever 'twixt that darkness and that light . . . . [2]

---

[1] Lord Byron, *The Destruction of Sennacherib*

[2] James Russell Lowell, *The Present Crisis*, st. 5 (see also Sec. ONE, HIS Story, p. 146 ff.

1. On the Nations, separating the Sheep from the Goats

(Matthew 25:31—46, Isaiah 11:3—4, II Timothy 4:1)

Matthew 25:31—46 will be a text for the remnant to use in the Tribulation period preaching which will show that when the Lord returns *after* the Tribulation, He will judge the nations on their treatment of the brethren of the Lord, and the judgment will be on the basis of benevolent works at that time (Matthew 16:27). Some of these works are suggested in *Hebrews* and the other epistles but they are not limited to these books. The remnant will be able to preach a trust in God for deliverance and the practicing of benevolent works.

It should be noted that this is not a judgment between *Christians* and *sinners*; the basis of judgment is on their works and not on their obedience to *the Gospel of Christ*.

a) Sheep (Matthew 25:34—40):

This is a recognition of the Tribulation martyrs, saints and remnant (Matthew 24:32):

(1) In the *First* resurrection are the Tribulation martyrs, those beheaded during the tribulation period who have been evangelists (Revelation 6:9—11 and 20:4—5). It is important that we distinguish between the "Out-ressurection from among the dead ones" (Philippians 3:11), and the "First resurrection" ones (Revelation 20:4—6). The "out-resurrection" occurs at the rapture when those who are asleep in Jesus are raised first, and then the Christians who are alive on the earth at the time of the Lord's coming, are "caught up" together with them to meet the Lord in the air (see I Thessalonians 4:13—28). The "first resurrection" occurs at the *end of the Tribulation period*, probably seven years after the rapture, and includes the Tribulation martyrs who will have been beheaded for the witness of Jesus and for the Word of God. These are those who are Christ's at His coming (I Corinthians 15:23).

(2) The Tribulation Saints are made up out of all nations (Revelation 7:9—14 and 5:9—10). They will be alive at the time that the Lord returns to the earth and are those who have been converted through the witnessing and preaching of the Tribulation martyrs and the Tribulation remnant.

(3) This Tribulation Remnant is made up of the 144,000 out of all of the living generation of the tribes of the children of Israel in that day (Revelation 7:4—8, 14:1—5, Isaiah 49:6, 54:5—8, Jeremiah 31:7—11, Isaiah 61:10, 62:5, Joel 1:16). This remnant will be the Bride of Christ. During the Tribulation period, the remnant evangelizes the rest of Israel and the nations (Micah 5:7—8).

"The Rest of the dead" (Revelation 20:5)

The above (Tribulation martyrs, saints and remnant) are distinct and separate groups from "the rest of the dead" which include all other men of all other ages, both Jew and Gentile, even the great saints and patriarchs of former ages beginning with Adam. "The rest of the dead" are to be resurrected at the second resurrection and are judged out of those things which are written in the books according to their works (John 5:28—29). The promises of God to all men of every age and dispensation will be fulfilled at this time. The promises to Abraham and his seed will come in to fulfillment as the new heaven and the new earth are revealed and as the Holy City, the New Jerusalem, comes down out of heaven from God. The "Old Testament Saints" do not share in the thousand year kingdom age but remain during this time in Abraham's bosom and thus the first, the Old Testament saints, shall be last; and the last, the Church, shall be first in resurrection.

b) Goats (Matthew 25:41—46):

The goats include Babylon and other persecutors of God's people. The living generation who persecutes the Tribulation remnant, the saints and the martyrs, are judged *immediately*, and are cast into the fire prepared for the devil and his angels.

The rest of the wicked—those who are dead—will be raised for judgment at the Great White Throne.

Note on II Timothy 4:1N.:

"I charge (earnestly testify to) thee therefore before God,
and the Lord Jesus Christ, who is about to judge the living
and the dead according to His *appearing* and His *kingdom*;"

The *Living* are judged at the *end* of the Kingdom, at the Great White Throne Judgment (Hebrews 6:2).

D. SATAN IS BOUND FOR ONE THOUSAND YEARS

(Revelation 20:1—3, Psalm 48:2, Matthew 5:35, Isaiah 14:12—14)

"And I saw an angel come down out of heaven, having the *key* of the abyss (bottomless pit) and a great chain in his hand. And he laid hold on the dragon, that old serpent, which is the Devil, (*Diabolos*, Accuser), and Satan, (Adversary), and bound him a thousand years, And cast him into the abyss, and shut him up, and set a seal over him, that he should deceive the nations no longer, till the thousand years should be fulfilled: and after that he must be loosed a little season."

For the use of this *key* see Isaiah 55:10—11, 61:1 "set at liberty" (Psalm 138:2). Jesus said concerning the lawyer (Luke 11:52), "Ye have

taken away *the key of knowledge*; ye entered not in yourselves, and them
that were entering in, ye hindered." Now that Word operates for a thousand
years, the millennium age, and during this time the Word of God rules (Revelation 19:15). The angel seized the dragon (monster), the cruel spirit, the
one full of subtlety; this is the devil, the accuser, the traducer, Satan the
adversary. He is cast into the pit which is sealed OVER him as the tomb
OVER the Lord at His burial.

Here during this millennium age, the Church enters in to the kingdom
with Christ as He is taking the place which Satan aspired to in this God's
foot-stool, the earth (Isaiah 14:12—14, Psalm 48:2). Just as kings are unseated and dethroned in these days, when Christ receives His kingdom
here, one of His first acts will be to bind Satan, the god of this world.

E. THE REIGN OF RIGHTEOUSNESS AND PEACE

(Revelation 20:4—6, Luke 1:32—33, Psalm 2:1—12, Daniel 7:13—14)

". . . The kingdom of the world is become of our Lord, and of
His Christ; and He shall reign for the ages of the ages."

Revelation 11:15 N.

The Kingdom of Heaven is at hand again. Once more the prayer is,
"Thy Kingdom come," and when Matthew 23:39 is fulfilled, it will come.
The Kingdom is from Armageddon to Magog; thus, God's will is to be done
on earth as it is in heaven."

1. The Church, the Body of Christ, reigns with Him in His Kingdom

(Luke 12:32, II Timothy 2:12)

In I Thessalonians 4:17a we read:
"And so shall we ever be with the Lord."

Thus the Church, the Body of Christ, returns with its Head when He
returns to earth. Wherever the Head goes, the Body must accompany (Colossians 3:4, Zechariah 14:5b). The place of the Twelve Apostles during
the Kingdom is announced by Jesus in Luke 22:29—30.

"The Lord Jesus Christ is yet to be established as king in a very
definite and literal sense. It should never be overlooked that He is not
yet on His own throne, but is on the right hand of the throne of His
Father. The teaching of the New Testament on this subject reveals
some significant facts. In the Gospels and also in the *Acts*, Christ's
kingship is clearly marked, but in the epistles it is singularly absent,
for our Lord is never described as *king* of His Church, but only as its
Lord and Head. Kingship is associated with his relation to the Jews
and to the universe. This gives an appropriateness to the fact that in
Revelation, Kingship is once more seen."

Anonymous

As we have noted in Section FOUR, (*Abraham to Christ's Spiritual Body*), [1] Christ fulfills a three-fold office of *prophet* during the Old Testament period; of *priest* during the time of His suffering and the Church Age; and as *king* when He returns to earth for His Iron-Rod-Reign.

While He was here on earth, they rejected Him as king:

> "When ye pray, say, 'Our Father who art in heaven,
> . . . THY kingdom come, THY will be done,
> on earth as it is in heaven'."

And when Christ's kingdom comes to earth, He will put away all sin and there will be a complete restoration of God's control on the earthly section of His kingdom as completely as it is in heaven (I Corinthians 15:24—28).

2. Israel is restored

> "Repent ye therefore, and turn ye, that your sins may be blotted out, so that times of refreshing may come from the presence of Jehovah; and He may send Jesus Christ, which before was preached unto you: Whom heaven must indeed receive until times of restitution (restoration) of all things, which God hath spoken by the mouth of all His holy prophets from of old."
>
> Acts 3:19—21N.

Following the healing of the man born lame (Acts 3:1—11), Peter now preaches the gospel of Christ to the people of Jerusalem, showing that the things which God had shown by the mouth of all His prophets—that Christ should *suffer*—He had so fulfilled. He calls them to repentance that their sins might be blotted out, and he assures them that the promise concerning *the glory* that shall follow of which the prophets wrote, the times of the restoration of all things, are yet to be fulfilled. This restoration of all things is accomplished in the Kingdom Age and an understanding of this restoration is made possible through the reading of the prophets.

In Isaiah chapter 60 is unfolded the glory that is to come upon Israel at the second coming of Christ to earth. This effulgent glory ought not be lightly esteemed for it is not to be a momentary experience, but will be an abiding one for the thousand years' duration of the Kingdom Age as is shown in this chapter:

Verse 1:
> ". . . The glory of the Lord is risen upon thee."

Verse 2:
> ". . . His glory shall be seen upon thee."

Verse 3:
> ". . . And the Gentiles shall come to thy light,
> And kings to the brightness of thy rising."

-----

[1] Section FOUR, *Abraham to Christ's Spiritual Body*, MY Story, VII. The Lord Jesus Christ, C. Distinctive Ministry, 4. Jesus as Prophet, Priest and King, pp. 259—260.

Verse 7:

". . . And I will glorify (beautify) the house of my beauty."

Verse 9:

". . . And to the Holy One of Israel, because He hath
beautified thee."

Verse 13:

". . . To beautify the place of My sanctuary;
And I will make the place of my feet glorious."

Verses 19—20:

"The sun shall be no more thy light by day;
Neither for brightness shall the moon give light unto thee:
But the Lord shall be thine everlasting light,
And thy God thy beauty.

Thy sun shall no more go down
Neither shall the moon withdraw itself:
For the Lord shall be thine everlasting light,
And the days of thy mourning shall be ended."

These verses indicate that the abiding presence of the Shekinah glory will
return to Israel when the Lord comes; and that the brightness of this glory
shall be witnessed by the nations of the Kingdom Age. The similarity of
the Kingdom Age will be a pre-view of the greater glory of the Day of God
—OMEGA.

For the general picture of the restoration of Israel, we should read
Ezekiel chapters 37 and 38, and Zechariah chapter 14.

There are at least four main parts to this restoration:

a) Israel is restored to the Land
Deuteronomy 30:3—5; Isaiah 62:1—7; Jeremiah 23:3—8; 24:6;
30:3, 10—11; 32:41; Ezekiel 11:17—18; 36:11, 24; 37:21; Zechariah 9:16; Amos 9:8—15, and Acts 15:15—18.

b) The King is restored to Israel
Psalm 110:1; Luke 20:41—43; Isaiah 9:6—7; 11:1; Jeremiah 23:
5—6; 30:9; Ezekiel 21:25—27; 37:22—25; 43:2—7; Hosea 3:4—5;
Zechariah 14:9; and Luke 1:32—33.

c) The Lord's protection is restored over Israel
Isaiah 11:11; Joel 3:1, 16—17; Zechariah 12:4—9

d) The Temple is restored
Ezekiel 37:26—28; Amos 9:11

The details of this temple are found in Ezekiel chapters 40—
48, and are herein discussed on page 37.

Thus will be fulfilled to the commonwealth of Israel, the covenants
of promise which were made by God to the fathers of Israel. The promises

of God are not given lightly and especially those which were given to Abraham are confirmed by two immutable things: the promise and the oath of
God (Hebrews 6:13—18, Genesis 15:5—6, and 22:16—17):

> "Thus saith Jehovah,
> Which giveth the sun for a light by day,
> And *the ordinances* of the moon and of the stars for a light
>   by night,
> Which divideth the sea when the waves thereof roar;
> Jehovah of hosts is His name:
> If *those ordinances* depart from before Me, saith Jehovah,
> Then the seed of Israel also shall cease from being a nation
>   before Me all the days.
> Thus saith Jehovah;
> If heaven above can be measured,
> And the foundations of the earth searched out beneath,
> I will also cast off all the seed of Israel for all that
>   they have done, saith Jehovah."
>   Jeremiah 31:35—37N.
> (cp. Jeremiah 33:7—26, especially vss. 20—26)

Upon the assurances of these Scriptures we conclude that God will bring
about the restoration of all things of which these prophets wrote.

3. A New Covenant is made with the House of Israel

When the Lord brought the children of Israel out of Egypt, He gave them
the covenant of the law of Moses, but when He brings about the restoration
of all things for Israel, He has promised them a *new covenant*. In Jeremiah
24:7 He states that He will give them a heart to know Him, and Jeremiah
31:32—34N. reveals how this new heart is brought about:

> "Behold, the days come, saith the Lord,
> That I will confirm a new covenant with the house of Israel,
> And with the house of Judah:
> Not according to the covenant that I confirmed with their fathers
> In the day that I took them by the hand to bring them out of the
>   land of Egypt;
> Which My covenant they brake,
> Although I acted with authority unto them, saith the Lord:
> But this shall be the covenant that I will confirm with the house
>   of Israel:
> After those days, saith the Lord,
> I will put My law in their inward parts,
> And write it on their hearts;
> And will be their God,
> And they shall be My people
> And they shall teach no more every man his neighbor,
> And every man his brother, saying, 'Know the Lord';
> For they shall all know Me, from the least of them

unto the greatest of them, saith the Lord:
For I will forgive their iniquity,
And I will remember their sin no more."

This same promise is given again in Ezekiel 11:19—20 and in Ezekiel 37:26. The results of the new covenant are found in Psalm 85:10:

"Loving kindness and truth are met together;
Righteousness and peace have kissed each other."

(Cp. also Isaiah 59:21)

It is to this same new covenant that Paul refers in Hebrews 8:7—13 which is a definite reference to this promise of the new covenant in Jeremiah 31. This is to be made with the living generation of Israel at the time the Kingdom of Christ is established at His second coming to earth.

To His disciples Jesus said:

"And I appoint unto you a kingdom, as My Father hath appointed unto Me; that ye may eat and drink at My table in My kingdom, and sit on thrones, judging the twelve tribes of Israel."

Luke 22:29—30

At this time He will fulfill the promises made in Matthew 26:28—29; Mark 14:24—25; and Luke 22:16—18. It is here that the blood of the new covenant is made effective in the removing of the sins of the nation of Israel in that day. In these passages in the Gospels, the Lord had brought to an end the old Passover and He points them to the new covenant of the Kingdom Age. This is carefully distinguished from the Communion Table and the New Covenant for the Church in Luke 22:19—20 and I Corinthians 11:25. Both Jew and Gentile participate in the New Covenant of the Church Age by becoming Christians; but during the Kingdom Age, both Israel and her Gentile converts participate in the new covenant which is made with them in that day when Romans 11:26 through 29 is fulfilled.

Some will ask, "will men die during the Kingdom Age?" And to this we would answer that death evidently continues during the Kingdom Age since the last enemy to be destroyed is death (I Corinthians 15:26) but with the binding of Satan and the diminishing of sin, man's natural life time will be extended during the Kingdom Age.

4. Ezekiel's Temple will be built at Jerusalem

The dimensions of the Sanctuary described by Ezekiel in chapters 40 through 48 are much larger than usually credited.[1] The basic standard of measurement is not stated but if it were cubits as is sometimes thought,

---

[1] A complete description of Ezekiel's temple and its measurements are given in *The Companion Bible*, App. 88, pp. 125—127.

the size of the city of the Great King would be less than two miles each
way, or less than four square miles. However if a *reed* is the standard of
measurement used (12 ft. 6 in.), then the measurement of the city, five
thousand reeds, will equal a city twelve miles square, with an area of one
hundred forty-four square miles which dimensions are befitting the metropo-
lis of the world.

Using this same basis of measurement, the total "Oblation" area in
which "The City" and "The Sanctuary" are located, is sixty miles square
or covering a total of thirty-six hundred square miles. The portion of "The
Oblation" for the Levites is sixty miles by twenty-four miles, an area of
fourteen hundred forty square miles; the portion of "The Oblation" for the
priests is the same, sixty miles by twenty-four miles, or an area of fourteen hundred forty square miles; and within "The Oblation" for the priests,
is located "The Sanctuary."

This leaves an area sixty miles wide and twelve miles long which is
divided into five equal sections: the center section being for the Prince's
portion, one on the west, and the other on the east of "The City."

The remaining two sections, twelve miles square on each side of the
City, between the Prince's portion and the City, are evidently the garden
portions of the City: "As the increase thereof shall be for food for them
that serve the City."

"The Sanctuary" is located in the center of the Oblation for the Priests,
and is enclosed within a wall measuring five hundred reeds each way (one
reed—12 ft. 6 in.), or a little more than a mile square. In the center of this
great square we have next the boundary wall enclosing the Outer Court,
measuring five hundred cubits each way (one cubit—21 in.), or about one-
fifth of a mile. Within this is the Inner Court, a square of three hundred
cubits or 625 English feet; inside the Inner Court is the Temple (or Palace,
Hebrew *heykal*) Court or the "separate place."

Finally, in the midst of the "separate place" stands the Altar, twenty-
five feet square, and the Altar stands before the house in the midst of the
"separate place" and is the actual center of the Millennial Sanctuary and
worship, rather than being the center of the building, the house or temple
immediately to the west of it. This indicates that the Millennial "Temple"
is really the Palace or Habitation of the Messiah in connection with "The
City of the Great King" (Psalm 48:2).

While some will object that the Oblation of sixty miles square will not
fit in to the present Holy Land, Palestine, we would call attention to the
dimensions of the land promised to Abraham[1] which so far exceed the

---

[1] See Section THREE, *Restoration to Terah*, HIS Story, II. Eden, God's Workshop,
pp. 177–183.

boundaries that are now applied to the Holy Land or that were ever occupied by the people of Israel up to this time. This Oblation for the Sanctuary and the City will be but a small part of the whole land which was promised to Abraham and his seed, and which will be occupied during the Kingdom Age. [1]

This Sanctuary and Temple will be the center of worship for the whole world and the nations will flow unto it during the Kingdom Age (Isaiah 2:2–4).

5. The Nations come up to Jerusalem to seek the favor of Israel

During the Kingdom Age, Israel will teach the nations; for Israel redeemed and blessed by the Lord, shall be sought out by the nations who shall flow unto it.

Today Christians evangelize by going out to the uttermost parts of the nations (Matthew 28:19); but during the Kingdom Age, the Lord shall so bless Israel that the nations shall come *to them*.

References: Psalm 2:8; Isaiah 2:2–4, 11:9, 19:18–25, 60:1–12, 64:2*b*; Zechariah 8:20–23, and 14:16–17.

In the Kingdom Age the problem of communication by means of different languages will be removed, for in Zephaniah 3:9 we find that the Lord said:

"For then will I turn to the peoples a pure lip (language),
That they may all call upon the name of the Lord,
To serve Him with one consent" (shoulder).

This is the same word (*lip*) which was used in Genesis 11:1, 6–7 and 9 when the whole earth was of one language before the confusion of tongues given unto them by the Lord.

6. Satan is loosed for a Little Season (Revelation 20:7)

"When the thousand years are finished," Satan is loosed for a little season and goes out to deceive the nations (Revelation 20:7).

7. Satan assembles Gog and Magog (Revelation 20:8–9)

Satan goes out to the four quarters of the earth and Gog and Magog are gathered for battle (Ezekiel chap. 38).

The events which are *announced* in Daniel chapter 10, and which are *revealed* and *written* in chapters 11 and 12, occur between Armageddon and Magog. The first great event of the Day of the Lord, Armageddon, is a great battle (Revelation 16:14–16). The second, Magog, is a great destruction (Revelation 20:9, Zechariah 14:12, Daniel 11:36—12:1).

---

[1] Section FOUR, *Abraham to Christ's Spiritual Body*, MY Story, II. The Growing Cloud of Testimony-Bearers, pp. 232–235. "Ezekiel limned a temple too large for even the Holy Land."

8. Fire from Heaven devours Gog and Magog (Ezekiel 39:6)

As they compass the camp of the saints about, and the beloved city, fire comes down from God out of heaven and devours them (Rev. 20:9b).

F. THE SEVENTIETH WEEK[1]

"Seventy weeks are determined (decreed) upon thy people,
And upon thy holy city, —
(1) To *finish* the *transgression,*
(2) And to *make an end of* (to seal up) *sins,*
(3) And to *make reconciliation for iniquity,*
(4) And to *bring in everlasting righteousness,*
(5) And to *seal up the vision* and the *prophecy* (prophet)
(6) And to *anoint the Most Holy* (holy of holies)."

Daniel 9:24N.

Somewhere in the seventy weeks occur the six events of Daniel 9:24; they did not occur in the sixty-nine weeks that are past (Hebrews 2:8) and therefore they must all be related to the last week, the seventieth, and to it alone. The first two groups of weeks (the seven and the sixty-two weeks) run up to the Triumphal Entry, A.D. 30. In Daniel 9:26 we read:

"After three score and two weeks shall Messiah be cut off, but not for Himself: and the people of the Prince that shall come, shall destroy the city and the sanctuary;"

Thus the king is crucified and the capital is destroyed *after* the sixty-ninth week.

It is important to note that all of Daniel 9:24 happens in the *last week,* As we have noted in the Sealed Division of *Daniel,*[2] there are two parentheses within the Seventy Weeks' prophecy: *The Church Age* and *The Kingdom of Christ.* There will be no "everlasting righteousness" until the end of the thousand years when Satan is cast into the Lake of Fire. Then can begin the Seventieth Week and Everlasting Righteousness.

As the outline indicates,[3] the time of the Seventieth Week is immediately following the judgment of fire upon Gog and Magog. The following are the events of this final week, the seventieth, which introduces the Consummation—OMEGA—when God shall be all in all.

---

[1] See SEALED DIVISION, I. *Isaiah* to *Malachi,* A. Group One, 4. The Prophecy of Daniel, *d)* Baseline of Prophecy, (1) Daniel's Seventy Weeks Prophecy, pp. 44–53.

[2] See SEALED DIVISION, I. *Isaiah* to *Malachi,* A. Group One, 4. The Prophecy of Daniel, *d)* Baseline of Prophecy, (2) The Church's Telescopic View of Israel's Seventy Weeks, pp. 50–52.

[3] *The Seven-Fold Chart,* page 140

1. Satan is cast into The Lake of Fire and Brimstone

(Revelation 20:10)

The devil is cast into the Lake of Fire and Brimstone where the beast and false prophet were already cast and here they are tormented forever (Matthew 25:41).

This final end of Satan is God's judgment upon this one who was a "covering cherub in heaven" "till iniquity was found" in him and he was cast down to the earth (Ezekiel 28:14—17).[1] The Lake of Fire and Brimstone was prepared for Satan and his angels (Matthew 25:41). The beast and false prophet had already been cast into this Lake of Fire at the beginning of the thousand years (Revelation 19:20).

That Satan is the ruler of hell, the place of fiery judgment, is most certainly NOT taught in the Bible, for he himself is judged by being cast into the Lake of Fire. His place in the church age is not in hell but in the earth and he is the god of this world. In Matthew 3:12 John the Baptist announces the purging with fire by the Lord, and here at the end of the thousand years' kingdom, Satan becomes a part of the chaff which is burned with unquenchable fire. Here we see the fulfillment of Matthew 10:28N.:

> "And fear not them which kill the body, but are not able
> to kill the soul: but rather fear Him (God) who is able to
> destroy both soul and body in Gehenna."

And in Luke 12:5N.:

> "But I will forewarn you whom ye shall fear: Fear Him (God)
> which after He (God) hath killed, hath authority to cast
> into Gehenna; yea, I say unto you, Fear *Him*" (God).

This harmonizes with Deuteronomy 32:39 and I Samuel 2:6. In these passages of Scripture we see that God has the power to kill, but in reading the context we find that this power is used in judgments. God used this power for judgment in Egypt (Exodus 12:12, 23), but He has committed to Satan the power of normal, physical death since Adam's sin.

> "Forasmuch then as the children are partakers of flesh and blood,
> He also Himself in like manner took part of the same; that through
> death He might render powerless him that has the power of death,
> that is, the devil; And deliver them who through fear of death were
> all their lifetime subject to bondage."

> Hebrews 2:14—15N.

> "The thief cometh not, but for to steal, and to kill, and
> to destroy: I came that they might have life, and that
> they might have it more abundantly."

> John 10:10N.

---

[1] Section ONE, *ALPHA*, SATAN'S Story, page 155

Satan, not God, brings death today, and for the Christian, there is no death because Christ delivered us from Satan's power and thereby has conquered death (John 8:52 and 11:25—26). We see in Revelation 20:10 that Satan who has had the power over death on earth, is now destroyed forever; and thus God makes an end of sin. This having been accomplished, the rest of the events of the Seventieth Week can be fulfilled.

2. The Land is cleansed (Ezekiel 39:9, Isaiah 24)

After Magog there is one week of seven years during which Israel is cleansing the land and Messiah is cleansing the people, and we see the Lion of the Tribe of Judah (Jesus) feeding the vultures with kings' flesh (Ezekiel 39:17—19). At the end of the Kingdom Age the great multitude out of the nations who are deceived by Satan (Gog and Magog) break the Everlasting Covenant (Isaiah 24:5). The resulting need for cleansing and judgment (The Great White Throne) is shown in Isaiah 24:1—22. The result of the cleansing is found in chapter 24:23 and chapter 25; (cp. Isaiah 25:8 and Revelation 21:4).

> The tumult and the shouting dies—
> The Captains and the Kings depart
> Still stands Thine ANCIENT sacrifice
> An humble and a contrite heart.
> Lord God of Hosts, be with us yet,
> Lest we forget—lest we forget! [1]

3. The Second Resurrection of *All* the Dead in the Graves (Revelation 20:11—15)

It is important in rightly dividing to note the distinctions in the events and persons referred to in John 5:19—29:

> John 5:24: here it is the Christian who passes from death unto life. In verses 25—26, John says, "the hour IS coming and NOW IS when the dead shall hear the Voice of the Son of God and they that hear shall live."

This indicates that John is writing at the close of the first century; he says that the hour now is, that is, during the Church Age when the dead shall hear the Voice of the Son of God; and those who hear the Gospel are those who pass from death unto life (cp. John 11:25—26, John 8:52). For them there is no death, only rapture. In verses 28—29 the reference is to the resurrection at the close of the Kingdom Age, "the resurrection at the last days" (John 11:24, Revelation 20:5, 11—15). This will be the resurrection of both Jew and Gentile and will include both those who have been faithful, and those who have done evil (Daniel 12:1—3). There are

---

[1] Rudyard Kipling, *Recessional.*

no Christians in this resurrection for they have been "caught up" to be with the Lord at the end of the Church Age (I Thessalonians 4:13—18 and I Corinthians 15:51 ff.).

4. The Great White Throne Judgment (Revelation 20:11—15)

The "Great White Throne" is a spectacle, not a movement. The Highway of Holiness is the path over which God moves from the beginning in carrying out His purpose and supervising the campaign that is going on until He arrives at the winding up of the Kingdom. Here at the Great White Throne Judgment, the division is made and then nothing is left ahead but the Holiness of the Beginning. You will understand the Highway of Holiness when you get the *ad quim pro* from the beginning to the ending, and are able to see the whole purpose.

At the Great White Throne Judgment, resurrected individuals but not Christians, out of every age and out of every nation are judged according to their works (Revelation 20:11—15, Daniel 12:1). Here will be fulfilled the parable of the wheat and tares which are allowed by the Lord to grow together until the harvest:

> ". . . And in the time of harvest I will say to the reapers,
> 'Gather ye together first the tares, and bind them in bundles
> in order to burn them: but bring together the wheat into my
> barn'."
>
> Matthew 13:30 N.

The interpretation of this parable is found in Matthew 13:36—43, and in Revelation 14:15*b*.

The Great White Throne has never been sullied by sin (Revelation 20:11):

> "And I saw the dead, small and great, stand before God; and the
> books were opened: and another book was opened, which is the
> book of life: and the dead were judged out of those things which
> were written in the books, according to their works. And the sea
> gave up the dead which were in it; and death and Hades delivered
> up the dead which were in them: and they were judged each man
> according to their works."
>
> Revelation 20:12—13 N.

This is the same "time of the dead" which is referred to in Revelation 11:18. Here the dead, both the righteous and the wicked of all ages, are judged, some for reward and some for condemnation.

5. The Second Death—The Lake of Fire
(Revelation 20:14, Matthew 13:42)

At the Great White Throne Judgment those whose names are not found written in the Book of Life will be cast into the Lake of Fire (Hebrews 12:29). These are those who are wholly irreconcilable. This is the *second* death for all those who are not named in the Book of Life; they include those referred to in Matthew 23:33—35. This becomes the fulfillment of the warning given in Luke 12:5. God who "kills" in the Great White Throne Judgment, casts these into the fire of Hell. Then Death and Hades are cast into the lake of fire; this is the *second* death.

6. The Earth is cleansed by Fire (II Peter 3:7—13)

The Seventieth Week begins with The Holy Land but now it will move on to the cleansing of the *earth* by fire. No more graphic description of this event could be given than that in II Peter 3:7—12N.:

> "But the heavens and the earth, which are now, by the same word are kept in store, reserved unto fire against the day of judgment and perdition of ungodly men. But beloved, be not ye ignorant of this one thing, that one day is with the Lord as a thousand years, and a thousand years as one day. The Lord is not slack concerning the promise, as some men count slackness; but is longsuffering to usward, not willing that any should perish, but that all should come to repentance.
> "But the day of the Lord will come as a thief in the night; in the which the heavens shall pass away with a rushing noise, and the elements shall be dissolved with fervent heat, the earth also and the works that are therein shall be burned up.
> "Seeing then that all these things shall be dissolved, what manner of persons ought ye to be in all holy behaviour and godliness, Looking for and hasting the coming of the day of God, by reason of which the heavens being on fire shall be dissolved, and the elements shall melt with fervent heat?"

*   *   *   *   *

> . . . These, our actors,
> As I foretold you, were all spirits, and
> Are melted into air, into thin air;
> And, like the baseless fabric of this vision,
> The cloud-capp'd towers, the gorgeous palaces,
> The solemn temples, the great globe itself,
> Yea, all which it inherit, shall dissolve;
> And, like this unsubstantial pageant, faded
> Leave not a rack behind.
>   We are such stuff
> As dreams are made on, and our little life
> Is rounded with sleep.[1]

7. The Vision's End; The Palin-Genesis of The *Prothesis* (Purpose) of God Almighty

The prophecy, "Seventy weeks are decreed upon THE PEOPLE (Israel)

---

[1] William Shakespeare, *The Tempest,* Act IV Sc 1

and upon THY HOLY CITY," reaches from the return from the captivity to
the bringing down of the new Jerusalem from heaven (Revelation 21:1—2)
at the introduction of the new heavens and the new earth. Peter looked
beyond the cleansing fire which came in preparation for the day of God,
and he said, "nevertheless we according to His promise look for—

'NEW HEAVENS AND A NEW EARTH,'

wherein dwelleth righteousness."

The Seventieth Week is the archipelago of Palin-Genesis into "The
Age of (all) the Ages" and the events of cleansing and making anew are
set forth in Revelation 20:11——21:8. Here within this week, the leaden-
footed ages are entered into the rapids and the six events of the Seventieth Week occur "quickly." The expectance of this week is found in the
dual interpretation of I Peter 1:1 to 2:12 when it is proclaimed by the
remnant during the Tribulation.

Out from this Seventieth Week
will open the mighty events of OMEGA
when I Corinthians 15:28 will come in to fulfillment.

Section SEVEN:

OMEGA

"'I am The Alpha and The Omega, beginning and ending,'
saith the Lord, 'which is, and which was, and which is
to come, the Almighty'."

Revelation 1:8 N.*

"But as it is written,
'Things which eye hath not seen, Nor ear heard,
Neither entered into the heart of man,
Things which God prepared for them that love Him'."

I Corinthians 2:9 N.*
(Isaiah 64:4 b)

"For, behold I create new heavens and a new earth;
And the former shall not be remembered, nor come into mind."

Isaiah 65:27 N.*

*See page *xiii*

575

Section *SEVEN: OMEGA*

TABLE of CONTENTS

OMEGA[1]

"I AM ALPHA AND OMEGA, THE FIRST AND THE LAST . . ."

Introduction

THE BIBLE is a miracle-laboratory where ordinary men become heroic. To name a few:

> Moses, the sheep-keeper
> Josiah, the boy-king
> Amos, "a herdsman, gatherer of sycomore—fruit."

Here in this Book, note the ascendancy:

> Sinners become saints
> Harlots become ancestresses
> Poets become prophets
> Shepherds become kings.

There is a power in operation which is nowhere else to be found, but it is here in this Book, reproduced upon its highest level from the very lowest of materials. There is an ascending apocalyptic ending (Gr. *telos*) all the way through:

> Moses said: "God shall raise up a prophet like unto me"
> Jesus Christ said: "Greater things than these shall ye do,
> for I go unto My Father."

And then appears the Church, that Mystery dwelling in the Heavenlies, of which Paul could say: "Till we all arrive at the unity of the faith . . ." and "that He might present it to Himself a glorious church . . ." (Ephesians 4:13, 5:27). Thus, no matter how surpassing any age may be, there is yet a *plus ultra* on ahead; from its highest there is yet a higher; or, "from glory unto glory."

Here in OMEGA comes the most glorious time for which the Ages were framed. God is revealed "without shadow of turning" as He moves into the new heavens and the new earth (Isaiah 51:16, 66:22) wherein dwelleth righteousness, there to be "THE All in All."

> "Then cometh the end, when He shall have delivered up the kingdom to God, even the Father; when He shall have put down all rule and authority and power.
>
> "The last enemy that shall be abolished is death.
>
> "For He hath 'put all things under His feet'. But when He saith

---

[1]
See also Section FOUR, MY Story, I. The Prophets beginning with Abraham, D. Abraham, the Visioner, pp. 323–329.

Chart No. 7

Section: SEVEN

O M E G A

"GOD ALL AND IN ALL"

I Corinthians 15:28

Revelation 1:8

1. THE TIME of OMEGA

a) Follows The Kingdom Age, I Corinthians 15:24—28

b) Begins with New Heaven and New Earth, Revelation 21:1—2

2. THE PURPOSE of OMEGA

The Consummation of all things for (Israel   — Psalm 23:6

(The Church   — John 14:1—3

(The Nations   — Revelation 21:24—27

3. THE GOD of OMEGA

Revelation 21:3—7, 22

4. THE DESTINATION of THE HIGHWAY of HOLINESS

The New Jerusalem, Revelation 21:2, 23—27

5. DISTINGUISHING THE THINGS THAT DIFFER

The City was *prepared* in ALPHA, *before* the Katabole (the casting down) since the works were finished *from* the Katabole, to be *revealed* in the Consummation (I Peter 1:3—5) in OMEGA

This Heavenly City must be distinguished from the earthly Jerusalem, the City of the Great King (Hebrews 11:8—16; John 8:56).

'All things are put under Him', it is manifest that He is excepted, which did put all things under Him.

"And when all things shall have been subdued unto Him, then shall the Son also Himself be subject unto Him that put all things under Him, that God may be alll in all'."

I Corinthians 15:24—28N.

With the opening of the twenty-first chapter of Revelation, we find that for the first time within the pages of the Word of God since Genesis 2, that we are looking upon a sinless earth again. The Kingdom of Christ has ended and the Seventieth Week has put away sin and we hear the Voice of the Great High God, the Almighty, speaking out of heaven saying, ". . . 'Behold, the tabernacle of God is with men', ..."

The heavenly rainbow reaches from Alpha to Omega with golden glories at *both* ends, but between are events which are *very* earthy. The first two chapters of the Bible and these two final chapters of *Revelation* tell a continued story when the interruption of sin has been removed from between them.

The four perfect ("sinless") chapters of the Bible

We find in Genesis 1 and 2:	And in Revelation 21 and 22:
1. New heavens and new earth: "In beginning God created the heavens and the earth"	1. New heavens and new earth: "I saw a new heaven and a new earth"
2. Beginning of Light	2. Eternal Light
3. Men in the image of God	3. Man restored to the image of God
4. No sin	4. Sin ended
5. The tree of life	5. The tree of life
6. The river	6. The river of life
7. No curse	7. No more curse
8. No death	8. No more death
9. No sorrow or tears	9. No more sorrow or tears
10. All things new	10. All things new
11. The Garden of Eden	11. The City, the Paradise of God
Genesis 2:8	Revelation 2:7

God was at Alpha and the Lord was at the beginning; and the Lord is at the ending and God again is at Omega. The Lord is in the prophecy of the Seventy Weeks of Daniel 9:24 and then God brings the two ends of the Kingdom of Christ and Omega together (I Corinthians 15:28*b*) above the events of Revelation 20:14 over the head of the old serpent.

I. THE PROCLAMATION

John heard "a great voice out of the throne" for only from the throne can come this unbelievable proclamation:

> ". . . Behold, the tabernacle of God is with men, and he
> shall dwell with them, and they shall be his peoples,
> and God himself shall be with them, and be their God:"

> Revelation 21:3 A.S.V.

First was Christ's incarnation; now comes God's tabernacle where He receives "His peoples":

> "And God shall wipe away every tear from their eyes;
> And there shall be no more death, neither sorrow,
> For the former things are passed away."

> Revelation 21:4N.
> (cp. Isaiah 25:8)

And in Revelation 21:5*a*:

> "And He that sat upon the throne said,
> 'Behold, I *make* all things new' . . ."

He is not stating that He will *create* them now, but that it is already done at this time (Revelation 21:1; Psalm 90:1–2).

To *the thirsty* is given the invitation of Revelation 21:6N.:

> ". . . 'It is done.
> I am Alpha and Omega, the beginning and the end.
> I will give unto him that is athirst of the fountain
> of the water of life gratuitously'."

> (cp. Matthew 5:6; Isaiah 55:1)

And to *the conqueror* is given the promise of verse 7N.:

> "He that overcometh shall inherit all things;
> And I will be his God, and he shall be My son."

But to *all others* is the judgment of verse 8.:

> "But the cowardly, and unbelieving, and the abominable, and
> murderers, and fornicators, and sorcerers, and idolators and
> all liars, shall have their part in the lake which burneth with
> fire and brimstone which is the second death."

II. THE HOLY CITY — THE NEW JERUSALEM

Introduction

John saw the Holy City descending, the arch-type of all buildings of God (I Chronicles 28:11–12, 19; Hebrews 8:5). There must be a super world of cities and peoples.[1] The New Jerusalem is described "as a bride

---

[1] See Section ONE, *ALPHA*, I. MY Story, *In re* Super World, p. 150

adorned for her husband" (cp. Luke 21:5). Here is demonstrated love's lavishment.

"The City" was "prepared" *before* the *Katabole* (casting down), since the works were finished *from* the *Katabole* (Hebrews 4:3), and this City was kept by the power of God "until the fulness of the times," "reserved in heaven" for this long-hoped for Age is "ready to be revealed in the last time" (I Peter 1:3—5; Revelation 19:7). God who prepared this City, showed it to Abraham; and it was described by Satan (Isaiah 24:12—14; Job 1:6) to Cain [1] and Nimrod; and now at the end of the ages, the Bride appears having the glory (Shekinah) of God as her bridal veil (I Timothy 6:16).

The heavenly, the new Jerusalem is the Bride's trousseau and dowry, and becomes the conclusion of the whole matter (Ecclesiastes 12:13 and Revelation 21:9——22:5).

A. THE DESCRIPTION OF THE GLORIOUS CITY

1. The Origin of The City (Revelation 21:10N.):

> "And he carried me away in the Spirit to a great and high mountain, and showed me that great city, the holy Jerusalem, *descending out of heaven from God.*"

2. The "light-giving" City (21:11N.):

> "Having the glory of God: and her *radiance* was like unto a stone most precious, even like a jasper stone crystallizing."

3. The Wall and its Foundations (21:12—13N.):

> "And having a wall great and high, and having twelve gates and at the gates twelve angels, and names written thereon, which are the names of the twelve tribes of the sons of Israel: On the east three gates; on the south three gates; and on the west three gates."

4. The Wall of The City (21:4

> "And the wall of the city had twelve foundations, and in (on) them the names of the twelve apostles of the Lamb."

5. Measuring of The City (21:15—17N.):

> "And he that talked with me had a golden reed to measure the city, and the gates thereof, and the wall thereof. And the city lieth foursquare, and the length of it is as large as also the breadth: and he measured

---

[1] See Section THREE, *Restoration to Terah, HIS* Story, II. Eden, God's Workshop, pp. 177—183

the city with the reed, unto twelve thousand fur-
longs.[1] The length and breadth and the height of it
are equal. And he measured the wall thereof, a hundred and forty four cubits, according to the measure
of a man, that is, of the angel."

6. The Building Materials of the Wall and The City (21:8N.):

"And the building of the wall of it was *jasper* (a stone
of various colors): and the city was *pure gold*, like
unto clear glass."

7. The Garnishing of the Foundations of the Wall (21:19—20N.):

"And the foundations of the wall of the city were garnished with *all manner of precious stones.*
>   The first foundation was jasper
>   The second, sapphire (celestial blue)
>   The third, chalcedony (gray)
>   The fourth, emerald (green)
>   The fifth, sardonyx (flesh color)
>   The sixth, sardius (blood-red)
>   The seventh, chrysolyte (gold-stone)
>   The eighth, beryl (sea-green)
>   The ninth, topaz (yellow)
>   The tenth, chrysoprasus (gold and a leek)
>   The eleventh, jacinth (purple)
>   The twelfth, amethyst (violet).*"

8. The Materials of the Gates and Street (21:21N.):

"And the twelve gates were *twelve pearls*; every
several gate was of one pearl: and the street of the
city was *pure gold*, as it were transparent glass."

9. The Temple of The City (21:22N.):

"And I saw no inner temple therein: for the Lord God
Almighty and the Lamb are the temple of it."

10. The Source of the Light of The City (21:23N.):

"And the city had no need of the sun, neither of the
moon, to shine in it: *for the glory of God did lighten
it, and the Young Lamb is the lamp thereof.*"

11. The Dwellers in The City (21:24—27N.):

'And *the nations of them which are saved* shall walk
in the light of it: and *the kings of the earth* do bring
their glory and honor into it.

---

[1] The Holy City, The New Jerusalem, will be a cube 1500 miles around: or in height,
breadth, and width, 375 miles.

"And the gates of it shall not be shut at all by day: for there shall be no night there.

"And they shall bring the glory and honor of nations into it. And there shall in no wise enter into it any thing that defileth neither whatsoever worketh abomination and maketh a lie: but *they which are written in the Young Lamb's book of life.*"

12. The Blessings of The City (22:1—5):

a) A river of water of life:
"And he showed me a pure river of water of life, bright as crystal, proceeding out of the throne of God, and of the Lamb."

b) A tree of life (22:2, 14):
"In the midst of the street of it, and on either side of the river, was there the tree of life, which bare twelve manner of fruits, and yielded her fruit every month: and the leaves of the tree were for the healing of the nations."
"Blessed are they that do His commandments, that they may have right to the tree of life, and may enter in through the gates into the city."

c) No curse (22:3*a*N.):
"And there shall be no more any curse:"

d) The throne located here (22:3*b*N.):
"And the throne of God and of the Lamb shall be in it;"

e) The Lord is present with His servants (22:3*c*—4N.):
"And His bond servants shall serve Him:
And they shall see His face; and His name shall be on their foreheads."

f) No night there (22:5*a*):
"And there shall be no night there; and they need no lamp, neither light of the sun;"

g) Eternal light (22:5*b*N.):
"For the Lord God giveth them light; and they shall reign for the ages of the ages."

*   *   *

Here within a Golden City at the rainbow about the throne,
God heads up all things in the Universe
Unsandal your soul!
Ye who would look with appreciation and understanding
Upon this glorious gem lying upon the bosom of God,
The Universe with its capital,
The Holy City prophesied in Hebrews 11:8—16.

*   *   *

B. THE FULFILMENT OF THE VISION
OF THE CITY SPLENDID

From the above description of the City, we must conclude that it incorporates more than just the nation of Israel, the restored wife of the Lord during the Kingdom Age (Isaiah 54:5—8; 61:10—11; 62:4, *et al*).

This City rests upon foundations with the names of
The twelve apostles of the Lamb, the nucleus of the Church;
Its Gates are named
For the twelve tribes of Israel, the chosen nation (Jews);
Its Inhabitants include
"The nations of them which are saved" (Gentiles)

(cp. I Corinthians 10:32)

Therefore, this City must be the abode of *the redeemed of all ages* (Revelation 21:27; Psalm 23:6; John 14:1—3), and here is brought into fulfilment, Matthew 8:11—12, Luke 13:28—30, when "Abraham and Isaac and Jacob and all the prophets are in the kingdom of God" and when unbelievers are kept out. It is here also that:

"And they shall come from the east, and from the west,
and from the north, and from the south, and shall sit
down in the kingdom of God."

There is nothing to indicate that Abraham, Isaac and Jacob have any share in the Millennial Kingdom for they are not resurrected until the Great White Throne Judgment. Therefore this term "the kingdom of God" in *Luke*, or "the kingdom of the heavens" in *Matthew*, as it is used in these passages, must apply to the Day of God which is the time of the New Jerusalem and the New Heavens and The New Earth.

Hebrews 11:8—16 summarizes the *waiting* by Abraham and his seed (vs. 10) for "the city which hath foundations whose builder and maker is God," and in this OMEGA time, we find the fulfilment of the promise which God gave and for which they waited: the prepared City. These in this eleventh chapter of Hebrews are not a part of the Millennial Kingdom for they are not raised until at the time of the "better resurrection" (Hebrews 11:35).

That Abraham is to be heir of the world was promised of God (Romans 4:13—24, esp. vs. 13). Abraham's vision[1] of our Lord's "My Day" (John 8:56) carried him forward through each age to this very last one—OMEGA— the Day of God, and the vision of this City Splendid made him willing to be a stranger and a pilgrim on earth. We as Christians are like-privileged through the gospel of Christ (I Corinthians 2:9—10). Our inheritance as Christians of the righteousness by faith *in Christ* confirms our relationship

---

[1] Section FOUR, *Abraham to Christ's Spiritual Body (The Church)*, MY Story, I. The Prophets beginning with Abraham, D. Abraham, the Visioner, pp. 222—226.

to Abraham in this present dispensation (Galatians 3:6—9, 13—14, 22—29). Abraham's earthly seed, the nation of Israel, receives the earthly promises given to this "friend of God," but through Christ, the promised Seed (singular), we, the Church, are "partakers of the heavenly calling" (Hebrews 3:11; 12:22—23; 13:14; Revelation 3:12). The new Jerusalem will thus be shared by all those who are waiting for the heavenly promise which is fulfilled when God is All in All. What glories lie ahead for His Body when we shall be forever with the Lord and shall be like Him!

THE ULTIMA THULE

This is the last, and the most solemn hour of God The Almighty's "Purpose" with man. At this point man has exhausted his every prerogative; the Abraham-s and the Dive-s have arrived at each one's *Ultima Thule*. This last of the inspired Writings is the ultimate effort of the All-Wise, Almighty, All-Compassionate God to save; nothing remains; destiny is now supreme.

> "Him that overcometh will I make a pillar in the inner temple of My God, and he shall go no more out: and I will write upon him the name of My God, and the name of the city of My God, which is new Jerusalem, which cometh down out of heaven from My God; and I will write upon him My new name."
>
> Revelation 3:12N.

> "Blessed are they that do His commandments, that they may have right to the tree of life, and may enter in through the gates into the city."
>
> Revelation 22:14

The gap between ALPHA and OMEGA has been closed; God's workshop has been garnished and swept clean. Thus we:

> ". . . Give thanks for Thy lovingkindness and for Thy truth: For Thou hast magnified Thy Word above all Thy Name."

"IT IS FINISHED"

from   to
ALPHA   OMEGA

"That God may be all and in all"

Therefore,

> "Unto Him be glory in the Church in Christ Jesus, Unto all the generations of The Age of The Ages."
>
> Ephesians 3:21N.

AMEN   and   AMEN!

APPENDIXES

THE AUTOBIOGRAPHY OF GOD

The Hebrew and Greek Languages and The Aorist Tense

C. G. Kindred

The exquisite nicety, precision and accuracy of the Hebrew and Greek tongues for the purpose of revelation is often noted by reverent scholarship; nor could these two languages be interchanged! If the two tongues were inspected as literature in the Bible, this would lack a smooth-flowing reading and irregularities would be noted; but tarry a while in its reading, and a whole world of beauty opens up. There is very good reason for us to ponder the use of the two tongues:

Languages were given to *mature* themselves "in the fulness of the times"; a miracle itself is never alone! The Greek tongue and the Hebrew race are best seen after this "fulness" has withered; these languages both came to their maturity unobserved of men, and for the purpose—just as that of Mary sitting at the feet of Jesus—of unveiling God's Mind. Quoting from the *Newberry Edition of the Bible* (p. *iii-a*2):

> "In the Hebrew and the Greek Scriptures, there are *Precisions* and *Perfections*, and *Beauties* which cannot be reproduced in any translation. The Greek prepositions express geometrical relationship and are mathematically precise."

The same is true of the Greek verb making the same precision, perfection and beauty of language by its AORIST TENSE. The Hebrew of the Old Testament uses the Short and the Long Tenses, but in the New Testament, we find the Aorist, this HORIZONLESS tense, particularly dominating the first section of the Book of Sanctification (*Ephesians*) where, "In the Heavenlies," the Christian is sealed and seated; and where "*In* Christ," this "eternal tense" is *producing* the perfect Church (Ephesians 3:10; 5:25*b* —27). "For I doubt not through the ages one unceasing (and increasing) purpose runs"; as Paul himself received not *from* men, nor *through* man, but through Jesus Christ, and God the Father who raised Christ from among the dead ones (Galatians 1:1N.). As an example, note the *ascent* of The *Glorious* Lord-Christ:

<pre>
                   (Pre-Historic
                   (Prophetic
     For He was   (Historic
                   (Ascended
                   (Glorified
</pre>

In the *Christian Century* magazine for February 22nd, 1939, the first paragraph of an article by Eleanor Slater headed, "We Need an Eternal Tense," expresses our own lack:

> "A few weeks ago I sat reading an article in *The Christian Century*; reading it with a curious complication of feelings because I had written it myself. It looked different in print, particularly the title, which stared up at me in heavy type: *"I Became a Quaker."* How wrong, how blunderingly, blatantly misleading! One does not become anything worth becoming so easily as that. I must write another

article, I thought. I must change the tense of that verb—into the present, into the future, into anything *but* the past. We need an eternal tense in our human speech to express the continual process of becoming which marks the soul in its highest endeavors."

There is "An Eternal Tense" in our *New Testament Greek*—The AORIST Tense; and this flowing Aorist Tense gears *us* into God; i.e. the preparation for Eternity by the Holy Spirit of God. God and man were meshed into the ascent of this tense together; and we see God moving from His Plan (Purpose) into the achievement through the Church; just as the Epistles move out and on:

> *Romans* proposing "The Gospel of God"
>> *Corinthians* moving onward "To them that are sanctified"
>>> *Galatians* rousing them into motion—to be seated with Him
>>> "In the heavenlies" of *Ephesians*.

Minutely and almost invisibly the precision of this tense can be told in the simple illustration of Michael Angelo who was chided by his student for spending time in his masterpieces over "trifles." The great master-artist replied: "Perfection is made up of trifles but perfection is no trifle."

The Aorist Tense in the New Testament stands among verbs just as Jesus did amidst men; it baffles grammarians and translators, for the Aorist refuses to be regular or equivalent to any translation; it is the one tense wholly out of step with any of our languages. Pastor Robinson said to the Pilgrim fathers: "God has yet further light to break forth from His Word"; and if this had to do with the minimizing of the Plan of Salvation, I would refuse it. But seven widely read teachers and translators have this to say of the problem:

THOMAS NEWBERRY, (*The Englishman's Bible,* p. *vii,* The Oxford Press, England 1885):

> "In respect to the verb, the Greek is the most wonderfully precise of all languages wrought out by Divine Providence for the purpose of being employed as the instrument of revelation in those portions of Scripture which require the nicest distinctions. In these portions especially, in order to clear understanding and sound theology, no distinction of tense *must ever be overlooked* . . . .
>
> "The Greek Aorist expresses an action, or event, rounded off and complete in itself: 'A point in the expanse of time'."

W. W. GOODWIN, (*The Harvard Greek Grammar,* 1892, pp. 91, 270):

> "The Aorist corresponds, *generally,* to the *indefinite* or *historical perfect* in Latin, and the *perfect* to the English perfect . . . . More commonly used in rapid narration (raised above normal); the imperfect in detailed description."

GEORGE RICKER BERRY, (*The Inter-Linear Translation of The Greek New Testament,* University of Chicago Press, 1896):

> "This (Aorist) tense of the Greek verb has been at all times the

most difficult to deal with, being translated in the A.V. (and by others) sometimes by the *present*, sometimes by the *past*, sometimes by the *perfect*. Grammarians say that, *in the main, it is the indefinite past.*"

RICHARD FRANCES WEYMOUTH, (Editor *"Resultant Greek Testament,"* 1929; and "On The Rendering into English of the Greek Aorist"):

"Aorist means indefinite, and we must bow to the authority of the Greek Grammarians who held that name to be a suitable one . . .; the *persistent* rendering of the Greek aorist by the English simple past in the R. V. of the N. T. has one very undesirable effect: *the translation is not English.*"

Professor A. T. ROBERTSON, D.D., LL.D., (of Southern Baptist Theological Seminary, *Greek Grammar*):

"The Greek Aorist covers much more ground than the English past. The Aorist in Greek is so rich in meaning that the English labors and groans to express it. As a matter of fact, the Greek aorist is translatable into almost every English tense, EXCEPT the Imperfect. The Aorist, strictly speaking, is *timeless.*"

WILLIAM HERSEY DAVIS, M.A., Th.D. (Associate of Professor Robertson, *Beginner's Grammar of The Greek New Testament*, 1924, pp. 80—91):

"The Greek aorist indicative is not the exact equivalent of any tense in English or *in any other language*. The translation given in the vocabulary is just to get the verb idea associated with the verb form. To translate the Greek aorist indicative, sometimes the English preterit is used, sometimes the perfect, sometimes the past. The Greek aorist indicative refers the action to the past without any *exact* specification as to antecedence of action or as to present results of action."

Ibid: Prof. A. T. ROBERTSON's *"Introduction to same"*; (pp. *vii, ix*):

"If one gets it into his head, that the *root* idea of tense is time, he may never get it out, and he will therefore, never understand the beauty of the Greek tense, *the most wonderful development in the history of language* . . . . The New Testament is the chief glory of the Greek tongue . . . . It is now known that the Greek of the N. T. is not literary Attic nor is it a peculiar Hebrew jargon or sacred Greek dialect. At bottom it is simply straight Koine of the first century . . . . Koine means the language common to people everywhere—not merely the language of common people . . . . It is the vernacular of men of great ability . . . ."

Ibid:

"The Greek was then the choicest language of the globe. Copious, flexible, polished, and widely diffused, *it had already done service for the Lord*. Centuries before the Christian era, *the writings of the Hebrew prophets were translated into the Greek*, thus filling it with the aroma and energy of a divine inspiration, and sanctifying it as a chosen vessel to contain the treasures of eternal wisdom, and convey the truths of revelation to the scattered sons of men."

These Hebrew Prophets gathered to themselves five thousand words out of this glorious tongue for a Temple (The New Testament) of Inspiration—and, "in their midst," the Aorist Tense stands as the Tabernacle for Him of John 1:14.

And, finally:

THE CONCORDANT VERSION, (Concordant Publishing Concern, Los Angeles, 1930), pp. 23—33:

> "The Greek language is capable of expressing with precision the finest and most delicate shades of meaning . . . . Greek is one of the most difficult of languages, the Verb is the most complex and most elaborate part of Greek grammar, and of the verb, the one unsolvable riddle has been the aorist. It is the most difficult of the most difficult . . . . After all the other forms had been assigned, and *tested,* the *Indefinite—Past—Future,* remained. Nothing was left but the so-called English present and it dawned upon the mind of the investigator that its name was a misnomer—it was not restricted to the *present* at all, but it, too, was *indefinite,* just like the Greek Aorist. We have named it "the English Aorist" . . . . It is a very (not quite) close equivalent English term—*Indefinite.*
>
> "The Indefinite changes an ACT into a (an abiding) FACT . . . . It transforms DEEDS into (age-abiding) TRUTH . . . . (Illustrations: Acts 2:36 and Ephesians 1:3—9).
>
> "This name Aorist was given by the ancients who used it continually in conversation and literature, and who ought to have known what to call it. It comes from two Greek elements, and is almost the same as our word *horizon*—without a horizon, i.e. indefinite.
>
> "*At times* the tense of a Word is of *greater* moment than its meaning. (See Acts 2:36 and Hebrews 6:6).
>
> "*The striking and distinctive feature of all true Aorists is that they contain the signs of past and future.*"

Again quoting Professor ROBERTSON:

> "The Greek Aorist . . . is not the exact equivalent of any tense in any other language."

The Aorist Tense may seem a trifle but through it God speaks with accuracy and perfection of His Purpose. The Bible came out from the Omnipresence and the Omniscient Mind of God and it is a Book that from the beginning to the end is in the AORIST TENSE—horizonless from ALPHA to OMEGA. There is no past nor future, it is all just one eternal "Present" and God is right here.

The only conclusion that can be drawn is that:

The Greek AORIST IS GOD'S ETERNAL TENSE.

The ICE AGES

1. The Bible and Modern Science   — Lt. Col. M. Davies
2. Frozen Mammoth in Siberia   — Smithsonian Institution
3. Mammoth Found in Ice   — *New York Times*

1. *The Bible and Modern Science,* (Pickering and Inglis, London, 1935,
   Third Edition) pp. 100—103, 108, 113, 117 and Davies Appendix,
   p. 190 and note 7.
   By Lt. Col. L. Merson Davies, M.A., F.R.S.E., F.R.A.I., F.G.S.
   Lieut.-Colonel late of Royal Artillery.

(From the *Foreword*: "The three great topics dealt with are
(the Astronomy, the Physics, and the Biology of the Bible.
(Major Davies adduces a glittering galaxy of facts from both
(Astronomy and Physics, showing how the Bible waits at
(the head of the paths of scientific progress to greet the
(discoverer with its Revelation of Prior Knowledge. The in-
(vestigator climbs upward through the twilight and finds
(Scripture illuminating the summit of his climb."

Harold C. Morton, B.A., Ph.D.

The Disaster

If it be objected that the Bible interpretation of nature can hardly be
held to apply, since the fossiliferous rocks bear witness to the fact that
similar sufferings and curses to our own must have existed at a date far
anterior to that of Adam, I reply that the Bible age for the earth is absolutely unlimited, and the second verse of *Genesis* clearly implies that at
least one former Creation had been wrecked before our own was brought
into existence during the Six Days. Besides this I very well know, as a
geologist, that fossil series are incapable, in themselves, of proving any
genetic connections; and I also know that the continuity of life between
our own world and the fossil one, so universally taken for granted today,
has simply to be assumed, for there is no way of establishing it. If the
Bible denies that continuity, it contradicts nothing that science can *prove*.

A very real difficulty, however, will here occur to some, who will
probably say: "But what of this break in life which you suppose to have
taken place between our present world of nature and former ones; must it
not be regarded as resulting from a most terrific convulsion of nature? You
are bound to admit that the wording of the second verse of *Genesis*, together with the events of the first three Days, would compel us to postulate,
upon your understanding of the chapter, a world-wide *physical* catastrophe
between our own Creation and the last one prior to it. Have you found
world-wide traces of such a catastrophe? And if not, how do you get over
such a fact?"

Now questions like these are obviously well-founded. The difficulty
is, at first sight, a most formidable one, for it is only too clear to a geologist that no great *physical* break seems to lie between our own creation

and fossil ones; and yet if the events of the Six Days are to be taken (as I believe they must) as describing the restoration of a *ruined* earth, then such a break is most certainly indicated by them.

I do not suppose that anyone could have felt the force of this difficulty more acutely than I have done; and I was long ago compelled, and in consequence, to make a special study of this particular problem. As a result of this study, however, I now not only insist upon the "restoration hypothesis" as the only one consistent to Scripture, but I also claim the literal truth and marvellous consistence to physics of the descriptions in the early verses of *Genesis*; and I further deny that any recognizable trace whatever of the disaster need be found in the rocks!

Such statements, of course, will require a good deal of justifying, and the whole of this chapter will be required for the purpose. Indeed, it will be very difficult to compress so big a subject into a single chapter! I may say, however, to begin with, that the key to this particular problem seems to lie in the fact that *the sun's light is withdrawn between the first two verses of Genesis*. Once grant that proposition, and everything else fits into place in the most remarkable manner. Let us, therefore, first look at the Scripture indications as to the *fact* of this occurrence, and then we will consider its *consequences*.

The Fact

Now the fact that the sun's light was withdrawn at this point was suggested long ago by Pember,[1] and others have shown that the complete "darkness" of Genesis 1:2 is foreign to the *pristine* creation of Job 38:4—7 where the morning stars, at least, are found to be already in existence, and presumably shining.[2] That this darkness was due to a *withdrawal* of the sun's light, and other lights, appears also to be indicated in Jeremiah 4:23—26, which is rendered by Driver[3] as follows:

23. "*I beheld* the earth, and lo, it was TOHU VA-BOHU: and the heavens and they had no light.
24. "*I beheld* the mountains, and lo, they trembled and all the hills moved to and fro.
25. "*I beheld*, and lo, there was no man, and all the birds of the heavens were fled.
26. "*I beheld*, and lo, the garden-land was a wilderness, and all the cities thereof were broken down before Yahweh, even before his fierce anger."

---

[1] "Earth's Earliest Ages" (p. 81)

[2] This passage, which clearly indicates the existence both of the stars and of the "Sons of God" (i.e. the Angels) before the earth, can be put in parallel with Genesis 1:1, which also clearly refers to the ORIGINAL Creation, and similarly mentions the "heavens" before the "earth"; but it cannot be put in parallel with the events of the Six Days, which seem to represent something quite different and altogether subsequent.

[3] "The Book of Jeremiah," pp. 23—24, Driver

Now this is the only other passage in the whole Bible in which the identical words "TOHU VA-BOHU" (rendered "without form and void") of Genesis 1:2 reappear; and the connection here is with a wrecked and ruined world, which has been the habitation of man, but whose *heavenly lights have been withdrawn* under the judgment of God. So if this passage does nothing else it clearly shows, as Skinner[1] himself allows that:

"The 'safest' way of regarding the second verse of Genesis is to take it as representing a 'darkened and devastated earth, from which life and order have fled . . .' .

"In any case, there is no escaping the fact that Jeremiah used the exact terms to describe a *ruined* world, as are used in Genesis 1:2 to describé the state of things on earth just prior to the Six Days . . . .

"*Chaos* is a Greek conception, not a Hebrew one. Its application to Genesis 1:2 seems wrong upon every count."

We could hardly, therefore, have a better warrant for so taking it. If, as a critic like Skinner admits, this view is the "safest," it is surely the one which cautious exegesis should accept before any other!

It also seems noticeable that this doctrine, that the darkening of the sun is a supreme mark of God's anger, runs right through Scripture and appears to be integral to it. For not only is it laid down as a general principle, in Job 38:15, that "from the wicked their light is withholden," but we find the same thing recurring over and over again in the prophecies regarding the coming wrath of God. Thus Isaiah, Ezekiel, Joel and Amos, all prophesy the darkening of the sun during the coming Day of the Lord; we find the same thing in our Saviour's own prophecies about His Second Coming; and it is prophesied again repeatedly in the Apocalypse. The darkening of the sun, then, appears to be integral to the greater demonstrations of God's anger; and it seems to be a deeply significant fact that when our divine Lord took upon Himself the wrath which our sins had earned, the sun was darkened from the sixth hour of the day. (Remember that this was at a time near the full moon, when an eclipse would not be even possible). (See another note here on earthquake and other terrestrial disturbances). Indeed, so far as we can see, it is only because He did die for us, that this judgment is never more than partial in the history of our own creation.

The Extinction of Life (p. 108)

In the first place then, let us repeat Pember's quotation from one of Herschel's "Familiar Lectures on Scientific Subjects":

"In three days," says Herschel, "from the extinction of the sun, there would, in all probability, not be a vestige of animal or vegetable life on the globe; unless it were among the deep-sea fishes and the

---

[1] *A Critical and Exegetical Commentary on Genesis*, pp. 16—17, Skinner

subterranean inhabitants of the great limestone caves. The first forty-eight hours would suffice to precipitate every atom of moisture from the air in deluges of rain and piles of snow, and from that moment would set in a universal frost such as Siberia, or the highest peak of the Himalayas never felt—a temperature of between two and three hundred degrees below the zero of our thermometers."

Thus one of the first results of an extinction of the sun would be the covering of the earth's surface with a universal mantle of ice and snow; the precipitation, in frozen form, of almost every atom of moisture in its atmosphere at the moment. All the higher forms of life, too, would be destroyed at once in this sudden appalling cold, which would kill them, as Herschel goes on to say, as effectively as boiling water would.

Bacteria and seeds, however, would probably not, as we now know, be killed off at once. They exhibit, indeed, a surprising power of resisting extremely *low* temperatures. Some experiments, however, have indicated that this power is by no means absolutely indefinite[1] and if a *tohou* period lasted, as it well might, without assignable limit, it is unlikely that any life would be found to survive it. As M. deCandolle has pointed out,[2] seeds do not retain vitality indefinitely, even under the best possible conditions for their preservation; and the extraordinary sterility of regions once occupied for long by ice, has been remarked on by many observers (for a discussion on this matter, see Geol. Mag. N.S., *vi* 420). On land, therefore, the great cold would probably in the end prove fatal to even the humblest and most tenacious forms of life.

The Physical Effects (p. 113)

We have now to consider the actual physical effects more closely. We have seen something of these from the fact that, as Herschel said, one of the earlier results of the extinction of the sun would be the precipitation of all water vapour present in the atmosphere, in frozen state upon the surface of the ground, over which it would thenceforth lie as a permanent mantle of snow and ice. But matters would not stop there, for this removal of all moisture from the air would itself involve the ultimate starvation of every body of water moving from land to sea. So, as the cold continued and increased, all streams and rivers would inevitably come to a final dead stop, being frozen both from their sources and in their beds. And, ultimately, the oceans themselves would freeze over. We seem to find some such calamity pictured in the words: "The face of the deep is frozen, and the waters are hid as with a stone" (Job 38:39). The whole world, in fact, would be reduced to a condition now faintly pictured by our present polar regions; so it is interesting to remember that Job refers to the latter as

---

[1]
   Davies gives note regarding freezing for long or short time, 5 yrs., 25 yrs., or to 300—409 yrs.

[2]
   M. de Candolle *Nature*, August 19, 1933, p. 276

tohu (26:7). He shows, therefore, that the word *tohu,* of the second verse of Genesis, is perfectly *applicable to a FROZEN world:* a point of peculiar interest to our present investigation.
(p. 117)

All animals and plants would be killed, whether on land or in the seas; the carcases of those that died on the land being held immovably in the position where they perished, much as the bodies of mammoths are preserved in the frozen soil of Siberia to this day, while those that died in the sea would be heaped together in shambles at the ocean bottoms, or locked in the freezing waters before they got there. Sea and land would be cased in ice; and the atmosphere itself would finally congeal on top of this. The earth would then roll on through space in utter darkness, ruined and desolate, with all its processes both of life and of geological action totally suspended.
(Davies Appendix, p. 190)

Thus it seems that the most literal and accurate rendering of the opening words of Genesis would be somewhat as follows:

"In the beginning God created the heavens and the earth.
And the earth had become (as) worthlessness and emptiness."

And perhaps there would also have to be adjustment of courses (in the restoration of light, after the nameless disaster which brought darkness down upon the world of the second verse of Genesis 1).

2. *Frozen Mammoth in Siberia* — Smithsonian Institution

(Annual Report of the Board of Regents of the Smithsonian Institution, Washington, D.C., Government Printing Office, 1904, pp. 611–619):

Extracts translated from report of O. F. Herz, chief of expedition of Imperial Academy of Science of St. Petersburg to the river Berezovka for excavation of frozen mammoth. Entire report in Russian in Bulletin of the Imperial Academy, St. Petersburg, April 1902 (fifth series vol. XVI, No. 4).

About the middle of April 1901, the Imperial Academy of St. Petersburg was informed by V. N. Skripitsin, governor of Yakutsk, of the discovery of a mammoth in an almost perfect state of preservation frozen in the cliff along the river Berezovka, the right tributary of the river Kolyma, about 200 miles Northeast of Sredne-Kolymsk—about 800 miles westward of Bering Strait and some 600 miles within the Arctic Circle. Thanks to the courtesy of Finance Minister Witte, 16,300 rubles were assigned for a prompt dispatch of an expedition to examine and secure this valuable find.

O. F. Herz, a zoologist of the Imperial Academy of Sciences, was appointed chief of the expedition: E. V. Pfizenmeyer, a zoological preparator of the same institution, and D.P.Sevastianoff, a geological student of the Yuryevck University, his assistants. The expedition started from St. Petersburg on May 3, 1902, and its chief reached the mammoth region on Sept. 9. On August 28 the expedition was joined by Mr. Horn, a police official from Sredne-Kilymak.

". . . Yavlovski tells me that rains during the summer had washed a mass of earth down the slope in which the mammoth lies, so that bones were torn from the hind part of the body, the entire back was exposed, and the most of the head skin was devoured by bears and wolves. At the first examination the trunk was already gone . . . . As he saw no hair or wool on the exposed parts, he thought that either there had been none or else it had been washed away by the rains.

"Sept. 11, 1901 . . . The body lies in a cliff that faces east and extends for a mile in a semicircle. The demolished portion of the cliff inclines toward the river at an angle of 35 degrees from the upper layer of earth, over which extends the "Taiga" or Siberian marshy forest. The body of the mammoth is 62 meters back from the bank of the river. According to measurements which I took in different places, the upper strata of earth covered with a layer of moss, is 30 to 52 centimeters thick. Beneath this is a loamy mass, one-third loam and two-thirds earth, averaging two meters thick, mixed with stones, roots, and pieces of wood, with lamellar plates of ice, 15 to 18 centimeters thick, stretching through the mass. Underneath this alluvial layer, there is a vertical wall of ice, which stands free for a distance of 5 meters, and in some places even 7 meters above the mammoth. This ice wall probably inclines to the river at the same angle as the entire cliff region which wall I intend to investigate later. Upon this supposed ice incline are huge shapeless earth masses and mounds, evidently moved downward during heavy rains by the gradual thawing of the ice wall, as well as by the water which falls from the upper "taiga" and from the hill 120 meters high, that rises in the rear of the wall about a sixth of a mile from the river bank. According to the Lamut natives of the region, (Mammoth was discovered by the three Lamuts and S. Tarabykin) the head of the mammoth was exposed two years ago by this downward movement, or by the breaking away of a considerable mass of earth; the rest of the body was exposed only at the end of August 1900.

"After taking some pictures, I commenced to open up the mammoth mound. The skull was soon exposed. Unfortunately most of the head skin had been devoured by carnivorous animals during the past summer. To my greatest surprise I found well-preserved food fragments between the teeth, which serves as proof that our mammoth, after a short death struggle, died in this very position. The fact that what we found was food and not substance carried in recently was later proved by comparing it with the stomach contents . . . . I could see marks of the ax which the Lamuts used in chopping off the tusk and could thus determine definitely that the tusk that I had seen in Sredne-Kolymsk was from this particular mammoth, for I had carefully measured and studied the cuts upon it . . . . The lower jaw, which was fast in the ground, lay upon a large piece of skin, which appeared later to belong to the upper part of the chest.

"I first gave orders to carefully remove the mound of earth about the mammoth beginning with the head. At a depth of 68 centimeters we found the left fore leg, still covered with hair on all sides up to the humerus. The epidermis had apparently completely rotted, but on account of the moist earth, the hair still clung to the skin. In a frozen condition we may perhaps succeed in getting to St. Petersburg . . . . The left fore leg is bent, *so that it is evident the mammoth tried to crawl out of the pit or crevice into which he probably fell,* but apparently he was so badly injured by the fall that he could not free himself . . . . Upon the left hind leg I also found pieces of decayed flesh, in which the muscular bundles were very easily discernible. The stench emitted by this extremity was unbearable, so that it was necessary to stop work every minute. A thorough washing failed to remove the horrible smell from our hands, and yet we were obliged to perform part of our task with bare hands . . . . From under the left leg the thick hair on the under side came to view, especially that on the fore joint. Some of this hair fell off with the earth, but the longer part will be saved by bandages . . . . Yellowish-brown under wool which in color resembles the summer coat of a young camel . . . . Thickly set hairs of a bristly coat 10 to 12 centimeters long . . . . Five hoof-shaped blunt nails could also be seen at the end of the digits . . . . In the mound, lying between upper layer of earth and the vertical ice wall, roots and other parts of trees and also boulders were found lodged. Under this layer of earth, two and one half meters thick, first we struck water ice 18 centimeters thick, caused by a thaw; then a thin layer of earth; under this again another layer of ice, and then the right fore leg of the mammoth came to view . . . .

The ice layer 71 centimeters at its thickest part, extends to the middle of the right side of the abdomen where it becomes 10 centimeters thick . . . .

The pit 4 meters square, dug with the spade after the mammoth was removed, showed that the ice wall must be quite deep . . . . At a depth of 1.7 meters in this pit I found ice similar to that of the upper part of the ice wall. About 100 meters north and even lower than the mammoth's grave there is an ice cliff covered by a layer of earth two and one half meters thick and structurally identical with the upper wall. The exposed ice is brownish earthy in color and contains numerous air bubbles, some of them elongated, averaging two to five millimeters in length; . . . . Among the bubbles which are connected, there are thin layers of sand or clay that in places form small lumps. Deeper down in the cliff the ice becomes more solid and transparent, in some places entirely white and brittle. After remaining exposed to the air even for a short time, this ice again assumes a yellow-brown color and then looks like the old ice. The ice on the other hand which is formed from melted ice and snow is always transparent, white and hard, and on account of the longer-vertical air bubbles which attain a length of over 20 millimeters, assumes a streaked appearance . . . stone ice which resulted from a previous glacial period . . . . Despite the fact

that the mammoth is in a frozen condition, the stench emitted is very disagreeable . . . . (Plate V. opposite page 618 shows picture with caption:
"Skull of the Mammoth with Food Remnants between the Molar Teeth";
Plate VI. shows left forefoot of Mammoth, about three-fourths the height
of a man.

(p. 619)

"There is also a small quantity of food upon the well-preserved tongue,
but I can secure this only when the lower jaw is removed . . . . When the
Lamuts discovered the mammoth they could not see the fragments of food,
for the lower jaw was then still in the ground. This was confirmed by Tarabykin's companions, whom I questioned closely on this point.

"Sept. 26. Today I took the principal measurements of the mammoth as
they are given in the accompanying drawings. I also collected the plants
that are partly under the snow.

"Oct. 3. After removing the last layer of earth from the back, the remains of food in the stomach were exposed. The latter was badly decayed.
We could not continue our work here owing to the solidly frozen condition
of everything . . . and then cleaned part of the stomach which contained
an immense quantity of food remnants . . . exposed several ribs, (three
broken), which were mostly very well preserved . . . . Then we skinned
the head, of which the following parts were preserved: the cheeks, the
right eyelid with the deep eyelash fold, part of the skin from the sinciput,
three-fourths of the upper lip, and the very well-preserved under lip. This
latter was also beset by scattered spines or bristles, which however, adhered to the ground and were mixed up with other hair, so that it was impossible to pick them out. Also the skin from the head which was already
decayed in several places, we immediately treated with alum and salt.
The flesh from under the shoulder, which is fibrous and marbled with fat,
is dark red in color and looks as fresh as well-frozen beef or horse meat.
It looked so appetizing that we wondered for some time whether we should
not taste it, but no one would venture to take it into his mouth, and horse
flesh was given the preference. The dogs cleaned up whatever mammoth
meat was thrown to them. The layer of fat beneath the skin is nine centimeters thick. It is white, odorless, spongy, and readily cut. The flesh between the ribs and skin, as well as the membrane under the ribs, could
easily be pulled off in separate layers without special effort. The skin on
the left shoulder is 19 millimeters thick, and on the right side 23 millimeters. The big bunches of hair that stuck in the frozen ground near the
lower lip, and which belonged to the chin and chest, are 36 centimeters
long, torn as they are, we may assume that these hairs were approximately
50 centimeters long . . . . From the stomach we removed about 27 pounds
of additional food remains . . . . We would gladly have transported the leg

intact, but for its too great weight for one dog sled. The flesh and fat are well preserved and will be packed for shipment. No hair was found on the outer and anterior sides of the right fore leg, and from the underside of this leg, I succeeded in saving only what I found in beautiful layers in the ice. I collected bits of blood, . . . resembled small pieces of potassium permanganate. When melted, these bits turned into dirty dark-red spots, which are easily washed off; to touch, resemble coarse dry sand. The stench is not nearly so intolerable as during the first two days, possibly because we have grown accustomed to it.

"October 10. After removing about 270 pounds of flesh, we started the raising of the abdominal skin which weighed about 470 pounds, we discovered to our greatest joy, the entire tail of the mammoth, and by means of it explained the other puzzling point . . . . The tail is short and consists evidently of 22 to 25 caudal vertebrae . . . the hard bristly hairs . . . end of tail covered with long hairs 20 to 25 centimeters long. The length of the tail measured on the under side, is only 36 centimeters, while its circumference at the base is 32 centimeters . . . ."

3. *Mammoth Found in Ice* (From *New York Times*, March 4, 1935, p. 8)

"Moscow, March 3, 1935: A mammoth's carcass has been found in the ice near the mouth of the Siberian River, the Academy of Science reported today. The Academy plans to send an expedition to study it. Several specimens have been found in the ice of the Arctic glaciers where the continuous cold preserved them in a perfect condition through the centuries since their death."

PROPHECY, or TOMORROWISM

By C. G. Kindred

(written for Christian Endeavor publication *EtCEtera*,
Englewood Christian Church, 1940)

MAN IS A TOMORROWIST. He lives in the future. His nature is sur-charged with a divine discontent. Horizons are his inhibitions, against which he is constantly at odds. We are all the children of Abraham, who wearily climbed many a hill expecting to catch a view of "the City" which he all his life had sought (and did see it—John 8:56).

The Bible is uniquely The Book of prophetic urge. David voiced it for us all: "I shall be satisfied when I awake in Thy likeness." The tread of the army of To-Morrowists in Hebrews 11, shakes the world occupants into revivalist passion to "Arise and depart, for this is not your rest."

Amid the voices by which men are led, is easily first the Prophetic. Columbus' supposed cry of "Sail On," if not actual, still is the voice of humanity. And, amid the prophetic, the clearest note, nearest universal, is that of the Bible. It speaks in terms of centuries of "that far off divine event towards which all creation moves." That its utterer is our Creator, is proven by the peace-giving response it evokes from all, especially from Christians. Who can read unmoved, the last two chapters of the Bible without rising to ecstasy at the prospect?

The Bible prophet is a fore-teller. He peoples the present with the brilliant heavens over the tomorrow. The parable of prophecy is the Bible day: "Evening and morning, day." The present is the beginning—it is the evening. We move amid the twilight shadows—groping our way. Then comes the prophet, companioning us in the dark, but "seeing the invisible"—the morning part of our day. He speaks, and lo, the darkness gives birth to a light. The prophet's statements began a long, long time before fulfillment. So long ago, that many fell a-weary of waiting, and dropped by the wayside. Finally, came a caravan who waiting, expecting, had seen His Star in the east, and came to worship Him. As the time shortened, the very heavens were peopled by prophetic utterances. Then He came!

When He went away, once more prophecy began its ministry into the unfulfilled. Prophets went from the Lord's Presence to speak forth the facts, commands and promises of the Gospel. These messengers were the prophets, each speaking of The Coming One, as at Pentecost to the three thousand, and as Philip to the eunuch—and "there was much joy" following.

The modern prophet is not so picturesque, nor awe-inspiring, but the total results are. Not clothed in strange garb, but as her kind, she sits amid a group of opening minds, planting the seed of the Gospel that strange to them, is the strength of her life. At its highest and best, the prophecy for today is TEACHING.

APPENDIX "D"
THE SERPENT IN GENESIS THREE
By E. W. Bullinger, D.D., A.K.C., F.R.G.S.

The Companion Bible, (Oxford University Press) App. 19, pp. 24—25

(Used by permission, Reprint by The Lamp Press, Ltd., London)

IN GENESIS Three, we have neither allegory, myth, legend, nor fable, but literal historical facts set forth, and emphasized by the use of certain figures of speech (see app. 6).

All the confusion of thought and conflicting exegesis have risen from taking literally what is expressed by Figures, or from taking figuratively what is literal. A figure of speech is never used except for the purpose of calling attention to, emphasizing, and intensifying, *the reality of the literal sense,* and the truth of the historical facts; so that, while the words employed may not be so strictly true to the letter, they are all the *more true to the truth conveyed by them,* and to the historical events connected with them.

But for the figurative language of verses 14 and 15 no one would have thought of referring the third chapter of Genesis to a snake: no more than he does when reading the third chapter from the end of Revelation (20:2). Indeed, the explanation added there, that the *"old* serpent" is the Devil and Satan, would immediately lead one to connect the word "old" with the *earlier* and former mention of the serpent in Gen. 3; and the fact that it was Satan himself who tempted "the second man," "the last Adam," would force the conclusion that no other than the personal Satan could have been the tempter of "the first man, Adam."

The Hebrew for "serpent" (Gen. 3:1) is *nāchāsh* from *nāchash,* to *hiss, mutter, whisper* as do enchanters. Secondary senses are *to divine, enchant,* whence the frequent use of noun as "serpent." The allied Chald. word means *brass, copper,* from "an assumed root" meaning *to be bright.* Various passages tell us that Satan possesses a glorious appearance, and the Heb. term probably includes the sense of *fascinate, enchant* (see Deut. 18:10 *et al).* This element of *fascination* connects with the later use of *nachash* as "serpent."

The term *sārāph* (pl. seraphim) is derived from *sāraph,* a Homonym meaning (1) *to burn* (2) *to be elevated.* In Num. 21:8 "a fiery serpent"— *sārāph;* in the following v. "a serpent"—*nāchāsh;* while in v. 6 both words are given for "fiery serpents." The same word *sārāph* (*serāphīm*) is used of the heavenly ones of Isa. 6:2, 6.

Thus *sārāph* is used of a fiery serpent and of an exalted celestial being; *nāchāsh* being similarly used to designate a serpent and a glorious spirit-being.

Indeed, a reference to the structure of Gen. 3 (on p. 7) will show that the Cherubim (which are similar celestial or spirit-beings) of the last verse (Gen. 3:24) require a similar spirit-being to correspond with them in the first verse (for the structure of the whole chapter is a great Introversion).

The *Nãchãsh*, or serpent, who beguiled Eve (2 Cor. 11:3) is spoken of as "an angel of light" in v. 14. Have we not, in this, a clear intimation that it was not a snake, but a being of glorious aspect, apparently an angel, to whom Eve paid such great deference, acknowledging him as one who seemed to possess superior knowledge, and who was evidently a being of a superior (not of an inferior) order? Moreover, in the description of Satan as "the king of Tyre," [1] it is distinctly implied that the latter being was of a super-natural order when he is called "a cherub" (Ezek. 28:14, 16, read from vv. 11—19). His presence "in Eden, the garden of Elohim" (v. 13) is also clearly stated, as well as his being "perfect in his ways from the day he was created till iniquity was found in him" (v. 15), and as being "lifted up because of his beauty" (v. 17).

These all compel the belief that Satan was the "old serpent" (*Nãchãsh*) in Gen. 3, and especially because the following words could be addressed to him:—"Thine heart was lifted up because of thy beauty, thou hast corrupted thy wisdom by reason of thy brightness: I will cast thee to the ground, I will lay thee before kings, that they may behold thee" (v. 17).

Even supposing that these things were spoken to, and of, an exalted human being in later days (in Ezek. 28), still "the king of Tyre" is not compared to a being who was non-existent; and facts and circumstances which never happened are not introduced into the comparison.

There is more about "the king of Tyre" in Ezek. 28:11—19 than was literally true of "the prince of Tyre" (vv. 1—10). The words can be understood only of the mightiest and most exalted supernatural being that God ever created; and this for the purpose of showing how great would be his fall. The *history* must be true to make the *prophecy* of any weight.

• Again, the word rendered "subtle" in Gen. 3:1 (see note) means *wise*, in a good sense as well as in a bad sense. In Ezek. 28:12 we have the good sense, "Thou sealest up the sum, full of wisdom"; and the bad sense in v. 17, "thou hast corrupted thy wisdom" (referring, of course, to his fall). So the word rendered "subtle" is rendered "prudent" in Prov. 1:4; 8:12; 12:23; 14:8; and in a bad sense in Job 15:5; I Sam. 23:22; Ps. 83:3.

The word "beast" also, in Gen. 3:1, *chay*, denotes *a living being*, and it is as wrong to translate *zoa* "beast" in Rev. 4, as it is to translate *chay* "beast" in Gen. 3. Both mean living creature. Satan is thus spoken of as being "more wise than any other *living creature* which Jehovah Elohim had made." Even if the word "beast" be retained, it does not say that either a serpent or Satan *was* a "beast," but only that he was "more wise," than any other living being.

We cannot conceive Eve as holding converse with a snake, but we can

---

[1] Ezek. 28:11—19, who is quite a different being from "the Prince of Tyre," in vv. 1—10, who is purely human.

understand her being fascinated[1] by one, apparently "an angel of light" (i.e. a glorious angel), possessing superior and supernatural knowledge.

When Satan is spoken of as a "serpent," it is the figure *Hypocatastasis* (see Ap. 6) or *Implication*; it no more means a snake than it does when Dan is so called in Gen. 49:17; or an animal when Nero is called a "lion" (2 Tim. 4:17), or when Herod is called a "fox" (Luke 13:32); or when Judah is called "a lion's whelp." It is the same figure when "doctrine" is called "leaven" (Matt. 16:6). It shows that something much more real and truer to truth is intended. If a Figure of speech is thus employed, it is for the purpose of expressing the truth more impressively; and is intended to be a figure of something much *more real* than the letter of the word.

Other Figures of speech are used in vss. 14, 15, but only for the purpose of emphasizing the truth and the reality of what is said.

When it is said in vs. 15, "thou shalt bruise His heel," it cannot mean His literal heel of flesh and blood but suffering, more temporary in character. When it is said (v. 15), "He shall crush thy head," it means something more than a skull of bone, and brain, and hair. It means that all Satan's plans and plots, policy and purposes, will one day be finally crushed and ended, never more to mar or to hinder the purposes of God. This will be effected when Satan shall be bruised under our feet (Rom. 16:20). This, again, will not be our literal feet, but something much more real.

The bruising of Christ's heel is the most eloquent and impressive way of foretelling the most solemn events; and to point out that the effort made by Satan to evade his doom, then threatened, would become the very means of insuring its accomplishment; for it was through the death of Christ that he who had the power of death would be destroyed; and all Satan's power and policy brought to an end, and all his works destroyed (Hebrews 2:14; I John 3:8; Rev. 20:1–3, 10). What literal words could portray these literal facts so wonderfully as these expressive Figures of speech?

It is the same with the other Figures used in vss. 14, "On thy belly shalt thou go." This Figure means infinitely more than the literal belly of flesh and blood; just as the words "heel" and "head" do in vs. 15. It paints for the eyes of our mind the picture of Satan's ultimate *humiliation*; for prostration was ever the most eloquent sign of subjection. When it is said "our belly cleaveth unto the ground" (Ps. 44:25), it denotes such a depth of submission as could never be conveyed or expressed in literal words.

So with the other prophecy, "Dust shalt thou eat." This is not true to the letter, or to fact, but it is all the more *true to truth*. It tells of a constant, continuous disappointment, failure, and mortification; as when

---

[1] It is remarkable that the verb *nachash* is generally translated "to enchant, fascinate, bewitch"; or of one having and using occult knowledge. See Gen. 30:27; 44:5, 15; Rev. 19:26; 18:10; I Kings 20:34; 2 Kings 17:17; 21:6; 2 Chron. 34:6. So also is the noun in Num. 23:23; 24:1.

deceitful ways are spoken of as feeding on deceitful food, which is "sweet to a man, but afterward his mouth shall be filled with gravel" (Prov. 20:17). This does not mean literal "gravel," but something far more disagreeable. It means *disappointment* so great that it would gladly be exchanged for the literal "gravel." So when Christians are rebuked for "biting and devouring one another" (Gal. 5:14, 15), something more heart-breaking is meant than the literal words used in the Figure.

When "His enemies shall lick the dust" (Ps. 72:9) they will not do it on their knees with their literal tongues; but they will be so prostrated and and so utterly defeated, that no words could literally depict their overthrow and subjugation.

If a serpent was afterward called a *nachash*, it was because it exercised fascination over other creatures, and if it became known as "wise," it was not because of its own innate positive knowledge, but of its wisdom in hiding away from all observation; and because of its association with one of the names of Satan (that old serpent) who "beguiled Eve" (2 Cor. 11:3, 14).

It is wonderful how a snake could ever be supposed to speak without the organs of speech, or that Satan should be supposed able to accomplish so great a miracle.[1]

It only shows the power of tradition, which has, from the infancy of each one of us, put before our eyes and written on our minds the picture of a "snake" and an "apple"; the former based on a wrong interpretation, and the latter being a pure invention, about which there is not one word said in Holy Scripture.

Never was Satan's wisdom so craftily used as when he secured a universal acceptance of this traditional belief: for it has succeeded in fixing the attention of mankind on the *letter* and the *means*, and thus blinding the eyes to the solemn fact that the Fall of man had to do solely with the Word of God, and is centred in the sin of believing Satan's lie instead of Jehovah's truth.

The temptation of "the first Adam" began with the question "Hath God said?" The temptation of "the second man, The Lord from heaven" began with a similar question, "If Thou be the Son of God," when the Voice of the Father had scarcely died away, which said "This IS My beloved Son."

All turned on the truth of what Jehovah had said. The Word of God being questioned, led Eve, in her reply (1) to *omit* the word "freely" (3:2, cp. 2:16); then (2) to *add* the words "neither touch it" (3:3, cp. 2:17); and finally, (3) to *alter* a certainty into a contingency by changing "thou SHALT SURELY die" (2:17) into LEST ye die" (3:3).

---

[1]   Greater than that wrought by God Himself, who opened the mouth of Balaam's ass.

It is not without significance that the first Ministerial words of "the second Man" were "It is written," three times repeated; and that His last Ministerial words contained a similar threefold reference to the written Word of God (John 17:8, 14, 17).

The former temptation succeeded because the Word of God was three times misrepresented; the latter temptation was successfully defeated because the same Word was faithfully repeated.

The history of Genesis 3 is intended to teach us the fact that Satan's sphere of activities is in the *religious* sphere, and not the spheres of crime or immorality; that his battlefield is not the sins arising from human depravity, but the *unbelief* of the human heart. We are not to look for Satan's activities to-day in the newspaper press, or the police courts; but in the pulpit, and in professors' chairs. Wherever the Word of God is called in question, there we see the trail of "that old serpent, which is the Devil, and Satan." This is why anything against the true interests of the Word of God (as being such) finds a ready admission into the newspapers of the world, and is treated as "general literature." This is why anything in favour of its inspiration and Divine origin and its spiritual truth is rigidly excluded as being "controversial."

This is why Satan is quite content that the *letter* of Scripture should be accepted in Gen. 3, as he himself accepted the letter of Ps. 91:11. He himself could say, "It is written" (Matt. 4:6) so long as the *letter* of what is "written" could be put instead of the *truth* that is conveyed by it; and so long as it is misquoted or misapplied.

This is his object in perpetuating the traditions of the "snake" and the "apple," because it ministers to the acceptance of his lie, the hiding of God's truth, the support of tradition, the jeers of the infidel, the opposition of the critics, and the stumbling of the weak in faith.

In the following pages we have a clue to the importance of the astronomic signs of the Zodiac. These pages are marked quotations and notes by Brother Kindred, listing the pages from three books:

MAZZAROTH   By Frances Rolleston (1875)

GOSPEL IN THE STARS (Or Primeval Astronomy)
                              By Joseph A. Seiss, DD. (1882)

THE WITNESS OF THE STARS
                              By Ethelbert W. Bullinger, DD. (1893)

More complete information and explanation of the original meanings of the Signs of the Zodiac, may be found in these three books.

                                                      R.M.L.

APPENDIX "E"

MAZZAROTH; Constellations of The ZODIAC

"Canst thou bring forth Mazzaroth in his season?
Or canst thou guide Arcturus with his sons?
Knowest thou the ordinances of heaven?
Canst thou set the dominion thereof in the earth?"

Job 38:32—33

"And God said,
'Let there be lights in the firmament of the heaven
to divide between the day and between the night;
and let them be for signs, and for seasons,
and for days, and years': . . .'."

"And to rule over the day and over the night,
and to divide between the light and between
the darkness . . . ."

Genesis 1:14, 18 N.*
(cp. Luke 21:25)

*see page *xiii*

"We have seen His star,
and
are come to worship Him."

Matthew 2:2

GLORIA IN EXCELSIS DEO!

APPENDIX "E"

THE ZODIAC

"This majestical roof, fretted with golden fire."

Shakespeare,

Hamlet, Act II, Sc 2,
L. 312

"The stars are forth, the moon upon the tops
Of the snow-shining mountains—beautiful!
I linger yet with nature, for the night
Hath been to me a more familiar face
Than that of man; and in her starry shade
Of dime and solitary loveliness
I learned the language of another world."

Byron,
Manfred, Act III, S 4.

MAZZAROTH (The Signs of the Zodiac)

Job 38:

31: "Canst thou bind the sweet influences of Pleiades,
   or loose the bands of Orion?

32: "Canst thou bring forth Mazzaroth in his season?
   or canst thou guide Arcturus with his sons?

33: "Knowest thou the ordinances of heaven?
   canst thou set the dominion thereof in the earth?"

The stars are an highway from us to Adam,—divinely marked.
The Zodiac is prophecy for which inspired writings witness.

1. *Mazzaroth, or, The Constellations* (Frances Rolleston, Keswick, in Four Parts, Publishers: Rivingtons, London, Oxford and Cambridge, 1875).

A far higher purpose is latent in the names and emblems of ancient astronomy; from them we may learn the all-important fact that God has spoken, that He gave to the earliest of mankind a revelation, equally important to the latest, even of those very truths afterwards written for the admonition of those "on whom the ends of the world" should come. Then, as now, the heaven-guided spirit in man sought to trace the glory of the Creator in His works: then, as now, the best aid was found in His revelation. That there was a revelation is shown by the prophetic import of these names and emblems, even that revelation recorded in the book with which they correspond.

Without the history of the fall of man we should not know by what types it had pleased God to foreshow his restoration. The seed of the woman in the ear of corn, the enemy in the serpent, might have been in vain set forth in the constellations, as unintelligble from their beginning as they became in the lapse of ages, and even now are when not viewed by the light of revelation. Without the figures of the sphere, "the record in heaven," that revelation had wanted the witness of its being coeval with the calamity whose remedy it declared.

There are few who have not heard of the Twelve Signs of the Zodiac; but what they are is not always distinctly understood. It is sometimes imagined that the forms of a ram, bull, or lion may be traced among the stars; but none such can be recognized. Those stars said to belong to the Ram might as well be supposed to belong to the Bull or the Lion. Only one of the constellations has a definite figure: the Northern Cross.

The Northern Crown is circular, resembling a diadem. In all the others the names have no affinity with the natural position of the stars: they are what the inventors of astronomy thought fit to annex. They will be seen to convey prophecy, as regularly, as systematically arranged, as the stars to which they are applied, are apparently irregularly scattered over the dome of heaven. There must doubtless be Divine wisdom in this apparent confusion, but as yet the science of man has failed to trace it.

2. *The Star of Bethlehem:* "HIS STAR" (Seiss, p. 25)

. . . It is furthermore a matter of inspired New Testament record that certain wise men from among the Gentile peoples not only looked to the stars as by some means made to refer to and represent a coming Saviour, even the Lord Jesus Himself, but were so moved and persuaded by their observations of the stars, from what they saw there signified, that they set out under the guidance of those starry indications to find Him whom they thus perceived to have been born in Judea, in order that they might greet Him as their Lord and honor Him by their adoration and their gifts (Matt. 2:1–11). All that entered into this case we may not now be able to determine, but the fact remains that these wise men of the Gentiles did actually come to Jerusalem, and thence to Bethlehem, to· find and worship the new-born Saviour, moved and led *by astronomic signs*, which they never could have understood as they did if there had not been associated with the stars some definite evangelic prophecies and promises which they could read, and believed to be from God.

Gr. ". . . *Ta panta kai en pantin Kristos*"
"But Christ all, and in all"
Colossians 3:11*b*

3. *Astronomy in the Time of Job* (Seiss, p. 54)

. . . Who Job was we do not precisely know. That he lived before the Hebrew Exodus, before the destruction of Sodom and Gomorrah, and hence before Abraham, is evidenced from the character, style, contents and non-contents of his sublime book which is at once the oldest, and the broadest, most original, and most scientific in all the Bible . . . . And yet, already in the time of Job the heavens were astronomically laid out and arranged in the manner just described, with the Zodiac formed, the constellations named, the figures of them drawn and recorded, and the same accepted and celebrated by God's people as the particular adornment of the sky in which to read the Almighty's glory.

4. *The Divine Origin of the Zodiac* (Seiss, pp. 55–57)

. . . Very significant also is this word, "GARNISHED" (Job 26:13) here employed by our translators. Its main sense is that of ornament or decoration, something added for embellishment; but it has the further meaning of summons and. warning. And by these adornings God hath also summoned the heavens and filled them with proclamations and warnings of His great purposes. Perhaps it would be hard to find another word to fit so truly to the facts or to the original for which it stands. It falls in precisely with the whole idea of the celestial luminaries being used "for signs" of the Gospel being written in the stars, and of the adornment and beaming of the heavens with this brightness of sacred brightnesses. And when we come to the direct analysis of these frescoes on the sky . . . we will find the diction of the Bible from end to end most thoroughly conformed to these beautiful constellations.

But more remarkable and important is the positive testimony here given to THE DIVINE ORIGIN of these embellishments and significant frescoes. All interpreters agree that the text refers to the heavenly constellations. This is made the more certain by the designation of the Serpent in the second part of the parallelism. That "fleeing Serpent" must mean either DRACO, the Zodiac, or HYDRA. And the affirmation is clear and pointed that the thing referred to is divine in its formation. Of the Almighty and His wisdom and power Job is speaking; and of that Almighty it is declared, "By His Spirit HE hath garnished the heavens," and "HIS HAND formed the fleeing Serpent." If the frescoing of the sky with the constellations is meant, then HE caused it to be done "BY HIS SPIRIT" —by impulse and inspiration from His own almightiness. If the Zodiac is meant, then His own hand bent and formed it. And if the constellation of the Dragon, or HYDRA, is meant, then He Himself is the Author of it, and, by implication, the Author of the whole system of the constellations of which DRACO, or HYDRA, is a part. We may wonder and stand amazed and confounded at the assertion; but here, from the Book of God, is the unalterable voucher for it, that these astronomic figures, in their original integrity and meaning, are FROM GOD and as truly inspired as the Bible itself. And many are the facts which combine to prove that such is verily the truth.

. . . Who, of all the sons of men, can point out any other origin of these remarkable denotations of the starry heavens? Who can tell us when, where, or by whom else the Zodiac was invented, its signs determined, and the attendant constellations fixed? Historical astronomy is totally at a loss to give us any other information on the subject. Here is the Solar Zoad, with its twelve signs and their thirty-six Decans; here is the Lunar Zoad, with its twenty-eight Mansions, each with its own particular stars, and each with its very expressive name; and here are the noted seven Chiefs, (the Sun, Moon, Mars, Mercury, Jupiter, Venus, and Saturn), playing a part in the traditions, sciences, theologies, and superstitions of earth, as brilliant as their splendid display on the face of the sky; but whence and how they were framed into these systems or came to place so conspicuous, acceptation so universal, and life so commanding and imperishable, even the science which handles them most, is quite unable to explain. As seven cities claimed to be the birthplace of Homer, who most likely was born in neither, so men in their uncertainty have referred to names and widely different countries, times, and ages for the source and authorship of the primeval astronomy, with about equal reason for each, and no solid reason for either. The world has looked in vain for the origin of these inventions on this side of the Flood, or anywhere short of those inspired patriarchs and prophets who illumined the *first periods* of the race with their superior wisdom and exalted piety.

5. *Age of The Constellations* (Seiss, p. 59)

. . . One great commanding fact in the case is that, as far back as we have any records of astronomy, these sidereal embellishments and notations existed and are included. We know from the Scriptures, that they are older than any one of the books which make up the Christian and Jewish Bible. We have monumental evidence in the Great Pyramid of Gizeh that they were known, and were noted when that mighty science-structure was built, *twenty-one hundred and seventy years before* the birth of Christ, and a thousand years before *Homer* who also refers to them.

The learned DR. SEYFFARTH, than whom there is not a more competent witness living, affirms that we have the most conclusive proofs that our Zodiac goes back among the *Romans* as far as seven hundred and fifty-two years before Christ, among the *Greeks* seven hundred and seventy-eight years before Christ, among the *Egyptians* twenty-seven hundred and eighty-one years before Christ, and among the *Oriental peoples* as far as thirty-four hundred and forty-seven years before Christ—even to within the lifetime of *Adam himself.*

RICCIOLI affirms that it appears from the Arab astronomy that it is as old as Adam's time, and that the names preserved by it are antediluvian.

BAILLY and others have given it as their conclusion that astronomy must have had its beginning when the summer solstice was in the first degree of Virgo, and that the Solar and Lunar Zodiacs are as old as that time, which could only be about four thousand years before Christ.

Professor MITCHELL says: "We delight to honor the names of Kepler, Galileo, and Newton; but we must *go beyond the epoch of the Deluge, and* seek our first discoveries among those sages whom God permitted to count their age by centuries, and there learn the order in which the secrets of the starry world yielded themselves up."

According to DRUMMOND, "Origen tells us that it was asserted in the Book of Enoch, quoted by the apostle Jude (Jude 14–15) that in the time of that patriarch the constellations were already named and *divided.*"

ALBUMAZER attributes the invention of both Zodiacs to Hermes. And

HERMES according to the Arab and Egyptian authorities, was the *patriarch Enoch.*

JOSEPHUS and the JEWISH RABBIS affirm that the "starry lore" had its origin with the *antediluvian patriarchs,* Seth and Enoch.[1]

6. *The Sabbatic Week and The Stars* (Seiss, p. 61)

It is generally claimed that the Sabbath, and the week of seven days which it marks, date back to the beginning of the race, to the institution of God Himself at the completion of the great creation-work. But that the system of the seven days is essentially bound up with these selfsame astronomical notations. We find among all the ancient nations—Chaldeans, Persians, Hindoos, Chinese, and Egyptians—that the seven days of the week were in universal use; and what is far more remarkable, is that each of these nations named the days of the week, as we still do, after the seven planets, numbering the Sun and Moon among them. Hence we say SUN-day, MOON-day, TUISCO or TUVES'-day (Tuisco being the Anglo-Saxon name for Mars), WODEN'S-day (Woden being the same as Mercury), THOR'S-day (Thor being the same as Jupiter), FRIGA-day (Friga or Freiya being the same as Venus), and lastly, SATURN-day, anciently the most sacred of the seven. The order is not that of the distance, velocity, or brilliancy of the orbs, neither does the first day of the week always co-incide among the different nations; but the succession, no matter with which of the days begun, is everywhere the same. It is impossible to suppose this mere accident or chance; and the fact forces the conclusion that the devising and naming of the seven days of the week dates back to some primitive representatives of the race, from whom the tradition has thus generally descended, and who at the same time knew and had regard to the seven planets as enumerated in the primeval astronomy.

7. *The Alphabet and The Stars* (Seiss, pp. 62–65)

It is now mostly admitted that alphabetic writing is as old as the human family—*that Adam knew how to write as well as we, and that he did write.*[2] There certainly were books or writings before the Flood, for the New Testament quotes from one of them, which it ascribes to *Enoch,* and *Adam* still lived more than three hundred years after Enoch was born. All the known primitive alphabets had the same number of letters, including seven vowels, and all began, as now with A, B, C, and ended with S, T, U. But whilst we are using the alphabet every day in almost everything, how few have ever thought to remark why the letters appear in the one fixed

---

[1] JOSEPHUS: *Antiquities of the Jews,* Book 1, chap. 2, p. 36: "Seth and descendants inventors of that peculiar sort of wisdom which is concerned with the heavenly bodies and their order."

[2] *Ibid.* JOSEPHUS, Book 2, chap. 3, p. 37, para. 3.

order of succession, and why the vowels are so irregularly distributed among the consonants! Yet in the simple every-day *a, b, c*'s, we have the evidence of the knowledge and actual record of the seven planets in connection with the Zodiac, dating back to the year 3447 before Christ. If we refer the twenty-five letters of the primitive alphabet to the twelve signs of the Zodiac, placing the first two letters in Gemini as the first sign, and take the seven vowels in their places as representing the seven planets, *a* for the Moon, *e* for Venus, the two additional sounds for *e* for the Sun and Mercury, *i* for Mars, *o* for Jupiter, and *u* for Saturn, as Sanchoniathon and various of the ancients say they are to be taken, the result is that we find the Moon in the first half of Gemini, Venus in the first half of Leo, the Sun in the latter half of Virgo, Mercury in the first half of Libra, Mars in the latter half of Scorpio, Jupiter in the latter half of Aquarius, and Saturn in the first half of Gemini; which, according to Dr. Seyffarth, is an exact notation of the actual condition of the heavens at an ascertainable date, which can occur but once in many thousands of years, and that date is the seventh day of September, 3447 before Christ!

It would be very absurd to say that this was mere accident. But, if it was not accident, it proves what the *Arab and Jewish writers affirm, that the alphabet was in existence before the Flood,* and demonstrates that astronomy is coeval with the formation of the alphabet.

Other facts, equally striking, but rather complex for ready popular statement, exist, to some of which we may have occasion to refer, all going to show and prove that the notations of the heavens so fully recorded in all antiquity do unmistakably date back beyond the Flood; that they came into being by no long-forming induction of man; that the whole system appeared full and complete from the start, like Psalla from the brain of Jove; and that the only true answer to the question of its origin is the one given in the text, which unequivocally ascribes it to the inspiration of God, who by His Spirit garnished the heavens and with His own hand bent the traditional ring of their goings.

It thus appears that in treating of these starry groupings and pictures we are dealing with something very different from the inventions of paganism and mythology—with *something as sacred in origin, as venerable in import as anything known to man.* Corrupt religion and classic fable have interfered to obscure and pervert their meaning, and scientific self-will has crowded them with impertinent and unmeaning additions; but, in reality they constitute the primeval Bible—a divine record of the true faith and hope of man, the oldest in human possession. With solemn and jealous veneration does it become us to regard them, and with devout earnestness to study them, that we may get from them what God meant they should be to His children upon the earth—sure that what, by His Spirit, He caused to be written on the sky is of one piece with what, by the same Spirit, He has caused to be written in His Word.

Field of glories! spacious field,
And worthy of the Master: He whose hand
With hieroglyphics, elder than the Nile,
Inscribed the mystic tablet; hung on high
To public gaze, and said, Adore, O man!
The finger of thy God.

Seiss

8. *The Star Pictures of the Zodiac* (E. W. Bullinger, p. 19)

"He telleth the number of the stars;
He calleth them all by names."

Psalm 147:4

These pictures (the Zodiac) were designed to preserve, expound, and perpetuate the one great promise and prophecy of Genesis 3:15, that all hope for Man, all hope for Creation, was bound up in *a coming Redeemer*; One who should be born of a woman; who should first suffer, and afterwards gloriously triumph; One who should first be wounded by that great enemy who was the cause of all sin and sorrow and death, but who should finally crush the head of "that Old Serpent the Devil."

These ancient star-pictures reveal this Coming One. They set forth "the sufferings of Christ and the glory that should follow." Altogether there are forty-eight of them, made up of twelve SIGNS, each sign containing three CONSTELLATIONS. These may be divided into *three* great books, each book containing four chapters (or Signs); and each chapter containing three sections (or Constellations).

Each book (like the four Gospels) sets forth its peculiar aspect of the Coming One; beginning with the promise of His coming, and ending with the destruction of the enemy.

But where are we to *begin* to read this wondrous Heavenly Scroll? A circle has proverbially neither beginning nor end. In what order then are we to consider these signs? In the heavens they form a never-ending circle . . . .

As I have said, the popular beginning today is with ARIES, *the* Ram. But comparing this Revelation with that which was afterwards written "in the Volume of the Book," VIRGO is the only point where we can intelligently begin, and LEO is the only point where we can logically conclude. Is not this what is spoken of as the unknown and insoluble mystery—"The riddle of the SPHINX"? The word "Sphinx" is from (Gr.) *sphuggo, to bind closely together*. It was therefore designed to show where the two ends of the Zodiac were to be joined together, and where the great circle of the heavens begins and ends.

The SPHINX is a figure with the *head of a woman* and the *body of a lion!* What is this but a never-ceasing monitor, telling us to begin with VIRGO and to end with LEO! In the Zodiac in the Temple of Esneh in Egypt, a Sphinx is actually placed between the signs of Virgo and Leo. Beginning, then, with VIRGO, let us now spread out the contents of this Heavenly Volume, so that the eye can take them in at a glance. Of course we are greatly hindered in this, in having to use the modern Latin names which the Constellations bear today. Some of these names are mistakes, others are gross perversions of the truth, as proved by the pictures themselves, which are far more ancient, and have come down to us from the primitive times.

After the Revelation came to be written down in the Scriptures, there was not the same need for the preservation of the Heavenly Volume. And after the nations had lost the original meaning of the pictures, they invented a meaning out of the vain imagination of the thoughts of their own hearts. The Greek Mythology is an interpretation of (only some of) the signs and constellations after their true meaning had been forgotten. It is popularly believed that Bible truth is an evolution from, or development of, the ancient religions of the world. But the fact is that they themselves are a *corruption* and *perversion* of primitive truth!

9. Mazzaroth—The Twelve Signs of the Zodiac

Isaiah 13:10 N.:

"For the stars of heaven and the constellations thereof shall not give their light: The sun shall be darkened in his going forth, And the moon shall not cause her light to shine."

Daniel 4:3 N.:

"How great His signs! and how mighty His wonders! His kingdom is an everlasting kingdom, and His dominion is from generation to generation to generation."

(The following outline of the Zodiac is presented with Scripture references from *"The Witness of the Stars,"* from study notes by C. G. Kindred with added Scripture references; also, the following extraction of the TWELVE SIGNS from *"The Gospel in the Stars"* :)

(Seiss, pp. 413—417):

. . . And to this EXTERNAL testimony, the INTERNAL substance and conditions correspond. In three grand parts, or books, each with four grand chapters, and each chapter divided into four distinct sections, is this record given. Set out in brief, the contents would run thus:

SIGN I

BOOK FIRST – THE REDEEMER PROMISED

(Note: * The asterisk each time indicates
(the interpretation of the foregoing sign).

CHAPTER FIRST—VIRGO, the Virgin: the figure of a young woman lying

prostrate, with an ear of wheat in one hand and a branch in the other.
* The seed of the woman. Isaiah 4:2; 7:14; 11:1; Jeremiah 23:5–6; Zechariah 3:8; 6:12 (9:9).
The Decans (piece or division) of Virgo:
1. COMA, the Infant, the Branch, the Desired One
   * "The Desire of all nations" Haggai 2:7
2. CENTAURUS, a centaur, with dart piercing a victim.
   * The man of double nature in humiliation, Isaiah 53:3.
3. BOOTES, or Arcturus, the great Shepherd and Harvester, holding a rod and sickle, and walking forth before his flocks.
   * The exalted Shepherd and Harvester, Job 9:9; John 4:34–38; John 10:11.

SIGN II—LIBRA

CHAPTER SECOND—LIBRA, the Scales; the figure of a pair of balances,

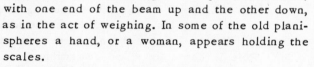

with one end of the beam up and the other down, as in the act of weighing. In some of the old planispheres a hand, or a woman, appears holding the scales.
* The Price to be paid; Revelation 5:9.

1. THE CROSS, over which Centaur is advancing, the Southern Cross.
   * The Cross endured; Daniel 9:26.
2. VICTIM of CENTAUR, slain, pierced to death.
   * The victim slain; John 10:15–18; Hebrews 9:11, 26.
3. THE CROWN, which the Serpent aims to take, called the Northern Cross.
   * The Crown purchased; Hebrews 2:9; Revelation 5:9.

SIGN III—SCORPIO

CHAPTER THIRD—SCORPIO, the Scorpion: the figure of a gigantic, noxious, and deadly insect, with its tail and sting uplifted in anger, as if striking.
* Cleft in the conflict; Genesis 3:15.

The Decans (piece or division) of Scorpio:

1. THE SERPENT, struggling with Ophiuchus.
   * The serpent's coils; Isa. 27:1; Job 26:13; Ps. 91:13
2. OPHIUCHUS, wrestling with the Serpent, stung in one heel by the Scorpion, and crushing it with the other.
   * The struggle with the enemy; Matthew 4:1—11.
3. HERCULES, wounded in his heel, the other foot over the Dragon's head, holding in one hand the Golden Apples and the three-headed Dog of hell, and in the other the uplifted club.
   * The toiling Vanquisher of evil; Hebrews 2:14—15.

SIGN IV—SAGITTARUS

CHAPTER FOURTH—SAGITTARUS, the Bowman; the figure of a horse with the body, arms, and head of a man—a centaur—with a drawn bow and arrow pointed at the Scorpion.
* The double-natured One triumphing as a Warrior; Ps. 38:2; Isa. 53:4—5; Gen. 21:20.

The Decans (piece or division) of Sagittarus:

1. LYRA, an Eagle holding the Lyre, as in triumphant gladness.
   * He gladdens the heavens; Ps. 65:1; Rev. 11:15.
2. ARA, the Altar, with consuming fires, burning downward.
   * He builds the fires of punishment; Ps. 21:9; Matt. 3:12.
3. DRACO, the Dragon, the old Serpent, winding himself about the Pole in horrid links and contortions.
   * He casts down the Dragon; Rev. 12:9—10; Ps. 91:13.

SIGN V—CAPRICORNUS

BOOK SECOND—THE REDEEMER'S PEOPLE

CHAPTER FIRST CAPRICORNUS: the Goat; the figure of a goat sinkdown as in death, with the hinder part of its body terminating in the vigorous tail of a fish.
* Life out of Death; Lev. 10:16—17; 16:22.
The Decans (piece or division) of Capricornus:

1. SAGITTA, the Arrow, or killing dart sent forth, the naked shaft of death.
   * The Arrow of God; Isa. 53:4—5; Ps. 37:2; Job 6:4.
(Shakespeare understood the truth about this constel-
(lation picture, which has been so long covered by the

(modern inventions. In his *Titus Andronicus, Act IV,* (Sc. 3, he speaks of an arrow being shot up to heaven (to the "Good boy in Virgo's lap."

2. AQUILA the Eagle, pierced and falling.
 * Pierced and falling; Ps. 37:10; Zech. 13:6.
3. DELPHINUS, the Dolphin, springing up, raised out of the sea.
 * Springing up again in abundant life; Ps. 42:7; Rom. 4:25.

SIGN VI—AQUARIUS

CHAPTER SECOND—AQUARIUS: the Waterman: the figure of a man with a large urn, the contents of which he is in the act of pouring out in a great stream from the sky.
 * Life-waters from on high; Num. 24:7; Isa. 35:1, 6; Isa. 41:18; 44:2–3, 6.

The Decans of Aquarius:

1. THE SOUTHERN FISH, drinking in the streams.
 * Drinking in the heavenly flood; Isa. 44:3; Joel 2:28.
2. PEGASUS, a white horse, winged and speeding, as with good tidings.
 * Carrying and speeding the Good News; Mark 16:15–16, 20.
3. CYGNUS, the Swan on the wing, going and returning, bearing the sign of the Cross.
 * Bearing aloft the Cross over all the earth; Matt. 28:18–20.

SIGN VII—PISCES

CHAPTER THIRD—PISCES, the Fishes; the figures of two large fishes in the act of swimming, one to the northward, the other with the ecliptic.
 * Swimming in the heavenly waters; Num. 24:7; Jer. 31:9.

The Decans (piece or division) of Pisces:

1. THE BAND, holding up the Fishes, and held by doubled end fast to the neck of Cetus, the Sea-Monster.
 * Upheld and governed by the Lamb; Hos. 11:4; Heb. 11:4; Isa. 41:8–10.
2. CEPHEUS, a crowned king, holding a band and sceptre, with his foot planted on the pole-star as the great Victor and Lord.
 * Head over all things; Ps. 146:10, Ps. 93:1; Isa. 52:7.
3. ANDROMEDA, a woman in chains, and threatened by the serpents of Medusa's head.

* The intended Bride bound and exposed on earth; Isa. 52:1–3; 54:11–14; Jer. 14:17; Rev. 21:1–2; 9, 10.

SIGN VIII—ARIES

CHAPTER FOURTH—ARIES, the Ram, by some nations called the Lamb; the figure of a strong sheep, with powerful curved horns, lying down in easy composure, and looking out in conscious strength over the field around it.

* The Lamb entered on dominion; John 1:29; Rev. 5:12; Gal. 4:4; Rom. 5:6.

The Decans of Aries:

1. CASSIOPEIA, the woman enthroned.

    * The Bride released and making ready; Isa. 54:5–8; 62:3–5; Jer. 32:3–12; Isa. 61:10–11; Ps. 45:9–17; Rev. 21:10, 2.

2. CETUS, the Sea-Monster, closely and strongly bound by the Lamb.

    * Satan bound; Job 41:1–10; Rev. 20:1–3; Isa. 26:21; 27:1; Ps. 74:12–14.

3. PERSEUS, an armed and mighty man with winged feet, who is carrying away in triumph the cut-off head of a monster full of writhing serpents, and holding aloft a great sword in his right hand.

* The Breaker triumphing; Micah 2:12–13; Eph. 4:8; Ps. 68:18.

SIGN IX—TAURUS

BOOK THIRD—REDEMPTION COMPLETED.

CHAPTER FIRST—TAURUS, the Bull; the figure of the shoulders, neck, head, horns, and front feet of a powerful bull, in the attitude of rushing and pushing forward with great energy.

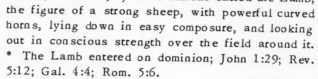

* The invincible Ruler come; Job 9:9; Jude 14–15; Deut. 33:17; Ps. 44:5; Isa. 13:11–15; 34:2–8; 26:21

The Decans of Taurus:

1. ORION, a glorious Prince, with a sword girded on his side, and his foot on the head of the Hare or Serpent.

    * The sublime Vanquisher; Job 38:31–32; Amos 5:8; Mal. 3:2; Isa. 60:1–3 (Ps. 19:1).

2. ERIDANUS, the tortuous River, accounted as belonging to Orion.

* The River of Judgment; Daniel 7:9.–11; fire *poured* out Ps. 97:3–5; 1:3; Hab. 3:5; Isa. 30:27, 33; II Thess. 1:7–8; *Nahum 1:16.*

3. AURIGA, the Wagoner, rather the Shepherd, carrying a she-goat and two little goats on his left arm, and holding cords or bands in his right hand.

* The all-ruling Shepherd; Isa. 40:1, 11; Ezek. 34:22; 27:24;Jer. 23:4; John 10:11; I Pet. 5:4; Isa. 45:22.

SIGN X—GEMINI

CHAPTER SECOND—GEMINI, the Twins, or a man and woman sometimes called Adam and Eve: usually, two human figures closely united, and seated together in endeared affection. In some of the older representations, the figure of this constellation consists of two goats, or kids.

* The marriage of the Lamb; also interpreted the Two-fold nature of Christ—God and Man; Acts 28:11; Isa. 4:2; 32:1–2; Jer. 28:5–6; 33:14–15; Ps. 72; John 17:22; Phil. 2:5–11.

The Decans of Gemini:

1. LEPUS, in some nations a serpent, the mad enemy under Orion's feet.

* The Enemy trodden down; Mal. 4:3; Ps. 60:12; Isa. 63:3–4; I Cor. 15:25–28.

2. CANIS MAJOR, SIRIUS, the Great God, the Prince coming
* The Prince coming in glory; Isa. 9:6; 55:4; Dan. 8:23, 25; II Thess. 2:8; Rev. 19:16.

3. CANIS MINOR, OROCYON, the Second Dog, following after Sirius and Orion.

* The Redeemed or Redeeming One; Isa. 49:24–26; 59:19–20; 53:12

SIGN XI—CANCER

CHAPTER THIRD—CANCER, the Crab; the figure of a crab, in the act of taking and holding on with its strong pincer claws. In Egyptian astronomy the scarabaeus beetle grasping and holding on to the ball in which its eggs are deposited, takes the place of the crab.
* The Possession secured; Deut. 33:18–19; Gen. 49:10–15; Ps. 57:6; Jer. 1:34; Ps. 89:19.

The Decans of Cancer:

1. URSA MINOR, anciently the Lesser Sheepfold, close to and including the Pole.
   * The first-born, the rulers; Gen. 22:17; Heb. 11:10–16; Eph. 1:14; John 10:1, 16.
2. URSA MAJOR, anciently the *Greater* Sheepfold, in connection with Arcturus, the guardian and keeper of the flock.
   * The Greater Fold, the after-born; Ezek. 34:12–16; Ps. 95:7; 100:3.
3. ARGO, the Ship or Two Ships, the company of travellers under the bright Canopus, the Prince, *the Argonauts returned* with the Golden Fleece.
   * The Heroes landed from their expedition, their toils and trials over; Isa. 43:14; Jer. 31:11–12; 30:10–11; Isa. 35:10. (Ships: Isa. 60:4–5, 8–9).

SIGN XII—LEO

CHAPTER FOURTH—LEO, the Lion; the figure of a great rampant lion, leaping forth to rend, with his feet over the writhing body of Hydra, the Serpent, which is in the act of fleeing.
   * The King aroused for the rending; Rev. 5:5; Isa. 42:13; Num. 24:8–9; Gen. 49:8–9.

The Decans of Leo:

1. HYDRA, the fleeing Serpent, trodden under foot by the Crab and Lion.
   * The Serpent fleeing; Rev. 20:2, 12:9; Isa. 27:1.
2. CRATER, the Cup or Bowl of Wrath on the Serpent.
   * The Bowl of Wrath upon him; Rev. 14:10; 16:19; Ps. 75:8; 11:6—(has *13* stars in it!)
3. CORVUS, the Raven or Crow, the bird of doom, tearing the Serpent.
   * His carcass devoured; Prov. 30:17; I Sam. 17:46; Rev. 19:17–18; Jer. 25:30–33.

That Christ and His work of Redemption are foretold in the Zodiac cannot be denied. Dr. Bullinger says (*The Witness of the Stars*, p. 174):

In Ophiuchus we see HIM in dread conflict with the Serpent, and we see HIS foot upon the Scorpion's heart (*Scorpio*). We see HIM, the Risen Lamb (*Aries*), binding *Cetus*, the great Monster of the Deep; we see HIM in the glorious *Orion*, whose foot is coming down on the enemy's head (*Lepus*); we see HIM in the

Lion of the Tribe of Judah (*Leo*), about to tread down that Old Serpent (*Hydra*) the Devil; we see HIM in the mighty Hercules, who has his foot on the head of the Dragon (*Draco*), and his uplifted club about to inflict the long-threatened blow; we see HIM crowned in *Cepheus* with all His enemies subdued, and His right foot planted upon the Polar Star.

SEISS (p. 417) concludes with these words:

Here is a marked order and symmetry of construction, a thoroughness of digestion, an assortment of elements, an evenness of balance, and an exhaustive comprehensiveness, not excelled by the highest inspired genius whose writings have come to us—an order befitting the God of order, and bearing in itself, in its three and fours, the expression of eternal Godhead moving and doing with reference to earth and man; whilst every topic in the twelve and twelve times three is a genuine Gospel topic, handled exactly as we find it in the writings of the Prophets and Apostles. There is nothing added and there is nothing left out. The whole story is complete—more complete than half the ministers in Christendom can tell it today with the whole volume of both Testaments before them, and after all the prophesying and preaching and fulfilling that has occurred in the five thousand years and more since these star-pictures were made.

INEVITABLE INFERENCE (Seiss)

"What shall we say, then, to these things? Was primeval man a gorilla, a troglodyte, a brutish savage, a wild man without knowledge? The Zodiac and the constellations as arranged upon the ancient sphere furnish the foundations of all astronomy. No man since they were made has been able to improve upon them. All subsequent touches of them have been bungles and absurdities. They stand today securely planted among the profoundest stabilities contained in human science. And yet the evidences are that they have come down to us from that selfsame primeval man. Then primeval man knew the visible starry heavens as well as any other man since. Then primeval man could draw maps, and make pictures, and write books, and teach wisdom, and transmit thought and intelligence, just as successfully as the remoter progeny sprung from his blood. Then the doctrine that modern man is a mere evolution from savageism, the result of a self-moved activity to become, his makership his own, his intelligence a mere self-efflorescence, IS A LIE."

To the testimony of SEISS and BULLINGER, is added that of FRANCES ROLLESTON's *Mazzaroth*, (Rivingtons, London, 1875, pp.6—7):

10. WHAT ARE THE REAL MEANINGS OF THE EMBLEMS OF THE SIGNS?

One of the greatest of uninspired teachers, the Socrates of Plato, is said to have always appealed to the common sense of his hearers. There is an appeal to the common sense of mankind as to the meanings of the emblems of ancient astronomy, which it was apparently intended they should make. The aid of history, languages, and traditions may have been required to ascertain what these meanings were; but when pointed out, any one acquainted with the Holy Scriptures can judge of their suitability to express the prophecies there recorded, as given to the first parents of mankind. The seed of the woman shall bruise the serpent's head, the serpent shall bruise his heel. There is a tradition that at the creation of man, the sun at the summer solstice was among the stars called the sign of the Virgin. In that place was figured, long before the Christian era, in the

VIRGO

Egyptian zodiac, the figure of a woman with an ear of corn in her hand, and below another female figure holding an infant. Here, then, is recognized the seed, the offspring of the woman.

LIBRA

In the next sign, the scales at once convey the idea of a purchase. He comes to buy, to redeem. (Deut. 32:6; II Peter 2:1; Ps. 91:13).

SCORPIO

Then there is the figure of a man grasping a serpent as in conflict, his foot on the head of a scorpion, whose reverted sting appears to have wounded his heel. Here the seed, the offspring of the woman, is bruising the enemy's head, after having received the predicted bruise in the heel. The first prophecy is thus fully figured out: the first part of it is as fully accomplished; the heel of the virgin's Son was bruised when nailed upon the Cross.

SAGITTARIUS

In the next sign an arrow is coming forth from the bow. Can anyone fail to see here expressed, that He shall come, speedily, surely? (Deut. 49:10; 33:29; Exod. 4:13).

CAPRICORNUS

Then a kid or goat, sinking down as the sacrifice appointed to be slain for sin. (Leviticus 16).

AQUARIUS

Then the promised seed, the man, is arising, and pouring out waters as to purify, sustain life. (Ezek. 47; Hab. 1:19).

PISCES

Two fishes, joined together by a band, come next: water is their element, abundantly multiplying is their characteristic. To the Christian there is but to name the Church of Christ, and the fitness of the emblem will at once be recognized. (Isa. 44:3; John 3).

ARIES
The primitive institution of sacrifice was equally of a kid or a lamb. The lamb, or young ram, is next, as it had been slain, but now living on high. (Exod. 12:5; Rev. 5:6).

TAURUS
The bull, also a sacrificial animal, but living, and in an attitude of victory. He who died in the kid is now alive again, and to Him all power is given. (Exod. 29:10; Heb. 9:13; Matt. 28:18).

GEMINI
The twins, the closest visible image of two natures in one person, are next; and the Scriptural believer will not fail to recognize their import. (Zech. 6:1, 3).

CANCER
The crab holds fast what it has once grasped. (John 10:28).

LEO
The lion rends apart whatever he seizes, as at the last awful day the Judge will separate good from evil. (Gen. 49:10; Matt. 25:22).

"Take and read," as the voice cried to the saint of old.[1] "Search the Scriptures," as the Lord Himself has enjoined, even if never searched before; and see if these simple and expressive emblems are not faithful interpreters of the prophecies there contained. The coincidences cannot be overlooked; they are too complete to be unintentional; the common sense of mankind at once recognizes the marks of design. To that universal faculty the appeal is made: are there not here those marks, and in the correspondence with Scripture the proof of what was that design? Was it not indeed in another, yet consistent, record to show forth the glory of God?

This appeal to the ordinary faculties of the human mind, to its powers of comparison and judgment, may well hope for the verdict that the signs[2] were intended to symbolize prophecy, as recorded in the Holy Scriptures. A connecting link is the signification of the ancient names in the original[3] language of mankind, as transmitted in the Hebrew of the Holy Scriptures and the most ancient Arabic: but to appreciate this additional evidence there must be either a knowledge of the languages, or a due estimate of the force of testimony. Those acquainted with the original Scriptures will testify to the occurrence of the root[4] of the name in those writings, as shown by the references given in the subsequent Tables.

---

[1] Augustin, *Confess.*

[2] The Zodiac in its present forms and order, as beginning with Aries, is transmitted by Hipparchus and Ptolemy, who lived about the time of the Christian era, as "or unquestioned authority, unknown origin, and unsearchable antiquity." The explanation here given follows the course of prophecy, and the order of the stars arising in the evening, with the sun in Aries.

[3] Part II (Rolleston) p. 76.

[4] "The Root" may be explained by Eng. examples: as, "family—familar" etc.

THE TWELVE SIGNS OF THE ZODIAC[1]

as connected with the Primitive Prophecies.

The antiquity and wide diffusion of these emblems, and the mystic veneration in which they were ever held, are traced in the accompanying pages: it is also shown that the notion of the signs having any reference to the seasons is of comparitively late origin, and could not at any time have been sustained consistently with the times and climates of their well-known previous existence.

It was not till the diffusion of the light of Christianity had cast into shade these dim foreshowings of its great events, that the vague awe with which these emblems were formerly regarded gave place to indifference and neglect, or was only preserved in the reveries of astrology. This reverence, in some cases leading even to idolatry, indicated a tradition that their message was divine. They each represented an action, still to be traced in the fables connected with them, a type, of which the true anti-type is to be found in the great subject of the ancient prophecies contained in the Hebrew Scriptures. The primitive year began in the sign Virgo, the stars of which were seen most strikingly in the evening sky when the sun was in Aries, the splendid star still by us called Spica, the ear of corn, in the woman's hand, marking the foundation of the hopes of fallen man. In the next sign Libra, we have His work, which was to be to buy, to re-deem, figured in the balance weighing the price against the purchase. Then in Scorpio follows the indication of what that price was to be; the conflict, in which the seed of the woman receives the wound in his heel, while his other foot is on the head of the enemy, here figured by the scorpi-on, a venomous reptile, who can sting even while his head is bruised.

Next we find the Archer, with his arrow in the act of going out from the bow, expressing that the promised Deliverer should be sent forth.

Then Capricornus, the goat, the victim or sacrifice sinking down as wounded, showing that the promised Deliverer must be slain as a sacrifice.

In Aquarius we see the rising up and pouring forth of water, as to cleanse and fertilize, showing that the sacrifice was to bring purification and benediction by means of the risen Messiah.

In Pisces two fishes are bound together by a band, which is continued to and held by the fore-feet of Aries, figuring the leading idea of union. The fishes, a well-known emblem of the Church among the early Christians, represent the redeemed and purified multitudes of the Church before and after the first coming, in union with each other and with their Redeemer.

The subsequent sign, the Lamb or ram of sacrifice, here not dying, but as it had been slain, is now reigning triumphant, with one foot on the

---

[1] Rolleston, *Mazzaroth*, p. 9ff.

head of the enemy, bound also by a band, which that foot holds.

We then see Taurus, the bull, showing forth the dominion of Him who had been a sacrifice for sin, now reigning over all.

In Gemini, the twins, whether human or of the sacrificial goat or sheep, the leading idea of combining, entwining, is equally conveyed, expressing the union of the divine and human nature in the promised seed.

Cancer, the crab or beetle, holding fast its prey or its nest, well conveys the image of tenacious possession by Him who has assured us, as to His purchased flock, that no man can pluck them out of His hand.

Leo, the majestic lion, rending the prey, represents irresistible strength, and final separation between good and evil. His foot is over the head of the prostrate serpent, closing the series as we are told by the Apostle that the dispensation must be closed: "For He shall reign till He has put all things under His feet."

Here, then, we have represented in action twelve leading ideas, twelve principal truths of Divine revelation,—

1. The seed of the woman shall come.
2. There shall be a price paid by Him for a purchased possession.
3. The price shall be a conflict with the serpent-foe, and a wound in the conqueror's heel.
4. He shall be sent forth swiftly, surely, as an arrow from the bow.
5. He shall be slain as a sacrifice.
6. He shall rise again and pour out blessings on His people.
7. His people shall be multitudes, and held in union with each other and Himself.
8. He who was slain, whose heel was bruised, shall rule, and shall tread His enemy under foot.
9. He shall come in power, triumphant, and have dominion.
10. He shall be the Son of GOD and the son of man, the victim and the ruler.
11. He shall hold fast His purchased possession, the reward of His work.
12. He shall finally put all enemies under His feet, coming with ten thousand of His saints to execute judgment upon all, separating the evil from the good.

These leading ideas are to be traced in the yet extant names of the signs as preserved in the Hebrew and Arabic appellations. Eight of these agree: of the other four, two are in Arabic different names of the same object, the other two contain the leading idea here attributed to the sign.

Two of the Syriac names from *Ulugh Beigh* differ from the Hebrew, as being other names of the same thing. Where the Hebrew and Arabic agree, there can be little doubt but that they preserve the name originally given: as where the words differ they still express the same idea, it seems that the emblems were invented, and universally known to the children of Noah, before the dispersion from Babel.

From ancient authorities we find that in the Aramaean and Coptic or early Egyptian names the same ideas are presented. They are also found in the Sanscrit.

The ancient Rabbins said that the astronomy of the Jews was in the Babylonish captivity corrupted by the astrology of the Chaldeans; but as the Chaldean dialect differs so little from the Hebrew, the names would not be materially altered. Slight Chaldee changes may be traced in one or two names of stars; but in the names of the twelve signs they do not occur, even where the interchangeable letters are found.

The existence of primitive roots in Arabic words, common to the Hebrew and other Semitic dialects, (however the usage of these words may have been varied and extended) is evident to Hebraists, though sometimes disputed by the scholar whose Oriental acquirements have not included the Hebrew. Such may be compared to the traveller in the desert, who, delighted with the fruit and shade of the palm-tree, thinks not of the source of strength and nourishment below, the deep and steadfast root hidden in the sand that has gathered around it in the lapse of ages. The root is obvious in these antique appellations of visible objects as in the proper names of persons and places contained in the Scriptures, and, though less obviously, may be traced even in those of other nations. Proper names, however corrupted in the spelling, generally retain something of the sound of the root whence they were formed: words used in expressing the varying actions and feelings of common life are much more subject to be perverted from their original meanings. The appellations of visible objects, if less *fixed* than proper names, are less liable to variation than those; accordingly we find these twelve names to have corresponding Arabic ones, even if in some places other, but synonymous, names are now used in Arabic astronomy.

The mythological fables attached to these emblems, and the titles under which they were worshipped, contribute to throw light on these meanings. All are connected with an offspring of the Deity; all say with the Evangelical Prophet, "Unto us a child is born, unto us a son is given: and the government shall be upon his shoulder."

If indeed Seth and his family were the inventors of these emblems and the givers of these names, intending to express in them the prophecies known to the ante-diluvian Church, such might well be their figures and their meaning. If the intention was what it is here considered to be, it is consistently developed by comparison with the written records of the

Hebrew prophecy, as delivered to the patriarchal Jewish Church; and is preserved for the Christian by those faithful witnesses for the authority and integrity of Scripture, and the yet unconverted Jews. As the Jews have kept the word of prophecy, the Arabs have preserved the names of the stars which so remarkably correspond with it, while the Greeks and Egyptians have transmitted the figures to which they belong.

These independent but concurring testimonies not only witness to the purpose of the long misunderstood emblems, but to the existence of a revelation anterior to their formation; for if their purport be prophetic, He who seeth the end from the beginning had already given to man that knowledge of future events which He alone can impart.

It is not doubted that about eighteen centuries ago there arose a re-markable person claiming to have no father but Him in heaven, who was put to death at the time of the slaying of the paschal lamb at Jerusalem. His death, the time and manner of it, were not in his own power. If pre-dicted by the prophets, prefigured in these ancient emblems, and then indicated in their primitive names,—that death, its manner and its time, must have been revealed by Him who by the mouth of Isaiah appeals to prophecy as the proof of His power and His Godhead, saying to the idols of the heathen, "show the things that are to come hereafter, that we may know that ye are gods." (Isa. 41:23). By prophecy and its fulfillment God speaks to man, at once displaying His foreknowledge and His sovereignty. So He spake to our first parents in Eden; and the echo of that voice was in the ears of the fathers of mankind, when these emblems were framed in memorial of the revelation.

NOTES (Rolleston)

In the sacred year, as ordained by Moses, beginning when the sun was in Aries, the signs would appear in the evening sky in the progression commencing with Virgo. In this succession coming events were to be accomplished. In the earlier ages, when the year naturally began from the anniversary of the creation, at the junction of Leo and Virgo, Aries, the first sign of the patriarchal zodiac, arose in the evening twilight, beginning at once the day and the year, the day with its evening, the year with its decline. As the night drew on, the Lamb as it had been slain, but arising in power, was followed by the other signs proclaiming His glory, His Kingdom, and His final victory.

Always and everywhere the series of the signs has begun with Aries, whether in Latium, in Egypt, in Arabia, India, or China. Some ancient nations began their year with this sign, but others, as the Chinese, from Aquarius, where the winter solstice took place about the time of the dis-persion at Babel; even these, however, began the zodiac with Aries.

Before the time of Moses the year of the Hebrews had begun, as the civil year of the Jews still begins, with the entrance of the sun into Virgo; so it seems probable that originally the woman, as now figured in the Egyptian zodiac of Dendera, held the ear of corn in one hand, the palm-branch in the other; while as Albumazer records in the ancient spheres, a woman as the first Decan of Virgo, was figured nursing an infant. The Arabians figured Virgo herself holding the infant, but these may have been the Christian Arabs, as it is said the ancient Arabs admitted no figures, human or animal, but represented Virgo by a branch.

It is not known how the ancient Hebrews figured the signs, except by the blessing of Jacob and that of Moses; but from these records it is evident that animal and even human forms were on the banners of Israel, —the Man form was that of the tribe of Reuben, the Lion borne by Judah, the Bull by Joseph, the Eagle or Basilisk by Dan. Balaam also evidently had the Lion of Judah before his eyes. Moses, speaking after the giving of the second commandment, dwells on the Lion of Judah and the Bull of Joseph without disapprobation. It was, therefore, the worshipping of these "likenesses" that was forbidden. The Jews in after times, warned by the idolatry of their forefathers, are said to have abstained from making any "likenesses" whatsoever; and the early Arabs are said to have followed their example. In the temple of Solomon, besides the consecrated cherubic images, there were pomegranates and flowers of lilies and palm-trees, but no animal likenesses, except the cherubic lions and oxen. There is here a proof that not the making of the likeness, but the worshipping of it, was the sin. Israel had been punished for desiring the golden calf to go before them, but Solomon was unblamed for forming the twelve oxen that upheld the molten sea. (I Kings 7; II Chron. 3:16).

(E. W. Bullinger, *Witness of the Stars,* The Lamp Press, London, pp. 17—19)

Ancient Jewish authorities declare that each tribe had one of the signs as its own, and it is highly probable, even from Scripture, that four of the tribes carried its "Sign"; and that these four were placed at the four sides of the Camp.

If the Lion were appropriated to Judah, then the other three would be thus fixed, and would be the same four that equally divide the Zodiac at its four cardinal points. According to Numbers 2, the camp was thus formed:

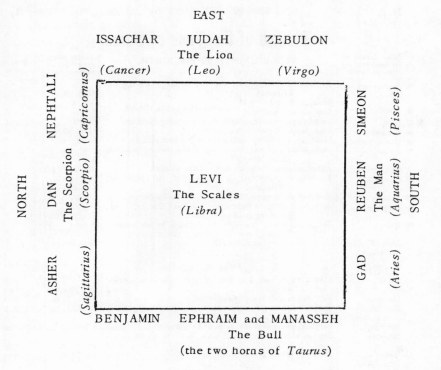

E. W. Bullinger
The Witness of The Stars
The Lamp Press, London

If the reader compares the above with the blessings of Israel and Moses, and compares the meanings and descriptions given below with those blessings, the connection will be clearly seen. Levi for example had no standard and he needed none, for he kept "the balance of the Sanctuary," and had the charge of that brazen altar on which the atoning blood out-weighed the nation's sins.

*   *   *

(The chart on the following page is taken from Frances Rolleston's *Mazzaroth*, Part II, p. 37, and gives the summary of the information concerning the Zodiac and the signs of the tribes of Israel):

Names of the Sons of Jacob,

ACCORDING TO THEIR BIRTH.

Signs borne on the banners of the tribes of Israel.		Texts where the word or its root occurs.	Hebrew roots.
♒ AQUARIUS,	Reuben, *behold a son*, the son, arising, pouring out blessings.	Gen. 29. 32.	
♓ PISCES, }	Simeon, *heard*, } characteristics of the Church. Levi, *bound, united*, }	Ib. 33. Ib. 34.	
♌ LEO,	Judah, *praise to the Lord*, for the coming Messiah.	Ib. 35.	
♏ SCORPIO,	Dan, *judging, ruling*, his people.	Gen. 30. 6.	
♑ CAPRICORNUS,	Naphtali, *wrestling*, sufferings at the first coming.	Ib. 8.	
♈ ARIES,	Gad, *good fortune*, blessings at the second coming, (Arab. use.)	Ib. 11.	
♐ SAGITTARIUS,	Asher, *happy*, the going forth of the Gospel.	Ib. 13.	
♋ CANCER,	Issachar, *recompense, or reward*, of the Messiah's sufferings.	Ib. 18.	
♍ VIRGO,	Zebulon, *dwelling*, as the promised seed at his first coming.	Ib. 20.	
♉ TAURUS,	Joseph, *adding*. Ephraim; *fruitful*, Gen. xli. 52; gathering in the Gentiles.	Ib. 24.	
♊ GEMINI,	Benjamin, *son of the right hand*, called by his mother, Ben-oni, *son of sorrow*, the suffering and triumphant Messiah.	Gen. 35. 18.	
(*Aben Ez. Com. Calmet.*)			

Stones of the Breastplate.

1st Row. Judah,	Odem, ruby, *red*, Isa. lxiii. 2 (*bloodshedding*, Arab. sense). *blood*	Ex. 12. 13.	דם
Issachar,	Pitdah, *reward, price of redemption.*	Num. 3. 49.	פרה
Zebulon,	Bareketh, *shining;* carbuncle. *lightning*	Ezek. 1. 13.	ברק
2nd Row. Reuben,	Nophek, *pouring forth*, as light or water. *flask*	1 Sam. 10. 1.	פק
Simeon,	Saphir, *numbered*, as multitudes, Rev. vii. 9; sapphire. *count*	Ps. 87. 6.	ספר
Gad,	Jahalom, *which breaks;* diamond. *break*	Ps. 74. 6.	הלם
3rd Row. Ephraim,	Leshem, *tongues*, of fire, Isa. v. 24. nations, *tongues*	Gen. 10. 20.	לישן
Levi,	Shebo, *dwelling;* agate. *dwellest*	Ps. 80. 1.	ישב
Benjamin,	Achlama, *which restores;* amethyst. *recover*	Isa. 38. 16.	הלם
4th Row. Dan,	Tarshish, *a possession*, Ephes. i. 14. *possession*	Num. 24. 18.	ירש
Asher,	Shoham, *lively, strong* (as a horse, Arab. use); onyx.		
Naphtali,	Jasphè, jasper, *which shall bruise, and be bruised.*	Gen. 3. 15.	שף

The Breastplate of the High Priest, with the Names of the Twelve Tribes and Signs engraven on the Stones; according to the Encampment ordered in Num. ii. (*Josephus, Antiq.*)

1st Row.	Bareketh, Zebulon, VIRGO.	Pitdah, Issachar, CANCER.	Odem, Judah, LEO.	
2nd Row.	Jahalom, Gad, ARIES.	Saphir, Simeon, PISCES.	Nophek, Reuben, AQUARIUS.	Exod. 28. 15—22, compared with Num. 2.
3rd Row.	Achlama, Benjamin, GEMINI.	Shebo, Levi, LIBRA.	Leshem, Ephraim & Manasseh, TAURUS.	
4th Row.	Jasphè, Naphtali, CAPRICORNUS.	Shoham, Asher, SAGITTARIUS.	Tarshish, Dan, SCORPIO.	

NOTE.—Libra was not borne on the banners of any of the Tribes of Israel, Simeon and Levi being united under the emblem of Pisces, but would be on the breastplate.

TABLE XVIII.

Mazzaroth (Rolleston) Cont'd. (pp. 22—23)

In the beginning of Genesis it is declared that "God made lights in the firmament of heaven, to divide between the day and the night, and to be for signs,[1] and for seasons,[2] and for days and for years." It is not said that on the fourth day God *created* them, but that He made them to appear as lights in the firmament, where previously vapours might have obscured their orbs. The word "signs" should lead us to ask, what do they signify? The primitive word *Othath*,[3] rendered *signs* in Gen. 1:14 and *mark* in Gen. 4:15, is something that testifies, foreshows. Their prophetic import may thus be seen, as implied in their name from the beginning. These *signs* in the firmament of heaven may then be expected to teach, to instruct, to foreshow. If these emblems, the signs of the zodiac and other constellations, are calculated to set forth important truths fitted to rule the hope of man as well as the computation of his earthly time, this declaration seems to authorize the conclusion, that the patriarchs, desiring to act according to the mind and will of God, so devoted them to show forth His glory. If the inventors of astronomy were indeed acquainted with truths of the utmost importance to the whole human race, might they not wisely desire to connect the remembrance of them with those memorials, those signs, by which they measured the path of the sun in the heavens, thus with the observations of earthly time associating the revealed glories of eternity beyond? They, whose accurate knowledge of the movements of the celestial orbs still astonishes posterity, might well desire to annex the message of everlasting mercy with which they had been entrusted, to the only visible works of creation that at all times and in all places present the same aspect of unalterable splendour. Adam, to whom the first revelation was made; Seth, in whose time it was begun to proclaim[4] the name of the Lord; and Enoch, walking with God, who prophesied of His final victory, might well be led to express the promises and predictions they had received in the very figures, and even words, constantly recurring in the written records of the subsequent revelations to patriarch and prophet, from the dying Jacob, who spake of the Lion of Judah, to him who saw the Lamb, the light thereof, in the holy city of the Apocalypse.

---

[1] Jer. 10:2: "Be not dismayed at the *signs* of heaven, for the heathen are dismayed at them" unduly venerating, being influenced by them. There appears here an allusion to the idolatrous use of them. The same word is rendered *token*, as applied to the rainbow (Gen. 9:12); and by it Korah and his company are said to be a *sign* unto the children of Israel. Again, it is said of the lights of heaven, that they were to *rule* the day and night.

[2] The original word means "periods," having no reference to summer, winter, etc.

[3] The original word "oath" evidently derived from it.

[4] The word is so rendered in Exodus 34:5—6.

Mazzaroth (Rolleston) Part I, pp. 13–14

Geology, showing that the earth was once a molten mass, on which nothing that now lives on it could have existed, proves that there must be a Creator. Astronomy not only manifests the existence, but the unity, the omnipotence, the omnipresence of that Creator. If this mind-exalting study can be freed from desecrating incumbrances, over which many of its most gifted students have lamented, they will surely rejoice in its rescue.

If a high, pure, and spiritualizing purpose can be shown to have suggested the invention of the names and symbols of ancient astronomy, will it not gladden all who love to contemplate the glory of God as made known in His magnificent creation?

If we may connect with every constellation, and each remarkable star, some divine truth, some prophetic annunciation, how adequately grand becomes the contemplation, how congenial the interpretation!

[1]If we there find recorded some hope, some promise given to the first parents of mankind, to support them under the loss of innocence and of Eden, will not that memorial be equally precious even now, shining like the stars that bear it, with undiminished lustre, on us their remote descendants? So read, the "poetry of heaven" will become its Scripture, and its line once more go out to the ends of the earth, declaring the glory of God to every nation.

Now that the hieroglyphics of Egypt are interpreted, and the characters of Babylon and Assyria deciphered, should those far more ancient and more widely diffused, the primitive hieroglyphics of the whole human race, be neglected? Those, the great enigma of ages, transmitting far more important intelligence, shall they not seem worthy of investigation? The Egyptian, belonging to a peculiar people, in a most peculiar climate, numerous and complex as they are, yield up their meaning lost for so many centuries. Those of the constellations, few and simple, formed from familiar objects and conveying ideas intelligible to all, should they be left hopelessly obscured in the darkness that has gathered around them?

The sculptures of Assyria in their stern grandeur have great analogy with the leading symbols of astronomy, but have corrupted in imitating them. Still it may be seen whence they originated. Those Egyptian hieroglyphics hitherto explained inform us only of the names and conquests of a race of half-forgotten monarchs. The Assyrian inscriptions seem mostly of the same nature. Both, however, corroborate historical allusions in the Holy Scriptures, thus warning unbelievers to respect what they cannot fathom, and encouraging believers to trust what they cannot as yet explain.

---

[1]
This paragraph included also in Section THREE, *Restoration to Terah, MY Story,* II. The Everlasting Gospel, p. 193.

HOUSES OF THE PLANETS (Rolleston, *Mazzaroth*, p. 26)

PLANETS   SYMBOLS   TWELVE SIGNS of ZODIAC and SYMBOLS:

PLANETS	SYMBOLS						
MARS	♂	Aries	and	Scorpio	♈	♏
VENUS	♀	Libra	and	Taurus	♎	♉
JUPITER	♃	Sagittarius	and	Pisces	♐	♓
SATURN	♄	Capricornus	and	Aquarius	♑	♒
MERCURY	☿	Virgo	and	Gemini	♍	♊
MOON	☽	Cancer	♋			
SUN	☉	Leo	♌			

From remote antiquity such have been called "the houses," or appropriate stations of the five planets, the sun and the moon. Belonging to Mars, who bruises and is bruised, are Aries, the Lamb bruised and wounded in sacrifice; and Scorpio, where He who should come is shown as bruised.

Venus: Libra, redemption   Taurus, deliverance
Jupiter: Sagittarius, deliverance by Him coming forth
           Pisces, whose are the congregation
Saturn: Capricornus, the sacrifice slain
           Aquarius, the water of purification
Mercury: Virgo, the branch   Gemini, the two comings

It seems probable that these agreements must have been arranged by the discoverers of the planets, the inventors of the emblems of the signs.

11. *The Witness of The Stars* (E. W. Bullinger, p. 27)

Such are the contents of this wondrous book that it is written in the heavens. Thus has God been speaking and emphasizing and developing His first great prophetic promise of Genesis 3:15. Though for more than twenty-five hundred years His people had not this Revelation written in a book as we now have it in the Bible, they were not left in ignorance and darkness as to God's purposes and counsels; nor were they without hope as to ultimate deliverance from all evil and from the Evil One.

Adam, who first heard that wondrous promise, repeated it, and gave it to his posterity as a most precious heritage—the ground of all their faith, the substance of all their hope, the object of all their desire. *Seth* and *Enoch* took it up. Enoch, we know, prophesied of the Lord's coming, saying, "Behold the Lord cometh with ten thousands of His saints to execute judgment upon all" (Jude 10). How could these "holy prophets, since the world began," have recorded their prophecies better, or more effectually, or more truthfully, and powerfully, than in these star-pictures and their interpretation? This becomes a certainty when we remember the words of the Holy Spirit by Zacharias (Luke 1:67—70):

> "Blessed be the Lord God of Israel;
> For He hath visited and redeemed His people,
> And hath raised up a horn of salvation for us
> In the house of His servant David;
> As He spake by the mouth of HIS HOLY PROPHETS
> WHICH HAVE BEEN SINCE THE WORLD BEGAN."

The same truth is revealed through Peter, in Acts 3:20—21. These words have new meaning for us, if we see the things which were spoken "since the world began," thus written in the heavens, which utter speech, (i.e. prophecy), and show forth this knowledge day after day and night after night, the heritage of all the earth, and their words reaching unto the ends of the world.

This revelation of the stars, coinciding as it does in all its facts and truths with that afterwards recorded "in the Volume of the Book," must have had the same Divine origin, must have been made known by the inspiration of the same Holy Spirit, and comparing the two, we can see how they agree at every point, proving that the source and origin of this Divine Revelation is one and the same.

This is the Revelation recorded in the heavens. This is the prophetic testimony inspired in the Book. And this is the heart-cry prompted by both:

> "Come, Lord and tarry not,
> Bring the long-looked-for day;
> Oh, why these years of waiting here,
> These ages of delay?
>
> Come, for Thy saints still wait;
> Daily ascends their cry:
> 'The Spirit and the Bride say, Come';
> Dost Thou not hear their cry?
>
> Come, for creation groans,
> Impatient of Thy stay;
> Worn out with these long years of ill,
> These ages of delay.
>
> Come, for Thine Israel pines,
> An exile from Thy fold;
> Oh, call to mind Thy faithful word,
> And bless them as of old.
>
> Come, for Thy foes are strong;
> With taunting lips they say,
> 'Where is the promised advent now,
> And where the dreaded day?'
>
> Come, for the good are few;
> They lift the voice in vain;

Faith waxes fainter on the earth,
And love is on the wane.

Come, in Thy glorious might;
Come, with Thine iron rod;
Disperse Thy foes before Thy face,
Most mighty Son of God.

Come, and make all things new,
Build up this ruined earth;
Restore our faded paradise,
Creation's second birth.

Come, and begin Thy reign
Of everlasting peace;
Come, take the kingdom to Thyself,
Great King of Righteousness."

                    Dr. Horatius Bonar